Between Arabia and the Holy Land

This volume is a general survey of the history of Jordan from ancient times to the present.

The author covers the major events that took place in this region since ancient times. Starting with the history of the region in Biblical times, the author discusses the major developments in the ancient kingdoms of Edom, Moab, and Amon, which shared common borders with the Hebrew kingdoms. He then provides a detailed coverage of the events that took place during the Nabatean period.

The author demonstrates how the character of this region had changed with the rise of Islam and the expansion of the Arabs and their encounter with the Byzantines. In addition, the author demonstrates how the rise of the Mamluk Sultanate affected the region. The author provides a detailed analysis explaining how the Hashemite Kingdom Jordan emerged and how the Ottomans and the British contributed to its rise. In addition to the political developments that took place in this region, the reader will become familiar with the economic, social, and cultural developments which contributed to the emergence of the modern Hashemite Kingdom. The book's audience includes college undergraduates, graduates, postgraduates, scholars, as well as lay readers with interest in this strategically important region.

The book is based on primary and secondary sources written in several languages.

Dr Jacob Abadi taught at the United States Air Force Academy in Colorado from 1994 to 2023. In addition to numerous articles, he is the author of the following books: *Britain's Withdrawal from the Middle East, 1947–1971*; *Israel's Leadership*; *Israel's Quest for Recognition and Acceptance in Asia*; and *Tunisia since the Arab Conquest.*

Between Arabia and the Holy Land

Jordan throughout the Ages

Jacob Abadi

Routledge
Taylor & Francis Group
LONDON AND NEW YORK

Cover credit: © sllmnhyt / Shutterstock.

First published 2024
by Routledge
4 Park Square, Milton Park, Abingdon, Oxon OX14 4RN

and by Routledge
605 Third Avenue, New York, NY 10158

Routledge is an imprint of the Taylor & Francis Group, an informa business

British Library Cataloguing-in-Publication Data
A catalogue record for this book is available from the British Library

Library of Congress Cataloging-in-Publication Data
Names: Abadi, Jacob, author.
Title: Between Arabia and the holy land : Jordan throughout the ages / Jacob Abadi.
Other titles: Jordan throughout the ages
Description: Abingdon, Oxon ; New York, NY : Routledge, 2024. | Includes bibliographical references.
Identifiers: LCCN 2023041099 (print) | LCCN 2023041100 (ebook) | ISBN 9781032584874 (hbk) | ISBN 9781032584881 (pbk) | ISBN 9781003450313 (ebk)
Subjects: LCSH: Jordan—History.
Classification: LCC DS154 .A23 2024 (print) | LCC DS154 (ebook) | DDC 956.95—dc23/eng/20231208
LC record available at https://lccn.loc.gov/2023041099
LC ebook record available at https://lccn.loc.gov/2023041100

ISBN: 978-1-032-58487-4 (hbk)
ISBN: 978-1-032-58488-1 (pbk)
ISBN: 978-1-003-45031-3 (ebk)

DOI: 10.4324/9781003450313

Typeset in Times New Roman
by codeMantra

Contents

List of figures *vii*

Introduction 1

I Jordan in antiquity 13

II Jordan under Byzantine and Arab rule 36

III The political history of Jordan under Mamluk rule 67

IV Administrative, social, economic, and cultural developments in Jordan during the Mamluk period 94

V Jordan in the Ottoman age 114

VI Jordan during World War I 153

VII Minorities, Bedouin tribes, and the challenge of integration 170

VIII The formative years of the Hashemite Kingdom 204

IX World War II and the Hashemite quest for national identity 238

X King Hussein's challenges 259

XI Jordan, the West Bank, and Jewish settlement plans 289

XII Jordan and its Muslim neighbors 310

Figures

0.1	Map of Modern Jordan	viii
1.1	Petra, capital of the ancient Nabatean Kingdom	32
8.1	King Abdallah I	234
10.1	King Hussein	285
14.1	King Abdallah II	380

Map 0.1 Map of Modern Jordan

Introduction

The region between the Arabian Peninsula and the Holy Land on which the present Hashemite Kingdom of Jordan is located had been occupied by numerous foreign powers and civilizations since antiquity. This land that connected the Arabian Peninsula with Egypt in the southwest, and Greater Syria in the north, had strategic and commercial value, which conquerors throughout history did not fail to appreciate.

Archaeologists found that during the fourth millennium BCE, the region's inhabitants were sedentary. They engaged in agriculture, domesticated plants, and painted and used metals to fashion their tools. The first settlement that flourished in that region was the village of Teleilat Ghassul where the inhabitants cultivated the land, and fashioned tools from the copper deposits found in Feynan, about 150 miles south of present-day Amman. Cities such as Pella and Tall al-'Umari were settled during the Bronze Age (3300 BCE–1200 BCE). The Iron Age, which began at about 1200 BCE, ushered in a new period in the region's history when the kingdoms of Moab, Edôm, and Ammon emerged in that region.

Biblical sources mention the Moabites who inhabited the Dead Sea region. Their capital was Dhiban and their king was Mesha who became known from the writing on a stele that mentions his exploits. Their kingdom flourished during the ninth century BCE. The Biblical story tells us that the Edomites were the descendants of the Biblical Esau, brother of Jacob and son of Isaac. They inhabited the area south of the Dead Sea, and their kingdom included the towns of Boṣra, Petra, and other small settlements. According to the Biblical account, the Israelite King Saul fought against them, his successor King David turned them into slaves, and many of them converted to Judaism. At the same time, the Ammonites inhabited the area between the Zarqa River and Wadi Mujib, and their capital was Rabbath Ammôn (Amman).

The Nabatean kingdom with its capital Petra was founded sometime in the fourth century BCE, and it flourished until 106 CE when it was incorporated into the Roman Empire. The Nabatean kingdom connected Arabia and Syria and thereby created an unprecedented commercial exchange where numerous merchants sold and bought their wares. Moreover, by providing protection to caravans that passed through its territories, the Nabatean kingdom amassed unprecedented fortune that

DOI: 10.4324/9781003450313-1

enabled its inhabitants to live in comfort, and it was only when the northern Syrian city of Palmyra (Tadmor), which gained control over the trade routes in this region during the second century CE that it started to decline.

Sassanid Persians and Byzantines fought over Jordan prior to the rise of Islam and when the Arab successors of Prophet Muhammad embarked on their conquests, decisive battles such as Mu'ttah (629), and Yarmouk (636) left them in control, and Jordan was incorporated, first into the Umayyad caliphate (661–750), and then into the Abbasid (750–1258). After the Fatimids conquered Egypt in 969, they extended their rule to Jordan, which they controlled, until the First Crusade in 1099, when the celebrated Kurdish conqueror Salah al-Din al-Ayyubi (Saladin) restored Muslim rule. Established by Salah al-Din, the Ayyubid Caliphate (1171–1260) controlled Jordan from its center in Egypt until the arrival of the Mamluks in 1250. Following their victory at the Battle of Marj Dabīq in 1516, the Ottomans controlled Greater Syria, which included Jordan until their empire collapsed in 1918. In 1921, Winston Churchill held a conference in Cairo where Britain granted the area dubbed 'Transjordan' to the Hashemites who were recognized as its legitimate rulers and Amir Abdallah became its monarch. Ever since, the consensus among historians is that Jordan is an artificial state and a product of colonial rule, and that its borders were determined according to Britain's commitments to the local players in the region.

This view that Jordan is an artificial state was particularly common among the opponents of the Hashemites who regarded Jordan as a country created by the circumstances that Britain found itself in the aftermath of World War I. For example, leaders of the Jewish community in Palestine such as Menachem Begin, who led the Jewish paramilitary group known as the Irgun, saw Jordan as part of the state promised to the Jews in the Balfour Declaration of 1917 and called for settling it. Following the establishment of the State of Israel, its first Prime Minister David Ben Gurion claimed that "Jordan is an artificial state with no future."[1] However, while many agree that the Sykes-Picot Agreement of 1916 produced artificial states like Jordan, Syria, and Iraq, some deny the validity of the term. Disputing the argument that Syria and Iraq are artificial state Asli Bâli writes:

> The trouble with the artificiality thesis, then, is twofold. First, the states that are deemed most precarious in the post-Ottoman region today-Syria and Iraq-have historical antecedents that predate Sykes-Picot and other Anglo-French agreements that partially defined their modern borders. Second, these geographic designations were sources of identity for the populations living on the territories, as is made plain by the history of nationalist mobilizations they engendered beginning in the 1920s.[2]

This argument can be applied to Jordan as well, particularly since most of the regions that now constitute the Hashemite Kingdom of Jordan such as Ajlun and Karak had separate character prior the state's formation and were sources of identity for the population living on them. Ever since Jordan's creation, the artificial state argument has been loosely utilized to describe most states in that region. States like

Syria, Iraq, Israel, and even Saudi Arabia were often described as artificial. For example, a recent commentator writes,

> Both the Zionist State of Israel and the Wahabi Kingdom of Saudi Arabia could be regarded—and are regarded by many in the Middle East—as artificial states imposed upon the region and kept in place by Western powers (primarily Washington) for the purpose of a long-term agenda of God-knows-what.[3]

According to the study *Artificial States* by Alberto Alesina, William Easterly, and Janina Matuszeski, "artificial states are those in which political borders do not coincide with a division of nationalities desired by the people on the ground."[4] Jordan was created in order to fulfill Britain's promise to Sharif Hussein of Mecca who agreed to join it in its campaign against the moribund Ottoman Empire. According to the authors of this study, there are three ways in which those who drew the borders created problems that could not be resolved. First, they granted territory to one group while ignoring the fact that another claimed it. Second, they drew boundaries and divided ethnic, religious, or linguistic groups with disregard to their national ambitions thereby causing dissatisfaction and unrest in the states that they formed. Third, a single country combined other groups that aspired to become independent.[5] Jordan is an example of the third category since it included Bedouins, Chechens, Circassians, Christians, and other small groups. As time went by the problem was compounded by the arrival of Palestinians who found refuge in Jordan following the establishment of the State of Israel in 1948, and the Six-Day War of 1967. Complicating the problem was the arrival of Palestine Liberation Organization (PLO) guerrilla fighters who established a base of operation in Jordan in order to fight Israel, until they were evicted by King Hussein in September 1970, and even more so when the Syrian Civil War erupted in 2011, causing many more refugees to seek haven in that country.

The authors of *Artificial States* argue that Jordan's borders are straight and therefore artificial.

They write, "straight borders are more likely to be artificial and less likely to follow geographic features or the evolution of hundreds of years of border design."[6] A straight line separates Jordan from Syria, Iraq, and Saudi Arabia in the east and south. It is noteworthy that over the years, the Hashemites who became the recognized family in Jordan negotiated with their neighbors with a view to obtain better borders for their kingdom. In 1965, they obtained some 5,000 kilometer square miles from Saudi Arabia and thereby gained wider access to the sea. A similar agreement was concluded with Iraq in 1982. By contrast, Jordan's border with Israel was determined by the geographical features that separated the two countries. The rivers Yarmouk and Jordan, and the Arava depression separated the country from Palestine. Following the establishment of the state of Israel, the Green Line placed the Jerusalem-Haifa railroad in it.[7]

Churchill's decision to establish an entity called "Transjordan" was unprecedented, and it was described as "a southerly extension of the province of Syria."

This according to Ash U. Bali was perhaps the only example of a wholly artificial state created under the mandates. Curiously enough, recent scholars who tried to construct new borders, which in their view reflected the ethnic composition of the population more accurately and therefore were likely to provide better opportunities for peace in the Middle East, did not find it necessary to make significant changes in Jordan's borders in their revised versions.[8] This makes the argument of the authors of *Artificial States* that there is a positive correlation between border delineation and economic prosperity tenuous at best. Jordan's precarious economy is an outcome of factors that have little to do with the way that its borders were determined. It is primarily the arid nature of its terrain, the paucity of water and oil, and the lack of significant amounts of raw materials, which prevent it from becoming an economic powerhouse.

Paul Belien mentions Iraq as an artificial state incapable of generating what he calls a genuine "civic glue" since it was formed by the Sykes-Picot Agreement. This creation combined three large groups (Kurds, Arabs, and both Sunnis and Shi'is) who were randomly thrown together, in addition to a small Assyrian community. Such combination, he argues, made it impossible to establish a democratic form of government.[9] Similarly, Jordan was created by the stroke of a pen, with total disregard to the composition of its population, or to the Ottoman administrative division in that region. It needs a strong monarch and establishing a democratic regime in it remains a daunting task.

It is the author's conviction that Jordan is no more artificial than any country even though its borders were determined by its former colonial occupier. Except in cases where the geographical features or the existence of an overwhelming national, ethnic, or religious majority in the border region determined the boundaries between two countries the dispute continued, and each side attempted to gain more territory at the expense of the other. The border conflict was usually resolved by compromise and normally the stronger country gained more territory that its weaker opponent. Moreover, boundaries were determined largely by the interests of the states involved in the dispute and by their ability to defend them.

After the right-wing Likud party came to power in Israel in 1977, many of its members found it convenient to embrace the idea that Jordan is Palestinian state. This argument was raised in order to delegitimize the Palestinian claim to statehood, and it reappears whenever the issue is discussed. Its main advocates were Likud Prime Minister Menachem Begin and his Defense Minister Ariel Sharon.[10] King Hussein's decision in 1988 to disown the West Bank came partially in an effort to invalidate this claim.

A major question that puzzles observers is Jordan's ability to survive in a volatile region where many regimes collapsed. One of the answers is the robustness of its foreign policy, which enabled it to obtain foreign support that is vital to its survival. The conviction that one can benefit from studies done by social scientists is now shared by more scholars than ever. Scholars such as Lisa Anderson and Rashid Khalidi found that theories and models built by political scientists can be useful to Middle East historians.[11] Others like James Rosenau, Michael Gordon, Jack Levy, Richard Rosencrance, and Arno Mayer are among many who found linkage between domestic developments and the conduct of foreign policy. Although their assumptions are based primarily on European and American history, they can be instrumental in examining Jordan's foreign policy behavior patterns and the way they contributed to its strength. Levy notes that the traditional focus of historians on official diplomatic files has given way to greater emphasis on the internal social, economic, and political determinants of foreign policy. Rosencrance associates internal stability with peace, and domestic instability with war, and argues that this relationship holds, regardless of the political structure or ideology of the regime. This can explain why the Hashemites were successful in remaining in power for so long. The county has not been engaged in foreign wars for most of the years of its existence, with the exception of two that it fought against Israel, and the peace accord that the two countries signed in 1994 left the Hashemites free to address their domestic problems. Mayer argued that domestic politics have the greatest impact on foreign policy by providing incentives or disincentives for war, especially under conditions of internal instability.[12] By dealing with domestic issues, the Hashemites provided disincentives for war. Jordan's foreign policy is analyzed in this study by applying the thesis that one ought to examine the social, economic, and political developments in the country in order to understand the nature of its foreign policy. This study assesses to what an extent relative domestic tranquility or instability in Jordan had impact on the Hashemites' behavior pattern toward neighboring and distant states.

Certainly, not all scholars accept such theses. For example, Marc Trachtenberg argues that reliance on traditional diplomatic history cannot help the historian understand the social determinants of foreign policy. Similarly, Mayer's thesis, which regards foreign policy as an outcome of manipulating domestic politics, was contested by Donald Lammers who rejected his application of the theory to Britain's behavior on the eve of World War I.[13] However, its application to the Jordanian monarchy's behavior in times of crisis can be of some use.

Bassel F. Salloukh's analysis of Jordan's political history from the mid-1950s through the early 1970s is based on theoretical models, which indeed help the reader to better understand the reasons why the Hashemites managed to remain in power against all odds. He examines the domestic determinants of foreign policy and their instrumental use for the purpose of gaining legitimacy. He argues that the Hashemites managed to retain power by neutralizing the impact of transnational ideologies such as Pan Arabism spread by Egyptian President Gamal Abd al-Nasser in the 1950s on Jordan. According to his analysis, four factors account for the survival of the Hashemites: their ability to insulate regional pressures; their successful attempt to form a state; their control over economic resources; and their unrestricted ability to use coercive methods.[14] Basing his analysis on Max Weber's thesis that a strong state is characterized by centralized and rationalized bureaucracy capable of operating without effective social opposition, Joel Migdal argued that a strong state is a social organization constantly in a struggle for social control over its population in an existing environment of conflict. Salloukh argued that a strong state can penetrate the society, regulate social relationship, extract resources, and appropriate or use resources in a determined way.[15] The Hashemites' performance in all these aspects was quite robust over the years, but many difficulties remained. Jordan's foreign policy has been affected by the incoherent nature of its society. In addition to its indigenous population, the country has Palestinian, Syrian and Hejazi, Chechen, and Circassian communities and the task of assimilating them remains daunting. According to Moroccan philosopher, sociologist, and historian Ibn Khaldun (1332–1406), a group develops an unconscious psychological bond among its members, which leads them to defend the entire group when its economic interests are threatened. Known as *'asabiyya* (group solidarity), this bond is essential for the group's survival. Ghassan Salamé argues that the state derives its power from its actual capabilities and their recognition by others. He goes on to say that *'asabiyya* and strong leadership are the two necessary conditions for a viable state. Every group within the state develops its own *'asabiyya* in addition to the one developed by the state. In order to function effectively the state's *'asabiyya* must have superiority over the local ones. Such superiority can be achieved only when all the inhabitants coalesce around the state's *'asabiyya*. According to this view, the local *'asabiyya*s in Jordan do not coalesce around the state's *'asabiyya* and therefore the different segments of the population continue to undermine the regime's leadership, expose it to threats from its domestic opponents and thereby cause insecurity dilemma.[16]

According to Brian Job, "insecurity dilemma" emerges when the state cannot provide security to the population or some of its sectors; when its institutions fail to provide service or maintain order; and when the state becomes vulnerable to foreign influence.[17] These were the conditions in Jordan in the 1950s when regional pressures such as Nasser's appeal to Pan Arabism acted as constraints on Jordan's foreign policy behavior.

One of Jordan's main problems was its undefined boundaries that exposed it to pressure by the surrounding countries (Iraq, Syria, Saudi Arabia, and Israel) and the paucity of its natural resources, which compelled it to rely on foreign aid. Nevertheless, the support of the army and the ability of the Hashemites to integrate individuals from among the Bedouins as well as from the Palestinians helped the regime stay in power. Moreover, by relying on foreign aid, the regime could concentrate on fighting against its domestic opponents. This occurred in 1957, when the regime managed to enlist the Bedouin tribes in the attempts to crush the nationalists who were inspired by Egypt and Syria. It was largely by relying on U.S. aid that the regime managed to crush the opposition. This scenario reoccurred in 1958, when the regime was under threat from the nationalists. King Hussein appealed to the United States and Britain for help and once it arrived, he embarked on cleansing the army and the administration from all anti-Hashemite elements. However, when the King had to face the Palestinian threat in 1970, it took much more effort to save the regime, and it was only the assurance of intervention by the United States and Israel that helped the Jordanian army and air force to prevent Syria from invading the country. The Hashemite regime resorted to several tactics in order to survive. It tried to avoid acting against the states in the region when the domestic arena was weak but once it gained control of the domestic situation, it adopted more aggressive measures. Moreover, the King found it prudent to act as a mediator in regional conflicts and appointed prime ministers who identified with their constituencies.

What accounts for the ability of the Hashemites to stay in power was their political acumen, which was aimed at integrating the tribes. They not only distributed benefits to their supporters but also showed consideration to political opponents. Furthermore, they restricted the activities of the opposition parties by introducing parliamentary measures and defense regulations, but when they felt incapable of controlling the country, they went to the extreme and disbanded all parties. In addition, they introduced changes in the electoral laws, which were designed to guarantee that the inhabitants of the East Bank and the members of the armed forces, which supported the regime, would be over-represented. Moreover, they cultivated relations with loyalist Palestinians such as the Nashashibi family notables who supported them and granted citizenship to its loyalists. Coercive measures were used as well. The intelligence services were relied upon to report on disturbances and disloyalty throughout the country. The army served as an instrument of integration, and in order to guarantee adequate supply of manpower, the Hashemites introduced conscription in 1976.

In addition to these practices, the regime relied on religion in order to support its claim to legitimacy. In his incisive study *State Power and the Regulation of Islam in Jordan*, Quintan Wiktorowicz argues that in Jordan, "the patterns of administrative practice in the regulation of Islam are designed to produce a depoliticized and unthreatening interpretation of Islam that reifies state power."[18] Among the most powerful factors, which allowed the regime to gain legitimacy and survive, was its ability to claim descent from Prophet Muhammad. Moreover, the fact that the Hashemites had been the custodians of the holy shrines in Mecca and Medina from 1201 until the rise of the House of Saud in 1925; that they had the important role of protecting the Dome of the Rock and the al-Aqsa mosque from which the Prophet is believed to have ascended to Heaven; and that King Abdallah was a martyr assassinated in that shrine in 1951 constituted an additional confirmation that the family has lasting religious functions and therefore sacred legitimacy. And most importantly, the Hashemites' policy of controlling all religious personnel, institutions and religious symbols enabled them to become closely associated with Islam and rule virtually without opposition. The ability of the Hashemites to forge a sense of Jordanian statehood and to use the regional umbrella to protect it from domestic opposition and foreign enemies was helpful as well. Even more remarkable was their ability to isolate the Palestinian population and to create a hierarchical political apparatus capable of penetrating the society and generously reward its supporters with material benefits.

While Jordan can be regarded as a weak state according to Ibn Khaldun's definition of *'asabiyya*, it is strong according to that of Weber-Migdal since the Hashemites had an uncanny ability to penetrate the society, keep control over their enemies and reward their supporters. In sum, the success of the regime's integrative survival strategy depends on a successful insular policy, the process of state formation, the availability of foreign aid that could compensate for the lack of natural resources, and the ability to use coercive methods, which it can use without hindrance.[19] And lastly, the Hashemites managed to strengthen their hold over the country by establishing institutions that had a central role in the country, by creating a strong security force and a military that could protect them, and by ensuring that key tribes and notables are part of the state apparatus and the military.[20]According to Michael R. Gordon, a government cannot function effectively without a strong sense of common national identity that can bind classes and groups together. In the absence of a common identity, the government may be tempted to resort to demagogy or repression.[21] Although the Hashemites used coercive measures on several occasions, they managed to stay in power by virtue of their ability to distributed benefits to sections of the population that remained loyal to it.

Crown Prince Hassan's famous statement to a Kuwaiti newspaper "My Israeli friends complain that they are surrounded by enemies; our problem is that we are surrounded by friends"[22] is an apt description of Jordan's dilemma in the Middle East. As one of the weakest countries in the Middle East, Jordan plays a role disproportionate to its resources. This, in a large measure is a result of its geographical location. Surrounded by Syria, Iraq, Saudi Arabia, and Israel, the country's only access to the sea is at the Gulf of Aqaba. Its meager resources and its location at the heart of the Arab-Israeli conflict compelled it to conduct a highly aggressive foreign policy. Moreover, domestic instability caused by the existence of aggressive Bedouin tribes and a large population of Palestinians made it necessary to maintain robust armed forces and supply them with sophisticated weapons and equipment, which can be procured only through active foreign policy. It was for that reason that the task of establishing the necessary connections with foreign countries had always remained in the hand of the royal family.

The Hashemite Kingdom of Jordan was formed in 1921 by Britain as a fulfillment of a promise made to Sharif Hussein of Mecca. Accordingly, Sharif Hussein's son Amir Abdallah was crowned king of Transjordan. Domestic problems continued to determine the course Jordanian foreign policy. The country continued to depend on foreign sources for help. Oil from Egypt and financial assistance from Saudi Arabia were constantly needed, especially due to the rising influence of the Muslim Brotherhood and the advocates of reform who lost their faith in the government's ability and willingness to modernize the country. The resentment against the Bedouin clans whom many regard as unproductive and the existence of a large Palestinian community continue to haunt the Hashemite regime and increase its dependence on foreign donors.[23] So far, the Jordanian government was capable of investing funds and energy that allowed it to conduct a robust foreign policy which earned it handsome dividends. Moreover, the ability of the Hashemites to gather intelligence has turned them into valuable allies of the United States and the Western powers. Known as the Mukhabarat, the state intelligence agency takes an active part in shaping the Hashemites' foreign policy. There are those who argue that many countries tend to bypass the government and deal directly with that agency, which turned into a ruthless instrument serving the state.[24]

Another issue that continues to puzzle observers was King Hussein's decision to sign a peace accord with Israel. After all, Jordan is an Arab country and the Hashemites already witnessed what happened to President Anwar Sadat who broke the psychological barrier between the Egyptians and the Israelis and addressed their House of Representatives (Knesset) asking for a peaceful settlement and withdrawal from the occupied territories. This radical *volte face* brought all the Arab states to expel Egypt from the Arab League and caused a major crisis in its relations with Syria and the Palestinians. In order to understand this radical step, one ought to trace the Israeli-Jordanian relations to the early days, when both countries were under a British mandate. Both countries were influenced by Anglo-Saxon culture, and both looked to the West for inspiration, and when the Cold War erupted, both regarded the United States as an ally. Moreover, it was already in its formative years that Israel began looking at Jordan as a country worth preserving and as a buffer with Syria. Numerous contacts between Israeli officials and King Abdallah I were made, with a view to establish normal relations. Agreements between the two states were reached with American mediation. One of the best examples of such agreements was the Johnston Plan, which determined the amount of water that each side was entitled to.

The Young Officers' Revolution which took place in Egypt in 1952 brought Nasser to power. The Pan-Arab ideology that emerged at that time swept the Arab world and led to rapprochement between Egypt and Syria. This tendency brought the two counties to establish the United Arab Republic in 1958, causing Jordan to feel insecure and to explore the possibility of establishing its own alliance. Moreover, it encouraged the pro-Nasser elements in Jordan to operate against the Hashemites. Under these conditions, King Hussein saw Israel as a lesser threat and the prospects of coexistence with Israel increased.

In May 1967, the Pan Arab sentiment reached one of its crescendos. Nasser's call for a war against Israel inflamed the Arab world and caused unrest in Jordan. This state of affairs put King Hussein between the hammer and anvil. Those who believed that this was a unique opportunity to do away with the Zionist state were in favor of war against it. King Hussein who sought to avoid war felt compelled to join it in order to maintain the popularity of his regime. Besides, the exaggerated stories regarding the superiority of the Arab armies, which emanated from Cairo, misled him to challenge the Israeli defense forces. The outcome was that in the Six Days' War, which erupted on June 5, 1967, he lost a significant part of his kingdom, including east Jerusalem to Israel. Seeking to recover his lost territories the king realized that neither Egypt nor Syria were capable of facing Israel in the battlefield again. Therefore, he met Israeli leaders in one of their cities, in various European capitals, and sometimes along the border, in order to reach a solution.

Even though King Hussein was one of the official enemies of the Jewish state, he gained the sympathy of many Israelis. Those who met him in foreign countries, communicated with him when he flew his private airplane, or spoke to him when he operated his shortwave radio were highly impressed with his warm and friendly personality. But it was primarily his conflict with Syria which brought him to regard Israel as the lesser evil. What made it so clear that he began to regard Israel as a potential defender was the fact that in 1970, he asked it to send forces against the Syrians who supported the Palestinians against him. At Washington's request, Israel sent forces to the Syrian border. Moreover, throughout the years, the Israeli-Jordanian agreements and meetings turned into a tradition, which eased the contacts between the two countries, and the last straw which led to the Wadi 'Araba accord in 1994 was the U.S. intervention and its promise that it would release him from all his financial obligations. King Hussein's acumen brought him not only to renounce his country's right to the West Bank, an act that detached his country from the Palestinian problem, but also to sign a peace treaty with Israel, which aggravated his relations with Syria.

This book is intended to provide the reader with an analysis of the major events that took place in the region that covers present-day Kingdom of Jordan, and it includes 15 chapters. Chapter I provides an overview of the political developments in Jordan during the ancient period. Chapter II deals with the political and military developments in that region during the caliphates established by the Umayyads (661–750) and the Abbasids (750–1258). Chapters III and IV are devoted to the political and administrative developments in that region under Mamluk rule (1250–1517). Chapter V is an analysis of the political, administrative, economic, and social developments in that region during the Ottoman Age (1517–1918).

Chapter VI explores the conditions in Jordan during World War I and Chapter VII discusses the emergence of the minority groups and their integration in the developing Jordanian polity.

Chapter VIII provides an analysis of the formation of the Jordanian state and the rise of the Hashemite family. Chapter IX explains the challengers that the Hashemites faced in the formative years of the Jordanian state and explores their struggle to find an identity to their state. Chapter X discusses the nature of the challenges that King Hussein faced, and the way he responded to them. Chapter XI deals with the West Bank and analyzes its relations with the East Bank. Chapters XII and XIII are devoted to Jordan's foreign relations. The first deals with Jordan's relations with the Muslim states in the region, and the second with foreign countries outside the Middle East. Chapter XIV deals with the challenges that King Abdallah II is currently facing, and Chapter XV provides an analysis of the cultural and artistic developments in Jordan.

While numerous books have been written on Jordan, the absence of a cumulative history on that subject is quite surprising. The purpose of this study is to provide the reader with one-volume account covering the history of that region from ancient times to the present. The author's purpose is not to criticize nor to refute any of the conclusions of the historians in this field. The sole purpose of this book is to introduce Jordan to experts and lay readers and explain the major developments, which had taken place in its territories throughout the centuries. The book is based on primary and major secondary sources written in Arabic, English, Hebrew, and French. Some of the repositories used in this book were the National Archive in London and the Israel State Archive in Jerusalem, in addition to sources found in special collections at the Firestone Library of Princeton University, Columbia University, New York University, the University of Jordan, and other institutions of higher learning. I wish to express my gratitude to all the individuals who assisted me in collecting material in all these repositories, and especially to my family whose cooperation and patience enabled me to complete this study.

Disclaimer: The views expressed are those of the author and do not reflect the official policy or position of the Department of Defense, the U.S. government, U.S. Air Force Academy, or U.S. Air Force.

Notes

1 Moshe Zak, "The Shift in Ben Gurion's Attitude toward the Kingdom of Jordan," *Israel Studies*, Vol. I, No. 2 (Fall 1996), p. 140.

2 Asli Bali, "Sykes-Picot and "Artificial States," *American Journal of International Law (AJIL Unbound)*, Vol. 110 (2016), p. 118.

3 Edward Morgan, "Israel and Saudi Arabia Are Artificial States, and the Cause of the Disastrous International Climate," July 15, 2018. https://prepareforchange.net/2018/07/15/israel-and-the-saudis-are-artificial-states- and-the-cause-of-the-disastrous-international-climate/, p. 14.

4 Alberto Alesina, William Easterly and Janina Matuszeski, *Artificial States*, http://www.nber.org/papers/w12328 National Bureau of Economic Research, Working Paper 12328, June 2006, p. 2.

5 *Ibid*, p. 3.

6 *Ibid*, p. 18.

7 Gideon Biger, "The Boundaries of the Middle East--Past, Present and Future," Studia z Geografii Politycznej i Historycznej, Tom 1 (2012), pp. 63–65.

8 Ash U. Bali, "Artificial states and the Remapping of the Middle East," *Vanderbilt Journal of International Law*, Vol. 53, No. 2 (March 2020), pp. 445–446.

9 Paul Belien, "Nations under Construction: Defining Artificial States," *The Brussels Journal*, June 13, 2006, p. 2.

10 According to former US Ambassador to Israel Samuel Lewis, "Begin and Sharon had the same strategic goal…that Jordan would become the Palestinian state." Even though Begin who never officially relinquished the Revisionist doctrine that both banks of the Jordan belong to the Jewish people later denied that he was in favor of this idea, Lewis insisted that he became more pragmatic and came to believe that the place of the Palestinians was in Jordan. David Landau, *Arik: The Life of Ariel Sharon* (New York: Alfred A. Knopf, 2013), pp. 174–175.

11 Bassel F. Salloukh "State Strength, Permeability, and Foreign Policy Behavior," *Arab Studies Quarterly*, Vol. 18, No. 2 (Spring 1996), p. 39.

12 Jack S. Levy, "Domestic Politics and War," *The Journal of Interdisciplinary History*, Vol. 18, No. 4 (Spring 1988), pp. 655, 668, 671.

13 Marc Trachtenberg, "The Social Interpretation of Foreign Policy," *The Review of Politics*, Vol. 40, No. 3 (July 1978), p. 341.

14 Salloukh, p. 40.

15 *Ibid*, p. 41.

16 *Ibid*, p. 43.

17 *Ibid.*

18 Quintan Wiktorowicz, "State Power and the Regulation of Islam in Jordan," *Journal of Church and State*, Vol. 41, No. 4 (Autumn 1999), p. 677.

19 Salloukh, p. 59.

20 Lawrence Tal, "Is Jordan Doomed?," *Foreign Affairs*, Vol. 72, No. 5 (November–December 1993), p. 47.
21 Michael R. Gordon, "Domestic Conflict and the Origins of the First World War: The British and the German Cases," *The Journal of Modern History*, Vol. 46, No. 2 (June 1974), pp. 209–210.
22 Cited in Peter Hinchcliffe, "Jordan's Relations with Her Neighbors: Victim of War or Casualty of Peace," *Asian Affairs*, Vol. 28, No. 3 (1997), p. 343.
23 "Jordan's Mukhabarat and 'Careless' Monarch Set Back Reform?," *Democracy Digest*, http://www.demdigest.net May 4, 2012.
24 Mohammad I. Aslam, "Jordan's Mukhabarat: Inside the Snakepit," *Foreign Policy Journal*, August 3, 2011. http://www.foreignpolicyjournal.com/2011/08/03/jordans-mukhabarat-inside-the-snakepit/.

I Jordan in antiquity

The geographical setting

Jordan is the region that lies between the eastern desert and the river that bears its name. In a geographical sense, it is the part of Arabia, which lies south of the Yarmouk Valley and Jabal al-Druze. The medieval historian William of Tyre (1130–1186) was the first to use the term *Ultra Jordanem*, which encompassed the Biblical regions of Gilead, Ammon and Moab to describe that country. He also named it *Trans Jordanem* and historians used the term 'Transjordan' thereafter. Established by the Ayyubid Emir al-Malik al-Nasir Dawud bin al-Mu'ẓam Isa (1206–1261), this region that lies east of the Jordan River constituted one geographical unit known as the Emirate of Karak, which later became the Hashemite Kingdom of Jordan.[1] The western boundaries of Jordan had changed as result of the Palestine War of 1948, and when East Jerusalem was annexed by Israel after the Six-Day War of 1967, the country's western boundary was drawn at the center of the Jordan River, the Dead Sea and Wadi Araba, and it extended to the Gulf of Aqaba. In the east, the country encompassed the Jabal al-Tuneiq massif, but the adjacent Wadi Sirḥan remained outside of its control. Transjordan's southern border is an imaginary line extending from south Aqaba to the south of al-Mudawara.[2]

Transjordan's scenery ranges from lifeless black basalt areas to fertile ones and from flat regions to mountains. The western part of the country is mountainous and fertile while the eastern part is a desert-like flat basalt plateau. The mountainous region of the west extends from the Sea of Galilee in the north to Aqaba in the south, along the border of the Jordan Valley and Wadi Araba. The main streams from north to south are Wadi Yarmouk, Wadi al-Zarqa, Wadi Shaib, Wadi al-Mujib, and Wadi al-Ḥasa. The first three flow into the Jordan River and the last two into the Dead Sea.[3] In his description of the Dead Sea, the Ayyubid geographer Abu al-Fida (1273–1331 AD) noted that the sea has no animals nor fish, but it had a substance called *ḥumr* (bitumen or asphalt), which the inhabitants of the region made use of in addition to apple and palm trees.[4]

The country's length covers the area between Mount Hermon in the north to the Gulf of Aqaba in the south. It is a plateau the peak of which is the Syrian-African Rift in the west, and it gradually turns into a desert in the east. The region is partially

DOI: 10.4324/9781003450313-2

mountainous. Hermon and the Golan in the north, Gilead at the center, and Edom in the south are all mountains above a thousand meters each. Rainfall is abundant in eastern Transjordan. The Seir Mountains, which extend from the Dead Sea to the Gulf of Eilat, get about 400 millimeters of rain annually. The main settlements in that country were located on the ancient Via Regis (The King's Way), which extended from Damascus in the north to Eilat in the south. Settlements could be found also at the mouths of the Jordan River's tributaries. Another group of settlements was found at the Yarmouk River and its tributaries.

The Jordan Valley was always connected with "Western Palestine" and never constituted a separate ethnic or political entity.[5] The valley was formed during the Lower Pleistocene Age, which expanded roughly from two million to seven hundred thousand years ago. It was connected to the Esdraelon Valley for several million years. Then it was severed from the sea. Basalt layers. The name applied to the valley through which the river flows below the Sea of Galilee is al-Ghôr, a low tract of land that extends along the Dead Sea and beyond. It was not until the nineteenth century that the region from Jericho to Tiberias was frequented by travelers, and we have no account of the valley's upper part in Tiberias' vicinity. We hear about pilgrims such as Antonius Martyr who at the end of the sixth century passed through the entire length of the valley from Tiberias to Jericho. We also know that St. Willibald (700–786 AD) followed a similar route. We know that in 1100 King Baldwin of Jerusalem accompanied pilgrims from Jericho to Tiberias, but except for the Crusaders who occasionally passed through the Ghôr, very little is known to us until the modern age, except for the account of the pilgrim Denis Possot who traveled to that region in the early sixteenth century, saw the medieval Montreal Castle, and the location where according to Biblical story, Lot's wife had turned into a column of salt.[6]

As we reach the modern period, the sources become more abundant. We know that in 1799, Napoleon Bonaparte reached the southern end of the Sea of Galilee, and that in 1806, the German explorer Ulrich Jasper Seetzen crossed the valley in the south but the description that he left is very general and says very little. In 1812, John Lewis Burckhardt visited the northern part of the country.[7] He traveled from Beisan to al-Salt. In 1818, Charles Leonard Irby and James Mangles went from Tiberias to Beisan, and then to Jarash and returned from al-Salt to Nablus across the Jordan Valley. At about the same time, William John Bankes and James Silk Buckingham crossed the Jordan Valley from Jericho.[8]

The prehistoric age

Sedentary life in the Jordan Valley began sometime in the Neolithic period, between the eighth and fifth millennium BC. Animals and plants were domesticated by then. Sheep and goats were widely used and crops such as wheat, barley, olives, lentils and grapes were plentiful. However, the image of the enormous grapes, which the Hebrew emissaries took from the valley of Hebron may have been nothing other than a bunch of bananas.[9] Archaeologists believe that a climate change, which occurred sometime between the middle of the seventh and the middle of the sixth millennium BC, caused the weather to turn drier and warmer.

In the sixth millennium BC. Jericho was already a town with a countryside that could be called modern.[10] Archaeologists found evidence of clay-made pottery and tools dating from the Neolithic period. In all likelihood, these were borrowed from Mesopotamia where sedentary life had already begun.

Situated north-east of the Dead Sea, the village known as Tuleilat Ghassul became the largest and most prominent of the settlements in that region at the middle of the fourth millennium BC. Archaeologists found evidence of houses with a rectangular shape and several rooms. We also hear about a settlement known as Ein Ghazal in Rabat Ammôn. Villages were also found in Nablus and al-Far'a. Human habitations expanded into remote areas and the caves of the Jordan Valley had often served as their places of residence. The widespread use of clay vessels and mud bricks led archaeologists to the conclusion that the culture of the inhabitants of that region was akin to the Ghassuli civilization which followed.

Recent archeological digs were made at Wadi Faynan that links the Dead Sea to the Gulf of Aqaba. Archaeologists found evidence that sedentary people engaged in farming and hunting, lived in that region, and that they domesticated animals and cultivated white barley. Fragments of tools and structures for storage of grain attest to highly sophisticated methods of food processing and preservation. The findings at Wadi Faynan show that the Agricultural Revolution, which marked the transition from hunting and gathering to crop-raising by sedentary people, took place in southern Jordan earlier than previously thought. Archaeologists date the findings at Faynan to a period, which extended between 10,000 and 8500 BC. These findings were the earliest discovered in the Middle East. In 2010, an archaeological expedition unearthed a large 22 by 19 meters amphitheater at Wadi Faynan, which dates from about 9700 BC. Another important Neolithic site was discovered in Jericho in the West Bank. Among the discoveries made, there was an eight-and-a-half meter tower, a massive stone wall and other structures similar to those found at Wadi Faynan.

Archaeologists refer to the Neolithic site at Wadi Faynan as WF-16 to distinguish it from other sites in southern Jordan. Another site was unearthed at the entrance to Wadi Faynan, half a kilometer from WF-16 where there is evidence of another Neolithic settlement dating back to 8500–6250 BC. A large mound nearby, dating back to 5500 BC shows that both farming and mining were practiced in that region. Wadi Faynan became the largest copper mine in the Roman Empire and during the Byzantine era the bishopric of *Palestina Tertia* was founded there. Caravanserais and other facilities were built there during the Mamluk era (1250–1517 AD). Archaeologists debate whether WF-16 was a permanent or temporary abode of humans who gathered for social and economic activities, such as harvesting and hunting. Wadi Faynan was an arid region where cereals could grow wild. Archaeologists estimate that WF-16 was abandoned around 10,500 years ago, and that another site nearby, at the entrance to Wadi Ghuwayr became a center of intense human activity. Remnants of buildings found in this site attest to the fact that its inhabitants cooperated on major projects, and that communal life became gradually more sophisticated.

Among the findings at Wadi Faynan were broken seashells from the Mediterranean and the Red Sea as well as raw materials such bitumen, and there is evidence of long-distance trade route, which connected Wadi Araba to other regions in Transjordan. In addition to Wadi Araba, there was Wadi Namla along the Sharah Mountains, which connected Faynan to Petra, 50 kilometers to the south. Prior to Petra's establishment around the fourth century BC. There was a road that linked Neolithic sites, such as Shkarat Msaied, Beja, and Beidah to Faynan. Though rugged, Beidah was not as parched as Wadi Faynan and vegetables could grow more easily there. A complex of circular and rectangular structures was discovered at this site, but there is evidence that unlike Wadi Faynan where the inhabitants settled continuously since the early Neolithic Age, the immediate area around was abandoned from about 6500 BC until the early Nabatean period, some 6,000 years later.[11]

The Israelites and their neighbors in Transjordan

More settlements were established in the Jordan Valley during the Bronze Age. Between the nineteenth and the sixteenth centuries BC, Jericho was the most important city in that region. An archaeological survey taken in the 1970s revealed the existence of several settlements in the regions of Ezôr and al-Ghôr. Tel a-Sarīm was the most important settlement north of the Jordan Valley followed by city of Beit Sh'an. According to the survey, these settlements were quite crowded.[12] It was largely as a result the economic activities and commercial needs of the time that cities developed in the desert region, as the eminent historian Fernand Braudel remind us saying,

> It is clear that in the western Mediterranean the great cities were all near the sea. But in the south and east of the Mediterranean, the great cities of Islam are a clear response to the demands of the roads through the desert.[13]

Settlements in present-day Jordan are mentioned in ancient Egyptian inscriptions. The kingdoms that thrived in Transjordan at that time were Edôm, the border of which extended to southern Wadi al-Hasan and included Wadi Araba, Petra, and Shaba; the Kingdom of Ammôn, which extended from the Zara River to Wadi al-Mujik and its capital was Rabat Ammôn and; the Kingdom of Moab, which bordered Ammôn in the south. Moab's center was Karak and it reached the peak of its development under King Mesha who expanded its territory and annexed the city of Ma'an. In the eight century BC, the Assyrians conquered Syria, Palestine, and Transjordan. They ruled over Moab until 626 BC when their empire began to decline. The Neo-Babylonians who succeeded them dominated Edôm and Ammôn until 586 BC, when they exiled the Jews and destroyed their First Temple in Jerusalem.

Following the destruction of their temple, the people of Jerusalem sought refuge in Transjordan (2 Kings, 24–25; Jeremiah 39–41). According to the Biblical account the people of Ammôn, Moab and Edôm were reprimanded by the prophets for rejoicing at the destruction of Jerusalem (Psalm 83; Isaiah 11; Jeremiah 49; Ezekiel 25; Zephaniah 2). In all likelihood, Transjordan flourished during the time of Nabonidus, the last king of the Neo-Babylonian Empire (556–539 BC) who resided in Teima in northwest Arabia, since the route to Jerusalem was important and he probably guarded it closely.

Transjordan fell under foreign rule once again in the sixth century BC. Cyrus the Great who became king of the Persian Empire in 539 BC extended his rule to the Fertile Crescent and Egypt and allowed the Jews to return and build their temple. Upon their arrival to Judah, the Jews are said to have found hostile neighbors such as Tobiah the Ammonite, Sanballat of Samaria, and Geshem the Arab, in addition to the Ashdodites, the Idumeans, and perhaps the Moabites. It seems that the Ammonite Kingdom continued to exist until after the conquests of Alexander the Great in the late fourth century BC. The Tobiads were present at that period until the second century BC when they were wiped out at Araq el-Amir. The Ammonites are mentioned in the books *Maccabees* 1, 2, and 5. Their capital changed to Philadelphia, but the old name Amman just like Dhiban and Boṣra the capitals of Moab and Edôm respectively, reappeared when the Arabs conquered the region in the seventh century AD.[14]

The Nabateans whose civilization flourished in the southern region of the country at that time established their capital in Petra and extended their influence to Transjordan all the way to northern Syria. The origin of the Nabateans remains controversial. Some scholars argue that they originated from Nabaioh, the eldest son of Ishmael. There are those who maintain that they originated in Iraq, and that they accompanied the Babylonian King Nebuchadnezzar during the sixth century BC when he was on his way to liberate Palestine, and later settled in Petra. There are also those who maintain that they originated from the heart of the Arabian Peninsula, while others argue that they originated from Yemen.[15] The Nabatean civilization reached its apogee under King Aretas IV (9 BC–40 AD).

The settlement process in the Golan was sparse during the early Iron Age (twelfth through the eleventh centuries BC) and it did not reach its peak until Roman and Byzantine times. The Seïr Mountain region, which had almost no settlements in the Bronze Age was becoming slowly settled by the beginning of the Iron Age. However, many of the cities in that region such as Boṣra, Tawilan, and Umm al-Biyara emerged before the ninth and eighth centuries BC. The Biblical Kingdoms of Ammôn, Moab and Edôm belong to the Iron Age and were founded sometime at the end of the second millennium BC. Rabat Ammôn was Ammôn's capital. Moab's capital was Kīr Moab (Karak) and Edôm's capital was Boṣra. Both Moab and Edôm were absorbed by the expanding Assyrian Empire, and lost their independence, whereas Ammôn remained free, not only from Assyria, but also from the Israelite Kingdom. According to the Biblical account, Moab was subjugated by the Israelite Kingdom to which it paid tribute. We are told that Mesha King of Moab sought to put an end to this state of affairs, and rose in rebellion. The Biblical account reads as follows:

> For many years the country of Moab had been controlled by Israel and was forced to pay taxes to the kings of Israel. King Mesha of Moab raised sheep, so he paid the king of Israel one hundred thousand lambs and the wool from one hundred thousand rams.
>
> (Kings, 3:4)

The story of that episode, which took place around 850 BC, was recorded on Mesha's stele was found in Dhiban, Jordan, in 1868.

A significant transformation occurred in Gilead and Moab at the beginning of the Iron Age.

A survey taken in northern Gilead, between the Yarmouk and the Jabbôk, demonstrates that during the Bronze Age, there were only about ten settlements. These were big Canaanite cities, most of which were on the Irbid Plateau, between the Yarmouk River and the Ajlun Plateau, and a few in the vicinity of the Jordan Valley, close to Pella. During the Iron Age, there were more than 70 settlements in that region. This mountainous region was known in Biblical times by the name Ephraim's Forest. Extending from Jabbôk to Irbid, west of Via Regis, this region which had only four settlements in the late Bronze Age expanded to more than 40 during the Iron Age, but it was much later that new settlements were established on its lower parts, close to Pechel.

During the late Bronze and early Iron ages, the central east Jordan Valley region (Deir Alla region) was relatively densely populated. This area connected western Palestine with the Transjordan plateau. With the decline of the Egyptian Empire, this west-to-east route with its socioeconomic structure disintegrated, causing the inhabitants of the region to return to a more egalitarian economy based on agriculture, pastoralism and settlement of marginal areas. Most settlers migrated from the plateau to Wadi Zarqa and settled in the Jordan Valley, and some may have crossed the Jordan River and settled on the other side.[16]

During the period between the late Bronze Age and the beginning of the Iron Age, there was a significant rise in the number of settlements in Ammôn and Moab and the population continued to rise. Some of the 12 Israelite tribes settled in the region upon their Exodus from Egypt, which took place sometime between the fifteenth and the thirteenth centuries BC. They tended to settle in the vicinity of the Jordan River, between the Yarmouk River in the north, and the Arnôn in the south. The most prominent among these were the tribes of Gad and Reuben who settled and mixed with each other in the southern part of that region, from Divon to Heshbon. Northward, Gad settled southern Gilead (Balqa) and many of its members settled all along Jordan's eastern valley, all the way to the city Tell-al-Sa'diyeh. Evidence to that effect can be found both in the Bible and Mesha stele. The Bible tells us that Israel's neighbors did not recognize their right to settle in the land that they conquered from Siḥon King of the Amorites (Judges, 11; 12–27). The evidence suggests that the two tribes lived together peacefully until the era of the Judges, when the region turned into a bone of contention between the Ammonites in the east and Moabites in the south. The weakness of Reuben Tribe and the fact that it resorted to life of wandering in the desert's periphery was in all likelihood a result of pressure exerted by Moab and Ammôn, which compelled it to abandon the area.

The settlement of Ajlun apparently began after that of Balqa and the plane north of Arnôn, between Divôn and Madaba. The Israelite tribe of Machīr or Half-Manasseh settled in Ajlun. Northeast of Ajlun in the Irbid Plateau and the regions called Ashterot and Bashan, lived the nomads of Gilead. Among the most prominent of the Israelite residents of that region were the Yaīri family that resided in northern Gilead, and the Novach family, which resided in the southern margins of the Bashan, close to Ajlun Mountain where there was a large Israelite settlement. The most prominent place given to the Israelite tribes in Transjordan was Gilead, which included Ajlun, Balqa, and the adjacent plane where their main settlements were found.

Despite the close family ties, the Israelite tribes of both sides of the Jordan River were often at odds. The Biblical account (Joshua, 22) tells us about the altar that the tribesmen of Gad and Reuben erected in the eastern side of the Jordan and the consternation, which the Sons of Israel in Canaan had upon learning about the event. It was with great difficulty that a rift between the two parts of the Israelite nation was avoided. The entire chapter is devoted to explaining the ideological basis of the nation's unity despite the Jordan River that separated them. The altar's name was not mentioned in the Biblical account but one of the verses gives us a hint. For example, we hear about the altar built by Jacob in Mount Gilead named Gal-Ed (Genesis 31; 44–63). It is evident from the Biblical accounts that the Gilead region included other tribes such as Ephraim and Benjamin, simply because the western region of the Jordan was overly crowded. Three nations, Ammôn, Moab and Edôm that settled the central and southern part of Transjordan were linguistically close the Israelite tribes. According to the Biblical narrative, these nations existed prior to the arrival of the Israelites to Canaan. Therefore, their lands were not included in the land promised to the People of Israel. Egyptian writing dating from the time of Ramses II (1279–1213 BC) mentions the Shasu from Edôm who in all likelihood were nomads that roamed that region.

Edôm consisted of independent tribes who were connected by bond of allegiance and interacted with each other both in Arabia and the Negev. These tribes controlled the trade routes leading to these regions. By the ninth century BC, the trade in copper mining turned Edôm into an independent kingdom with a major administrative and religious center in Boṣra, which paid tribute the Assyria. However, Edôm was not a monolithic nation-state but a kingdom consisting of numerous pastoral and agricultural tribal groups, tied to each other by bonds of cooperation and allegiance and ruled by a monarch.[17]

Archaeological evidence shows that the settlement process in Mount Seïr did not gain momentum until the eighth and the ninth centuries BC and that very few settlements date from the thirteen and twelve centuries, when the Israelites arrived in Canaan. Furthermore, the settlements found were mostly in the northern part of Moab. We also hear about the Sons of Esau who are mentioned in the Bible. These are said to have inhabited Edôm and Mount Seïr and they resided in the region, at least since the thirteenth century BC. Archaeologists found a string of fortresses on the borders of the Edomite and Moabite territory, which they date to the early Iron Age. This seems to support the Biblical narrative that these kingdoms were already in place when the Israelites arrived from Egypt to the land of Canaan.[18]

It was only during the period of the Israelite monarchy that there was a significant contact between Israel and Edôm. The outcome of this contact was that Israel ruled Edôm whose inhabitants made repeated attempts to break away and invade

Judah. This was a long drawn out struggle the objective of which was to control the Gulf of Eilat and the outlet to the Red Sea, and it did not end until the Hasmonean age (140–37 BC) when the Edomites disappeared and some of them mixed with Judah's population.

We have little knowledge about Moab and its northern neighbor Edôm. This knowledge comes to us from an inscription on the wall of the palace of Ramses II in Luxor. There was a sparse population in Moab during the late Bronze Age and the number of settlements increased during the Iron Age. This expansion took place near the settlements of the Israelite tribes of Gad and Reuben, on the plane north of Arnôn, between Divôn and Madaba, and on the planes of Moab. We learn from the Biblical account that there were frequent clashes between Moab and Israel. We also hear about the Midianites, denizens of the eastern desert. They appear in connection with the Moabites, but it is difficult to determine the nature of this connection. However, in Bil'am's Episode in the Bible (Numbers, 22, 7), there is a hint that the Moabites used Midianite mercenaries in their war against the Israelites. It seems that the Moabite Kingdom, which expanded mostly between the rivers Zered and Arnôn, still did not control large areas in the north and that the Israelites settled there with their herds. The fact that during the era of the Hebrew Judges the Moabites were the real power west of the Jordan River is evident from Ehūd Ben Gera's episode in the Bible, during which the Moabites took control of Jericho and its environs and thus constituted a threat to the Israelite tribes of the mountains. Despite the frequent clashes, the northern parts of Moab were settled by Israelites, and there were numerous cases of intermarriage and mixing with the local population.

Among the peoples of Transjordan, we learn about the Sons of Ammôn who settled in the region uninterruptedly throughout the second millennium BC. According to articles found at a temple in the vicinity of the capital Rabat Ammôn, this city prospered and maintained commercial connections with the civilizations in the region during the fourteenth century BC. The Ammonites referred to them as aboriginal giants whom they called *zamzumim*, and according to the Biblical account, the ancient people that resided here were called *refa'im* (Deuteronomy, 2, 20). This ties in with the tradition that maintains that Ammôn was closely connected to Israel, due to its origin from Lot. It is also the basis of the argument that the Israelites did not conquer the land of Sons of Ammôn because the two were relatives, and that they inherited their land rightfully by prevailing over the indigenous peoples.

It is conceivable that the Sons of Ammôn settled the region close to Rabat Ammôn and there is archaeological evidence that the area was densely populated by the beginning of the Iron Age. A large settlement was discovered in Sakhab, southeast of Rabat Ammôn. This settlement reached its apogee during the Iron Age but later its population diminished considerably.

This unusual pattern of development can be explained by the fact that the Sons of Ammôn began settling in Rabat Ammôn, Jabbôk Heights (Wadi Amman), and the periphery of the desert. They expanded to southern Gilead and tried to take control of the northern part of that region where the Israelite settlement was dense.

We also learn about the struggle between the Israelites and the Ammonites over Gilead and the Land of Siḥon in particular. During the late period of the Judges, the Ammonites are said to have invaded Yavesh Gilead, a city located in Ajlun.[19]

The conflict with the peoples in the region continued during the monarchial period. According to the Biblical account, King Saul fought against his enemies in Moab and the Sons of Ammôn and Edôm, in addition to the Philistines (Samuel I, 14, 47). We hear about Saul's campaign against the Sons of Ammôn whose aim was to save the people of Yavesh Gilead from Naḥash King of Ammôn (Samuel I, 11). When David sought to become king of Israel, he sent emissaries from his headquarters in Hebron inviting the people of Yavesh Gilead in East Transjordan to recognize his rule. Once he managed to eliminate the Philistines, he turned against Edôm and Moab. However, the war against the Ammonites proved to be difficult for him since they were supported by Aram, which he managed to defeat and thereby gain control over both Via Maris and Via Regis, the highways which connected Egypt with Mesopotamia through Palestine and Syria.

When King David (993–965 BC) conquered Edom, he turned it into a province ruled by an Israelite governor. This conquest set the Arnôn line as the border between Moab and Israel. The plane of Moab was annexed to the Kingdom of Israel. The defeat of the Ammonites and the Edomites solidified the Israelite hold on Gilead and Ammôn became subservient to King David. It is not clear how David dealt with Ammôn. It is hard to believe that he crowned himself king of Ammôn since the Biblical account (Samuel I, 11, 1) tells us that certain Shovi who was probably the son of Naḥash King of Ammôn, welcomed David who fled from his son Absalom to Machanayim. It seems plausible that David left a measure of self-government to the Ammonites, while solidifying the ties between Jerusalem and Rabat Ammôn. King Solomon's marriage to Na'ama, the Ammonite mother of Rehoboam, is a testimony to this tie. David's wars against the Ammonites who were allies of the Aramaeans caused conflicts between Israel and Aram, which David managed to control. The borders between Israel and Ammôn did not change significantly during the monarchial age. The Kingdom of Ammôn centered around Rabat Ammôn whose kings aspired to expand their borders in Gilead and thereby clashed with Israel.

After the division of the Israelite Kingdom into Israel and Judah (926–922 BC) both attempted to control the Eastern Jordan. It is not clear why Jeroboam King of Israel (928–907 BC) abandoned Shechem and transferred the capital of his kingdom to Penuel in Eastern Jordan (Kings I, 12, 25), and then to Tirzah in northern Tell al-Far'a (Kings I, 14, 17). Apparently, he recognized the importance of this strategic region in preventing the marauders from the desert from infiltrating his newly established kingdom, and he sought to bolster its position vis-a-vis the Kingdom of Judah in the south.

Jeroboam's successors remained concerned about the developments in that region. Omri King of Israel (882–871 BC) transferred the capital from Tirzah to Shomron. He established new settlements in the western side of Mount Shomron such as Khirbet Jama'in east of Qalqilya. Mesha's stele tells us that Omri inherited Madaba, north of the Arnôn, and even managed to subjugate Moab. Omri's achievements were largely due to the normalization in the relations between the two Hebrew Kingdoms, and the fact that Israel managed to conclude a peace with Sidon. We also hear about the victories of Ahab King of Israel (873–852 BC) in that region. Following his victory over Aram, Ahab took steps to strengthen his kingdom's hold on Moab. He built several fortresses such as Yaḥatz, and thereby secured the connection between his kingdom and the plane of Moab, and fortified Jericho, which controlled the Jordan River Valley. However, the Syrian threat prevented him from dominating Moab. It seems that by the time Ahab died, Mesha took control of the entire plane, and reached as far as Nebo north of Madaba. Likewise, the joint campaign of Jehoram son of Ahab (852–842 BC) and Jehoshaphat King of Judah (870–846 BC) against Mesha failed (Kings I, 3, 4–27). After further campaigns, Jehoshaphat managed to overcome the Moabites, the Ammonite, the Philistines, and the Arab tribes. His control over Edom enabled him to secure the southern borders of Judah. Gradually, the Kingdom of Judah began to adopt a firm policy toward that region. We hear of King Amaziah of Judah (798–769 BC) introducing reforms in the army and waging war against Edôm. He managed to defeat the Edomites in Salt Valley north of Araba, and then conquered the "Rock," which was probably Salah, south of La-Tafilah (Kings II, 14, 7). Moreover, he settled some of Judah's inhabitants in that location which he renamed Yakt'el.

According to the Biblical account, Jeroboam, son of Joash, King of Israel (789–748 BC), prevailed over the Arameans and expanded his kingdom to such an extent that the entire East Jordan was in Israel's hands. By the eighth century BC, the Kingdom of Israel began imploding due to frequent coups. It was at that time that King Retzin of Aram-Damascus who sought to dominate the land of Israel by helping Pekaḥ ben Remaliahu (the claimant to the crown in the Kingdom of Israel) came from Gilead to dominate Shomron (Samaria) in the Kingdom of Israel. Likewise, Rezin tried to crown a certain Ben-Tabeal from East Jordan in Judah. By doing so, Rezin hoped that the kings of Israel and Judah would become subservient to him.

During the campaigns of Tiglath-Pileser III King of Assyria (745–727 BC), Transjordan was conquered and its Israelite population was exiled. The provinces that were established in the region, according to the stele of King Sargon II, included those of the Phoenician coast and Transjordan, which paid a tribute to Assyria. The Biblical account tells us that King Uzziah of Judah (758–743 BC) continued the policy of expansion and that his son Jotham (750–735 BC) defeated the Ammonites and exacted heavy tribute from them (Chronicles II, 27:5). We do not know whether this was done in collusion with King Jeroboam II of Israel (786–746 BC) but there is a reason to believe that such was the case.[20]

Assyrian rule brought prosperity to the peoples of Transjordan by providing them defense against the nomads. Auxiliary forces were stationed along the borders and in the main cities in Edôm, Moab's and Ammôn. One of the inscriptions of Assyria's King Ashurbanipal (685–627 BC) mentions a delegation of the king of Moab who was a loyal vassal of the king of Assyria and who managed to repel repeated attacks by Amalek King of Kadar.[21]

The Bible tells us that when the Neo Babylonians destroyed the First Temple of Judah in 586 BC, the Edomites were the first to take advantage of the situation, and they invaded the southern parts of the country. We learn from the scriptures that the kingdoms in Transjordan made efforts to limit the expansion of the Israelites. At that time, Edôm extended from River Zered to the Red Sea, and it bordered the eastern desert (Kings I, 9, 26). Its main cities were Taiman, Boṣra, and Sellah. Edôm had numerous grazing grounds and its inhabitants maintained pastoral way of life. Araba with its plentiful minerals, its metallurgic industry, the roads that went through it, and the port of Eilat was vital for the Edomites and their prosperity, but they constituted a serious bone of contention with the Israelites.

The plane of Moab that extended from the Arnôn River to the desert in Jericho's vicinity became a bone of contention between the Israelites and the Moabites. The boundary between the two countries moved southward toward the Arnôn River, or northward toward Madaba and Nebo. The archaeological evidence shows that there were numerous settlements in Moab that survived between the thirteenth and the sixth centuries BC. Moab's royal court was in Kīr Ḥaroshet known also as Kīr Moab (Kings II, 3, 25), or al-Karak and it was located south of the Arnôn. According to the Biblical account the Moabites were pushed out of the region north of the Arnon by Siḥon King of Ḥeshbon, and the Israelites took the district from them, but even after this conquest several Moabite enclaves remained. This course of events demonstrates that the Moabites did not give up their attempts to control the area north of Arnôn and that it continued to be contested by both sides. The stele of Mesha in Divôn describes one of the wars that took place between Moab and the Israelites in that region. Another kingdom, which began its rise at that time, was that of the Nabateans who acted as middlemen in the trade between southern Arabia and Syria. The smooth trade depended on the Nabateans and there can be little doubt that it passed northward into Transjordan and then the west across Araba to Gaza and El Arish.[22]

During the Persian period, we hear about the "states" of Shomrôn, Judah, Ashdôd, and Edôm in the west, and Ammôn and Moab in Transjordan. An indication that the northern part of Transjordan was divided into administrative provinces can be found in the Bible (Ezekiel 7, 8) but some scholars believe that these were already formed by the Babylonians. Little is known about Transjordan during the period; however, from a survey taken in the 1940s, it becomes evident that the kingdoms in that region were destroyed in the sixth century BC and that their resettlement began much later. Ammonite graves were discovered in Mekablin date from that time. Archaeological excavations in Hebron, Boṣra, and the discovery of a cemetery in Tell-Mazar provide some knowledge about the region during the Persian period. The fortress and the settlements discovered in Tell-Sa'diyeh are similar to those found in Beit Sh'an Valley and cannot be regarded as typical Jordanian types.

Ammonite graves found in Rabat Ammôn reveal that the city thrived until the sixth century BC. Josephus Flavius tells us that the Babylonian King Nebuchadnezzar fought against the Ammonites and the Moabites in 582 BC and defeated them. It is plausible that both Ammôn and Moab became Babylonian provinces. The books of Ezra and Nehemiah mention both Ammôn and Moab as Persian provinces. The Book of Nehemiah mentions Tobias the "Ammonite slave" (3;19, 4;1 and 6;1) and the term *slave* is usually interpreted as "the king's slave," or an employee of the Persian king. We know that Jews resided in the western part of Ammôn, and in Gilead as well however, it is not clear whether these Jewish settlements were rebuilt during the Persian period, or whether those Jews who did not leave after the destruction of the First Temple constituted the nucleus, which allowed the community to survive.

The Hellenistic period

During the Hellenistic period, Transjordan was inhabited by the Nabateans. Historians regard the Nabateans as the precursors of the inhabitants of present-day Kingdom of Jordan and those who shaped its national Arab identity.[23] By the end of the fourth century, Alexander the Great established three military settlements in Transjordan; one in Nablus, one in Bayt Ras (Capitolius) in the north, and one in Jarash. Following his death, the region was contested by his successors, the Seleucids who controlled Syria, and the Ptolemies who ruled Egypt. The latter were the ones who gained control of Palestine, the Phoenician towns on the Mediterranean coast, and Transjordan.

In addition to the old towns that were expanded during the Hellenistic period, there were forts and towers built in strategic locations to protect that region from the desert nomads. A round tower was built in one of these cities, probably by Perdicas, one of Alexander's successors, and it can be traced back to the Ptolemaic period. The upper part of each city (*acropolis*) was refortified in the Seleucid age by walls defended by square towers. These cities were founded as Hellenistic fortress and expanded thereafter. Archaeological findings show evidence of Seleucid rituals and numerous coins, both Seleucid and Ptolemaic. The most common among the Ptolemaic coins were those of Ptolemy II Philadelphus (309–264 BC) and Ptolemy III Euergetes (246–222 BC). Among the coins of the Seleucid period, the most common were those of Antiochus III (241–187 BC) and Antiochus IV (215–164 BC). The ceramic objects found in Samaria were similar to the ones discovered in other cities of that period. Numerous utensils were imported from other Greek cities. Other items discovered were fragments of statues such as the bronze-made one of Heracles, and a terracotta athlete leaning on his right foot.[24]

Among the Hellenistic cities of Transjordan was Gadara, which became famous due to the outstanding figures that originated from it. Situated south of the Yarmouk in a place known as Umm Qais the city had hot water springs that became famous already in antiquity. Gadara was conquered in 218 BC during the Fourth Syrian War. The Greek historian Polybius (200–118 BC) tells us that Gadara was quite formidable among the cities in the region. We learn from Stephanus of Byzantium, the sixth-century author of the geographical dictionary *Ethnica* that profound changes occurred in that city, and that it had a Seleucid name. Gadara's resilience manifested itself clearly during the days of King of Judaea Alexander Jannaeus (103–76 BC) when it managed to withstand a ten-month siege.

Northeast of Gadara was Abila, which was one of the cities jointly known as the Decapolis. Abila was situated on two hills, Tell Abil in the north and Tel Umm-al-Ammad in the south. The city was famous for its wines. It was conquered by the Seleucid King Antiochus III in 218 BC. He conquered the city before reaching Gadara and managed to overcome a Ptolemaic army that came to its rescue. Abila was conquered again in the Fifth Syrian War (202–200 BC). During the Seleucid period, Abila's name was changed to Seleucia and its citizens became the "Seleucids of Abila," according to coins from the Roman period that were found at that site. Even though the city was quite important strategically, it had little cultural impact on the Hellenistic and Roman periods. Another city of the Decapolis was Dion. Like Gwerasa (Jarash) or Pella, Dion one of the cities founded during Alexander's reign or his successors, and it was essentially Macedonian. The city's location is still unknown, but archaeologists believe that it is Tell al-Ash'ari located south of Nahr al-Ihrayr.

Close to Dion, Pella was the second city in Transjordan that had a Macedonian name. It is clear, however, that the city's name had an ancient eastern origin known as Pechel that appears in the Egyptian hieroglyphics of the eighteenth and nineteenth dynasties, and that by the Hellenistic period it was renamed after the famous Macedonian city. The city's name was preserved in Khirbet Faḥl, about 12 kilometers east of the Jordan River, southeast of Beit Sh'an and the name is familiar from Talmudic sources (Talmud Yerushalmi, Shvi'it, 36, 73). During the middle-late Bronze Age, the city functioned as a 'gateway' community or a corridor through which essential and exotic goods passed from other autonomous communities in the eastern Mediterranean to the interior regions of the west.[25] The main archaeological findings of that city such as a temple, a theater-like building, a road with columns, and a nymph temple are mainly from the Roman period but the handles of the Rhodian jars belong the Hellenistic period. In all likelihood, there was a Macedonian settlement at the beginning that warrants the name Pella. The Greco-Macedonian character of that city becomes clear when one takes into account the negative response of Pella's inhabitants to Alexander Janneus' proposal to convert to Judaism.

The book *Maccabi I* gives the impression that there was a total war between the Jews and the peoples of Transjordan. It states that "the sons of Ammôn" and "the peoples in Gilead" rose against the Jews to liquidate them. However, a close look at the identity of those enemies of the Jews undermines this assumption; the sons of Ammôn could not have been the enemies of the Jews because there were no such people at that period. Thymotius who was the main figure in the wars of Transjordan and who is said to have led these enemies against the Jews was probably a Seleucid officer.[26]

There are about 500 archeological locations between Aqaba and Madaba the remains of which show that there were Nabatean towns and villages in that region.[27] That Petra was considered valuable becomes clear from a letter sent by the

Seleucid Antiochus I (324–261 BC) to his general (*strategos*) Meleagrus ordering him to provide a land gift to Aristodicides of Issus. It reads in part, "Thus you will make an inquiry as to whether Petra has not been given to someone else." As it turned out "Petra and the adjacent territory had already been given to Athenaeus,"[28] In his description of the campaign that Demetrius, a lieutenant of Antigonus, the One-Eyed who was one of Alexander's satraps (382–310 BC), launched against the Nabateans from Idumea, the Greek historian Diodorus of Sicily (60–30 BC) author of *Library of World History*, writes:

> While there are many Arabian tribes who use the desert as pasture, the Nabateans far surpass the others in wealth…; for not only few of them are accustomed to bring down to the sea frankincense and myrrh and the most valuable kinds of spices, which they procure from those who convey them from what is called Arabia Felix.[29]

The Nabatean Kingdom was also a military power that could not easily be defeated. In his study of Nabatean military power, Salah bin Ibrahim bin Saleh al-Daghim writes:

> In the description of the of the campaigns, which the Nabatean army embarked upon, and which were repeated in several ancient literary sources, the military power of the Nabateans was effective and influential on the battlefields ever since their written history commenced. These sources add, that their army constituted a powerful force capable of withstanding extreme hardships, and that it was difficult to defeat it in the battlefields, and in fact none of the great powers of that time such as the Assyrians, the Persians or the Macedonians were capable of subduing them or ruling over them.[30]

Antigonus became engaged in a fight with the Nabateans. Three confrontations between him and the Nabateans followed, and his son Demetrius led an army that managed to inflict a crushing defeat on them. Antigonus was interested in the Dead Sea region, which had many sites containing bitumen, which was highly prized in the ancient world. However, the Nabateans defeated him and offered his son Demetrius who commanded the army a tribute, if he agreed to withdraw his army. He agreed and the hostilities came to an end. Clearly, the Nabateans were not tributaries even though they presented gifts to the Persian authorities. The author of *Persian History*, Heraclides of Cumae (500 BC) referred to one Nabatean king saying that he was "independent and subject to nobody".[31] By the end of the second century BC, the coalition of cities known as Decapolis was established in the region, which extended from northern Transjordan to Damascus. These cities, according to Pliny the Younger were Skitopolis (Beisan), Pella (Fiḥl), Gadara (Umm Qays), Habbus (al-Hasan), Diyum (Edôm), Kanatha (al-Qanawat), Philadelphia (Amman), and Ghraza (Jarash). It seems that Damascus joined the alliance in addition to Capitolis (Bayt Ras) and Arbela (Irbid).

Moab was a Babylonian province that withstood Arab attacks, which continued during the Persian periods. As for Edôm, it seems that this country was destroyed by Arabs, Sons of Kedar. There is little archaeological evidence, but we know that by the beginning of the Hellenistic period, the Sons of Kedar were repulsed by the Nabateans who turned Edôm into their center and headquarters.[32] In 93 BC, the Nabatean King Obodas (96–85 BC) defeated the Hasmonean King of Judaea Alexander Jannaeus (103–76 BC) at the city of Gadara near the Golan. According to Flavius, domestic pressures forced Jannaeus to give up his conquests in Transjordan. He surrendered the territories which he had conquered in Moab and Galaditis, and the strongholds there "in order that he might not aid the Jews in the war against him."[33]

Transjordan under Roman rule

The Nabatean Kingdom managed to maintain its independence by paying tribute to Rome. Flavius tells us how King Aretas III (87–62 BC) deemed it prudent to pay the Roman commander three hundred talents, to prevent him from marching on Petra.[34] The Jewish kings of the Hasmonean dynasty had control over portions of Transjordan. John Hyrcanus I (135–104 BC) and his two sons, Judah Aristobolus (104–103 BC) and Alexander Jannaeus (103–76 BC), expanded their kingdom eastward. Hyrcanus I took Madaba and Esbus (Ḥeshbon) across the Jordan River and captured Idumea. Alexander Janneus captured Hippos (Sussita), Gadara (Umm Qais), Abila (Qalibah), Dium, Pella (Fiḥl), Tel Ammata, Gerasa (Jarash), and Gedor (Ain Jedur). Only Philadelphia (Amman) remained independent.[35] There were incessant raids across the Nabataean borders and Aretas was defeated by Alexander Jannaeus.[36]

The conflict persisted when Alexander Jannaeus' sons, Hyrcanus and Aristobulus fought over the throne after the death of their mother Alexandra Salome in 67 BC. It was precisely at the moment when it seemed that Aristobolus was about to move against his brother and depose him that Antipater the Idumean appeared at the scene, and persuaded Hyrcanus to called upon the Nabatean king for help. Supported by Arab troops Hyrcanus managed to defeat his brother Aristobolus. The Roman legate Marcus Aemilius Scaurus who arrived at the scene from Damascus decided, after receiving substantial bribe, that Aristobolus should be crowned king. However, Antipater took the case to the Roman general Gnaeus Pompey who was in Damascus at that time. Upon hearing the case, Pompey decided in favor of Hyrcanus and went in person to dislodge Aristobolus from his position.[37] The tension persisted during King Herod' reign (33–4 BC). In his *Antiquities of the Jews*, Flavius describes how robbers found refuge in this land, saying that Herod was forced to pursue them by attacking the kingdom.[38]

At that time, Judah east of the Jordan River encompassed Livias in the eastern Jordan Valley and Klirohi, in Moab. It is difficult to determine the exact border that separated Palestine and Arabia. This is largely because the geographer Ptolemy (100–170 AD) anachronistically lumps together many cities such as those of the Decapolis of Coele-Syria, and some that were part of Palestine such as Hippos

(Sussita). Herod who sought to increase the size of his kingdom was engaged in a battle with the Nabatean general Elthemos in Philadelphia's vicinity. Although Herod managed to inflict a major defeat on the Nabateans, this triumph had no significant consequences for the region's future due to the changes that took place in the east in the wake of Octavian's victory over his rivals Mark Anthony and Queen Cleopatra VII of Egypt at the Battle of Actium (31 BC). Realizing that it was more beneficial to have Octavian on their side, both Herod and the Nabatean King Malichus I (59–30 BC) took steps to ingratiate themselves with him. This meant that the entire region was at the mercy of the young general who was about to become the Roman Emperor, and that the inhabitants of the territories on both sides of the Jordan River had to confront Roman governors.[39]

During the Augustan period, the Nabatean Kingdom flourished under King Aretas IV (9 BC–40 AD) who became Rome's client. In order to prevent Rome from taking over Transjordan, he built fortifications along the border in places like Jawf and Mada'in Salih. According to Pliny, the Younger, when the Roman Emperor's grandson Gaius Caesar was sent to the Arabian Peninsula, he turned back at Aqaba.[40] Following King Herod's death, his kingdom was divided. Philip the Tetrarch ruled the area north of the Yarmouk, which included Jabal Druze, Leja, and Ḥawran in which the Nabatean culture continued to prevail. Another battle took place in Gamala, north of the Yarmouk sometime after 27 AD when Herod Antipas fell in love with Herodia who was his niece and the wife of Philip the Tetrarch. Seeking to recover Gamala, Philip expelled the bride who happened to be the daughter of Aretas who invaded that town.

Flavius' account is not very clear on that point; however, one can assume that Aretas moved through the Yarmouk into Philip's territory, with a view to control the Golan and the regions east of it and thereby threatened Herod's territory. After Herod's defeat, Emperor Tiberius (14–37 AD) sent his general Vitellius and the region that included Jabal Druze, Leja, and Ḥawran were incorporated into the province of Syria.[41]

The Nabatean state that served as a buffer between Judah, which constituted the south-eastern border of the Roman Empire, and the desert tribes which posed a threat to the southern frontiers of the Roman Empire, became extremely valuable in the eyes of the emperors. Upon the death of last Nabatean King Rabbel II (70–106 AD), Emperor Trajan annexed his kingdom to the Roman Empire (106 AD). The annexation was carried out by Syria's governor Cornelius Palma and as far as we know, without resistance from the local population.[42] The first capital of the annexed kingdom was Petra but later it moved to Boṣra. The importance of the new capital stemmed from its location on the trade route, which Trajan established during the years 111–115 AD along the Transjordan Plateau. This route, which became known as Via Traiana, or Via Traiana Nova started on the Red Sea coast and ended in Damascus. Boṣra was also the home of the Rome's Third Cyrenaica Legion.[43]

There is no consensus among historians regarding the exact borders of the Roman Arabia province. It is clear however, that cities such as Philadelphia (Amman), Gerash (Jarash), Moab, Madaba, and Ḥeshbôn occupied the central Transjordan

Plateau. At the same time, Palestine encompassed the Jordan Valley, the western parts of the Golan, Gilead, and Moab. Arabia Petraea, which was named after its capital Petra, extended over the central and eastern parts of Transjordan, all the way to the desert. Its capital Boṣra was at the northeastern part of the Bashan. Its boundary in the south was Eilat and the Red Sea. It included the entire Mount Edôm region, Petra, central and southern parts of the Sinai, and the Faran village.[44] Following the Roman conquest, the major cities of Roman Arabia were Boṣra, Petra, Characmoba, and Rabbathmoba. It seems that the golden era of Hegra (Mada'in Salih) was already over and based on the assumption that Philadelphia (Amman) had a special exemption from Roman interference due to its membership in Coele Syria district,[45] it was quite prominent city at that time. There were some cities, which appear to have been important in the eyes of the Romans in Transjordan. For example, we learn from the Roman historian Ammianus Marcellinus (330–395 AD) that the family of a certain Jewess named Babatha moved during the Bar Kokhba rebellion (132 AD) from Zoar in the southern part of the Dead Sea, to Ein-Geddi and the fertile Lisan that were subject to the Roman magistrate of Arabia. Apparently, she fled together with her family and died in the caves of the Judean desert.[46]

The boundaries of Transjordan continued to be in a state of flux and they were altered by successive Roman emperors who sought to provide greater security to the empire. Fundamental changes in Arabia's boundaries occurred during the reign of Emperor Diocletian (284–305 AD). That province, which until then expanded all the way to the Bashan and Jabal Druze, lost much of its territory. Mount Edôm, the Negev, and the central and the southern parts of the Sinai were incorporated into the province of Palestine. The boundary between the two provinces was the Zered River. The city known as Tzoar, which was situated at the mouth of that river at the southeastern side the Dead Sea was also incorporated into Palestine.[47]

The southern part of Transjordan bordered on the Negev and the Sinai deserts. This border was designed with a view to reduce the power and the responsibilities of the provincial governors but it resulted in the enlargement of Palestine. This step was accompanied by the transfer of the Tenth Legion southwards. The new arrangement led to a division of responsibilities between the two provinces of Arabia and Palestine. The military commander of Arabia who had at his disposal the Third Cyrenaica Legion that was stationed in Boṣra, and at a certain period the Fourth Legion in Beitoro (apparently Ajlun), was in charge of the Syrian desert frontier in the northeast, and the military commander of Palestine was in charge of protecting the southeast region. The decision to transfer the southern parts from Arabia to Palestine was apparently meant to prevent concentration of excessive power in the hands of one general.[48]

Among the cities of Arabia mentioned by the Roman historian and Christian publicist Eusebius (363–339) in his book *Onomasticon* (On the Place Names in the Holy Scriptures) are Boṣra the capital in the vicinity of Jabal Druze in Trachon, Neveh Vaadraa (Edre'i) in the Bashan, Avila (Evel), Gerasa (Jarash), Philadelphia (Rabat Ammôn) at the Transjordan Plateau, Esbos (Ḥeshbôn), Madaba, and Arioplois (Rabat Moab) in Moab. Arabia's western border with Palestine passed through the Transjordan Plateau above the crests that descend to the valley. That valley and the cities around it became known as Transjordan (Ferrea) and it was part of Palestine. Among the settlements of that region were Hippos (Sussita), Gadara, Pella (Pahal), and Yavesh-Gilead. The easternmost point of Palestine's border in the Transjordan Plateau was Be'ezer-Ye'ezer, situated about ten miles west of Philadelphia (Rabat Ammôn).[49]

In his book *Geography*, the Roman scholar Claudius Ptolemaus (90–170 AD) makes a distinction between Judah west of the Jordan River, which encompassed Shomrôn, Galilee, Skitopolis (Beit Sh'an), and the cities of Arabia such as Philadelphia, Gerasa (Jarash), Damascus and Avila de Lisianias. The fact that Ptolemaus mentions Gerasa together with Krak Moab, Madaba, Ḥeshbon, and other places demonstrates that the Roman province of Arabia occupied the center of the Transjordan Plateau, and that Palestine included the Jordan Valley and the western part of the Golan, Gilead, and Moab. In these areas, there was a large Jewish community since the time of the Second Temple (516 BC–70 AD) and they became known as part of the province of Judah (Jewish Transjordan, or the Ferrea).

Arabia Petrae expanded from the central and eastern part of Transjordan to the desert. Its capital Boṣra was situated on the northeastern part of the Bashan province. In the south, its boundary extended to Eilat or Elena, as Ptolemaus called it, and the Red Sea, including the Edôm Mountain and Petra. In addition, Arabia Petrae included the central and southern part of the Negev with the Farran village in southern Sinai. More cities emerged in Arabia during the second and third centuries. Among these were Ariopolis (Rabat Moab) Karkhmuba (Krak Moab), Esbos, and Philipolis at the Ḥawran. Units of the Roman Tenth Legion and other auxiliary forces were stationed in camps along the border, on the road leading from Eilat through the Transjordan Plateau to Syria. This was part of the system of Roman defense known as the *limes*.

In order to defend the frontiers of Via Trajana, the Romans built fortresses from Elana to Boṣra. This was a network of 20–25 posts some of which were fortified camps, which extended from Ma'an to Kastel at the border of Rabat Ammôn in the north. These fortified positions that were sometimes surrounded by walls were built in the Roman tradition. The best preserved among these *limes* were those of Odruh or Adroh, less than a three-hour camel ride from Petra, on the other side of the mountain range in the direction of Ma'an, probably build by Trajan prior to the annexation of the province to Rome. Odruh was known to have been a customs station, which brought handsome revenues to the empire.[50] The Palestinian part of the *limes* was called *Limes Palaestinae* and the Arabian part was called *limes arabicus*. This source of our knowledge regarding the location of the Tenth Legion comes from the *Onomasticon* as well as from the book *Notitia Dignitatum* (The Respected Position). This book tells us about the location of the Tenth Legion and the deployment of its units along the Transjordan Plateau, the Negev and some regions of Palestine all the way to the southern city of Eilat.[51]

In Roman times the province of Arabia consisted of the Nabataean Kingdom of Jordan that flourished at that time and whose capital was Petra. Included in this province, in addition to Transjordan, was the southern part of modern Syria, northwestern Saudi Arabia and the Sinai Peninsula. The province was annexed to the Roman Empire during Emperor Trajan (97–118 AD). Describing its unique nature, the eminent historian Theodor Mommsen writes,

> A peculiar civilization was developed from the mixture of national and Greek elements in these regions during the five hundred years between Trajan and Muhammad...In contrast to the customary repetition elsewhere usual of traditional forms there prevails here an architecture independently suiting the exigencies and the conditions, moderate in ornamentation, thoroughly sound and rational, and not destitute even of elegance. The burial-places, which are cut out in the rock-walls rising to the east and west of Petra and in their lateral valleys, with their façades of Doric or Corinthian pillars often placed in several tiers one above another, and their pyramids and propylaea reminding us of Egyptian Thebes, are not artistically pleasing, but imposing by their size and richness. Only a stirring life and a high prosperity could display such care for its dead.[52]

When the Roman Empire began disintegrating in the West, Transjordan remained chaotic. Paganism and superstition prevailed until the Arab conquest. Describing the state of affairs in the region during that time, the eminent historian Jacob Burckhardt writes:

> Aside from external danger because of plundering Saracens whose raids reached the very gates of Jerusalem, paganism persisted with desperate stubbornness in the vicinity of Arabia Petraea and in Coele-Syria; furthermore, daimonic activity, which had so long been native to Palestine, was as vigorous as ever. We have already seen St. Hilarion as an exorciser of daimones. Jerome himself takes us to the tombs of the prophets not far from Samaria, where a large number of possessed persons waited for relief; they could be heard at a distance, howling with the cries of various animals. These were the stray spirits who hovered over the battlefield of all religion, the land between the Jordan, the desert, and the sea.[53]

Following the transfer of the Roman capital to Constantinople the Christian population in the eastern part of the empire increased considerably in the Greek cities while the other cities remained relatively unaffected by the new faith. From the list of bishops who attended the Council of Nicaea in 325 AD, we learn that in these provinces, including Transjordan, there were Christian communities led by bishops. Apart from the cities of Palestine, this list includes Napolis (Shechem), Sebastia (Samaria), Jericho, and Gadara Capitolias (Beit Risha) in Transjordan. This constitutes a testimony to the fact that the expansion of Christianity was still limited to the Greek cities, and even in those cities the Christian communities were small.[54]

Figure 1.1 Petra, capital of the ancient Nabatean Kingdom.

Notes

1 Yūsuf Darwīsh Ghawānmah, Tarīkh Sharqi al-Urdun fi ʻasr Dawlat al-Mamālik al-Ullah, *Al-Qism al-Siyāsi* (History of East Jordan in the early Mamluk Period, the Political Part), Arabic text (ʻAmman: Wizārat al-Thaqāfah wa-al-Shabāb, 1979), pp. 37–38.
2 Frederick G. Peake, *History and Tribes of Jordan* (Coral Gables, FL: University of Miami Press, 1958), p. 1.
3 G. Lankester Harding, *The Antiquities of Jordan* (New York: Thomas Y. Crowell Company, 1959), p. 1.
4 Geograhie d'aboufida, *Abū al-Fidā, Kitāb Taqwīm al-Buldān* (Book of the countries' Evaluation), Arabic Text with title in French, edited by M. Reinaud and Mac Guckin de Slane (Paris: L'imprimerie Royale, 1840), p. 228.

5 *Historia shel Eretz Yisrael: mehatkufot ha-prehistoriyot ad sof ha-elef hasheni lifnei hasfira* (History of Israel: From the pre-historic periods until the end of the 2nd millennium B.C.), Hebrew text, Vol. I, Edited by Yisrael Ef'al. (Jerusalem: Keter, 1982), p. 14.
6 Denis Possot, *Le Voyage de la Terre Sainte*, 1532 (The Voyage to the Holy Land, 1532) French text (Paris: Ernest Leroux, 1890), p. 182.
7 John Lewis Burckhardt, *Travels in Syria and the Holy Land* (London: John Murray, 1822), p. 509.
8 Edward Robinson and Eli Smith, "Biblical Researches in Palestine and in the Adjacent Region," *A Journal of Travels in the Year 1838*, Vol. I (Boston, MA: Crocker and Brewster, 1874), pp. 537–538.
9 Maguelonne Toussait-Samat, *History of Food* (Malden, MA: Blackwell Publishing Ltd., 1992), p. 679. The Biblical reference to the gigantic bunch of grapes carried by the Emissaries reads as follows: "And they came unto the brook of Eshcol, and cut down from thence a branch with one cluster of grapes, and they bare it between tow upon a staff…the place was called the brook of Eshcol, because of the cluster of grapes which the children of Israel cut down from thence…" Numbers, 13; 23–24.
10 Fernand Braudel, *The Structures of Everyday Life: Civilization & Capitalism, 15th–18th Century*, Vol. I (New York: Harper & Row, 1979), p. 484.
11 Gail Simmons, "Jordan long before Petra," *Saudi Aramco World*, Vol. 65, No. 6 (November/December 2014), p. 8.
12 Ofer Bar-Yosef and Ram Gofnah, "Ertez Yisrael batkufa haprehistorit: hatkufa hapaleolitit, hatkufa the neolitit ve hatkufa the khalkolitit ad ha'elef harevi'i lifnei hasfirah," (Israel in the Prehistorical, Neolithic and Chalcolithic periods, until the fourth millennium B.C.), *Historia shel Eretz yisrael*, Vol. I, pp. 33, 82–87, 168–169.
13 Fernand Braudel, *The Mediterranean World in the Age of Philip II*, Vol. I (New York: Harper & Row, 1972), p. 316.
14 James A. Sauer, "Transjordan in the Bronze and Iron Age: A Critique of Glueck's Synthesis," *Bulletin of the American Schools of Oriental Research*, No. 263 (August 1986), pp. 18–19.
15 Khālid al-Hammūri, *Mamlakat al-Anbāṭ: Dirāsah fi al-aḥwāl al-Ijtima'iyya wa-al-Iqtiṣadiyya* (The Nabatean Kingdom: A Study in the Social and Economic Conditions), Arabic text (Al-Batrā': Bayt al-Anbāṭ, 2002), pp. 22–23.
16 Eveline J. Van Der Steen, "The Central East Jordan Valley in the Late Bronze and Early Iron Ages," *Bulletin of the American Schools of Oriental Research*, No. 302 (May 1996), p. 51.
17 Pioter Bienkowski and Eveline J. Van Der Steen, "Tribes, Trade, and Towns: A New Framework for the Late Iron Age in Southern Jordan and the Negev," *Bulletin of the American Schools of Oriental Research*, No. 323 (August 2001), pp. 21, 40.
18 Max Miller, "Ancient Moab: Still Largely Unknown," *The Biblical Archaeologist*, Vol. 60, No. 4 (December 1977), p. 200.
19 Moshe Kochavi, "Tekufat ha-Hitnachalut (mi-sof ha-meah ha-shlosh-esrei ad sof ha-meah ha-achat-esrei lifnei hasfirah," (Period of the Settlement, from the end of the thirteenth until the end of the eleventh century B.C.), Hebrew text, *History of Israel: Israel and Judah in the Biblical Period*, Vol. II, Edited by Yisrael Ef'al. (Jerusalem: Keter, 1984), pp. 69–71, 72, 73, 74, 75, 76, 77.
20 Hayim Tadmor, "The Period of the First Temple, the Babylonian Exile and the Restoration," *A History of the Jewish People*, Edited by Haim Hillel Ben Sasson (Cambridge, MA: Harvard University Press, 1994), p. 132.
21 Zvi Gal and Oded Bustanai, "Mamlakhot Yisrael ve-Yehudah 1020 bekeiruv, ad 586 lifnei Hasfirah," (The Kingdoms of Israel and Judah from about 1020 B.C. until 586 B.C.), Hebrew text, *Historia shel Eretz Israel*, Vol. II, pp. 116, 118, 119, 137, 141, 142, 143, 144, 150, 152, 153, 154, 158, 176, 193, 194, 195, 198, 199.

22 Glen Warren Bowersock, *Roman Arabia* (Cambridge, MA: Harvard University Press, 1983), p. 15.
23 Na'īf al-Nuwaisah, "Sikūlūjīyat al-Anbāṭ," (Psychology of the Nabateans), Arabic text, Min al-ma'ālim al-thaqāfīyah wa-al-ḥaḍāriyah fī-al-Urdun 'abra al-'usūr ('Ammān: al-Markaz al-Thaqāfi al-Malaki, 2002), Vol. I, p. 345.
24 Menachem Stern, "Eretz Yisrael batekufa ha-Helenistit (332–360 lifnei hasfirah)," (The Land of Israel in the Hellenistic period, 332–360 B.C.) Hebrew text. *Historia shel Eretz-*Yisrael: Hatekufa Ha-Helenistit u-medinat ha-Hasmonaïm (332–337 lifnei hasfirah), Vol. III (Jerusalem: Keter, 1981), pp. 79–80.
25 Bernard Knapp, "Complexity and Collapse in the North Jordan Valley: Archaeometry and Society in the Middle-Late Bronze Ages," *Israel Exploration Journal*, Vol. 39, No. 3/4 (1989), p. 145.
26 A. Rappaport, "Ha-'arīm ha-Helenistiyot be-Yehudah ve Eretz Yisraël bi-tkufāt ha-Ḥashmonaīm," (The Hellenistic cities in Judah and Israel during the Hasmonite period), Hebrew text, Doron: Meḥkarīm be-tarbūt klasīt: Essays in honor of Professor Benzioni *Katz* (Tel Aviv: Tel Aviv University, 1967), p. 221.
27 Yasmīn Zahrān, *Isada min tarīkh al-Urdun* (Echos from Jordan's history), Arabic text ('Ammān: Dar al-Kitāb, 1960), p. 59.
28 Cited in Pierre Briant, *From Cyrus to Alexander: A History of the Persian Empire* (Winona Lake, IN: Eisenbrauns, 2002), p. 414.
29 Cited *Ibid*, p. 717.
30 Sāleh bin Ibrahīm bin Sāleh al-Daghīm, *Al-tanẓimāt al-'askariyya al-Nabaṭiyya* (The Nabatean Military Reforms), Arabic text ('Ammān: Madrasat 'Abd al-Raḥmān al-Khayrīya, 2002), p. 49.
31 Cited in Briant, *Ibid.*
32 Ephraim Stern and Chaim Tadmor, "Shilton Paras (538–332) lifnei hasfirah," (Persian Rule, 538–332 B.C.), Hebrew text, *Historia shel Eretz Yisrael*, Vol. II, p. 231.
33 Cited in Bowersock, p. 24.
34 Josephus Flavius, *The Complete Works of Josephus: Antiquity of the Jews* (Grand Rapid, MI: Kregel Publications, 1981), p. 293.
35 Peter Richardson, *Herod: King of the Jews and Friend of the Romans* (Columbia: University of South Carolina Press, 1996), pp. 73–74.
36 René Grousset, *L'empire du Levant: histoire de la question d'orient* (Empire of the Levant: History of the Eastern Question), French text (Payot: Paris, 1979), p. 44.
37 Francis E. Peters, *The Harvest of Hellenism: A History of the Near East from Alexander the Great to the Triumph of Christianity* (New York: Simon and Schuster, 1970), pp. 295, 323.
38 Flavious, p. 350.
39 Bowersock, pp. 43–44.
40 *Ibid*, p. 58.
41 *Ibid*, pp. 65–66.
42 Yoram Ttsafrir, "Ha-provintziyot be-Eretz Yisrael--Shemot, Gevulot ve-Tekhumei min-hal," (The provinces in Israel--Names, boundaries and administrative divisions), Hebrew text, Eretz Israel: from the Destruction of the Second Temple to the Muslim Conquest, *Political, Social and Cultural History*, Vol. I, Edited by Z. Baras et al. (Jerusalem: Ben Zvi, 1982), p. 352.
43 *Ibid*, p. 352.
44 *Ibid*, p. 358.
45 Bowersock, p. 88.
46 *Ibid*, pp. 88–89.
47 Tsafrir, p. 361.
48 *Ibid*, p. 365.
49 *Ibid*, p. 362.

50 A. Kammerer, *Pétra et la Nabatène: L'Arabie Pétrée et les Arabes du Nord dans leurs rapports avec la Syrie et la Palestine jusqu'a l'Islam* (Petra and the Nabateans: Arabian Petra and the Arabs of the North, and their connection with Syria and Palestine until the rise of Islam), French text (Paris: Librairie Orientaliste Paul Geuthner, 1929), pp. 269–270.
51 Tasfrir, pp. 365–368.
52 Theodor Mommsen, *The Provinces of the Roman Empire: From Caesar to Diocletian*, Vol. II (Chicago, IL: ARES Publishers, 1909), pp. 156–157.
53 Jacob Burckhardt, *The Age of Constantine* (Garden City, New York: Doubleday, 1956), pp. 362–363.
54 Joseph Geiger, "hitpashtut ha-Natzrut be-Eretz Yisrael me-reshitah ad yemei Yulianus," (The Expansion of Christianity in Israel from its origins until the days of Julian), Hebrew text, *Eretz* Israel: from the Destruction, Vol. I, pp. 225–226.

II Jordan under Byzantine and Arab rule

Jordan under Byzantine rule

Following Emperor Trajan's conquest, the Nabatean city of Petra underwent a period of decline. However, it emerged once again as a prosperous city following fall of Rome in the West. Recent archaeological studies show that during the Byzantine era, the city achieved a remarkable state of prosperity due to its agricultural growth and the expansion of its commerce carried by the merchants of the caravans that crossed the desert and established markets where they sold their wares.[1] Prior to the Arab conquest, the region between the Jordan Valley and the Mediterranean that was controlled by the Byzantine Empire underwent a period of expansion and revival. This was due to the fact that the Byzantine and the Persian empires had weakened each other in the process of competition over that region. Consequently, the number and size of the settlements in the Jordan Valley increased significantly. For example, the fortified village of Herbat Masad, which was situated on the road between Jerusalem and the Mediterranean, at the altitude of 530 meters, reached its maximum level of density by the time that the Arab conquerors appeared. A similar level of expansion occurred in the same region, especially in Ramat Matred where there is evidence of continuous agricultural activity from the fifth to the twelfth century. At the same time however, the central Negev in southern Palestine was neglected and abandoned.[2]

From the description provided by the eminent historian Edward Gibbon, we learn that the region east of the Jordan River had a long tradition of prosperity. He writes:

> One of the fifteen provinces of Syria, the cultivated lands to the eastward of the Jordan, had been decorated by Roman vanity with the name *Arabia*, and first arms of the Saracens were justified by the semblance of a national right. The country was enriched by the various benefits of trade; by the vigilance of the emperors it was governed with a line of forts; and the populous cities of Gerasa, Philadelphia, and Bosra were secure, at least from a surprise, by the solid structure of their walls.[3]

DOI: 10.4324/9781003450313-3

The fortified city of Petra provided a formidable challenge for the Byzantines who captured it with great difficulty. Gibbon explained why it was so difficult for the Byzantines to take over city by saying,

> The siege of Petra, which the Roman general with the aid of the Lazi immediately undertook, is one of the most remarkable actions of the age. The city was seated on a craggy rock, which hung over the sea, and commanded by a steep and narrow path with the land.... Seven hundred had perished in the siege, two thousand three hundred survived to defend the breach. One thousand and seventy were destroyed with fire and sword in the last assault...
>
> The instant demolition of the works of Petra confessed the astonishment and apprehension of the conqueror.[4]

Byzantine sources throw light on the way that the Jordanian regions, cities, and villages were administered during the pre-Islamic period. In the provincial list *Laterculus Veronesis* from 312 to 314, we find two provinces called *Arabia*, one which was in all likelihood the northern part of *Arabia* province that was established by Trajan in 106 with its capital Boṣra. This province included Dion (Tell As'ari), Madaba (modern Madaba), Gerasa (Jarash), Philadelphia (Amman), and Esbos (Tell Ḥisban).[5] The other, *Item Arabia* encompassed the southern part of eastern Jordan, including Petra, Galilee, and parts of eastern Jordan such as Pella (Tabaqat Faḥl), Gadara (Umm Queis), Abila (Tell Abil), and Capitolia (Bayt al Ras).[6] It is possible that Petra was the capital of the southern province and that the Negev and some other areas were part of the *Arabia* province.

According to the sources, there were three provinces named *Palestina* and each encompassed Jordanian territories at one time or another. The first (*Palestina Prima*) was formed in 314. Its capital was Caesarea, and it included Samaria, Judea, and western Idumea.[7] The second (*Palestina Secunda*) comprised the southern parts of Jordan that were already incorporated into Palestine in the time of Constantine the Great (306–337) and its capital was Beit Sh'an (Skytopolis).

During Emperor Diocletian's reign (284–305), south Jordan, which constituted a part of the *Arabia* province, was incorporated into Palestine. This was part of an administrative change, which brought Mount Moab in Jordan, Zoar, the Negev Desert, and half of the Sinai Peninsula under the jurisdiction of what became *Palestina Salutaris*.[8] In the beginning, its capital was Khalutza and it was only in the beginning of the sixth century that it moved to Petra. It is possible that *Palestina Salutaris* turned into *Palaestina Tertia*.[9] *Palestina Tertia* encompassed southern Edumea, Nabatia, and Arabia. Running through these regions was Wadi Araba, which connected the Dead Sea with the Red Sea. This district was governed by *praeses* who probably ruled from Petra, and it comprised the following cities and regions: Augustopolis (Udruh), Arindela (Gharandel), Characmoba (Kerak), Areopolis (er-Rabba), Soar or Zoara, (Ghor es-Safi), Betthorus (probably Lajjun), Ayla (Aqaba), and Mamopsara (Boṣra).[10]

Ayla (Aqaba) appears in the list of bishops who attended the Council of Nicaea in 325.[11] A clear picture of the administrative division of these districts is nearly impossible to construct. It is obvious, however that the southern part of *Arabia* was already incorporated into Palestine at the time of the Council of Nicaea. Palestine remained a unified province until 358, when it was divided into two parts under governor Clematius who was sent by Emperor Constantius II to monitor the activities of the Persians along the border. This was part of a new drive by the emperor to provide efficient governors to this region.[12]

The sources that shed light on these developments are the letters of the rhetoric teacher Libanius of Antioch (314–393), the lists of the geographer Hierocles author of the *Synekdemos* (sixth century) and those of the ecumenical patriarch of Constantinople, George of Cyprus (1241–1290).[13]

During the fourth century the eastern provinces of the Byzantine Empire were controlled by civilian commissioners and military figures known as *duces*. An official known as *defensor* whose task was to defend the weak and the downtrodden was nominated in the cities. Gerasa (Jarash) was known to have had such official. We also hear about royal estates known as *saltus* in the northern parts of Jordan, in cities such Jericho and Livias (Julias), east of the Dead Sea.[14]

If one follows the account of the fifth-century ecclesiastic historian Salamanes Hermias Sozomenos (Sozomen), it is very likely that the remarkable Arab Queen Mavia, who ruled the semi nomadic Tanukhid tribes of southern Syria, managed to defeat the Romans in the second half of the fourth century, and reached the Transjordanian part of *Palestina Prima* where its boundaries met with those of Phoenicia.[15] In addition to this administrative division, the Byzantines divided the region into military commands. An official known as *Dux Palaestiniae* was in command of the troops stationed in Zadocatha (Khirbet es Sadaqa), Hawra (Khirbet al-Khaldeh), Veterocaria [Vetrocania], and Ayla (Aqaba).[16]

The sources tell us about a struggle, which took place over the Jotabe Island, which was apparently Jazirat Far'un, also known as the Corals Island in the Gulf of Eilat. Jotabe Island was a place through which goods from India passed and the levies imposed on them constituted a source of considerable income for those who ruled the island. According to the sophist Malchus of Philadelphia (fifth–sixth centuries) an Arab leader by the name of Amru Elkis or Amorkesos took control of the island. At first, he was a protégé of the Persians but then he changed sides and served the Byzantines. After taking control of the island, he expelled the Byzantine tax collectors and took the revenues for himself. In time, he managed to improve his relations with the Byzantines Emperor Leo I (440–461) who recognized him as leader of this island, and granted him the *phylarchia* of all the Arabs that inhabited Arabia Petraea.[17]

Jordan was not entirely neglected by the Byzantine authorities. Churches and monasteries were often beautified and repaired and we are told for example that after the suppression of the Samaritan rebellion Emperor Justinian (527–565) helped rebuild them, probably from tax levied in Palestine. The sixth-century historian Procopius attributed to Justinian the construction of numerous establishments such as hostels, cisterns, and pools. He is said to have built a church and a hostel in Jericho, reconstructed the walls of Bethlehem, and helped erect the walls of

Tiberias.[18] The sources tell us that Justinian suppressed the Samaritan rebellion in Mount Gerizim. According to Gibbon, "It has been computed that one hundred thousand Roman subjects were extirpated in the Samaritan war, which converted the once fruitful province into a desolate wilderness."[19]

In his *Life of Saint Saba*, Cyril of Scythopolis who lived in mid-sixth century mentions how the commanders (Dux) John and Theodore of Palestine were ordered in 529–530 to raise an army to attack the Samaritans, and how the latter crushed their rebellion.[20] In order to suppress the Samaritan rebellion of 529, the Byzantines used thousands of Arab prisoners whom they later sold in the markets of Persia and India.[21] According to Irfan Shahid, mercenary Ghassanid troops based in Jordan's vicinity prior to the Arab conquest were the ones who helped crush the Samaritan revolt of 529. John Haldon reminds us of a later tradition, saying that Byzantine and allied troops were stationed to the west of Jordan and the Dead Sea during the 630s, and that by the time of the Byzantine victory at Mu'ta (situated east of Araba, between Arindela, and Zoara) in 629, the Ghassanids and other tribes joined the Byzantine side. Naturally, the Arab conquerors exerted considerable efforts to detach these tribes from their Byzantine allies.[22] The Battle of Mu'ta is mentioned in *Chronographia* by Theophanes the Confessor, and in *Chronicla* of George Cedrenus. Theodore, Vicarius Cubicularius from *Palestina Tertia* is said to have participated in a battle where three Muslim emirs sent by Prophet Muhammad were killed.[23]

As the Arabs began proving their remarkable military ability, the Byzantines lost control over these allies. Even though the *Book of the Ceremonies* of Emperor Constantine VII Porphyrogennetos (908–913) mentions a certain lord of Arabia, saying "To the kyrios [lord], of blessed Arabia. A gold bull. Constantine and Romanos, faithful to Christ the Lord, Great autocrats and emperors of the Romans, to…[name] ruler of Arabia," there was no lord of Arabia in the tenth century comparable to the old Roman province of *Arabia Petrae*.[24]

Although the Byzantines had political and ecclesiastical organization in town such as Ayla (Eilat) and Ma'an, their real authority seems to have reached only as far as the most north-easterly regions of Palestine.[25] The Arabic sources tell us that the region bordering the eastern Mediterranean was divided into four *ajnād* or army-districts. These were from south to north, Filasṭin (Palestine), al-Urdun (Jordan), Dimashq (Damascus), and Ḥimṣ. According to Haldon, the *ajnād* bear little resemblance to the old Roman *themata* organized by Emperor Heraclius during 629–634 in order to provide better defense to the Byzantine Empire in the face of the Arab assaults.[26] The boundaries of these *ajnād* are not clear. According to the sources, the *jund* of al-Urdun was part of Dimashq on the desert side, and it included Boṣra and Amman before reaching the Filasṭin *jund*.[27] According to the description of the Iraqi historian al-Baladhuri (d. 892), the *jund* of Dimashq included the province of Arabia, with its capital Boṣra and Amman to the south.[28] In his *Kitab al-Buldan*, the tenth-century geographer Ibn al-Fakih al-Ḥamdani tells us that the *jund* of al-Urdun included the districts (*kurah*s) of Tabariyyah (Tiberius), as-Samirah (Samaria or Nablus), Beisan (Beit Sh'an), Fiḥl (Pella), Jarash, Akka (Acre), al-Kadas (Kadesh Naphthali) and Ṣur (Tyre).[29]

According to the early nine-century *Chronographia* of Theophanes who followed the Syriac chronicle of Theophilus of Edessa, some of the districts under the purview of the *duces* of Palestine and Arabia were referred to as "Jordan" during the early seventh century. A reference to "Jordan" is made also in the thirteenth-century chronicle of Michael the Syrian. Syriac sources also use the term "Jordan."[30] Of the four mentioned *ajnad* that of al-Urdun was the least similar to the administrative and military units formed by Emperor Heraclius (610–641).[31] The district of Jordan was later expanded to include north Samaria and Galilee in order to meet the security requirements of the time. Both areas had a population hostile to the Byzantines, and for a while, they supported the Persians but they surrendered peacefully to the Arabs during Heraclius' reign. The boundaries of the military districts of Jordan were determined primarily by the need to control a potentially hostile population. The fact that the Persians have encouraged the Jews to attack Acre and Tyre before the capture of Jerusalem in 614 and that these two ports were later incorporated by the Arabs into the *jund* al-Urdun demonstrates that strategic requirements were the main considerations which determined the boundaries of these military districts.[32]

Jordan in the age of Prophet Muhammad

Prophet Muhammad's advance northward from the Arabian Peninsula to the southern part of Greater Syria, which included the territories east and west of the Jordan River began shortly after the Hijra, when he and his followers left Mecca on their way to Medina in 622. Occasional raids were conducted where the Prophet's small contingents of converts invaded southern Syria and Wadi Sirḥan with a view to spread Islam, reconnoiter, and assess the military potential of the Byzantines, which he was about to meet in the battlefield. In addition, there were Bedouin tribes whose raids on the caravans that passed through Jordan on their way from Damascus to Mecca and Medina disrupted the Hejaz trade and caused economic hardships for the Muslims.

The first major campaign took place in the autumn of 626 when a Muslim force of a thousand men descended on Daumat al-Jandal (Jauf) in order to conquer the region, turn it into a base of operations for the imminent campaigns against the Byzantines, and convert its inhabitants. Little is known to us about the precise direction of this invasion but in all likelihood the Muslim expedition passed through Tabbuk and Hausa where the mosque known as Masjid Du al-Gifa was later built. However, the small size of the expedition and the paucity of its provisions compelled it to return to Medina without attacking Jauf. Muhammad's fear was that his force was too small to attack the al-Kirda tribe whose chief Akidir Ibn Abd al-Malik fought on behalf of the Ghassanid princes of Boṣra who relied on Byzantine help. Initially, the Ghassanids settled in the Jordan in the fourth century and the Byzantines chose them as allies but they did not prove capable of fighting Persian Sassanids. Yet the fact that they could count on Byzantine help deterred the Muslims. Another Muslim expedition followed in November 626 when 700 men under the command of Abdul Raḥman Ibn 'Auf advanced toward Jauf. Although this was just another minor campaign, it boosted the morale of the Muslims who managed to win converts from among the Bani Kalb tribe who inhabited the region.

Jordan's inhabitants were subjected to treatment similar to those in other regions that fell under Muslim rule. Christians and Jews (*dhimmi*s) who did not embrace the new faith were subject to the poll tax (*jizya*). The Arab conquerors established marital relationships with the local inhabitants and thereby created a wider base of support. Thus, for example, Abdul Raḥman Ibn 'Auf married Tomadhir, daughter of Isbagh Ibn Amr, chief of Bani Kalb who converted to Islam. The campaigns expanded deep into the region of present-day Jordan and the conversion process continued unabated.

In 627–628, Farwa Ibn 'Amr of the al-Judzam tribe who governed Ma'an on the Byzantines' behalf converted to Islam and was crucified by them as a result. In July 629 a group of fifteen Muslims who were sent to Dzat Atlah on the border of southern Transjordan to obtain information about the Byzantines was captured and killed. At the same time, Ḥarith Ibn Omeir who was on the Prophet's mission to meet the Ghassanid prince at Boṣra was killed by Shuraḥbil Ibn 'Amr, chief of the Mu'attā who resided south of Karak. Soon afterward, reports came from the north that Emperor Heraclius appeared in Karak where he made agreements with the local tribes of Bahra, Lakhm, Judzam, Billi, and Balqawiya.[33]

Seeking to avenge the death of a messenger that he sent and to assess the strength of the Byzantine forces, Muhammad sent another expedition of about 3,000 men to the Jordanian frontier, under Zayd Ibn Ḥaritha who died in the campaign as did J'afar Ibn Abu Ṭalib and Abdallah Ibn Ruwaha who succeeded him as commanders of the Muslim forces.

When Muḥammad heard that Ghassan called upon the tribesmen of Transjordan to help him recover Boṣra, which the Muslim army had already captured, he sent an expedition against him. The two armies faced each other at Mu'tta and Khalid Ibn al-Walid saved the day. In the campaign, which took place in 630. Muhammad's expeditionary force passed through Thamud on its way to Tabbuk, Daumat al-Jandal, and the Dead Sea district. The Muslims attempted to convert the Christians and Jews of Daumat al-Jandal and the Gulf of Aqaba as far north as Ma'an to Islam, promising them protection. However, the Muslims could hardly protect the new converts, given the fact that both Ghassan and the Byzantines were close by. The tribute collected was so irregular that Muhammad found it necessary to send another army to hold on to that region.[34]

When the first Arab invaders arrived in Ma'an, Heraclius who was in Balqa at that time gathered a large army of 100,000 men from Lakhm, Jaddham, Qayn, and other tribes. Hearing about this huge army, the Muslim commanders went to inform the Prophet, while Ibn Rawaḥa, one of his companions, encouraged the Muslims to stand and fight. The fighting took place in Mu'atta village in the Balqa region. This campaign ended in a Muslim victory and it opened the way to Greater Syria (*bilad al-Sham*). Since it was their first campaign against a great foreign power, it was crucial for the Muslims to win. The conquest led to the conversion of many of the region's inhabitants and it demonstrated the potency of Islam. Moreover, it had enormous impact on the tribes that fought alongside the Byzantines, and it encouraged the Muslim armies to continue moving northward.[35]Although the Muslims prevailed over their Byzantine enemies at the Battle of Mu'atta, it remained for Khalid ibn al-Walid to drive them out of Syria completely. The raids continued under Abu Ubaidah and Amr Ibn al-As who succeeded him and advanced toward the territory with 20,000 foot soldiers and 10,000 cavalry. This force started moving northward by the end of September 630.

When the danger of the Byzantine advance toward Hejaz subsided Muhammad accepted the submission of the Christians and the Jews in southern Transjordan and sent several expeditionary forces to control the conquered region. Khalid moved toward Daumat al-Jandal; Ḥamza Bin 'Abd al-Mutalib proceeded toward the Red Sea coast; Sa'd Ibn Abi Waqqās moved toward Al-Kharrar in the Jordan Valley and Abdallah Ibn Jaḥsh moved toward Nakhla, between Taif and Mecca. Muhammad concluded treaties with the Christians and the Jews of Jordan the most famous of which was with John Ibn Ruyah and the chiefs of Ayla (Aqaba), exhorting them to embrace Islam or pay tribute and threatening to punish them severely if they failed to comply. John complied and went to meet Muhammad. The treaty granted John and his followers freedom of movement in the territories conquered by the Muslims, and unrestricted their use of water resources. The annual tribute agreed upon was 300 golden dinars, a sum which was not increased during the reign of caliph Umar II (99–101). Muhammad made similar treaties with the Jewish villagers in Maqna, Udhrah, and al-Jarba who agreed to pay by coin, cattle, or by portion of their harvests.[36]

Khalid's next expedition fared better than the previous ones. A small contingent of 420 horsemen arrived in Jauf, an oasis 200 miles from Tabbuk, and prevailed over Akidir Ibn Abd al-Malik who was forced to pay tribute, which included 2,000 camels, 800 sheep, and 400 suits of mail and arms. Akidir who was brought before Muhammad embraced Islam and was allowed to return to Jauf. However, soon after the Prophet's death in May 632, he rose in rebellion in Jauf and made contacts with the Byzantines.

The Samaritans of Jordan

The Samaritans resided mostly in Mount Shomron in the West Bank. Their communities were scattered over several areas such al-Bira, close to Ramallah in the northern Judean mountains, and in Mount Carmel region. We hear about their conflict with the Jews in 535 BC when they built their Second Temple in Jerusalem. The Samaritans sought to take part in building the temple but they met stiff resistance. And when the spiritual leader Ezra the Scribe insisted that Jews who were married to Gentiles, including Samaritans, abandon their wives, the tension between the two communities reached its climax.

The Samaritans experienced persecution during Roman times. The persecution was particularly intense during the late Roman Empire, when they lent their support to the Roman candidate Pescenius and thereby alienated Septimius Severus (193–198). In retribution, Severus decided to deprive the city of Shkhem,

(Napolis or Nablus) of its rights and to promote its rival Sebastia (Shomron) whose population supported his candidacy. Further persecutions followed during the reigns of Decius (250–251) and Diocletian (286–305). Under Roman rule, the Samaritans continued to suffer persecution. From what we learn from Samaritan sources, their synagogues were destroyed and they were prevented from practicing their traditional customs such as circumcision. Like other pagans, the Samaritans were persecuted but the fact that some autonomic institutions such as the high priesthood continued to exist suggest that the description in the Samaritan sources is highly exaggerated.[37]

The resentment, which they had toward the Romans led the Samaritans to cooperate with the Jews of Palestine in the rebellion against governor Gallus, which took place in Antioch in 351 AD When Julian, known as 'The Apostate' became emperor (361–363) paganism was allowed and the Samaritans took part in the anti-Christian revolts. These revolts resulted in atrocities and considerable destruction of property. Priests were murdered, priestesses raped, churches burnt, and tombs of saints desecrated. These events are described in a legend recorded in the Samaritan chronicles regarding a certain Baba Raba, a Samaritan leader who rebelled against the authorities. According to the story, he was not defeated but "invited" with great honor to Constantinople where he was placed in "preventive custody."[38]

By the end of the fourth century, the Samaritans were persecuted again. Those who could not bear the persecution converted and some were integrated into the Byzantine administration and reached senior positions. Not only Christians accused the Samarians of false conversion but also their coreligionists such as the fourth century Amram Dara who complained about those who betrayed the faith in the face of persecution.[39] The fact that by the end of the Byzantine period, there were only a few Christian settlements shows that conversions were common mainly in the urban areas and in those outside Mount Samaria. The persecution of the Samaritans continued during the fifth and sixth centuries causing several rebellions. The first erupted in 484 when rumor spread that Emperor Zeno (474–475 and 476–491) intended to build a church on Mount Gerizim and banned ancient Samaritan rituals. Another rebellion erupted at about 495 when Emperor Anastasius was in power (491–518), and it was suppressed by the Byzantine army.

The sources tell us that when Emperor Justinian (527–565) sought to conclude a peace treaty with the king of Persia a Samaritan delegation had promised Palestine, including Jerusalem and 50,000 Jews to the king. Both Jews and Samaritans served in the Persian army and some of them fled to Persia during the great Samaritan rebellions.[40] Under Justinian, the conditions worsened and the persecution of the Samaritans is described by the Byzantine historian Procopius (500–565 as excessive. These resulted in further rebellions the most destructive among which occurred in 529 and in 556). Although the rebellions were a result of religious differences they had an agrarian aspect. Procopius tells us that the Samaritan peasants rebelled against their Christian landlords. The revolt, which began as a campaign to liberate Mount Gerizim, spread to other cities and villages. In the revolt of 484, the Samaritans rebelled in Caesarea, the capital of the province and the seat of the Byzantine governor in Palestine, and in the rebellion of 529, they took control of

Beit Sh'an, Ashkelon, and other regions, but the center of the rebellion was Mount Samaria, which bore the brunt of Byzantine reprisal.

Perhaps the Samaritans expected Persian help when they rebelled. However, the Byzantine army which was stationed in Jericho suppressed the rebellion and according to Procopius, Samaria turned into a heap of rubble. Samaritan resistance was considerably reduced after that time and there are no indications that they rose in rebellion during the Persian invasion of 614–617 nor during the Arab invasion in 637–640. Although some accounts talk about Samaritan resistance to the invading Arabs, the Samaritans tended to stay out of conflicts between Arabs and Christians despite their sympathy to the latter.[41]

Jordan under the rightly guided Caliphs

Prior to his death, Muhammad ordered his followers to assemble an army and to move against the Byzantine forces that were stationed in the ancient city Abil ez-Zeit in Jordan. However, it was not until Abu Bakr became the caliph in 632 that the campaign against the Byzantines began. Upon his rise to power, the caliph ordered one of his generals Osama Ibn Zayd to assemble an army at al-Jorf, outside Medina and move northward against the Byzantines but after reaching Yibna (Yavneh) in Palestine, the army was ordered to return to Medina to fight the rebels in that city. In 633, Abu Bakr ordered Khalid Ibn Sa'id to move northward where he faced the Byzantines who assembled an army at Zizya, in the Balqa region. The Muslims won in the first encounter but when a large Byzantine army advanced toward them, they suffered a crushing defeat. Then the caliph ordered the Muslim armies to move north. One of the armies commanded by Khalid Ibn al-Walid and al-Muthanna Ibn Ḥaritha was ordered to move northward to Mesopotamia, while the other under 'Iyad was ordered to capture Daumat al-Jandal and then move toward Mesopotamia. However, 'Iyaḍ who had to face several local enemies such as Akidir of al-Jauf, al-Jundi of Bani Kalb, Jabala prince of Boṣra, and the Ghassanid mercenaries was forced to call for help. Hearing about the attacks by these opponents, the caliph sent Khalid Ibn al-Walid who came and defeated them. The attacks in the north resumed soon afterward and the rebellions in Arabia were suppressed. On their way to the north, the Arab conquerors defeated their Byzantine enemies in Jordan. Describing the first encounter of the Arabs with the Byzantines in that region, Abd al-Muta'al al-Sa'idi writes,

> Khālid bin Sa'id advanced until he reached Qastel on the way to the Dead Sea, and he destroyed the Byzantine army on its eastern shore. He then moved forward until he encountered the Byzantines whose numbers far exceeded his own.... The Byzantine soldiers were led by one of the most skilled of their commanders who sought to bring Khalid bin Sa'id to expose the rear flank of his army in order to attack and defeat him....[but] Khalid bin Sa'id turned back, surrounded him, cut his line of retreat, and nothing was left of him other than [the fact] that he ran away with his comrades.[42]

Jordan was conquered at the onset of the Arab conquests and it was designed to enable the Arab conquerors to move further north with greater force. The illustrious general Amr Ibn al-As had the ambition to become the supreme commander of the Muslim forces but Abu Bakr denied him that post. Four armies formed in the spring of 633 to take control of Greater Syria. They were commanded by Abu Ubaidah Ibn Jarraḥ; Yazid Ibn Abi Sufyan; Shuraḥbil Ibn Ḥasanah, and Amr Ibn al-'As. Abu Bakr is said to have instructed his commanders to move northward in three directions. Amr Ibn al-As was ordered to move from Ayla (Aqaba) into southern Palestine through Gaza. The second column, under Yazid Ibn Abi Sufyan, was ordered to move from Tabbuk up to the eastern side of the Dead Sea, and Shuraḥbil Ibn Ḥasanah was told to move to Bosra and then to Damascus.[43] The supreme command was given to Abu Ubaidah Ibn Jarraḥ. Abu Bakr determined that each army would be in charge of one major region. Abu Ubaidah's army was in charge of Ḥims, Yazid's in charge of Damascus, Amr in charge of Palestine, and Shuraḥbil's in charge of Jordan. Abu Ubaidah departed with his army northward, passing through Wadi al-Qurrah, through Dath al-Manar, Zizya and then Ma'ab.[44] It was there that they encountered a Byzantine army, which they defeated and then gave amnesty to the people of Ma'ab. According to the eminent historian al-Ṭabari (838–923) this was the first truce, which the Arab conquerors concluded in Greater Syria. The next encounter with the Byzantines occurred shortly afterward. Yazid advanced toward Balqa, Abu Ubaidah moved toward Jabiyah, and Shuraḥbil toward Bosra. The Byzantines sent three thousand troops to Wadi 'Araba, south of the Dead Sea. This Byzantine force threatened the Arab armies that moved on the eastern route from Tabbuk to southern Damascus, 50 kilometers from al-Jabiyah. This Byzantine force was stationed behind the Arab armies and was in a position to sever the road leading from Medina and the Arabian Peninsula. There was another Byzantine force stationed in Bosra. The Battle of Wadi Araba erupted in a place called al-Ghamr. The Byzantines were defeated, and the Muslims pursued them to al-Dubbaya, 16 kilometers south of Rafaḥ. The Byzantines fled to Dathin and the Arabs pursued and defeated them and thus managed to conquer Gaza. It was the army of Abu Ubaidah that won that victory. The events that took place during that battle were described by Abu Amamah al-Bahali. He writes:

> I was with the force that Abu Bakr dispatched under Abi Ubaidah, and his group and the first battle took place at Araba and Dathnah that day. These were not the greatest days. Six Byzantine commanders advanced toward us, with five-hundred men each....
>
> Abi Ubaidah sent me with five-hundred men. Yazid's column followed us, and when we saw the Byzantines we defeated them and killed one of their commanders. They fled and we followed them.[45]

Jordan was exposed to invasions by tribes that migrated from southern Arabia before the rise of Islam. Among these were the Ghassanids whom Khalid Ibn al-Walid had to defeat at the Battle of Daumat al-Jandal in August 633 in order to protect Transjordan, which constituted the southern border region of Greater Syria. This battle was part of the *Riddah* campaigns, which the Rightly Guide Caliphs (*Rashidun*) waged against those who turned their back on Islam.[46] There is no consensus regarding the chronological order of the campaigns that took place in that region as the eminent historian Ibn Khaldun tells us. He writes:

> Al-Waqidi determined that the Yarmouk campaign took place in the fifteenth year (after the *hijra*), that in that year Heraclius moved from Antioch to Constantinople, and that the Yarmouk campaign was the last to take place. Sayf tells us that the Yarmouk campaign took place in the thirteenth year, that the message regarding the death of Abi Bakr arrived before the day that the Greeks fled, and that after the Yarmouk campaign the *amir*s proceeded to Damascus and conquered it. Then came the Fiḥl campaign, and then came other campaigns against the troops of Heraclius, and Allah knows.[47]

The campaigns are said to have been closely supervised by Abu Bakr who ordered the commanders to refrain from devastating the lands that they conquered. The Muslims armies benefited from the fact that Heraclius was in no position to pay the Ghassanid mercenaries and also from the weakness of the monarchs of the Sassanid dynasty of Persia. Moreover, the local populations who were fleeced by the Byzantines regarded the Muslim conquerors as saviors. The armies of Shurḥabil, Yazid and Abu Ubaidah moved from their base at Zizya in the Balqa region to Wadi Araba in order to clear the way for Amr Ibn al-As to move northward from Aqaba. In the battle which took place in the valley south of the Dead Sea, the Muslim armies dealt a crushing blow on the Byzantines and 3,000 of their soldiers fled. The three commanders returned to Balqa and captured Karak. This cleared the way for Amr Ibn al-Aṣ to move toward Gaza and then to Ain Ghamr in Wadi ‘Araba. There he awaited reinforcements, while Shuraḥbil and Abu Ubaidah remained in the Balqa region. Thus, Transjordan fell easily in the hands of the Arab conquerors. Undoubtedly, this can be attributed to the generous terms imposed by the conquerors.[48] Soon afterward, Khalid Ibn al-Walid joined the campaign with a force of 9,000 men that moved across the desert from Ain al-Tamr, close to Mesopotamia, to Qaraqir, either directly, or through Daumat al-Jandal and Wadi Sirḥan. From Qaraqir, he moved through the harsh and waterless desert in the east to Suwa, and then to the neighborhood of Damascus.

In the battle, which took place in Marj Raḥit in April 634. Khalid defeated a Ghassanid force and then proceeded to Thaniyat al-Okab where he could see Damascus but he refrained from attacking the city and moved to Bosra instead. There he met Yazid, Shuraḥbil, and Abu Ubaidah, and the four generals moved south to join ‘Amr Ibn al-As at Wadi ‘Araba. At Wadi Araba, the Muslim armies were faced with a new threat from the Byzantines when the emperor’s brother Theodorus moved his forces to Ajnadayn, near Ramla in Palestine in July 634. The battle ended with a victory for the Muslims and Theodorus fled to Ḥims where he met Heraclius.

Umar Ibn al-Khattab who became the next caliph after Abu Bakr in 634 continued the Arab expansion northward. Amr Ibn al-Aṣ remained in Palestine to complete its conquest while Khalid continued the conquest of Syria. He moved toward Beisan and forced the Byzantines to retreat to Fiḥl (Pella), a fortified town overlooking Transjordan. Khalid moved toward the town and captured it. This victory brought the Decapolis and al-Jaulan (Golan) under Muslim control. At that point, the road to Damascus was virtually opened to the Muslims, and in July 635 it fell into their hands.

When the commander in-chief Abu Ubaida Ibn al-Jarraḥ did not know whether to take over Damascus before conquering Fiḥl, he wrote to Caliph Umar who ordered him to conquer Damascus before Fiḥl because, as he put it, "it is the fortress of the Sham [Greater Syria) and the residence of their kingdom."[49] Baladhuri tells us that the Battle of Fiḥl in Jordan was one of the bloodiest of all Muslim campaigns. The battle occurred sometime in January 635. The commander-in-chief was Abu Ubaidah Ibn al-Jarraḥ. Describing the events in this battle Baladhuri writes:

> They [the Byzantines) met the Muslims at Fiḥl in Jordan, and the Muslims killed many of them until Allah made them prevail. Their patricians were killed along with and ten thousand men, the rest were distributed in the towns of Syria, and some of them joined Heraclius. The inhabitants of Fiḥl retired to the fortifications where they were besieged by the Moslems until they sought amnesty, agreeing to pay tax and *kharaj* on their lands.[50]

He added to his account saying,

> Shuraḥbil conquered all the towns and fortifications of Jordan, which, according to this agreement [surrendered], without bloodshed. He conquered Beisan, Susiyah, Afiq, Jarash, Bayt Ras, Qadas and al-Jaulan, and subdued the district of Jordan and all its land.[51]

Describing the conquest of that region, which opened Syria to the Arab conquerors Umar's biographer elaborated further saying,

> The Muslim forces advanced toward Sham-the western front-with a view to embark on a second campaign against the Roman forces. These forces advanced and crossed the Yarmouk until they reached Fiḥl where they camped and faced the Romans at Beisan....But as soon as the Romans attacked, the Muslims killed them...eighty thousand were killed and only few fled.[52]

Islamic sources seem to agree that the conquest of these lands was bloodless for the region's inhabitants.[53] Umar is said to have received a hearty welcome from the people of Adhri'at. Baladhuri tells us that one of the witnesses to that event, Abdallah Ibn Qays said,

> I was one of those who went with Abu-Ubaidah to meet Umar as he was coming to Syria. As 'Umar was passing he was met by the singers and tambourine players of the inhabitants of Adhri'at with swords and myrtle.[54]

The Battle of Yarmouk

When the Arab commanders saw that the Byzantines were facing them, they began debating what steps they needed to take next. After discussing the matter with Amr Ibn al-As, they wrote to Abu Bakr and assembled at Yarmouk. Abu Bakr confirmed what 'Amr told them, "Move forward with all the armies in the Muslim invasion. You are Allah's helpers…assemble at Yarmouk, with the necessary support and pray for each other."[55]

Khalid and Abu 'Ubaidah who already moved northward and captured Ḥims had to abandon Damascus and move southward to meet the Byzantine army which was commanded by Theodorus. The Byzantine army, which was estimated to have been between 100,000 and 200,000, moved toward the Yarmouk Valley. Recounting the Battle of Yarmouk, the sources state that 60,000 lightly armed troops of Ghassanids reinforced the army of the Byzantine commander.[56] The Ghassanids who guarded the Byzantine Empire in that front were crushed by the Arabs.[57] For years these Christian mercenaries were guarding this frontier and as Mark Whittow reminds us, they were as effective in pitched battles against the Persians as any of the Byzantine troops.[58] The combined Byzantine-Ghassanid army was camped at Deir Ayyub, on the north bank of the river while the Muslims occupied the southern bank, at Wadi Khalid. When the campaign began, Khalid bin al-Walid inflicted a crushing defeat on the Byzantine army, which suffered from dissensions among its ranks and whose Armenian soldiers were reluctant to continue fighting. One of the main Byzantines commanders, Baanes fled from the battlefield and the morale among the soldiers plummeted. The Arab armies continued their advance despite occasional resistance in the small towns and villages.

Following their victory at Ajnadayn in 634, the Muslims had high hopes that they could win the battle at Yarmouk. At the caliph's order, the Muslims armies advanced toward Yarmouk and the Byzantine army was led by Tidor. This was a convenient location in which an enemy could be trapped. The Muslims had 40,000–45,000 warriors under Khalid bin al-Walid. The Byzantines had 140,000. The Muslims arrived at Yarmouk and camped there while the Byzantines camped on the southern bank of the river. Khalid arranged his armies in a new fashion. He distributed them to divisions as follows: *firqat al-qalb* that consisted of 18 regiments under the command of Abi Ubaidah bin al-Jarraḥ, Ikrimah bin Abi Jahl, and al-Qa'qaa' bin Amr; *firqat al maymanah* that consisted of 10 regiments under the command of Amr ibn al-Aṣ and Shuraḥbil Ibn Ḥasanah; *firqat al-Maysarah* that consisted of 10 regiments under Yazid bin Abi Sufyan; *firqat al-talī'a* (*al-muqqadimah*) or front regiment, which consisted of cavalry and a small and mobile police force for intelligence-gathering and observation and; *firqat al-mu'akhirah* or rear regiment, which consisted of 5,000 warriors (five *kardus*) under Sa'id Ibn Zayd, and it was in charge of administrative matters. It had special personnel in charge of specific administrative matters. Every commander endeavored to encourage his troops to fight. They were all aware of the fact that Yarmouk was a decisive campaign, which they must win in order to conquer Syria.[59]

The Muslim commanders who sought to win the battle against the Byzantines understood all too well that the support of the local population, and especially the

Christians among them, was indispensable. They left the Christian Patriarchates in the hands of the Monophysites and granted freedom of worship to the Orthodox population. According to the Arab historian al-Mas'udi (896–956), all four sacred mountains, Mount Sinai, Mount Horeb, Mount Olive, and Mount Jordan (Mount Thabor), remained in the hands of the Orthodox Christians who exerted considerable influence on the Muslims who gradually adopted the cult of Jerusalem and the holy places from the Orthodox Christians.[60]

Dominating Jordan was crucial for the Muslim conquerors. The objective of Khalid Ibn al-Walid who led the campaign to conquer Greater Syria was to capture Ḥira where he sought to establish as his headquarter. He moved through the villages and towns such as Tadmor (Palmyra), Ḥawran and Adhri'at before reaching Yarmouk.[61] The decisive campaign that let the Muslims to take over the region is known as the Battle of Yarmouk, and it took place in 636. According to Muslim sources, which apparently provide an exaggerated picture of the Byzantine force, it was enormous compared to what the Muslims had until then. Seeing the Byzantine forces one of the Arab commanders Aṭiyya bin Amir is reported to have said that their number could be compared to a widespread locust.[62] The results of the encounter were equally staggering. It is difficult to provide a precise number of the casualties in that campaign. The estimates however, are that the Byzantines had 105,000 casualties and 40,000 captives while the Arabs had only 4,000 altogether.[63]

Then the Muslims continued their conquest of Jordan before moving northward toward Syria. While Damascus was under siege, the Muslim commander Abul Aur kept a watch over the Jordan Valley, near Fiḥl, on the eastern slope of the Jordan Valley, six miles south of the Sea of Galilee. One by one, the cities of Beisan, Tiberias, Adhri'at, Maab, Jarash, Amman, Boṣra, and the Ḥawran capitulated and Muslim garrisons were stationed in them. The two Muslim generals left in Jordan were Amr ibn al-As and Shuraḥbil. This was an easy task to accomplish due to the Byzantine weakness and the fact that the region's inhabitants were receptive to the new conquerors. As William Muir put it

> Shorahbil and Amru were left to reduce to order the province of the Jordan. The task was easy. The fire of patriotism had never burned brightly anywhere in Syria; and what there might have been was now extinguished by the listless cowardice of the Byzantine Court. To the Bedouin class, weary of Roman trammels, the prospect of an Arabian rule was far from unwelcome. Neither were the Jews and Samaritans unfavorable to the invaders; indeed, we find them not infrequently giving aid and information to the enemy. Even the Christians cared little for the maintenance of a government which by courtly and ecclesiastical intolerance had done its best to alienate their affection.[64]

Following the bloody Battle of Fiḥl, the Arab conquerors continued to Beisan to which they laid a siege and then attacked and killed many while giving amnesty to those who surrendered.[65]

Damascus fell a month after the Battle of Yarmouk and Tabaqat Fiḥl where a Byzantine detachment was stationed was captured after a short campaign. Meanwhile, Yazid bin Abu Sufyan captured Amman. He continued moving southward and took Gharandal near Tafila and thereby subdued the tribes in Shera Hills, west of Amman. The population in these areas had no close ties to the Byzantines and offered no resistance to the Muslims.[66]

Following the conquests, Abu Ubaidah was nominated governor of Greater Syria, which extended from the Mediterranean in the west to the Euphrates River in the east, and from the Byzantine border in the north to Sinai in the south. This vast region was divided into military districts called *jund*s. The first was the *jund* of Palestine, which included Jaffa and Amman in the north and Rafah, Shera Hills and possibly Ma'an in the south. The second was the *jund* of Urdun with its capital in Tiberias, and it included Deraa, Irbid, Beisan, Acre, and Sidon. The third was the *jund* of Damascus and Ḥims in the north. Special attention was given to the creation of an efficient tax and justice system. Muslims were required to pay tithes, those who submitted to the Muslims paid tax on land (*kharraj*) and non-believers were required to pay head tax (*jizya*). There seems to be a consensus among historians that Umar's attitude toward other religions in the areas conquered by the Muslims was remarkably tolerant, and this helps explain the survival of these communities in the present-day kingdom of Jordan. During the reign of Caliph 'Umar Ibn Khatab, (634–644), a restructuring took place and there were four *jund*s: Damascus, Hims, Filasṭin, and Urdun, with Tiberias as its center.

The year 639 in which Jordan was exposed to famine and plague exacerbated by severe drought became known to history as the "Year of the Ashes." During that year, Abu Ubaidah and other Arab commanders perished. Umar passed through Jordan on his way to tour the devastated region in Syria and he arrived in Aqaba on his way back.[67] When the succession to Muhammad took place during the caliphate of Ali, Jordan became a battleground and a place where the followers of Ali and the Umayyad general Mu'awiya contested the throne of Islam. Daumat al-Jandal was chosen as the place where the two sides decided to settle their differences.[68]

Jordan under the Umayyads (661–750)

By the beginning of the Umayyad period, Kinasrin was detached from Hims and Greater Syria consisted of five *jund*s.[69] We know that the first Umayyad caliph Mu'awiya Ibn Abi Sufyan (661–680) transferred Persians from Baalbek, Ḥims, and Antioch to the coastal regions of Jordan.[70] During the Umayyad period, Jordan became a resort of the caliphs. Caliph Marwan I (684–685) spent most of his time among the Bedouins and Yazid II son of 'Abd al-Malik (720–724) spent much time in Balqa. Yazid died in Beit Ras, north of Irbid. Buildings that were found in Jordan can be dated to the time before Yazid III (744). Qasr al-Khoraneh and Qasr Amar can be dated to the early eighth century. Mowaqqar was probably occupied by Yazid II. His son lived at al-Qastal and al-Azraq in the desert. Other castles in that region were Hammam as-Sarakh, Bayir, Meshetta, and Qasr al-Tuba, which had been occupied by al-Walid II (743–744).

Jordan was also the place where the Umayyads built two mints in which copper coins were struck. The mints seem to have stopped operating at about 710. When Caliph Abd al-Malik faced a danger from 'Abdallah Ibn Zubayr, he sent an army to secure the region between Ayla and the Hejaz in order to prevent him from deploying his forces in that region.[71] Archaeological evidence shows the remains of forts built by the Umayyads throughout Jordan, a land to which the caliphs sent their opponents and those who had to be kept at a safe distance from Damascus.[72]

The Umayyad caliphs tended to retire to the desert. They had appreciation for the Greek culture as it was known in Syria and Palestine, and they endeavored to build palaces in a combined Greek and Syrian-Palestinian style. Six such palaces were built in Jordan alone. One of the palaces was Qasr Amrah, which was a resting place and preparation for hunting and it was situated some fifty miles east of Amman. It was built with all the amenities, including a bath. Its walls are covered with pictures showing the caliph in all his glory, accompanied by his entourage. Standing behind him are the Persian king Khosroes, the Byzantine emperor, the Negus of Ethiopia and Roderick king of the Visigoths. Their names are engraved in Arabic as well as Greek. The other one is Qasr al-Kharanah, on the way that leads to Qasr Amrah. This two-story palace was built with stones and it had towers and special quarters for slaves and beasts of burden. Other, less-known palaces are al-Qasr al-Azraq to the northeast of Qasr Amrah and al-Qasr al-Ṭaubi, which was situated some forty miles south east of Amman.[73]

The Umayyad caliph Walid II who never took his duties seriously had established his residence in the district east of the Jordan. When Yazid III fought for the crown, he sought refuge from his opponent Mansur bin Jumhur who wished to eliminate him. Luckily for Yazid, the Kalbite commander of the Syrians in Ḥira, Sulayman bin Sulaim saved him by facilitating his flight to Balqa. He was hidden in a woman's apartment until he was dragged by a Kalbite who brought him to Damascus where he was arrested and ridiculed for his long beard.[74] Like the Arabs in the other parts of Greater Syria, the inhabitants of Jordan sided with Muhammad Ibn Abd al-Malik and sought to eliminate Yazid. However, Yazid prevailed, many of his opponents were killed and others were compelled to pay him homage.[75]

When the Umayyads came to power, Jordan was not only their retreat but also the place where they built impressive Muslim monuments that left their mark on Islamic civilization. The discovery, in 1992 of a 32 dinar treasure in Aqaba, containing 29 Umayyad coins minted in Sijilmasa on the Trans-Saharan route in North Africa (when that city was ruled by the Banu Wanudin, clients of the Caliph of Cordoba at the end of the tenth and the beginning of the eleventh centuries) demonstrates not only that the Caliphate of Cordoba had influence on the economic and monetary affairs in that city and the interest that the Andalusi merchants had in controlling Fes-Sijilmasa route but also the fact that the Jordanian cities maintained lively commercial contacts with the countries of the Mediterranean coast. The discovery of these coins that were minted in the name of the Umayyad caliph is the most ancient trace of money diffusion from Sijilmasa, via the Maghreb and Andalusia. The diffusion of dinars increased considerably when the sultans of the Almoravid dynasty, which ruled northwest Africa during the eleventh and twelfth centuries, minted their own coins and the Egyptian merchants acquired them from those who came from the Maghreb to trade in Alexandria. The commercial connection with the Red Sea and the Arab east increased the diffusion further.[76]

It was also in that period that the pilgrimage road from Damascus to Ma'an developed. This route lost its importance after the Abbasid revolution of 750 when the center of the caliphate shifted from Damascus to Baghdad. The caliphs of the new dynasty developed the road from Baghdad to the holy cities, and thus neglected the old road that passed through Jordan. When the Abbasid caliphate began to disintegrate Jordan became a target for the ambitions of the Egyptian Fatimids who regarded it as an area that had to be guarded against the ambitions of the Seljuk sultans in the north.

Attempting to explain the reasons for the fall of the Umayyad dynasty, historians mention several factors. The orientalist Van Floten mentions factors such as the hatred, which the downtrodden peoples had toward the regime and the opposition of the Shi'i community. The Shi'is who believed that the true leader of the Muslim community was the Mahdi who would bring justice and peace to the world distrusted the Umayyads from the very beginning. Van Floten argued that the reasons for the Abbasid revolution was the resentment of the local population to the Arab conquerors and the ability of the Shi'i sect to become the pioneer in leading the downtrodden against the Umayyads. Julius Wellhausen stressed the role that the tribes played in the revolution. Others dwell on the role that the inhabitants of Khurasan played in the revolution. These historians, however, paid little or no attention to the fact that there were centers of resistance in Greater Syria, including Jordan and the tribes within its domains. It is true that the Abbasid Revolution erupted in Khurasan. There were numerous rebellions of Shi'is, Kharijites, and Umayyads in Iraq as well as in Khurasan, but they all failed. The Abbasid revolution would not have been possible without sound leadership that came from Jordan. This was the place where the call for the revolution began to spread and the Umayyad dynasty was brought to an end by those who came from Jordan. If we follow the manner by which the Umayyad caliphs endeavored to establish peace and order in their domains, we can understand that only by establishing peace among the traditional factions of Qays and Yaman, they could hope to restore order. Mu'awiya ibn Abi Sufyan relied on help the Yamani tribes and he brought them to his side. He benefited from their service and managed to establish a balance between the two factions. This brought stability to the Umayyad caliphate during his reign and that of his son Yazid and it was not until the battle of Marj Rahit in 684 AD that these tribes began raising their voice and clashed again. The Qaysites were represented by al-Ḍaḥak bin Qays and the tribes who supported him while the Yamanites were represented by Khas Ibn Baḥdal and his followers.

When Caliph al-Walid (668–715) came to power, he deemed it necessary to side of the Qaysites, the most prominent among whom were al-Ḥajjaj Ibn Yusuf and Qutaybah bin Muslim al-Bahali. When Sulayman bin 'Abd al-Malik (674–717) came to power, he was concerned about the stability of his regime and sided with the Yamanites. And when 'Umar ibn Abd al-'Aziz (717–720) came to power he found it necessary to reconcile them but the feud reemerged after his death. When Yazid II (720–724) came to power chaos prevailed as a result of the tribal feuds. He maintained close ties with Hajjaj ibn Yusuf, the former governor of Iraq who was a Qaysi. At the same time, there was hostility toward Yazid bin al-Muhalab, the governor of Iraq, during the time of Sulayman bin ‘Abd al-Malik. The militancy among the tribes intensified and the caliphs had to allow the members of the tribes to participate in the government. Yazid continued the reconciliation process. Caliph Hisham bin Abd al-Malik (724–743) who was described by historians as an efficient administrator with robust qualities was just as incapable of extracting himself from the tribal conflict. First, he sided with the Yamanites who suffered under the previous caliph, and then he decided to support the Qaysites and thereby alienated his former allies.

When al-Walid II (743–744) came to power after a period of stability the strife between the two sides reemerged and he found it necessary to side with the Yamanites. This strife led to bloodshed and weakness which manifested itself not only at the center of the caliphate but also in the periphery, and the tribes in Jordan took a significant part in the conflict. After Walid's death, the caliphate fell into the hands of Yazid III known as al-Naqis who relied on help from the Yamanites to prevail over the Qaysites who refused to recognize him as caliph. He came to power in 744, remained caliph for six months, and was followed by his brother Ibrahim who had little popular support. At that point, the Umayyad officer Marwan bin Muhammad staged a revolution on the pretext of taking revenge on behalf of al-Walid II. He relied on the Qaysites, fought against his brother Ibrahim, entered Damascus with his forces, and declared himself caliph. He then moved the capital to Haran where his Qaysites allies had their power base. However, he came too late to take control and the strife intensified. The process of decline continued and the civil war spread to Palestine and Jordan.

Jordan under the Abbasids (750–1258)

Seeking to avoid a conflict with the Shi'is, the Umayyad Caliph Abd al-Malik Ibn Marwan contacted Ali Ibn Abdallah Ibn al-Abbas who sought to become caliph and gave him the village of al-Ḥamima (Ḥawra) in the Balqa as a land grant (*iqtā'*). Al-Ḥamima, close to Nagb al-Shatr on the road between Ma'an and Aqaba, came into prominence shortly prior to the Abbasid revolution. It became the residence of the followers of Ali, son in law of Prophet Muhammad who called for the overthrow of what he regarded as the unholy Umayyad usurpers. The reason for Abd al-Marwan's act was political. The Umayyads regarded al-Ḥamima as a place where resistance to their regime was likely to emerge, and therefore sought to place it under close observation. When caliph al-Walid came to power, he imprisoned Ali, flogged him, and paraded him in the streets of Damascus. He blamed him for killing his brother Saliḥ bin Abdallah bin al-Abbas and then sent him to exile in Sharah in southern Jordan. Then Ali established himself in al-Ḥamima, which he turned into his headquarters and stayed there until his death in 763. Thus, the Abbasid faction settled in al-Ḥamima and after his death, his son Muhammad bin

Abdallah al-Abbasi remained in that village. All sources agree that the Abbasid call to overthrow the Umayyads began with Muhammad bin Ali al-Abbasi and he is considered the most powerful among the Abbasid family. The al-Ḥamima-Kufa-Khurasan axis was the place where the Abbasid message began to spread and al-Ḥamima was the first place where the movement to overthrow the Umayyads began to take shape. From there, it spread to Kufa, and then to Khurasan where the revolution began.

Muhammad bin Ali al-Abbasi benefited from the mistakes of the previous Shi'i rebellions, most of which had wide support in Kufa. It was impossible for any secret movement to start in Kufa because the Umayyads sent their agents who managed to nip any such movement in the bud without major difficulties. Stifling the movement in Kufa meant that the entire rebellion was doomed. Muḥammad bin 'Ali al-Abbasi's plan was different that those who preceded him because he selected a headquarters in Greater Syria, which was the center of Umayyad power and over which they had little control. By doing so, he avoided Iraq and the Hejaz, which were constantly monitored by the Umayyads. Al-Ḥamima became the center of the movement and its activities. Its isolation from other villages and its location at the heart of Greater Syria where one would not even think that it was possible for such movement to rise made it possible for the revolutionists to act freely. Moreover, al-Ḥamima's location between Syria and the Ḥejaz, close to the road leading to Iraq made it easy for those who spread the message to arrive there without being noticed.

Historians divide the period of struggle against the Umayyads into two parts: the period in which the call to revolution was secret but had no real force, and the second in which the idea was implemented and the Umayyads were overthrown. The first period started sometime in beginning of the eighth century and lasted until 744–745. During that time, al-Ḥamima was the center from which the movement began. From there, the word reached Iraq and Khurasan by merchants known for having originated from the House of the Prophet (*ahl al bayt*). These were the callers (*dai'*s) who spread the message. During that time, the *shaikhs* of al-Ḥamima were writing to those of Khurasan and thereby spreading the message. Muḥammad bin Ali al-Abbasi remained in charge of the movement in al-Ḥamima. He kept in touch with the events in Kufa and Khurasan where their inhabitants kept the matter secret. After Muḥammad bin Ali al-Abbasi died his son Ibrahim continued his mission. Unlike his father who remained a propagandist Ibrahim was the one who started the uprising and his brothers benefitted from it.

The second phase of the revolution started in 744–745 when the political elite in al-Ḥamima wrote to Abu Muslim al-Khurasani, asking him to lead the revolt against the Umayyads. The revolution was carried out in the name of al-Riddha from the House of the Prophet. Ibrahim bin Muḥammad was seen by many as the rightful candidate and the Umayyads discovered the connection between Ibrahim and other leaders of the revolution. Consequently, Marwan bin Muḥammad wrote to the governor of Damascus, Walid Ibn Muawiya and ordered him to tell the governor of Balqa to go to al-Ḥamima to capture Ibrahim. Al-Walid complied and Balqa's governor came and apprehended Ibrahim who sat in the city's mosque in 749–750.

Then Marwan imprisoned Ibrahim and put him to death shortly afterward. Prior to his death, Ibrahim transferred the imamate to his brother Abi al-Abbas and told him to go with his brothers and the entire family from al-Ḥamima to Kufa. They departed the town secretly arrived in that town where they found more supporters for their cause.[77]

Al-Hamima was situated in the Sharah region south of Ras al-Naqb in Jordan in the ancient kingdom of Edom, approximately 40 kilometers south of Petra, and 55 kilometers north of Aqaba, a place through which the caravans passed between Aqaba and the northern part of the Arabian Peninsula in the south and Petra and Syria in the north. Al-Ḥamima was established during the reign of the Nabatean king Aretas III (62–87). Its original name was Hawra, which meant "white." Legend has it that Aretas III had a dream that his son Rabel I (86–87) would establish Hawra and that he had to find a white location for that purpose. As he began looking for a white location, he saw an apparition of a man clad in white and riding a white camel. The apparition quickly disappeared. He then saw a tree with many roots and ordered the building of a city in that location. The name al-Ḥamima is associated with the white color, due to the white hills that extended north and east. Ptolemy mentions al-Ḥamima in his *Geography*. Aretas IV expanded the city and its agriculture base. He paid much attention to the commercial road between Aqaba and Petra. Efforts were made to settle nomads and houses and aqueducts were built to accommodate the settlers.

In 106, al-Ḥamima fell into Roman hands when Emperor Trajan conquered it and it became part of Provincia Arabia. The Trajan Road passed through the village. The village became part of the Legion III Cyrenaica, and a fortification was built there during Emperor Diocletian's time. Roman bathtubs and a variety of utensils were found, indicating that Roman manners were prevalent in that village. During the Byzantine age, the facilities were widely used and soldiers abandoned their barracks to engage in agriculture and trade. There is an indication that the taxes were increased in the sixth and seventh centuries and that several churches were built in the village. Five of these churches were discovered. These were Greek-Orthodox churches, which competed with other branches of Christianity such as the Melkite, Nestorian, and Jacobite to win souls in that region. During the seventh century, al-Ḥamima was a center of a bishopric that was under the jurisdiction of the church in Boṣra.

Al-Ḥamima fell under Abbasid control already during the days of the Umayyad caliph Abd al-Malik ibn Marwan when Abdallah Ibn Zubair refused to recognize him as caliph and declared himself caliph of the Muslims in Mecca and Medina instead. Prior to his death, Abdallah Ibn al-Abbas told his son Ali to reach Abd al-Malik bin Marwan in Damascus. Ali bin Abdallah made his way to Damascus where he met Abd al-Malik who welcomed him, placed him above Ibn Zubair, and sent him to the Sharah region of Jordan. He arrived at Adhraḥ, east of Petra and then settled in al-Ḥamima which he purchased. This is how al-Ḥamima became a center of Abbasid propaganda. This act increased the reputation of that town. Moreover, al-Ḥamima was the center of the *hajj* route, which connected Syria and the Hejaz. It was connected to Daumat al-Jandal (al-Jauf) and Kufa. This was the road that Abul Abbas al-Saffaḥ passed through when he left al-Ḥamima on his way to Kufa.

Al-Ḥamima became Ali's center and he built a mosque and a residence with all the necessary amenities in that town. It is said that he used to pray on a board, which he brought from the Zamzam in Mecca, and that he had five hundred kinds of olives toward which he prayed two bows every day, and therefore became known by the sobriquet al-Sajjad.[78]Ali stayed in al-Hamima until his death in 735. His son Muhammad succeeded him and the sources tell us that that Muḥammad bin Ali ibn Abdallah was the one who spread the Abbasid message.

The sources are not clear regarding the exact sequence of events or the personalities involved. We are told that Abdallah Ibn Muhammad Ibn Ḥanafiyah the grandson of Imam Ali Ibn Abi Talib who was not the son of Fatima al-Zahrah, stopped over in al-Hamima on his way from Damascus to Medina. He was sick on his way to see Muḥammad Ibn Ali al-Abbasi at al-Ḥamima. The Abbasid claim that he was poisoned by the Umayyads cannot be confirmed but we know that he was welcomed and died soon afterward. It is said that Abu Hashim transferred the imamate to Muḥammad Ibn Ali al-Abbasi upon his arrival to al-Ḥamima. The Abbasids were the ones who assumed the task of fighting against the Umayyads, and they succeeded where the Alids failed. This is how Muhammad Ibn Ali and his son Ibrahim began spreading one of the most crucial revolutionary messages in the Islamic world. The imam who sat at al-Ḥamima was the one who began the process that eventually led to the fall of the Umayyads. Muḥammad had around seventy propagandists (*da'i*s), the most outspoken of which was Bakir bin Mahan who called for the downfall of the unjust Umayyads. Bakir was from a Sijistani family and he was called Abi Hashim. His father lived in Jordan. Bakir lived with the Arab tribe of Bani Masila in Kufa. The first *dai*s of Kufa sent him to meet Imam Muhammad at al-Ḥamima. Dressed as a merchant, he rode to Damascus and then to al-Ḥamima with some of his followers.

It was Ibrahim, son of Muhammad Ibn Ali, who ordered Abu Muslim al-Khurasani to call for a rebellion against the Umayyads. He told his comrades that they need to wear black clothes and hoist black flags and the revolution began in June 747. However, Ibrahim did not reap the benefit of what he had done because the last Umayyad caliph caught him at al-Ḥamima and brought him to Damascus and then to Ḥaran where Marwan II was stationed. He imprisoned him and he died in 748–749. With some of his ardent supporters Abul Abbas al-Safaḥ left al-Hamima secretly and went to Kufa. His uncle Dawud Ibn Ali and his son met him at Daumat al-Jandal (Jauf) and they kept him abreast of the unrest in Khurasan. Abul Abbas made his way to Kufa and from the stage (*minbar*) of its mosque, he declared himself caliph thereby establishing the Abbasid caliphate.

Following the departure of the Abbasids, al-Ḥamima began losing its importance even though it was the birth place of many of the Abbasids and some of them were buried there. It was the birth place of Abdallah Ibn Muhammad al-Abbasi and Ja'far al-Mansur. Also born there was caliph Muhammad al-Mahdi Ibn al-Mansur and several other prominent Abbasids. Al-Ḥamima was the home of the Abbasids for six decades from 687 to 750. Archaeologists found remains from that period the most prominent among them were an old mosque. The magnificent palace built there by Ali Ibn Abdallah was 50 by 61 square meters. It has a big gate facing east, and close to it, there are houses for guests. Some of the houses have frescoes with geometrical designs and some were inlaid in ivory. Also found in that place was a silver dirham dates back to the early Islamic age.

No major construction works were carried out in al-Hamima by the Abbasid dynasty, apart from some mosques and tombs. This move marked the beginning of Jordan's decline. The forts and palaces in Jordan were neglected and the roads fell into disrepair. The pilgrims' road moved eastward and they departed from Mesopotamia to Mecca.

We are told that in 770, the Abbasid caliph al-Mansur sent a fleet against pirates who found refuge in Karak. They were said to have terrorized the Red Sea and that the caliph sent a naval force to eliminate their threat to Basra. The Abbasids established a naval power that accompanied the ships on their way to the Red Sea and guarded the Persian Gulf. They had to deal with numerous rebellions throughout the empire, and the region of Jordan was no exception. For example, when Ibrahim Ibn al-Mahdi was the governor of Damascus, he was informed about three bands that terrorized the region: Da'amah and Nu'man who were the clients (*mawali*) of Bani Umayya, and Yaḥya bin Armiyya who was from the Jews of Balqa. Two of them capitulated, but the third remained recalcitrant and was eventually killed in a campaign with the army. Ever since, there were no such incidents during Ibrahim's rule.[79]

In 878, the Egyptian governor Aḥmad Ibn Tulun took control of Damascus and thereby Syria fell under his rule. This was the beginning of the disintegration of the Abbasid Caliphate. Egypt, Syria, Mecca, and Medina all were controlled by Caliph al-Muttaqi Billah (940–944). Syria, Jordan, and Palestine were in a state of turmoil and instability due to frequent changes that occurred in Egypt, which fell in the hands of the Fatimids in 969, and its governors were incapable of providing effective administration to these areas.

Fatimids, Mamluks, and Crusaders in Jordan

Among the most active regions in Jordan prior to the Fatimid occupation were Wadi Sirḥan, Daumat al-Jandal, Balqa, Ma'an, Amman, al-Salt, Ḥisban, and Jarash. The Wadi Sirḥan route appears to have been neglected during Roman times. When Roman rule came to an end, the Ghassanids took control of it in 531, and by the time of the Prophet, they extended their rule over the entire route, as far as Jauf where they nominated a governor. When the Muslim conquest began this area was dominated by Bani Kalb and Bani Udhra. In pre-Islamic times, Daumat al-Jandal maintained an annual fair and the idol Wadd was worshipped. This area is believed to have been called Wadi al-Azraq, until sometime in the middle of the eighteenth century when the Sirḥan tribesmen moved from Ḥawran and settled around Jauf.[80]

The history of Amman is closely tied with that of the Balqa. Amman, al-Salt, and Ḥisban competed over which one of them ought to be have been Balqa's capital. The name Balqa appears in the Islamic geographical and the historical sources but there is no agreement among scholars regarding its meaning. The name could have originated from the mineral *balaqa* (mica) or from *balaq* (conquest), among the many terms that were mentioned by geographers and historians. It could have come from the word *baluqa* (wasteland) or from *balqa'* (tent or plane). It is also possible that it originated from a historical figure such as Balaq bin Ma'ab, or Balaq Ibn Suwairiyah of Bani Amman, or from Balak Ben Tzipor whose name is mentioned in the Bible and who brought Balaam Ben Pe'or to curse the Sons of Israel (Numbers: 22–24). The Balqa region was exposed to invasions by the inhabitants of the Arabian Peninsula since the dawn of history. The Yamani states in the region established commercial stations on the road, which extended from the Arabian Peninsula to Syria. Some of these stations such as Ma'an became commercial centers for the inhabitants of that town. Among the tribes that migrated from the Arabian Peninsula in the beginning of the first millennium BC and came in greater number in the third century AD were the Qaḍa'a who dominated most of Balqa. The region had white mountainous areas but it also had arable land.

Jarash, which played an important role in the Byzantine period, loomed large in Islamic history as well. Whereas the archaeological research conducted by James Sauer held the view that most major cities occupied during the Umayyad period such as Jarash, Umm el-Jimal, Quweilbeth, Umm Qais, Pella, and Umm al-Rasas were almost abandoned by the end of the Umayyad period, new research carried out in Pella, Jarash, and other Jordanian cities, all the way to Aqaba, revealed that urban settlement in these areas continued at least until the ninth century, and that both Abbasid and Fatimid cities existed in Jordan. These cities were not affected immediately by the fall of the Umayyads and the rise of the Abbasids in 750. The archaeological evidence suggests that urban life in Jarash continued from the sixth to the ninth century AD. This becomes evident mainly from the pottery forms found on that site. One of the most prominent findings confirming this view is a unique type of oil-lamp with an animal head that was used as a handle, and which evolved at about 640 and continued to be made until the middle of the eighth century. Many of the lamps found could be traced to the last quarter of that century and they were often inscribed and dated according to the Muslim *hijri* calendar. These lamps confirm that Muslims and Christians interacted and urban life continued uninterruptedly until the ninth century, when the settlement began to decline, probably as a result of severe economic recession. The Circassian refugees who arrived in Jarash in 1878 found nothing but ruins and began laying the foundation of another town on that site.[81]

In 969, al-Mu'izz al-Fatimi sent his commander Ja'far bin Falaḥ to Greater Syria and he captured Ramlah from the Ikhshidids who controlled it from their base in Egypt. He then moved toward Tiberias which was the capital of the *jund* of Urdun, and from there to Damascus where the Friday Noon Sermon (*khutbah*) was read in the name of al-Mu'izz and no longer in the name of the Abbasid caliph. The house of Jaraḥ had considerable influence in the Fatimid court after it supported them against the Qarmatians who arrived in Ramla.[82]

The Fatimids nominated Daghfal Ibn al-Jarah a commander of that city and provided him with a group of Ikhshidids and Kafurites supporters. The position of the Jarah family became even more secure when the Fatimids recognized them as the rulers of Ramlah in return for 100,000 dinars. Following the death of the city's commander al-Mufrij, Ibn Da'ghal was nominated as his successor. The new commander, however, exploited the turmoil in the region to expand his borders and he captured most of south Jordan and some areas of Palestine. The turmoil was such that the Bedouin tribes around Damascus managed to capture that city in 972. Consequently, the Damascenes sought help from the Qarmatians in order to recapture their city. Ibn al-Jaraḥ took this opportunity to gain support among the region's inhabitants. This state of affairs did not please the Fatimid Caliph al-Aziz and he sent one of his commanders, Baltakin al-Turki who assembled an army and with help from the Arabs of the region and the Qaysis in particular, and thereby managed to defeat Ibn al-Jarah in 980. The house of al-Jaraḥ established themselves in Sharah south of Jordan, due to its strategic location and there they fortified themselves whenever they felt a threat from the Fatimids.

In 982, Amman became a center where Fatimid forces concentrated under the command of Munir al-Khadim in order to eliminate Bakjur the *wali* of Damascus. Munir managed to assemble the Qays, the Aqil and other tribes from Balqa and the Hawran and moved with them to Damascus. At that time, Amman was ruled by Nasiḥ al-Ṭabakh. The Fatimid vizier Ya'qub ibn Kilis sent him a message demanding that he go to Ḥims and capture those who were loyal to Bakjur and who found refuge in that town after they were defeated by Munir al-Khadim. Nasiḥ left for Ḥims, managed to capture Bakjur's followers, and sent them to Damascus. One of the governors of Amman during the Fatimid period was Badr Ibn Ḥazim. When the turmoil spread in Greater Syria in 1067–1068, the Fatimid caliph al-Muntasir bi-llah nominated Qutb al-Dawlah Bazṭaghan as governor of Damascus, and dismissed Badr al-Jamali on the pretext that he oppressed the population. Badr al-Jamali established himself in Acre in an attempt to take revenge of the governor of Damascus al-Sharif al-Alawi Abu Ṭahir Ḥaydarah. When Ḥaydarah felt the danger, he fled to Balqa. However, Badr al-Jamali managed to convince Badr bin Ḥazim to help him catch Ḥaydarah in return for the sum of 12,000 dinars. Badr bin Ḥazim caught Ḥaydarah and sent him to Badr al-Jamali in Acre where he was flayed alive.[83]

At that time, Greater Syria was a battleground in which the Fatimids and the Bedouin tribes were fighting for domination. The Kalb tribe was stationed in Damascus and its environs, and it was led by Sinan Bin Alyan al-Kalbi. The Ṭayi tribe dominated southern Palestine and Jordan, and thereby occupied Amman and Balqa.

Despite the warfare in that region, there were settlements in many areas such as Amman, al-Salt, Zizya, and Zarqa. When al-Muqqadisi divided Greater Syria into six regions. He used the term *kawr* instead of *Jund.* These *kawra* were Qinasrin, Ḥims, Damascus, Urdun, Filasṭin, and Sharah. According to al-Muqqadisi, Sharah had a *qasbah* and its cities were Ma'ab, Ma'an, Tabbuk, Adhraḥ, Ayla and Madin in addition to numerous villages. Talking about Amman, he said that it bordered the desert and that it had villages and plantations. Its rural region was Balqa and it was replete with grains and cattle. It had several rivers, water mills, and a mosque in the vicinity of the market ornamented with mosaic tiles. The city had a castle and the tomb of Uriah on which there was a mosque and there was also a playing ground. He added, that the prices were cheap and the fruits were plentiful. However, its inhabitants were ignorant and there was no easy road leading to it. Al- Muqqadisi's description of the city's inhabitants as ignorant had its origin probably in Shi'i beliefs, which prevailed when it was under Fatimid rule. Al-Muqqadisi mentioned the Raqim region and said that it was a village close to Amman at the desert's edge and that it had a cave with two gates, one big and one small. The prevailing belief was that whoever could enter the big one but could not enter small was a bastard. The cave had three tombs. Al-Muqqadisi mentioned that Amman was connected to a road network: the first from the Jordan River to Amman and Marḥalah; the second from Nablus to Jericho, Bayt Ram, and then to Amman; and the third from Amman to Ma'ab, Zarqa, Idhr'at, and Damascus.

Due to the fact that Amman and Balqa were under Fatimid rule, Shi'ism spread to the region, primarily to Amman. The Dead Sea (*buḥayrat saghr*) was a place where the sick came to treatment. Trade flourished in this region and cultural life blossomed. In the eleventh century, Amman and its environs were exposed to invasions and wars, not only as a result of the conflict between the Fatimids and the Abbasids but also as a result of the Crusades, which began at the end of that century. The Crusaders who came in the eleventh century sought to control the region by defeating the Fatimids and establishing fortresses in Jordan, a strategic region which connected Egypt and the Hejaz to the heart of the Middle East. The governor of Damascus, Zahir al-Din Tughtikin, aimed at establishing a force that would separate him from the Crusading armies. He nominated al-Aṣfahid al-Turkomani to rule Jordan and he gave him Balqa, Moab, Sharah, and Wadi Musa as land grants (*iqta'āt*) in order to prevent the expansion of the Crusaders' territories in the region and to maintain the line of communications with Egypt. In addition, he sought to stop the hostile acts of the Crusaders against inhabitants of the region. But the Crusaders managed to inflict a defeat on Asfahid. This defeat compelled Zahir al-Din to conclude truce with the Crusaders in 1108. According to Ibn al-Qalanisi, the Sawad, which consisted of the region of Jarash and Jabal Awf (Ajlun), was divided into three areas, third of which was taken by the Turks, third by the Franks, and third by the Fatimids. The truce between the governor of Damascus and the Franks included the region north of the Zarqa River, which probably extended to al-Salt, while Amman and Balqa were not part of these regions.

According to Abu Shama, Nur al-Din arrived in Karak, spent several days in Amman, and then laid a siege to Karak. When Ṣalaḥ al-Din left Egypt on his way to Karak, Nur al-Din heard the news and headed to that city, reaching Raqim (Dir al-Kahf) in the vicinity of Amman. Following the death of his father, Ṣalah al-Din began the conquest of Greater Syria. After the conquest, he bequeathed Karak to his brother al-Malik al-Adil who obtained Balqa and al-Salt as well. The *iqta'* given to al-Adil included the region from the Zarqa River north to Aqaba in the south. When al-Adil asked his brother to give him the eastern parts, the sultan agreed to grant him all the territories that he had in Greater Syria, including Karak, Shawbak, al-Salt, Balqa, and half of his *iqtā'* in Egypt. In return, al-Adil had to bring six thousand bags of money that were to be carried annually from Balqa to al-Salt, and then to Jerusalem. Thus, Balqa and Amman became part of the Ayyubid sultanate, which was ruled from Karak and turned into an area where the armies were recruited and trained.[84]

The Fatimids who moved from Ifriqiya (Tunisia) in 969 invaded southern Syria. The harsh rule and the mismanagement of the Fatimids caused much discontent in Jordan and led to the outbreak of rebellions that were suppressed with utmost cruelty in 1021, but after 1043, Fatimid rule was no longer effective, and following the invasion of the Seljuk Turks in 1071 into the region, the Fatimid rule came into an end. This was the situation when the Crusaders appeared in the Holy Land.

By 1071, Jordan fell under Seljuk control when one of Malik Shah's generals took it over. The area between Jordan and the Ḥawran fell to the Crusaders. Their leader Baldwin I (1060s–1118) built a fortress on the southern bank of the Yarmouk River. This was the first fortress built by the Crusaders in Jordan. In 1115, he stationed a garrison in the ancient Suwayt fortress in Wadi Musa. Moreover, he took control of Aqaba and built fortresses in places such as Jazirat Far'un in Egypt, Tafilah, and Ma'an in Jordan, with a view to guard the trade route between Cairo, Damascus, and Mecca.

There were several invasions of Jordan during the time of Baldwin II (1118–1131) and Falk of Anju (1131–1143) during whose reigns castles and fortresses were built in Palestine and Transjordan. Taj al-Muluk Buri built the Karak fortress in 1124. Karak became one of the most important fortresses on the eastern side of the Jordan River and the Dead Sea. It became known as the 'Desert Stone'. During the reign of Baldwin III (1143–1163), Philip de Milly managed to become the emir of Karak, Shawbak, Ma'an, Wadi Musa and the adjacent planes but Hebron was not part of his emirate. The mountainous region of Beni Auf (Ajlun) in northeast Jordan remained unconquered due to the difficulties involved in such operation. Therefore, its inhabitants remained neutral. When Salah ad-Din became the master of Egypt he built ships that were carried by camels to the Red Sea and took over Aqaba.[85] In 1173, he laid a siege to Karak but left for Egypt after hearing about his son's illness, which led to his death in that year. Salah ad-Din exploited the turmoil caused by the rise of Nur al-Din Zangi to march toward Syria, which he took over and declared himself sultan in 1174. In 1182, when Reynold ruler of Karak attacked a Muslim caravan, confiscated its merchandize, and arrested its members, Salah ad-Din attacked him from the Sinai and southeast Jordan. He chose this route because the Crusaders were in control of the entire coast region from Gaza to Alexandria. He then inflicted a heavy blow on the crusades at the Battle of Ḥattin in 1187, taking Reynold prisoner and capturing Jerusalem. The fortresses in southeast Jordan were the last fall in Salah ad-Din's hands. Karak fell into his hands in October 1188, Kawkab al-Hawah and Shawbak fell in the following month, thus bringing the presence of the Latins in Jordan to an end.

Following the death of Salah al-Din, his empire was divided among his relatives. Of all claimants to the throne, it was al-Adil who took control of most of the empire. At that time, Ajlun was ruled by Izz al-Din Usama. A dispute erupted between the two in 1211, and al-Adil sent his son, al-Mu'azzam Isa, who conquered the region and nominated one of his Mamluks named Aybak Ibn Abdallah. During that period, the people of al-Salt rebelled and after quelling the rebellion Aybak built a fortress on one of its hills, in order to watch over the entire region. Ḥisban was the capital of Balqa and then it was moved to al-Salt. To secure the road to Mecca, Aybak built the Azraq Castle. He remained governor of Balqa, Ajlun, and al-Salt, which were dominated by the Ayyubid Sultan al-Kamil of Egypt until 1239.

There were conflicts between the sultans of Damascus and those of Egypt in addition to the fight against the Crusaders. When the Egyptian general Rukn ad-Din Baybars invaded Jerusalem the victorious Egyptian army moved to Jordan and took control of Izz al-Din Usama's castle of Ajlun in 1245. This made it possible for the Egyptian sultan to capture Damascus. Fakhr al-Din Yusuf Ibn al-Shaikh who commanded the Egyptian army rose against his sultan al-Nasir and took control of all its fortresses and castles, including Karak, which did not surrender until 1249. Following al-Nasir's reign Egypt went through a period of instability when Ibn Turan Shah became the sultan. Then the Mamluks gave the throne to Shajara ad-Dur, a woman of Turkish descent. Soon afterward, the kingdom was divided into two parts: Damascus, Ajlun, and Balqa were ruled by the king's friend al-Nasir Yusuf and the southeastern part of Jordan remained part of the Egyptian kingdom. Ajlun remained in the hands of al-Nasir Yusuf until the Mongols evicted him from Damascus, and forced him to retreat to Izz al-Din Usama's castle, which he was forced to surrender in 1260, after they conquered al-Salt and destroyed its castle which was rebuilt later by the Mamluk Sultan Baybars. The Mongols were defeated by Baybars at the Battle of Ain Jalut later that year, and therefore their control of Jordan was short lived. Mamluk rule over Jordan requires further discussion and this would be the topic of the next two chapters.

Notes

1 Geroges Tate, "La Syrie-Palestine," (Syria-Palestine), French text, *Le Monde Byzantine, Tome I: L'Empire romain d'Orient 330–641*, Edited by Cécile Morrison (Paris: Press Universitaires de France, 2004), p. 386.
2 Michel Kaplan, *Les hommes et la terre à Byzance du VIe au XIe siècle* (The People and the Country of Byzantium from the Sixth to the Eleventh century). French text (Paris: Publications de la Sorbonne, 1992), pp. 528–529.
3 Edward Gibbon, *The Decline and Fall of the Roman Empire*, Vol. III (New York: The Modern Library, No Date.), pp. 146–147. [Italics are in the original].
4 The Lazi were a tribe from the northern region of Colchis, in the western part of present-day Georgia. Gibbon, Vol. II, pp. 619–620.
5 Pawel Filipczak, *An Introduction to the Byzantine Administration in the Syro-Palestine on the Eve of the Arab Conquest* (Lodz, Poland: Lodz University Press, 2015), p. 13.
6 *Ibid*, p. 9.

7 *Ibid*, p. 8.
8 Eyal Ben-Eliyahu, *Identity and Territory: Jewish Perception of Space in Antiquity* (Oakland: University of California Press, 2019), p. 92.
9 Yaron Dan, "ha-minhal ha-Bizanti be-Eretz Yisrael," (The Byzantine Administration in Israel), Hebrew text, Eretz Israel: from the Destruction of the Second Temple to the Muslim Conquest, Vol. I: *Political, Social and Cultural History*, Edited by Z. Baras et al. (Jerusalem: Ben Zvi, 1982), p. 390.
10 Filipczak, pp. 10–11.
11 Yaron Dan, "Palestina Salutaris (Tertia) and its Capital," *Israel Exploration Journal*, Vol. 32, No. 2/3 (1982), p. 134.
12 Walter Stevenson, *The Origins of Christian Diplomacy: Constantius II and John Chrysostom as Innovators* (London: Routledge, 2021), p. 82.
13 Yaron Dan, pp. 388–389.
14 *Ibid*, p. 395.
15 Ifran Shahîd, *Byzantium and the Arabs in the Fourth Century* (Washington, DC: Dumbarton Oaks Research, Library, 2006), p. 145.
16 Filipczak, p. 20.
17 Yaron Dan, pp. 408–409.
18 *Ibid*, pp. 410–411.
19 Gibbon, Vol, II, pp. 838–839.
20 Filipczak, pp. 55–56.
21 Yaron Dan, p. 418.
22 John Haldon, "Seventh-Century Continuities: The Ajnād and the "Thematic Myth," *Arab-Byzantine Relations in Early Islamic Times*, Vol. 8, Edited by Michael Bonner, *The Formation of the Classical Islamic World, Laurence I. Conard*, General Editor (Trowbridge, Wiltshire, UK: Ashgate, Variorum, 2004), pp. 405–406.
23 Filipczak, p. 45.
24 Edward N. Luttwak, *The Grand Strategy of the Byzantine Empire* (Cambridge, MA: Harvard University Press, 2009), p. 197.
25 Haldon, p. 406.
26 *Ibid*, p. 386.
27 *Ibid*, p. 389.
28 *Ibid*, 407.
29 *Palestine under the Moslems: A Description of Syria and the Holy Land from 650 to 1500, Translated from the works of the Medieval Arab Geographers by Guy Le Strange* (London: 1890), p. 30.
30 Haldon, p. 393.
31 *Ibid*, p. 403.
32 *Ibid*, pp. 409–410.
33 Peake Pasha, *History and Tribes of Jordan* (Coral Gables, FL: University of Miami Press, 1958), p. 45.
34 David George Hogarth, *Arabia* (Oxford, UK: The Clarendon Press, 1922), pp. 44–45, 50.
35 Bāsim Ṣaliḥ al-Jayshī, "Ma'rakat Mu'ātta, bawābāt al-Islām naḥū bilād al-Shām," (The Mu'ātta Campaign, Islam's Gates to Greater Syria), Arabic text, *Min al-ma'ālim* al-thaqāfīyah wa-al-ḥaḍāriyah fī-al-Urdun 'abra al-'usūr ('Ammān: al-Markaz al-Thaqāfi al-Malaki, 2002), Vol. I, p. 489.
36 Peake, p. 48.
37 Zeev Safrai, "Ha-Shomronim," (The Samaritans), Hebrew text, *Eretz Israel: from the* Destruction of the Second Temple to the Muslim Conquest, Vol. I: *Political, Social and Cultural History*, Edited by Z. Baras et al. (Jerusalem: Ben Zvi, 1982), p. 261.
38 *Ibid*, p. 262.
39 *Ibid*.

40 Zvi Baras, "Ha-kibush ha-Parsi be-shalhei ha-shilton ha-Bizanti," (The Persian Conquest at the end of the Byzantine rule), Hebrew Text, Eretz Israel: From the Destruction of the Second Temple to the Muslim Conquest, Vol. I, pp. 326–327.
41 Safrai, pp. 263–264.
42 'Abd al-Muta'āl al-Ṣa'īdī, Al-Siyāsah al-Islamīyah fi 'ahd al-khulafā al-Rashīdīn (Islamic Politics during the Age of the Rightly Guided Caliphs), Arabic text (No place of publication: Dar al-Fikr al-'Asrī, 1961), pp. 99–100. [Parentheses are mine].
43 John Bagot Glubb, *The Great Arab Conquests* (New York: Barnes & Noble Books, 1995), p. 134.
44 Al-Ṭabari tells us that Ma'ab was a village in Balqa. Contemporary historians refer to it as Moab. The kingdom of Moab was in Transjordan and one of its ancient towns was Qir Ḥāritha (Kir Hareshet) where the town of Karak was established. 'Abd al-Sattār al-Shaykh, *Abū Bakr al-Ṣadīq:Khalīfat Rasūl Allāh* (The Righteous Abu Bakr: Deputy of Allah's Messenger), Arabic text (Dimashq: Dār al-Qalam, 2011), p. 678.
45 Cited *Ibid*, p. 682.
46 The Ghassanids migrated from Yemen when agriculture declined in that region. 'Abd al-'Azīz Salīm, Tarīkh al'Arab fi al 'asr al-Jāhili: mundhu aqdam al-'usūr ḥāttah qiyām al-dawlah al- *Islamīyya* (History of the Arabs during the Age of Ignorance: From the Earliest periods until the establishment of the Islamic state), Arabic text (Beirut: Dar al-Nahdah al-'Arabīyya, 1970), p. 223.
47 'Abd al-Raḥmān Ibn Khaldūn, *Tarīkh Ibn Khaldūn* (History of Ibn Khaldun), Arabic text, Vol. 2 (Fez: Dār al Ṭab'i wa-al-Nashr bi al-Māghreb, 1936), pp. 308–309.
48 Niqulah Ziyādah, "Al-taṭawwur al-Idārī li-bilād al-Shām bayn Bizānṭah wa-al-'arab," (The administrative development of the cities of Greater Syria between the Byzantines and the Arabs), Arabic text, Bilād al-Shām fī al-'ahd al-Bizānṭī, Al-Nadwah al-ulah min a'amāl al-mu'tamar al-dawlī al-rābi' li-tarīkh bilād al-Shām, Vol. I ('Amman: Jam'īyat al-Maktabāt al-Urduniyah, 1986), p. 124.
49 Cited in Muḥammad Husayn Hāykal, *Al-Fārūq 'Umar*, Arabic text, Vol. I (Al-Qāhirah: Maṭba'at al-Miṣr, 1945), p. 131.
50 Aḥmad Ibn-Yaḥyā Ibn Jābir al-Balādhuri, *Al-būldān wa-futūhuhā wa-aḥkamuhā* (The countries, their conquests and their rule), Arabic text (Beirut: Dār al-Fikr, 1992), pp. 2646–2647.
51 *Ibid.*
52 Maḥmūd Shalabī, *Ḥāyāt 'Umar* (Umar's Life), Arabic text (Al-Qāhirah: Matba'āt al-Qāhirah, 1968), pp. 112–113.
53 'Abdallāh al-Ḥamāwi Ibn Yāqūt, *Mu'jam al-Buldān* (A Dictionary of Countries), Vol. I, Arabic text (Beirut: Dar Ṣādir, 1955), p. 148.
54 Philip K. Hitti, *The Origins of the Islamic State, being a translation from the Arabic, accompanied with annotations geographic and historical notes of the KITĀB FUTÛḤ AL-BULDÂN of al-Imâm abul 'Abbâs Aḥmad ibn-Jâbir al-Balâdhuri* (New York: Longmans Green & CO., 1916), pp. 214–215.
55 Cited in 'Abd al-Sattār al-Shaykh, p. 682.
56 John Bagnell Bury, *A History of the Late Roman Empire: From Arcadius to Irene* (395 A.D. to 800 A.D.), Vol. II (London: Macmillan and Co., 1889), p. 264.
57 Luttwak, *Ibid.*
58 Mark Whittow, *The Making of Byzantium 600-1025* (Berkley: University of California Press, 1996), p. 87.
59 'Ali Muḥammad al-Ṣalābi, *Abū Bakr al-Ṣidīq, shakhṣiyatuhu wa 'aṣruhu* (Abu Bakr the Righteous, his personality and his time), Arabic text (Dimashq: Dār Ibn Kathīr, 2003), pp. 396–397. Cited in 'Abd al-Sattār al-Shaykh, p. 682.
60 Alexander Alexandrovich Vasilev, *History of the Byzantine Empire, 324–1453*, Vol. I (Madison: The University of Wisconsin Press), p. 217.
61 Maḥmūd Shīt Khattāb, *Qādāt fatḥ al-'Irāq wa-al-Jazīrah* (Leaders of the conquest of Iraq and the Peninsula), Arabic text (Beirut: Dar al-Fikr, 1973), pp. 143–145.

62 Abī 'Abd Allāh bin 'Umar al-Wāqidī, *Futūh al-Shām* (The Conquest of Greater Syria), Arabic text (Beirut: Dār al-Jīl lil-Nashr wa-al-Tawzī'wa-al-Ṭibā'ah, 1970?), p. 166.
63 Ahmad Ibn-Zayni Daḥlān, *Al-Futūḥāt al-Islāmīya* (The Islamic Conquests), Arabic text (Al-Qāhira: Al-Maṭba'a al-Husaynīya al-Misrīyya, 1905), p. 32.
64 William Muir, *Annals of the Early Caliphate: From the Death of Mahomet to the Omeyyad and Abbaside Dynasties, A.H XI-LXI (A.D. 632–680)*, from original sources (Amsterdam: Oriental Press, 1968), p. 153.
65 Abī Ja'far Muḥammad bin Jarīr Al-Ṭabari, *Tarīkh al-Umam wa-al Mulūk* (History of the Nations and the Kings), Arabic text, Vol. II (Al-Qāhirah: Matba'āt al-Istiqāmah, 1939), p. 630.
66 Peake, p. 53.
67 *Ibid*, pp. 54–55.
68 Some historians identify the place as Udhruh in today's southern Jordan. Hugh Kennedy, *The Caliphate, A Companion to the History of the Middle East*, Edited by Youssef M. Choueiri (Malden, MA: Blackwell Publishing Ltd, 2005), p. 56.
69 Taysīr al-Fāris, *Al-'alāqāt al-Urdunīyah al-Filasṭīnīyah: wāqi'uhā wa-mustaqbaluhā* (Jordanian-Palestinian Relations: Their Present and Future), Arabic text ('Ammān: al-Maktaba al-Waṭtanīyah, 2002), pp. 6–7.
70 Abū Nāsir 'Umar, *Mu'āwiyah Ibn Abī Sufyān wa-'aṣruhu* (Mu'awiya Ibn Abi Sufyan and His Time), Arabic text. (Beirūt: al-Maktabah al-Ahlīya, 1962), p 159.
71 Iḥsān Ṣidqī al-'Amad, Al-Ḥajjāj Ibn Yūsuf al-Thaqafī: ḥayyatuhu wa-ārā'uhu al-siyasīyah (Al-Hajjaj Ibn Yusuf al-Thaqafi: His Life and His Political Views), Arabic text (Beirut: Dar al-Thaqāfa, 1973), p. 117.
72 Shukah Ravek and Avi Shemida', *El Kenyone Mo'av ve-Edom* (Canyon Moab and Edom, Hebrew text (Tel Aviv: Teva' ha-Devarim, 2000), p. 55.
73 Dimitrī Barāmki, Āthār al-Ḍiffah al-Sharqīyah min al-Mamlakah al-Urdunīyah al-Hāshimīyah:*dalīl mujaz muṣawwar* (Archeological Sites of the East Bank from the Hashemite Kingdom of Jordan: A Short Illustrated Guide), Arabic text (Al-Quds: matba'ah al-Tijārīyah, 1947), pp. 73–77.
74 Julius Wellhausen, *The Arab Kingdom and Its Fall* (Calcutta: University of Culcutta, 1927), pp. 356, 368.
75 'Umār Abū al-Nāṣir, *Al-Ayyām al-Akhīra lil-dawlah al-Umawīyya* (The last days of the Umayyad state), Arabic text (Beirut: al-Tarikhīyah, 1962), p. 195.
76 Christophe Picard, L'océan Atlantique musulman De la conquête arabe à l'époque almohade: Navigation et mise en valeur des côtes d'al-Anadalus et du Maghreb occidental, *Portugal-Espagne-Maroc* (The Muslim Atlantic Ocean from the Arab conquest to the Almohad period: Navigation and development of the coasts of al-Anadalus, and the Western Maghreb, Portugal-Spain-Morocco), French text (Paris: Maisonneuve & Larose, 1997), pp. 143–144.
77 Ḥusayn 'Āṣī, "Ishām al-Urdun fī al-da'wah al-'Abbāsīyah," (Jordan's contribution to the Abbasid appeal), Arabic text, Min al-ma'ālim al-thaqāfīyah wa-al-ḥaḍāriyah fī-al-Urdun 'abra *al-'usūr* ('Ammān: al-Markaz al-Thaqāfi al-Malaki, 2002), Vol. I, pp. 461–465.
78 Ṣālih al-Ḥamarnah, "Al-Ḥamīmah al-Urdunīyah, Mawṭin al-Dā'wah al-'Abbasīyah," (Jodanian al-Hamimah, Abode of the Abbasid appeal), Arabic text, *Ibid*, p. 473.
79 Muṣtafā Shākir, *Dawlat Banī al-'Abbās* (State of Bani al-Abbas), Arabic text (Kuwait: Wakālat al-Maṭbu'āt, 1973), Vol. I, pp. 346, 724; Vol. II, p. 34.
80 Peake, p. 59.
81 Michael Galikowski, "Jerash in Early Islamic Times," *Oriente Moderno*, Nuova serie, Anno 23 (84), No. 2 (2004), pp. 469–470, 472–473. http://www.jstore.org/stable/25817944.
82 The Qarmatians (Qārāmiṭa) were a radical ascetic group and a branch of the Sevener Shi'i sect in Islam. Their base was in al-Hasa in Eastern Arabia where they claimed to have established a religious utopian state at the end of the ninth century. They were

sworn enemies of the Abbasids whom they regarded as materialistic and profane. Led by Abū Ṭāhir al-Jannabi they sacked Mecca, stole its Black Stone, and desecrated the Zamzam by hurling corps into it during the Hajj month in 930 AD.

83 Muḥammad 'Abd al-Qādir Khuraysāt, *'Ammān fī al-'ahd al-Islāmī* (Amman in the Islamic Age), Arabic text ('Ammān: Amānat 'Ammān al-Kubrah, 2004), p. 88.

84 *Ibid*, pp. 94–95.

85 Aḥmad Muḥāmmad Khalaf al Mūmani, Al-Urdun Tarīkh wa-Ḥadhārah: Dirāsah fi al-Tarīkh *Al-Siyāsi wa-al-'Askari* (Jordan's History and Civilization: A Political and Military study), Arabic text ('Ammān: 'Umun lil-Dirasāt, 2003), p. 33.

III The political history of Jordan under Mamluk rule

In September 1260, Jordan fell under the rule of the Mamluks who took control of Egypt after defeating of the Mongols at the battle of Ain Jalut in Jezreel Valley in Palestine, and it remained under Mamluk rule until the Ottoman conquest in 1516. Although Jordan was located at the periphery of the Mamluk Empire, the political, economic, social, and cultural developments in that county had considerable impact on the empire's welfare and its stability. Jordan had strategic importance, which the Mamluk sultans could hardly afford to ignore during both its early Turkish or Baḥri phase, and the late Circassian or Bourji stage (1260–1382 and 1382–1517 respectively). Most Mamluk sultans were keen on guarding the strategic roads, ramparts and strongholds in Jordan such as the castles in Karak, Shawbak, al-Salt and Ajlun, which remained practically intact after they were built by the Crusaders. They also recognized the strategic and commercial value of the Aqaba harbor, situated across from the old town of Ayla (Eilat) and served as the main outlet to the Red Sea.

In addition to its important geostrategic position connecting the Arabian Peninsula with Iraq, Syria, and Egypt, the port of Aqaba played a vital commercial role, and it turned into one of the most important commercial stations in the Islamic world during that period. Jordan absorbed numerous waves of immigration from all over the Middle East. Many refugees who fled from persecution of the numerous conquerors such as the Persians, the Byzantines, and the Crusaders found refuge there. When the Mongols invaded the region in the mid-thirteenth century, many Ayyubids emirs found shelter in the country's mountainous regions. Many came to places such as Ajlun, al-Salt, Shawbak, and Karak where they could hide in the castles and the fortresses. The influx of refugees continued during the subsequent assaults of the Mongols led first by Hülegü Khan, and later by the Ilkhanid Maḥmoud Ghassan and the great Mongol overlord Tamerlane whose threat to that region did not end until his death in 1405. The Jordanians provided assistance, both material and moral, to the Ayyubids and the Mamluk sultans who ruled Egypt and faced the Mongol invasions.[1] The purpose of this chapter is to explain the importance of Jordan's towns and villages and their contribution to the stability of the Mamluk sultanate.

DOI: 10.4324/9781003450313-4

The Ayyubid Interlude

Ibn al-Athir (1160–1223) tells us that when Ṣalaḥ al-Din was on his deathbed, he summoned his sons Afḍal and his brother al-Adil to discuss the future of the Ayyubid dominions. He told Afḍal to proceed to Khilaṭ in the northwestern side of Lake Van, in present-day Turkey, stressing that this was a strategically located town in the vicinity of the great city of Constantinople, and that its occupation could stop invaders coming from the west. He then ordered his brother al-Adil to go and occupy Karak.[2]

The Ayyubid sultans considered Jordan an important defense line that could not be entrusted to a disobedient vassal. In their eyes, the entire region east and west of the Jordan River was strategically important and required extreme vigilance. When the governor of Karak, al-Mughith Umar, sent a force under the command of Rukn al-Din Khass-Turk to occupy Nablus, sultan al-Malik al-Naṣir Ṣalah al-Din Yusuf (1169–1193) sent an expedition to recapture it. However, unwilling to alienate al-Mughith whom he regarded as a reliable governor capable of preventing that vital region from falling into foreign domination, he bequeathed to him several other places, which hitherto formed the principality of the Ayyubid sultan of Damascus, al-Naṣir Daud (1227–1229); the Balqa, Bayt Jibril, and possibly Hebron.

Karak continued to provide refuge for many dissidents who fled from Mamluk and Syrian rule and it was there that al-Malik al-Ẓahir Baybars and his supporters from the Baḥri Mamluks prepared to invade Egypt. Aided by al-Mughith Umar, they moved toward Egypt, and brought the Ayyubid dynasty to an end in 1260. When the Baḥri Mamluks moved toward Egypt, they met resistance from a military contingent sent by al-Naṣir Yusuf. They were forced to cross the Jordan River and then retreated to Balqa down the eastern shore of the Dead Sea, until they reached Zughar on its southern tip. Then they contacted al-Mughith to whom they pledged their loyalty. Delighted by the fact that these troops could buttress his position vis-á-vis the emir of Damascus, he lavished on them enormous wealth, which the previous sultan of Egypt al-Ṣaliḥ Ayyub (1240–1249) stored in Karak Castle eight years earlier. He then joined his army to theirs but the entire force, which included many mercenaries, including Shahrzuri Kurds, suffered a crushing defeat by the Egyptian army, which was led by Faris al-Din al-Musta'rib and Sayf al-Din Kutuz, at the battle that took place in March 1258.[3]

The Mongol invasion had such a profound impact on the balance of power in the region that some of the Ayyubid emirs became desperate and allied themselves with the Mongols and the Crusaders against other Ayyubid amirs. This accelerated the decline of Ayyubid influence in the region, and led to the fall of Ḥims, Ḥama, Aleppo, and Damascus in 1260. Many of the Ayyubid princes found refuge in Jordanian towns. For example, al-Malik al-Naṣir, ruler of Aleppo, fled southward and found refuge at the Karak Castle. After the Mongols laid a siege to Karak, al-Naṣir surrendered to Hülegü and asked for amnesty. Ibn al-Wardi (d. 1348) tells us that al-Naṣir was caught by Hülegü after he left Birket Ziziya because one of his men betrayed him and informed Hülegü on his whereabouts. He was found in

Karak and brought to Ajlun, which resisted the Mongol assault and was forced to order the defenders to surrender the castle, which the Mongols destroyed.[4]

Birket Ziziya was a haven to several Ayyubid sultans. When sultan al-Malik al-Ashraf Musa al-Ayyubi (1250–1254) came to this region to find shelter from the Mongols, Hülegü sent Amir Sarim al-Din Uzbek bin Abdallah al-Ashrafi with soldiers and cavalry to Birket Ziziya where he found him.[5] This mountainous region and particularly Ajlun and its castle provided shelter to those who fled from the assault of the Mongols who eventually captured it in 1260. They occupied the castle and looted the town until they were defeated at the battle of Ain Jalut later that year. The castle was liberated by Sultan Qutuz who rebuilt and refortified it.

Al-Salt was the last to fall under Mongol rule and like other regions it provided shelter to Muslim warriors who sought refuge from Mongol savagery. In this castle, there was a stiff resistance to Mongol rule led by Badr al-Din Muhammad bin al-Ḥaj al-Nahiḍh Abi Bakr al-Atabaki. The resistance lasted long but was eventually subdued. The sources do not tell us whether, or not the Mongols committed atrocities in that place. Qutuz regained it from the Mongols after defeating them at Ain Jalut and al-Atabaki occupied it.

Although the Mongols managed to conquer these strongholds, the distant mountainous regions of Jordan remained unoccupied. All the Ayyubid emirates collapsed when the Mongols advanced, except for Karak, which was ruled by al-Malik al-Mughith Umar. Despite their fame as marauders who relied solely on force, the Mongols tried to capture Karak by diplomacy and peaceful means. They conducted negotiations and send diplomatic missions until they managed to convince al-Mughith to join and fortify the castle for them. Meanwhile, Shawbak fell under the influence of Karak, and was incorporated into the territory ruled by al-Mughith. Ṣarim al-Din Qaimaz al-Naṣiri became al-Mughith's deputy in Shawbak. Under al-Mughith, Karak became one of the principal Ayyubid emirates and it constituted a threat to the Mamluk state, especially when al-Mughith made it clear that he intended to help the Mongols extend their influence in the region. This led sultan Qutuz who already defeated the Mongols at Ain Jalut to allow al-Mughith to retain Karak but he deprived him of al-Salt, Balqa and al-Khalil.

Following the death of Qutuz and the rise of Baybars, al-Mughith resumed his hostile acts against the Mamluk state. Ibn Shaddad (1145–1234) tells us that his hostility to the Mamluks and his connection with the Mongols stemmed from his envy and hatred of Baybars whom he regarded as a tyrant who attempted to monopolize power.[6]

Jordan's towns and castles under the Baḥri Mamluks

The Mamluks began ruling Egypt following the death of al-Malik al-Mu'aẓẓam Turan Shah, the last sultan of the Ayyubid dynasty (1249–1250). In 1254, some of Mamluk emirs realized that they were in danger and fled to other regions of Greater Syria. One of them was Baybars who fled to Gaza asking for protection from al-Malik al-Nasir who allowed him to operate freely along the Egyptian border. Their regiments had robbers who attacked areas dominated by Muslims and

Franks. It is possible that al-Malik al-Nasir and later the Ayyubid emir Mughith al-Din of Jordan contemplated the possibility of an invasion to Egypt with the help of such Mamluk rebels.[7]

In 1258, Hülegü stormed Baghdad and brought the Abbasid Caliphate to an end. Hülegü's invasion came at the time that the Mamluk regime was only beginning to establish itself in Egypt. The Ayyubid emirs who fought over the towns of Greater Syria did not manage to settle their differences and thereby not only enabled Hülegü to benefit from the chaos that prevailed there but also paved the way for the rise of the Mamluks who proved more equal to the task of facing the Mongol threat, to rise in Egypt.

In 1259, al-Malik al-Manṣur Ali Ibn Aybak Izz al-Din Nur al-Din (1257–1259), who was incapable of controlling the recalcitrant emirs in his court, nominated his father's vizier al-Muẓaffar Saif ad-Din Kutuz al-Mu'izzi who fought against the Mongols and liberated Jordan, Syria, and Palestine, as his successor.

During the Baḥri epoch (1260–1382), all the lands of Greater Syria were exposed to Mongol invasions. The conquest of Damascus took place in 1260, following the flight of its ruler al-Malik al-Naṣir Yusuf to Shawbak, and then to Balqa where he found refuge with one of the tribes. Damascus surrendered to the Mongols and was taken over by Hülegü Khan who then sent his forces, which took over Palestine, Ajlun, Balqa, Birket Zizya, and al-Salt. Following the Mongol defeat at Ain Jalut, Baybars became the sultan in Egypt (1260–1261) and began fortifying the northern region of Jordan, particularly Ajlun and Balqa. Moreover, he ordered the refortification of al-Salt. By refortifying the string of castles and fortifications, which passed through al-Salt, Ajlun, Karak, and other towns in Jordan, he began forming the core of Mamluk defense line in the north, which protected the state against invasions by Mongols and Crusaders. In the winter of 1266, Baybars ordered the construction of a bridge over the Jordan River at Damiah. This bridge connected al-Salt, through Karawa with Nablus and it was designed to facilitate the transfer of supplies to the Mamluks just like Jacob's Daughters Bridge in the north, which as it turned out, did not facilitate the transfer of heavy equipment. Stores with massive supplies were built in Ajlun and Karak.[8]

When Baybars came to power and perceived Jordan's importance to the security of his kingdom, he nominated Izz al-Din Aybak Bin Abd Allah al-Alani as governor of Ajlun and ordered him to repair the castles of Izz al-Din Usama and that of al-Salt. Concerned that the cities along the coast would fall into the hands of the Crusaders, Baybars reached an agreement that left them in control of a few sites on the coast. He regarded Jordan as a vital region connecting Syria and Egypt. His objective was to secure the road between Ajlun and Syria, in order to facilitate the movement of his troops and their equipment when needed. He built stations for pigeon posts and towers in order to transmit news between Iraq and Egypt on the route that passed through Irbid and Ajlun. This was a route through which news arrived to the sultan in Cairo twelve hours after the events took place.[9]

The inhabitants of Greater Syria and the Jordanians among them were astounded by the change of regime that took place in in Egypt on October 24, 1260, when Baybars came to power, after killing Qutuz who ruled Egypt during that time

(1259–1260). They were gripped by fear and began thinking about rebellion. Petty rulers at the margins of the Mamluk Empire began asserting themselves as independent leaders and recruited soldiers to achieve that aim.

Of all the fortresses and castles in that region, Karak with its fortified castle was the most prominent, and it was there that most military encounters between the Mamluk sultans of Egypt and the local rulers took place. The rise of Baybars as the sultan of Egypt and Syria constituted a new phase in the history of the conflict between Cairo and Karak, which lasted for more than two and a half years (1260–1263). This conflict ended with Baybars' domination over Karak, which he took from al-Mughith whom he imprisoned and killed at the Cairo Castle. Thus, the Mamluk state managed after its victory at Ain Jalut and its domination of both banks of the Jordan River to subdue Karak and incorporate it into its dominions.

Major changes occurred in Jordan during Baybars' reign when Amir Alam al-Din Sanjar al-Ḥalabi, the governor (*naīb*) of Damascus assumed the title 'sultan of Damascus', declared *jihad* and extended his influence southward to Ajlun.[10] Baybars' attempts to dissuade him from his intent were to no avail. Meanwhile, the Mongols and the Crusaders agreed to collaborate against the Mamluks but they failed to achieve their objectives. While the Mongols lost the battle against the Muslim forces stationed in Aleppo and Ḥama, the Crusaders who attempted to recover some of their former positions in the Near East lost the battle against the Turcomans of the Jawlan, south of Damascus, and were forced to pay them tribute. The prospect of an alliance between the Mongols and the Crusaders against the Mamluk state that dominated Greater Syria from its center in Cairo did not materialize; however, it was frequently discussed in Europe, and the Papacy did not relinquish the idea throughout the entire Mamluk period.[11]

Noticing al-Ḥalabi's weakness in Damascus and his inability to extend his influence southward Baybars embarked on a campaign aimed at detaching the northern areas of Jordan from his orbit. His objective was to capture the fortresses in that region, defend them from the Crusaders, and fortify the communication line between Damascus and Cairo. He began expanding his control over Ajlun, knowing well that this was a superb defensive line. Baybars was no stranger in Ajlun where he was stationed in 1246 with his commander Ala al-Din al-Bandaqdar whom the Ayyubid sultan Najm al-Din Ayyub (1169–1193) sent in order to fortify his position in that region. At that time, Ajlun's chief judge (*qaḍi*) was Aḥmad bin Abd al-Samad bin Abdallah who was one of the prominent personalities with connections to the town's most influential dignitaries. Baybars' connection with him proved useful and it helped him to obtain legitimization of his acquisition of al-Salt and other strategically located areas in Jordan such as Balqa and Ajlun. However, the southern part of that region was still under the control of al-Mughith Umar, last of the Ayyubid emirs who ruled Karak. Seeking to increase his influence in Jordan, Baybars contacted the Damascene emirs with a view to incite them against al-Ḥalabi. Encouraged by the Egyptian support, they besieged al-Ḥalabi at Damascus Castle and forced him to flee to Baalbek, Lebanon, where he was imprisoned. Thus, Baybars managed to take control of most of Greater Syria. The only area that he still needed to capture was the Emirate of Karak, which remained under the emir of the previous Ayyubid dynasty that ruled Egypt. It was not until 1263 that Baybars took control of this emirate and turned it into an integral part of the Mamluk Empire.

Aware of the strategic significance of this region, Baybars began constructing a defense line from the castles of Transjordan to Ḥims, and from al-Asia Castle northward. He repaired the fortifications of Shaba, al-Salt, Ajlun, and Karak, which he also turned into a central district and a headquarters for his administration and armed forces. He then raised an army and recruited skilled personnel to serve in his administration, granted land (*iqtā'*s) to Bedouin tribes who yielded to his authority and gave amnesty to the people of Karak. In addition, Baybars invested efforts in maintaining the region in order and he delegated powers to local emirs who submitted to his rule and proven their loyalty. In 1263, messengers from Khaibar in the Ḥejaz arrived at the sultan's court and asked him to free some of the refugees that were in his custody. Seeking to secure his friendship with the local tribes, he honored the request, entrusting Amir Amin al-Din Musa Ibn al-Turkumani to carry out that task. At the same time, he instructed the governor of Karak, Izz al-Din Aydamar al-Ẓahiri, to gather a naval force in order to protect the coastal regions of the Mediterranean that were laid astride Jordan's fortifications. Baybars sought to benefit the most from Jordan's strategic location. In addition to the ramparts, which he established and fortified, he built a caravanserais (*khan*s), mills, bakeries, and other facilities, with a view to expand the settlements that were close to his line of defense in Jordan. He also used lands and building given as endowments by Muslim benefactors (*awqāf*) to establish shops and workshops that served his armed forces and his bureaucratic apparatus. He expanded the area under Mamluk control northwards as well as in the south. In 1265, he laid a siege to Arsuf castle on the Palestinian coast and sent many of its prisoners to the Karak castle. He then ordered the destruction of the towers of Arsuf. The land and the spoils taken during his campaign were given to the warriors who participated in the *jihad* against the Crusaders.

Most Mamluk sultans were keen on guarding the main castles such as those in in Karak, Shawbak, al-Salt, and Ajlun. The Egyptian historian and Hanafi scholar Ibn al-Furat (1334–1405) tells us that in 1285/1286, sultan al-Manṣur Qalaun (1279–1290) sent governor Amir Ḥasam al-Din Ṭarnṭai al-Manṣuri "with a huge army of Egyptian troops and ordered him to go to Karak and lay a siege to it."[12]

In 1281, Qalaun was in Jericho and he was in a process of negotiations with the Franks while his other Mamluk opponents conspired to assassinate him in a place called Khamra Beisan. The chief conspirator Kundakh who was interested in collaboration with the Franks told them about the conspiracy. However, the Franks alerted Qalaun who already found out about the conspiracy. Some of the conspirators were drowned at the Sea of Galilee. This was a pragmatic decision made by the Franks who were motivated by fear rather than an act of chivalry.[13]

After the ceasefire of 1283, Qalaun signed a treaty with the Franks, which gave him control over Karak, Shawbak, Hebron, Jerusalem, Lajjun, Jenin, Ajlun, and numerous other regions.[14]

Jordan continued to loom large in the eyes of the Mamluk sultans who followed Baybars and despite periods of neglect, which stemmed from over-confidence, financial crises, competition among the claimants to the throne, corruption, and other factors that weakened the Mamluk Empire, the fortifications were generally kept in good repair. Sultan al-Naṣir Muhammad bin Qalawun (1293–1294; 1299–1309; 1310–1341) paid attention to Jordan and did utmost to fortify the region against the Mongol invasion. He regarded the region as an essential springboard to the towns of northern Syria. The occupation of Karak from which he sought to proceed toward the Syrian towns of Ḥama and Aleppo occupied an important part of his strategic thinking.[15] It appears from the sources that local opposition to Mamluk control was minimal at best. The sources do not tell us about major resistance from Jordan's inhabitants who apparently preferred to be under Cairo's tutelage than that of Damascus. In fact, Ibn Kathir (1301–1373) provides a detailed description of al-Naṣir's entry into Karak, the warm welcome that he received when he stopped on his way to Damascus and the unease, which the governor of Damascus felt when it became obvious to him that the Mamluk sultan enjoyed such popularity in an area where he had territorial ambitions.[16] Al-Naṣir refortified the Shawbak Castle and improved the pilgrims' road southward to Aqaba. Moreover, he strengthened the fortifications in Aqaba and built a fortress on Mount Harun, which stands to this day. To ease the movement of troops and encourage commerce, he built caravanserais, which served the merchants and their beasts of burden. The most prominent among these were built in Aqaba, al-Ḥasa, and several other regions.

Following the Battle of Ain Jalut, Jordan remained under Mamluk rule until the Ottoman conquest in 1516. That Baybars' successors did not wish to neglect Jordan was largely due to the fact that the Mongol assaults did not cease after Ain Jalut and it was not entirely clear whether or not the Crusaders would resume their campaigns in that region.

By the time that the Mamluks took over Egypt, the Orders of the Templars and Hospitallers, which played a major part in the Crusades, were in a state of weakness and disarray, unwilling to resign to the fact that their days of glory were over. Their military castles in the Levant, which included Arsuf, Safed, Belfort, Chastel Blanc, Crac de Chevalier, Akkar, Belda, Marga, and others, all fell in Mamluk hands between 1265 and 1285. The Orders fought valiantly to defend the last strongholds of the Crusaders in the region, and during the siege of Acre of 1291, the Master of the Templars was killed, and that of the Hospitallers was seriously wounded. Nevertheless, many Europeans became skeptical about the usefulness of the Orders. Thus, for example, the French knight Philippe de Nanteuil who was captured by the Mamluks at the Battle of Gaza in 1239, went to the extent of expressing his distrust of the Templars, saying that they were cowards. The reluctance of the Orders to assist individual Crusaders in the conquest of lands that could not be defended had alienated many of their supporters. Moreover, there were those who suspected that the Orders amassed fortunes, which they were not willing to share with others. Yet, despite their declining fortunes, the Orders kept their resolve to fight the Mamluks. There were indications that the Hospitallers were bent on building up a naval squadron for that purpose and when James of Molay, the Master of the Templars, toured the West in 1294–1295, he revealed his plans to conduct naval raids on Mamluk coastal towns.

There were other signs that new crusades were about to start at any moment.

There was correspondence between king of France Philip IV (1285–1314) and the Ilkhan of Persia regarding the possibility of a common action against the Mamluks, which both sides saw as feasible and beneficial. A letter from the Ilkhan from 1289 quotes Philip IV as saying, "If the armies of the Ilkhan go to war against Egypt, we shall set out from here to go to war and attack [the rear enemy] in common operations." The Ilkhan's response was:

> Now, We make it known to you, that in accordance with Our honest word, We shall send our armies [to arrive] at the [time and place] agreed, and if by the authority of heaven, We conquer those people, We shall give you Jerusalem.[17]

In 1306, Pope Clement V asked James of Molay and Fulk of Villaret the Master of the Hopsitallers for advice regarding the crusade that he intended to declare. He received two messages from them stating that they understood the importance of maintaining an embargo on Egypt, but Molay rejected the idea of uniting the two Orders, which Clement regarded as a *sine qua non* for embarking on a new crusade.

The hostility between the Mamluks and the Crusading orders did not abate until 1403 when a treaty was signed between them, which restored the status quo of 1370, allowing the orders to maintain a hospital in Jerusalem, keep consuls in places such as Jerusalem, Ramla and Damietta, and maintain custody of the pilgrimage to the Holy Land.[18] The threat of a new crusade compelled the Mamluks to maintain their positions not only along the coast of the Levant but also in the hinterland and the areas close to Jerusalem. The string of fortifications, which stretched along Jordan, remained a vital part of the Mamluk defense system, and it constantly had to be maintained and reinforced. These were the imperatives, which dictated Mamluk policy throughout the entire period between the conquest of these fortresses by the Crusaders until the beginning of the fifteenth century, and it was unlikely that they deemed it prudent to abandon their vigilance over the fortifications of Jordan immediately following the conclusion of the peace accord. Moreover, the idea of a European collaboration with the Mongols became a cardinal point in the Papacy's foreign policy, and it was frequently proposed by Christian propagandists of the later medieval period who shared its hostility to the Mamluks.

In addition to the debâcle suffered by the Europeans at the Battle of Ḥattin in 1187, the fall of Acre in 1291 and the fall of Constantinople in 1453, the presence of kings and former crusaders from the Near East reminded the Europeans of their defeat and made them more determined to renew the fight against the Muslims. It was no mere coincidence that the presence the King of Cyprus, Peter I de Lusignan in Europe came shortly before the sack of Alexandria in 1365. Clearly, not all calls for a renewed crusade were directed against the Mamluks, and after the fall of Nicopolis to the Ottomans in 1396, the Byzantine Emperor Manuel II Paleologus called on the Europeans to save the beleaguered city of Constantinople. His call, however, kept the crusading spirit alive in Europe and the Mamluks remained the target of European aspirations and feelings of revenge.

Aziz S. Atiya reminds us that the Europeans were far from abandoning the idea of a renewed crusade and he emphasizes the fact that "the fourteen century in particular is marked by an avalanche of literary propaganda covering almost all the countries of Europe." The Mamluks remained highly vulnerable to this campaign. Typical of that sort of propaganda was the passionate appeal (*Epistola*) of Thaddeus of Naples who was evicted from Acre along with other Christians following the city's fall in 1291, exhorting the Europeans to go on a new crusade. Both Charles II of Anjou, King of Naples who inherited his father's claim to the crown of Jerusalem, and the Franciscan friar Fidenzio of Padua who assisted Pope Nicolas IV were sympathetic toward the idea. References to the Mamluks were made on numerous occasions by secular as well as religious figures in Europe. For example, in his essay *Liber recuperationis Terre Sancta*, Fidenzio highly recommends a maritime blockade of the Mamluk Empire from bases on the coast of Cilician Armenia that could serve for military operations against Syria and Palestine. Furthermore, the news about the famous Catalan propagandist Raymond Lull (1232–1316) who was stationed in Tunis while he was on a mission to convert the Muslims kept the crusading spirit alive. It was also during that period that Philip IV who humbled the Papacy by transferring its seat from Rome to Avignon envisioned the establishment of an eastern empire encompassing Byzantium, the Holy Land, and the entire Mamluk sultanate to be ruled by one of his sons.

Among the most powerful advocates of another crusade against the Muslims were Peter Dubois and William of Nogaret, two prominent jurists who had considerable influence in the French court. In addition, powerful personalities who were associated with the crusading movement such as Molay, Villaret, Henry II de Lousignan, and the Genoese admiral Benedict Zaccaria popularized the crusading idea and some of them expressed their thought in treatises that circulated in Europe at that time. In his treatise *De recuperatione Terre Sancta*, Dubois advocated not only missionary work in the Near East but also a ban on trade with the Mamluks by imposing a blockade that would cripple their commercial ties with the rest of the world. This was one of the numerous propaganda pieces in Europe at that time, and they were instrumental in leading Peter I de Lusignan the Latin king of Cyprus (1359–1369) and his close associates Peter Thomas and Philip of Mézières who managed to convince the Venetians to supply the necessary ships to invade Egypt in 1365. The 165 ships, which departed to Alexandria on October 4 of that year came from Cyprus, Rhodes, Venice, and Genoa, and the entire force was led by king of Cyprus Peter I de Lusignan founder of the Order of the Sword whose mission was to liberate Jerusalem. Although the city was fortified, the weakness of the Mamluks was obvious for all to see. The reigning sultan was the seven-year-old Sha'ban who was manipulated by his guardian emir Yalbogha.

The Mamluk army was not prepared for the attack and the damage that the invaders inflicted on the city was immense. The looting and plundering lasted for about a week and the assailant spared no one. The fleet is said to have sailed away with some five thousand men and women of all creeds, in addition to plundered objects which filled the ships to the brim.[19] The Mamluks never forgot this calamity.[20] It is hardly surprising therefore that the maintenance of strong military presence in Greater Syria and the fortifications in Jordan, which provided protection from foreign invasion coming from north and west, remained a high priority on the foreign policy agenda of the Mamluk sultans.

Jordan continued to loom large in Mamluk foreign policy not only due to its strategic importance but also for the fertile regions in it.[21] Realizing that the economic prosperity of their empire depended on steady imports of grain the Mamluk sultans could not ignore that region and the string of castles were regarded vital for both their defensive as well as economic value. In addition to guarding the fortifications that crisscrossed Jordan, the Mamluk sultans ensured that the Aqaba harbor, which was the main outlet to the Red Sea remain in their hands. Jordan played an important administrative role in the Mamluk state. The Mamluk sultans turned Karak into a special administrative unit dominating large areas, which extended to the Mediterranean, the Iraqi border and the Arabian Peninsula. During the Mamluk period, Jordan was divided between the provinces of Karak and that of Damascus. It was a corridor between Syria and Egypt and it was refortified during the reign of the Ayyubid sultans who dominated the castle, penetrated the adjacent Bedouin territory, and established the Karak emirate. During the reign of the Ayyubid amir al-Naṣir Daud (1229–1248), this emirate was unified and operated independently from Damascus and Cairo and its borders reached roughly those of present-day Kingdom of Jordan.[22] This emirate was incorporated into the Mamluk state and its borders and its administrative division fluctuated according to the changing circumstances. Major changes in the emirate were already made by Baybars who turned it into the defensive line of the Mamluk state. Al-Naṣir Muhammad developed it further, and introduced financial and tax reforms. His sons tried to turn it into an imperial capital and the Bourji sultans (1382–1517) continued the trend.

In her study of Mamluk rule in Jordan, Bethany Walker identifies two events that shaped the course of events in the Mamluk dominions during that time; the cadastral surveys (*rawks)* of sultan al-Nasir Muhammad I in southern Syria (1313), Egypt (1315), Tripoli (1317), and Aleppo (1325), and Barquq's financial reform at the end of the fourteenth century.[23] These measures had a profound impact on the territories constituting present-day Jordan. In addition to its strategic importance Jordan was a place where some of the Mamluks sultans, their sons and commanders found refuge. Moreover, it was a place where they kept their arsenals and treasures and where they detained their enemies.

The Jordanian population contributed not only to the security of that region but also to its cultural development during that period. Many Jordanians served in important positions in the great Arab capitals. There were scholars, religious and secular, poets and other men of letters who had considerable impact on the intellectual life of the Mamluk Empire. In addition, Jordan contributed to the commercial and agricultural development of all Mamluk territories. Jordan had a considerable supply of agricultural products such as olives, grapes, figs, vegetables, sugarcanes, and a variety of cereals. The Ghor region played an important role in supplying many of these products to the country's inhabitants. Jordanian industry was also important due to the abundance of its workshops, which produced olive oil, soap, sugarcane, and arms, particularly lances, bows, and arrows. Jordan was also the place through which the commercial caravans and those of the pilgrims passed regularly and it connected the Arabian Peninsula with Iraq, Syria, and Egypt and the port of Aqaba with its outlet to the Far East turned into one of the most important commercial stations in the Islamic world during that period.

Jordan was a place where many uprisings took place. The sons of Baybars, al-Sa'id, and al-Mas'ud were the first to start their uprisings in that region. Jordan served as a refuge to al-Naṣir Muhammad bin Qalaun who embarked on his campaign to take over the Mamluk Empire. It was also the place where Barquq rose in rebellion with the assistance of the region's inhabitants. Numerous other attempts to overthrow the Mamluk regime, some of which were successful, erupted in that region. The descriptions of Ibn Ḥajar al-Asqalani (1372–1449) reveal that chaos reigned on both sides of the Jordan River. In 1409–1410, there was a power struggle in Mount Nablus, which started when Ibn Abd al-Satir and his cousin Abd al-Qaḍir Shaykhi al-Ashir fought against each other. The turmoil that ensued was such that the roads were blocked and life was disrupted for quite some time.[24]

During the Mamluk period, Jordan absorbed numerous waves of immigration from the Middle East and beyond. Many Ayyubid emirs found refuge in Jordan when the Mongols invaded the region and numerous refugees came to seek shelter in its mountainous regions. They came to places such as Ajlun, al-Salt, Shawbak, and Karak. Those who fled from the conquests of Mahmoud Ghassan (1271–1304) and Tamerlane (1336–1405) arrived at these locations as well. The Jordanian population provided material and moral assistance to the Mamluk sultans who faced the Mongol invasions.[25] Greater Syria, which included the territories of present-day Jordan, was profoundly affected by the coming of the Mongols. In 1299, the Mongols invaded Damascus again. They were led by Ghassan whose armies defeated the Mamluks at Wadi Khazandar in December that year. They captured Damascus and the Friday noon prayer (*khutba*) was read in Ghassan's name. His armies reached the Ghor and invaded Jerusalem, Hebron, Gaza, and Karak where they looted and destroyed all that was in their way. Ghassan sent a force of 20,000 warriors to the Jordan Valley and they moved toward Ajlun and Ṣarkhad, forcing the region's governor Palawan to retreat to Egypt. The mayhem did not cease until Ghassan decided to turn back. In 1303, Ghassan invaded once again, and there was a massive immigration of refugees from the Syrian towns. The Jordanian towns had ample supplies and food for the newcomers. The Mongol threat to Greater Syria did not end until 1321, when the Mamluk sultan al-Naṣir Muhammad bin Qalaun concluded a truce with Abi Sa'id the Ilkhan of Persia. Following the death of Abi Sai'd in 1335, the Mongol states in Iran collapsed.

The Mongol invasions caused many of the inhabitants of Greater Syria to move toward the Jordanian towns. The first major influx of refugees came in 1299, when the Mongols defeated a Mamluk army in Majmau' al-Muruj, near Ḥims. This invasion led to a major migration, which included not only the elite members of Greater Syria but commoners as well. They fled toward the mountains of Ajlun and Balqa. This migration caused major concern in Damascus where the governor called for an emergency meeting in order to bring it to an end. It was at that time that the eminent Muslim scholar Ibn Taymiyya (1263–1328) met Ghassan and obtained from him a personal guarantee that the harassment of the Syrian people will cease. However, the Mongol assaults resumed and another wave of migration of Syrians to Jordan ensued. This happened in 1302, when Ghassan returned to Syria. Ibn Aybak al-Dawadari (d. 1313) tells us that the people of Damascus were alarmed, the prices went up, and the Mamluk regime prohibited them from leaving the town and ordered them to prepare for *jihad*.[26] All Jordanian towns that were close by were affected by the turmoil, which the Mongol invasions caused in Greater Syria. Recognizing the strategic value of towns such as Ajlun, al-Salt, Balqa, Karak, and Shawbak with their citadels and fortifications Ghassan was determined to capture them.

During the entire period, the inhabitants of the Jordanian towns contributed to the Mamluk effort to throw off the Mongol yoke. They provided shelter, supplies, and even arms to the refugees who arrived in their towns. Aḥmad al-Qalqashandi (1355–1418) tells us that the Jordanian tribes fulfilled an important role in the campaign against the Mongols. Among these were Ahl al-Mara' who inhabited the towns of the Ḥawran—such as Ajlun, Zarqa, and al-Khalil—Boṣra, and even al-Ḥarrah in the vicinity of Medina. They joined the Mamluk army and played an important role in the victory over the Mongols at the Battle at Shaqḥab (Marj al-Saffar) in 1303. According to al-Qalqashandi, they fought with remarkable heroism.[27] Once again, the Mongol invasion had a direct impact on the Jordanian towns. There was a massive emigration of refugees from the Syrian towns whose inhabitants provided supplies and food to the newcomers.

The power struggle in Jordan did not come to an end even when the Mongol assaults ceased. Karak was one of the strongholds, which the amirs and the tribal chiefs sought to control. The sources tell us that in 1383, the governor of Karak, Amir Taghai Tamr al-Qablawi, fought against Khatir who led the Bedouins in that region and captured his supporters. They fought each other ferociously. The governor was defeated, many of his supporters were killed, and Khatir managed to free the captives held by his rival. However, the governor was bent on taking revenge. He embarked on another campaign against Khatir, and after inflicting a defeat on his forces, he gave him the impression that he was willing to resolve the conflict amicably but when Khatir came to him with his two sons, the governor gave the order to kill them.

Towns and castles in Jordan during the Bourji Mamluk age

Sultan al-Ẓahir Saif al-Din Barquq who ruled for two reigns (1382–1389; 1390–1399) introduced administrative reforms in Greater Syria and applied them to Jordan as well. His son and successor al-Naṣir Faraj bin Barquq who ruled for two reigns as well (1399–1405; 1405–1407) had to face several rebellions in Jordan and was compelled to reinforce the Mamluk presence in that region. Jordan continued to play an important role in the second (Bourji) part of Mamluk rule (1382–1517). It was during that period that Barquq obtained the support of the people in Jordan in his effort to return to power. Jordan was also the place where many uprisings took against Mamluk rule occurred. Nevertheless, the Bourji Mamluks did not pay as much attention to the region as their Baḥri predecessors and Jordan's fortresses were not kept in good repair as they were earlier. Moreover, causes such as drought, locust, pestilence and floods had direct impact on region's demography. Tamerlane's invasion, the struggle for the Mamluk crown, the rebellions of the local governors and the frequent raids of the tribes in the towns and villages, all contributed to the decline of the region, especially in the political and economic realms, and it was not until the sixteenth century that the region regained its former prominence.[28]

Soon after he began his first reign (1382–1389), Barquq faced competition from the Yalbughawiya Turks and especially from Yalbugha al-Naṣiri the governor of Aleppo. This governor took advantage of the fact that the sultan did not pay much attention to the Turkish princes whom he imprisoned, exiled some, and murdered others. Barquq was one of the youngest of the Yalbugha Mamluks, while al-Naṣiri was among the older ones. What sparked the revolt was apparently the unwillingness of the Turkish Mamluks to be ruled by the Circassians who had recently risen in the ranks. As it turned out, Barquq prevailed over his rival, and after imprisoning him in Alexandria, he restored him to his position as governor of Aleppo.

The relations between al-Naṣiri and his rival, the former governor of Aleppo, Sawdun al-Miẓfari deteriorated after the latter informed the sultan about al-Naṣiri's plans to undermine his regime. Al-Nasiri followed a similar tactic. Concerned about al-Naṣiri's designs the sultan called him for clarifications. Al-Naṣiri failed to report, arguing that the uprising of the Turcomans in his region prevented him from coming to Egypt. Meanwhile, he managed to bring the Turcoman princes to his side and thereby took over many towns in Greater Syria, with the exception of Damascus, Baalbek, Karak, and Shawbak. Karak's governor, Amir Sayf al-Din Ma'mur al-Qalmaṭawi, did not rush to take side until he saw who the winner was likely to be. He then chose to ally himself with al-Naṣiri. Consequently, the sultan sent against him a force of five hundred Mamluks, led by several commanders such as Jarkas al-Khalili who arrived in Gaza, captured the commander Ala al-Din Aqbaghah al-Safawi and imprisoned him at the Karak Castle. The Mamluk troops continued northward to meet their enemy but after a ferocious battle, they were defeated by al-Naṣiri's army in 1388. Al-Qalmaṭawi announced his decision to join forces with al-Naṣiri and those of Gaza's governor, Hisam al-Din bin Bakyash. As a precondition for joining the alliance, al-Qalmaṭawi had to surrender the Karak Castle with all the arms, money, and the provisions that it contained to al-Naṣiri.

For those who heard the news, this was a sign that the Mamluk state was in a process of decline and it was an indication that Karak occupied a prominent place in the strategic thinking of the Mamluk sultans. The consequence of the Egyptian defeat was that the commanders fought each other. Jarkas al-Khalili was killed. Another commander, Yunis al-Nawruzi al-Dawadar tried to flee with a group of five hundred followers but he was caught and killed by Anqa bin Shaṭi in the vicinity of the Yarmouk, while he was on his way to Egypt. Bin Shaṭi caught some other commanders who were on their way to Egypt and sent to them Karak Castle as prisoners. Then al-Naṣiri gathered arms and provisions from all regions, including Karak, imprisoned the Circassians in castles such as Ajlun, Ṣarkhad, and other places in Jordan, and prepared to move toward Egypt.[29]

In 1388, Barquq began preparing for the encounter with al-Naṣiri and his allies after hearing about the defeat of his army in Greater Syria. He fortified the castles in Jordan and raised the taxes on its inhabitants. Responding to this threat al-Naṣiri called upon his allies, left Damascus and headed for Egypt. Aided by Gaza's governor Hasam al-Din bin Bakish who informed him regarding the level of readiness among the Egyptian soldiers, he moved toward Saḥliya. When the battle began, it became clear to the sultan that he would not be able to defeat his rival and therefore asked for amnesty, which al-Naṣiri agreed to grant and told him to disappear "until the intensity of his hostility subsides."[30] The hostilities ended and the sultan was spared. After hiding in the citadel, he went to meet al-Naṣiri and they both agreed to let al-Ṣaliḥ Amir Ḥaji bin al-Malik al-Ashraf whom they gave the name al-Malik Al-Manṣur to come to power. Al-Naṣiri became the state's chief administrator, and assumed the title 'The State's Controller' (*muddābir al-mamlaka* and the commander (*atabeg*) of the soldiers. This marked the end of Barquq's first reign.

Fearing that Barquq would come to reclaim his throne al-Naṣiri gathered the chief Mamluks who debated the issue. Some of them, like Minṭash, sought his execution while others were in favor of imprisonment. The final decision was to imprison him in the Karak Castle that was under the control of governor Ḥasam al-Din al-Kujkani. Al-Naṣiri ordered his men to watch over his captive and to release him if Minṭash had no objection. Barquq was imprisoned with his son Amir Yalbugha al-Amri al-Khaski and other family members. However, al-Kujkani befriended his captive. He promised to release him from captivity and told him that he would introduce him to the Turcoman emirs who would protect him. Based on his good relationship with the governor of Karak and the sympathy, which its inhabitants had for him, it seems that Barquq did not try to escape from the castle and waited for the events to unfold.

The rivalry between Minṭash and al-Naṣiri reached its climax in 1388 when Minṭash climbed the citadel. He managed to attract some of the Mamluk amirs to his side and prevailed over al-Naṣiri whom he imprisoned in Alexandria with those who remained loyal to him. He then summoned al-Shihab Aḥmad al-Baridi and they wrote a letter to al-Kujkani telling him to kill Barquq, sever his head, and send to him. Al-Shihab was a Karaki and there was considerable hostility between him and the people of that town because he attempted to confiscate their possessions. In addition, he was married to the daughter of the *qadi* of Karak, Imad al-Din Aḥmad Isa al-Muqairi al-Karaki. A dispute between them erupted when her father tried to convince him to divorce and marry her to someone else. Al-Shihab returned to Egypt and tried to convince Minṭash to allow him to go to Karak and kill Barquq. Minṭash agreed and wrote to the governor of Karak, asking him to help accomplish the mission and provide al-Shihab access to the castle. Arriving at a nearby village, Shihab made his hatred of Imad al-Din known. This alienated the inhabitants of Karak who had sympathy toward the *qadi* and they warned him about al-Shihab's intentions.

The governor refused to carry out the execution even when al-Shihab came to Karak to hasten Barquq's demise. When told to carry out the execution the governor said,

> This is something that I will not do under any circumstances. I will write to Egypt about what I know, I will ask the friendly amirs whom I trust, and I will send an effective message saying: if you want him killed then send someone to kill him.[31]

Barquq was fortunate to have loyalists such as the youth Abd al-Raḥman al-Baba who informed the inhabitants of Shihab's intent. Consequently, they climbed the castle and killed al-Shihab. At that moment, the governor was dining with Barquq. They entered and took him by his hand, brought him out of the tower in which he was imprisoned and told him "step on the head of your enemy!" and showed him al-Shihab's corps. Seeing the frightened governor, they thought of killing him too but the sultan prevented them from doing so. Barquq was declared sultan at the Karak Citadel and the people came to pay him homage.

Meanwhile, Barquq gathered his supporters from among the Circassians and others who agreed to join. One of those who joined him was Na'ir the amir of Ahl Faḍl who feared Barquq who gained popularity among the inhabitants of Karak, Shawbak and their armies. The chiefs of the tribes in the region joined him as well. His power increased considerably when Haytham bin Khater, the amir of Beni Uqbah decided to join him with his 7,000 combatants. The Bedouins of Jarm decided to join after Gaza's governor Hasam al-Din bin Bakish sent a letter to Barquq asking for a reprieve. Even the Christians of Karak and Shawbak hurried to send their support and messages of good will to the freed sultan. Ibn Furat tells us that one Christian merchant hurried to come to Barquq's aid. He writes,

> A Christian merchant from Shawbak came to serve al-Malik al-Zahir Barquq. He met Malik a-Zahir Barquq and told him, "I have a hundred thousand dinar that I wish to give his majesty the sultan so that he will distribute it among the soldiers and the armies who need it. And if they need more, I will bring it, and all of my property and my children would be a hand to his majesty the sultan.' And he thanked him for that and left.[32]

It seems that when Barquq was leaving Karak its dignitaries feared the wrath of Minṭash and Sultan al-Manṣur Ḥaji. They rallied around Imad al-Din Aḥmad bin Isa al-Muqairi, the *qadi* of Karak, whom they convinced to arrest Barquq with help from Minṭash and Ḥaji. They argued that they did not let Barquq out of prison and apologized for releasing him. The *qadi* agreed to the plan to arrest Barquq and sent his brother Naṣir al-Din Muhammad to close the city's gate. The news regarding that scheme reached Barquq who was on his way out of the city. It so happened that Ala al-Din Ali who was in charge of the Office of Karak's Secrets was the brother of *qadi* Imad al-Din who remained devoted to Barquq after his release from Karak Castle. After hearing about the scheme, he went to Barquq and convinced him to accompany him to the city's gate.

Upon their arrival, they found the gate locked. Ala al-Din managed to convince his brother Naṣr al-Din who stood at the gate to open it. Barquq left the city with his allies and all the Mamluks who arrived from the distant regions of Greater Syria in addition to Bedouins, Turcomans, and many of Karak's inhabitants. Ibn Qadi Shuhba (d. 1448) tells us that

> Ẓahir Barquq left Karak on his way to Damascus. Those who went with him were from among the people of Karak, from his Mamluks, those who served him and from among the amirs. There were those who rode and those who walked and they were six hundred or less. Those who went with him sacrificed their lives and some of them had wives that gave up their dowries. They paid their debts and were prepared to kill.[33]

Barquq made his way to Damascus and when he stopped in Lajjun on his way Beni Mahdi came to pay him homage. In 1388, he arrived at Ḥisban where its inhabitants received him warmly. It was at that point that Gaza's governor Ḥussein bin Bakish came with his soldiers and faced Barquq who inflicted a crushing defeat on his army. When Barquq reached Zarqa, notables such as Qasim al-Harathi, Isa bin Faḍl, and al-Ghazawi pledged their allegiance to him. Ibn Sasra (d. 1397?) tells us that "the sultan had taken the cauldrons of Ḥisban and Balqa and all of these towns. His greed intensified, and every day he gained more."[34] When he reached Idhra'at, the Bedouins and the Turcoman tribes came to express their loyalty to him. Amir Naṣr al-Din bin al-Shaikh Ali and his brother Shihab al-Din Aḥmad came to greet him. There are numerous stories about the loyalty and the respect that the people of Jordan had toward Barquq. Ibn Sasra relates a story about the cooks who slaughtered a lamb for the sultan and had among them one who took the lamb's head and put it on a loaf a bread saying, "this is Barquq's head and we shall eat it today." Upon hearing this remark, a Karaki who was standing nearby killed him instantly with his sword.[35]

Barquq managed to meet Jantmar, the brother of Ṭaz, the governor of Damascus, at his home in Shaqḥab, close to Damascus where he defeated him. He obtained reinforcements from other governors such as Kamshabgha al-Ḥamawi the governor of Aleppo who came to his aid with troops and supplies. Upon hearing of his victories in Syria, his rival Minṭash sent a force against him and brought with him al-Manṣur Ḥaji and other dignitaries. In 1389, they met Barquq at Shaqḥab. Kamshabgha retreated to Aleppo and was followed by al-Kujkani the governor of Karak and his men. Then Barquq managed to inflict a crushing blow on Minṭash and his force and proceeded to Egypt to assume the throne for the second time after al-Malik al-Manṣur Amir Ḥaji gave it up while he was still in Shaqḥab. Barquq ruled Egypt again until his death (1390–1399).

It seems that after Barquq became sultan for the second time, he continued to maintain such close ties with Karak's inhabitants, which he could rely on their assistance whenever he faced his opponents. When two Mamluk leaders fought over the governorship of Karak, the sultan intervened but he had to yield to the demand of the inhabitants to install the candidate of their choice. This happened in 1391, when Ṭaghitmar Ibn Abd Allah al-Ala al-Qablawi, the governor of Sa'is, rebelled against his master. Barquq incited the inhabitants of Karak to complain about their governor on the day that sentences were carried out. They rose against their governor and asked that Taghitmar be installed instead.

In 1393, one of the tribes of Karak plundered 3,000 sheep from merchants who passed by their town. When the merchants complained to Sharaf al-Din al-Qashtamri who was the governor at that time, he managed to recover 1,700 but was killed by the tribes in the process of recovering the rest. In 1396, Barquq managed to kill Iyas al-Jarkasi, one of the powerful amirs in Egypt who maintained troops in Damascus. When Naṣiri staged his rebellion, Iyas who was then the governor of Gaza managed to suppress it and imprisoned him in the Karak Castle.[36] Following the sultan's return to Egypt, Iyas was nominated as governor of Safed. He was then transferred to Tripoli where he sought the good will of the Christians by elevating them to high positions at the expense of the Muslims. When he became the governor of the Ghor, he fleeced the population and ruled with iron hand, committing atrocities in the process. Ibn Sasra said about him

> in the towns of Ghor he severed seventy cruel hands, including the foot of a Muslim who stepped on a western cross, and he devastated Ghor, causing its inhabitants to flee. He was the cause of his ruin, one of the cruelest [rulers] who would not be merciful to anyone who complained. [37]

Iyas remained in the Ghor until the sultan recalled him. In 1394, a merchant by the name of Naṣir al-Din bin Abd Allah became the governor of Damascus. He was notorious for his avarice. He is said to have hoarded flower, which he bought when the price was low and sold it when it rose. The popular unrest that ensued led to his assassination by the Damascenes. In the previous year, there was a quarrel between the people of Karak and Amir Naṣir al-Din bin Mubarak, the grandson of Karak's governor Ibn al-Muhmandar. The incident ended in many deaths and injuries. The people of Karak became involved in the reconciliation process and some went to complain to Barquq about their governor.

Barquq was followed by his son Faraj who was named al-Naṣir. During Faraj's reign, there was much turmoil and instability in Greater Syria, which had a negative impact on Jordan. In 1399, Abd al-Rahman al-Mihtar came to Karak with money and gold which he was ordered to place at the Karak Castle and he addressed the *shaikh*s of the region with a view to incite the soldiers against Amir Tanam, the disobedient governor of Syria. Hidden behind this move was the fact that the Egyptian amirs sent al-Mihtar to Karak in order to seize Sawdun al-Ẓarif, the governor of Karak, without his knowledge. What spurred them to act was the conviction that the governor became subordinate to Tanam who ruled Syria. When al-Mihtar arrived at

Karak, Sawdun pursued him but he managed to flee. This led to a division among the people of Karak along the traditional Qays and Yaman pattern; the Yamanies supported Sawdun while the Qaysis supported al-Mihtar. The Qaysis were led by Sharaf al-Din Musa bin Qadi al-Qudah and Imad al-Din Aḥmad al-Karaki, and the Yamanies by the chamberlain (*ḥājib*) Sha'ban bin Abi al-Abbas. They fought each other ferociously and in the encounter, which took place at the Ghor in 1399, there were several deaths and many injured. Ibn Abi al-Abbas and the Yamanies emerged as winners, and al-Mihtar fled to Egypt. Some of the leading Qaysis died and their bodies were dumped into ditch without ablution and all their belongings were confiscated.

Shortly afterward, al-Mihtar returned to Jordan and asked the emir of Beni Uqbah, Munjid bin Khatir to provide him four hundred camels and provisions to help recapture Karak. He later arrived in Karak and blamed Amr bin al-Hadhbani the governor of Karak of disobedience to the sultan. He gathered forces and killed the governor and many of his supporters. Shortly afterward, however, al-Mihtar suffered a defeat at the hands of Amir Shaikh al-Maḥmoudi who came from Safad with his army to Nablus and killed him. The reason for his defeat was that he rose against al-Naṣir Faraj and came to an agreement with Amir Nawruz who sacked Nablus. Al-Maqrizi (d. 1442) tells us that "Abd al-Raḥman al-Mihtar "raided Karak and ruined it by incessant wars."[38]

In 1399, Amir Jarkas al-Sawduni, also known as Abu Tanam, arrived at Karak to take the town after Amir Bitkhas al-Sawduni failed to do so. Jarkas moved toward the town causing mayhem, without opposition from Sha'ban bin Abi al-Abbas the *ḥājib* of Karak, and he established himself there. The destruction caused by the intense strife was immense. The reason for the conflict was that in 1398, the governor of Karak, Sawdun al-Ẓarif, went to meet Sultan Faraj in Damascus after designating Sh'aban as his successor. Following Sawduni's arrival in Damascus, Sha'ban was dismissed, and the sultan nominated Amir Saif al-Din Bitkhas al-Sawduni who rushed to meet him. However, the people of Karak prevented the newly appointed emir from entering the town. They pleaded with the sultan to replace him and he nominated Jarkas instead, but there was intense opposition from some of the people of Karak who supported Sha'ban, and the civil war that ensued brought the city to the verge of ruin.

Another wave of immigration came with the rise Tamerlane who invaded the Syrian towns in 1399. The Mamluk sultan al-Naṣir Faraj bin Barquq (1389–1412) was the one who facilitated the flight of the people who lived in the Syrian towns to Jordan and Egypt. When the army that accompanied Faraj on his way to the Hawran was defeated, many of its officers and soldiers fled to Jordan, which became a place of refuge for those who fled from the Mongols and the Mamluk authorities.[39] Ibn Ḥajar al-Asqalani (d. 1449) relates how refugees who sailed through the Dead Sea passed through Transjordan on their way to Cairo. Others fled to the rural region of the Ḥawran and the northern regions of Jordan such as Irbid, Ajlun, and it villages. These regions were attractive because they were fortified and inaccessible. There were occasions, however, when newcomers encountered difficulties and raids by the local tribes in Jordan. This happened after the sultan Faraj left Damascus and returned to Egypt with his amirs. Those who headed for Jordan were caught by the local tribes who robbed and massacred them.

The group that came to this region in 1400 included the Amir Shihab al-Ḥalabi, Jamal al-Malkawi, and others who headed toward Arafat and Ajlun. Jordan's inhabitants provided them with all their needs and they joined the Mamluks in the efforts to defeat the Mongols. We are also told that one of the local chiefs, Amir Shihab al-Din Aḥmad bin al-Shaikh, made his way to the Jordan Valley and recruited followers among which was Isa bin Faḍl of Ahl Ali and Beni Mahdi, in addition to the Bedouin Ḥartha and their chief, Ibn al-Qan al-Ghazawi, who managed to gather more than a thousand horses to defeat the Timurids.

According to Badr al-Din al Ayni (1360–1453), Tamerlane's assault caused considerable alarm not only in the northern cities of Syria such as Aleppo, Damascus, Ḥama, and Ḥims, but also in Jerusalem, Nablus, Beisan, and even Ajlun. Following Tamerlane's death in 1405, those who took refuge in the Jordanian towns returned to their homes, finding that nothing was left after of the Timurid invasion.

From the Arabic sources, we gather that the people of Karak were the guardians of the sultan's authority in their region and that they opposed his enemies. For example, in 1401, Ṣuraq, the governor of Gaza rebelled against his master and he gathered around him bandits who blocked the roads. The sultan decided to nominate Salamish as governor instead but Ṣuraq imprisoned the nominee. Salamish managed to escape and obtained support from the Bedouins of Jaram whose amir Amr bin Faḍl al-Jarami joined his rebellion. They followed Ṣuraq and caught him. Gaza was exposed to looting and it was only after the intervention of Amr bin Faḍl that the town was spared. Ṣuraq who managed to escape took control of the Ghor and defended it from the tribes who invaded it.

In 1404, the governor of Syria, Shaikh Maḥmoudi, ordered the Ghazawi tribe of Ajlun to bring camels and supplies to the town of Idhra'at. Feeling that they did not fulfil their obligations when he was away, he destroyed their houses in Ajlun and Ṣakhra. The members of the Ghazawi tribe became powerful in that region when they obtained *iqṭā*'s from Barquq following his departure from Karak. They became too independent and cared for no one else thereafter, but when they were punished by the governor, they regretted what they had done and asked for amnesty.

The Mongol threat reappeared during the Bourji period and the conflict with the Mamluks resumed in course by the end of the fourteenth century, during Barquq's reign, when Tamerlane attacked Tabriz and defeated its leader Aḥmad bin Aways who fled to Baghdad. According to al-Aṣqalani, Tamerlane's assault on Greater Syria started in 1399. The Mongol assault continued when Aḥmad bin Aways who ruled Baghdad killed some of its amirs and persecuted others. In return, they complained to Tamerlane's governor who came and captured the city. Some historians argued that the imprisonment of Aṭlamish, a relative of Tamerlane, by Yusuf al-Turkmani who ruled Tabriz, was the reason for the Mongol invasion of Syria. The Hungarian traveler and Orientalist Arminius Vámbéry (1832–1913) notes that the need to rescue the captives who were tormented by their oppressors drove Tamerlane to conquer Khorasan and to save the rulers of Persia, Iraq and

Syria from the anarchy that reigned there.[40] To this, one needs to add the economic importance of Syria and Egypt and the strategic and religious value of the region. In addition, the Mongols' desire to recover their losses and to restore the pride lost at Ain Jalut played a major role in the renewed assault on Greater Syria. The hostility of the Mongols did not cease even when many of them adopted Islam and others converted to Christianity.

The Mongol invasion was unrelenting. They captured Malṭiya, Bahsana, and Aleppo, which according to al-Asqalani was taken because its ruler Damardash collaborated with Tamerlane. At the same time, Miran Shah, son of Tamerlane, attacked Hama in 1400. Tamerlane advanced toward Ḥims and Baalbek on his way to Damascus. Amirs all over the state called upon sultan Faraj to save them from the Mongols and he sent his army to Gaza and then continued to Damascus where he arrived later that year and forced Tamerlane to withdraw. From what al-Maqrizi tells us, it becomes evident that the inhabitants of Jordan were sympathetic to their Muslim brethren. He writes,

> Amir Shihab al-Din Aḥmad bin al-Shaikh headed toward the *aghwar* and assembled many followers among whom were Isa bin Faḍl amir Ahl-Ali, Beni Mahdi and the Bedouins of Ḥartha, and Ibn Alqan and the Ghazawi, and they found in Tamriya more than a thousand horsemen, killed most of them and took from them gold and many pearls.[41]

Al Asqalani reminds us that Jordan was the place into which many refugees who fled from the Mongols passed. He mentions the fact many of them sailed through the Dead Sea from Jordan and then fled to Egypt. Other historians, such as Aḥmad Ibn Arabsha (1370–1389), tell us that the refugees passed through that region without mentioning the places. They found refuge in the northern and eastern parts of Jordan. The anonymous historian of the work *Qiṭ'ā min Tarikh al-Qarn al-Tasi' al-Hijri* (*A Fragment from the History of the Ninth Hijri Century*) writes,

> On the night of 28 Rabi' al-Akhir, a group from them reached us when we were sowing, before sunset, among them were Shihab al-Din al-Ḥalabi and Jamal al-Malkawi, and told us that the rest of the caravans were heading toward the towns of Idhra'at and Ajlun.[42]

Just like Jordan, the Nablus Mountain became a refuge to those who fled from the Mongols and a place where the Mamluk troops were stationed. It was there that the inhabitants of Nablus prevailed over a Mongol force sent by Tamerlane. They were defeated near a narrow canyon that lies between two mountains by the inhabitants who used mostly stones and daggers. Al-Maqrizi informs us of the demographic changes that took place in the region in 1400, when Tamerlane's troops invaded and caused many of the al-Ghazawi and other tribes to move toward the Ḥawran, which at that time included Irbid and Ajlun. It seems that the al-Ghazawi, which settled in Ajlun played an important role in the struggle of the second Mamluk state against the Mongols.

In 1400, Tamerlane's soldiers captured and sacked Damascus. Shortly afterward, Jordan was exposed directly to the assaults of the Mongols. Al-Badr al-Ayni tells us that the fear drove the inhabitants of Jerusalem, Nablus, Beisan, and Ajlun to flee. The sources for that period make it clear that Jordan was exposed to Mongol invasion just as much as the northern parts of Greater Syria, and that the inhabitants of that region played an important role in its defense. Furthermore, it seems that the region's economy was severely affected by the invasions, especially if one takes into account the fact that this was the road, which the pilgrims took on their way to Mecca and Medina. Al-Fasi (d. 1428) mentions the fact that due to Tamerlane's invasion no pilgrims came from Syria in 1400 through the way that they were accustomed.[43]

Meanwhile, in Egypt, the Bourji Mamluks were dissatisfied with Sultan Faraj who promoted the Greco-Romans (*Rums*) personnel at their expense. They attempted to drown him and sought to replace him with Baybars, son of sultan Barquq's sister. Fearing for his life, Faraj went to hide in the house of Sa'd al-Din Ibn Ghurab. In response, the Mamluk amirs sought to promote the ten-year-old crown prince Abd al-Aziz bin al-Sultan al-Ẓahir Barquq to whom they paid homage in 1405. Shortly afterward, however, the boy was overthrown and al-Naṣir Faraj ascended the throne. The weakness of the central government in Cairo was such that Jordan and other regions of Greater Syria were adversely affected by it. In 1405, Amir Sawdun came from Damascus to overthrow Emir Yashbak al-Mawsawi who occupied the Karak Castle and refused to surrender it. Consequently, Sawdun invaded the Balqa region and terrorized its inhabitants. This, in turn, compelled the governor of Syria, Amir Nauruz, to call upon Gaza's governor Ḥasan bin Bakish to go to Karak in order to replace al-Mawsawi. During the same year, Sha'ban Azbak Dawadar al-Amir Nauruz came from Damascus with his soldiers to overthrow Karak's governor al-Mawsawi who managed to assemble the Bedouins of Jarm and their amir Amr bin Faḍl tried to take over Gaza and overthrow its governor Salamash. It seems that Amr ibn Faḍl sent a message to Salamash informing his about the event. When they arrived, the governor of Gaza was ready to meet them and the fighting ended with the capture of al-Mawsawi whose horse's feet sunk in the mud.

Sawdun al-Muḥammadi who was sent by Nauruz to Gaza tarried in Ramla and did not arrive. Then Salamsah sent a message to Nauruz informing him that al-Mawsawi was captured, and he ordered his imprisonment at the Damascus Castle. Amr bin Faḍl the amir of Jarm who was stationed in Ajlun was killed later that year, and the sultan sent Muhammad al-Turkmani to Karak instead of Sawdun al-Jalab. Al-Turkmani advanced toward Karak, captured Ibn Faḍl, beheaded him and sent his head to Cairo. Afterward, this emirate was ruled by Faḍl bin Isa al-Jarmi who appealed to the sultan to grant him the position for the payment of 50,000 silver dirhams.

In 1403, Amir Shaikh al-Maḥmoudi who lost the governorship of Damascus to Sawdan al-Ḥamzawi rebelled against the sultan and tried to release Amir Nauruz from Ṣubiba prison, in present-day Banias, but he failed to do so. Concerned about the potential threat posed by al-Maḥmoudi, the sultan, pursued him to Damascus and imprisoned him in its castle. However, al-Maḥmoudi managed to flee and take over Damascus from Nauruz. Then two rivals reconciled and al-Maḥmoudi seized the governorship of Tripoli. Together they dominated Greater Syria and decided to march toward Cairo. However, sultan Naṣir Faraj proved to be wiser. He broke the alliance, bringing al-Maḥmoudi to his side by granting him the governorship of Damascus. This enabled the sultan to isolate Nauruz and to send him to exile in Jerusalem. Then the sultan became engaged in another campaign against al-Maḥmoudi who refused to extradite some of the amirs, which the sultan ordered him to send to Cairo. During the campaign, al-Maḥmoudi found refuge at Ṣarkhad Castle to which the sultan laid a siege for an entire month. Eventually, however, they came to an agreement that terminated the hostilities.

The Jordanian tribes took the opportunity to benefit from the fight between al-Maḥmoudi and Nauruz. Led by Muhammad bin Haiza', the amir of Beni Mahdi, they brought mayhem to the region. Al-Maḥmoudi who was on his way to fight the governor of Safad, Shahin al-Zardakash defeated bin Haiza'. Al-Maḥmoudi and Nauruz dominated Greater Syria and the tension between them resumed. However, when the sultan marched against them in 1405, they decided again to settle all their differences. Accordingly, al-Maḥmoudi obtained control over Damascus and its environs, while Nauruz took Aleppo and the adjacent areas. This state of affairs allowed them to act independently and ignore the sultan.

Determined to teach his vassals a lesson the sultan sent another expedition under Sawdun al-Jalb who marched toward Karak and captured it. While the sultan was in Aleppo, al-Maḥmoudi and Nauruz moved toward Damascus. They passed through Tadmor, Ṣarkhad, Balqa, Jerusalem, and Gaza on their way to Cairo in an attempt to capture it, but they were defeated by the sultan's army and headed back toward Karak through the Sinai Peninsula. Upon their arrival at Nakhl, they split into two corps; one force under Nauruz who was accompanied by Yashbak bin Azdmar and Sawdum Baqja, and the other by al-Maḥmoudi and Sawdan al-Muḥammadi. Each group was accompanied by Mamluks who acted as soldiers of fortune willing to profit from the mayhem. Upon their arrival in Shawbak, its inhabitants resisted and they made their way to Karak, while Sawdun al-Jalb let them enter the town where they remained.

In 1410, the chief *qadi* Shams al-Din al-Akhnai and the military commander Taj al-Din Rizq Allah proceeded to Ajlun to prepare for the sultan's arrival to Karak. Many Egyptians were killed in the encounter that ensued, and the shortage of food affected both sides. Al-Maḥmoudi and Nauruz established themselves at the Karak Castle and fortified it. Then al-Maḥmoudi came with Amir Sawdun Baqja and Qani Bai al-Muḥammadi. They made their way to Karak's public bath. When the chamberlain of Karak, Amir Shihab al-Din Aḥmad, heard of their arrival, he gathered many of the town's residents and incited them to kill al-Maḥmoudi and his comrades. However, some of the Mamluks who heard of the scheme informed al-Maḥoumdi who prepared to leave the bath before their arrival. In the violent encounter that ensued, many were killed on both sides, until Nauruz managed to defeat them. Sawdun Baqja was killed and al-Maḥmoudi was hit by an arrow, which left him out of commission. When Nawruz heard of Sawdun's death, he killed many of Karak's residents. The men fled the town, leaving only their women and children behind. Meanwhile, Sawdun al-Jalb, the governor of Karak, who feared for his life fled to Mardin in northern Syria.

This state of affairs divided Karak into two camps: the Shaykha and Nauruziyya. The Shaykha sided with al-Maḥmoudi and the Nauruziyya with Nauruz. Both al-Maḥmoudi and Nauruz were in control of Karak until 1410, when the sultan laid a siege to the town and captured them. They pleaded for mercy until the sultan decided to spare them, on the proviso that they will not grand land (*iqṭā*) or an office to anyone without his permission, that they surrender the Karak Castle to him, and that the amirs agree to divide the territories among them. Accordingly, Tughri Bardi took Damascus, al-Maḥmoudi took Aleppo and Nawruz took Tripoli. He then returned to Cairo.

In 1413, a highly educated and charismatic figure Uthman bin Aḥmad bin Uthman bin Maḥmoud bin Muhammad bin Ali bin Faḍl bin Rabi'a who was also known by the name Sultan al-Malik al-A'ḍam al-Sufyani gathered around him supporters in Ajlun and its environs, and took control of that region. He reduced the taxes, and his name was read in the Friday noon prayer (*khutba*) in Ajlun. As fate would have it; however, a rebel known by the name Ghanem al-Ghazawi, from the tribe ruled by Khattab bin Amr assembled an army, rose against al-Sufyani in the spring of that year, and killed him at a mosque in Ajlun. Some of al-Sufyani's supporters were imprisoned at Ajlun Citadel. They were later taken to Safad Citadel at the order of the Mamluk sultan al-Mu'ayyad Shaikh (1412–1421). Al-Sufyani's wife who claimed that she bore his child and that the fetus was talking from her belly, was caught and imprisoned for seven years. The sources differ regarding her fate. While Ibn Iyas says that she was killed al-Sakhawi argues that she was spared.

In 1439, the governor of Karak, Aqbagha al-Turkmani killed Jabir the amir of Beni Uqbah who had considerable influence at the court of Sultan al-Ẓahir Jaqmaq (1438–1453). Upon his return from the sultan's court, the governor of Karak who felt that he had no control of Jabir ordered his arrest and execution. Infuriated by the governor's action the sultan demanded his arrest. He was brought before the sultan and was imprisoned until his death in 1440. Amir Ṭawghan Iqbardi al-Munqar who became Karak's next governor suppressed the tribes in that region in Jaqmaq's name. He oppressed Beni Uqbah who eventually rose up and killed him. He was followed by Tawghan al-Sayfi Aqbardi al-Munqar whom Ibn Tughri-Bardi described as "negligent, mean, recklessly cruel and immoral" but that "he was also known for his bravery that was [mixed] with rashness and levity."[44]

The power struggle among the local amirs did not remain confined to Transjordan. The West Bank had its share of strife during the Mamluk period. The Bedouin tribes in that region became involved in the struggle for power. In 1486, the inhabitants of Mount Nablus were involved in a civil war (*fitna*) that led to the killing of Amir Aqbardi bin Bakhshaish al-Inali in the Ghôr region and many were killed in the encounter, including Abu Bakr chief of the Bedouins of Jarm and Yusuf bin al-Jayushi who was one of Nablus' notables. The sultan sent Aqbardi al-Dawadar to restore peace in that region. The disorder spread again through the region in 1489, when the governor of Damascus ordered the execution of rebels at the Ghor who killed the governor Amir Khadr Beg.

In 1493, the governor of Damascus Qanswa al-Yaḥyawi caught Shaikh Ibn Sa'd and Shaikh Ibn Isma'il who came from Nablus to Ajlun where they were accused of disobedience to the governor. He was about to inflict punishment on them but the heavy snowfall in the Ḥawran and Ajlun in that year prevented him from accomplishing his goal. This was also the year when the conflict between the governor of Damascus and his opponent Ibn Sa'd was raging. In 1494, the governor of Damascus, Kurtbai al-Aḥmar, planned to build a citadel in Ṣakhra. Ibn Sa'd who sought to curb his power sent his son with money to bribe him but governor refused to receive him, insisting that Ibn Sa'd himself appear before him. When Ibn Sa'd refused, the governor went to search for craftsmen in Damascus for the construction project but many of them fled fearing his wrath. He oppressed the people in his district and many had to flee.

In 1498, the governor returned from Ajlun to Damascus after building the citadel at Ṣakhra. He stopped at the village of Ibn Sa'd where he arrested many of his supporters. Ibn Sa'd gathered people around him and they besieged the castle and managed to capture those who tried to flee. However, the governor managed to regroup. He captured Ibn al-Aṭar al-Ṣaghir whom he regarded as the leader of the insurgents and beat him for trying to escape. Moreover, he destroyed the Ṣakhra village and laid waste to the adjacent areas. He also robbed the Bedouins of Beni Hadhim at Qaṣr Shabib, close to Zarqa, and stole their flock. Many of them were imprisoned until the chief *qadi* implored him to set them free.

In 1505, the governor of Karak, Amir Qaytabi al-Ramaḍani, summoned all those whom he suspected of disloyalty, including the chamberlain, and sought to demonstrate his authority by threats and executions. The response was fast and furious, the people of Karak rose in rebellion and he had to flee to Gaza. Upon hearing the news, the sultan decided to send him to exile in Jerusalem.

The area under Ibn Sa'd's control remained tranquil until 1509, when a group sent by Sibai, the governor of Damascus who came from Egypt with order to destroy Ibn Sa'd's towns, appeared. In the following year, he went to the Ḥawran to carry out the mission that the sultan entrusted him. He came with a vengeance and caused destruction in Ibn Sa'd's towns. This brought the son of Amir Ibn Sa'd to surrender. He declared his loyalty to the governor and asked for amnesty. In 1510, Amir Ibn Sa'd al-Ghazawi entered Damascus to see the governor and the two reconciled.

It becomes clear from all these developments that there were no major rebellions against the central government in Jordan in the period between 1403 and 1516 and that the tribes in the region played a major role in the politics of that time. The governors of Karak were entrusted with the defense and maintenance of the fortresses against foreign enemies and unruly tribes within. This leads one to following conclusions: First, the inhabitants of Karak played no role in the selection of their governor and that the nomination remained the monopoly of the Mamluks, with the exception of Amir Muhammad bin Abi al-Jawd Naṣir al-Din al-Karaki who was known as Ibn al-Gharabili and who was born in Karak, and Amir Khalil bin Shahin al-Ẓahri who was born in Jerusalem. The Arabic sources available for that period do not say whether they were Circassians or Turks. Second, there was a constant rivalry between the governors of Karak and the Mamluks on the one hand, and the Arab tribes on the other for controlling the region or for establishing presence in it, especially after it became clear that the tribes were playing a political role, which resulted from the eclipse of the Mamluk state at the beginning of the fifteenth century. Testimony to the importance of their political role was the murder of Amir Khatir by Amir Sayf al-Din al-Qablawi, and that of Amir Jaber of Beni Uqbah by Amir Aqbagha al-Turcomani, as well as the murder of Amir Ṭawjan al-Sayfi by the Karaki tribes. Third, it is evident that some of Karak's governors acquired their position by graft and bribery. This can be understood if one takes into consideration the state of the economy that was adversely affected by years of draught, pestilence, floods, and other natural disasters, in addition to the rivalry among the Mamluks and the corruption within their ranks. All these led to instability, which manifested itself in the chaos that prevailed during the time of Amir Ḥaj Iyal al-Jakmi. Fourth, the Karak region was exposed to destruction and the cruelty of some of its governors who took advantage of the fact that the Mamluk sultans were occupied trying to take control of the resources of Greater Syria, especially during the period when al-Maḥmoudi and Nauruz conspired against Sultan Faraj. Fifth, Karak's governors were exposed to imprisonment by the Mamluk sultans and that lead to division among the population, between those who favored the governors and those who favored the sultans, and it further intensified the conflict between and Qaysis and Yamanis in that region. Furthermore, this strife led to emigration and severe economic crises. Sixth, the conflict among the governors of Karak and the Arab tribes stemmed from the fact that they were incapable of carrying out their mission. The fact that the Mamluk sultans were weak and busy defending themselves against foreign enemies increased the involvement of tribes in politics and their threat to the commercial caravans did not cease. Seventh, the governors were often forced to decide whether to defend the sultan or his enemies and thereby found themselves between the hammer and the anvil. Eighth, the governors of Karak were sensitive to the demands of their people and they were accustomed to complain to the sultan against anyone who was unpopular. Nineth, it is evident that Amir Amr Shah al-Turkmani remained in his office as governor of Karak for the longest period, while Amir Aqbagha al-Lakash al-Ẓahiri for the shortest one. Tenth, it appears that after 1453, historians no longer paid much attention to the list of governors who ruled Karak. The reasons for that are that the historians of the period such as al-Maqrizi, Badr al-Din al-Ayni, and Ibn Qadi Shuhba had long passed away, that those who lived after that time tended to concentrate on political affairs, and that the region had become marginal.

In the end, the weakness of the Mamluk sultans brought the governors of Karak to attempt to dominate their regions and its tribes, but they failed to achieve their goal.[45]

Notes

1 Aḥmad al-Jawārinah, *Tarīkh al-Urdun fi al'Asr al-Mamlūki* (History of Jordan in the Mamluk Age), Arabic text ('Ammān: Lajnat Tarīkh al-Urdun, 1999), p. 5.
2 Īzz al-Dīn Ibn al-Athīr, *Al-Kāmil fi al-Tarīkh* (The Perfect in History), Arabic text, Vol. 12 (Bayrūt: Dar Ṣāder, 1966), pp. 95–96.
3 R. Stephen Humphreys, *From Saladin to the Mongols: The Ayyubids of Damascus 1193–1260* (Albany: State University of New York Press, 1977), pp. 321, 331–333.
4 al-Jawārinah, p. 16.
5 *Ibid*, p. 18.
6 *Ibid*, p. 19.
7 Joshua Prawer, *Toldot mamlekhet hatsalbanim beeretz Yisrael* (A History of the Latin Kingdom of Jerusalem), Hebrew text, Vol. II (Jerusalem: Bialik Institute, 1963), pp. 337–338.
8 *Ibid*, pp. 458–458.
9 Al Mūmani, p. 41.
10 Yūsuf Darwish Ghawānmah, *Tarīkh Sharqi al-Urdun fī 'aṣr al-Mamālik al-Ulah, al-Qism al-Siyāsi* (History of East Jordan in the First Mamluk Age, the Political Part), Arabic text (Ammān: Wizarat al-Thaqāfah wa-al-Shabāb, 1979), p. 69.
11 Bertold Spuler, *The Mongol Period: History of the Muslim World* (Leiden, Netherlands: E.J. Brill, 1969), p. 29.
12 Muḥammad Ibn, *Abd al-Raḥim Ibn al-Furāt, Tarīkh Ibn al-Furāt* (History of Ibn Furat), Arabic text, Vol. VIII (Beirut: Al-Maṭba'a al-Amirkāniyah, 1942), p. 35.
13 Prawer, pp. 507–508.
14 *Ibid*, p. 510.
15 Aḥmad bin 'Ali bin,' *Aḥmad Al-Qalqashāndi, Kitab Ṣubḥ al-A'shā fi Ṣinā'at al-Inshā* (Book of the Daybreak for the Blind regarding the composition of Chancery Documents), Arabic text (Al-Qāhirah: Al-hay'a al-Miṣriyya lil-Kitāb, 2006), p. 204.
16 Isma'īl Ibn 'Umar Ibn Kathīr, *Al-Bidāyah w-al-Nihāyah fī al-Tarīkh* (The Beginning and the End in History), Arabic text, Vol. 14 (Miṣr: Maṭba'at al-Sa'ādah, 1932), p. 51.
17 Letters of the Ilkhan to King Philip IV of France (called 'The Fair' 1285–1314), Bertold Spuler, *History of the Mongols: Based on Eastern and Western Accounts of the Thirteenth and Fourteenth Centuries* (New York: Dorset Press, 1968), p. 142. [Parentheses are in the text].
18 Norman Housley, *The Later Crusaders: From Lyon to Alcazar 1274–1580* (New York: Oxford University Press, 1992), pp. 207–208, 225.
19 Mustafa M. Ziada, "The Mamluk Sultans, 1291–1517," *A History of the Crusades: The Fourteenth and Fifteenth Centuries*, Vol. III, Edited by Harry W. Hazard (Wisconsin: the University of Wisconsin Press, 1975), p. 489.
20 Aziz S. Atiya, "The Crusades in the Fourteenth Century," *Ibid*, pp. 4–6, 17–18.
21 Maqrizi tells us that several Baḥri Mamluks fled from Cairo in the year 652H (1254–1255) and they wandered five days in the desert until the sixth day, when they saw a magnificent city with walls and gates made of green marble. They entered the city and walked its streets. However, a sandstorm came and the city and its walls and gates were covered by sand. They found utensils and garments, a tray and nine dinars on which there was an image of a deer and Arabic script. They met Arab tribesmen, which they took with them to Karak. Then they came across money changers to whom they sold the dinars. They were told that the coins were minted in the time of Moses, and they paid them a hundred dirhams for each dinar. They were told that this fertile land was exposed to sand floods, which only those who come there could see. Maḥmūd al-'Abidī, *Al-Batrā'* (Petra), Arabic text ('Ammān: Maktabat al-Ṭāhir Ikhwān, 1956), pp. 39–40.
22 Bethany J. Walker, *Jordan in the Late Middle Ages: Transformation of the Mamluk Frontier* (Chicago: Middle East Documentation center, 2011), p. 9.
23 *Ibid*, p. 18.

24 Ibn Ḥajar al-ʻAsqalāni, *Anbā' al-Ghumr bi-Anbā' al-ʻUmr* (the News of Immersion is the News of a Lifetime), Arabic text, Vol. II, Edited by Ḥasan al-Ḥabashi (Al-Qāhirah, 1971, No Publisher), p. 462.
25 A-Jawārinah, p. 5.
26 *Ibid*, p. 23.
27 *Ibid*, pp. 23–24.
28 Shawkat Ramaḍān Ḥujjah, Al-Tarīkh Al-Siyāsi li-Mintaqat Sharqi al-Urdun (Min Janūb al-Shām), fi ʻAṣr Dawlat al-Mamālik al-Thānya (Political history of Eastern Jordan (from Southern Syria) in the Second Mamluk Age), Arabic text (Irbīd: Muasasat Ḥamādah lil-Dirasāt al-Jami'iyya wa-al-Nashr wa-al-Tawzī', 2002), p. 9.
29 *Ibid*, pp. 68–69.
30 *Ibid*, p. 70.
31 *Ibid*, p. 84.
32 *Ibid*, p. 86.
33 *Ibid*, pp. 76–77.
34 *Ibid*, p. 77.
35 *Ibid*, p. 78.
36 *Ibid*, pp. 79–80.
37 *Ibid*, p. 81.
38 Cited *Ibid*, p. 116.
39 Al-Jawārinah, pp. 29–30.
40 Ḥujjah, p. 121.
41 Cited *Ibid*, p. 123.
42 Cited *Ibid*, p. 125.
43 *Ibid*, p. 127.
44 *Ibid*, p. 164.
45 *Ibid*, pp. 185–187.

IV Administrative, social, economic, and cultural developments in Jordan during the Mamluk period

Jordan's administrative division

The Mamluks who controlled the territories of present-day Jordan were aware of the strategic and economic importance of that region. Therefore, they incorporated that region into their empire and established an administrative order that tied it to Cairo. Karak, Shawbak, Ajlun, al-Salt, and the Jordan Valley region attracted the attention of most of Mamluk sultans and they tried to incorporate them into the Mamluk orbit, preferably without invading their borders.

During the Mamluk period (1250–1517), Greater Syria was divided into six administrative units, each called a province (*niyaba*). These units were Damascus, Aleppo, Ḥama, Tripoli, Safad, and Karak. Damascus was the largest, and it encompassed central Syria, a large part of Palestine, and the northern part of East Jordan. The East Jordan district (*wilaya*) was divided into two administrative units; the southern part, which included Karak, and the northern, which encompassed Ajlun, Balqa, and the adjacent valleys. The Karak district was divided into four smaller provinces (*a'mal*). These were Burha, which included the areas surrounding Karak, Shawbak, Zaghr, and Ma'an. Sometimes the Balqa region was added to Karak, depending on the political imperatives that prevailed or the strength, or weakness of its governor. Karak enjoyed total freedom and it managed its own domestic affairs. Each district was controlled by a governor (*wali*) who was nominated by the general governor (*naïb*) of Karak. Each district had its own army and its own judge who resided in the center. In addition, each had an official called *wali al-bar* who resided in Karak, and dealt with issues that had to do with its surrounding areas. Another position was later added to the Karak district. This was the governor (*naïb*) of the citadel. The holder of this position was nominated directly by the center of the Mamluk state in Cairo. He was sometimes chosen from among the amirs of the *tablakhana* (house of the drums) who had the privilege of having drums played at their citadels. Baybars was the one to create this position in the Karak castle in 1275, when he conferred it on Amir Shams al-Din Sawab al-Sahily. There were other positions in the district of Karak such as governor (*wali*) of the city, the chamberlain (*ḥajib*), the chief of the army (*naqib*), the master of ceremonies (*mahamandariyya*) and the postmaster. Al-Qalqashandi mentions additional positions held by individuals who assisted the judge with the implementation of

DOI: 10.4324/9781003450313-5

the Islamic law, such as the *ḥajib al-qadi*, *naqib al-qadi*, *amna'al-qadi* and the witnesses. He also mentioned positions such as the inspector (*nathir*) of Karak, the official in charge of secrets (*katib al-sir*), the army inspector, and the treasury supervisor.[1]

The boundary of the Karak province extended southward from Ula, to Aqabat as-Sawan and then to Ayla. Then it extended northward from the Mujib River until it reached Ziziya. In the east, it passed through al-Jafr, Bayr, al-Azraq, and Badiyat ash-Sham, to a line between the Dead Sea and Aqaba, and then to Wadi Araba and the Sinai in the west. Despite its importance to the Mamluks, Karak was often incorporated into other districts. This was due to the weakness of the central government and the endemic raids of the tribes in that region. In 1506, Karak was incorporated to the district of Jerusalem, in 1510 to Safad, and in 1516 to Gaza.

As for the district of Balqa, it was incorporated into that of Damascus and sometimes into Karak. This is what happened during Baybars' reign, when Karak extended northward at Balqa's expense. At the same time, al-Salt was incorporated into Balqa, which extended from the Mujib River southward to Wadi al-Zarqa in the north, and from the *Ajwar* in the west to al-Azraq and the desert to the east. These borders contained several important towns such as Ḥisban, al-Salt, Moab, and Amman. As for al-Salt, it was sometimes independent, incorporated into Balqa or to the Ajlun district.

Unlike Balqa, Ajlun was small. It was incorporated into the district of Damascus and was controlled by a governor. After 1411, Ajlun became so important that it was ruled directly from Cairo. It extended from the Zarqa River southward to the Yarmouk River in the north, and from the *Aghwar* in the west to the Syrian Desert in the east. The central and base of this district was al-Bauniya. This district included several towns and villages such the Suwayt (situated between Ajlun Mountain and Jarash and extended eastward to Umm al-Jamal), Irbid, Ḥabras, Bayt Ras (Jadara), al-Ḍalil, al-Mafraq, Aydun, Ramtha, and other smaller towns and villages.

The historian Shams al-Din Ibn Tulun (1475–1546) tells us that in 1471, the sultan nominated Ibrahim bin Shadbak as governor of al-Salt and Ajlun. The *Aghwar* were incorporated into the district of Damascus. This area bordered the Dead Sea and at some point, the governor of Damascus gave it up and nominated an official responsible for its administration.[2]

Commerce, industry, and agriculture

Jordan played an important role in the economic life of the Mamluk sultanate. This was due to the abundance of its trade routes, both on land and at sea. Its importance stemmed from its location as a region connecting the cities of the Hejaz, Egypt, Syria and Iraq. The existence of numerous markets and workshops contributed to its importance to the Mamluk state.

Several roads converged on land and sea in Jordan. The most ancient was the China road, which began in that country and passed through India, the Persian Gulf and thence to Basra. From there the road extended on land to Baghdad where it divided into two sections. The first extended from Damascus to the ports of the

Mediterranean, then southward to Egypt along the shore to Gaza. This road to Egypt passed through the northern parts of Jordan. Then it continued through the desert to Cairo. The second extended to Aleppo, then to Asia Minor in the west, where it connected to Constantinople and to Europe by sea. In the east, this road connected Greater Syria to Central Asia.

The second road was through the sea. It started from the Far East, continued to the Indian Ocean and then to the Red Sea and its ports, and then to Aqaba where it divided into two sections. The first extended from Aqaba through East Jordan and then continued to Damascus. The second went through the Sahara Desert to the great cities along the Nile, and then to Europe.

Following the Mongol invasion and the fall of Baghdad in 1258, the merchants had to rely more heavily on the naval road that passed through the Red Sea, which began to play a major role in the flow of goods from Greater Syria to other ports. In addition, there was a domestic trade network, which connected Egypt with Greater Syria. Jordan played an important role in that network, which connected the great cities of Baghdad, Damascus, to the Hejaz. The road passed through Jordan was used for mail delivery, and it was through it that the commercial caravans passed. This road was divided into two sections. The first was from Egypt to Gaza and Karak. The second started in Egypt, passed through Gaza and Hebron, then continued to Damascus by way of Jisr al-Majami', Zaḥr, Irbid, and Damascus through al-Ṣanmin and al-Kaswah. Camels were used to transport merchandize from Syria to Egypt, through the Jordanian regions of Irbid and Beisan.

The land road from Aqaba in which merchandize was transported from the Far East led to Greater Syria through Yemen, Tahama, Asir, and the Hejaz. In addition to the roads that lead to the Hejaz there were others; the Wadi Taym road, which led to Ma'an and northward to Damascus; the ancient Wadi Araba road, which led to Petra; and the Jerusalem road that passed through the Negev and Hebron.

The internal commercial roads, which connected Egypt to Greater Syria, played a crucial role in the economic life of the Mamluk state. Ibn Fadl-Allah al-Umari (d. 1349) tells us that Jordan constituted an important trade network because it connected Baghdad with Damascus, Cairo, and the Hejaz. It was a place where the roads were used by the commercial caravans and those of the pilgrims who headed for Mecca, and it was there that the mail and the correspondence of these great cities passed through. Al-Qalqashandi provides the directions which that route took; from Egypt to Gaza, then to Karak through Hebron, and from Egypt and Gaza to Damascus through al-Jami' to Zaḥr, then to Irbid and from there to Damascus through the al-Ṣanmin village in the Hawran and the al-Kaswa village in Damascus. He mentioned that the camel was the main beast of burden and the means of transport.[3]

There were also commercial roads from the port of Aqaba that were used to sell the products of India and China in all regions of Greater Syria. The merchants used to pass through Yemen, Aṣir and the Hejaz and from there to Wadi Yatam that reached Ma'an and then to Damascus and Wadi Araba to Jerusalem through the Negev Desert and Hebron. The roads that passed through Jordan were the only outlets to the caravans and their pilgrims who came from Syria, Iraq, and other regions in the north to the Hejaz and back. These caravans met in the Mazirib region in the vicinity of Idhr'at and the Ḥawran. The caravans, which sometimes consisted of 13,000 camels, passed through Jordan from the north, through Ramtha, then to Zarqa where they stayed a day or two and continued to Ziziya, where they camped for three of four days, continued to Jaun and then to Karak where they spend several more days. Then the caravan continued to al-Ḥasa where the merchants replenished their water supplies, and continued to Ma'an where they stayed several more days, and then proceeded to walk on land in the direction of Aqaba, Sawan, and Tabbuk, until they reached Medina and Mecca. These caravans, which carried merchandize of all kinds from Greater Syria and the neighboring countries, contributed to the expansion of the Mamluk economy in Jordan and beyond.

The sources for that period show that the caravans carried a wide variety of items such as rugs, furs, horses and works of fine craftsmanship. The caravans returned from the Hejaz with numerous items. Spices such as pepper, ginger, nutmeg, and other items such paper, indigo, iron, copper, tin, lead, gold, ivory, and a wide variety of minerals were traded on the journey. We are told that the Ayyubid sultan of Damascus, al-Malik al-Mu'ẓam Isa (1218–1227), was the one to undertake the task of improving the pilgrims' road in the year 1224, when he sent a special unit to pave the road from Bab al-Jabiya to Jabal Arafat. Rugged areas where rocks and dunes slowed down the journey were paved. He also provided them with sources of supply in places such as Karak, Shawbak, Tabbuk, Ala, and Medina.

The Mamluk authorities took great care of this region in order to protect commerce. There were numerous markets that had to be protected against foreign invasions such as those of the Mongols and the Timurids. There were also natural disasters such as plagues and years of meager harvests, that had adverse effect on the economy, and the Mamluk authorities were aware of their impact. The markets of Jordan were similar to those that one could find in the Islamic world as that time. There were permanent markets as well as fairs, which merchants held occasionally to sell their wares. The typical market (*souk*) specialized in a certain item. The historian and administrator of the Baḥri Mamluk era Shihab al-Din Ahmad bin Abd al-Wahhab al-Nuwayri (d. 1333) tells us how the markets operated; it contained a *souq* of leather dyers, *souq* of vegetables, *souq* of the mat makers, *souq* of the butchers, *souq* of linen, *souq* of headgear makers, and the like.[4]

The Mamluks built caravanserais (*khans*), which provided lodging for the merchants. Caravanserais were built in Aqaba, al-Ḥasa and other places. The most prominent among these were Khan Qatrana and Khan Qiyad (Ḍab'a), which provided food and facilities that merchants needed.[5] Among the important places were the *qisariyya*, which had a food center and leather- and fur-dyeing facilities and workshops, which merchants needed. In addition, the *qisariyya* served as a storage place for merchandize. A market was established in Zarqa, which served the pilgrims who came from Greater Syria, and it was one of the most important in the region. In this market, one could find fruits such pear, grapes, plums, peaches, and cucumbers. Lambs, goats, horses, barley, hay, and a wide variety of linen were sold or exchanged. There was also a market in Irbid and others places along the caravan road from Damascus to Cairo. Merchants from faraway places such as Bukhara,

Samarqand, Shiraz, and Iraq came to these markets to sell their wares. Irbid had caravanserais that provided the merchants with all their needs. There was also a market in Ma'an, which provided hay for the beasts of burden. Cattle were sold in this market in addition to a variety of fruits. This market became one of the major sources of livelihood for Irbid's inhabitants, and it developed largely as result of the pilgrimage to the holy cities of Islam.

Another market, which emerged as result of the pilgrimage, was the one in Aqaba, which became a center of trade for merchants who came from all parts of the Islamic world during the pilgrimage season. The Muslim scholar and engineer al-Jazari (1136–1206) tells us that there were big markets in Aqaba, replete with merchandize, fruits, and vegetables that one could not find elsewhere, and that merchants from Greater Syria came to them in large numbers.[6] Among the numerous items, which al-Jazari said to have existed in the markets of Aqaba, were fruits such as dates, raisins, nuts, apples, pears, honey, and all kinds of grains and cheeses, in addition to sheep, lambs, and blocks of salt, which came from the Dead Sea. He tells us that a wide variety of merchandize was brought from other regions, and that the trade in Aqaba was cheaper than anywhere in Greater Syria or Egypt. Ibn al-Sirafi (d. 1494) tells us that the prices in Aqaba were lower than any other places, and that the pilgrims enjoyed prosperity in the year 1469, due to the abundance of markets and the merchandize that came from other countries.

Due to the importance of these markets, the Mamluk sultans established centers for levying custom duties and registering merchandize. One such center was established in al-Ḥasa, which was part of the Karak district. This center was situated midway between the Hejaz and Greater Syria, and it brought revenue of ten thousand *mithqal* every year.[7] The Mamluk sultans provided means to secure this road. This concern about the security of these roads manifested itself from Baybars' time through the entire Baḥri and the Bourji periods. The sultans were keen on protecting the tribes of Beni Aqaba, Beni Mahdi, al-Mara and those of Karak.

Mamluk commerce suffered a serious setback as result of the discovery of the route to India by Vasco da Gama in 1498. The importance of Aqaba and the Red Sea diminished considerably.

In addition, the arrival of the western countries to that region constituted another problem for the Mamluk trade. Consequently, Sultan Qansu al-Ghuri (1501–1516) sent a fleet to the coast of India to attack the Portuguese and clear the sea of pirates who constituted a major threat to Mamluk trade with India and China. Four years later, the Mamluk fleet joined the navies of Gujarat, Calicut, Venice and the Ottoman Empire in a joint encounter with the Portuguese, which the latter won and it became known to history as the Battle of Diu. The Mamluks built towers on the coasts of Jeddah and other places along the Red Sea to provide protection for the merchants and a garrison was stationed in Aqaba in 1499. Mamluk governors had often abused their power, confiscated merchandize, and monopolized items such as sugar, which brought them handsome profit. In addition, Jordan experienced plagues and periods of meager harvests, which had adverse effect on commerce. The mainstay of the economy in Jordan was agriculture, which declined as result of natural disasters.

The expansion of agriculture depended heavily on rainfall that was needed for the cultivation of grain, barley, and other food items, which grew on the planes of Ḥawran, Shawbak, Karak, and Balqa. The region that lies between the Ghor, which extends from south of the Sea of Galilee to the Dead Sea, was one of the most fertile in Jordan, and it had a wide variety of products such as sugarcane, banana, dates, indigo, esparto, and rice. There was a wide variety of trees, some of which had fruits in the region that extended from Ajlun Mountain northward to Mount Moab, where grapes, figs, nuts, and lemons were grown. In addition, there were numerous kinds of non-fruit bearing trees and that were used mainly for their lumber. The farmers used the traditional two-field system practiced since Roman times. Normally, they cultivated the land by using an iron plough pulled by two oxen. The small industries that were widespread in the Mamluk era in Jordan were those in which sugar, indigo, olive oil, soap, tobacco, balsam, textiles, rugs, charcoal, flower, and wines were produced. Also widespread were the workshops where swords, daggers, bows, arrows, and other implements were made. In addition, there were workshops where metal, glass, wood, and other raw materials were fashioned to create exquisite art works.

The sugarcane industry was the most important in that region at the time of the Mamluks who promoted its expansion. The sugar industry was widespread in the north and the southern region of the Ghor. The sugar production in this region was so important that the Crusaders introduced it to Europe and the Holy Roman Emperor Frederick II (1197–1250) brought it with him to Sicily. Archaeologists found numerous implements in Jordan that were used in the sugar industry. The Mamluk sultans attached great importance to the Ghor region, and they appointed a special governor known by the title *Istidar al-Ghor*, which became one of the most important positions in the Mamluk bureaucracy, and it came under the supervision of the governor of Damascus.

Not only did the Mamluk sultans monopolize the sugar industry, they also became involved in its marketing and determined its price. We know that in 1481, the Damascenes protested against the rise in the price of sugar, and they came to the markets to express their resentment. The price went up from 14 to 28 dirhams for one *ratl*, and then went up again to 30.[8] Moreover, the Mamluk sultans were keen on encouraging the production of oil and soap. They encouraged the planting of olive trees in the region that extends from the Ajlun and Shawbak to Shara in the south. The olive trees were vital to the economy. Olives were used for the production the oils and their pits were ground and used for cooking. Grinding stones were widely used close to rivers and streams. These were common in Amman, Ḥisban, Ajlun, Karak, Shawbak, and the Jordan Valley. In addition to the charcoal industry, textile production and weaving were common in Balqa, Ajlun, and throughout all the rural areas of Jordan. There was an industry that manufactured wooden carts at Zaghr, south of the Dead Sea, and rug industries at Shawbak and Karak. We are told that when the Mamluk sultan al-Malik al-Ashraf Sha'ban (1363–1377) went to the *hajj* he stopped in Aqaba where he was received by Karak's governor. The sultan asked him to make rugs, which he brought with him to Cairo.[9]

Jordan was a place with workshops in which all kind of utensils and jars were made with exquisite decorations. Workshops for framing and molding metal works were common in places such as Ajlun and Karak. The ceramics industry was common as well. Ceramic dishes and jars were in common use during that period. The arms industry was so developed during that time that the Karak castle contained shops for the production of items such as swords, bows, lances, coats of mail, and naphtha. Mu'ata became famous for its iron swords while the city of Zaghr earned a big reputation for its production of bows and arrows. The Amta village in the Jordan Valley became famous for the production of arrows that were known for their superb quality. Jordan had iron ores that were used in the arms industry. Iron was primarily taken from Ajlun and the Jordan Valley and smelted to remove impurities. Archeological evidence shows that ovens were used in the smelting process. White sulfur was extracted from the northern regions of the valley and the eastern shore of the Dead Sea. Also found in this area was red bitumen, also known as asphalt or pitch, which was taken from the Dead Sea to produce naphtha that was used in weapons production. The red bitumen was taken from the surface of the Dead Sea and transported to the Karak castle where the production took place. It seems that bitumen was also used as a repellent to protect trees from the damage by mosquitos. In addition, copper was discovered in the vicinity of Aqaba in 1508, and in 1510 gunpowder was found. The Mamluk sultan is said to have been so pleased with the discovery of the gunpowder that he granted ten dinars to the one who brought it and asked him to bring more. This was a major discovery for the Mamluks, given the fact that gunpowder was rare in Egypt and they had to import it from Anatolia and Europe. Moreover, the European powers put a ban the shipment of weapons to the Mamluk state. Another mineral that proved useful for the Mamluks was bromide, which was extracted from Jabal al-Shara.

Ajlun became a market where merchandize from the entire region came. Normally, the Mamluk state imposed heavy taxes on the merchants, but sometimes sultans who did not wish to hinder the economic growth, refrained from collecting them. For example, in 1465, an ordinance that was issued by sultan al-Malik al-Ẓahir Sayf al-Din Khushqadam (1461–1467) abolished all dues that were imposed by Amir Jarbak al-Daraki on the people of Ajlun. Qadi Abd al-Basit (1388–1450) boasted that Karak was in the pinnacle of its glory, and that it had all the money and the products known at that time.[10]

Jordan's geographical location on the road that led to Egypt and North Africa, Syria, Iraq, and the Arabian Peninsula turned it into an important region connecting all these countries. This was the place through which the commercial caravans that came from the Arabian Peninsula on their way to Damascus, Iraq, Persia, and the Byzantine Empire passed. They came with a variety of items such as pearls, silver, fine linen, brass utensils, pinewood, Arabian horses, and numerous other items that were sold in the bazaars of the Muslim world. They also brought a wide variety of spies such as pepper and nutmeg, perfumes such as musk and sandalwood, and precious stones and metals such as iron, copper, mercury, gold, and ivory.

The caravans of the pilgrimage to Mecca began their journey from Damascus to Kaswah, Ṣanamin, Boṣra or Ras al-Ma' in Muzairib, close to Dar'a. Then they arrived at Ramtha where they stayed for a few days. Archaeologists of Yarmouk University found thousands of clay pieces scattered around a wide area in the vicinity of Ramtha and several places, proving that the caravans used to stop at this area for rest and trade. Then they continued to al-Mafraq (al-Fadin). The name al-Mafraq was given to that place because the pilgrims who returned split from that point and went to their countries. From there they proceeded to al-Ḍalil, which was located between al-Mafraq and Zarqa, and then they arrived in Zarqa where they stayed for a day or two. This was the location on which the Shabib bin Malik palace was built. A big market was opened in Zarqa, and it had a wide variety of items and numerous sellers and buyers who arrived from Damascus and the regions nearby. This market had a wide variety of fruits such as figs, apples, pears, grapes, peach and cucumbers. There were all kinds of meat—such as lamb, goat, and chicken—grain, barley, flower, and numerous other items. These items were then transported from Ajlun to Zarqa.

Sometimes the caravans came from Boṣra to Hasan al-Azraq, a place that had water for the pilgrims, and then they made their way to Zarqa. Their next station was Zaizah in the Balqa region and then they passed through Qatrani where there was a great citadel in which they stayed and sold their merchandize, which consisted of beasts of burden, barley, hay, chicken, sour cream, and numerous other items. Sometimes the caravans passed through Zaizah al-Lajjun where they found running water. Then they continued to Karak where they stayed three or four days. It seems that the town had a market for the pilgrims where they bought food and items necessary for their journey. Then they continued on their journey to al-Ḥasa, which was known for its grazing areas and wells. The Arabs gathered in this region and they sold a variety of grains, figs, raisins, chicken and other items. Nevertheless, the pilgrims did not stay there. They made their way to Khan Anizah where they could stop, rest, and wash in its pool. Then they arrived at Ma'an, which had wells and abundance of running waters. A big market was established there, which had a wide variety of items that they needed for their camels, in addition to numerous kinds of meats, fruits, and vegetables, which came mostly from Hebron. This gave Ma'an the revenues that it depended on for the entire year. Then the pilgrims made their way to Aqaba and Sawan, Tabbuk, and Ala' on the way to Medina and Mecca.

The road, which the caravans used to reach the holy places of the Hejaz, changed over the centuries. Sometimes the caravans went from Damascus to Kaswa and then to Ṣanmin, Dar'a, and Boṣra. During the Frankish conquest the caravans changed course; from Boṣra, they went to south Jordan and then to al-Azraq, Bayr, and Jafr, until they reached Ma'an, or they went from Boṣra to Zizya Rasan and then to Lajjun, Ma'an, Aqabat al-Ṣawan, and then to Medina. Sometimes the pilgrims used to go from Ma'an to Ayla and then to Tabbuk on the way to the holy shrines. However, sometimes the journey to Mecca did not materialize because the region was exposed to foreign invasions. This happened in 1400, when Damascus was conquered by Tamerlane and his armies. The chaos that prevailed in 1402 led the pilgrims to avoid the caravan road of Greater Syria. In 1405, the Damascenes did not go on the pilgrimage to Mecca with the exception of some merchants who went to Gaza and from there to Ayla and the holy cities. Not only the pilgrims but also the local residents in all these stops benefited from the trade and the markets that sold numerous products. All along the way, there were custom stations and places where the merchants and their merchandize were registered. One of the most famous of these stations was Markaz Jisr al-Ḥasa, which was part of the Karak district. This was the main center between the Hejaz and Damascus. The annual revenue collected in this spot was estimated to have been ten thousand gold *mithqal*.[11]

During the pilgrimage season, markets were established in Ayla where those who came from Egypt, the Maghreb, and Greater Syria sold their wares and bought what the markets had to offer. These includes a variety of fruits, fresh as well as dried, honey, barley, meats of all kinds, blocks of salt brought from the Dead Sea, a wide variety of cheeses, and those of Hebron and Karak in particular. Caravans that went to Ayla often encountered difficulties and shortages of food and animals. The Mamluk sultans often came to their aid and are known to have shipped them the necessary supplies. In addition to building caravanserais along the trade routes, the Mamluks kept the roads in good repair.

The Mamluks attached gre.at importance to the trade in that region. Commerce in the Red Sea was particularly important in the thirteenth century, after the Mongol invasions. The Suez route and Ayla were the commercial centers and the only outlets north of the Red Sea. The fall of Constantinople in 1453 played an importance role in the emergence of Ayla as an important port and it increased the volume of trade passing through it. This port became important for all the goods, which came from Great Syria. The port had a station, which levied taxes and customs on the merchants. The annual income from the taxes imposed on the merchants is said to have reached 3,000 dinars. From there, the merchandize was transported by caravans to Damascus and Aleppo and then to the ports of Antioch, Tripoli, Beirut, Sidon, Tyre and Acre, and then it was exported to Europe.

Commercially, Jordan was closely connected to Europe. The sources mention a variety of facilities where the European merchants stayed. These merchants came from Pisa, Venice, and other places. The governor of Karak had to comply with all the commercial agreements, which the Mamluks had with the European countries. For example, during the reign of sultan al-Muayid Shaikh al-Maḥmoudi (1413–1421), a decree was issued to the governors of Tripoli, Hama, Alexandria, Safad, Gaza, and Karak to comply with the agreement that was concluded by the ambassadors Santo Feniro and Lorenzo Calbo, which determined that if the contracting parties agreed to trade by barter, they could not use cash.[12]

The Mamluks built towers on the shores of the Red Sea, in Jeddah and other places and they provided protection to ships that left Aden. A tower was built in Aqaba in 1509, and it was protected by a garrison. The arrival of European merchants who often competed with the local ones had adverse effect on trade in places such as Jeddah and Ayla. This competition often led to instability and sometimes to sharp fluctuations of prices of many items throughout Greater Syria.

Although the Mamluks made efforts to protect commerce and promote economic growth the people of Jordan were often fleeced by the sultans and the governors. For example, in 1395, the Jordanian tribes suffered a loss of three million dinars as result of confiscations. In 1409, the villages of Marj and Ghawṭa and the towns of the Hawran were forced to supply to the central government a certain amount of barley, and in 1428, the sugar that was manufactured in the Ghor was confiscated. In addition to these confiscations and dues, which the inhabitants had to pay, the value of the coin fluctuated and counterfeit money was circulated. Some of the sultans monopolized certain items that came from Jordan and brigandage was a major obstacle that hindered trade. For example, a commercial caravan that came from Iraq was robbed in 1397 by the Arab Na'ir Amir, and in 1485, a Syrian merchant was lost in Ma'an after his caravan returned from the pilgrimage to Mecca. Often there were quarrels among the leaders of the caravans, which caused much bloodshed. In addition, there were natural causes such as pestilence, draught, snow and other disasters, which had negative impact on trade in Jordan. For example, in 1392, pestilence spread in the northeast and the valley and caused numerous deaths. In 1410, the pestilence hit Ajlun, Palestine, Hawran and Tripoli and by 1411, most Greater Syria's towns were exposed to it. Then the pestilence reappeared in 1437 and killed many. The plague reached its peak in 1491.

The Mamluks sultans were not unaware of the impact of poor health conditions and they made efforts to find the appropriate solution. They built hospitals throughout the empire and some of which were in Jordan. The most famous among them was the one built in Karak by sultan al-Naṣir Muḥammad. It became known as *Bimarstan al-Naṣiri* and was built by Amir Sanjar Bin Abdallah al-Jawali. Al Maqrizi tells us that 1422 was a year of drought, which had a devastating impact on the Hawran, Karak, Jerusalem, Ramla, and Gaza. This led to migration of many farmers from these areas. The draught of 1468 caused prices to rise sharply everywhere in Greater Syria. A heavy snowfall in 1483 caused difficulties in al-Ḥasa. Many were killed while others lost their possessions. In 1512, the pilgrims could not go on their way to Mecca due to the heavy snow. Karak had floods that caused considerable damage to agriculture. Moreover, occasional earthquakes caused havoc in Jordan. In 1458, an earthquake caused many deaths and damage to property in Karak. Locust fell on that region in 1410, and the damage to agriculture was considerable. To all these, one needs to add the local wars and the rivalry among the governors, all of which led to chaos, which had adverse effect on the farmers, the merchants and the rest of the inhabitants in that region. Evidence to the impact of all these factors can be found in the writings of al-Maqrizi, al-Asqalani, al-Sakhawi (1372–1449), Ibn Ayyas (d. 1523/1524), and Muḥammad bin Khalil al-Asadi (fifteenth century).[13]

Bethany Walker's conclusions regarding the Mamluks' commissions and omissions, and their impact on Jordan are useful to mention. They are as follows: (a). The Mamluks invested in southern Syria, primarily for security reasons and this investment provided a catalyst for the establishment of an efficient infrastructure, which benefited agricultural and commercial growth. (b) By the end of the fifteenth century, the Mamluk sultans purchased entire villages in places such the Jordan River Valley and the Karak plateau, which they turned to religious endowments (*awqaf*) in order to finance a variety of projects such as the construction of qur'anic schools outside Jordan. (c). By the fifteenth century, the Mamluks reduced their investments in Jordan and therefore caused a decline which was exacerbated by drought and insecurity along the trade routes. (d). While most villages in Jordan remained small and agriculture was maintained on a subsistence level, there were numerous large estates on the eve of the Ottoman conquest. (e) While land management opened new markets, it caused soil exhaustion and accelerated the deforestation process. (f). Climatic and political changes, rather than urban violence or high taxation, had the most adverse effect on village life; drought and civil unrest caused by the struggle among the emirs of Karak had the most negative impact on the economic development of the villages. (h) The fact that the Mamluk state purchased large estates and turned into religious endowments allowed for better management, which encouraged agricultural development.[14]

Education in Mamluk Jordan

The Mamluks were keenly interested in learning and they invested efforts in establishing qur'anic schools in their dominions. They were primarily motivated by religious reasons but learning expanded far behind that. The number of scholars and men of letters increased significantly during the reign of both Baḥri and Bourji dynasties. Learning spread in the towns of Greater Syria and expanded to Jordan. Towns like Ajlun, al-Salt, Amman, Ḥisban, and others became places where Islamic jurists and scholars gathered. Moreover, scholars from Jordan were active virtually in all the towns and villages of Greater Syria such as Damascus, Aleppo, Ḥims, Ḥama, Tripoli, Safad, Nablus, Jerusalem, Hebron, Nazareth, Gaza, Ramla, Alexandria, and Damietta. Jordanians took part in the effort to spread the faith by establishing religious foundations, schools, rooms where Sufis met (*zawiyya*s) and other institutions, whether religious or judicial, and these activities encouraged the expansion of learning. The Mamluks sought to expand the Sunni form of Islam throughout the empire, and Jordan became an important center for disseminating the knowledge of the Qur'an, the *hadith*s, and the commentaries on these sources. These activities led to an increase in the number of schools. Some of the early scholars and scientists in Karak made enormous contributions, even before many schools were established. For example, the physician Abu al-Faraj bin Ya'qub bin Isḥaq Bin al-Qaf al-Karaki (1286), a Christian from Karak who was taught by his father's friend Ibn Abi Asib'a went to serve in Ajlun Castle and then in Damascus castle. He became an instructor in medicine and among his publications are *Kitab al-Shafi fi al-Tib* and *Sharḥ al Kuliyat min Kitab li-Ibn Sina*, and *Sharḥ al-Fusul Li-ibqarat*, and *Kitab al-'Umdah fi sina'at al-Jaraḥ*. Al-Asqalani mention the Shafi'iyya school in Karak, which sultan al-Naṣir Muḥammad decided to open in 1311, and he appointed Amir Sanjar bin Abdallah al-Jawali to launch that project.

Al-Maqrizi mentioned the Salaḥiyya School of Karak but the sources do not tell when it was founded. We hear about the Yaqiniyya School in Ajlun, which was destroyed in a flood, and the Sarghatmash School, built by Amir Sarghatmash al-Naṣiri in 1356. It promoted the teachings of the Ḥanafi School of jurisprudence (*madhhab*), like the one that he established in Cairo. Also known were the Sayfiyya schools built by Saif al-Din Bhaktamar al-Hasami in al-Salt and Ḥisban. These schools taught according to the method of the Shafi'i *madhhab*, and both had rich libraries that were available to scholars.

The number of Jordanian scholars who occupied high positions in the Mamluk state was by no means negligible. For example, Sultan Barquq (1382–1398) appointed Qadi Ala-Din Ali al-Muqayri al-Karaki al-Shafi'i as writer in the Chamber of Secrets in Cairo. We also hear about Shaikh Abu Abdallah Muhammad bin Salama al-Nuwayri al-Karaki whom Barquq brought to his home, where he put him in a prominent place among the state's dignitaries. One of the highest positions occupied by a Jordanian in the Mamluk period was the supreme judge of the Shafi'i *madhhab* in Egypt. Sultan Barquq's choice for that position was the remarkable jurist and scholar Imad al-Din Ahmad Bin Isa al-Karaki. In addition to his preference for experts in Islamic jurisprudence, Barquq sought competent judges many of whom were found in Jordan's towns and villages. One of the most prominent among them was Ala al-Din Ali bin Isa bin Ḥamid al-Azraqi al-Muqairi al-Karaki al-Shafi'i whom he nominated judge. In addition to his keen sense of justice, this judge was known for his skills as an extraordinary writer and a secretary in the government offices of Karak and in Egypt. Another judge who attracted Barquq's attention was Shaikh Abu Abdallah Muḥammad bin Salama al-Tawzari al-Maghribi al-Karaki. Barquq thought so highly of him that paid him a hundred dinar for reciting the Qur'an on his grave for several weeks.[15]

Barquq was not the only sultan who showed reverence and appreciation for Islamic scholars.

We hear about Sultan al-Malik al-Ashraf Abu al-Naṣir Qa'itbay (d. 1496) who nominated Shaikh Ibrahim bin Abd al-Rahman Ibn Muhammad al-Majd al-Karaki to be his private *imam*, in addition to his role as the chief Ḥanafi judge in Cairo. Another prominent scholar who served as supreme judge of the Hanafi *madhhab* in Qa'itbay's time was Shaikh Zayd al-Din Abd al-Raḥman bin Ahmad al-Ḥaṣbani.[16] We also find the scholar al-Burhan al-Karaki occupying the position of "supreme sheikh" (*shaikh al-shuyykh*) during Qa'itbay's time. The most prominent center of Islamic scholarship was located in Karak. Riad Nasser reminds us that this town became a center of brilliant scholarship, and it attracted numerous scholars, experts not only in Islamic studies but also in the sciences, literature, philosophy and medicine. He writes:

> In Karak there were a few prominent scholars and scientists, especially, during the era of the Ayyubi king, al-Nasser Da'oud who surrounded himself with men of science, jurisprudence, literature and philosophy-among its most prominent scientific physicians was Abed al-Hamid ibn 'Aissa al-Kharushahi, 1185–1254. Also [well known, was] abu al-Fajr ibn Muwafaq al-Din ibn Izhaq ibn al-Qoff, 1233–1286, who was a famous physician and who wrote [the book] *al-Sahfi fi al-Teb*...And among its most distinct men [was] the jurist Ahmad ad-Din al-Karaki (1341–1398).[17]

Prominent men from Jordan distinguished themselves in the numerous towns of Greater Syria. We hear about Imad al-Din al-Ḥaṣbani who became the judge of Damascus by the end of the Baḥri Mamluk period, and Shaikh Ahmad bin Isma'il al-Ḥaṣbani who occupied that position several times during the reign of Barquq and his son Faraj.

Yusuf bin Danyal bin Mankali al-Karaki (1329) who was famous for his knowledge in Islamic law served as *mufti* and Shawbak's principal judicial authority. Yusuf bin Israïl bin Usuf Abi al-Ḥasan al-Naṣri al-Karaki (1333) was a prominent lecturer who had numerous disciples such al-Dhahbi and Ibn Rafi' al-Barzali occupied that position. We also hear about Imad al-Din Ahmad bin Isa al-Azraqi al-Ameri al-Karaki al-Shafi'i (1398) who served as chief judge in Karaq, and then in Egypt during the reigns of Barquq and his son Faraj. Scholars who did not occupy positions in the Mamluk bureaucracy were encouraged to study and write commentaries.

Shaikh Muhammad bin Muhammad bin Abi al-Jawad al-Karaki (1431) was a prolific scholar who wrote on numerous aspects of Islamic jurisprudence. He collaborated with al-Asqalani in writing commentaries on Islamic jurisprudence. Muhammad al-Karaki (1436), Ali bin Ibrahim al-Rabawi al-Karaki (1437), and Shaikh Muhammad bin Ḥamd bin Ma'tuq al-Karaki who was a Ḥanbali scholar (1447) were renowned scholars with many followers. Persons with proven judicial and administrative skills had little trouble obtaining positions in the Mamluk administration. For example, Shaikh Imad al-Din Yusuf bin Aḥmad al-Ba'uni was nominated supreme judge of Damascus several times between 1444 and 1466. Shaikh Ibrahim Ibn Musa bin Balal bin Damj al-Karaki (1449) was a Shafi'i scholar who taught in Karak and contributed significantly to the study of Islamic law. He was in charge of Al-Ẓahiriya School in Cairo and wrote numerous works among them are *Al-Is'af fi Ma'rifat al-Qat'wa-al-Isti'naf*, and *Al-Aalah fi Ma'rifa al-Fatḥ wa-al-Imamla*. Shaikh Burhan al-Din Ibrahim Ibn al-Karaki (1516) who was active in Egypt as a teacher and a judge, and Ibrahim ibn Abd al-Rahman bin Muhammad bin al-Majd al-Karaki (1516) who studied under al-Asqalani and contributed to the interpretation of Islamic law and to the development of the Arabic language are worthy of mentioning. The latter became a confidante of sultan Qa'itbay and his personal *imam*. Among his publications were *Fatawa Mubawaba*; *Ḥashiya 'ala Tawḍiḥ Ibn Hashim* and, *Fayḍ al-Mawla al-Karim*.

While Karak provided many scholars of fame, Ajlun did not fall far behind and its scholars occupied high positions in numerous areas. We hear about Qasim bin Abi Bakr al-Ajluni (1348) who was a great scholar of the Shafi'i *madhhab*. Other prominent figures from this region were Abu Abdallah al-Ajluni (1371) who lectured in Damascus and taught at the Atabakiyya School.

There were also poets among the *literati* of Ajlun such as Muḥammad bin Usuf bin Ali al-Ajluni (1348) who was one of the most gifted among them and inspired numerous followers. Shaikh Isa bin Ahmad bin Manṣur al-Ajluni (1410) was a Shafi'i jurist who excelled in Arabic calligraphy and interpreted the Nawawi *hadiths*. He wrote commentaries on *Al-Ḥawi al-Ṣaghir* and *Alfiyah Ibnu Malik*. Shaikh Muḥammad bin Ali bin Ja'far al-Shams al-Ajluni (1417) served in important government positions in Egypt, and wrote commentaries on hadiths and on the thoughts of prominent scholars such as Abu Ḥamid al-Ghazalli (d. 1111). Shaikh Ibrahim bin Muḥammad bin Isa Abu Isḥaq al-Ajluni (1422) was a chief judge in Safad during Barquq's reign. He taught in several schools and wrote a commentary on Nawawi. Sharaf al-Din al-Kafiri al-Ajluni (1427) taught in schools around Damascus and wrote commentaries on the *hadith*, including those of Al-Bukhari. Others scholars such as Shaikh Abd al-Raḥman bin Amr bin Abd al-Salam bin Dawud bin Uthman al-Ajlani (1446) were brilliant interpreters of Islamic law. Shams al-Din Abu 'Abdallah Muhammad bin Sa'id al-Ajluni (1470) taught in several schools of Damascus. Najm al-Din Ibn Qadi Ajlun (1472) was a great teacher of Islamic jurisprudence. He wrote commentaries such as *Sharḥ al-Minhaj al-Musama bil Taḥrir*; *Al-Taj fi Zawi'd al-Rawḍa ala-al-Minhaj*; *Taḥrim Dibaḥ al-Yahud wa-al-Naṣara*; *Sharḥ al-Aqidah al-Shaibaniyya*; and *Taḥrim labs al-Sinjab*.

To this impressive gallery of Ajluni personalities whose knowledge contributed to the development of the Islamic sciences, one can add other names such as Shaikh Khattab bin Amr bin Mihna bin Yaḥya al-Ghazawi al-Ajluni (1473) who lectured in the schools and the mosques of Damascus; Shaikh Ala-Din Ibn Qadi Ajlun (1477) who taught Islamic law in Damascus.

Shaikh Taqi al-Din Ibn Qaḍi Ajlun (1522) was a famous instructor in Damascus who attracted many scholars of the Shafi'i school.

Other regions of Jordan such as Ḥisban had their own class of *literati* who contributed to the Mamluk civilization. For example, Imad al-Din al-Ḥasbani was a prominent Islamic scholar who served as chief judge in Damascus and taught at the Amniyya School in Damascus. Taj al-Din al-Ḥasbani (1377) was said to have been one of the most famous judges during the first Mamluk age. He taught at the Iqbaliyya Mosque in Damascus, then at the Amniyya, and eventually became a prominent judge in Ḥisban. We also hear about Qadi Isma'il bin Khalifa bin Abd al-Ḥasbani (1377) who was the director of the Shafi'i school in Damascus, taught at the Fatḥiyya and other schools in Damascus, and became a famous author. Among his writings was the book *Sharḥ al-Minhaj* and thereby contributed to the development of Islamic law. Another prominent figure was Shaikh Ḥaji Ibn Musa Aḥmad al-Sa'di al-Ḥasbani who was head of the Shafi'i *madhhab* in Damascus where he lectured and then became a judicial consultant. In addition, one has to mention the prominent scholar Shihab al-Din Aḥmad al-Ḥasbani (1413) who was a Shfi'i scholar and a jurist in Damascus who taught in its schools. He also delved in astronomy. Other scholar of note was Shaikh Zayn al-Din al-Ḥasbani (1495) whose knowledge in Islamic studies made him famous in the schools of Damascus where he taught.

Some of these *literati* originated from al-Salt. For example, Muhammad bin Ibrahim bin Raḍi al-Salti was a prominent Shafi'i jurist who taught at the al-Shamiyya school, and later occupied important judicial positions in Egypt. To this impressive gallery of scholars, one can add Muhammad Ibn Abdallah bin Ahmad al-Hakari al-Salti (1384) who was Shafi'i jurist that occupied top positions in many capitals of the empire. He was the author of *Mukhtasir Maydan al-Fursan*. Shams al-Din Muḥammad bin Abbas bin Muḥammad bin Abbas al-Salti (1404) served as supreme judge in Damascus, Baalbek, Ḥims, Ḥama and Gaza. Also known was Shaikh Muhammad bin Abbas al-Salti (1404) who was one of the major jurists of the Maliki *madhhab*. He was a chief judge in Damascus and then served in similar capacities in Egypt, Jerusalem, and Ḥama. Both Taj al-Din bin al-Salti (1516) and Shaikh Zayn al-Din ‘Abd al-Raḥman bin Aḥmad al-Ḥasbani occupied judicial posts in Damascus during the later Mamluk age.[18]

Also famous was Shaikh Badr al-Din Muhammad bin al-Burhan bin Wahaybiyh al-Salti who served as judge in Nablus, Damascus, Tripoli, and other places and Ibrahim bin Musa al-Sayid Burhan al-Din al-Salti (1528) who taught in some of these towns.

Scholars who originated in Balqa were relatively few. We hear about Shaikh Muḥammad bin Khaydar bin Dawud al-Balqawi (1489) who was an Islamic scholar who interpreted *hadiths*. Among his publications were *Al- Barq al-Malmu' li-Kashf al-Ḥadith al-Mawḍu'* and *Al-Manhal al-Jari min fatḥ al-Bari bi-Sharḥ al-Bukhari*.

Although not as prominent as Karak or Ajlun, many other regions of Jordan provided scholars who contributed to the fecundity of the age and some of them are worthy of note. For example, Qasim Muhammad al-Irbid al-Shafi'i who taught Islamic law at the Atabakiyya School in Damascus, and became the chief judge of Idhr'at; Shihab al-Din al-Ḥabab (1398) who served as chief judge in Shawbak, and taught in the Assadiya School in Damascus; Shihab al-Din Abu al-Abbas Aḥmad bin Rashid bin Ṭarkhan al-Malkawi (1400), who taught in several schools in Damascus, and Sharaf al-Din bin Musa bin Aḥmad at Ramthawi (1413) who was of the greatest jurists of his day and taught in several schools in Damascus. Shihab al-Din al-Bau'ni (1413) filled several posts in the judicial system in Damascus and in Egypt and taught in their schools and Shaikh Sharaf al-Din al-Samaqi (1423) was active in the schools of Damascus and Ḥims.

To this list of outstanding personalities who became famous for their contribution to the development of Islamic law, one needs to add Imad al-Din Yusuf bin Aḥmad al-Ba'uni (1466) who was a chief judge in Damascus. Although few women were preoccupied with issues affecting Islamic jurisprudence, some invested efforts in this field. For example, Aïsha bint Usuf bin Aḥmad bin Naṣir al-Ba'uniyya (1516) was a prolific writer and a poet who made noteworthy contribution to the literature on the subject. Among her publications were *Al-Malamiḥ al-Sharifa wa-al-Aathar al-Munifa*; *Al-Fatḥ al-Ḥanafi*; and *Dur al-Ghaïṣ bi Baḥr al-Mu'jazat wa-al-khaṣaïṣ* and other works.

Jordan's contribution was not limited to religious matters. In addition to their contribution to the Islamic tradition, these men of letters served in secular capacities. We hear about scholars, physicians, and other professionals who were active not only in Jordan but outside as well.

We hear about Abu al-Faḍaïl Danyal bin Mankali al-Karaki (1296), one of the scholars in Damascus and Shawbak who had enormous impact on the scholars of his day such as Ibn Rafi' al-Barzali and Amir Sanjar al-Jawali. He was the governor of Karak and Shawbak where he died. Tuma bin Ibrahim al-Tayïb al-Shawbaki (1324) was a famous physician during the Mamluk age who classified medical information. Among his works was the treatise *Ikhtisar Masa'il Hanin*, which sultan al-Naṣir Muḥammad bin Qalauun became interested in, and he was one of his best physicians. There were numerous other scholars, whose contribution to Islamic learning and interpretation was valuable, especially in those years of domestic strife and foreign invasions, and the reader ought to bear in mind that even under such dire circumstances, cultural activities in the Mamluk sultanate continued and learning did not cease.

Tribes and social classes during the Mamluk age

Conflicts and warfare among the Jordanian tribes were common during the Mamluk age. The Mamluk authorities intervened occasionally and often managed to settle the differences among them. The fact that the Mamluk state had a strong and centralized character allowed it to play such a role. Moreover, the Mamluk regime managed to obtain support from the powerful tribes by incorporating them into its bureaucracy and delegating powers to them. The tribes obtained high positions in the government. Tribesmen who obtained such position usually cooperated with the Mamluk regime, albeit reluctantly. Al-Omari and al-Qalqashandi tell us that the Mamluks made used the military rank 'Arab prince' (*amir al-'Arab*), which became part of the state apparatus, that the owner of that title had high status, and that he was valued for his swordsmanship skills. Generally, the princes of the Mamluk period were skilled in swordsmanship and were directly under the control of the sultan who nominated them to such positions. They were selected from among the most distinguished warriors and from the tribes of the Mamluk state. The Mamluk sultans took great care in selecting competing princes, particularly in strategically located regions such as Jordan, where it was essential to have men skilled in warfare and loyal to the sultan. Apart from cases of nepotism, such titles were usually given sparingly to reliable local leaders. These princes held different ranks. Some tribes, such as the Jordanian Ahl al-Mara'i obtained from the sultan positions of considerable influence.

Those tribes, which had proven their loyalty to the sultan, were usually rewarded by such titles. For example, Banu Uqba and Banu Mahdi who helped sultan Muḥammad bin Qalawuun in his coup in 1309, were rewarded with such titles when he came to power the second time. Both Amir Shati bin Uqbah and the amirs of Ahl Mara'i who succeeded him were given such titles. Al-Umari tells us that the Mamluk sultans used these tribes to provide protection to the pilgrims and to safeguard the trade routes throughout the empire. They were assigned the task of maintaining the postal system, and they provided horses for that purpose. Moreover, they were also given positions as guards in strategic locations and narrow passes. Qalqashandi mentions the positions, which were given to Ahl Mara'i and other Jordanian tribes, saying that they obtained positions of considerable influence, which they were trained to perform. Ahl Mara'i is said to have furnished a thousand horses to the Mamluk sultan. Moreover, this tribe had the authority to control the Hawran and the Balqa, and it contributed to the maintenance of the trade and to the security along the pilgrimage roads by protecting the caravans from brigandage. The tribe lost its influence during the reign of the Baḥri Mamluks but regained it 1501, during the reign of the Bourjis who followed them, when the Amir of Ahl Mara'i was given the task of organizing the defense of the Syrian pilgrimage route that passed through Transjordan, all the way to the town of Idhar'at in the vicinity of Damascus. Then in 1505, the Ahl Mara'i tribe under Amir Janabi helped protect the pilgrims' roads from Ḥasa to Damascus.

Similarly, the Banu Mahdi and Banu Uqbah tribes were responsible for defending the roads leading to the Hejaz. Banu Mahdi provided military assistance to the Mamluks. Together, the two tribes provided a thousand horses to the Mamluk sultan. The amir of Banu Uqbah was given the task of preparing his military contingent for a *jihad* whenever the Mamluk sultan asked for it. They provided assistance to sultan Barquq after he was released from the prison in Karak, and when he was on his way to Damascus. Moreover, the Banu Uqbah tribe was entrusted with protecting the roads from Medina and Gaza and Balqa to the Hejaz. They helped Barquq following his departure from Karak, providing him with armed protection, which included 7,000 horses under their leader Haytham bin Khatir.

The Banu Lam tribe was one of the most powerful in Jordan at that time. This tribe exhausted the Mamluk regime and was a thorn in its throat. The Mamluks guarded the Banu Lam carefully, and eventually brought them to cooperate by nominating them as guardians of the caravans of the Syrian pilgrimage and the trade routes. In 1505, their emir ordered them to protect the caravan route from Lu'la to al-Ḥasa. They fulfilled their obligation faithfully and obtained rewards from the sultans such as land, robes of honor, titles, gems, young slaves, horses, saddles, and other objects of considerable value. The wild and recalcitrant tribes were coaxed into cooperating with the government by rewards that consisted for the most part of land grants (*iqtā*), which often extended over large areas, and included towns and villages. Sometimes, the Mamluk sultans had to resort to coercive measures to subdue the tribes by intimidation and military force. For example, when the tribes of Karak under Shaikh Mubarak of Banu Uqbah attacked pilgrims in Aqaba in 1467, the sultan decided to send a force commanded by several amirs who managed to defeat him and kill many of his followers.[19]

In 1392, Banu Khalid attacked Egyptian pilgrims on their way to Aqaba and many died in the encounter. Many other towns in Jordan were subject to invasion and robbery. Karak and Shawbak were among the regions, which suffered the most from brigandage. In 1493, the two regions experienced major raids. These raids spread into Ma'an and al-Ḥasa where a caravan of pilgrims was attacked before its arrival to Ma'an. In 1492, Banu Khalid attacked an Iraqi caravan of 3,000 camels that was on its way to Damascus, and took all its possessions and in 1494, they raided the region between Aleppo and Ḥama, and stole the belongings of a commercial caravan, which headed toward Damascus. These raids continued throughout the entire period of Mamluk rule in Jordan, and they gave the sultans the excuse to tighten their grip over the region. In 1418, Sultan al-Malik al-Mu'ayyad Shaikh al-Maḥmoudi (1412–1421) wrote to Amir Shanin the governor of Karak, asking him to join the governors of Gaza, Ramla, and Jerusalem in the campaign against Banu Uqbah, and to confiscate their possessions. The amir ordered them to assemble in Karak and to prepare for the campaign.

Al-Maqrizi tells us that there was hostility between the Mamluk government and the Jordanian tribes and that Banu Uqbah were the most recalcitrant among them. This caused the sultan to act against them. In 1418, he sent the governors of Gaza and Jerusalem to help the governor of Karak who was attacked by Banu Uqbah. Then in 1498, the governor of Damascus Anyal or Anil raided the tribe of Amir Mashlab of the Banu Lam who attacked a caravan, which was on a pilgrimage to Mecca. In the following year, the governor of Damascus killed many of the raiders but did not manage to put an end to the assaults.

There were several social classes in Jordan during the Mamluk period. The Mamluks constituted the ruling elite. This was a social class whose members were soldiers and landowners. Its role was to fight and defend the state. This group, which remained isolated, regarded the other classes as inferior, and did not mix with them. The other class whose members had a high position in the society was that of the learned people who served in religious positions (*ulama*). This included the scholars of Islam, men of letters, writers, members of Sufi orders, and students. The members of this class benefited from the fact that the sultans had high regard for learning, and they were rewarded for their services. The third class was that of the commoners most of which were traders, artisans, and farmers. This class was the largest numerically and it resided in towns and villages. It contributed to the society by their innovations, discoveries, and development in numerous fields. Generally, this class was loyal to the sultans who provided the security and the peace on which its livelihood and welfare depended. The commoners demonstrated their loyalty to al-Malik al-Naṣir Dawud and supported his amir al-Malik al-Mughith Amr. They served in the Mamluk armed forces and helped al-Sa'id al-Mas'ud, the son of Baybars in taking over the government. They also stood beside al-Malik al-Naṣir Muhammad and Barquq whom they took out of his prison in Karak, placed him on the throne, and sent him aid.[20]

Jordan attracted a mixed population of urban people and villagers during the Mamluk period. Most of them were villagers who resided in the northern, central and southern regions of the country. The vast majority were farmers and anglers, and the land on which they toiled were usually military land grants that belonged to Mamluk amirs. Jordan and its northern part in particular provided means of livelihood for the soldiers. It also had religious endowments with their administrations. Many institutions such as mosques, schools, and caravanserais were built during that time. An example for the practice of endowing such institutions with the money and land that they needed was that of Sultan al-Ashraf Sha'ban (1363–1377) who endowed a school in Cairo in 1375. Moreover, there was a wide variety of facilities that were built on these lands, such as the baths and the garden in Wadi Karak.

The Bedouins constituted a major part of the Jordanian society at that time. Many of them were spread throughout the country, from the desert region in the south to the north. They were mostly shepherds who sold their products in the towns and the villages and regarded themselves as a warrior class, superior to the peasants who suffered from their depredations. Their relations with the authorities underwent frequent changes, according to the circumstances. Many of these tribes resided in East Jordan. Banu Uqbah resided in Karak and Shawbak, Banu Mahdi resided in Balqa, Ahl Mara'i in Zarqa, al-Ḍalil spread from north Jordan to the Hawran and the Golan, and Banu Gham resided in Karak and Shawbak, while Banu Sakhr inhabited most of regions of East Jordan.

Most of Jordan's inhabitants were Muslims of the Sunni branch. Christians lived throughout the entire country as well, and for the most part, they respected the law and came to defend the country from invasions when needed. We hear, for example, of a monk who lived in Shawbak and who went on behalf of al-Malik al-Mu'ẓam Isa to Sicily to investigate the rumors regarding the Sixth Crusade, which Frederick II was planning to embark on to the Holy Land. The Christians helped Sultan Barquq maintain his troops in that region. The sources tell us that Christians from Shawbak gave Barquq a thousand dinars to distribute among the soldiers. The Christians of Karak were highly regarded by the Mamluk sultans who encouraged and promoted them in an effort to gain their loyalty and contribution to the security of their frontiers. It was precisely the insecure nature of the region, and the need to defend it against foreign invasions, that brought the Christians and the Muslims together. Al-Qalqashani tells us that the Mamluk sultans endeavored to maintain cordial relations between the two religious communities. Sultan al-Naṣir Muhammad is said to have written to his son Amir Ahmad when he nominated him to be the governor of Karak, to treat the Christians and other *dhimmi*s well. As for the Jews, they were scattered throughout the country. They were engaged in commerce, artisanship, and industry and lived mainly in villages. Al-Maqrizi tells us that they resided in Aqaba due to its commercial importance. There was also a minority of Jews in Ajlun (Gil'ad).[21]

According to recent archaeological findings, significant demographic changes had taken place in Jordan during the late Mamluk period. These changes began already during the Mongol and Timurid periods. During the Mongol advance in Syria in the mid-thirteenth century, many of the inhabitants of Damascus migrated to Karak, and did not return to their city until the Mongols moved away more than a month later. The villagers of Adhri'at migrated toward Ajlun during Timur's invasion and returned only when he and his army left. Political conflicts in fortified centers such as Karak forced many residents of the Jordan Valley to migrate to the neighboring areas at the end of the fourteenth century. A significant change in settlement took place in Jordan during the fifteenth century. The collapse of the Mamluk state resulted in disorder and Bedouin attacks on villages intensified. In the southern plains of the Jordan Valley as many as 60–85 percent of the sites that were occupied during the Mamluk period had been abandoned and in the central plains, the rate is estimated to have been around 30–50 percent. Substantial demographic recovery did not take place until the twentieth century. Many sites in central and southern Jordan were abandoned by the sixteenth century and many smaller ones were established. The dispersal of large villages to smaller ones was an outcome of imperial collapse. The migrants often resorted to pastoralism and subsistence agriculture. Surveys in the Jordanian plains in places like Karak, Madaba,

Dhiban, and other locations demonstrate that there was a general abandonment of the plains. The areas into which the migrants came tended to be smaller and had gardens, orchards, or small plots of grain. These demographic changes affected central and southern Jordan much more than the regions north of Irbid. There is also evidence of years of drought, pestilence, and famine during the late fourteenth and fifteenth centuries, which contributed to such migration. The collapse of the Mamluk Empire had a negative impact on large-scale production of staples, such as grain and sugar. The *iqta'* system collapsed and the settlers returned to more traditional farming methods.[22]

Notes

1 Al-Jawārinah, p. 35.
2 *Ibid*, p. 37.
3 *Ibid*, p. 56.
4 *Ibid*, p. 59.
5 *Ibid*, p. 63.
6 Cited *Ibid*, p. 61.
7 A *mithqal* is equal to 4.25 grams and normally used when weighing precious metals.
8 Al-Jawārinah, p. 67.
9 *Ibid*, p. 68.
10 Ḥujjah, p. 202.
11 *Ibid*, p. 255.
12 *Ibid*, p. 258.
13 *Ibid*, pp. 264–265.
14 Bethany J. Walker, "Sowing the Seeds of Rural Decline? Agriculture as an Economic Barometer for the Late Mamluk Jordan," *Mamluk Studies Review*, Vol. 11, No. 1 (2007), pp. 181, 207.
15 Al-Jawārinah, p. 48.
16 *Ibid*, p. 43.
17 Cited in Riad Nasser, *Recovered Histories and Contested Identities: Jordan, Israel, and Palestine* (Lanham, MD: Lexington Books, 2011), p. 147.
18 Al-Jawārinah, p. 55.
19 *Ibid*, p. 74.
20 *Ibid*, p. 78.
21 *Ibid*, p. 81.
22 Bethany Walker, "The Phenomenon of the 'Disappearing' Villages of Late Medieval Jordan as Reflected in Archaeological and Economic Sources," *Bulletin d'Études Orientales*, Vol. 60 (2011), pp. 161–162, 164–167, 170–171.

V Jordan in the Ottoman age

The towns that constitute modern-day Jordan were essentially defenseless separate entities in ancient times. Their efforts to defend themselves against foreign conquerors and Bedouin invaders led to the creation of a league known as the Decapolis.[1] The European crusaders who arrived at the end of the eleventh and the beginning of the twelfth centuries built castles and fortresses to defend their kingdoms. However, under the Arabs, the Ayyubids, and the Mamluks who dominated this region in the medieval period, the inhabitants were forced to fend for themselves. They formed tiny settlements governed by Bedouin *shaikhs* who provided protection to the population, its land, and its flocks. Settlements were established in Karak, Tafila, Ma'an. and other places along the *hajj* road, which provided all the pilgrims' needs.

By the end of the fifteenth century the Ottoman Empire faced competition from the rising Portuguese empire in the Red Sea and the Persian Gulf region. Lacking hulls sturdy enough to carry big guns, the Ottoman merchant ships of that time were practically useless for warfare. Nor were there any places around the Indian Ocean where vessels could be obtained. Consequently, the Ottomans were compelled to rely on Red Sea ports such as Aqaba or Ayla from which they could sail to the Persian Gulf and engage in battle against the Portuguese.[2] The need to rely on these ports prompted the Ottomans to occupy Jordan, and station garrisons in its towns and castles, in order to establish bases of operations from which they hoped to deploy forces capable of securing their access to these ports.

The Ottoman domination of Jordan began shortly following the fall of Constantinople in 1453. Following the Battle of Chaldiran in 1514 against Safavid Persia, the Ottomans became masters of Anatolia and began expanding toward Greater Syria. The attempt made by the Mamluk Sultan Qansu al-Ghuri to stop the Ottoman advance failed when he was defeated by Selim I at the Battle of Marj Dabīq, near Aleppo in 1516. This conquest brought an end to Mamluk rule, which began in the mid-thirteenth century and enabled the Ottomans to control the towns and villages on both side of the Jordan River.

After occupying Aleppo, the Ottomans advanced toward Damascus and other Syrian cities such as Safad, Nablus, Jerusalem, Ajlun, and Gaza. The sultan reorganized his armies, made efforts to gain the support of the Bedouins of these regions, and then moved toward Egypt, which he conquered after his victory at the

DOI: 10.4324/9781003450313-6

Battle of Raydaniyah in January 1517. Following the conquest, he embarked on administrative reforms, creating administrative units known as *sanjaks* or districts, which were part of larger administrative units called *eyalet*s. The Ottoman documents of that period help shed light on the new administrative order in Jordan at that time. The seventeenth-century traveler Evliya Celebi tells us that when Selim I conquered Jerusalem from the Mamluks he installed a governor (*pasha*) in Jerusalem. According to the sultan's register, the province of Palestine comprised five *sanjaks*. These were Izzat al-Hashim (Gaza), Jabal Ajlun, Lajun, Nablus, and Jerusalem.[3]

Ever since, the Ottomans controlled the *hajj* road to Mecca and Medina through the chiefs of the local tribes who provided protection to the pilgrims in return for tax reductions, special payments or sinecures. The 'Porte' as the Ottoman imperial government came to be known, provided security to the pilgrims, not only by paying the local Bedouins to avoid raiding the caravans on their way to and from the *hajj* but also by building fortresses and caravanserais along the road. The most famous among these fortresses were built in 1563 by Suleiman II in Wadi Ḥasa and Saqiyat Ma'an. However, despite these measures, instability and chaos prevailed in the country, and the Bedouins continued to invade the fertile regions and plunder the villages and towns.

With the arrival of the Ottomans, the Mamluks lost control over the Jordanian towns and villages. Selim I nominated a Mamluk official, Janbirdi al-Ghazali as governor of Greater Syria with the exception of the *eyalet* of Aleppo. The governor demonstrated his concern for the *hajj* road as soon as he came to power. Hearing about the intention of the Bedouin tribes of Jordan to attack the caravan on its return from Mecca, he changed its course to an alternative road leading from Damascus to Gaza. Moreover, in the summer of 1520, he crushed a rebellion staged by the governor of Nablus, and hanged several notables from that town.

Even though the Porte established a new administrative system, local notables throughout Greater Syria were often left in their position. A case in point is Turabay bin Karajah, head of the Bedouin tribe in northern Samaria whom the sultan re-nominated to the position of *amir al-darbayn*, or 'prince of the two roads' (Damascus-Uyun al-Tujjar-Cairo; Damascus Uyun al-Tujjar-Jerusalem). As such he was also the governor of the Jezreel Valley. In return for providing security to the region and its inhabitants, he was given the right to collect taxes from several regions to the north and west of Nablus. This privilege allowed his family members to expand their influence during the next hundred years, and they occupied key positions in that region. One of the dominant figures during the second half of the sixteenth century was Assaf, son of Turabay who was in charge the King's Highway to Damascus, and later executed by its governor. Other members of the family such as Aḥmad bin Turabay who became governor of Lajjun in the second half of the seventeenth century continued to have influence in that region. However, the family began losing influence in the century that followed.[4]

At the beginning of the Ottoman age, Greater Syria comprised the *eyalets* of Aleppo and Damascus. Aleppo was entrusted to an Ottoman governor and Damascus to a Mamluk. However, the Ottoman authorities treated both *eyalet*s as one. This state of affair continued until the end of Suleiman the Magnificent's reign in 1566. In the administrative division of *sanjaks* and *eyalets*, Greater Syria was called *Eyalet Arab*. It later became known as *Eyalet Sham* and Jordan became part of it. It is regrettable that we know so little about the administrative conditions, which prevailed there prior to 1525, except for the fact that between 1517 and 1521, the Arab regions consisted of 19 *sanjaks*.

When the Ottoman Empire conquered the region of southeast Syria, the country's inhabitants became Ottoman subjects, and as such they were subjected to heavy taxes, were required to abide by the Ottoman law, and to serve in the Ottoman army. Furthermore, they were not allowed to form a militia for self-defense or to keep arms. Jews and Christians were treated as Peoples of the Book (*dhimmis*) and as such were subjected to a poll tax (*jizya*).

The first time that the name "Transjordan" was mentioned in the Ottoman archives was in 1525, following the conquest of al-Salt and Ajlun. One can find documents relating to the Ghor, but there is no mention of other regions, with the possible exception of one document that refers to Ajlun (register number 970, which was published by the scholars Muhammad Adnan al-Bakhith and Nawfan al-Hammoud but bears no date). One document mentions the *liwa* of al-Salt-Ajlun among the 15 *liwa*s of *wilayat al-'Arab*. According to this document, the *amir* of that *liwa* was Iskander Beg whose annual salary was 200,000 *aqjah*. There is no doubt that the *liwa* of al-Salt-Ajlun contained the Karak region. It appears from the documents that this state of affairs continued until the mid-seventeenth century. The only area of Transjordan mentioned in a register of Diyar Bakr and *Wilayat al-Arab* from 1530 was al-Salt-Ajlun. It is possible to conclude in light of what we find in the Ottoman documents that the *liwa* al-Salt-Ajlun contained all the lands of present-day Jordan. According to Register 970, this *liwa* contained the following regions: al-Salt, Ajlun, Alan, Taifat Arab, Karak, Ghor, Shawbak, Wadi Musa, and Jabal Ḥamida. This confirms the view that *liwa* Salt-Ajlun included all the areas of present-day Jordan.

A document from the mid-sixteenth century (1550–1551) mentions the *liwa* of al-Salt-Ajlun, which included Karak and Shawbak. This *liwa* was among the eight in Greater Syria, which included Syria, Jerusalem, Gaza, Nablus, Safad, Tripoli, al-Salt-Ajlun with Karak and Shawbak, and the Arab *liwa* of Tarabay. The *liwas* of Aleppo, Ḥama, and Ḥims were separated from it in order to form the *eyalet* of Aleppo, which included the *liwa*s of Aintab and Birecik.

According to a register from 1568 to 1574, Transjordan was divided into two *liwa*s: the *liwa* of Ajlun and that of Karak and Shawbak. It seems that the administrative division of the *wilaya* of Greater Syria contained 14 *liwa*s: Syria which was the seat of the *pasha*, Jerusalem, Gaza, Tripoli, Safad, Nablus, Ajlun, Karak and Shawbak, Lajun, Ḥims, Salkhad, Beirut, Sidon, and Jabala. Despite the fact that the Ottomans made changes (according to registers of 1573–1588) to some of the *liwa*s such as Salkhad, Beirut, and Sidon, the administrative arrangement of the *liwa*s of Ajlun and Karak remained the same.[5]

During the seventeenth century, Ottoman rule in Transjordan was lax and the peasants were left exposed to the depredations of the Bedouins. Between the end of the sixteenth century and the beginning of the nineteenth century, the Hawran plane lost 60 percent of its population, while the Ajlun Mountain lost only 30 percent.[6] The Druze amir of Lebanon and governor of Sidon and Safed, Fakhr al-Din II al-Ma'ni (1572–1635) managed to extend his rule to Nablus, Hawran and the Ajlun district east of the Jordan. In 1622, he obtained the imperial title to the lands "from the borders of Aleppo to those of Jerusalem."[7]

The Ottomans faced major difficulties in their fight against the Bedouins in Transjordan and the surrounding regions. Danger existed mainly in the Biqa' Valley and on the *hajj* road, which connected Damascus and the Hejaz. Nevertheless, they managed, sometimes by force, and sometime by bribes and persuasion, to obtain the cooperation of the Bedouins in the attempt to guard the road against the marauders. Normally, the agreements with the tribes were short-lived due to the frequent changes and the rise of new leaders among the tribes. The ability to control the region also depended on the extent to which the Porte was capable of exercising its authority. Local leaders capable of facilitating the Porte's task of controlling the Bedouins occasionally emerged in these regions. A case in point is Fakhr al-Din of the Ma'n family who gained control over the Bedouin tribes in the Biqa', Ḥawran, Palestine, and Transjordan during the first half of the seventeenth century. His influence extended from the rural regions of northern Syria to Antioch and Aleppo in the north, and to the desert regions of the east, all the way to Tadmor (Palmyra). Sultan Murad IV (1623–1640) granted him the title 'Amir Arabstan' and he named himself 'Sultan of the Land'. In order to understand how Fakhr al-Din II obtained such position, it is necessary to trace his campaign against Harfush family and their allied, which began in 1623.

In 1623, Yunus al-Harfush prohibited the Druze of the Shouf region of Lebanon from cultivating their lands in the Beqaa valley, and thereby incurred the wrath of Fakhr al-Din II who evicted him and his family from the region. Displeased with his action, the Porte dismissed his sons Ali, Hussein and Mustafa Kethuda from their positions as *sanjak-beys* of Safad, Ajlun, and Nablus respectively, and nominated new ones from among Fakhr al-Din's enemies. Soon afterward, however, the Porte allowed Fakhr al-Din II and his sons to regain Ajlun and Nablus, but not Safad. When the Ma'ns moved to take control of Ajlun and Nablus, Yunus called upon on the Janissary leader Kurd Hamza, to help him block their advance. With Hamza's help, Yunus managed to became the *sanjak-bey* of Safad.

Following his defeat by the Turabays and the Farrukhs at the Battle of Ajwa River, near Ramla in Palestine, on November 1 of that year, Fakhr al-Din learned that the Porte decided to restore all the three *sanjaks* to his family. The Porte's decision was a result of a bribery, which Fakhr al-Din's agent in Constantinople had paid Sultan Murad IV, who ascended the throne on that year, and his Grand Vizier, Kemankeş Ali Pasha. Nevertheless, the Harfushes continued the assaults against the Ma'ns. Disgruntled by his losses in Palestine, Fakhr al-Din who arrived in Qabb Iliyas on October 22 was determined to recover his losses by raiding the villages of Karak, Nuh, and Sar'in, which were controlled by the Harfushes. He then continued his campaign against the Harfushes and their allies whom he managed to defeat. However, despite the fact that he obtained the consent of the *beylerbey* to retain several regions, he did not manage to regain Gaza, Nablus, and Lajjun due to opposition by local landowners.[8] Complaints against the Ma'ns eventually brought the sultan to order Fakhr al-Din's execution in the spring of 1635.

The French traveler Jean de Thévenot who visited that region at the end 1650s had noted that following the execution, the Porte faced enormous difficulties prevailing over the tribes.[9] Consequently, more administrative changes followed when Lajun and Ajlun became two separate *sanjaks* in the *eyalet* of Damascus, and from what Evliya Celebi tells us, this arrangement continued at least until the middle of that century. However, sometime in the beginning of the eighteenth century, these two *sanjaks* became a single administrative unit known as Sancak Jabal Ajlun ve-Lajun or simply Sancak Ajlun or Sancak Lajun. One ought to conclude then that the two *sanjaks* were combined sometime during the second half of the seventeenth century, perhaps in order to bolster governor's position and to enable him to prevent the incursions of the Bedouins in that region. In March 1702, the *sanjak* of Ajlun and Lajun was transferred from the *eyalet* of Damascus to that of Tripoli and three year later, it was incorporated into the *eyalet* of Sidon. Most of the *sanjak* consisted of areas west of the Jordan such as Jabal Nablus-the Issachar Heights, the Jezreel Valley, the Carmel Range, the Plain of Dothan, and the northern part of the Sharon Plain. The eastern boundary of the *sanjak* (excluding Jabal Ajlun) ran along the Samaritan Hills and reached the Yarkon River in the south. The *sanjak* was divided into a number of *nahya*s, four east of the Jordan and three in the west. Those in the west were Naḥiyat Haifa, Naḥiyat Saḥil Atlit (which comprised the coastal plain of the Carmel Range, as far as Wadi Zarqa), and Naḥiyat Sha'ra, which extended along Wadi Ara as far as the Nablus Hills.[10]

The governors sent by the Porte resorted to harsh measures, which intensified in the early nineteenth century, when the region fell under Muhammad Ali Pasha of Egypt and his son Ibrahim whose ruthless measures against the Bedouins brought order to that region. Commenting on the Egyptian ruthlessness toward the Bedouin tribes in Jordan, the English traveler Alexander William Kinglake, who visited the region in 1835, had this to say about Ibrahim's methods:

> Ibrahim has craftily sent a body of troops across the Jordan. The force went warily round to the foot of the mountains on the East, and then surrounded them as they lay encamped in the vale; their camels, and, indeed, all their possessions worth taking, were carried off by the soldiery, and moreover then Sheik, together with every tenth man of the tribe, was brought out and shot.[11]

Like other imperial powers, the Porte had to resort to the time-honored method of collaboration with reliable individuals or groups to guarantee the safety of the pilgrims who passed through Transjordan. Utilized by all imperial powers at that time, this method was later applied to their colonies. This was an indispensable method for efficient rule by any imperial power, as the eminent historian Ronald Robinson who explored the tools of imperialism put it, "Imperialism was as much a function of the victims' collaboration or non-collaboration-of their indigenous politics-as it was of European expansion."[12]

The task of protecting the *hajj* road was entrusted to a tribe or an individual who could provide intelligence, or organize a force to fight unruly tribesmen and it often yielded positive results. Tribes continued to arrive from neighboring regions and maintaining order in that region remained a problem for Ottoman and the Egyptian governors. For example, we hear about the Ḥawara tribe, which came from Egypt at the end of the eighteenth century when Aḥmad Jazzar was the governor. This tribe that once rebelled against Ibrahim Pasha had turned into an important instrument of collaboration with the Ottoman authorities following the pasha's withdrawal and it served them well in the district of Acre. Heading this tribe was Akili-Agha who managed to rise to prominence, particularly during the Druze rebellion of 1852. He was entrusted with maintaining peace in Palestine. He was a Bedouin and as such, he knew how to establish ties with other clans, and keep them under control. Known for his tolerance toward foreigners and minorities such as Christians and Jews, he saved the members of the American exploration Lynch team, which came to visit Jordan and the Dead Sea in 1848 from assaults by unruly tribes.[13] In addition to paying those who agreed to collaborate with them, the Ottoman authorities had made use of the traditional method of bribes (*bakhshish*), in order to entice the tribal chiefs. This became obvious to travelers who arrived in that region, as William Libbey and Franklin E. Hoskins noted:

> For some forty years or more, the government has found bakhshish the most potent weapon, and every year a sum of one hundred pounds has been distributed among the tribes who line the route. As the government has gradually strengthened its position in Damascus, it has coveted the rich lands of the Jordan, and has slowly extended its hold on the highlands, by building fortresses and occupying ancient sites and garrisons. Irbid (Arbela) was sieged some thirty years ago. Then Salt and Madeba fell. Kerak held its own semi-independently until twelve years ago. About that time the government hastened to stretch a line of telegraph from Damascus through this eastern highland, and southward to Medina and Mecca, making its occupation more easy and certain.[14]

Transjordan had no government to speak until then and when the Ottomans returned, they began to establish an efficient administration in it. The imperative of the moment was to protect the *hajj* road from the Bedouin threat, and to establish an orderly government with regular taxation system that could cover the daily expenses.

The construction of the Hejaz Railway in 1902 enabled the Ottomans to control these regions more effectively, and they introduced reforms, which considerably improved the social and economic conditions. However, the ferocity in which the Porte's agents collected taxes and the rapacity of its officials led to resentment, which caused frequent rebellions such as the one which erupted in Karak in 1910, spread to Tafila and Ma'an and forced the Ottomans to send troops to that region. Among the reasons for the outbreak of the rebellion was the Porte's decision to disarm the tribes, introduce military conscription, impose land registration, and stop the payment to tribal leaders who were accustomed to be compensated for their cooperation.[15]

The administrative division

The region which extended from Ma'an to 'Aqaba in the south remained unoccupied after the Ottoman conquest and the caravans traveling along the *hajj* road were often attacked by Bedouin tribes. In addition to providing protection to the pilgrims along the *hajj* road, the Porte's main concern was to maintain security along the main route to Egypt and to protect the major urban centers, but apart from maintaining security along the *hājj* road, little attention was paid to Greater Syria.[16] This administrative organization survived with minor changes until 1831–1833 when Ibrahim, son of Muhammad Ali conquered Syria, which he was forced to evacuate following intense uprising. But while Syria and Palestine experienced domestic turmoil, which led to intervention by the great European powers and to drastic decline in population, which decreased from four million to a million-and-a half Transjordan, and the region which bordered it in the south remained relatively unscathed.

Although the reforms implemented by the Porte in Transjordan were basic and largely inadequate, they helped lay the foundations of a modern society, which gradually evolved in that country. Ottoman elementary schools where the Turkish language was taught were established in the major urban areas, and the religious and ethnic groups had their parochial educational system. Just like in any other region of Greater Syria, there was a certain measure of westernization among the elites in Transjordan, but there was no western education to speak of. The improvements that were later introduced by the Porte as part of the *Tanzimat* reform movement accelerated the process, and even though their scope remained limited, they were instrumental in the creation of a modern state.

Situated in the northern part of Transjordan the Ajlun district was the first to come under Ottoman rule. In 1851, Ajlun turned into an administrative unit known as *kaza* and it constituted part of the Nablus district known as *mutasarrifiya*. Its governor sat at Irbid. That Ajlun was one of the first areas in which the Ottomans chose to establish an administrative center was largely because this region was under constant threats of raids by Bedouins and there was always need to send military expeditions in order to suppress the unruly tribes. In 1868, the Porte brought the central district of Balqa under its control, and like Ajlun, it turned into a *kaza* entrusted to the governor of Nablus who sat at al-Salt. Similarly, Karak and Ma'an in the south came under the jurisdiction of the *mutasarrifiya* of Nablus. In his effort to maintain order, the official who was in charge of Nablus (*mutasarrif*) obtained assistance from Karak whose inhabitants were granted amnesty for past transgressions. Later, Ajlun district was expanded to include Ma'an, al-Salt, Tabbuk, and Medain Saleh. Aqaba, which remained under Egyptian control, was not included in these arrangements but following Ibrahim's withdrawal from Syria, it was incorporated into the Medina district.

This arrangement was far from being permanent. Ajlun was first attached to Nablus, but in 1861, it was incorporated to Hawran. In 1893, the status of Ajlun changed again and it became a *liwa* of the *vilayet* of Syria with its center in Damascus. Similarly, al-Salt was first attached to Nablus, but in 1893, it was incorporated to Karak.[17] Palestine, which included some of the areas of present day Jordan, was divided as follows: the Ajlun district was placed under the *mutasarrif* of Nablus and the Zarqa River became its northern boundary; Ramtha was cut off from the rest of Ajlun and it was included in the *sanjak* of Hawran, while the Ghor came under the *mutasarrifiya* of Tiberias. Then Palestine was divided again. Galilee and Samaria became two *sanjaks* of the *vilayet* of Beirut called the *sanjak* of Acre and that of Balqa respectively. The rest of Palestine, including Judea and the south down to the Gulf of Aqaba, became the independent *sanjak* of Jerusalem. At the same time, the East Bank was divided into the districts of Hawran, Jawlan, Amman, al-Salt, Karak and Aqaba.[18]

By the late Ottoman period, Transjordan was sparsely populated. A few areas were cultivated and the peasants lived on a subsistence level, with little or nothing to export. Transportation methods were primitives, and the mail delivery was slow and uncertain. Most roads used by passengers with their merchandize and their beasts of burden, were not paved, except for those used by the Ottoman troops or those leading to the major towns. Likewise, there were very few educational establishments and these were usually Qur'anic schools, which provided little more than elementary education.

The attempts of the Ottoman authorities to protect the *hajj* road from the encroachments of the Bedouins by 'divide and conquer' tactics and often by persuasion were not always successful.[19] The only remaining solution was to pay a special payment known as *khuwah* to the Bedouin *shaikhs* who agreed to provide protection to the pilgrims. The early *hajj* road passed through Karak, Dera'a, Mafraq, Zarqa and Ma'an. The pilgrims who passed through this road could obtain the supplies and the food that they needed in these areas. An official known as 'prince of the *hajj*' (*amir al-hajj*) was responsible for maintaining security along this road and a special annual budget of 100,000 sovereigns were allocated for that purpose. A significant part of that sum was used to pay the tribal *shaikhs* who agreed to keep peace along the road, and to provide camels for the *amir al-hajj* and his men. The *shaikh*'s cooperation was deemed essential for the task of maintaining order along the *hājj* road, and for the most part his men fulfilled their duty as expected. They were committed to protect the pilgrims and to maintain adequate supply of water. Failure to pay the stipend normally meant that the *shaikh* would not honor his part of the bargain. Although the Porte kept a small garrison to protect the pilgrims, it could not expect to guarantee safety along the road without honoring its obligation to the *shaikh*.

The sources tell us that attacks on pilgrims were rife during the Ottoman period. For example, Aḥmad al-Budayri (1741–1762) tells us that in 1756, Banu Sakhr attacked the pilgrims' caravan and "committed deeds that even worshippers of fire would not commit."[20] We are also told that in 1909, the *amir al-hajj* did not did not dare return by land from the Hejaz to Damascus and that Sharif Hussein of Mecca had to send his son Abdallah and his brother Naṣir to accompany the pilgrims.

Safety was of major concern not only along the *hajj* road but throughout the entire country.

The accounts of nineteenth-century travelers provide an insight into the difficulties which one had to encounter upon arriving at the region. For example, the cleric Selah Merill (1837–1909) who served as the American consul in Jerusalem, tells us about the difficulties of mail delivery, saying that it was hard to find anyone willing to carry a letter from Ajlun to al-Salt. We are also told that a young man from al-Salt who sought to enroll in the American College in Beirut was prevented from doing so due to concern over his safety. The lack of amenities and the shortage of supplies in al-Salt forced the population to rely on outside help. No medical equipment was available in that town, and a stretcher had to be brought from Jerusalem to carry a sick man to the hospital. Robinson Lees who traveled to that region in that period relates how he and his companions were looking for someone to accompany them on the road from Amman to Hawran, saying that only after a long deliberation, two Circassians agreed to make the journey for a payment of two pounds.[21]

Relations between villagers and Bedouins in Transjordan were often tense. Normally, villagers agreed to pay *khuwah* in order to obtain guarantee that the Bedouins will not attack them. Prominent among these tribes were the Ḥuwaiṭat under Audeh Abu Tayeh and the Adwan under the Majala family, who normally allied themselves with al-Salt and the adjacent villages. Banu Sakhr operated in Madaba, and they constituted a threat to the Christian tribes in that region. It was not until 1921 that Banu Sakhr were defeated by the villagers of Madaba. In addition to the Bedouins, there were local Druze *shaikhs* who exerted power over the villagers. They provided protection to numerous villages, both Muslim and Christian in the *sanjak* of Hawran, which included the sub-districts (*kaza*s) of Kunaitra, Jabal Ajlun, and Jabal Druze. Seeking protection for their land and flocks, villagers were compelled to pay fees for many of their activities and even for permission to marry. For the most part, villagers preferred to pay these protectors rather than to pay taxes to the Ottoman authorities on whose support they could not count.[22]

Bedouins had considerable impact on life in Transjordan. By the second half of the nineteenth century, their impact in Ajlun and its environs was such that the inhabitants resolved to emigrate from their villages. This state of affairs caused concern in Constantinople and the Porte sent a military force to assist the inhabitants against Bedouins who invaded Wadi al-Arab where they built a castle from which they attacked the villages. The Ottoman campaign against the Sa'idi tribe resulted in major massacre, which resulted according to eyewitnesses in bloodshed that caused the waters of Wadi al-Arab to change color.[23] Consequently, Banu Sakhr migrated to Balqa and the Jordan Valley where they felt safer and gained more confidence. The only spots in the Ajlun district, which the Bedouins did not manage to dominate, were Mount Ajlun, al-Kawra, and al-Kufarat. In the other parts of that district, the destruction was such that the size of the population decreased considerably. Only three villages remained: al-Iraq, Kathrabah and Khuzïra. Madaba was destroyed, and it was not until 1876 that some tribes emigrated from Karak to settle there. The relative ease by which Ajlun could be defended can be explained by the fact that its rulers who migrated from the eastern and northern parts of Hawran where they had control over the Bedouins were determined to maintain order in Ajlun as well. Furthermore, the rugged nature of the terrain made it easy to defend the villages in that district.

Villagers in places such as al-Salt, Karak, Tafila, and Ma'an defended themselves by forming alliances with powerful tribes nearby. We are told that the oppression of the Bedouins was such that when they prevailed over their enemies, they prohibited weddings from taking place, and did not let their enemies bury their dead before they took their share of the spoils. Another story is told about a Bedouin who asked a peasant from Karak to be his partner but only appeared in the harvest season to take his share.[24] Scattered and divided among themselves villagers could hardly defend themselves, even though they used guns against the Bedouins who were armed with swords and lances.

The Porte's failure to establish security in Transjordan made the task of providing protection harder for the local governor, the chief of the tribes and the heads of the families. So accustomed were the *shaikhs* to receive payment from foreign travelers that they rarely allowed freedom of passage without them. For example, the British traveler Gray Hill who passed through Karak in 1887 could not do so without payment. The inability of foreign travelers to pass through Karak without payment shows the extent of the power, which a local chief could exercise at that time. The same can be said about the areas further south. We are told that the traveler Captain Shakespeare was not allowed to pass through Aqaba on his way from Mecca to Transjordan without giving *shaikh* Audeh Abu Tayeh the required fee.[25]After all the administrative changes, the division of Transjordan could be more accurately defined and by the second half of the nineteenth century these were the main districts in Transjordan:

Ajlun

In 1851, the region between the Yarmouk in the north and the Zarqa River was called *sanjak* and it was governed by an official known as *qaimaqam*. The center of this *sanjak* was Irbid and it included Kaura, Beni Jahmah, al-Sur, Wusṭiyya, Beni Abid, al-Kafarat, Jabal Ajlun, and Jarash. Ramtha, its surrounding villages, and those in the east of Wadi al-Shalala were part of the *sanjak* of Hawran. The northern Ghor region of Transjordan was part of the *qaimaqmiya* of Tiberias. This *sanjak* became part of the *mutasarrifiya* of Hawran. Jarash and Ajlun were incorporated into the *qamaqamiya* of Irbid, while Ramtha was incorporated into Dar'a.

Jabal Ajlun district combined several mountain villages which constituted a commune (*naḥya*) each ruled by a leader (*za'im*). There were eight such communes in the nineteenth century only two of which, Bani Juhma and Kafarat survived from the seventeenth century.[26] This hilly district, which has the highest rainfall in Transjordan, 500 millimeters annually, had enough land and water for cultivation of olive and fruit trees, in addition to vegetables and grain. The abundance of agricultural produce and the security, which the terrain provided, turned Jabal Ajlun into the most populated area in Transjordan. The southwest part of that district known as al-Jabal or Ajlun was the largest of the eight *naḥyas* of Jabal Ajlun and the most populated in the district. Ajlun was governed by the Furayhat family from the village of Kufrinja.

Bordering Ajlun in the north was the *naḥya* of al-Kura ruled by the Shurayda lords from their center at Tibna village. There was much hostility between them and the Furayhat and they rarely lived in peace. The Shurayda came to power after evicting the Rushdan family that had long ruled Tibna. This change took place in the early eighteenth century when Abd al-Nabi of the Shurayda gathered around him supporters who helped him overthrow the Rushdan. After a period of common rule over al-Kura the Shurayda prevailed, and they continued to rule by the time-honored reliance on hospitality and by force, when necessary. The fact that the areas north and east of the district were hilly and flat made it possible for Bedouin horsemen and pastoralists to invade. This forced the inhabitants of the region to come to terms with them. Consequently, the six *naḥyas* became controlled jointly by the *za'ims* and the Bedouin *shaikhs*.

By the end of the nineteenth century, these parts of Jabal Ajlun fell under the domination of the Zaban, Hamid, and Khadir branches of the Banu Sakhr tribe. Each village had a brother (*akh*) who acted as a protector and a judge. With the exception of external defense, the *za'im* dealt with all aspects of the district's administration. The Ajlun district was open to northern commercial influence and its merchants looked to Ḥawran and Damascus as places where they could sell their wares or find shelter.[27]

Hawran

In antiquity, the Hawran region was part of the Kingdom of Zobah and its capital was Anjar. In addition to Hawran, the kingdom included the Biq'a region and the eastern Lebanese mountain chain, Qalmun and Damascus. By the tenth century BC, the Kingdom of Zobah became part of Aram-Damascus. Assyrian inscriptions tell us that King Shalmaneser III (859–824 BC) attacked Syria and moved toward Hawran where he sacked and burnt many towns. We are also told that Tiglat-Pileser III (745–727 BC) conquered Damascus, and the adjacent areas which included Hawran with its capital Ashterot Farnin (Shaikh Sa'd). He divided the regions to sixteen districts one of which was Hawran, which included the Hawran Mountain (733 BC). In 88 BC, the Nabateans incorporated southern Syria to their kingdom after their victory over the Seleucids. Then the region fell under Roman rule and was incorporated into the Kingdom of Herod the Great (37–4 BC). Prior to the rise of Islam, Hawran fell under the Ghassanids who served as mercenaries of the Byzantine Empire in its wars against Sassanid Persia until the Battle of Yarmouk in 636 AD when it was conquered by the Arabs.[28] During the Ottoman period, the province (*liwa* or *mutasarrifiya*) of Ḥawran was the most southerly part of the province of Syria. It was subdivided into three smaller units (*qaimaqamliks*);

Kunaitra at the foot of Jabal al-Shaikh (Mount Hermon) and Mount Ajlun, and its governor (*mutasarrif*) resided at Shaikh Sa'd village.

Karak

Karak was a fortress located in the Balqa region, between Ayla, Baḥr al-Qulzum, and Jerusalem, close to as-Sarat, on a mountain surrounded by valleys on all sides, except at the entrance. On his way to Boṣra, Ṣalaḥ al-Din stopped there after hearing about Arnaṭ's governor intension to attack the pilgrims. In the encounter that ensued, the governor attacked the pilgrims and then turned toward Ṣalaḥ al-Din and his Egyptian troops. Ṣalaḥ al-Din moved toward Boṣra where he stopped the governor and saved the caravan.

By the mid-seventeenth century, this region was inhabited by the Amamiyah and the Amru tribes. Jalal bin Shadid who came from al-Khalil brought the Majali tribe along, and they clashed with the Amru. Then the Majali formed alliances with other tribes of Transjordan such as Beni Ḥamida and al-Ḥajaya, and together they defeated the Amru. However, this did not bring an end to the tribal warfare, and the Porte found it necessary to intervene by sending an army that was well-received in Karak, which they turned into a *mutasarrīfīya* with Hussein Ḥilmi Pasha as its *mutasarif*. In 1790, Amir Ibn Saud took control of Jauf and he reached Karak in 1806. However, the tribes in Karak refused to pay the taxes that he imposed on them. The Wahhabis advanced to Hawran and drove the Turkish army away, but they were forced to evacuate Karak when the Egyptian viceroy Muhammad Ali Pasha invaded Arabia.

During the eighteenth century, Karak was dominated by the Majali tribes. Most of the tribes were members of one of the two alliances—the Eastern (*Sharaqa*) and the Western (*Gharaba*)—which included most of the tribes in that region. Generally, the *Gharaba* occupied the western and northern lands of the district, while the *Sharaqa* occupied those of the south and east of the town of Karak, which was divided in a similar fashion, except for the central markets that were regarded as neutral, and where members of both tribes used to meet. Tribes that did not belong to either of these groupings were at the lower end of the social rung. The *Sharaqa* were led by the Tarawneh family, while the *Gharaba* were led by the Majalis.

By the last quarter of the eighteenth century, the Majali family dominated the town of Karak but they faced a serious challenge by the Tarawneh and the *Sharaqa* in addition to nomadic tribes such as Banu Sakhr and the Ḥuwayṭat who did not belong to any of these alliances. The *shaikh* of Karak did not have complete authority over his people. In 1808, the Saudi-Wahhabi confederation, which dominated the Arabian Peninsula, extended its rule over Karak whose ruler Yusuf Majali obtained from Ibn Saud the title "Emir of all the Bedouins to the south of Damascus, as far as the Red Sea."[29]

When the inhabitants of Palestine rebelled against Ibrahim Pasha in 1834, the rebel Qasim al-Aḥmad fled to Karak. Ibrahim laid a siege to Karak, which lasted seventeen days, and it was not until 1840 that the Egyptians were forced to evacuate the town in the wake of a joint campaign, which the European powers and the Porte carried out against the Egyptian force. Karak's inhabitants took revenge on their besiegers by pursuing them on their way to Egypt and by the time Ibrahim reached Gaza, he had lost most of his army and its supplies. The Egyptian danger ended with the London Convention of 1840, when the great European powers agreed to let his father Muhammad Ali maintain Egypt as his family's domain, in return for his consent to withdraw from Syria. Majali remained in power, and he managed to prevail over his opponents, which included the Banu Sakhr, the Ḥuwayṭat, the Tarawneh, and the Sharaqa. He even used Ottoman arbitration when he saw fit. For example, when a dispute between the Christian inhabitants of Karak and the Sharaqa erupted in 1861, he called upon the governor in Jerusalem who sent a commission of inquiry that resolved the case in his favor.[30]

Karak played central role in commerce and it served as a major entrepot between the deserts of the Arabian Peninsula and the towns of Palestine. Its trade with Hebron was particularly robust, and other towns such as Jerusalem benefited from it. The trade was mostly barter based. During the Napoleonic period, the Arab provinces of the Ottoman Empire were devastated by foreign conquests. Upon returning to Egypt from his military campaign Napoleon Bonaparte left his general Jean Baptiste Kléber who prevailed upon the Syrian tribes. He entered Nazareth and Tiberias and brought the tribes in that region under French control. Soon afterward, Muhammad Ali sent his son Ibrahim who conquered Syria and laid a siege to Karak whose governor Ibrahim al-Dammur refused to surrender.[31] Following his withdrawal, the tribes resumed their fights and the region plunged back into turmoil. Occupied with the need to pacify Palestine and to resist Russian encroachments on its territories in the north, the Porte was in no position to control the tribes in Transjordan. Therefore, in 1850 it established the independent *sanjak* of Ajlun, which initially was part of the *mutasarrifiya* of Nablus and nominated a *qaimaqam* as its governor. This *sanjak* included Kura, Saru, Wusṭiya, and Beni Ubayd in the north, and it extended to the Zarqa River in the south. The Ramtha district was separated from Ajlun, and was incorporated into the *sanjak* of Hawran. The Ghor became part of the *qaimaqamiya* of Tiberias.[32]

In 1893, Ḥussein Ḥilmi Pasha became the *mutasarrif* of Karak. He granted amnesty to its residents, and agreed to provide regular payment to its notables on the proviso that they collaborate with his officials, and help impose the necessary security measures. The Porte decided that Ma'an would be the center of the *mutasarrifiya* and that Karak, al-Salt, and Tafila would form the *qaimaqamat* of Ma'an. The boundaries of this administrative unit were Wadi al-Sirḥan in the east; the Jordan River, the Dead Sea and Wadi Araba in the west; Wadi al-Zarqa in the north; and Madaïn Salah in the south. The center of this administrative unit was Damascus, and it was placed under the purview of its governor. However, when the inhabitants protested, the government realized that Karak's location was more appropriate. It issued a decree stating that Karak would become the center of this administrative unit, and incorporated Ma'an, al-Salt, Tafila, Tabbuk, and Madaïn Salah to it. Ḥilmi Pasha established a residence for the government near the castle, which he fortified and built a military camp. He imposed taxes on the residents in order to finance the agricultural, educational and other projects. His was one of the first elementary school established in that district. His successor, Ṣadiq Pasha, was corrupt and much less efficient. During his tenure, the government ceased paying the notables. This led to dissatisfaction and the tendency to rebel intensified. Consequently, the governor sent a cavalry force under the command of Khusrow Pasha the Circassian who was known for his legendary ferocity. Fearing the inevitable, the inhabitants armed themselves as best as they could. Thereupon, the *mutasarrifiya* was governed by Rashid Pasha who was determined to establish order in it. He too embarked on major construction projects. He built another school in Karak with public contributions, and embarked on a campaign to renovate mosques. Moreover, he established residences for the government in al-Salt and Tafila, and encouraged the inhabitants to establish new villages. Unfortunately, Rashid was relieved from his position before the government responded to his request to establish a local government in Karak. He was followed by Mustafa Beg al-Abid, brother of Izzat Pasha al-Abid who was a friend of Sultan Abd al-Ḥamid II. Mustafa was arrogant and corrupt. He cared for no one other than himself but it was during his incumbency that a local government was finally established in Karak in 1902.[33]

Meanwhile, the Adwan continued fighting over Balqa and the Ottoman authorities tried to restore order in this region. But the tribal warfare continued and the chaos prevailed. By then, the Ajlun district was part of the *mutasarrifiya* of Hawran and the Balqa district was part of the *mutasarrifiya* of Nablus. However, in 1905, the administrative order changed and both Balqa and Ajlun became part of Karak. The heavy taxes imposed on the population led to uprisings the most famous among them erupted in Shawbak in 1905 and in Karak in 1910. These rebellions led to new legislation that enabled the Porte to rule the area more effectively. The Ottoman authorities confiscated arms and laid a siege to Karak castle. Sami Pasha arrived with his army from Jabal al-Druze and entered Karak, which he ruled with iron hand. He was known for inflicting heavy punishments on those who resisted his measures. Among the methods he used against the rebels was tying a heavy stone around their necks and throwing them from the castle.[34]

Ma'an

Ma'an was the southernmost part of Transjordan. This hot and arid region extended to Egypt and the Hejaz. Shaikh Qutb al-Din al-Nahrawali who was sent in 1557 by the Sharif of Mecca to plead for the removal of a local Ottoman official tells us that he stopped in Ma'an "where the water was not good," and where he found "supply caravans (*mulaqat*) with fruits and provender."[35] However, Ma'an was a major stop on the caravan route linking southern Arabia with Damascus. Its location at the junction of major transport routes uniting the surrounding areas and the abundance of water made this town survive the assaults of the nomads, which devastated the surrounding settlements. The geographer Alois Musil who visited Ma'an in 1910 described it as a place where several trade routes converged, saying that it would have been surprising had the settlement in Ma'an not been of considerable importance during that period, given the fact that so much merchandise passed through its routes.[36] The Umayyads settled in that district prior to the establishment of the caliphate that bore their name in 661. The fort of Ma'an along with those of Ḥajar, Tabbuk, and Qaṭranah were built in 1559. By the 1660s, the fort was occupied by the inhabitants who turned against the troops that were sent from Damascus. Water resources were discovered in the area but their quality was poor. A Roman cistern was situated three kilometers from the town, and there was a market where the pilgrims could purchase provisions and merchandize imported from Hebron and Gaza. By 1904, the Hejaz Railway reached the Ma'an station, which had buildings that included a hospital, a hotel and other facilities for the merchants and the pilgrims who stopped there on their way to the *hajj*.[37]

The fortress which stood on the *hajj* road constituted the southern boundary of the land-locked Ma'an district. Ma'an was divided into two townships the small one of which was known as Ma'an al-Shamiyya, and the bigger as Ma'an-al-Ḥejaziyya.[38] The earliest inhabitants of that town were the Midianites who revered Prophet Shu'āib. Administratively, Ma'an was part of the district (*jund*) of Palestine whose capital was Ramla. Separating the Ma'an district from Karak was Wadi al-Ḥasa. The western boundaries of the Ma'an district were Wadi Araba and the Egyptian frontier to the west. In the south, Ma'an district bordered the Ḥejaz at Aqaba al-Shamiyya. Situated in this district were the settlements of Tafila, Shawbak, Shara, and Ma'an. Tafila was the home of the regional tribes of Bani Hajaya, Salayt and the Ḥuwayṭat who fortified themselves in that town. The town consisted of some 600 houses, and it had close trade links with Gaza and Hebron. Close by there were three villages of the Bani Ḥamida tribes. The settlements of the Shara were controlled by the Ḥuwayṭat. Included in these settlements was the Shawbak castle, which contained a hundred families who lived in tents or homes. The inhabitants of Shawbak secured their trade by paying *khuwah* to the Ḥuwayṭat. The Shawbak castle was linked to Aqaba al-Shamiyya by a road that passed through Wadi Musa. At the same time, the village of al-Jiy in the vicinity of Petra was separated from Ma'an by desert, and it contained some 200–300 houses. Its agriculture was robust and its connections to the markets of Gaza and the *hajj* road had turned it into a village of considerable importance.

Ma'an constituted an important station on the pilgrimage road. Its trade was robust and it turned into an important center of Islamic culture. However, its location made it vulnerable to the political and social upheavals that took places in that region. This became abundantly clear in 1807, when the Saudi-Wahhabi confederation occupied the holy cities of the Hejaz and imposed a ban on the caravans sent by the Porte on their way to the *hajj*. This occupation had a serious impact on Ma'an's economy. George August Wallin who visited the region in 1845 provides a description of a small village northeast of Ma'an called al-Shamiya or al-Maghara whose main features were similar to those of Ma'an.

Despite the fact that the Ottoman rule lasted for more than four hundred years, this region was neglected and little was done other than the introduction of minor administrative, educational and medical reforms. Despite the presence of Ottoman military forces, the population suffered from invasions and strife among the tribes who fought for supremacy over the region. Ultimately, the *shaikhs* of the Bedouin tribes were in control and they were the ones that the Porte could rely on to defend the pilgrimage road. However, the need for search for food and water led the Bedouins to invade agricultural land, and the local peasants were compelled to repel these invasions by their own means. Alliances between Bedouin tribes were often formed and the villagers reacted by creating alliances of their own. But the Bedouins prevailed in most cases. The villagers were left without choice but to pay *khuwah* to the invaders, in order to prevent them from stealing their land, flocks, and water. It was only after the villagers managed to overcome the Bedouin threat with the assistance of neighboring villages, that stability was brought to the region and order was restored.

Following Ibrahim Pasha's withdrawal from Syria, the southern part of Transjordan remained virtually without a government until 1894, when the Porte nominated Raouf Pasha as governor of Damascus. For quite some time, the Porte paid little attention to this region. When Rashid Pasha appealed to the central government to attach Ma'an to the new Balqa district his request fell on deaf ears. In 1872, his successor Abd al-Laṭif Subḥi Pasha established a new administrative center in Ma'an, which included the districts of al-Salt, Karak and Jawf in Central Arabia. However, budgetary constraints and lack of resources led to its closure. In time, however, this region began to loom larger in Ottoman strategic thought. The British occupation of Egypt and the need to secure the passage to the Arabian Peninsula brought home to the Ottoman government the need to establish order in that region. But the Porte did not act with alacrity. When the governor of Damascus proposed in 1884 that the government create a new *vilayet* of southern Syria that would combine the districts of Jerusalem, Balqa, and Ma'an as a buffer against foreign invasions, his proposal fell on deaf ears in Constantinople.

Another proposal to create an administrative unit centered in Ma'an with the districts of Karak, Tafila and the *naḥyas* of Amman, Banu Ḥamida, and Wadi Musa was discussed in 1886 but still no action was taken. In 1888, a new *vilayet* based on Beirut was created by detaching northern Palestine and the Lebanese coast from Syria whose governor protested and called again for the establishment of an administrative center in Ma'an under his authority.[39]

In May 1892, the governor of Syria, Osman Nuri Pasha, proposed the creation a regional government centered in Ma'an, including the districts of Karak and Tafila. The Porte approved the plan, but since Ma'an was sparsely populated, Karak became the administrative center even though the efforts to turn Ma'an into an administrative center did not cease. This change came as a result of pressure by the *shaikh* of the Karak, Ṣaliḥ al-Majali who felt threatened by Banu Sakhr. On the other hand, Banu Sakhr felt threatened by the alliance between the Majalis and the Ruwala tribes, and they appealed to the Porte to intervene. In October 1893, the Porte sent troops to Karak. After lengthy siege, the city was captured, and in 1895, it became the capital of that *mutasarrifiya*. At that time, the al-Salt district was detached from Hawran and incorporated into Karak and district governors were appointed to Tafila and Ma'an. Thus, through a combination of force and politics, the Porte managed to bring Transjordan under control.

Balqa

After the fall of the Mamluk regime in Egypt, the Balqa district northwest of Amman was dominated by warring tribes that did not cease fighting each other. The dominant tribe was that of Nawfal al-Ajrami, which migrated from Ala in the Hejaz and settled in the Balqa district. They were followed by the Radha and the Mahdawiya who emerged as the leading tribes in that region around the year 1640. The Adwan tribe that originated in Kinda in the Arabian Peninsula also moved northward, and managed to dominate parts of the Balqa district. Another tribe that came from Ala was that of Banu Sakhr who subdued the Sardiya and the Sirhan tribes in the Hawran. In 1730, the struggle over the Balqa district resulted in a clash between the Adwan and the Banu Sakhr, which took place at Waqi'at Lib in the Hawran. Banu Sakhr managed to prevail over the Adwan and the tribes who allied with them from Mount Ajlun such as the Mumaniya. At the same time, the Ibad tribe managed to dominate a big part of the Balqa district. This brought the Adwan to ally themselves with Beni Ḥasa and the inhabitants of al-Salt. Together, they fought against the Ibad tribe and forced them to flee to Beisan. In 1867, the Porte turned al-Salt into the capital of the district of Balqa, which was later incorporated into the *sanjak* of Nablus. By 1882, the 'Adwan managed to become dominant in the Balqa district but the tribal warfare persisted.

The Balqa extended from Wadi al-Zarqi northward to Wadi al-Mujib, and by the second half of the nineteenth century, the Porte nominated a *qaimaqam* to this region. Its center was the town of al-Salt. This district was incorporated into the *mutasarrifiya* of Nablus, and a military unit was stationed at the al-Salt citadel. In 1915, the Balqa district was separated from the *mutasarrifiya* of Nablus and incorporated to that of Karak.

The Balqa district included the town of al-Salt where commerce and agriculture flourished. This town was built on a steep slope and it had a castle. Three clans inhabited the town; the Akrad, the Qatishat and the Awamila, and each had its leader and its quarter. Ruling the entire town was the 'town leader' (*shaikh al-balad*). Sometimes this position was shared by heads of two or more clans. The head of the town resided in the castle and he in charge of its defense. The area east of the Balqa district where the Zarqa River and the abundant rainfall provided water for grain cultivation was a battleground of rival pastoralists and cultivators who fought over the plains. The inhabitants of al-Salt who sought access to farming land came to agreements with the neighboring tribes to whom they paid annual tribute. By the 1810s, Banu Sakhr displaced the Adwan as "lords of the Balqa'" and collected tribute from al-Salt.[40] Gradually, al-Salt turned into the most important commercial center in Transjordan. Merchants traveled in caravans for protection and traded with numerous items that included garments, wool and butter. Particularly important were the *summaq* that tanners in Palestine used, and the *qili*, or ash that was used for soap manufactured in Nablus. In the south, the Balqa district extended from al-Salt to Wadi Mujib. There were no permanent settlements between al-Salt and Karak, and the land between them was contested between the tribes of the Balqa district and those of Karak.

The inhabitants of the Balqa district were victims not only of Bedouin depredation but also of corruption by local officials. Reporting on the abuses that the inhabitants of the Balqa district were subjected to, a consular officer writes,

> In the south, however, chiefly in Belka, cases of injury by encroachment and petty pillage of the settled districts became more frequent, but they tended principally to the enrichment of local officials by the exercise of arbitrary acts of imprisonment and spoliation to the little satisfaction of the actual sufferers.[41]

Aqaba

Aqaba was a village situated on the gulf that bears that name, across from Ayla. The Egyptian side of Aqaba was known as "Egyptian Aqaba" (*aqaba al-misriyya*) as opposed to "Syrian Aqaba" (*aqaba al-shamiyya*). Aqaba changed hands throughout history. At times, it was part of the Ḥejaz and at other times part of Syria or Egypt. When Muhammad Ali Pasha withdrew from Syria and Palestine, he did not evacuate Aqaba and it remained part of Egypt until 1892, when the Egyptians left it, and it was incorporated into the Ḥejaz. A dispute emerged at that time between the Porte and the British government over the Sinai Peninsula, which the latter insisted on incorporating into Egypt. Although the sultan threatened to use force, he was compelled to accept the inevitable. A commission was set up to determine Aqaba's boundaries. On October 1, 1906, the two sides agreed that the border would extend from Rafah in the northeastern part of the Sinai Peninsula, to Wadi Taba at the tip of the Gulf of Aqaba. At that time, Aqaba was part of Medina, and its importance increased significantly during the Ottoman invasion of Yemen and Asir, and even more so after the outbreak of World War I. In 1915, Aqaba turned into a supply center, and it was connected to Ma'an by telegraph. The dispute between the Porte and Great Britain increased the tension that reached its peak when the former sent thousands of troops to Aqaba, forcing the British to send their battleships from Egypt to the Gulf.[42]

The Suez Canal and the Hejaz Railway

A major development that had adverse effect on Bedouin life in Transjordan was the opening of the Suez Canal in 1869. Increasing reliance on sea routes and the neglect of those which passed through the desert caused the Bedouins to lose their role as protectors who could benefit from the traditional *khuwah*. Among the tribes that lost the *khuwah* was the Ḥuwayṭaṭ of Ibn Jad. The unrest that ensued made the task of pacifying that region difficult for the Ottoman authorities who had to yield to local pressures. For example, in 1898, the *shaikhs* of Bir al-Ṣabi who did not receive the customary *khuwah* for protecting pilgrims who crossed their territory southwest of Ma'an rebelled and declared their intention to abandon their Ottoman citizenship and become Egyptian. Seeking to restore peace in that region the Porte yielded to the pressure and they regained the *khuwah*.[43]

Another major development that had considerable impact on life in Transjordan was the construction of the Hejaz Railway. Work on the Hejaz Railway began in Damascus in 1900. The line reached Amman, Dar'a, and Haifa in 1903, Ma'an in 1904, and Medina in 1908. The railway made it possible to travel quickly from Syria to Arabia and back. Naturally, objection to the project came from Bedouins who felt that their traditional role as vendors and *khuwah* collectors would be adversely affected. Nevertheless, the objection subsided overtime and the railway had considerable impact on the prosperity and security in that region. Merchants reached their destination safely with their wares and Ottoman forces could be deployed quickly with their arms and supplies to restore order to any trouble spot. When the railroad was completed, it extended to the main towns of Transjordan such as Irbid, al-Salt, Karak, and Aqaba and it facilitated the extension of the telegraph line to these towns.

The improvement in communication brought tighter Ottoman control in addition to numerous taxes and dues. Taxes were levied on land and all real estate. In addition, there were taxes on agricultural produce, cattle and beasts of burden. Income tax was levied on merchants and artisans, on service rendered and business transactions of all kinds. Individuals unwilling or incapable of military service were made to pay special payment known as *bedeli askeri*.

The Karak revolt

The outbreak of the revolt in Karak on November 21, 1910, can be attributed to the general lack of trust, which the people of that region had in the Turkish government. In addition to the heavy taxes, the harsh measures applied by the Young Turks who came to power in 1908, such as census taking, land registration, and conscription of young men to the army, alienated the people who were already fed up with the conduct of the ruthless and often corrupt Turkish officials who had little concern for their welfare. But there were also specific incidents, which sparked the revolt. The first took place in 1905, when troops stationed at the Shawbak castle ordered the local women to bring water from a spring in a valley nearby. The villagers protested and demanded that the garrison be removed from that place. The Turkish authorities responded with vengeance, and when the troops came to disperse the crowd, several villagers were killed. Furthermore, the central government's decision to cease the payment of stipends to the *shaikhs* of Karak and its refusal to appoint Shaikh Qadr al-Majali as member of the Administrative Council, despite the fact that he obtained the majority of the votes in the elections, infuriated the inhabitants. The main motive for the rebellion, which erupted in 1910 however, was the government's decision to conduct a census in order to determine who should be enlisted and whose land had to be registered. This measure was followed by an attempt to enforce conscription and to disarm the inhabitants. The rebels were joined by Bedouin tribesmen and the revolt quickly spread to Ma'an and Tafila. A government force commanded by General Sami al-Farouki moved quickly, and quelled the rebellion in Hawran and Jabal al-Druze and then proceeded to Karak. Led by Qadr al-Majali, the rebels operated mainly in the Karak castle where they raided the governor's office, the railway stations, and other facilities. Arriving through the Hejaz Railway, the Turkish troops crushed the rebellion, causing deaths and injuries on both sides. Ten people were condemned to death and executed while Qadr al-Majali was forced to pay half the fine imposed on the rebels. It was only in 1912, when the Turkish leaders were preoccupied with Italy's attack on Tripoli that amnesty was granted to the people of Karak and the conscription cancelled. Qadr al-Majali who came out of his hiding place died soon afterward, apparently by poisoning.

The rebellion of 1910 did not represent an Arab challenge to Turkish authority. The rebels reacted against the increased taxation, and there was no attempt to create a conflict between the Arabs and the Turks and as P.J. Vatikiotis observed,

> It would be a mistake therefore to associate this local rebellion with the wider political developments among the Arabs at that time and soon thereafter in the First World War. The latter reflected themselves in the demands made by the Arabs for a measure of decentralization and local autonomy within the Ottoman Empire.[44]

Agricultural and educational reforms

There seems to be a consensus among historians that agriculture in Transjordan was in decline in Greater Syria during the Ottoman period. According to Khalil al-Ẓahiri, at the beginning of the Ottoman conquest, there were 1,500 towns and villages in Hawran, 350 in Ghawta, and 360 in Wadi al-Tim. Muhammad Kurd Ali tells us that prior to the departure of the Ottomans the number of villages in Hawran did not exceed 400, Ghawta had 50 and Wadi al-Tim had between 30 and 40.[45] Munib al-Madi and Sulayman Musa attribute the decline of agriculture during the Ottoman period to the following factors: the excessive reliance on traditional methods of farming out or granting land; the frequency by which governors were appointed and relieved their subordinates from their position, which left little or no time to introduce substantial reforms; the lack of security measures that could protect the inhabitants and their property from the raids of the desert nomads; the endemic shortage of capital and skilled personnel; the absence of a steady and orderly tax system; the transfer of property owned by farmers to government officials and influential persons who had little or no incentive to cultivate it and; the absence of sufficient roads to distribute the harvests. In addition to the domestic strife and the Bedouin raids, foreign invasions by conquerors such as Ali Bey al-Kabir, Bonaparte, Ibrahim Pasha, and the Wahhabis all had adverse effect on the decline of agricultural in that period.[46]

Despite their limited scope, the educational reforms introduced by the Porte during that period had a positive impact in Transjordan. The Ottoman authorities paid considerable attention to cities such as Amman and other major urban centers. The first elementary school was established in Amman in 1900, and soon afterward towns such as al-Salt, Ajlun, Karak, Wadi al-Sir, and Na'ur, all had had their own schools. The arrangement made by the Ottoman authorities was that families who wished to send their children to school had to bear part of the financial burden. However, while this arrangement benefited children of wealthy and middle-class families, it prevented the indigent from attending school. Moreover, the inhabitants of Transjordan were hesitant to send their children to these schools, out of fear that the authorities would monitor their activities, and recruit them to the army. Another factor that discouraged many was the fact that the language of instruction was Turkish, while they insisted on instruction in Arabic. It was only after a long and hard campaign that the Ottoman authorities yielded to the pressure and began providing instruction in Arabic. Among the instructors recruited to teach in the Arabic language were Circassian graduates of al-Azhar University-Mosque in Cairo such as Shaikh Musa and Yusuf Afendi from Wadi al-Sir, and Muhammad Ali Janbulad from Amman. Gradually, more elementary schools were opened in the major cities. However, it was not until the rise of Amir Abdallah and the imposition of the British Mandate that significant educational reforms were introduced.

It was not until after the Great War that all schools were placed under one administration and the Education Law was introduced. By then, there were 18 elementary schools in Amman alone. These elementary schools taught the children to read and right. Arithmetic and calligraphy were part of the curriculum as well. These reforms however were far from satisfying the entire population. The schools that were established by the Ottomans were subject to criticism of the traditional *shaikhs* who felt threatened by the new teachers and argued that they had neither the skills nor the knowledge necessary to teach. There were also those who saw in these schools a threat to the values of the traditional Islamic society. Nevertheless, this state of affair changed overtime and the teachers in the newly established schools managed to gain the respect of the students whose numbers expanded by leaps and bounds.[47]

The educational system in Transjordan during that period had two tiers: the first consisted of three-year elementary schools in which the students were taught religious studies, calligraphy, and arithmetic, and the instruction was in the Arabic language; and in the secondary tier, students attended classes for three years, and learned geometry, history, geography, and biology. The instruction in this level was in Turkish in addition to Arabic. There were four such schools in Karak, al-Salt, Irbid, and Ma'an, but there were no more than ten in the entire country. In addition, there were some private schools where the teachers taught the rudiments of religion and the Arabic language, and some parochial schools in which the minorities provided education for their children at their expense.

Minorities and the Bedouin assaults

During the first half of the nineteenth century, about three quarters of the population in Transjordan were Muslims and the rest were mostly Greek Orthodox Christians. There were very few mosques in Irbid, Ajlun, and al-Salt, but these were old and in a state of disrepair, while Karak had one that was in ruins, and it was not until the end of the nineteenth century that the Ottomans erected a new one. The churches in the countryside were in a similar state of neglect and disrepair. There were two churches in Karak, and one in al-Salt, which was one of the most attended in Transjordan. Popular religion and veneration of local saints were common practices as well. Saints such as St George and Nabi Yusah' (the prophet Hosea) had shrines in places such as Karak, al-Salt, and the adjacent village of Mahis where visitors came to worship and merchants sold their wares.

The contact between the Christian communities and the Muslims resulted in a cultural diffusion, and there were cases where Christians adopted Muslim practices such as polygamy or baptized their children. The tolerant nature of the Jordanian society encouraged interaction, allowing Muslims and Christians to interact and dress in a similar fashion. With the exception of Ma'an that was closely linked to the pilgrimage road, there was virtually no religious tension in the urban areas.[48] The most common cultural feature of the towns and villages in Transjordan was that hospitality played important role in all of them. Guesthouses (*manzil* or *madafa*) were common especially in the southern part of Transjordan. Normally, the cost of hosting guests was covered by the upper classes. Burckhardt tells us that the hospitality of the inhabitants in the places that he visited had no bounds. For example, when Yusef Shurayda, a local chief in Ajlun sought to serve his guests with a large tray that did not fit his door, he ordered his men to bend it in the middle in order to pass through. Hospitality was not only a time-honored custom, which the inhabitants practiced from time immemorial, but also a means by which one gained respect and political power in that region.[49]

In many areas of Transjordan, the inhabitants were either oblivious or indifferent toward their Ottoman overlords and it was only in the Ajlun district that the sultan's authority was recognized. All Ottoman subjects were required to pay taxes and even the Bedouins had to pay a yearly tribute from their flocks and herds. In addition to the Ottoman taxes, the *khuwah*, which the residents had to pay, the Bedouins for their protection constituted a burden, which they could hardly bear. Pressed by their inability to pay the tax collectors the peasants often left and moved elsewhere, after crossing the Zarqa River to Balqa, where the Ottomans authorities had little control. The Bedouins of Balqa did not recognize the Ottoman authorities and they avoided paying the tribute whenever possible. This was the case in Karak as well. While the inhabitants of Karak had a modicum of respect for the sultan, they regarded the provincial governors as lackadaisical, corrupt and avaricious. There was even less respect for Ottoman rule in the district of Ma'an. Witnessing the sultan's attempts to subdue local rebels in places such as Mount Lebanon and Palestine, the inhabitants of Transjordan were in no mood to tolerate abuse by local governors.

Pressed by the need for revenues and the desire to control Transjordan, which linked Damascus and the Hejaz, the Ottomans extended their sway southward toward the steppe lands of Ajlun and Balqa. One of the factors, which prompted them to move in that direction, was the fear that the British might occupy Transjordan in order to secure their hold on Egypt.

However, the Porte's attempt to establish effective rule in the southern part of Transjordan required settlement building and control over the Bedouins, and it proved to be a painstakingly slow process, which began in Ajlun district. By that time, Jabal Ajlun was dominated by the Adwan tribe and some branches of the Anaza confederation who taxed the peasants in that region so heavily causing many to flee. This put the burden of protecting the peasants on the Porte's shoulders, and in 1844, it decided to send Muhammad Sa'id Agha Shamsdin with a force of 50 cavalrymen to and restore order, but the mission was not accomplished. Likewise, the plan adopted by the Porte in 1846 to appoint a district governor with a force of 600–700 soldiers to the village of Il'al in northeast Irbid fell through.

In 1851, the Ottomans established a district center in Irbid but this proved to be a short-lived attempt. This move came as result of large deficit in the finances of the governor of Damascus.

In effort to put an end to the Bedouin assaults, the military commander of Damascus raided the areas controlled by the Banu Kilab and Banu Sakhr tribes and confiscated their herds of sheep and camels. At the same time, he conceived of a plan to employ exiled Algerian refugees to establish an administrative post in Irbid. In October of that year, the Porte nominated Aḥmad Efendi Salim as district governor of the *Sanjak* of Ajlun. He was stationed in Irbid and the Algerian immigrants were put in charge of guarding the region from Bedouin assaults. However, the plan to settle the Algerians as watchdogs over the Bedouins faltered due to the poor living conditions in Irbid, which they left and moved to other areas. In 1852, the Ottomans were losing control over Ajlun whose inhabitants opposed their attempt to introduce military conscription. Furthermore, the changes caused by the interference of the Administrative Council in Damascus in the local affairs led to dissatisfaction which resulted in the abandonment of the project. For the next 12 years, the Ottoman provincial government combined Karak, al-Salt and Ajlun as one *liwa*. However, Ajlun was neglected. Security in that region was left to local leaders (*za'ims*) of the villages and the Ottoman presence was restricted to the annual visits of the tax collectors. This situation changed as result of the Vilayet Law of 1864, which reorganized the provincial administration in the empire and nominated a *wali* to Damascus whose term of service was limited to five years.[50]

The Vilayet Law laid the foundations of the Ottoman administration in Greater Syria. According to this law, the basic administrative unit known as *kaza* was to be ruled by a district governor, a *mufti* in charge of religious affairs, and a judge. To assist the governor in his task, the law made provision for elected councils that participated in the process. The governor elected in 1866 was Mehmet Rashid Pasha who managed to subdue the tribes in the northern towns and extended Ottoman control over Transjordan by creating administrative districts in Ajlun and al-Salt. His five-year tenure enabled him to implement his project with consummate efficiency. In May 1867, he managed to subdue the tribes of Balqa with help from the local tribes such as Ruwala, Wuld Ali, Beni Ḥasan, and the Druze inhabitants of the Hawran. His force advanced from Jabal Ajlun to Balqa and then entered al-Salt unopposed. Dhi'ab al-Humud, head of the Adwan tribe who had the Sirḥan, the Sardiya and the Banu Sakhr on his side, retreated southward to Ḥisban in attempt to regroup. Meanwhile, Rashid remained in al-Salt, which he managed to control. Faris Agha Kardu was appointed governor and an administrative council was formed to assist him. He then moved southward and defeated Dhi'ab who retreated to Karak, and was captured in October that year. In the administrative changes that ensued Ajlun was incorporated into Hawran and al-Salt to Nablus, which was part of the *mutasarrīfīya* of the Balqa, which extended over the two banks of the Jordan River. Muhammad Sa'id Agha became the first governor of the Balqa. In 1867, Banu Sakhr and Adwan resumed their collaboration. They defied Rashid and insisted on collecting *khuwah* payments from the villages in the Hawran. Consequently, the Ottomans sent another expedition to Balqa, which defeated them and forced them pay a fine of 225,000 piasters to cover the cost of the campaign. This campaign made it abundantly clear that the Ottomans came there to stay.[51]

In 1869, the Ottoman governor Rashid Pasha sent an expedition to subdue the Bedouin tribes in Moab, and he put one of the *shaikhs* in charge, providing him a stipend as compensation. In one of the incidents that occurred in that region, tribesmen attacked government buildings and the damage to property was considerable. In 1873, Bedouins from Leja raided buildings of the Hawran's government center at Edhra'at. They expelled the soldiers and the government employees, destroyed the archives, and whatever else they found. Consequently, the commander in the region was recalled and the seat of the government was moved to Shaikh Sa'd. A new governor, Essaa Pasha was nominated, but he failed to establish order. He was soon recalled and the region fell again into the hands of the Bedouins who terrorized the Christian villages. The influx of Druze to eastern and southern parts of Leja contributed to the disorder, since the newcomers occupied arable land and dispossessed its inhabitants. This caused the central government to be concerned about the ability of the sedentary population to continue paying taxes.

By the early 1870s, ethnic groups such as Circassians, Chechnians, and Armenians began settling in Transjordan. A few Jewish settlements were established afterward, but they were soon abandoned. The Ottomans encouraged the migration of Circassians and Chechnians from the eastern part of the empire to Transjordan, where they established their own settlements and multiplied. Some measure of stability was gradually achieved following these migrations. However, the southern part of Transjordan remained unstable and required constant vigilance. Britain's growing interest in that region caused concern in Constantinople and the fear that Saudi tribes such as Ibn Rashid would subdue the Bedouin tribes of Transjordan intensified. Consequently, regions such as Ma'an, Wadi Ram and Karak, were placed under direct Ottoman control.[52] This southern region became a *mutasarrifiya* tied to Syria, and it was governed by a *mutasarrif*. By such means, the Ottomans managed to control Karak, Ma'an, Tafila, Wadi Sirḥan, and even northern Madaba. The *mutasarrif* was Hussein Ḥilmi and Ma'an became his political headquarter. This headquarter was later moved from Ma'an to Karak. This was in response to a request by Karak's inhabitants and the governor of Syria who supported their demand for greater share in the government. Shortly afterward, al-Salt, Tafila, and Madaba were added to Karak. The Porte appointed individuals who helped to administer the region. It nominated Arab officials to positions in the local government, and recruited soldiers from among the region's inhabitants. Furthermore, the Ottomans introduced reforms that enabled them to control the tribes that lived in that region. The local leaders obtained some measure of autonomy that was beneficial to the public. After its separation from Karak, Ajlun became a separate administrative unit, and the Ottomans distributed its agricultural land among the inhabitants in return for their loyalty, and provided education and other vital services.

Most of Ottoman Transjordan consisted of *liwa* Ajlun, which was a sub province of *liwa* Dimashq. The northern regions, which encompassed the tribes Banu Kinanah, Banu Kafarat, Banu Jahm and Banu al-Asar, were administered as *naḥiya*s of *liwa* Dimashq.[53]

The Porte encouraged local leaders to assume the task of defending the region. This happened in the previously mentioned attack on Edhra'at in 1873, when the Arabs of Leja appointed a Druze *shaikh* to protect them. This appointment was approved by the Ottoman governor of the Hawran, and when he was caught by the military authorities and transferred to Damascus, the governor ordered his release and he was restored to his position. That the inhabitants of Edhra'at continued to enjoy respite from Bedouin assaults afterward was largely due to the presence of a few Druze individuals who carried out a mission which the government failed to do despite the fact that it had a battalion stationed nearby. However, the Bedouin raids never ceased entirely and the villagers continued to suffer. Another village whose inhabitants suffered from Bedouin attacks was Khubab where Greek Catholics resided. Situated in the vicinity of Edhra'at and on the edge of Leja, this village became prone to Bedouin attacks. Their appeal for protection was answered when the Porte sent 80 soldiers, but they failed to restore order.

Realizing that order could not be restored without the presence a substantial military force the Porte responded by stationing a battalion in Leja, and embarked on negotiations with some of the local *shaikhs*. However, lethargy and corruption prevented any decisive solution to the problem. The Porte faced a similar problem in Mount Ajlun where the inhabitants evaded taxation. An armed expedition was sent to the region in 1877, in an attempt to recover the revenues but with little the success. Although the government introduced better methods of land registration the people's opposition, the indifference and the corruption of local officials prevented more efficient tax collection. Intervention by state's officials rarely saved the victims from these depredations.

In 1879, Hawran's population included Muslims, Druze, Christians, and several Arab tribes, including a population of some 300 Circassian families. Jabal Ajlun was overwhelmingly Muslim. Most Druze lived in Jabal Druze and some in south Leja. As for the Christians, they resided in the west and the southwest, mainly in the villages of Leja and in Mount Ajlun. Leja was inhabited by Bedouin tribes among which were the 3,000 members of the Sloot tribe who were governed by thirteen *shaikhs*. They lived largely by herding and brigandage, and the Ottoman attempts to establish order in that region met with limited success.

The Young Turks sought to centralize their regime by introducing new reforms. The result was a sharp increase in taxes and a substantial reduction in payments to local notables. The deteriorating conditions, the high taxes, the forced recruitment to the army, and the hostility of the tribes to each other, all contributed to discontent among the inhabitants and the uprisings became more frequent. The rebellion of

1910 was suppressed with utmost brutality by Sami al-Faruqi, but when the great Arab rebellion erupted six year later and the Hashemite forces began moving northward, Jemal Pasha tried to meet the demands of the rebels. Furthermore, he made an attempt to create a military force from among the inhabitants of Transjordan in order to fight against the rebels. However, neither the inhabitants nor the tribes were willing to cooperate and they waited for the Sharifi emirs to come and lead them in the struggle against the Turks.

The Jewish settlements

The potentialities of the seemingly arid regions of Transjordan captured the imagination of numerous western travelers. For example, the reverend Henry Maundrell who traveled to the region in 1697 tells us that

> the great plain joining to the Dead Sea, which by reason of its saltiness, might be thought unserviceable both for cattle, corn, olives, and vines, has yet its proper usefulness for the nourishment of bees and for the fabric of honey, of which Josephus gives us testimony.[54]

In 1878, the British traveler Laurence Oliphant visited Balqa and envisaged a plan to settle Jews in it. He remarked that the region was endowed with superb land, and that it could provide livelihood for hard-working immigrants who would be a great asset to the sultan and to foreign investors. He argued that the Land of Gilead was more fertile than many areas west of the Jordan River, that it was sparsely populated by nomadic people who had no legal right to it, and that Jews could be settled there without clashes with the Arab inhabitants. He tells us that the Bedouins of south Balqa that bordered on Karak cultivated their land only once in every three or four years. His impression was that the Karak region, which had a town with the same name (Karak or Kir Moab), was extremely fertile, that the *qaimaqam* ruled the district in an arbitrary fashion, and that he frequently disobeyed the Porte's orders. He argued that that this region could be made very productive, that its resources were not developed, and that the climate was suitable for European settlers.

Oliphant reassured his readers that there was no opposition to Jewish settlement in Karak among Ottoman government officials, and that there was no need to be concerned about the rights of the Arab inhabitants to that region. He provided examples of successful settlements in similar regions by other minorities such as the Chechens who established villages in Kunaitra and Amman. Furthermore, he argued that that with only a handful of soldiers the *qaimaqam* evicted the Banu Sakhr tribe from Ajlun, and that he even managed to collect taxes from the most recalcitrant *shaikhs* in that region. He argued that one could visit Qal'at Zarqa, Amman, and Iraq al-Amir, without paying the customary *bakshish*, and that one Protestant farmer had already settled in the region, and enjoyed handsome revenues from a tract of land for which he did not have to pay, and over which he had no legal right. Furthermore, he dismissed the notion that the Arab inhabitants of that region would raise objection to Jewish immigration, which could only bring investments and skills, and he argued that the Porte could provide protection for the Jewish settlers.

Oliphant suggested that the entire Balqa region from the Arnon River in the south to the Jabbok River in the north, all the way to the Hejaz Railway in the east, parts of the Ajlun district north of Jabbok, and the western coast of the Dead Sea could all be settled by Jews, and he called for the acquisition of a million or million-and-a-half acres to implement the project. He also argued that the western coast of the Dead Sea was rich in mineral resources, and that it had abundant water supplies from natural reservoirs and pools. Indeed, significant reservoirs of were found in Um al-Raṣaṣ, Mseitbah, Zizya and other places.[55] However, it was the region north of Gilead that captured his imagination the most, since most of its Arab inhabitants had no legal ownership of the land that they cultivated. The difficulty of including the entire Ajlun district north of the Yarmouk in the borders of the proposed settlement was that a large part of it was rural property registered in the Ottoman cadastral list known as *Tabu*, while in the Balqa region that was not the case. Any individual or a company seeking to acquire land in the north had to buy it from its owners while in Balqa which was the property of the Ottoman state it was possible to purchase land directly from the government, and without infringement on individual rights, with the exception al-Salt where one could acquire land only by special negotiations. Oliphant believed that the Balqa region could be owned by a land company authorized by the Porte with a bank that would provide good credit terms to cultivators. His proposal included the hot water springs around the Dead Sea, and the region of Ghor Seisaban, which was inhabited by the Ghawarini tribes. He argued that the variety of climates in the Jordan Valley could facilitate the growth of numerous kinds of fruits and vegetables. He also mentioned the phosphates and other resources of the Dead Sea that could be extracted and used.

Oliphant argued that the implementation of such plan required investments and manpower; that Banu Sakhr and other Bedouins could provide the manpower necessary for the project and; that the peasants could be easily enticed by good working conditions. Moreover, he argued that foreign labor could be brought from the poor countries of the Balkan Peninsula. He believed that the short distance between Balqa and Jerusalem would facilitate the transfer of the necessary supplies for the settlers, and that the Mediterranean ports would provide an easy outlet to agricultural exports.[56]

The drive to settle Jews in Transjordan was part of the agenda of several Jewish youth movements in the Diaspora prior to the establishment of the State of Israel. Among the places that the socialist Mapai party began to settle was the Dead Sea coast. Settlement in Transjordan was one of the main objectives of the Zionist Labor movement whose goal was to transform the petty Jewish merchant of the Diaspora into a productive farmer in Palestine.[57] There were those who feared that the Jewish settlement of Transjordan would detract the Zionist movement from its main mission, to settle Palestine but even they did not rule out that possibility. For example, the prominent leader of Labor Zionism, Chaim Arlozoroff, expressed his conviction that this region will have to become an area of a Jewish settlement, arguing that the Jordanian parliament had repealed the law prohibiting the sale of land to Jews, and that the *shaikhs* in that region welcomed that possibility.[58] The drive to settle Jews in Transjordan was not limited to the socialists among the Zionist movement. Prominent leaders of Revisionist Zionism such as Vladimir Jabotinsky saw Transjordan as suitable location for Jewish settlement and members of the Betar youth movement had repeatedly called for settling Jews in Jericho, Ramala, Tul Karem, and other towns.[59]

Although initially Oliphant's project was studied seriously in Constantinople, it was eventually dropped from the agenda. In 1889, Baron Edmond de Rothschild sent agents to purchase land in Transjordan for that purpose. A few Jews arrived in al-Salt and Gilead was selected as a place for Jewish settlement, but nothing came out of this project. Rothschild's only purchase was in the Golan, to the north of the Yarmouk River but since that area was isolated from the other settlements that were built by the Jewish immigrants, it was abandoned soon afterward. Another attempt was made in 1891 by Mordechai Ben Hillel who was one of the Lovers of Zion movement and who argued that the previous attempts to settle Jews in Transjordan failed due to lack of mass participation. He therefore called for the formation of groups of hundreds of Jewish immigrants to accomplish that mission. Like Oliphant and others, he argued that Transjordan was sparsely populated, that its land was fertile and cheap, and that one of the most prominent *shaikhs* of the Balqa region was favorable toward the idea.[60]

In 1892, Claude Reignier Conder who visited the region a decade earlier told the members The Lovers of Zion of his doubts regarding the possibility of settling Jews in Transjordan. Yet in the eyes of the many of the early Zionists, settling Transjordan was the imperative of the moment and they were not willing to forfeit their right to do so. For example, Eliahu Eilath who was the Jewish Agency's representative in Washington, DC, stated that Gilead or Moab in Transjordan "were in my eyes not any different from the rest of the places in western Palestine" and that most Jews did not wish to forfeit their right to settle Transjordan.[61]

In 1920, the prominent Zionist leader Max Nordau went to the extent of arguing that the lands in Transjordan were more valuable than those in Palestine, and that they were large enough to absorb millions of Jews who must demand that they be handed over to them.[62] The Zionist attempts to settle in Transjordan came as result of two major factors: the persecution of Jews in Europe and the drought conditions in Palestine by the end of the 1920s and early 1930s.[63]

When the Jewish engineer Pinhas Rutenberg submitted a plan to use the waters of the Jordan and the Auja rivers for electrical power, British officials, including Winston Churchill, looked favorably at the proposal.[64]

The Circassian settlements

Between 1878 and 1884, there was a large wave of Circassian immigrants who arrived from Anatolia and the Balkans where they were accused of stirring trouble.[65] The newcomers settled in three villages; Amman and Wadi Sir in the Balqa, and Jarash in Jabal Ajlun. A Turcoman settlement was established at al-Ruman during that period as well. A second wave of Circassian and Chechen immigrants arrived in 1901–1906, and they established the villages of Na'ur, Zarqa, Sukhna, Rusayfa, and Suwaylih. Amman which by 1893 had more than a thousand souls was the first Circassian settlement. Like other ethnic minorities, the Circassians were exposed to frequent assaults by Bedouins, and they were not welcomed by the local population who regarded them as intruders, but they slowly began occupying important positions in the Ottoman administration, primarily as tax collectors and policemen in the *jandarma*. In time, they acquired considerable influence and power, which brought Banu Sakhr to form an alliance with them. Thus, the Circassians gained the support of Banu Sakhr when they had a conflict with the Baqawiyya confederation in 1906–1910. By the first decade of the twentieth century, there were between 5,000 and 6,500 Circassians in Balqa and Jarash.[66]

The Christian settlements

Christians came to settle in al-Salt in 1867, when the Ottomans occupied that area. Even though some settled in the area long before, most began to settle once they began enjoying security and stability. Some left al-Salt and settled in regions such as al-Fuhays and al-Rumaymin which were administered by al-Salt. The Christians of Rumaymin encountered Bedouin resistance. Nevertheless, the village continued to grow and in 1870 the Catholic missionary Jean Morétain arrived in the hope of converting its residents from the Greek to the Latin rite. By 1875, there were 150 residents and a Latin mission was established in the village. According to the Christian missionary Don Gatti, the Al-Fuhays settlement, which had no more than 16 tents inhabited for no more than three months a year, expanded to 400 settlers in 1873. A Protestant missionary claims that by 1875, there were 25–30 houses in that settlement.

By the mid-1870s, three Christian tribes emigrated from Karak to Madaba. There was tension between the Uzayzat Christian clan that converted to Roman Catholicism, and the ruling Majali family in Karak. The abduction of a married woman from the Latin community in 1879 caused tension between the Christians and the Muslims, which resulted in the emigration of the Christians of Karak to Madaba in 1880–1881. Although the Ottoman governor Midḥat Pasha favored the idea of settling Christians in Madaba, Banu Sakhr opposed the move and its shaikh Sattam al-Fayiz demanded that they return to Karak. The Majalis who felt that their position was weakened in that town supported the effort to drive the Christians out of their newly found home. In turn, the Christians made a protection agreement with the Beni Ḥamida tribe. Thus, the Uzayzat became a recognized tribe and their leader Ṣaliḥ al-Marar obtained the title *shaikh*. Al-Marar called upon the leading tribes to form alliances with their rivals, and thus came to be regarded as an arbiter. This prevented Shaikh Sattam from operating against the Uzayzat settlers in Madaba. Midḥat Pasha whose main concern was that the lands in this region would be cultivated, that its occupiers pay taxes regularly and have their land registered, was sympathetic to Shaikh Marar's request and he rejected the claim of Sattam Fayiz that Shaikh Marar did not register the land in this region and failed to pay taxes on a regular basis. Unlike the Circassians and the Turkoman refugees, the

Christians in Madaba were required to pay annual taxes on their land as well as on their harvests. Shaikh Marar's struggle paid off, and the Christians remained settled in Madaba, which became the southernmost settlement in Balqa.[67]

Hebron, the West Bank, and Jerusalem

Located in the Judean Mountains and in the southern part of the West Bank, some 30 kilometers from Jerusalem, the city of Hebron is known for the burial ground of the Biblical patriarchs Abraham, Isaac, Jacob, and their wives. The city flourished during the Bronze Age, several hundred years before the arrival of the Israelites to the land of Canaan. Archaeological evidence show that the city was destroyed and then resettled. According to the Biblical account, Abraham purchased the burial ground from Ephron the Hittite, and a small Jewish community flourished there ever since. The city was taken by the Israelites upon their entry to the Promised Land. By the end of the second millennium Hebron was the seat of David King of Israel, and it was there that his son Absalom rose in rebellion and declared himself king. Hebron is also mentioned in the Bible as one of the Six Cities of Refuge. Its location astride the land routes leading to Jerusalem gave it unique importance. Following the fall of Jerusalem and the destruction of First Temple in 586 BC the Jewish population was exiled, and the city fell to the Edomites. In 167 BC, the city was plundered by Judah the Maccabee.

During Baybars' reign, the city was connected to the main Damascus-Cairo road. However, it came under the administrative jurisdiction of Jerusalem, and thereby lost its strategic importance. Qalauun is known for rebuilding the Machpelah Cave. His follower sultan al-Naşir Muhammad continued the reconstruction process in this sanctuary, which became a place of pilgrimage for Jews, Muslims, and Christians who used the caravanserais and soup kitchens built by the sultans. But the city's leaders were often incompetent and corrupt and were known to have embezzled the treasury on numerous occasions.

The Mongol invasions brought many refugees to Hebron, but many left in the late 1340s, when rumors spread that the Bedouins were about to attack the city. In 1472, disturbances erupted in the city when the Kurdish inhabitants and the ad-Darriyah clan, named after ad-Darri who according to tradition obtained the city from Prophet Muhammad, fought against each other. Both sides sought Bedouin support and the devastation caused by the feud did not cease until the end of the century. Among the city's inhabitants were the Tamir al-Darri, a clan of Kurdish origin that resided in the vicinity of the cave. In addition, there were powerful families such as Tadmuri and Ja'bari who originated from Syria, and came to Hebron in the aftermath of the Mongol invasion. They occupied key positions in the city. There were also Sufis who came and built facilities such as hostels and places for prayer and meditation.

The Jewish community in Hebron remained small. This was largely a result of the limited commercial opportunities, the city's distance from the main trade routes, and the hostility of the Muslim population. The Jews were attached to the Machpelah Cave, particularly to the sites associated with Abraham such as his residence in Elonei Mamrai, and the stone on which he was circumcised. Other sites which the Jewish pilgrims frequented were Abraham's Well, Sarah's Well, and the tombs of David's father Yishai, and Abner Ben Ner. Rabbi Meshulam of Voltaira tells us that in 1481, there were 20 Jewish households in Hebron. This number was confirmed by Ovadia of Bartnura who remarked that they were all rabbis, and that half of them came to reside "under the shadow of the Holy Spirit (*shekhinhah*)."[68]

By the mid-sixteenth century, many of the villages in Hebron's vicinity lost their population. It is possible that Hebron's location on the edge of the desert, the climatic conditions and the difficulties involved in cultivating the land caused many to migrate to other cities such as Jerusalem and Nablus. The Christian inhabitants also left Hebron to cities nearby. At the same time, the Muslim population increased until it reached 6,000 in the mid-sixteenth century. However, by the last third of the century, the number decreased to 4,000. Christian communities continued to exist in Hebron, particularly in Majdal Bani Fadhil where they managed to maintain their identity.[69]

Like other Muslim cities, Hebron's population was divided along the traditional Qaysi-Yamani lines. Both sides fought for influence in the city, and the tension often culminated in a feud. For example, we hear that in 1565, the dispute reached a point where there was a need for cancelling the Friday prayers in the Machpelah Cave. The city's inhabitants tended to favor the Qaysis when these fought against the Yamanis of Bethlehem.

Jews came to Hebron at the end of the fifteenth century in the wake of the Catholic persecution in Spain and their subsequent expulsion. Some were rabbis while others were merchants and artisans. By the fourth decade of the sixteenth century, Rabbi Malkiel Ashkenazi settled in Hebron where he established the Karaite Courtyard, which became the center of the Jewish community. Jewish scholars arrived from Safad. Some of them were followers of the messianic Shabtai Zvi movement. The Jews of Hebron maintained ties with their co-religionists in Italy who supported them.

By the eighteenth century, the Jews of Hebron were victims of the feuds among the Muslim clans and the general decline in the Ottoman Empire, which lessened its ability to administer its territories efficiently. In 1733, the Porte nominated a special committee for the city but the disturbances did not cease, and the Jews remained scapegoats. For example, in 1775, they were accused of murdering the 'grand shaikh king of the land' but the danger subsided thereafter.[70] By the end of the eighteenth century, the Jewish community experienced a severe financial crisis, and they had to rely on assistance from their brethren in Jerusalem.

A popular uprising erupted in Hebron in 1834 against Egyptian rule causing all religious minorities, including Jews to suffer. Ibrahim's harsh rule, the taxes and the practice of conscripting young men to the Egyptian army led to this rebellion, which was crushed with utmost severity. Many of the city's inhabitants fled to Jerusalem and other towns nearby.

A.D. Wenger who visited Hebron in 1901 estimated that there were about 1,000 Jews and 15,000 Muslims "of a most fanatical type" and that the town's main branches of industry were glass, pottery and water skins made from goats' hides.[71] The mainstay of Hebron's agriculture was barley and wheat, in addition to a variety of fruits and vegetables such olives, figs, and pomegranates. However, the hilly nature of the terrain and the irregular rainfall made cultivation difficult. By the early nineteenth century, the Yamani family of Amr was the most influential in Mount Hebron. Suleiman, the slave and assistant of Jazzar Pasha was the governor of the *eyalet* of Damascus and as such he ruled Hebron in addition to Nablus and Jerusalem. Hebron's population had gradually increased from 6,000 in 1800 to 16,557 in 1922.[72]

The Ottoman military forces that operated in the provinces of Greater Syria consisted of regular Janissary and feudal units of *sipahi* knights who received *iqta'*s or *muqata'a* where they had to right to collect taxes, in return for providing military service when called upon to do so. In Palestine, the *sipahi* was exempt from military service. Instead, he had to participate in the effort to protect the *hājj* road from the depredations of the Bedouin tribes. Thus, the *sipahi*s of the districts of Nablus, Lajun, Jerusalem, and Gaza had to enlist in units known as *Jerda* whose task was to protect the pilgrims that passed through Transjordan and the commander of these units had to provide the necessary supplies to the pilgrims.[73]

The Ottomans left the al-Ma'n family in control in Mount Lebanon. Fakhr al-Din al-Ma'ni who ruled that region expanded his boundaries, and during 1590–1634, he managed to incorporate most of Syria and Palestine to his domain. He later incorporated the districts of Ajlun and Nablus, Gaza and all of Palestine, except Jerusalem. His attempt to capture Jerusalem failed when he was defeated by Aḥmad Turabay the governor of northern Samaria and Jezreel Valley in 1624–1625.

Another governor who played an important role in Nablus during the seventeenth century was Farukh Ibn Abdallah, an officer of Circassian origin who served the governor of Gaza. In 1603, he embarked on promoting his personal interest. In addition to obtaining the title *amir al-hajj*, he became the governor of the *sanjak* of Jerusalem and Nablus. Following his death in 1621, his son Muhammad Ibn Farukh obtained the same title in addition to the governorship of the districts of Jerusalem and Nablus, which he had on and off, until his death in 1639. The fact that Farukh was not a Bedouin was an indication that the Porte was bent on suppressing the Bedouin tribes. Shortly before Farukh's nomination as governor of Jerusalem the city's Muslim notables who were disturbed by the Bedouin raids drafted a letter to the sultan saying, "Unruly Bedouin tribes are surrounding Jerusalem from all sides. They are preventing the pilgrims and all those coming to visit (it) and pass through (there). They dominate the people who are at their mercy in that region."[74] When Farukh was nominated as governor, he invested considerable efforts in stopping the invasions of the Bedouin tribes. He relied on the Ta'amrah tribe which helped him fight the Bedouins who were on their way to Transjordan. He killed some and imprisoned others and thus fulfilled his role successfully as *amir al-hajj,* protecting the caravans that passed through the region controlled by the Bedouins in Transjordan. He was generous toward the tribes who agreed to cooperate with him, and in the beginning of 1624 he fought against the chiefs of the tribes of Ḥawran and Ajlun. Farukh's marriage ties with the Turabay family, his successful campaigns against the Bedouins of Transjordan and against Fakhr al-Din al-Ma'ni helped him gain control of Nablus. On the other hand, he brutalized the inhabitants of Jerusalem and many fled to the Nablus Mountain.[75]

By the beginning of the eighteenth century, Tiberias came to be dominated by Ẓahir al-Umar who originated from the Zaydan tribe, which emigrated from the Arabian Peninsula to the Lower Galilee region. Ẓahir who began his career in Tiberias managed to expand his domain westward, and by 1733, he captured villages near Nablus and Ḥawran which was considered the bread basket of Damascus, and reached he as far as Kunaitra. However, when his Egyptian ally Ali Bey al-Kabir was deposed by Abu ad-Dhahab, Ẓahir's position was no longer tenable. The new Egyptian pasha was his enemy, and he gave the southern parts of Palestine to Zahir's long time enemy Mustafa Tukkan who was the governor of Nablus. In 1773, Ẓahir managed to gather his forces and after conquering Jaffa, he moved toward Nablus, defeated the Tukkan family, and brought the town under his rule. By 1774, Ẓahir's son Aḥmad was recognized by the Porte as the legal governor of Ajlun district. Ẓahir, who expressed his willingness to pay his debts to the Ottoman treasury and remain obedient if he obtained the official Ottoman title of *beylerbey*, agreed to give up his original demand and was satisfied with being confirmed as governor of the *ayelet* of Sidon, Nablus, and Jaffa. By the end of January 1774, the Porte agreed to grant Ẓahir rule over Nablus, Ajlun, Jaffa, and Gaza. However, before the official nomination was made, Sultan Abdul Hamid I who came to power following the death of Mustafa III replaced many of the previous officials, including the *wali* of Damascus. The previous agreement made by the Porte was no longer valid, and Ẓahir was not recognized as the governor of Gaza, Jaffa and Nablus. Nevertheless, he managed to rise again after the sudden death of the Egyptian governor Abu Dhahab in 1775. Confident that he could rely on Egyptian support or at least neutrality, he expanded his rule over western Palestine and captured Ajlun. Prior to his death, he bequeathed his domains to his sons; Tiberias was given to Salibi; Dir Ḥanna to Aḥmad; Shefar'am to Uthman; Zippori to Sa'id, and Safad to 'Ali. However, after 'Ali consolidated his rule in Dir Ḥanna, Aḥmad occupied Ajlun. This led to quarrel among the family and a short-lived rebellion against Ẓahir. In the reconciliation that followed Ẓahir bequeathed Nablus to Sa'id.[76]

When Napoleon's forces landed in Palestine in 1799, Aḥmad Jazzar Pasha who was the governor of Acre and the Galilee convinced the inhabitants of Nablus by payments and gifts to divert the attention of the French troops in order to prevent them from moving northward from Jaffa, which they conquered in March 1799. The inhabitants of Nablus embarked on skirmishes that turned the attention of the French troops to the Shomron region and delayed their advance northward. Jazzar's cavalry unit which obtained aid from the inhabitants of Nablus ambushed a French column near Kakun, but the attempt failed and Acre came under siege on March 19, 1799. During the following month, cavalry forces from Nablus fought the French in the Carmel region, but they were defeated by the French. Reinforcements of infantry and two light canons, which arrived from Nablus joined an Ottoman force that arrived at the scene but the French troops managed to defeat them at the Battle of Tabor, in the neighborhood of Fuleh, or the village of Afulah close by. This allowed the French to reoccupy Tiberias and resume the siege of Acre. But when Napoleon was forced to withdraw as result of the British military campaign and the epidemic that spread among his troops, all that Jazzar had to do was to encourage the Bedouins and the inhabitants of Nablus was to harass his troops on their retreat to Egypt. In October 1790, Jazzar was nominated again as *wali* of Damascus. The nomination decree issued by the Porte stated specifically that he was nominated as governor of the districts of Nablus and Jerusalem, and he continued to serve in that capacity until the end of 1795.[77]

One of the regions, which constituted a major problem for the Porte, was Jabal Nablus where local families vied for power, acted with considerable freedom and were far from being subordinated to the Ottoman governor. Just like in the other Arab regions of the Ottoman Empire, the population of Jabal Nablus was divided along the old factional pattern of Qays and Yaman, and both had allies among the Bedouin tribes. Initially, the district of Nablus was part of the *eyalet* of Damascus. Following the Egyptian withdrawal in 1841, the *sanjaks* of Nablus just like those of Jerusalem and Gaza were transferred to the *eyalet* of Sidon. These three *sanjaks* formed a larger unit known as *mustasarriflik* within the *eyelet* of Sidon, and it was governed by a *mutasarrif* or a pasha who was subordinated to the *wali* of Sidon or directly to the Porte.

Nablus remained a troublesome area and the Porte's traditional methods of persuasion, conciliation, and 'divide and conquer' were never sufficient to guarantee control. It was only with help from the emir of Lebanon Bashir Shihab II that the *wali* of Sidon, Abdallah Pasha was capable of capturing the Ṣanur stronghold in Nablus in 1829–1830, but he failed to control the region. This state of affairs encouraged the local forces who took advantage of the Porte's weakness. Powerful families vied for power in that region; the Ṭuqan, al-Jarrar and al-Rayyan on the Qaysi side, and the al-Nimr, Qasim, and Abd al-Hadi on the Yamani. The most ferocious fight was between the al-Nimr family, which lost its supremacy by the end of the eighteenth century and Ṭuqan, which came to prominence. This fight that erupted at the end of that century lasted more than two decades.

Both the Qaysis and Yamanis had their Bedouin allies, but they often had disputes among themselves. Families, such as the Ṭuqan and Jarrar who were both Qaysis, often clashed during the early nineteenth century. The Yamani al-Nimr family changed sides on several occasions. First, it supported the Ṭuqans against their rivals. Then it sided with the Jarrars, and organized a coalition against the Ṭuqans who nevertheless managed to establish their supremacy in that region. This state of affairs continued, until the arrival of Ibrahim Pasha when the Yamani families of Abd al-Hadi and Qasim replaced the Jarrars as their chief rivals.

Upon his arrival, Ibrahim Pasha appointed the Yamanis as leaders in Nablus and the Abd al-Hadis reigned supreme due to their loyalty to the Egyptian pasha, and the abortive rebellion of May 1834, which was led by the Qasim family. The suppression of this rebellion kept the al-Hadis in power. The Qasims lost their power and prestige, and the al-Nimrs who remained neutral during the rebellion, managed to improve their position. With the backing of the al-Nimrs the Abd al-Hadi family remained in control until the end of the Egyptian occupation.

With the Ottoman re-conquest of Jabal Nablus, the status quo was reversed and the defeated families regained their power. The factional struggle resumed along the Qays and Yaman loyalties; the Abd al-Hadis gained the support of the al-Nimrs, the Qasims and some other Yamani families. Against this coalition stood the Qaysis led by the Ṭuqans, the Jarrars and the Rayyan. Neither the Abd al-Hadis nor the Ṭuqans agreed to compromise and the warfare continued throughout the mid-nineteenth century. Attempting to restore order and bring the region under control, the Ottoman authorities faced resistance by armed peasant militia of 20,000 (*jarud*) and many Bedouins. Consequently, the Ottomans were forced to choose a local governor in order to restore order, and collect taxes in this area, which they considered as one of the best in the empire. However, the selection of the governor was influenced by considerations other than what was best for the Porte or for the region's inhabitants. Corruption and political bias were always factors determining the selection process. Moreover, intervention by the British and the French played role as well; the former supported the Ṭuqans, while the latter supported the Abd al-Hadis. As for the Ottomans, their preference was for the Ṭuqans, but when they were unable to impose their will, they acquiesced to the rule of the Abd al-Hadis. Bribery and the Porte's desire to maintain the Egyptian system for a transitional period led to the nomination of an Abd al-Hadi candidate as governor of Nablus and nearby villages such as Jenin and others. Resistance from local families brought the Porte to dismiss Maḥmoud Abd al-Hadi from his position in 1842, and to nominate Sulayman Bey Ṭuqan as *qaimaqam*, but he failed to restore order even though he was nominated twice, and remained in his position until 1851.

The upshot was that the hostilities between the Abd al-Hadis and the Ṭuqans were resumed with vengeance. Following a short interval where the Ottoman authorities arrested members of both factions the Abd al-Hadi's candidate Maḥmoud was nominated *qaimaqam* of Nablus. This nomination came as result of the Porte's desire to mitigate the impact of the conscription it was about to introduce in 1852. However, once this measure passed, it sought to replace Maḥmoud by a Turkish governor. Following Maḥmoud's replacement by a member of the Ṭuqans, a Turkish *qaymaqam* was installed by the end of 1853, but he did not have sufficient forces to control the region, and the position was contested by Maḥmoud Abd al-Hadi, Ali Bey Ṭuqan and other Turkish candidates. Eventually, bribery and the weakness of the central government led to the nomination of Shaikh Abd al-Hadi who remained in his position from 1856 until 1858, when the Porte managed to assert its control over Jabal Nablus. What made it possible for the Porte to control that region was the weakening of the local forces, and the pressure applied by the European powers in the wake of the disturbances that erupted in that region in 1856. Furthermore, new administrative measures facilitated tighter Ottoman control over that region; the district of Nablus was transferred from Jerusalem's jurisdiction and placed under the *wali* of Sidon. A Turkish governor, Ziya Bey was nominated as *mutasarrif* and he had at his disposal considerable military force which enabled him to overcome the local forces and to arrest Maḥmoud Abd al-Hadi. Displeased to see their family member deposed the al-Hadis rebelled in their stronghold in Araba, and it was not until 1859 that the rebellion was quelled with help from the Ṭuqans and the Jarrars.

Further reforms introduced by the Ottomans in Jabal Nablus led to resistance by the end of 1859. The Ottoman authorities crushed the resistance soon afterward with reinforcements from Palestine. Ever since, the Ottomans managed to establish reasonable level of order in that region, even though the local families who now sat in the *majlis*, were capable from time to time to voice their opinions and challenge their rule.[78] The relative peace in the region brought some measure of prosperity and the population of increased from 8,000–10,000 in the beginning of the nineteenth century to 11,000–12,000 in 1880, and to 16,000–17,000 on the eve of World War I.[79]

By the eighteenth century, the Ottoman authorities encountered difficulties in subduing the local chiefs who controlled Jerusalem. These chiefs managed to expel the Ottoman authorities in 1808–1809 and again in 1825. By 1854, Jerusalem became an independent *eyalet* governed by a pasha who was responsible directly to Istanbul. A small garrison was stationed in Jerusalem, and for the most part, it was sufficient to maintain order. For example, in the period between 1858 and 1860 when rebellions erupted there the pasha managed to subdue the mountainous regions with a military force whose number did not exceed 1,000.[80]

Notes

1 The Decapolis included Gerasa (Jerash); Scythopolis (Beith Shean); Hippos (Sussita); Gadara (Umm Qais); Pella; Philadelphia ('Ammān); Capitolias (Beit Ras); Canatha (Qanawat), Raphana and Damascus).

2 Richard Hall, *Empire of the Monsoons: A History of the Indian Ocean and its Invaders* (London: HarperCollins, 1996). p. 208.

3 Robert Dankoff and Sooyong Kim, Translation and Commentary on *An Ottoman Traveler: Selections from the Book of Travels of Evliya Celebi*, (London: Eland, 2010), pp. 317–318.

4 Amnon Cohen, Shmuel Avitzur and Mina Rozen, "Eretz Yisrael ba-imperia ha-uthmanit al saf ha'et ha-hadashah," (The Land of Israel in the Ottoman Empire on the threshold of the New Age), Hebrew text, The History of Eretz Israel under the Mamluk and Ottoman Rule (Jerusalem: Keter, 1981), pp. 114–115.

5 Faḍil Bayāt, "Sharqī a-Urdun fī al-Niẓām al-Idārī al-'uthmāni fī ḍaw al-wathāiq authmāniyah," (Eastern Jordan in the Ottoman administrative order in light of the Ottoman documents), Arabic text, Min al-ma'ālim al-thaqāfīyah wa-al-ḥaḍāriyah fī-al-Urdun'abra al-'usūr ('Ammān: al-Markaz al-Thaqāfi al-Malaki, 2002), Vol. II, pp. 11–12.

6 Marc Lavergne, *La Jordanie*, French text (Paris: Editions Karthala, 1996), pp. 59–61.

7 Frank Ronald Charles, Bagley, "Egypt and the Eastern Arab Countries in the First Three Centuries of the Ottoman Period," *The Last Great Muslim Empires: History of the Muslim World*, Edited by Hans J. Kissling et al. (Princeton, NJ: Markus Wiener Publishers, 1996), pp. 70–71.

8 Abdul-Rahim Abu-Husayn, *Political Leadership in Syria, 1575–1650* (Beirut: The American University of Beirut, 1985), pp. 114–117.

9 ʻAbd al-Karīm Rāfeq, *Al-ʻArab wa-al-ʻUthmāniyyūn* (The Arabs and the Ottomans), Arabic text (Dimāshq: Maṭābi' Alif Bā', 1974), pp. 320–321.
10 Amnon Cohen, *Palestine in the 18th Century: Patterns of Government and Administration* (Jerusalem: The Hebrew University, The Magnes Press, 1973), pp. 158–159.
11 Alexander William Kinglake, *Eothen* (New York: D. Appleton and Company, 1898), p. 111.
12 Ronald Robinson, "Non-European Foundations of European Imperialism: Sketch for a Theory of Collaboration," *Imperialism: The Robinson and Gallagher Controversy*, Edited by W.M. Roger Louis (New York: New Viewpoints, 1976), p. 129.
13 Itzhak Ben Zvi, *Eretz Israel under Ottoman Rule*, Hebrew text (Jerusalem: Bialik Institute, 1955), p. 349.
14 William Libbey and Franklin E. Hoskins, *The Jordan Valley and Petra*, Vol. I (New York and London: G.P. Puntam's Sons, 1905), p. 210.
15 Fathi, p. 83.
16 Amélie Marie Goichon, *Jordanie réelle* (Real Jordan), French text (Paris: Desclée De Brouwer, 1967–1972), Vol. I, p. 53.
17 Sulayman Musa, *Cameos: Jordan, Arab Nationalism, Sharif Hussein, King Abdullah, T.E. Lawrence* (Amman: Ministry of Culture, 1997), p. 138.
18 Anne Sinai and Allen Pollack (Eds.), *The Hashemite Kingdom of Jordan and the West Bank: A Handbook* (New York: American Academic Association for Peace in the Middle East, 1977), pp. 20–21.
19 Moshe Ma'oz, "The Impact of Modernization on Syrian Politics and Society," *Beginnings of Modernization in the Middle East: The Nineteenth Century*, Edited by William R. Polk and Richard L. Chambers (Chicago: The University of Chicago Press, 1968), pp. 343–344.
20 Cited in Musa, p. 87.
21 Cited *Ibid*, p. 88.
22 Shimon Shamir, "The Modernization of Syria: Problems and Solutions in the Early Period of Abdülhamid," *Beginnings of Modernization*, p. 371.
23 Tarīkh al-Urdun fi al-Qarn al-ʻIshrīn, p. 4.
24 *Ibid*, p. 5.
25 Musa, p. 146.
26 Eugene L. Rogan, *Frontiers of the State in the Late Ottoman Empire* (Cambridge, UK: Cambridge University Press, 1999), p. 24.
27 *Ibid*, p. 25.
28 Aḥmad ʻAlī Isma'īl ʻAlī, *Tarīkh al-Shām al-Qadīm* (History of Ancient Syria), Arabic text, Vol. I (Dimashq: Markaz al-Shām lil-Khidmāt al-Ṭiba'īyah, 1998), p. 525.
29 Jonathan Ludwig Burckhardt, *Travels in Syria and the Holy Land* (London: 1822), pp. 382–383. Cited in Rogan, p. 31.
30 *Ibid*, p. 32.
31 Rūkus Ibn Zā'id Al-ʻUzāyzi, *Ibnā al-Ghasāsinah wa-Ibrahīm Bāshā: Qissah Ḥaqīqīya waqa'at hawadithuhā sanat 1832 fi al-Karak min a'māl Sharqi al-Urdun* (Ibna al-Ghsasinah and Ibrahim Pasha: A true story, which occurred in 1832 in al-Karak, from the deeds of East Jordan), Arabic text (Rāfāt: Matba'at Maytam Sayyidat Filasṭine, 1937), p. 17.
32 Al Mūmani, p. 45.
33 Tarīkh al-Urdun fi al-Qarn al-ʻIshrīn, pp. 8–9.
34 Al Mūmani, p. 46.
35 Journey to the Sublime Porte: The Arabic Memoirs of a Sharifian Agent's Diplomatic Mission to the Ottoman Imperial Court in the era of Suleyman the Magnificent: The Relevant Text from Quṭb al-Dīn al-Nahrawālī's al-Fawā'id al-sanīyah fī al-riḥlah al-Madanīyah wa al-*Rūmīyah*, Introduced, Translated and Annotated by Richard Blackburn (Beirut: Orient-Institut, 2005), pp. 28–29.

36 Alois Musil, *The Northern Hejaz* (New York: AMS Press, 1926), p. 5.
37 Journey to the Sublime Porte, p. 29, note 87.
38 Rogan, p. 33.
39 *Ibid*, p. 52.
40 *Ibid*, p. 28.
41 "Report of a Journey made by Vice-Consul Jago of Damascus during portions of May and June 1879, to the Hawran; comprising the Lejah, the Jebel Druze, or Druze Mountain, and the Mountains of Ajloon," Arabic text, Jawdat Ḥilmi Nāshkhū, *Tarīkh al-Sharkas (al-Adīghah)* wa-al-Shishān fī liwā'ay Haurān wa-al-Balqā, 1878–1920 (Ammān: Manshurāt Lajnat Tarīkh al-Urdun, 1998), pp. 300–301.
42 Tarīkh al-Urdun fi al-Qarn al-'Ishrīn, p. 9.
43 Musa, p. 147.
44 Panayiotis J. Vatikiotis, *Politics and the Military in Jordan: A Study of the Arab Legion 1921–1957* (New York: Praeger Publishers, 1967), p. 36.
45 Tarīkh al-Urdun fi al-Qarn al-'Ishrīn, p. 6.
46 *Ibid*, pp. 6–7.
47 Hind Ghassān Abū al-Sh'ar, and Nūfān Rajā al-Sawārīyah, *Ammān fī al-'ahd al-Hāshemi, 1916–1952* (Amman in the Hashemite Period), Arabic text, Vol. I ('Ammān: Amānat 'Ammān, 2004), p. 52.
48 Rogan, p. 38.
49 *Ibid*, p. 40.
50 *Ibid*, p. 48.
51 *Ibid*, pp. 51–52.
52 Sulaymān Mustafa al-Samādi, *Al-Urdun, miat 'ām min al-taḥaduth wa-al-'atā'* (Jordan, a Hundred years of Challenge and Bid), Arabic text (Irbīd: Matba'at al-Ruznah, 1999), p. 16.
53 Jordan in the Late Middle Ages, p. 15.
54 Early Travels in Palestine, Comprising the narratives of Arculf, Willibald, Bernard, Saewulf, Sigurd, Benjamin of Tudela, Sir John Maundeville, *De La Brocquière and Maundrell*, Edited by Thomas Wright (London: Henry G. Bohn, 1848), p. 438.
55 Reverend James Aitken Wylie who visited the Jericho region in 1883, tells us that there was a copious spring known as the Fountain of Elisha, and that "It bubbles up in a gravely basin at the foot of the mountain, and as we drank its waters at table, we can attest that they are still sweet." Reverend James Aitken Wylie, LLD., *Over the Holy Land* (London: James Nisbet & CO, 1883), p. 191.
56 Sefer Hatzyonūt, Tekufat Ḥibbat Tsiyōn: Hatenuah aḥaray 'ha-re'amīm', 'ha-Alīyah ha-Rishonāh' ve-yissūd ha-moshavōt ha-rishonōt, teḥilāt mifa'lōt'Hanadīv'ba-aretz (The Book of Zionism, The Lovers of Zion's Period: The movement after 'the thunderbolts', The First Aliyah, and the establishment of the first settlements, the onset the Nadiv enterprises in the Land of Israel), Hebrew text, Vol. I (Jerusalem: Bialik Institute, 1961), pp. 90–96.
57 For example, the prominent leader of Labor Zionist, Yitzhak Tabenkin told members of the Histadrut (The General Federation of Labor) in February 1933, in Tel Aviv that the purpose of his movement was to turn the Jew to a proletarian in the harsh conditions of places such as the Huleh Lake and Transjordan. J. Tabenkin, *Devarim* (Collected Speeches), Vol. I, Hebrew text Vol. 1 (Tel Aviv: Hakibbutz Hameuchad, 1967), p. 146.
58 Chaim Arlozoroff, *Ktavim VI: Rashuyot* (Writings VI: Authorities), Hebrew text (Tel Aviv: A.J. Stybel Publishing House, 1934), pp. 131–132.
59 Ch. Ben-Yerucham, *Book of Bethar: History and Sources*, Vol. II, Hebrew text with title in English (Tel-Aviv: Hamerkaz Press, 1975), p. 546.
60 Qaḍīyat shirā' *al-arāḍi wa-al-istiṭān al-Ṣihyūnī fī al-Urdun wa-Ḥawrān wa-al-Jawlān 1871–1947* (The problem of land purchase and the Zionist settlement in Jordan, Hawran and Golan), Arabic text ('Ammān: Dār al-Jalīl lil Nashr wa-al-Tawzī', 2003), pp. 33–34.

61 Eliyahu Elath, *Zionism and the Arabs*, Hebrew text with title in English (Tel Aviv: Dvir Co. Ltd, 1974), pp. 108–109, 112.
62 Max Simon Nordau, *Ktavim Tsiyuniyim: Neumīm u-ma'amarīm (1915–1920)* (Zionist Writings: Speeches and Articles, 1915–1920), Hebrew Text (Yerushalayim: Hasifriyah ha-Tsionīt, 1962), pp. 152–153.
63 Sulaymān Bashīr, *Judhūr al-Wiṣayah al-Urdunīyah: Dirāsāh fī wathā'iq al-arshīf al-Ṣahyūnī* (The Roots of Jordanian Tutelage: A study in the documents of the Zionist archive), Arabic text (Beirut: Shirkat Qadmus lil-nashr wa-al-tawzī', 2001), pp. 11–12.
64 Martin Gilbert, *Winston S. Churchill, Vol. IV, 1916–1922: The Stricken World* (Boston, MA: Houghton Miflin, 1975), p. 536.
65 There is no sufficient evidence to implicate Circassians in the civil unrest, which took place during the 1860s and 1870s. Brad Dennis, "Patters of Conflict and Violence in Eastern Anatolia Leading Up to the Russo-Turkish War and the Treaty of Berlin," *War and Diplomacy: The Russo-Turkish War of 1877–1878 and the Treaty of Berlin*, Edited by Hakan Yavuz with Peter Sluglett (Salt Lake City: The University of Utah Press, 2011), p. 277.
66 Rogan, p. 76.
67 *Ibid*, p. 81.
68 *Ibid*, pp. 88–89.
69 *Ibid*, pp. 161, 163.
70 *Ibid*, pp. 216–217.
71 Amos Daniel Wenger, *Six Months in the Bible Lands and Around the World in Fourteen Months* (Doylestown, PA: J.B. Steiner Printing House, 1901), pp. 318–319.
72 Rogan, p. 70.
73 Eretz Yisrael ha-imperia ha-uthmanit al saf ha'et ha-hadashah, p. 108.
74 *Ibid*, p. 117.
75 *Ibid.*
76 *Ibid*, pp. 120, 126–130.
77 *Ibid*, pp. 142, 145–147, 149.
78 Moshe Ma'oz, *Ottoman Reform in Syria and Palestine 1840–1861: The impact of the Tanzimat on Politics and Society* (London: Oxford University Press, 1968), pp. 113–118.
79 Shmuel Avitsur, Joshua Ben-Arieh, Alex Carmel, David Kushnir and Ya'acov Shavit, *Hashilton ha-Othmāni: Korot ha'Aretz ve-demutah* (The Ottoman Rule: History of Land of Israel and its Image), The History of Eretz Israel: The last phase of Ottoman rule, Hebrew text with title in English (Jerusalem: Keter, 1983), p. 87.
80 Ma'oz, pp. 7, 32–33, 52.

VI Jordan during World War I

World War I ushered in a period of major difficulties for the inhabitants of Transjordan, not only by the mere fact that it was waged on former Ottoman territory, which the Allied European belligerents sought to dominate, but also due the restrictive measures that the Turkish regime imposed on the population. The Turkish authorities imposed military conscription on all towns and villages of Transjordan, with the exception of Karak, where the rebellion was crushed. Strict regulations were imposed on the population throughout the country, stores were looted, food was confiscated, and trees that could be used in the construction of Hejaz Railway were cut. However, the main event that took place during the war was the Arab Revolt of 1916, which made it obvious that the Turkish authorities had lost control over the territories of the former Ottoman Empire.

The Arab revolt of 1916

The bitter experience of the Karak revolt remained so ingrained in the mind of the inhabitants of Transjordan that when the great Arab uprising of 1916 erupted, some of them became willing participants in the effort to overthrow the Turkish regime. Recognizing the strategic importance of Transjordan, the Turkish regime went to great length to buy the loyalty of the Arab notables to whom they bestowed honorific titles and grants. On the other hand, the Christian notables were suspected of maintaining ties with foreign powers, and they were persecuted by the Turkish authorities. For example, the Christian notables of Karak and Madaba were sent to prisons in Damascus and later to Anatolia. Churches were desecrated and mission centers were closed. Although some tribes joined the rebellion, most of the Bedouins remained loyal to the Turkish authorities. A Circassian regiment was stationed in Balqa and its task was to provide information regarding the activities of the rebels.[1] Nevertheless, some of the tribes were captivated by the idea of rebellion against their repressive masters. Audeh Abu Ṭayih who lead the Ḥuwayṭat tribe was the first to answer the call. He met Amir Faiṣal to whom he swore allegiance, and promised to start a rebellion in Transjordan. Shortly afterward, he accompanied a small expedition led by Sharif Naṣir, Nasib al-Bakri, the British officer T.E. Lawrence, and a few Syrian leaders. They all headed toward Wadi Sirḥan, which became a recruitment depot for the volunteers who joined the revolt.

DOI: 10.4324/9781003450313-7

The subsequent victories would not have been possible had it not been for Abu Ṭayih. The Arab rebels moved toward Abu al-Lason, west of Ma'an where they defeated a Turkish army, and on July 6, 1917, they captured Aqaba and the surrounding heights. While the Syrian and Iraqi troops were engaged in major operations on the Jordanian front, Abu Ṭayih and his men remained in their positions, fighting the Turkish army for a month-and-a-half and when Faiṣal's army made its way toward Aqaba, they moved northward and began playing an active role in the revolt. Meanwhile, Faiṣal met his brother Zayd, and their forces moved together northward and captured Petra, Shawbak, and Ma'an. In September 1918, the Arab forces freed Dera'a, and on October 1, they reached Damascus and thereby brought an end to Turkish rule. The Ḥuwayṭat, Banu Sakhr and the Ruwalla tribes took part in major operations, including attacks on railway stations, bridges, trains, and other vital facilities. Villagers as well as nomads participated in the battles of Tafila and Wadi-al-Ḥasa.[2]

This victory brought immediate relief to all inhabitants of the Arab regions of the former Ottoman Empire, including those of Transjordan, and the degradation, which they were exposed to during that period, was deeply ingrained in the minds of that generation. In 1917, Taqi al-Din Affendi, a man of Lebanese extraction known for his unusual cruelty, was nominated governor of al-Kawrah. His harsh measures included arrests without due process, torture, and humiliation by shaving the beards and mustaches of the victims who opposed Turkish rule. When the inhabitants complained to the *qaimaqam* of Irbid, Maḥmoud Rajab Raghib, he rejected the complaint saying, "perhaps their chins are dirty and they will become pure after the shave."[3]

The outbreak of World War I brought many of the recruits to desert and the Turkish authorities resorted to forced recruitment, which began in the small village of Safar Barlik and expanded to other locations of Greater Syria. The resistance caused led to bloodshed, confiscations, and rape among the population, and the events became known in the collective memory of the people of Greater Syria as "the days of Safar Barlik."[4] Many of the recruits of Transjordan recruits remained in prisons where the living conditions were intolerable. Moreover, villagers became victims of locust that descended on their land and destroyed their agriculture. The Turkish authorities recruited children to collect the locust eggs, which they bought cheaply and set fire to. This resulted in the spread of typhoid, cholera, and other diseases. Recalling the experience, an eyewitness Abd al-Qadir al-Saliḥ noted in his memoirs that "the memory of Safar Barlik still causes horror in the hearts of those who lived at that time."[5] Recalling his experience as a recruit in the Turkish army, a young man, whose attempt to redeem himself from military service by paying the recruiting officer a sum of 50 *lira* yielded no results, writes

> I joined the rest of the recruits on the 19th day and we took the train to Damascus....We could not find a place to sleep so we decided to cover the floor with some blankets and sleep despite the cold weather. We were moved the next morning to Daraa, a small village next to the Hejaz railway...We

> were suffering from the cold so we asked our commanding officer to allow us to leave Daraa. He did and we left with no food or water and walked around 9 hours before we reached the village of Salkhat near Jabal al-Druze.... We got really scared every time an Ottoman officer insulted us. He would even beat us. My friend couldn't take it anymore so he escaped and never returned back.[6]

This period is also known as the time when the Arab nationalists began their rebellion against the Turkish regime. When Sharif Hussein of Mecca began his rebellion on June 8, 1916, he moved his forces from Jeddah and Mecca, with the intension of joining the British forces tasked with the mission of conquering the southern region of Greater Syria and moving toward Damascus. This move came following his correspondence with the British resident in Cairo, Sir Henry McMahon who promised that if the Arabs were to join the British forces in their fight against the Turks, the British government would recognize all the territories conquered by them as an independent Arab state. The Arab forces assembled in Medina, at the vicinity of the Hejaz Railway terminus. Hussein's son, Amir Faişal, took control of the ports of Hejaz and turned them into military strongholds. He then moved northward, until his army gained control of a significant part of the Hejaz. However, the entire railway from Damascus to Medina still remained in Turkish hands. The main road connecting Syria and the Hejaz was also the one that connected Damascus with Dara'a. The Hejaz Railway split westward from Dara'a to Haifa in Palestine, and the Turks used it to supply their troops west of the Jordan River. The other section of the railroad extended 50 miles to Amman and from there 150 miles to Ma'an, where a garrison of between 3,000 and 4,000 Turkish troops was stationed. The Turkish garrisons were deployed in the rugged terrain north of Ma'an and had no access to the railroad, except through the Ma'an-Medina line. This was largely due to the relentless Arab assaults on the railway stations. Initially, however, the Arabs controlled no more than two bases between Aqaba and Ma'an, and there was much to be done in order to evict the Turks from that region.[7]

The first Arab objective was to conquer Aqaba, which provided an outlet to the Arabian Sea. The conquest of Aqaba, which began on July 6, 1917, required control over the road leading from Ma'an, and it was necessary to rely on the support of the Bedouin tribes in that region.

Recalling why the participation of the local tribes was so essential for the operation, T.E. Lawrence who participated in the operation writes:

> If we wanted to get beyond Tebuk or toward Ma'an or Aqaba (and we did, badly) it was clear that we must find a way round by the east, and for this we should require the favour of the nomads there. Our route would run first through the Billi and Moahib country as far as the railway: and would then cross part of the district of the Fejr. We had the Fejr. Beyond them lay the various tribes owing obedience to Nuri Shaalan, the great Emir of the Rualla, who after the Sherif and ibn Saud and ibn Rashid was the fourth figure in the desert.[8]

Guided by Lawrence, the Arabs planned to attack the Turkish battalion that was stationed in Ma'an and whose task was to send a weekly caravan to a garrison of three hundred men that was stationed in Aqaba, in addition to other three hundred Turks who guarded the road to it.[9] The conquest of Aqaba had long been the objective of the British officers in Egypt who estimated that at least six divisions would be necessary for such operation.[10] The success of the operation was due to the element of surprise used by the Arab force, and to the local tribes on which they could count for assistance. As Lawrence recalled in his memoirs:

> Unfortunately for the enemy, they had never imagined attack from the interior, and of all their great works not one trench or post faced inland. Our advance from so new a direction threw them into panic, and wisely they did not progressively resist us. The attempt if made would have availed them nothing, for we had the hill tribes with us, and by their help we could occupy the sheer peaks with riflemen whose plunging fire would render the gorge untenable for troops without overhead cover....Our numbers had swollen till we were much more than a thousand strong....Next day at dawn fighting broke out on all sides, for hundreds more hillmen, again doubling our numbers, had come about us in the night and, not knowing the arrangement, began shooting at the Turks, who defended themselves....the surrender went off quietly after all.[11]

The next few months were spent in consolidating their position. Hussein's son Amir Zayd was tasked with organizing an Arab army to replace Lawrence in case the latter died in the war. In the Tafila campaign, which took place on January 25, 1918, Zayd won an overwhelming victory over the Turks. This battle was one of the most important after the one that ended in the capture of Aqaba and the engagements, which the Arabs had in the struggle to capture Dera'a in the Hawran. Twenty-one Turks were killed in that campaign and the prisoners taken included 12 officers and 200 soldiers. In addition, his force managed to sink six enemy sail boats loaded with grain and supplies that were on their way from Karak to Jericho. During the Tafila campaign, the Arabs won victories virtually without casualties. From the correspondence between Zayd and his brother Faiṣal, we learn that the Arab commander Ali bin Arid was in Rashadiyah at that time and that Zayd planned to take over the Aniza station prior to capturing Karak. He was concerned that the Turks would attack before he had enough troops to meet that threat. We also learn that Zayd warned the people of Karak that he would arrest all their dignitaries, unless they reassured him that they were on his side. Realizing the magnitude of the forthcoming campaign, Zayd asked Ja'far al-Askari to send him reinforcements, supplies, ammunitions, and some experienced officers. According to al-Askari, their plan consisted of the following steps:

- a Zayd was to establish his operation center at Wadi Musa or al-Haysha.
- b After the Arab entry into Tafila, the Algerian troops were to remain in it.
- c The people of Shawbak were to guard their town.

d The infantry corps with the Turkish mortars and canons captured in Jarf al-Darawish was to remain in al-Haysha.
e The remaining troops were to assemble at Basṭa, and their task was to sever the railroad south of Ma'an prior to the assault on that town.

Supplying the force was not an easy task for the high command due to the shortage of beasts of burden. Moreover, the long distance between Tafila and Faisal's headquarters made it difficult for the Arab contingents to communicate. Faişal believed that Zayd could solve this problem by capturing Karak. He asked that Zayd seek the help of Shaikh Dhiyab al-Awdan in order to obtain enough troops to attack the railroad. In addition, he asked Zayd to consult Bunu Sakhr's chief Awdah Abu Tayeh regarding the methods by which the assault on the railway was to be carried out. At the same time, Faişal advanced to take over the Mudawara station. However, the operation faltered when the volunteers failed to advance quickly toward the enemy's positions. In the following day, the Arabs were forced to withdraw due to lack of potable water. Fortunately, the size of the Turkish force did not exceed 200 officers and soldiers. Faişal promised to send ammunitions and money to his brother. He stressed the importance of attacking the railway north of Ma'an, saying that he would attack the line in the south. On January 28, 1918, Faişal sent a sum of 10,000 *lira* to Zayd, with a promise to send contributions from Banu Sakhr two days later, and said that he agreed to his plan to avoid going northward to Karak until the railway connection was severed.

On February 3, Zayd responded by saying that that while he agreed to Faisal's plan he was concerned about letting Tafila's inhabitants defend the town by themselves. He insisted on remaining in Tafila and leading the campaign from there. He asked for more supplies, saying that the Turks were concentrating troops in Karak and that three enemy airplanes were bombing Arab positions. He also requested mules to carry the cannons and the mortars of the Maghribi unit. Faişal sent him the sum he promised, in addition to the contributions of Banu Sakhr, and announced that he was ready to attack the railroad and move toward Tafila as soon as he had enough men and supplies. Following the Tafila campaign, Faişal wrote to his father telling him that Zayd had a decisive victory, and that the enemy had 400 dead, among them was the commander Hamid Fakhri and 320 prisoners. He mentioned the difficulties involved in the campaign, saying that only 500 camels remained in his possession, and that these were not sufficient to cover the seven-day distance between Tafila and Aqaba. In addition, Faişal mentioned that 62 prisoners were captured at Ghor al-Muzara'a, and that he was hoping to move beyond Jabal Druze.

When the Turks began concentrating their troops in Karak, Zayd asked his brother to send more supplies and money to pay his troops. He also asked him to send the cavalrymen of Banu Sakhr whom he considered indispensable for the campaign, as well physicians and other support staff. From one of his letters, we learn that Lawrence promised Zayd to send him additional sum of money to meet his needs.[12] Meanwhile, the Turks continued to assemble troops in Karak, Qatrana and Jarf al-Darawish, and started preparing for a campaign to recapture Tafila.

Another sum of 25,000 *junniya* to pay the warriors of Banu Sakhr arrived, but since Zayd needed to pay other volunteers, he was compelled to request additional 20,000.

The correspondence between Hussein's sons reveals that Faişal was not oblivious to his brother's requests, and he continued sending him money and supplies. Meanwhile, the Turks continued to station forces in Qatrana, Karak, and Jarf al-Darawish and the skirmishes did not cease. Led by al-Sharif Ali bin Arid, a group of Arabs who were on patrol encountered an enemy force in the environs of Ḥasa. The encounter resulted in a defeat for the enemy who lost 30 men. The enemy forces included German and Bulgarian mercenaries. The Arab high command nominated Amir Zayd al-Ẓabit Abdallah al-Dalimi as commander troops in Tafila.

Hussein remained keenly interested in the events, and his letters attest to that. Responding to a letter that he received from his father, Zayd explained the situation in the north, saying that his main tasks were (a) to prevent the enemy forces from coming to Ma'an from the north; (b) to capture Karak; and (c) to open a road between the Arab and the British forces that were stationed in Jerusalem in order to facilitate the transfer of supplies to the Sharifi army that moved northward to Syria. Zayd told his brother that more tribes (al-Ḥajaya, al-Nu'aymat, al-Kharishah, al-Qadha, al-Batush, al-Ṣarayrah, Banu Aṭiyah, and part of al-Majaliyah and al-Ṭarawanah) joined the rebellion and without further delay, Faisal sent additional 23,000 *junniya*.

Meanwhile, the enemy concentrated his forces east of Tafila. Zayd informed his brother that the force that concentrated in Jarf al-Darawish station consisted of 1,400 men, that the Turks gathered an army at Karak and that the Arabs expected invasion from both sides. In addition, he said that airplanes stationed at Qatrana and Ḥasa were bombing Arab positions, and that this had adverse effect on the morale on the soldiers, the Bedouins and others who contributed to the war effort. On March 1, Zayd assembled his forces with a view to attack the Hejaz Railway. He sent Ibn Arid with a Maghribi unit and weapons that included cannons and mortars, in addition to a force of regulars and a Bedouin contingent. These were sent to Tawana, midway between Jarf al-Darawish and Tafila. However, the enemy moved his forces westward. They consisted of infantry manned by Turks and Germans in addition to cavalry, cannons, mortars, and an airplane. In the ensuing encounter, the Arabs ran out of ammunitions and had to withdraw and establish another defense line. They lost 12 men and Ibn Arid was injured. Nevertheless, Zayd tried to convince his brother to exploit the opportunity to attack Ma'an. Then came Abdallah bin Ḥamza and his warriors and the joint force began preparing for combat. The battle continued day and night. The Turks entered Khirbet Abur west of Tawana, and on March 7, the Turks moved in the direction of Rashadiyah in order to encircle the Arab force. Zayd was compelled to evacuate Tafila and he moved to Rashadiyah before the enemy's arrival. He prepared to face the enemy, and asked that the force stationed at Shawbak join him. Again, he implored Faişal to take the opportunity to invade Ma'an. *Faişal* responded merely by sending a cavalry force that joined the Arab troops.

The Turks continued to resist, and on March 11, 1918, the Arabs were compelled to withdraw to Shawbak. A Turkish cavalry force moved toward Başirah village, but it was forced to retreat. In the following day, six enemy airplanes bombed Shawbak where Zayd was about to establish a defense line. The Turks stopped their advance and did not enter Tafila. Then on March 31, they began withdrawing from Rashadiyah and the Arabs entered that town. In a message to his father from Shawbak on March 31, Zayd stated that he lost 35 men, that some of them were injured and that the entire force did not exceed 100 soldiers, including Bedouins and villagers. He noted that the people of Tafila were cooperating with him; that he sent several men under Sharif Abd al-Mu'in's command to attack the railway station; and that he asked Banu Sakhr who were stationed south of Wadi al-Ghadaf, to occupy the attention of the Turks while this operation was taking place.[13]

The heavy rains of March 1918 caused the operations to halt for a few days. Then Faişal sent a force to attack the railway station south of Ma'an, but the heavy rains brought an end to that operation. By March 23, the weather conditions improved and the Turks withdrew from Tafila. Zayd wrote to his father that his force was moving toward Tafila, and that the enemy withdrew to Karak. By the end of the month, the British army attacked al-Salt. Zayd sent a force, which consisted of the tribes of al-Maṭir, al-Rawalah and al-Aqilat under the command of al-Sharif Naşir to Madaba. Shaikh Hussein al-Damur of Karak told Zayd that he was ready to assist the Arab forces. On March 30, a cavalry force consisting of men 250 commanded by Majali notables arrived at Zayd's headquarters at Shawbak. The Turks began withdrawing from Karak as soon as the British entered al-Salt. At that juncture, Faişal began preparing for Ma'an's invasion. On March 29, he wrote to Zayd from Aqaba about his intension to start the campaign within a few days. His plan was to establish headquarters in Karak, while sending Zayd to capture Madaba and al-Azraq and at the same time ordering Naşib al-Bakri to move toward Jabal Druze. In addition, Faişal asked Ali al-Ḥarithi to move with his contingent toward Amman and join al-Sharif Naşir and the British army.

The attack on Ma'an began on April 10. Faişal wrote to Zayd that the unit commanded by Nuri al-Sa'id carried out operations south of Ma'an that resulted in the destruction of 13 bridges and the capture of Abu Ṭarfa station where 150 Turkish soldiers were taken prisoners. The letter also stated that the capture of the hills nearby was accomplished at that night. On April 12, Faişal asked Zayd to move southward with a view to conquer Ma'an but the Arab army was incapable of moving as fast as planned, and the invasion was delayed to April 14. Al-Sharif Naşir announced that the Bedouins refused to attack the fortresses and asked for more troops to attack Ma'an from the north. On April 16, regular troops arrived at Ma'an railroad station. Gradually, the Arabs managed to capture railway stations south and north of Ma'an. They suffered losses and several officers and soldiers were killed. They had armored cars, which they obtained from the British but these were stationed far from the Turkish positions. At that time, the number of volunteers who joined Zayd increased significantly. Meanwhile, al-Sharif Naşir began his assault on Ḥasa railway, while enemy airplanes were bombing the Arab positions.

Awdah Abu Tayeh took a leading part in the Aqaba campaign, and his men joined Naşir but the Arabs did not manage to sever all railroads, since the Turks brought reinforcements and with the help of German and Austrian commanders, they managed to recapture some of them. Confusion and disenchantment among the Arab officers ensued when it was announced that no decision regarding their salaries was made, and some officers handed their resignation in protest. The crisis did not end until Orde Wingate, Edmund Allenby, and other senior British officers intervened to reassure them that their pay was forthcoming. On July 12, Zayd wrote to Hussein saying that Faişal left Abu Lissan and moved toward Azraq to lead the next campaign. Meanwhile, the Turks managed to recapture some of the lost territories. A Turkish force attacked an Arab unit stationed in Wadi Ḥasa on July 6, and after a three-day fighting this unit was forced to withdraw from Rashadiyah. The Turks resumed their campaign until they reached Tafila, which they captured on July 8. Zayd believed that these Turkish moves were designed to frustrate the Arab plans to move toward al-Azraq and the north. The Turks managed to take over Rashadiyah, but were later were forced to abandon it. Similarly, they had to abandon Tafila, and withdraw to al-Tawana. According to Zayd, the tribes of Ḥuwaiṭat, al-Ḥajayah, and al-Mana'in were the ones who took part in the campaign that caused the Turks to withdraw. He also mentioned that the skirmishes continued in Ma'an. Zayd estimated that the number of Turks who participated in the campaign was 6,200 soldiers and officers, and that 10 Arabs were killed.

When it became clear to the Turks that they were defeated in Palestine and that it was impossible for them to build new defense lines south of Damascus, they began withdrawing from Ma'an as well. The retreating Turkish troops were pursued on the way from Jardunah to Jarf al-Darawish by the Arabs and the tribes among them, especially Banu Sakhr who distinguished themselves in the battlefield. The retreating Turks reached Zizya where they were caught and besieged. Meanwhile, the British conquered Amman before the Turks could arrive. The upshot was that all the Turkish forces from Zizya to Amman were forced to surrender to the British army. The last telegrams that Zayd sent to Faişal were written in October 1918. Soon afterward, he made his way from Ma'an to Damascus, which turned into the center of gravity of the Arab national movement.

The Turkish leader Jemal Pasha selected Ma'an, which was the most important station on the Hejaz railroad between the Dead Sea and Medina, as a point of departure for three Turkish columns comprising over 7,000 men, several light cavalry units, and a squadron of German airplanes. According to the plan, one column camped at Shawbak, another arrived from the south, while the third came from Ma'an in the east. These forces were all scheduled to meet in Petra on October 21.[14] The rugged terrain near Petra and Wadi Musa allowed Lawrence and his troops the opportunity to harass the Turkish enemy. It was in a narrow gorge at the hills of Petra that his men ambushed the Turkish troops. Describing the event Lowell Thomas who accompanied Lawrence writes:

> When the Turks wedged into the narrowest part of the gorge, near to the entrance to the city, one of his aides fired a rocket into the air as a signal for the

> Arabs to attack. A moment later pandemonium broke loose in the mountains of Edom. The Arabs poured in a stream of fire from all sides. The crack of rifles seemed to come from every rock. With shrill screams the women and children tumbled huge boulders over the edge on the head of the Turks and Germans hundreds of feet below. Those stationed behind the columns of the Temple of Isis kept up a steady fire. Utterly bewildered, the invaders became panicky and scattered in all possible directions, while the Arabs on the ridges continued to devastate their broken ranks.[15]

It was in this region that Allenby implemented his plan to lead the Turks into thinking that he was moving along the Jordan River from the Dead Sea toward Galilee. Staging this hoax, he brought equipment from southern Palestine to the banks of the Jordan valley. Describing the preparations for this camouflage Thomas writes,

> The sacred valley of the Jordan was filled with all the properties for a sham battle of the ages. Never since the Greeks captured Troy with their famous wooden horse has such a remarkable bit of camouflage been put on a credulous enemy.[16]

On August 1918, Lawrence's camel corps attacked the Turkish garrison at Mudawara. He then led a force against Amman. Seeking to confuse the enemy, Lawrence sent one of Banu Sakhr's chiefs to Damascus with 7,000 pounds in gold to purchase barley. This led the Turks to believe that this purchase was intended for Allenby's forces in the Jordan Valley. Meanwhile, Lawrence began spreading rumors that Faiṣal's army was about to attack the Dera'a railway junction, between Amman and Damascus. Commenting on this plan Lawrence said,

> As a matter of fact, we had every intention of attacking Deraa, but we spread the news so far and wide that the Turks refused to believe it. Then in deadly secrecy we confided to a chosen few in the inner circle that we really were going to concentrate all of our forces against Amman. But we were not.[17]

Led to believe that the attack was going to be in Amman, the Turks sent their troops to that region. Only Faiṣal, Colonel Joyce and Lawrence knew that the attack was going to take place in Dera'a. In September 1918, Lawrence moved from the Gulf of Aqaba to assist Allenby. On his way north, he recruited a new army from among the desert Bedouins. In addition, Joyce brought deserters from the Turkish army to join this force. When Laurence arrived at Wadi Araba, his force consisted of 2,000 camels, 450 mounted racing camel riders, 400 machine-gun units, two airplanes, and three Rolls Royce armored cars. In addition to these Arab forces, there were some foreign elements such as men from the Egyptian camel corps, a battalion of Gurkah camel riders from India and Algerian gunners. He also had a bodyguard, which consisted of 100 Bedouins. The total force amounted to 1,000 mounted camel riders. The troops moved across the desert where there were difficulties supplying their needs, and the warriors suffered from dire thirst. Moreover, some of the wells in this region were contaminated. Nevertheless, after a fortnight of exhausting march, the army reached Dera'a. Lawrence's primary mission was to prevent the Turks from communicating with the main cities in that region, and to ease Allenby's advance from the south. He therefore ordered his men to sever the Turkish railway and telegraph lines around the town. Leading the Turks to believe that the attack would take place in the Jordan Valley, the British generals carried out their operations elsewhere; Lawrence in Dera'a and Allenby north of Jaffa.[18]

Transjordan was a crucial line of communications for the Turks during World War I. All the supplies and the ammunitions had to be brought from northern Syria through the Damascus-Palestine-Amman-Medina railway. Lawrence's plan was to operate in this region in order to sever the Turkish supply lines. Severing the communication lines around Dera'a was part of an ambitious plan, which eventually paid off. The 290-mile journey from Aqaba to Azraq demanded water and supplies, which the army lacked, and there were only few oases where water could be found. When the army reached Tafila, the Bedouin chief Abu Irgeig of Beersheba invaded a Turkish naval base located at the southern end of the Dead Sea. Lawrence's original plan was to engage the Rualla tribe in his campaign. He planned to move toward the Hawran hills and thence attack Dera'a. However, disagreement among the senior officers led him to modify his plan. He decided to attack the railroads north, west, and south of Dera'a with his regular troops who were supported by Druzes from the Hawran, and a handful of Rualla cavalrymen commanded by Shaikh Khalid and Trad Sha'alan. Once again, Lawrence sought to divert the attention of the Turkish enemy by leading its commanders into thinking that an assault on Amman and al-Salt was imminent. Consequently, he asked the chiefs of Banu Sakhr tribe to concentrate forces near Amman. This came at a time when Allenby was giving the Turks the impression that the Jordan Valley would be the place where the real attack was going to take place. The upshot was that the Turks paid considerable attention to the Jordan Valley, while neglecting the Mediterranean coast north of Jaffa.

Upon reaching Azraq, the armies came across an old castle, which Lawrence sought to turn into headquarters. He moved from the Azraq oasis to the foothills of al-Salt and then arrived at Umtaiye, 13 miles southeast of Dera'a where he managed to recruit many young men to the Sharifi army, among them was Shaikh Tallal al-Khair al-Din of Tafas, who accompanied him on his spying expeditions in the Hawran. Lawrence sought to place his army between Dera'a and the Turkish armies in Palestine, in order to lead the Turks into thinking that Dera'a needed reinforcement, and thereby to allow Allenby advance with greater ease along the coast. Severing the railway lines south and west of Dera'a was imperative since it could reinforce the notion that the real attack was going to be against the Turkish Fourth Army in the upper Jordan Valley. According to Allenby's plan, two expeditions were to be sent, one in March and other in April, to capture Amman and the Hejaz Railway, and to take control of the road from Damascus in the north, to Mecca in the south. Both raids failed causing many casualties.[19]

Meanwhile, Faişal established his headquarters at Wahirah, close to the Turkish positions overlooking Ma'an. The Turkish forces confined to the towns and the railway stations south of Ma'an consisted of 17,000 troops. In addition, there were about 3,000 in Ma'an itself, and between 3,000 and 4,000 who guarded the line connecting Ma'an and Amman. Other contingents of Turkish troops were spread along the railroad and the Dead Sea. Faişal's plan was to occupy the Turkish troops whose total number was between 20,000 and 25,000 troops, in order to prevent them from joining their comrades who confronted Allenby's army. Faişal's army consisted of 3,000 volunteers supplied by Allenby's army. In addition, he managed to obtain camels, an aircraft squadron, a few armored vehicles, canons, and submachines. Several units arrived from Arabia and Egypt and they were commanded by British officers. Not all the forces arrived since Aqaba had several camps on the sandy hills at Wadi Araba, and these had to be defended.

In November 1918, an Arab force under Zayd invaded Karak and Tafila. A Turkish force moved forward but failed to stop the invasion. Then the question was whether the Arab force would be able to hold on to the positions overlooking Ma'an, or would have to retreat to al-Qawirah. Faişal was determined to stay in his new position. The commander in charge of the combined forces of Hejazis, Syrians, and Iraqis was Ja'far Pasha.

On November 16, 1918, Faişal sent a message to Zayd asking him to lead the troops who were advancing northward, to remain in Ţafila after capturing it, and not to leave until he had enough resources. Fearing a clash between Awdeh Abu Tayeh and Ḥamd bin Jazi, he asked his brother not to let the Ḥuwaiṭat attack Ţafila by themselves. He also asked him to tell al-Fa'r to move toward the Ghor and occupy it. Zayd arrived with his troops to Wadi Musa on November 18, 1918, while Naşir took control of Jarf al-Darawish station and continued westward to Ghadir Abu Safah. From there he moved toward Tawana where he met Shaikh Dhyab al-'Awaran and they discussed the strategy of taking over Ţafila. Dhyab sent his son Abd al-Salam to reassure Faişal regarding his father's loyalty, and the willingness of Ţafila's people to welcome the Arab troops. Accompanied by Ja'far al-Askari and other senior officers, Zayd moved toward Tafila after asking Faişal to send reinforcements to him and to Sharif Ali al-Hussein al-Ḥarithi who was in Azraq at that time. Following his arrival into Tafila on November 22, Zayd wrote to Faişal saying that the enemy concentrated his troops at the railway station. He added that according to his plan, al-Sharif Naşir and his volunteers from the Ḥuwaiṭat and Banu Sakhr tribes were to confront the enemy at the railway station, while contacts were being made with the Bedouins south of Karak. He was convinced that the capture of the railway station would automatically lead to the fall of Karak.

The domination of the Arab rebels over Tafila had serious impact on the position of the Turks in the Jordanian front and they were determined to recover it. In order to achieve that a special force under Ḥamid Fakhri moved from Amman but the Arabs managed to defeat it in the vicinity of Tafila. On November 25, 1918, Zayd notified Faişal that the campaign lasted 24 hours and that more than 100 prisoners fell into their hands, in addition to weapons and equipment. He asked for supplies and money because, as he put it, "We were emptied of everything, especially money."[20] Two days later, Zayd sent a message saying that his forces captured nine officers, 150 soldiers, 200 mules, 17 mortars and two canons. He also mentioned in his message that Abdallah bin Ḥamza managed to sever the railway line between Karak and the Ghor. He repeated his request for aid, saying, "if you don't give us all that I asked for, especially money and war supplies we will be in great danger."[21]

It was only in the fall of 1918, that the hardships associated with Safar Birlak came to an end. The relief in Jordan as in all regions in Greater Syria that were affected by the horrors of the event was such that the people felt grateful to the British who brought the abominable Turkish rule to its knees. A poem from that period illustrates the joy that overwhelmed these regions. It reads as follows:

> On October first, the year 1918, A wonderful sight in our village was seen: Guns popping, flags flying, sky rockets went up: We were so excited we hardly could sup: The Turks had all left us, the British were near: Our troubles were over, we knew peace was here. Hurrah for the Arab nations--three cheers! Away with all sorrows and sighing and tears: The people are happy because they all know that their Arab nation in freedom may grow.
>
> (Anonymous ten-year-old American girl).[22]

The Ottoman legacy

M. Goichon mentions three decisions made by the Porte during the nineteenth century that had particular impact on modern Jordan; the legislation concerning property; the settlement of the Circassians, and the construction of the Hejaz railroad.[23] The modern history of Jordan ought to begin not with the British creation of the Hashemite rule in the aftermath of World War I, but in the second half of the nineteenth century, when the region was under Ottoman rule. The Ottomans were the ones who established new settlements and repopulated old ones. They settled many of the Bedouins and brought large areas under cultivation. They introduced reforms that transformed the primitive agrarian society into a modern one. All this was accomplished as part of the Tanzimat reforms whose value is still debated by historians.

The Ottomans extended their rule over Transjordan in the 1850s through military campaigns. It was not until 1867, however, that the northernmost districts of Ajlun and Balqa were incorporated into the province of Damascus. Karak and Ma'an were incorporated in 1893. The Porte embarked on a policy designed to subordinate the pastoral nomads and to settle them. Uncultivated land was distributed among settler communities, which included Chechen and Circassian refugees. The Land Law of 1858 regulated the rights of land tenure based on cultivation and tax payment rather than on traditional rights. The Ottoman authorities encouraged trade by maintaining the roads in good repair, and facilitated the growth of a healthy merchant elite. The Ottomans made a serious attempt to introduce an efficient administration with responsible officials and to eliminate corruption. For example, Ahmed Şefik Midḥat who was Syria's governor in the 1880s made the effort to hold the Ottoman officials accountable and to promote honest practices. Among the officials whose records he investigated for corruption was the *qaimaqam* of Ajlun but no evidence was found to incriminate him.[24]

Another factor that accelerated the growth of a modern society in the territories that were later incorporated into the Hashemite Kingdom of Jordan was the arrival of the British missionaries of the Church Missionary Society, and the Italian and French priests of the Latin Patriarchate of Jerusalem. In addition, the Greek Orthodox Church sent missionaries to Transjordan where it had little influence. These missionaries hoped to proselytize among Muslims and Christians. Although their efforts to convert many inhabitants had limited success, they played a major role in Transjordan by disseminating knowledge and promoting education. Furthermore, they established schools, clinics, and other facilities that promoted welfare among the population. It was largely through their efforts that the local population became aware of its rights and obligations and often it expressed its discontent when these rights were trampled upon, by revolting, as the revolt in Karak in 1910 demonstrated.

World War I was a major ordeal for the inhabitants of Transjordan. The Ottomans' attempt to crush the Arab Revolt by encouraging the local notables to cooperate with them failed. Antagonized by the brutal methods, which the Ottoman officials used to maintain order in the country the inhabitants of Transjordan were hardly in a mood to cooperate. Yet despite the harsh measures and the inefficiency of its officials, the Ottoman government laid the foundations of the modern state of Transjordan, and contributed to its development as a distinct nation by the order that it maintained and the occasional reforms that it introduced.[25]

Generally speaking, Transjordan hardly mattered to the Ottoman authorities. Apart from securing the road for the pilgrims, which they entrusted in the hands of the local tribes who provided camels and basic necessities required for the *ḥajj*, the Ottoman authorities did little other than establishing *khan*s or caravanserais along the road to facilitate the journey. To the best of our knowledge, the region remained neglected. Apart from a few elementary schools in which religious subjects were taught, there was little that could help spread literacy among the public. Much of what we know about the society at that time comes from the accounts of travelers such as William John Bankes, Irby and Magles, J.S. Buckingham, Burkhardt, and W.F. Lynch but what they had to say is superficial, and shades little light on life in that region.

The region that included the districts of Ajlun, Balqa, Karak, and Ma'an was part of what later became known as *Transjordan*, a term that was not used by the Ottomans at that time and it has little resemblance to the modern Hashemite Kingdom of Jordan. Ottoman control extended to the pilgrimage road, but not to the eastern desert region, which the Bedouins controlled. None of these districts had an outlet to the sea, and even the Gulf of 'Aqaba was surrounded by the Hejaz in the south and Egypt in the southwest. The Ottoman way of calculating distance in time gives us a rough indication of the size of that region. It took eight days to walk the length of Transjordan's frontier and its width ranged from 22 hours in Ajlun to 12 hours in the Balqa, and to 20 hours in Ma'an.[26] There was no common or national Jordanian identity to speak of, even though most of the residents of these areas were Sunni Muslims. Every one of these regions had its political institutions and its special relations with the tribes in that region.

The reputation of the Ottoman officials in Transjordan was based on their generosity, their integrity and on the type or projects, which they carried out. These officials occupied a variety of posts and they lived in close contact with the inhabitants. Preference was given to Turks who had extensive experience in other parts of the empire, knew the Arabic language, and had experience dealing with the local population. Although many of these officials were corrupt and sought to enrich themselves during their tenure in office there were some who had a genuine desire to introduce reforms. For example, the district governor of al-Salt, Yunis Agha was described as someone who "spoke with great enthusiasm of the reforms which would be introduced" and how "the Turkish government would do its best to educate these regions."[27] Similarly, the Druze Amir Arslan who served as a district governor of Irbid is described in Ṣaliḥ Tall's memoirs as an incorruptible and magnanimous. According to Ṣaliḥ Tall, the district governor of Irbid, Isḥaq Bey, worked tirelessly to eliminate corruption, even though the local press portrayed him in a negative light. Service records compiled by the Ottoman Civil Functionaries Commission provide details about the distinguished careers of individuals such as Mehmet Arefi Bey who served as governor of Karak in 1907, and held numerous positions in which he served with distinction. Another example of individuals who served with distinction was that of Aḥmet Ḥamdi Efendi, an Iraqi Kurd who was appointed to serve as a treasurer in Karak, and was later dismissed for misappropriation of 21,369 piasters of state funds.[28]

Ottoman presence in the towns of Transjordan was visible through the buildings that were erected, and occupied by the governor and his bureaucracy. Buildings were erected in places such al-Salt, which had an impressive two-story structure. In addition to facilities used by the government employees, the building had a court and a house of detention. More modest buildings were built in Ma'an, Shawbak, Wadi Musa, near Petra, and al-Iraq, near Karak. Facilities such as mosques, clinics, prisons and other structures were built according the need but overall, only structures deemed essential were built.

The Ottomans invested in keeping roads in good repair and paving new ones. The two main roads in Transjordan were *Darb al-Hajj* that linked the settlements at the desert's edge mainly Ramtha, Zarqa and Ma'an and the King's Highway (*Darb al-Sultani*) that started in Bursa Eski Sham in east Hawran, passed through Mafraq and reached Zarqa and Amman. The King's Highway extended southward to Ḥisban, Madaba, Dhiban, Karak, Petra, and Aqaba. Rural as well as urban roads were improved significantly by the end of the nineteenth century. A ferry service was established in the Red Sea, which connected Jericho to Karak and the Hejaz railroad and thereby made the communication among the cities easier. By 1900, the telegraph line passed through the entire length of Transjordan, and it linked the towns of al-Salt, Madaba, Karak, Tafila and Ma'an and ended in Aqaba.

Additional stations were built in remote areas and these helped the Porte tighten its control over the county. However, the cost of safeguarding the network from attack by Bedouins who regarded it as representing the Porte's authority was a major drawback. Built in beginning of the twentieth century, the Hejaz railroad connected cities such as Zarqa, Qatrana, and Tabbuk. It constituted a major stimulant to economic growth, but it was also a security risk that the Porte had to assume. To provide security to the inhabitants in Transjordan, the Porte established local police stations in the main towns such as al-Salt, Karak, Tafila, and Ma'an and recruited mounted *jandarma* to be in charge of patrolling important sites such as military camps and telegraph stations. Circassians as well as Chechens joined that force.[29] The Ottoman legacy remained strong in Jordan. Many Jordanians were employed in the Ottoman bureaucracy, and seven prime ministers were graduates of Ottoman civil and military schools.

Transjordan became the center of the Arab revolt after the capture of Aqaba by Faisal in July 1917. In November, Jerusalem was captured by the British expeditionary force that was sent from Egypt, and by February 1918, Jericho was taken despite the effort of the German commander Otto Liman von Sanders. However, when the British expeditionary force entered al-Salt on March 25, 1918, the Germans managed to stop it. Consequently, the inhabitants of that town paid dearly for assisting the British. During this first Transjordan campaign, over 6,000 al-Salt civilians fled and many were transported by the British to Jerusalem.[30]

Christian elders from Madaba and al-Salt show the Turkish authorities requisitioned agricultural products and livestock from them while those of al-Fuhays remember the raids on their grain fields. An elder from al-Rumaymin remembered how the houses were searched to ensure that the residents follow the rationing regulations, and some even remembered severe hunger saying, "We who were once well-fed, during the war were desperate, and used to search for grain in the dung for our bread."[31]

World War I caused major difficulties to Jordan's inhabitant who resided in Jerusalem. Christian churches suffered from lack of provisions and pilfering by Turkish soldiers were rife. When the United States declared war on Germany in April 1917, the soup kitchens run by the American Colony were closed, and the poor had nowhere to go. It was only after Bertha Vester Spafford and her husband who ran the facility appealed to the Minister of the Marine Jemal Pasha to resume the charitable work that he agreed to let them to use the Grand New Hotel inside Jaffa Gate as a hospital, that they resumed their activities.[32]

On Easter Sunday 1918, the inhabitants of al-Salt witnessed the retreat of the British forces that were repulsed by the Ottomans whose return caused them considerable hardships. The Christian communities in the region were affected the most by this change. However, the solidarity, which the Muslim families demonstrated toward them, mitigated the impact of the persecution that ensued.[33] The British waged three campaigns against the joint Ottoman-German force. Al-Salt inhabitants still recall the year that years as *Sanat al-Hijra* (The Exodus Year) when 6,000 civilians, the majority of whom were Christians, fled from the region after the first raid, which took place in March 25–April 1 of that year. The inhabitants of al-Salt who welcomed the British feared retribution by the Ottomans and many of them who returned to their homes found that they were vandalized.

In his analysis of the impact of World War I on Greater Syria's inhabitants, Mathew Madain argues:

a The Muslims of Transjordan had demonstrated greater solidarity with the Christians than any other region.
b Those Muslims who helped the Christians in 1918 were largely members of tribes with whom the Christian clans were allied long before 1867, when the Ottomans began to administer the region directly and they lasted after the outbreak of World War I
c The inhabitants of Transjordan suffered largely due to economic burdens that were imposed on them by the Ottomans, and less due to forced recruitment.[34]

Notes

1 Mathew Madain, "Remembered One Hundred Years Later: Al-Salt, Transjordan, and the First World War," *Oxford Middle East Review* (July 3, 2020/August 9, 2021), p. 4. https://omerjournal.com/2020/07/03/remembered-one-hundred-years-later-al-salt-transjordan.
2 Sulayman Musa, p. 76.
3 'Abd al-'Azīz al-Kulayb al-Sharīdah, *Al-Ḥajj Kulayb al-Yūsuf al-Sharīdah: Sīrat Ḥayāt 1865–1941* (Al-Ḥajj Kulayb al-Yūsuf al-Sharīdah: Life Story 1865–1941), Arabic text ('Ammān: Wizārat al-Thaqāfah, 2000), pp. 55–56.
4 For explanation on the origins of this practice see Abdallah Hanna, "The First World War according to the Memories of 'Commoners' in the BILAD AL-SHAM," *The World in World Wars: Experiences, Perceptions and Perspectives from Africa and Asia*, Edited by Heike Liebau, Katrin Bromber, Katharina Lange, Dyala Hamzah and Ravi Ahuja (Leiden, The Netherlands: Brill, 2010), pp. 299–300.
5 'Abd al-Qādir al-Ṣāliḥ, *Dhikrayāt* (Memoirs), Arabic text ('Ammān: Matba'at Rafīdī, 1985), p. 11.
6 Cited in Leila Tarazi Fawaz, *A Land of Aching Heart: The Middle East in the Great War* (Cambridge, MA: Harvard University Press, 2014), p. 165.
7 Sulayman Musa, *Al-Thawrah al 'Arabīyah al-Kubrah wa-al-ḥarb fī al-Urdun 1917–1918: Mudhakkirāt al-Amīr Zayd* (The great Arab Revolution and the war in Jordan, 1917–1918: Memoirs of Amir Zayd), Arabic text (Amman: Markaz al-Kutub al-Urduni, 1990), p. 217.
8 Thomas Edward Lawrence, *Seven Pillars of Wisdom* (Fordingbridge, UK: Castle Hill Press, 1997), p. 180.
9 *Ibid*, p. 309.
10 *Ibid*, pp. 241, 243, 244. [Parentheses are in the text].
11 Lawrence, pp. 338, 339, 340, 341.
12 Sulayman Musa, *Al-Thawrah al 'Arabīyah al-Kubrah wa-al-ḥarb fī al-Urdun: Mudhakkirāt al-Amīr Zayd*, p. 38.
13 Ibid, p. 43.
14 Lowell Thomas, *With Laurence in Arabia* (New York: The Century Co., 1924), pp. 223–224.
15 *Ibid*, pp. 227–228.
16 *Ibid*, p. 256.
17 *Ibid*, p. 258.
18 *Ibid*, pp. 258–260.

19 Edward C. Woodfin, *Camp and Combat on the Sinai and Palestine Front: The Experience of the British Empire Soldier, 1916–1918* (New York: Palgrave Macmillan, 2012), p. 114.
20 Sulayman Musa, p. 34.
21 *Ibid.*
22 Cited in Melanie Tanielian, *The War of Famine: Everyday Life in Wartime Beirut and Mount Lebanon (1914–1918)*, Unpublished Dissertation, University of California, Berkeley (Fall 2012), p. 1.
23 Goichon, Vol. I, p. 55.
24 Shimon Shamir, "The Modernization of Syria: Problems and Solutions in the Early Period of Abdülhamid," *Beginnings of Modernization in the Middle East: The Nineteenth Century*, Edited by William R. Polk and Richard L. Chambers (Chicago: The University of Chicago Press, 1968), p. 358.
25 Eugene L. Rogan, *Frontiers of the State in the Late Ottoman Empire* (Cambridge, UK: Cambridge University Press, 1999), pp. 1–2, 17–20.
26 *Ibid*, p. 23.
27 Cited *Ibid*, p. 56.
28 *Ibid*, p. 59.
29 *Ibid*, p. 67.
30 Madain, p. 5.
31 Cited Ibid, p. 6.
32 Roberto Mazza, "Churches at War: The Impact of the First World War on the Christian Institutions of Jerusalem, 1914–1920," *Middle Eastern Studies*, Vol. 45, No. 2 (March 2009), p. 215.
33 Madain, p. 1.
34 *Ibid*, pp. 2–4.

VII Minorities, Bedouin tribes, and the challenge of integration

By the early 1870s, ethnic groups such as Circassians, Chechens, and Armenians began settling in Transjordan. A few Jewish settlements were founded thereafter but were soon abandoned. The Ottomans encouraged the migration of Circassians and Chechens from the eastern part of the empire to Jordan, where they founded their own settlements. Some measure of stability was gradually achieved following the migrations. However, the southern part of Jordan remained unstable and required constant vigilance. Britain's growing interest in that region caused concern in Constantinople, and the fear that Saudi tribes such as Ibn Rashid would subdue the Jordan's Bedouins intensified. Consequently, regions such as Ma'an, Wadi Ram, and Karak were placed under direct Ottoman control.[1] This southern region became a district (*mutasarrifiya*) tied to Syria, and an official known as *mutasarrif* was its governor. By such means, the Ottomans managed to control Karak, Ma'an, Tafila, Wadi Sirḥan, and even northern Madaba. The *mutasarrif* was Ḥussein Ḥilmi, and Ma'an became his headquarters. This headquarters was later moved from Ma'an to Karak. This was in response to a request by Karak's inhabitants and the governor of Syria who viewed with favor their demand that they were marginalized. Shortly afterward, al-Salt, Tafila, and Madaba were added to Karak. In addition to nominating a *mutasarrif*, the Porte appointed individuals who helped administer the region. It nominated Arab officials to positions in the local government and recruited soldiers from among the region's inhabitants. Furthermore, it introduced reforms beneficial to the public. After its separation from Karak, Ajlun became a separate administrative unit, and the Porte distributed its agricultural land among the inhabitants and the tribes who lived in that region. The local leaders obtained some measure of autonomy, and in return for their loyalty, the Porte provided them education, medical care, and other vital services.

The Young Turks who came to power in 1908 sought to centralize their regime by introducing new reforms. The result was a sharp increase in taxes and a substantial reduction in payments to local notables. The deteriorating conditions, the high taxes, the forced recruitment to the army, and the hostility of the tribes to each other, all contributed to discontent among the inhabitants, and the uprisings became more frequent. Sami al-Faruqi suppressed the rebellion of 1910 with utmost brutality, but when the great Arab rebellion erupted in 1916, and the Hashemite forces began moving northward, Jemal Pasha tried to meet the rebels' demands. Furthermore, he

DOI: 10.4324/9781003450313-8

attempted to recruit a military force from among the Jordan's inhabitants in order to crush the rebellion. However, neither the inhabitants nor the tribes were willing to cooperate, and they waited for the Sharifi emirs to come and lead them in the struggle against the Turks.

Most of Ottoman Jordan consisted of Ajlun, which was a sub-province (*liwa*) of the *mutasarrifiya* of Damascus (*dimashq*). The northern regions inhabited by Banu Kinanah, Banu Kafarat, Banu Jahm, and Banu al-Sar were smaller administrative units (*naḥiya*s) of *liwa* Dimashq.[2] The *mutasarrifiya* of Ḥawran was the most southerly part of the province of Syria. It was subdivided into *qaimaqamlik*s; Kunaitra at the foot of Jabal al-Shaikh (Mount Hermon), and Mount Ajlun. The *mutasarrif* resided at Shaikh Sa'd village. In 1879, its population included Muslims, Druze, Christians, and several Arab tribes, including a population of some 300 Circassian families. Jabal Ajlun was overwhelmingly Muslim. Most Druze lived there and some in south Leja. As for the Christians, they resided in the west and the southwest, mainly in Leja and Mount Ajlun. Leja was also inhabited by Bedouin tribes, among which were 3,000 members of the Sloot tribe who were governed by 13 *shaikh*s. They lived largely by herding and brigandage, and the Ottoman attempts to establish order in that region met with limited success.

In 1869, the Ottoman governor Rashid Pasha sent an expedition to subdue the Bedouin tribes in Moab, and he put one of the shaikhs in charge, providing him a stipend as compensation. In one of the incidents that occurred in that region, tribesmen attacked government buildings and the damage to property was considerable. In 1873, Bedouins from Leja raided buildings of the Hawran's government center at Edhra'at. They expelled the soldiers and the government employees, destroyed the archives, leaving nothing behind. Consequently, the commander in the region was recalled, and the seat of the government was moved to Shaikh Sa'd. The Porte sent a new governor, Essaa Pasha but he failed to establish order and the region fell again into the hands of the Bedouins who terrorized the Christian villages. The influx of Druze to eastern and southern parts of Leja contributed to the disorder by occupying arable land and dispossessed the inhabitants. This caused the central government to be concerned about the ability of the sedentary population to continue paying taxes.

The Porte encouraged local leaders to assume the task of defending the region. This happened in the previously mentioned attack on Edhra'at in 1873, when the Arabs of Leja appointed a Druze shaikh to protect them. That the inhabitants of Edhra'at continued to enjoy respite from Bedouin assaults afterward was largely due to the presence of a few Druze who managed to restore order; a task, which the Porte failed to perform despite the fact that it had a battalion stationed close by. However, the Bedouin raids never ceased entirely, and the villagers continued to suffer. Another village whose inhabitants suffered from Bedouin attacks was Khubab where Greek Catholics resided. Situated close to Edhra'at, and on the edge of Leja, this village became prone to Bedouin attacks. They appealed to the Porte who sent eighty soldiers, but they failed to restore order.

Realizing that order could not be restored without the presence a substantial military force, the Porte responded by stationing a battalion in Leja, and embarked on negotiations with some of the local shaikhs. However, lethargy and corruption prevented any decisive solution to the problem. The Porte faced a similar problem in Mount Ajlun, where the inhabitants failed to pay taxes. An armed expedition was sent to the region in 1877, in an attempt to recover the revenues but with little the success. Although the government introduced better methods of land registration, the people's opposition, the indifference, and the corruption of local officials prevented more efficient tax collection. Intervention by state's officials rarely saved the victims from these problems.

During the first half of the ninteenth century, about three quarters of the population in Transjordan were Muslims and the rest were mostly Greek Orthodox Christians. There were very few mosques in Irbid, Ajlun, and al-Salt, but these were old and in a state of disrepair, while Karak had one that was in ruins, and it was not until 1896 that the Ottomans erected a new one. The churches in the countryside were in a similar state of neglect and disrepair. There were two churches in Karak and one in al-Salt, which was one of the most attended in Transjordan. Popular religion and veneration of local saints were common practices as well. Saints such as St. George and Nabi Yusha' (Prophet Hosea) had shrines in places such as Karak, al-Salt, and the adjacent village of Mahis, where visitors came to worship and merchants sold their wares.

The contact between the Christian communities and the Muslims resulted in a cultural diffusion and there were cases where Christians adopted Muslim practices, such as polygamy or baptized their children. The tolerant nature of the Jordanian society encouraged interaction, allowing Muslims and Christians to interact and dress in a similar fashion. With the exception of Ma'an, which was closely linked to the pilgrimage road, there was virtually no religious tension in the urban areas.[3]

The most common cultural feature of the towns and villages in Transjordan was that hospitality played important role in all of them. Guesthouses known as *manzil* or *madafa* were common, especially in the southern part of Jordan. Normally, the cost of hosting guests was covered by the upper classes. Burckhardt tells us that the hospitality of the inhabitants in the places that he visited had no bounds. For example, when Yusef Shurayda, a local chief in Ajlun sought to serve his guests with a large tray that did not fit his door, he ordered his men to bend it in the middle in order to pass through. Hospitality was not only a time-honored custom, which the inhabitants practiced from time immemorial but also a means by which one gained respect and political power in that region.[4]

In many areas of Jordan, the inhabitants were either oblivious or indifferent toward their Ottoman overlords, and it was only in Ajlun district that the sultan's authority was recognized. Taxes were imposed on all Ottoman subjects, including the Bedouins who had to pay a yearly tribute from their flocks and herds. In addition to the Ottoman taxes, the *khuwah* which the residents had to pay the Bedouins for their protection constituted a burden, which they could hardly bear. Pressed by their inability to pay the tax collectors, the peasants often left and moved elsewhere after crossing the Zarqa River to Balqa, where the Ottomans authorities had little control. The Bedouins of Balqa did not recognize the Ottoman authorities and they avoided paying the tribute whenever possible. This was the case in Karak as well.

While the inhabitants of Karak had a modicum of respect for the sultan, they had contempt toward the provincial governors whom they regarded as lackadaisical, corrupt, and avaricious. There was even less respect for Ottoman rule in the district of Ma'an. Witnessing the sultan's failed attempts to subdue local rebels in places such as Mount Lebanon and Palestine, the inhabitants of Jordan were in no mood to tolerate abuse by local governors.

Pressed by the need for revenues and the desire to control Jordan, which linked Damascus and the Hejaz, the Ottomans extended their sway southward toward the steppe lands of Ajlun and Balqa. One of the factors, which prompted the Ottomans to move in that direction, was the fear that the British might occupy Jordan in order to secure their hold on Egypt. However, the Porte's attempt to establish effective rule in the southern part of Jordan required settlement building and control over the Bedouins, and it proved to be a painstakingly slow process, which began in the Ajlun district. By that time, Jabal Ajlun was dominated by the Adwan tribe, and some branches of the Anaza confederation, which taxed the peasants so heavily, causing many to flee. This put the burden of protecting the peasants on the Porte's shoulders, and in 1844, it decided to send the commander Muhammad Sa'id Agha Shamsdin with a force of fifty cavalrymen to restore order, but the mission failed. Likewise, the plan adopted by the Porte in 1846 to appoint a district governor, with a force of 600–700 soldiers to the village of 'Il'al in northeast Irbid, fell through.

In 1851, the Ottomans established a district center in Irbid, but this proved to be a short-lived attempt. This move came as result of large deficit in the finances of the governor of Damascus.

In effort to put an end to the Bedouin assaults, the military commander of Damascus raided the areas controlled by the Banu Kilab and Banu Sakhr tribes, and confiscated their herds of sheep and camels. At the same time, he conceived of a plan to employ exiled Algerian refugees to establish an administrative post in Irbid. In October of that year, the Porte nominated Aḥmad Efendi Salim as district governor of the *Sanjak* of Ajlun. He was stationed in Irbid and the Algerian immigrants were put in charge of guarding the region from Bedouin assaults. However, the plan to settle the Algerians as watchdogs over the Bedouins faltered, due to the poor living conditions in Irbid, which they left and moved to other areas. In 1852, the Ottomans were losing control over Ajlun whose inhabitants opposed their attempt to introduce military conscription. Furthermore, the changes caused by the interference of the Administrative Council in Damascus in the local affairs led to dissatisfaction, which resulted in the abandonment of the project. For the next 12 years, the Ottoman provincial government combined Karak, al-Salt and Ajlun as one *liwa*. However, Ajlun was neglected. Security in that region was left to local leaders (*za'ims*) of the villages, and the Ottoman presence was restricted to the annual visits of the tax collectors. This situation was reversed as result of the Vilayet Law of 1864, which reorganized the provincial administration in the empire, and nominated a *wali* to Damascus whose term of service was limited to five years.[5]

The Vilayet Law laid the foundations of the Ottoman administration in Greater Syria. According to this law, the basic administrative unit known as *kaza* was to be governed by a district governor, a *mufti* in charge of religious affairs, and a judge. To assist the governor in his task, the law made provision for elected councils that participated in the process. The governor elected in 1866 was Mehmet Rashid Pasha who managed to subdue the tribes in the northern towns, and extended Ottoman control over Jordan by creating administrative districts in Ajlun and al-Salt. His five-year tenure enabled him to implement his project with consummate efficiency. In May 1867, he managed to subdue the tribes of the Balqa with help from local tribes such as Ruwala, Wuld Ali, Beni Ḥasan, and the Druze inhabitants of Hawran. His force advanced from Jabal Ajlun to Balqa, and then entered al-Salt unopposed. Dhi'ab al-Humud, head of the Adwan tribe who had the Sirḥan, the Sardiya and the Banu Sakhr on his side, retreated southward to Ḥisban in an attempt to regroup. Meanwhile, Rashid remained in al-Salt, which he managed to control. Faris Agha Kardu was appointed governor, and an administrative council was formed to assist him. He then moved southward and defeated Dhi'ab who retreated to Karak and was captured in October that year. In the administrative changes that ensued, Ajlun was incorporated into Hawran and al-Salt to Nablus, which was part of the *mutasarrifiya* of the Balqa, which extended over the two banks of the Jordan River. Muhammad Sa'id Agha became the first governor of the Balqa. In 1867, Banu Sakhr and Adwan resumed their collaboration. They defied Rashid and insisted on collecting *khuwah* payments from the villages in Hawran. Consequently, the Ottomans sent another expedition to Balqa, which defeated them and forced them to pay a fine of 225,000 piasters to cover the cost of the campaign. This campaign made it abundantly clear that the Ottomans came there to stay.[6]

Nowadays, Jordan has a mixture of nationalistic, religious, and ethnic groups the largest of which are the Palestinians. The Circassians who came to the country in the mid-1870s constitute a large minority. The Christian communities resided in the country since the first century of the common era. In addition to these sedentary inhabitants, there were several nomadic Bedouin tribes. Jordan's ruling family is Hashemite and it has a Saudi origin. It is for that reason that most Jordanian textbook books dwell on the origins of the kingdom's rule, rather than on the origins of its population.[7] Jordanian citizenship was never confined to one group and it was in a constant state of flux. For example, when Jordan annexed the West Bank in Palestine War of 1948, several thousand Palestinian refugees became Jordanian citizens. King Hussein's decision to disengage from the West Bank in 1988 meant that the Palestinians who were incorporated into the Jordanian state in the aftermath of the Six-Day War of 1967 and represented by the PLO meant that they were no longer Jordanian citizens. Such drastic changes invalidate any argument by contemporary Jordanians that they are direct descendants of their ancestors. It is for that reason that Jordanian textbooks tend to deal more with the origins of the Hashemite dynasty than with Jordanian people.[8] The tendency to promote the Hashemite family, both as Muslim and Arab, was motivated by the desire to legitimize the regime, and to overcome ethnic diversity. Jordanian textbooks tend to emphasize the Hashemite connection to Prophet Muhammad. In addition, the pan-Arab ideology promoted by Egyptian President Gamal Abd al-Nasser in the 1950s was highly attractive to the Hashemites. Since pan-Arabism was an ideology that sought to erase the boundaries among the Arab states, any Arab had the freedom to move from one country to another, to vote as well as run for public office. The adoption of this ideology by the Jordanian regime provided legitimacy to a host of ministers and public officials whose origin was Arab but not necessarily Jordanian. In addition, the role, which the Hashemite family fulfilled as a champion of the Arab cause in the revolt of 1916, earned it the reputation of being pan-Arab and gave legitimacy to the regime. Such endeavor enabled the regime to link itself to major events in Arab history, particularly victories, and claim ownership of them.[9] An example for that is the Battle of Yarmouk of 636 AD in which Arab forces inflicted a major defeat on the Byzantine army.

There is no explicit claim in the Jordanian textbooks that the ancient peoples who inhabited the country such as the Ammonites, Amorites, Moabites, and Nabateans were the ancestors of the contemporary Jordanians, even though they are thought to have been Arabs. The official narrative leaves the contemporary Jordanians without roots and they cannot lay claim to continuity in the country. The regime is capable of overcoming this problem by relating Jordan to pan-Arabism and its monarchy to Prophet Muhammad.[10] However, before delving into the controversial issue of identity a discussion of Jordan's ethnic groups is in order.

Circassians and Chechens

In addition to its numerous Bedouin tribes, Jordan absorbed minorities that came and settled during Ottoman times. Both Circassians and Chechens found home in Jordan, as did Christians and Jews. The ability of the Circassians and the Chechens to integrate in the Jordanian society stemmed from previous encounters, which the Arabs had with them. Led by the Arabs, the commercial caravans brought items such as spices, precious stones, iron and silver utensils, and sold them in the towns and villages of the Caucasus where the Circassians lived. The Arabs were aware of the economic significance of this region since the days of Prophet Muhammad's successors. In 642, Caliph Umar ibn Khattab sent an army under Sarrakah bin Amr to Azerbaijan; a military force under Bakr bin Abdallah and Abd al-Raḥman bin Rabi'a made its way to Shirwan and Daghastan; and another force moved toward the towns of Karj and conquered Tiflis. Daghastan became Muslim and Derbend turned into headquarters of the Arab administration and a center of Islamic culture.[11] Following the Arab conquests, the commercial contacts continued, and when the Circassians and Chechens arrived in Syria between 1860 and 1914, and they settled in Jordan.

Between 1878 and 1884, there was a large wave of Circassian immigrants who arrived from Anatolia and the Balkans where they were accused of stirring trouble.[12] The newcomers settled in the villages of Amman and Wadi Sīr in Balqa, and Jarash in Jabal Ajlun. A Turcoman settlement was established at al-Ruman during that period as well. A second wave of Circassian immigrants arrived in 1901–1906, and they established the villages of Na'ur, Zarqa, Sukhna, Rusayfa, and Suwaylih. Amman, which by 1893 had more than a thousand souls, was the first Circassian settlement. Like other ethnic minorities, the Circassians were exposed to frequent assaults by Bedouins, and they were not welcomed by the local population who regarded them as intruders, but they slowly began occupying important positions in the Ottoman administration, primarily as tax collectors and policemen in the *jandarma*. In time, they acquired considerable influence and power, which brought Banu Sakhr to form an alliance with them. Thus, the Circassians gained the support of Banu Sakhr when they had a conflict with the Baqawiyya confederation in 1906–1910. In 1906, there were 2,250 Circassian families in Jordan compared to 1,949 in Kunaitra, and several hundreds, in other smaller towns and villages throughout Greater Syria.[13] They arrived in Jordan in the 1870s, and settled in the site of the ancient city of Philadelphia (Amman). When the newcomers arrived, the arable parts of that region were cultivated by farmers from al-Salt. Local tribes such as Banu Sakhr and others camped there and made use of the water supplies. Some 50 members of the Shabsugh family survived the disaster, which struck the ship *Sphinx*, which was on its way from Kavala to Latakia in March 1878, when fire erupted and killed 500 who were onboard. At first, they settle in Nablus and other areas in Palestine. Others joined the first group and thereby increased its size to about 500. However, they abandoned the settlement, and when the British South African author and traveler Laurence Oliphant visited Amman in the early 1880s, he found no more than 150. They cultivated the land and maintained herds of sheep. Their number increased when another 25 families joined them in 1880. Another settlement was established in that year at Wadi as Sīr. Alienated from the Arab population, the Circassians lived in abject poverty and were on the verge of extinction. Their condition did not improve until 1892, when another group of 75 families arrived. Initially, they encountered hostility from Sattam ibn Fayiz and Banu Sakhr tribe with whom they eventually allied. The number of the Circassians increased to about 1,000 in 1893, and they became involved in trade and construction.

The Circassian settlement in Jarash began probably in 1884. Jarash was settled by Circassians of the Kabarday family, headed by former officer Amir Nuḥ Bey who served in the Russian army and delegated some of his duties to his son Abdul Ḥamid. The community farmed the land and turned Jarash into a flouring trading center. Most of the 1,600 who lived there by 1900 were Circassians. In 1902, 1904, and 1906–1907, the Circassian community increased further when additional members of the Kabarday group joined them. The war veteran Mirza Wasfi Pasha became the recognized leader of Amman and its environs. Gradually, the Circassian community became organized and the distribution of land between the old settlers and the newcomers became regulated. Skirmishes with Arab tribesmen intensified in 1906 or 1907, when another group of Circassians arrived and started the Balqawiyah wars, by abducting a girl from the local tribes. The Circassians proved their ability to fight, and they participated in the campaigns against the Druze of Jawlan and Karak during the rebellion of 1909–1910. By the first decade of the twentieth century, there were between 5,000 and 6,500 Circassians in Balqa and Jarash.[14] They continued to fulfill important roles during World War I, and worked on the construction of the Hejaz railroad. By the beginning of the twentieth century, Amman was almost an exclusively a Circassian agricultural settlement, and it was only when immigrants from other towns arrived that its character began to change.

The Circassians managed to maintain their unique identity and tribal structure. Majd al-Din Khamash attributed their ability to maintain their unique identity to three main factors; their tendency to create political alliances with other tribes, their self-sufficiency, and the purity of their Adyghe-Xabze culture, which demanded loyalty and sacrifice from the members of the society.[15] Commenting on the change made by the arrival of the Circassians to Jarash the author of *The Vanished Cities of Arabia* writes:

> Gerasa, the modern Jerash, lay uncared for and deserted for a thousand years and more, before a new population was settled on the right bank of the river, among some of the ruins but away from the most important. These were the Circassians, flying, as those who made Amman their home, from troubles in their own country. They were posted there by the Turks to act as a barrier to prevent the Bedawins from raiding the neighborhood…They had to be armed against tribes who had found the ruins of Jerash a convenient place for their camps when on the march, or for flocks moving from one pasture to another. Little by little, the Circassians arranged their lives in this new setting, for which only their fervent Mohammedanism fitted them….they certainly took much from the ruins, as anyone can see who takes the trouble to inspect their houses.[16]

The first Chechen settlement was established in Zarqa in 1902, and they founded Rusayfah, Suwaylih, and Skhnah shortly afterward. They farmed and worked on the Hejaz Railway. Both Circassians and Chechens settled in villages in central Transjordan, and Jarash in particular. They were of considerable value to the Ottoman authorities as fighters and frontiersmen. There were 6,000 Circassians compared to 1,000 Chechens in the 1920s. Both groups played important roles during the formative years of the Jordanian state, both in the Arab Legion, the Transjordan Frontier Force and the government bureaucracy. Some of them rose to high positions as officers and administrators. Over the years, the Circassians lost their image as daring pioneers and fierce fighters, and they gradually assimilated into the Jordanian population in the urban areas.[17]

The Christian communities

Christians lived in Jordan since the time of Christ. Archaeological research shows that a Christian community prospered in Jarash well into Islamic times. The removal of figural subjects from some of the mosaic church pavements provides a proof to that. The Umayyad Caliph Yazid II (720–724) is said to have been particularly determined to remove Christian or pagan inscriptions. However, the recent discovery at Umm al-Rasas of a mosaic that was made in 756, mutilated by iconoclasts and repaired before its final abandonment, shows that Byzantine churches might have functioned there beyond the eighth century. Archaeologists believe that two churches were destroyed in that location by an earthquake, and that Muslims and Christians coexisted during the second half of the eighth century.[18]

Christians also lived in towns like Karak, Madaba, and Amman. Although their number decreased considerably when Islam spread, both the local inhabitants and the nomadic tribes practiced Christianity. The number of Christians remained small until the eleventh century, when the Crusaders arrived to liberate the holy places from the hands of the Seljuk Turks. The traveler Sir John Mandeville tells us about the Christians he saw in Karak. He writes:

> You need to know that as you travel east from the Dead Sea from the border of the promised land is a sturdy castle called, in the Saracen language, *Krak*, that is, in French, Réal-Mont. A French king called Baldwin, had this castle built for him, for he had won all this land and placed it in Christian hands for safekeeping. Below the castle is a fair town called Gabaon. Christians live around here under obligation to pay tribute.[19]

It seems that religious differences had little impact on peace in that region, as the British Ambassador to Jordan Alec Kirkbride noted in a memorandum from March 4, 1942.

> In Kerak in Trans-Jordan, Christian tribes have existed since the time of the Moslem conquest of Byzantine Syria. They were allied for all purposes with Moslem tribes at whose side they fought in tribal wars and by whom they were treated as men with equal rights in all things. No one heard of strife between Moslims and Christians on religious ground until after the Ottoman Government established an effective sway over that part of the country early in the twentieth century.[20]

Christians came to settle in al-Salt in 1867 when the Ottomans occupied that area. Some settled in the area long before, but most of them came at that time and remained once they began enjoying security and stability. Some left al-Salt, and settled in regions such as al-Fuhays and al-Rumaymin, which were administered by al-Salt. The Christians of Rumaymin encountered Bedouin resistance. Nevertheless, the village continued to grow and in 1870, the Catholic missionary Jean Morétain arrived in the hope of converting its residents from the Greek to the Latin rite. By 1875, there were 150 residents and a Latin mission was founded in the village. According to the Christian missionary Don Gatti the Al-Fuhays settlement, which had about 16 tents, inhabited for no more than three months a year, expanded to 400 settlers in 1873. A Protestant missionary claims that by 1875, there were 25–30 houses in that settlement.

By the mid-1870s, three Christian tribes emigrated from Karak to Madaba. There was tension between the Uzayzat Christian clan that converted to Roman Catholicism, and the ruling Majali family in Karak. The abduction of a married woman from the Latin community in 1879 caused tension between the Christians and the Muslims, which resulted in the immigration of the Christians of Karak to Madaba in 1880–1881. Although the Ottoman Governor Midḥat Pasha favored the idea of settling Christians in Madaba, Banu Sakhr opposed the move and its shaikh

Sattam al-Fayiz demanded that they return to Karak. The Majalis who felt that their position was weakened in that town supported the effort to drive the Christians out of their newly found home. In turn, the Christians made a protection agreement with the Beni Ḥamida tribe. Thus, the Uzayzat became a recognized tribe and their leader Ṣaliḥ al-Marar obtained the title *shaikh*. Al-Marar called upon the leading tribes to form alliances with their rivals and thus came to be regarded as an arbiter. This prevented Shaikh Sattam from operating against the Uzayzat settlers in Madaba. Governor Midḥat Pasha whose main concern was that the lands in this region be cultivated and that its occupiers pay taxes regularly and register their land was sympathetic to Shaikh Marar's request, and he rejected the claim of Sattam Fayiz that Shaikh Marar did not register the land in this region and failed to pay taxes on a regular basis. Unlike the Circassians and the Turkoman refugees, the Christians in Madaba were required to pay annual taxes on their land as well as on their harvests. Shaikh Marar's struggle paid off, and the Christians remained in Madaba, which became the southernmost settlement in Balqa.[21]

When the Emirate of Transjordan was formed in 1921, there were 230,000 people and less than 10 percent of them were Christians. According to the Ottoman statistics, most resided in the northern and central districts of Ajlun, al-Salt, and Karak. In addition, there were few Christians in the southern regions such as Tafila and Ma'an.[22] By the end of the Ottoman period, the vast majority of the Christians belonged to the Greek Orthodox Church, but the Roman Catholic clergy managed to convert about one-fifth of them. There were other groups such as Anglicans, Armenians and Greek Catholics, which had only a handful of followers. They were regarded as "Peoples of the Book" (*dhimmi*s), which according to tradition could practice their religion as long as they paid the required poll tax (*jizya*). Their autonomous status in the Ottoman Empire was confirmed first during the Tanzimat, and then by the Mandatory regime during the interwar period, and finally by the independent Jordanian state.

The Organic Law of 1928 established Islam as the state religion but guaranteed freedom of worship to all religious communities, as long as they did not disrupt public order and did not try to convert Muslims. Legislated in 1938, Law 22 recognized nine Christian communities in Transjordan; Greek Orthodox; Greek Catholics, or Melkites; Armenian Orthodox; Latin, or Roman Catholics; Arab Evangelical Episcopalians, or Anglicans; Maronites; Evangelical Lutherans; Syrian or Syriac Orthodox; and, Seventh-Day Adventists), all of which were to have the right to maintain courts, which dealt with a variety of personal status issues. The churches were allowed to set up special committees to administer their affairs and raise funds. They had the same jurisdiction as the Muslim *sharia* courts. However, the nomination of church members to high positions was subject to approval by a royal decree, and major acts such as marriage and divorce had to be entered into the national civil registry.

While the British Mandate's regulation of 1922 regarding inheritance determined that boys and girls inherit equal share, the Family Law of 1951 stated that the civil law of the country ought to determine the manner in which inheritance was to be distributed. However, since there was no civil law covering personal status, it was determined that the provisions provided by the *sharia* will also applied to Christians by their courts.[23] The constitution of 1952, guaranteed the same religious rights specified in the Organic Law of 1928, but it specified that the churches ought to abide by state regulations, and submit their teaching curricula for the state's approval. In 1953, the government legislated a law regarding the disposal of real estate, which gave it the right to supervise the amount of real estate possessed by religious organizations, and in 1955, it passed another law, stating that private schools must adopt the books of the public education system. Nevertheless, the government issued regulations respecting the specific requirements of the churches, such as allowing them to observe Sunday and holidays. Christians could practice their religion freely, as long as this did not cause disturbances. Thus, the adopted requirement was that the Christians who worship in their churches and other restricted areas must refrain from engaging in acts that are offensive to Muslims, such as eating and drinking in public during the fast of Ramadan, or selling alcohol to Muslims.

Since its establishment, the state made the efforts to control the Greek Orthodox Patriarchate of Jerusalem by Arabizing its members, and severing its relations with foreign countries such as Russia or Greece, which tended to support them in order to gain influence in the region. The relations between the state and the Orthodox religious establishment were complex. While seeking to control it and prevent it from establishing ties with foreign power, the Hashemites needed its blessing, in order to legitimize their role as guardian of the holy sites in Jerusalem. Consequently, a state of constant battle developed between the two sides. On the other hand, the Orthodox clergy sought ways to increase its influence. It insisted on having an Orthodox presence in the holy sites, maintained contact with Greece, and made profit by selling and leasing its property to foreigners, including Jewish organizations.

The churches became engaged in fundraising and charity activities. The intensity of their activities and their penetration of the state bureaucracy and especially their connections with foreign powers aroused suspicion among the population. Moreover, the organizations in which they operated, such as The Brotherhood of the Holy Sepulcher, were viewed as traitors to the Arab cause. This state of affairs was of major concern to the Hashemites who sought legitimacy for their claim to be the protectors of the holy sites, and they sought to play a mediating role between the church and the nationalists. The latter became especially vocal during the age of pan-Arabism, when many Jordanians called for an alliance with Egypt, and severing relations with the West. The accommodating attitude of the Hashemites resulted in a rapid growth of the Orthodox Church's influence. The Church became involved in charity and fund-raising activities, and many of its members became integrated into the society by virtue of their connections, and the offices which they held in the ever-expanding government bureaucracy. They fulfilled a wide variety of social and economic tasks, where the government failed to act and therefore were deemed essential.

Similar accommodation had to be made with the Roman Catholics in the country. In its treatment of the Roman Catholic Church, the Jordanian regime had to take into consideration the interests and the attitude of the Vatican. This limited the Hashemite ability to intervene in the Church's affairs. The Catholic churches, which never had a *dhimmi* status under Ottoman rule, enjoyed greater autonomy than the Orthodox Church under the Hashemite regime. The main reason for the influence, which the Catholic Church had in Jordan, stemmed from the fact that the Hashemites had less control over it. Neither the Latin Patriarch of Jerusalem who was nominated by the Pope, nor the bishop of the Melkites who was under the jurisdiction of Antioch, depended on ratification by the king. Furthermore, the Catholics in Jordan possessed more resources than those of the Orthodox, and they maintained a wider network of educational institutions, health care facilities, relief, and charity organizations. The attempt to control the activities of these organizations created tension between the government and the churches, which did not relish being regulated and monitored by the state. The upshot was that by the end of the 1950s, the Catholic charitable institutions withdrew from the Union of Voluntary Societies, and no longer registered with the Ministry of Social Affairs, but they continued to operate under the purview of the Latin Patriarchate. In order to legitimize its continued claim to Jerusalem, the Hashemite regime was compelled to accommodate the Catholic Church. This explains the cordiality in which the regime treated it and respected its rituals. Furthermore, the need to maintain cordial relations with the Vatican, which did not maintain official relations with the Hashemites until 1994, even though Pope Paulus VI already visited Jordan in 1964, made it necessary for the Hashemites to be tolerant toward the Catholic Church. One of the main bones of contention between the Hashemite regime and the Vatican was always the latter's insistence that it had the right to acquire property in Jerusalem, and dispose of it in the ways that it saw fit. This attitude stood in contrast to the state's tendency to limit the amount of property purchased by the Vatican. A special law was enacted in 1953, which allowed the state to supervise the purchase of such property, and which the Vatican tried to bypass in a variety of ways.[24]

By the nineteenth century, Christian missionaries arrived in Jordan, and both Catholic and Protestants took part in establishing strong Christian foundations in the country. By 1921, the Orthodox Patriarchate community was well-established. Christians who resided around the towns such as Irbid, al-Mafraq, Jarash, Zarqa, and El-Hosun were already integrated in the state, its bureaucracy and its economy. One of the main reasons for the ability of the Christians to prosper was that the state accepted them as *dhimmis*, and no oppressive measures against them were adopted.[25]

Another group of Christians arrived in the aftermath of the Palestine War. These Christians originated from central Palestine, the Galilee, south and middle Lebanon, southern Syria, and the Caucasus. The vast majority of Christians who settled in Amman and Zarqa were refugees who arrived after the Palestine War or other domestic or external migrations. About 60,000 Christians fled their homes at that time, and they settled in both the West Bank (mainly in Jerusalem, Bethlehem, and Ramallah) and the East Bank (mainly in Amman, Karak, al-Salt, Ajlun, and Madaba). The majority of the Christians were Orthodox with the exception of those in Madaba, which had a large concentration of Latin Catholics. In addition, there were smaller communities of Greek Catholics or Melkites, Protestants, Armenians, and Syrian Orthodox.

During Ottoman times, the Christians were heavily taxed, and with the rise of the State of Israel and its conflict with the Arabs, many of them were affected by the event and sought better living conditions in Jordan. Their number increased from 93,500 in 1951 to 115,000 in 1961 and to 175,000 in 1967.[26] When the liberal Renaissance (*al-Nahda*) movement emerged in the second half of the nineteenth century, many Christians took part in discussing and writing about the liberal trends of that time. The main idea discussed during that time was equality among the country's religious groups, and the impact of this idea was beneficial to the Christians. It was largely due to that movement that the Christian communities became involved in political affairs, and many embraced nationalist ideas. Yet, despite their tendency to identify with anti-Zionist ideologies, the Christians tended to be less militant and less in agreement regarding the role of Islam in these liberation movements. Consequently, many Arab nationalists regarded them with suspicion. However, since the Christians who moved to Jordan following the Palestine War had experiences similar to the Arab Palestinians, they tended to develop the same attitude toward the conquest and the Zionists. Some of them, such as the future leaders of the Palestinian resistance movement, George Habash, and Nayef Hawatmeth, became heads of radical groups the Popular Front for the Liberation of Palestine and the Popular Democratic Front for the Liberation of Palestine, respectively. Christians became so involved in the Palestinian struggle for statehood and the only difference between them and the Muslims, who opposed the arrival of the Zionists, was that they tended to be more secular. The Christians managed to integrate in the Jordanian society not only economically but politically as well. What helped the process of integration was that the Election Law of 1928 granted a certain degree of overrepresentation to all minorities, including Christians, Circassians, and Bedouins. Therefore, they always had representatives and ministers in the governments that were formed following the country's independence. Generally, the Christian Palestinians were not harassed for their religious beliefs but for fighting for the cause of those whom they believed had been evicted from their land.[27]

The Jewish settlement plan

The Jewish traveler Benjamin of Tudela, who arrived in the region sometime between 1165 and 1178 visited Kadish (Kedesh Naphtali) on the coast of the Jordan River where the tomb of the Biblical hero Barak Ben Avinoam is, recalled in his travel log that there were no Jews in it.[28] An anonymous traveler who came to Nablus in 1522–1523 wrote that the town was deserted, that it had hot springs, and that everything in it was cheap. He noted that it had a handful of Jews and that the Samaritans were performing their religious rituals.[29] The potentialities of the seemingly arid regions of Transjordan captured the imagination of numerous western travelers. For example, the reverend Henry Maundrell who traveled to the region in 1697 tells us:

> The great plain joining to the Dead Sea, which by reason of its saltiness, might be thought unserviceable both for cattle, corn, olives, and vines, has yet its proper usefulness for the nourishment of bees and for the fabric of honey, of which Josephus gives us testimony.[30]

These comments became of interest to those who in the late nineteenth century tended to look at this region as a potential settlement for Jews. The Samaritans who settled the Mount Gerizim region did not seem to interact with Arabs or with the Jews. According to Rabbi Eliezer Halevi who visited the town in 1838, "the Samaritans (*kutim*) in this town have nothing to do with the Jews, except for matters of negotiations."[31]

In 1878, the British traveler Laurence Oliphant visited Balqa and envisaged a plan to settle Jews in it. He remarked that the region had superb land, and that it could provide livelihood for hard working immigrants who would be a great asset to the Ottoman sultan and to foreign investors. He argued, that the Land of Gilead was more fertile than many areas west of the Jordan River, that it was sparsely populated by nomadic people who had no legal right to it, and that Jews could settled there, without clashes with the Arab inhabitants. He tells us that the Bedouins of south Balqa that bordered on Karak cultivated their land only once in every three or four years. His impression was that the Karak region, which had a town with the same name (Karak or Kīr Moab), was extremely fertile, that the *qaimaqam* ruled the district in an arbitrary fashion, and that he frequently disobeyed the Porte's orders. He argued that this region could be made productive, that its resources were not developed, and that the climate was suitable for European settlers.

Oliphant reassured his readers that there was no opposition to Jewish settlement in Karak among Ottoman government officials, and that there was no need to be concerned about the rights of the Arab inhabitants to that region. He provided examples of successful settlements in similar regions by other minorities, such as the Chechens who established villages in Kunaitra and Amman. Furthermore, he argued that with only a handful of soldiers the *qaimaqam* evicted Banu Sakhr from Ajlun, and that he even managed to collect taxes from the most recalcitrant *shaikh*s in that region. He argued that one could visit Qal'at Zarqa, Amman, and Iraq al-Amir, without paying the customary tip (*bakshish*), and that one Protestant farmer had already settled in the region, and enjoyed handsome revenues from land for he did not have to pay and over which he had no legal right. Furthermore, he dismissed the notion that the Arab inhabitants of that region would raise objection to Jewish immigration, which could only bring investments and skills, and he argued that the Porte could provide protection for the Jewish settlers.

Oliphant suggested that the entire Balqa region, from the Arnon River in the south to the Jabbok River in the north, all the way to the Hejaz Railway in the east, parts of Ajlun district north of Jabbok, and the western coast of the Dead

Sea, could be settled by Jews, and he recommended that they acquire a million or million-and-a-half acres to implement the project. He also argued that the western coast of the Dead Sea was rich in mineral resources, and that it had abundant water supplies from natural reservoirs and pools. Indeed, significant reservoirs of were found in Umm al-Raṣaṣ, Mseitbah, Ziza, and other places.[32] However, it was the region north of Gilead that captured his imagination the most, since most of its Arab inhabitants had no legal ownership of the land that they cultivated. The difficulty of including the entire Ajlun district north of the Yarmouk in the borders of the proposed settlement was that a large part of it was rural property registered in the Ottoman cadastral list known as *Tabu*, while in the Balqa region, that was not the case. Any individual or a company seeking to acquire land in the north had to buy it from its owners, while in Balqa, which was the Porte's property, it was possible to purchase land directly from the government, and without infringement of individual rights, with the exception al-Salt where one could acquire land only by special negotiations. Oliphant believed that the Balqa region could be owned by a real estate company, authorized by the Porte, with a bank that would provide good credit terms to cultivators. His proposal included the hot water springs around the Dead Sea and the region of Ghor Seisaban, which was inhabited by the Ghawarini tribes. Moreover, he argued that the variety of climates in the Jordan Valley could facilitate the growth of numerous kinds of fruits and vegetables. He also mentioned the phosphates and other resources of the Dead Sea, which could be extracted and used.

Oliphant argued that the implementation of such plan required investments and manpower; that Banu Sakhr and other Bedouins could provide the manpower necessary for the project and; that the peasants could be easily enticed by good working conditions. Moreover, he argued that foreign labor could be brought from the poor countries of the Balkan Peninsula. He believed that the short distance between Balqa and Jerusalem would facilitate the transfer of the necessary supplies for the settlers, and that the Mediterranean ports would provide an easy outlet to agricultural exports.[33]

The drive to settle Jews in Transjordan was part of the agenda of several Jewish youth movements in the Diaspora prior to the establishment of the State of Israel. Among the places that the socialist Mapai Party began to settle was the Dead Sea coast. Settlement in Transjordan was one of the main objectives of the Zionist Labor movement, whose goal was to transform the petty Jewish merchant of the Diaspora into a productive farmer in Palestine. For example, the prominent of Labor Zionist, Yitzhak Tabenkin, told members of the Histadrut (The General Federation of Labor) in February 1933, in Tel Aviv that the purpose of his movement was to turn the Jew to a proletarian in the harsh conditions of places such as Lake Huleh and Transjordan.[34] There were those who feared that a Jewish settlement in Transjordan would detract the Zionist movement from its main mission to settle Palestine, but even they did not rule out that possibility. For example, the prominent leader of Labor Zionism, Chaim Arlozoroff, expressed his conviction that Transjordan will have to become an area of a Jewish settlement, arguing that its parliament had repealed the law prohibiting the sale of land to Jews, and that the shaikhs in that region welcomed that possibility.[35]

The drive to settle Jews in Transjordan was not limited to the socialists among the Zionist movement. Prominent leaders of Revisionist Zionism such as Vladimir Jabotinsky, saw Transjordan as suitable location for Jewish settlement, and the members of his Betar youth movement had repeatedly called for setting Jews in Jericho, Ramallah, Tul Karem, and other towns, which were incorporated into the Hashemite Kingdom of Jordan.[36]

Although the Porte looked settlement project seriously, it was eventually abandoned.

As it turned out however, the idea still fascinated many prominent Jews who were concerned about the future of their people. In 1889, Edmund de Rothchild sent agents to purchase land in Transjordan for that purpose. A few Jews arrived in al-Salt and Gilead was selected as a place for Jewish settlement, but once again, nothing came out of this project. Rothschild's only purchase was in the Golan, north of the Yarmouk River but since that area was isolated from the other settlements that were built by the Jewish immigrants, the settlers abandoned it soon afterward. Another attempt was made in 1891, by Mordechai Ben Hillel who was a member of the Lovers of Zion movement and who argued that the previous attempts to settle Jews in Transjordan failed due to lack of mass participation. He therefore called for the formation of groups of hundreds of Jewish immigrants to accomplish that mission. Like Oliphant and others, he argued that Transjordan was sparsely populated, that its land was fertile and cheap, and that one of the most prominent shaikhs of the Balqa region was favorable toward the idea.[37]

Claude Conder Reignier who visited the region in 1892 told the members the Lovers of Zion of his doubts regarding the possibility of settling Jews in Transjordan. Yet in the eyes of the many of the early Zionists, settling Transjordan was the imperative of the moment, and they were not willing to forfeit that right. For example, Eliahu Eilath who was the Jewish Agency's representative in Washington, DC, stated that Gilead or Moab in Transjordan "were in my eyes not any different from the rest of the places in western Palestine," and that most Jews did not wish to forfeit their right to settle there.[38]

In 1920, the prominent Zionist leader Max Nordau went to the extent of arguing that the lands in Transjordan were more valuable than those in Palestine, and that they were large enough to absorb millions of Jews who must demand that they be handed over to them.[39] The Zionist attempts to settle in Transjordan came as result of two major factors: the persecution of Jews in Europe, and the drought conditions in Palestine at the end of the 1920s, and early 1930s.[40] When the Jewish engineer Pinhas Rutenberg submitted a plan to use the waters of the Jordan and the Auja rivers for electrical power, British officials, including Winston Churchill looked favorably at the proposal.[41]

There was, however, occasional tension between the Jews and the Arab inhabitants, which manifested itself as soon as the State of Israel was established. We are told, for example, that when the Minister of Justice, Ibrahim Hashem, authorized the registration of a Jewish company that sought the right to extract minerals in Transjordan, the public was outraged. Officials in the Ministry of Justice such as Abu al-Hadi and Sa'id al-Mufti resigned in protest. The consul of Transjordan in Egypt stated that the law compelled the Minister of Justice to register every company; that registration did not mean that the company obtained special rights; and that the government will cancel the registration if the company had connections with Jewish donors.[42]

The Kurds

Kurds had long resided in Transjordan where they engaged in farming and trade. The cooperation between the Kurds and the Hashemites dates back to the years prior to their rise to power. Kurds already participated in the Arab rebellion against the Turks in 1916–1917. In fact, Kurdish leaders throughout Greater Syria who aspired to overthrow the Ottoman yoke had long maintained connections with the Arab Jordan's inhabitants, with a view to incite them to rebel. Prominent figures such as Abd al-Raḥman Basha al-Yusuf in Damascus, Khalid al-Barzani in Ḥamah and As'ad al-Ayyubi in Mount Lebanon had once wrote a letter calling upon Sharif Hussein to declare a revolt against the Turks. Kurdish military figures such as Ja'far al-Askari, Jalal Baban, Jamil al-Midfa'i, Rashid Pasha al-Midfa'i, and others, played an important role in the revolt. About 2000 Kurdish troops participated in the Arab campaigns in the regions that were under Turkish rule, especially in northern Hejaz, Jordan, and Syria. King Abdallah I who aspired to rule over Greater Syria was known to have established contacts with Kurdish leaders. In the volume, *Al-wathaïq al-Hashimiyya: mashru' surya al-kubrah* (The Hashemite Documents: The Greater Syria Program), one can find the exchange of letters between King Abdallah I and several prominent Kurds, such as the historian and writer Muhammad Kurd Ali, General Sami al-Hinawi, Musa al-Ḥamuri, members of the Barzani, and other tribes in the Kurdish region of Syria.

Kurds played a significant role in Jordanian political life ever since the country was established. They participated in the formation of the political parties, took part in national conventions, fought with the Jordanian resistance against British rule during the Mandatory period, and took a firm stand in support of the Palestinian liberation moment. Among the Kurdish personalities who emerged in Jordan during the period of the Jordanian emirate (1921–1947) were Saydu Ali al-Kurdi, Ali al-Kurdi, Khayr al-Din al-Zarkali, Salim Agha al-Sa'dun, Fayïz al-Kurdi, Yahya al-Kurdi, Sa'd Jum'a, Hosni Saydu al-Kurdi, and Aḥmad al-Kurdi. Prominent Kurds continued to play an important role in Jordanian political life, in the government bureaucracy and in the army. The relations between the Hashemites and the Kurds became closer when King Talal's daughter, princess Basma, married the entrepreneur Walid al-Kurdi. Another marriage, which brought the two sides together, was that of Ayisha daughter of King Hussein to Zayd Sa'd al-Din Jum'a al-Kurdi. During the Six-Day War of June 1967, Mullah Mustafa al-Barzani told King Hussein that he was ready to enlist 10,000 Kurds to take part in the war against Israel.[43]

The debate over tribalism and the Jordanian tribes

For over two decades, tribalism (*'asha'iriyyah*) has been a major theme of discussion in the press and the Jordanians return to this issue when discussing the country's progress and the need for introducing reforms. While the proponents of tribalism extoll its virtues, opponents regard it as an impediment to the progress of the modern nation state. This became a major issue in the 1984 parliamentary by-elections. For the most part, the intelligentsia consider tribalism as a divisive force, and claim that family ties and allegiance to a tribe tend to undermine the state's centralization efforts. For example, in an article that appeared in the daily *al-Rai* on March 9, 1984, the writer argued that

> tribalism was appropriate and good at the time of no state, it was one of the means for peaceful existence in the absence of a state. But today tribalism is a kind of illness and affliction, which eats the fortunes and sustenance of the people.[44]

Furthermore, critics argue that tribalism constitutes a threat to the state's security, and they compare it to the pre-Islamic period known as the *jahiliya*, a chaotic period in which individuals had loyalty to a tribe or to blood relatives. They also argue that these loyalties are archaic and they impede progress. They insist that in the modern age, the individual ought to have pride in his own achievements, and most importantly, in the state and its organizations, while the advocates argue that the tribal society is the sources of noble qualities such as hospitality, generosity, courage, honor, and self-respect, and they compare them favorably with the Five Pillars of Islam. Moreover, they claim that life in the desert preserves the individual's noble qualities such as hospitality and group solidarity (*asabiyya*), and they argue that Prophet Muhammad acquired them while he was among the Bedouin tribes. The advocates often refer to the writings of the fourteenth-century Maghrebi historian Ibn Khaldun, who argued that it is precisely during the primitive or Bedouin stage that empires manage to maintain their vitality, and that these virtues are lost when urbanization begins and comfort becomes commonplace. Moreover, the argument that the Bedouin way of life was instrumental in preserving the purity of the Arabic language is still prevalent among the advocates.

One of the recent examples that illustrates the complexity of this issue is the claim of the Bedoul Bedouins that Petra represents their identity, and that their traditional way of life does not contradict the Hashemite regime's efforts to bring the kingdom into the modern age. Attempting to demonstrate that the Bedoul's claim to Petra as a source of its heritage does not contradict the vital interests state modern age, the anthropologist Layan Fuleihan writes,

> Urban nomadism…is much more compatible with Jordan's development goals than previously perceived because it locates the Bedoul within this mythology and consciousness of an urban paradigm. Urban nomadism is the lifestyle that embraces both the traditional and historical cultural practice and

> the contemporary standards of developed communities. Hence, the Bedoul Bedouin in claiming attachment to Petra while maintaining identification as pastoral nomads, are in fact resolving the opposing forces of international globalism and historical and cultural nostalgia.[45]

The Hashemites' tendency to promote Bedouin culture rather than to suppress its manifestations demonstrates that they are open to the idea of preserving it, while continuing the march toward the modern age. The heroic deeds of the Bedouins are paramount in the schools' curricula, in shows, in the media and in museums. These efforts emanate primarily from the Hashemites' need to secure the loyalty of the tribes on which the stability of the regime rests, but also from the need to boost the country's attraction to tourists. At the same time, however, the needs for the modern nation state compel the government to abolish practices, which stand in contrast to the need to promote authentic democracy. It is for that reason that in January 1985, the Upper House of Parliament called for a single law requiring allegiance to the state. Yet, King Hussein always stood firm as the defender of tribalism, and insisted that as a scion of Hashem and the Quraysh tribe, the comments of the critics offended him. On January 28, 1985, he told *The Jordan Times*, "Whatever harms our tribes in Jordan is considered harmful to us."[46] The tribalism debate emerged largely as result of the identity crisis, caused by the existence of the Palestinian majority in the kingdom. Yet, the progress toward modernization and the quest for authentic democracy require the adoption of new standards, which stand in contrast to tribal practices.

The Bedouin tribes

Jordanian history is inextricably tied to it tribal heritage. The tribes had constantly interacted with the inhabitants of the towns and the villages, and thereby introduced cultural change, stimulated the economy, and played an important role in the armed forces. Moreover, they became involved in the country's politics, and the Hashemites had always regarded themselves as their defenders. Unlike the other Arab states in the region, the tribal heritage became an integral part of Jordan's national identity, and the Hashemites exploited the pure and pristine qualities that are associated with the Bedouin way of life, such is endurance, ability to survive in a harsh environment, hospitality, and loyalty, to provide the regime a unique identity. As Linda Layne put it, "Jordan's tribal heritage has been expropriated by the state as a symbol of Jordan's distinctive national identity."[47] The general tribal structure in Jordan is such that its members are organized in groups, from the smallest to the largest in the following order *ahl*, *ḥamula*, *fakhdh*, *firqa*, *ashira*, and *qabila*. The tribes of Jordan who arrived from the Arabian Peninsula as result of the harsh conditions caused by lack of water and droughts, and later by the Arab conquest of the seventh century, can be divided into three categories: nomads who relied on their camels for most of their needs, from transportation to food, and lived in tents. This category of Bedouins conducted raids (*raziya*s) on other tribes for their livelihood, and did not regard this activity as necessarily nefarious or exceedingly harmful. They had better relations with the inhabitants of the towns than those of the villages whose land they coveted and often raided. These raids often ended with violence, and it was not until 1937 that the state intervened, and their relations with the villagers became normal. In his vivid portrayal of this cycle of warfare where Bedouins fought against villagers and then became sedentary, Kirbride writes:

> When these nomads, or bedouin, as they call themselves, first come into contact with cultivators, they prey upon them; next they adopt some of the habits of the despised tillers of the soil; and finally they abandon their roving life and settle on the land, to be replaced by other tribes which have moved up to fill the void. This process appears to continue indefinitely, to be expedited by conquests which accompany the rise and fall of empires but never to be stopped entirely.[48]

The second category often referred to as the "shepherd tribes" (*qaba'il al-ghnamah*) included semi-nomads who did not tend to move frequently, and relied heavily on sheep and what they could sell them for. The third category is the 'civilized tribes' (*qaba'il al-mutaḥaḍarah*) who used camels and sheep and lived in stone houses. They were called 'farmers' (*al-falaliḥ*) because agriculture was one of their main occupations.[49] The last group is divided into two sections: the aristocrats and the notables who had property, and the commoners who toiled and paid them taxes.[50]

When the Arab conquest began in the seventh century, there were between 3 and 5 million inhabitants in Jordan, many of whom were killed by pestilence. During the Umayyad (661–750) and Abbasid (750–1258) periods, many tribes moved to that region. According to one source, members of the Ṣaliḥ tribe came to Syria where it joined Ibn al-Sumayda bin Hazbar al-Imliqi. After they joined him, they settled in near Balqa, Ḥawirat, and Zaytun. We are also told that part of the Banu Lakhm who fought as mercenaries of the Sassanid Empire against the Byzantine-supported Banu Ghassan prior to the Arab conquest, reached Jabal al-Shirah and Jadham, and settled around Madin, Tabbuk and Adhruḥ, and some went to Tiberias, Lajjun, Yamun, and Acre.[51]

When the Ottomans occupied the region in the sixteenth century, they had to subdue powerful tribes who resided there. While doing so, they found local tribal leaders willing to collaborate with them in order to prevail over their rivals. Tribal leaders who collaborated with the Ottomans were compensated with gifts, positions in the government bureaucracy, and some of them were given the prestigious role of "guardian of the pilgrimage road" (*amir* al-*haj*), which began in Damascus, and ended in the holy cities of the Hejaz. The Ottomans found it necessary to contain ambitious local leaders in that region by using one against the other, and by granting a variety of gifts and titles. On the other hand, the Ottomans resorted to harsh punishments against recalcitrant leaders who refused to summit to their rule. Major urban areas in Jordan were entrusted to local families on which the Ottomans felt that they could rely to maintain peace and security. We know, for example, that the Qansuh family was firmly in control in Ajlun.

The Qansuh dynasty originated in Ajlun. It was founded by Naşir al-Din Muhammad Ibn Abi Sayf Mudallal, also known as Ibn Sa'id al-Ghazawi. He became governor of Ajlun in the last decades of the Mamluk rule. Ibn Sai'd was referred to as grand chief of Ḥawran and Ajlun. However, when the Ottomans began their conquest, he lost control over his Bedouin loyalists and the *hajj* was cancelled in 1517. Both the son and the grandson of Ibn Sa'id were executed for taking part in the disturbances or for not stopping them. To secure the *hajj* road the governor of Damascus, Janbirdi al-Ghazali led a campaign against the Bedouins in Ḥawran and Ajlun during the following year. He managed to capture a Bedouin chief called Jughayman who later managed to flee. An agreement with the tribes was reached subsequently, where they agreed to stop their assaults. Meanwhile, Ibn Sa'id lost control over the tribes and the Ottoman confidence in him waned. However, his family survived, and some of its members were appointed to protect the pilgrims on *hajj* road.[52]

In 1551, one of Ibn Sa'id's descendants, Qansuh Ibn Musta'ida Ibn Muslim Ibn al-Ghazawi, was appointed governor (*sanjakbeyi*) of Karak and Shawbak. In that capacity, he protected the *hajj* road in the rugged highland east of the Dead Sea. During the years 1564–1568, he served as the *sanjakbeyi* of Ajlun while apparently retaining Karak and Shawbak. However, he was accused of oppression, misappropriation of funds, and inciting the tribes to rebel. After they failed to arrest him, the Ottomans appointed him *amir al-hajj* in 1570, a task, which he carried with remarkable efficiency. However, two chiefs of the Mafarrija tribes, Naṣrallah and Salama Ibn Na'im, rejected his nomination and Salama's relative, Uqab occupied that post. Once again, this appointment met with opposition from tribes who feared that it would enhance the prestige of the Suradiyya faction of the Mafarija at their expense. Meanwhile, Qansuh regained his position as *sanjakbeyi* of Karak and Shawbak as well as that of *amir al-hajj* while his son Muhammad was charged with a similar task.

Qansuh continued to serve as *amir al-hajj* and the *sanjakbeyi* of Ajlun, Karak, and Shawbak until 1585. Ajlun appears to have remained his family's domain. He obtained funds and manpower to protect the *hajj* road. By 1585, however, the Porte decided to reassert its authority and subdue the local leaders. Consequently, Qansuh was ordered to surrender to the governor of Egypt. When he failed to appear, he was arrested but pardoned by the sultan soon afterward. Although he remained *amir al-hajj*, he was deprived of Ajlun, Karak and Shawbak. Then Ajlun was granted to Abu-Safyan. Unwilling to give up Ajlun, Qansuh rebelled and managed to defeat a Janissary force sent against him. This was largely because the chief of the Mafarija tribe Amr Ibn Jabr was on his side. The two allies attacked Shaikh Salama Ibn Na'im, chief of the Suradiyya faction of the Mafarija who competed with Shaikh Amr for the support of the upper class (*mashayakh*) of Hawran. Hearing that, Sinan Pasha the *beylerbeyi* of Damascus sent a force to defeat him and he fled to Aleppo. His attempt to regain his lost *sanjaks* failed, despite his popularity and the influence, which he had at the Ottoman court. After his death, Ajlun remained in the hands of his family, but they did not retain it for long due to internal rivalries.

One of the local leaders forced to submit the Ottomans was Mansur Furaykh who was arrested in Istanbul in 1585–1586, when they came to occupy southern Syria. During his absence, his son Korkmaz Furaykh collaborated with the Ottomans in the Biqa Valley against Yunus al-Ḥarfush who tried to seize Ba'albek from Aḥmad al-Aqra with help from the Druze. Upon his return from Istanbul, Mansur received from the Ottomans the *sanjaks* of Nablus, Safad and Ajlun in addition to the title *amir al-hajj*. He bequeathed Nablus to one of his sons, possibly Korkmaz, and Ajlun to another son, Dali Ali, or Cherkes Ali. Consequently, the Qanṣuh family, which governed Ajlun and held the post of *amir al-hajj*, was enraged. In 1592, Aḥmad Qansuh claimed Ajlun but Mansur was the one who kept it, in addition to Safad and the title *amir al-hajj*. In return, Mansur agreed to pay 500,000 *filoris*, but he submitted only 100,000, which brought the Porte to demand the balance, but neither he nor those who governed on his behalf met the payment's deadline set for December 1592–January 1593. Consequently, both Mansur and his son fell into disfavor in the Ottoman court. Mansur who misused the revenues from his territories and employed forced labor, was executed in December 1593. Korkmaz met a similar fate after attempting to flee. This marked the beginning of the family decline.[53] Thereupon, Mansur Furaykh became the bey of Ajlun, and his son Aḥmad was appointed shortly afterward. Aḥmad Qansuh was also the *amir al hajj* and one of his brothers became the governor of Karak and Shawbak. However, Mansur Furaykh managed to be reappointed as *amir al-hajj* and *sanjkbeyi* of Ajlun. Aḥmad Qansuh defeated Mansur Furaykh and obtained recognition from the Porte as the legitimate leader in that region. Mansur Furaykh was still recognized as the tax collector (*multazim*) of the *sanjaks* of Safad, Nablus, and Ajlun as well as *amir al-hajj* until early 1593. The upshot was that Aḥmad Qansuh turned into a rebel. He relied on help from the Mafarija and from a base in Hawran he tried to raid the caravan, which made its way to Mecca, but he was pursued by troops sent by the governor of Damascus and died shortly afterward. It appears that he was the *sanjakbeyi* of Ajlun during the reign of Murad III (1546–1595). He was probably poisoned by the order of the Ottoman authorities.[54]

The next to lead the Qansuh family was Aḥmad (1595–1616) whose son Ḥamdan was appointed as *sanjakbeyi* of Ajlun and Karak-Shawbak where he kept the Bedouins under control. He was still *sanjakbeyi* when the Ali Janbulad's rebellion erupted and Murad Pasha tried to suppress it. Ḥamdan seems to have taken part in the Ottoman fight to suppress Janbulad's rebellion.

By 1612, Ajlun, Karak, and Shawbak came under Farrukh who was also the *sanjakbeyi* of Nablus and the *amir al-hajj*. Hawran was assigned to Shaikh Rashid. When asked by Amr Ibn Jabr to dislodge Farrukh from his position, Ali Ma'an, son of Fakhr al-Din, managed to defeat Farrukh and his Damascene Janissaries. Consequently, Ḥamdun Qansuh was reinstated in Ajlun and Amr Ibn Jabr in Hawran. When Farrukh and the Damascene Janissaries pursued Ḥamdan he sought refuge with the tribe of al-Ayid in Gaza, while Amr accompanied Ali Ma'an to his home in Jabal Druze. The governor of Damascus, Aḥmad Pasha al-Ḥafiz, gave reprieve to Ḥamdan and reappointed him as the *sanjakbeyi* of Ajlun.

This state of affairs continued until the governor was recalled to Istanbul in April 1615. Then the Qansuh family began to lose their influence and Fakhr al-Din Ma'n had the opportunity to extend his influence as their ally. Ḥamdan was taking refuge with the al-Ḥayar Bedouins near Ḥama when his two brothers, Sayf and Bashir made peace with Banki Mustafa who was then the *sanjakbeyi* of Ajlun. Their brother Ḥamdan was reappointed as the *sanjakbeyi* of Ajlun in 1616. Upon his arrival in Ajlun, he killed his brother Sayf who fled to Shaikh Rashid who was Qansuh's traditional enemy, and who was in Balqa at that time. Rashid joined forces with Bashir Qansuh against Ḥamdan who died shortly afterward.[55]

Ḥamdan's death caused a division among the Qansuh family. His son Aḥmad managed to succeed his father as the *sanjakbeyi* of Ajlun. However, he had to struggle against his uncle and cousins. Relying on help from Shaikh Amr, he controlled Ajlun from 1616 until 1619, when Ibn Qalawun replaced him. At the same time, Shaikh Rashid replaced Amr in Hawran.

Ibn Qalawun had to rely on help from Bashir in order to enter Ajlun. Bashir then moved against his nephew Aḥmad. After losing Ḥawran, Shaikh Amr sought help from Fakhr al-Din Ma'n against his rival Shaikh Rashid, but he had to wait for the Porte's approval, which came in September-October 1619. Amr regained Ḥawran and Aḥmad was installed in Ajlun. Hearing about the Porte's decision, Ibn Qalawun fled to Damascus, while Shaikh Rashid went to find refuge with the Hayaris near Ḥama. Aḥamd Qansuh went to take Ajlun and Amr proceeded to the Hawran.

By the end of the eighteenth century, droughts, disease and other natural disasters pushed many of the tribes in Jordan's direction. This was the beginning of the conflict between the Bedouin tribes and the villagers, and then among the Bedouins themselves who fought for grazing land. When arable land fell into the hands of the tribal leaders, they found it difficult to motivate the Bedouins to cultivate the land. Consequently, they had to rely on the villagers. The process of recruiting Bedouins to work on the land proved to be difficult, since they disdained such work. At times, the Bedouins had conflicts with the authorities in Istanbul.

As in the previous centuries, the Ottomans used the Bedouin tribes in Jordan to protect the pilgrims on their way to the *hajj*. It often occurred, however, that they did not pay them for the service or that corrupt bureaucrats kept the reward money for themselves, as happened in 1753.

Normally, the Porte's reaction to such incidents was extremely harsh, especially when it was obvious that the *amir al-ḥajj* did not fulfill his duty as it happened in that year. When pressed by the Bedouins to return the money, the *amir al-ḥajj* complied, but the sultan who heard about the incident ordered their decapitation. In revenge, the Bedouins massacred 2,000 pilgrims at the Qatrana fort on the road to the holy sites.[56]

There is no consensus among historians regarding the origin and the movements of the tribes in Jordan. There seems to be a consensus, however, that the absence of a centralized government and the harsh conditions brought these tribes to villages and urban areas where they carried out their raids. One of the reasons mentioned for the intensification of their movement in the last decades of the eighteenth century was the Saudi-Wahhabi expansion. The occupation of Syria and Palestine by Ibrahim Pasha had a similar effect.[57] Some historians hold the view Banu Sakhr were among the early Bedouin tribes who arrived in Jordan in the mid-seventeenth century. Others believe that the Anazah were prominent in the area until the nineteenth century, when Banu Sakhr became the most powerful among them. According to M. Freiherr von Oppenheim, tribes began moving toward Jordan in the early seventeenth century. It was then that the Sardiya tribe settled in the region, which extended from Balqa southward, and they were predominant in that region until the eighteenth century. At the same time, Banu Sakhr continued moving north and reached Balqa.[58]

During the eighteenth and nineteenth centuries, Balqa became a battleground where the Adwan and Banu Sakhr fought for dominance. Other tribes such as Abbad, Banu Ḥassan made alliances with one of them. By the eighteenth century, another tribe, the Ḥuwaiṭat, moved northward from Aqaba and reached Wadi al-Ḥasa. The construction of the Hejaz railroad changed the status quo considerably. Deprived of their traditional role as providers of means of transportation for goods that passed through their territory, the Bedouins felt that their service was no longer necessary. Moreover, the camel, which constituted the principal transportation animal, lost its importance. Tribes had to raise sheep and goats and thereby tended to restrict themselves to a limited area and settle there. They began to adopt a more settled lifestyle when the Porte tightened its hold on that region. Not only were they under firm control of the government, which restricted their raiding activities, but they also faced competition by agriculturalists who extended their activities in areas adjacent to their grazing lands.

Jordan's population consisted of town dwellers, villagers, and Bedouins. The Bedouins dominated the desert region east of the *ḥajj* road (*darb al-hajj*) where the Hejaz Railway was later built. They moved to the area west of the Jordan Valley where they spent the summer months. They were nomads who moved constantly in search of water and grazing land. They lived in tents made of goat hair, raised camels, sheep, and horses. Tribes tended to ally with other tribes and they settled in an area that they could call their own. The Ḥuwaiṭat dominated the areas of south around Ma'an; Banu Sakhr lived in the middle and the north, and the Adwan in the Jordan Valley and the eastern plateau, around al-Salt and Amman. Villagers came to depend on these tribes and they often reached agreements for common defense. For example, the inhabitants of al-Salt became allies with the Adwan tribe.

Villagers often fought with the tribes, as the case of Banu Sakhr's war against the villagers of the north demonstrated. The payment (*khuwah*) became the time-honored method of obtaining protection. The tribesmen's skills as warriors and the mobility of their horses gave them superiority over the villagers who had little experience in warfare. Bedouins could attack and run with ease. However, they could not be effective in hilly or forested areas, and against villagers who used firearms against them. In the open terrain, however, only the intervention of the government and its forces could save the villagers from attacks by Bedouins. Even the Porte preferred to avoid an armed encounter by payment or by persuasion. When the Porte sent a military force, it usually exterminated the Bedouin assailants.

The German explorer Gottlieb Schumacher mentions in his *Northern Ajlun* that the Porte's military force and the villagers had massacred an entire Bedouin tribe.[59] The prominent Jewish journalist Mordechai Ben-Hilel Hacohen recalled in his diary how unruly the tribes could be. He writes:

> News came from the Lower Galilee that the Bedouins from Transjordan raid the villages and the settlement, and pillage the granaries. Some of the tribes complain and claim that in the olden days the residents of these places used to pay them a tax and therefore they claim what is "rightfully" theirs from the peasants who purchased this land; sometimes they arrive as brigands that are starved to death, and they take whatever they find, including from the shops of the [Jewish] settlement without old rights. And the Bedouins are hard-headed, all of them are armed…the government's hand will not reach them easily, [especially] with their light horses, and it seems from what Jemal Pasha has done in the Hawran and in the Druze Mountain, that the government is unwilling to antagonize the Bedouins and pursue them. There are always family ties among the various Bedouin tribes, and many of them are fighting now against the Turks under the banners of the new shariff in Mecca, the ally of the British.[60]

Yet despite the problems caused by the encounters between Bedouins and the chaos that ensued, the Bedouins became the backbone of the Hashemite regime when the Jordanian state was formed. In the words of Nahid Ḥattar, "If the monarchy in Jordan lasted until now, it owes its existence to the Jordanian tribes, which were and continued to be the backbone of the *asabiyyah* (group solidarity), on which the Jordanian state leans."[61]

A new tribal structure was formed in the second half of the nineteenth century, when the traditional conflict between the Bedouins and the peasants intersected with other concerns, such as the need to introduce reforms, to expand the agricultural base, and to develop the coastal regions of Greater Syria. Such development projects increased the demand for agricultural produce such as flower, grain, cattle, and sheep. To guarantee economic growth, it was necessary to end all domestic conflicts. This led to the establishment of hundreds of villages, towns, and independent tent communities, which became tribal fortresses. In the beginning of the twentieth century, the wars between the Bedouins and agriculturalists almost ended. The tribes became half Bedouins and half agriculturalists residing in well-knit areas. Although they were not entirely cohesive, their educated elites came after the French conquest of Syria in 1920, to Jordan where they thought they could establish a state prior to Amir Abdallah's arrival to the country in 1921.

The state's efforts to incorporate the Bedouin tribes

When Amir Abdallah announced that he came to liberate Syria, many of the inhabitants of Ma'an, Amman and other towns of Greater Syria joined him. The Jordanian tribes extended their hands to the amir and to his government, which consisted of politicians and bureaucrats of Faiṣal's royal family in Damascus. However, this harmony ended when the tribes had to pay exorbitant taxes, and their entry into government positions was blocked. As it turned out, the amir did not free all Greater Syria, and even the independence, which Transjordan gained was limited.[62]

During the 1920s and the first half of the 1930s, there was a conflict among the tribes and the Emirate of Transjordan that was established by Britain. This conflict ended in the following years. Realizing that they will not be able to control the country, the British understood that they needed to reach an understanding with the tribes. This meant that the Jewish settlement activities in Transjordan had to come to an end; that Britain would have to recognize the influence of the tribes; that they will have to recruit young Bedouins into their army; and that the bulk of the government's expenditure would have to be invested in public service and agriculture.[63]

The period between the mid-1920s and the outbreak of World War II witnessed the integration of the Bedouins into the Jordanian society but several events made the adjustment difficult. The technological changes, which took place in the 1920s, had a major impact on the Bedouin society. Their traditional occupations were threatened and they could hardly adjust to the changes. A series of droughts and the world economic crisis of 1929 had serious impact on their livelihood. Many became accustomed to raids on the settled society. One of the ways to absorb their energy was the creation of the Desert Patrol in which they were to play an important role. Thus, they fulfilled an important defensive task of providing protection. Normally, they accomplished their tasks, unless they were struck by drought or disease. Christina Phelps Grant who spent several years in the region relates an event, which helps throw light of the effectives of this system. She writes:

A certain shaykh in Trans-Jordan made a treaty with the British...

> he undertook to keep his tribesmen in order; to prevent their robbing foreigners resident in Trans-Jordan...He kept his word faithfully, to the letter, for many months: until, in fact, all the native inhabitants of Trans-Jordan began to suffer acutely from the effects of a severe drought (this happened in 1932). Finally, on one day, he and his men held up and robbed thirteen cars on the Jerusalem road, in a pass near Jericho... Of course he would guarantee that no more robberies should occur, unless Allah chose to prolong the terrible drought.[64]

As the state's needs increased and its apparatus expanded, the shaikhs lost their importance.[65] Consequently, the Bedouin tribes opposed King Abdallah's attempt to centralize the regime. They refused to submit to the state's authority and pay taxes. A major incident occurred in Kura in Ajlun in 1921, when Shaikh Klayb ash-Shrayda insisted on maintaining his local administration, and refused to be incorporated into the Irbid province. It was only after the intervention of the Royal Air Force (RAF) that his resistance was crushed. There were similar acts of rebellion during that year in Karak and Tafila. These rebellions, however, were local and they lacked nationalist characteristics, until 1923 when the Adwan uprising erupted. Local leaders such as Rufayfan al-Majali of Karak and Mithqal al-Fayiz of Banu Sakhr proved bold enough to challenge Abdallah's regime, and to press for the elimination of the Syrian influence. It was apparently for that reason that in April 1921, al-Majali made contacts with the British whose aim was to reduce Syrian influence in the Hashemite court. It is hardly possible, however, to conclude that these acts of resistance were manifestations of Jordanian nationalism, but they could be used to combat the threat of the Arab nationalist movement.[66]

When Abdallah gave preferential treatment to Banu Sakhr who constituted the backbone of his regime, the Adwan rose in rebellion. Sultan al-Adwan moved toward Amman with the Balqa tribes, and they demanded greater participation in the government. They obtained support from lower-middle-class professionals and voiced their objection to the nomination of non-Jordanians to government positions. The slogan "Transjordan for the Transjordanians" was heard for the first time. Although the rebellion was crushed, the Adwan obtained more government posts and there was greater emphasis on equality, efficiency and fair taxation. In addition, the most vocal among the Arab nationalists were expelled. Shaikh Adwan and Abdallah came to the conclusion that cooperation was in their best interest. Moving from the southern region whose tribal population was loyal to him, he continued northward, courting some tribes, cajoling others and showering gifts and benefits on them. His contacts with the local leaders and the notables were personal and informal, despite the existence of the state's bureaucracy. It was precisely because the tribes were initially hostile to Hashemite and Syrian rule that he found it necessary to coax them into cooperation. By nominating tribal leaders to government positions, he hoped to gain their support. The case of Mithqal al-Fayiz who was chosen to represent the northern Bedouins in the Legislative Council in 1929 serves to illustrate this point. Al-Fayiz obtained additional posts that increased his influence, and his son Akif followed that tradition. Abdallah's effort to recruit Bedouins to top positions in the Arab Legion should be viewed in a similar light.[67]

In preparation for the first elections of the newly established Emirate of Transjordan in 1929, the Bedouin Control Law replaced the Tribal Courts Law of 1924. It defined who was a Bedouin. Eleven tribes were identified, but many subsections of Banu Sakhr and Ḥuwaiṭat were listed as independent. In 1936, a new law was introduced, which divided the desert region into three parts at the center were Banu Sakhr; in the north were al-Sirḥan, Banu Khalid and al-Isa; and in south were the Ḥuwaiṭat, al-Ḥajaya, al-Saidiyeen, Banu Aṭiya, and al-Shararat. As the state assumed responsibility over providing basic services, the leaders of the tribes were absorbed and amalgamated into the system. This caused them to lose much of their influence, as the president of Mu'ta University, Adnan Bakhit, told Schirin Fathi:

> The state by virtue of providing security, spending and jobs is replacing gradually, not totally, all these loyalties…functions previously fulfilled by the tribe are now taken by the state and, more than that, the tribal leadership has been amalgamated within the system.[68]

Abdallah's efforts to win the loyalty of the tribes were crucial for the state-building process. As for the British, they were divided over the way to deal with the tribes. Whereas John Philby advocated greater representation for the tribes, which would have reduced the state's ability to control them, Fredrick Peake sought to exclude Bedouins from state institutions, a step which only alienated the tribal leaders and led to non-cooperation. By contrast, both John Glubb and Abdallah advocated Bedouin participation. While Glubb incorporated them into the Arab Legion, Abdallah courted them and thereby gained their subordination and loyalty to the state.[69]

The disorder in Transjordan caused agriculture to stagnate until the end of 1930, when several groups of Bedouins started giving it priority. It was then that the time-honored practice of raiding settled communities ended. This was the result of the educational renaissance, which gradually changed the Bedouin mentality. This period saw the beginning of the attempts to incorporate Bedouins into the country's social and cultural life. Education was the vehicle that allowed them to be incorporated in the society. Shaikh Awdah used to say that he believed in in defending his tribe and containing others so that they would not invade areas occupied by the Ḥuwaiṭat. He claimed that he conducted raids for self-defense, for preserving the honor of his tribe, and for providing protection to those who depended on him. This was a customary and legal practice in the Bedouin community at that time. A tribe that did not raid had to expect raids by others. Awdah who was known for his uprightness and moral principles did not raid to humiliate other tribes. In fact, at one time, he raided a tribe whose members rebelled against its leader and dismissed him from his position.[70]

No significant changes occurred in the lives and the customs of the Jordanian tribes during the Ottoman period. Tribes fought for survival and therefore raiding and killing was common. Most of what later became the Emirate of Transjordan was desert, which explains why the fight over arable land was so intense. Each tribe was led by a *shaikh* who represented an independent political unit. Every tribe constituted a mini state and its members had common origin and a patriarch, which all recognized. He was the founding father and the source of the tribe's legitimacy. Every tribe had other individuals that joined it at some point, such as clients (*mawali*) or common members of other tribes. The strong bond of each tribe was the instinct of self-preservation and protection against common enemies. This sentiment of solidarity, which Ibn Khaldun called *asabiyya*, promoted cohesion, and allowed the Bedouin tribes to survive in a hostile environment. These Bedouins were eventually integrated in the Jordanian society, confirming what Ibn Khaldun said about them. He writes:

> Evidence for the fact that the Bedouins are the basis of, and prior to, sedentary people is furnished by investigating the inhabitants of any given city. We shall find that most of its inhabitants originated among Bedouins dwelling in the country and villages of the vicinity. Such Bedouins became wealthy, settled in the city, and adopted a life of ease and luxury, such as exists in the sedentary environment.[71]

The tribes of Transjordan have contributed to the country's development. Some of the prominent tribesmen mentioned by historians were Muhammad al-Hussein, Mithkal al-Faiz, Hussein al-Tarawanah, Ṣaliḥ al-Awdan, Sa'id al- Mufti, Shams al-Din Sami, Awda al-Qasus, Ata Allah al-Saḥimat, Najib Abu al-Sh'r, Sulayman al-Rwasan, and Salim Abu al-Ghanam. Nevertheless, the relations between the Bedouins and the urban dwellers were sometimes tense even though the Hashemites regarded them as the backbone of their regime.

Several anecdotes will help to illustrate the devotion and sacrifice of the tribes. Sulayman Musa reminds us that when the armies of Ibrahim Pasha entered Syria he stopped at Karak where he met its Shaikh Ibrahim al-Dhamour, and asked him to surrender the keys to the castle. Al-Dhamour told him that he was entrusted with the key, and that he will not surrender it to anyone but the people of Karak. Ibrahim threatened him, saying that if he did not surrender the key he will put his son to death. Then al-Dhamour brought the matter to his wife who answered that the trust of the people of Karak was more important. Hearing that, Ibrahim Pasha put the son to death.

In 1910, the people of Karak revolted against the forced recruitment of their young men. Qadr Pasha al-Majali was the one who led the revolt. When asked why he sacrificed himself even though he did not have sons, his answer was that all sons of Karak were his. He was killed and many tribesmen fell victims to plunder. When Glubb asked the *shaikhs* of Banu Hassan permission to recruit their sons to fight against the Iraqi rebels, they refused. Glubb took revenge of Banu Hassan by denying them entry into the Jordanian army. When the first constitutional assembly met in 1928, six of its tribesmen refused to sign the treaty with Britain, while others demanded changes in its clauses. The tension between the Mandatory government and the tribes persisted, but the Bedouins demonstrated their devotion to the Hashemites on numerous occasions. The events of the stormy days of the late 1950s demonstrated that the Bedouins were reliable allies of the king. Describing the response of the Bedouins to King Hussein's predicament at that time Lu'ayy Fayiz al-Nu'aymat writes:

> The Bedouins are known for their discretion, and most of the words repeated on their lips are "Allah" and "honor." The officers of the military units were from among the sons of the Bedouin tribes in Zarqa, and other locations. They were debating among themselves regarding the conditions that prevailed. For weeks their loyalty was an object of trail. If they let the king who is the descendent of the Prophet, to be harmed, they would bring eternal shame on themselves and their tribes. In the hour that preceded breakfast, in the month of Ramadan, they gathered in circles and waited for the call for prayer and the breakfast which followed, and then it occurred to them that they needed to make a definite decision that they will stand beside the king.[72]

In a letter to his nephew Amir Ghazi bin Muhammad, King Hussein extolled the virtues of the tribes, saying that they have been highly appreciated for their service to the country.[73]

Following the Palestine War of 1948, the West Bank was incorporated into the Hashemite Kingdom of Jordan, which became independent two years earlier. This ended the first stage in the history of modern Jordan. By the 1950s, a new independence movement came out of the struggle for national liberation and clashed with the regime. At that point, the tribes became divided along the Bedouin-agriculturist line. The sons of the agriculturalists joined political parties, particularly the Ba'th and the Communists. Some of them became soldiers who followed the Egyptian example, and turned into the Jordanian Free Officers who failed in their mission because the sons of the Bedouin tribes sided with the king. With the rise of Wasfi Tall the Jordanian state became highly influenced by the populist and socialist Nasserite-Ba'thist ideology. The state was armed with strong intelligence, a large bureaucracy and an army, which incorporated the tribes. This is what enabled it to face challenges such as the one posed by the Palestinians in 1970.

With help from Syria in the 1970s and Iraq in the 1980s, and occasional grants from the Gulf countries, the regime proved capable of bolstering the alliance with Bedouin tribes, which enabled it to survive. This was done by expanding the state's apparatus and the public sector; absorbing the members of the tribes in most organizations and positions; building infrastructure in the Bedouin villages; and expanding the health and educational systems. Attempts to settle Bedouins were made normally after harsh conditions, which caused unrest among them. For example, in 1962, southern Jordan was hit by torrential rain, storms and snowfall. The government was faced with the need to provide relief, and a plan to develop the Jordanian desert was brought to the fore. The plan called for forming a Bedouin committee whose task was to establish model villages, with the help of industrial and construction executives. Then it was decided to choose a place where the new villages were to be built. They agreed that the location ought to have arable land and, be close to the main roads and to water resources. The plan was studied by architects who determined that the villages would have houses, mosques, markets, health facilities, places for social gathering, and schools. Within the next five years, eight model villages were established, with 227 homes, only three of which were large, and the rest had single rooms. These villages were built at Ḥasa, Qatrana, Adhra' Ayl, Abu-al-Lin, al-Qarin, al-Farzaḥ, and al-Qawirah. The plan had little success since the Bedouins had no desire to settle and there were not enough sources of income in the spot chosen for the project.[74]

The Jordanian government was never satisfied with symbolic relations with the Bedouin tribes. It started by incorporating them into the army and the security forces, and thereby facilitated their incorporation into the society. Thus, they became a force capable of deterring threats from one tribe to another. Moreover, the government established itinerary schools for the Bedouins, particularly for those who were about to enlist in the army. These steps accelerated the process by which the government incorporated the Bedouins into modern society. By doing so, the government not only managed to incorporate the Bedouin community into its army and political institutions but also left the tribal leaders with considerable autonomy as representatives of their tribes in the state.[75] All the external challenges, which the Jordanian state faced such as that of the threat of the Wahhabis in the 1920s, the

Nasserites in the 1950s and 1960s, and the Palestinians in the 1970s, were possible to overcome due to the internal cohesion of the Jordanian state and the positive role, which the tribes fulfilled in it. However, the relations between the regime and the Bedouins was far from being smooth and occasional periods of tension interrupted the harmony, which the Hashemites sought to achieve. The tribes were often blamed for disorderly conduct and for disrupting the election campaign.

In 1989, there were riots in Tafila, Karak, Madaba, and al-Salt, which resulted in many casualties. The prices of bread and animal feed rose. One of the tribesmen, Na'if al-Kharisha led the demonstration in front of the prime minister's office, but he was immediately arrested. Banu Sakhr demonstrated against the harsh measures taken by the government but they remained loyal to the regime.[76] In 1994, the Hashemite regime sent forces to Ma'an in order to disarm the tribes that helped to establish the state, stood against invasions of Wahhabis and riots of Palestinians, and acted as deterrent to an Israeli conquest in the east. In August 1996, the regime sent an army to capture tribal fortresses in Karak and in Ma'an. A similar attempt was made in February 1998. Moreover, the regime expelled political activists from among the tribes, which only lead to the development of independent political awareness and opposition to the state.

During the Ottoman age, the government maintained firm control over the region, which led to the emergence of permanent centers such as Karak, al-Salt, and Ajlun. At the same time, however, its hold on the desert region east of the Jordan River was far from being firm. When the region was divided following the collapse of the Ottoman Empire, new states with well-defined boundaries emerged, and the Bedouins found themselves residing in several countries. This state of affairs led to problems not only between the Bedouins and the political establishments of the various states in which they found themselves residing, but also among the tribes. The Bedouins of Syria and Iraq lost their independent judicial institutions as early as 1958. By contrast, the Bedouins in Transjordan continued to enjoy judicial freedom until 1976.

The secret of the state's ability to deal with domestic and foreign challenges is that it had the flexibility to build a bureaucracy that absorbed not only the traditional heads of the tribes but also the educated sons of the tribes, the nationalists and the leftists. The state continued to maintain a role of guardian of human rights and the welfare of all its citizens. It embraced the idea that Bedouins and agriculturalists are equal. It distanced itself from commerce and encouraged contempt toward wealth and extravagance. For those who were absorbed by the state's institutions, the new ideas of social justice were appealing and elevating the tribes seemed natural.[77] The tribes helped the Hashemite regime consolidate its power, but they were by no means the only pillar on which the regime leaned.[78] Nevertheless, their service remained indispensable.

Far from dissociating themselves from their tribal heritage, the Hashemites continued to construct a national ideology based of their association with the Bedouins.[79] These efforts manifested themselves by the regime's attempts to display tribal modes of behaviors and objects associated with them such as food, clothes, and ornaments, in a highly positive light. The Jordanian government, as Linda Layne has demonstrated in her study about the customs of the tribes in

Jordan, made an effort during the last few decades, to integrate all tribal identities into one, in order to promote Bedouinism in a general way, rather than encourage each tribe to develop on its own. To achieve that, the government took legal steps and used symbols from the material culture of all tribes, in order to transform them into one source of national pride and common heritage.[80]

Notes

1 al-Samādi, p. 16.
2 Jordan in the Late Middle Ages, p. 15.
3 Rogan, p. 38.
4 *Ibid*, p. 40.
5 *Ibid*, p. 48.
6 *Ibid*, pp. 51–52.
7 Riad Nasser, *Recovered Histories and Contested Identities: Jordan, Israel, and Palestine* (Lanham, MD: Lexington Books, 2011), p. 125.
8 *Ibid*, p. 126.
9 *Ibid*.
10 *Ibid*, pp. 128–129.
11 Muḥammad 'Abd al-Ḥamīd al-Ḥamad, *Tarīkh al-Sharkas wa-Al-Anzūr al-Adīghah wa-al-Shīshān wa-al-Daghistān, wa al-Astīn* (History of the Circassians, al-Anzur al-Adigha, the Daghastani Chechens and al-Astin), Arabic text (Syria: Al-Raqqah, 2001), p. 94.
12 There is no sufficient evidence to implicate Circassians in the civil unrest, which took place during the 1860s and 1870s. Brad Dennis, "Patters of Conflict and Violence in Eastern Anatolia Leading Up to the Russo-Turkish War and the Treaty of Berlin," *War and Diplomacy: The Russo-Turkish War of 1877-1878 and the Treaty of Berlin*, Edited by Hakan Yavuz with Peter Sluglett (Salt Lake City: The University of Utah Press, 2011), p. 277.
13 Norman N. Lewis, *Nomads and Settlers in Syria and Jordan* (Cambridge, UK: Cambridge University Press, 1987), p. 101.
14 Rogan, p. 76.
15 Majd al-Din Khemash, "al-Sharkas fī al-Urdun, al-indimāj al-ijtimā'ī," (The Circassians in Jordan, the Social Assimilation), Arabic text, *Min al-ma'ālim al-thaqāfīyah wa-al-ḥaḍāriyah fī-al-Urdun 'abra al-'usūr*, Vol. II, p. 51.
16 Steuart Erskine, *The Vanished Cities of Arabia* (London: Hutchinson & Co, 1925), pp. 250–251.
17 Lewis, *Nomads and Settlers in Syria and Jordan*, pp. 101, 107–108, 111–112.
18 Michael Galikowski, "Jerash in Early Islamic Times," *Oriente Moderno*, Nuova serie, Anno 23 (84), No. 2 (2004), pp. 470–472. http://www.jstore.org/stable/25817944.
19 Sir John Mandeville, *The Book of Marvels and Travels*, Translated with an Introduction and Notes by Anthony Bale (Oxford UK: Oxford University Press, 2012), p. 52.
20 Memorandum from the Office of the British Resident, Transjordan, 4 March 1942. The National Archive (TNA), Kew Gardens, London, FO 371/313/81/E2363.
21 Rogan, p. 81.
22 Géraldine Chatelard, "The Constitution of Christians Communal Boundaries and Spheres in Jordan," *Journal of Church and State*, Vol. 52, No. 3 (Summer 2010), p. 476.
23 *Ibid*, p. 480.
24 *Ibid*, pp. 495–497.
25 K. Louisa Gandolfo, "The Political and Social Identities of the Palestinian Christian Community in Jordan," *Middle East Journal*, Vol. 62, No. 3 (Summer 2008), p. 439.
26 *Ibid*, pp. 440–441.
27 *Ibid*, p. 450.

28 Yehuda David Einstein, *Otzar Masa'ōt: Kovetz tiyūrīm shel nos'īm Yehudīm be-Eretz Yisraël, Suryah, Mitzrayim ve-aratzōt acheirōt* (A Compendium of Jewish Travels) Hebrew Text with title in English) (Tel Aviv, No date and No publisher): p. 29.
29 *Ibid*, p. 133.
30 Early Travels in Palestine, Comprising the narratives of Arculf, Willibald, Bernard, Saewulf, Sigurd, Benjamin of Tudela, Sir John Maundeville, *De La Brocquière and Maundrell*, Edited by Thomas Wright (London: Henry G. Bohn, 1848), p. 438.
31 Einstein, p. 291.
32 Reverend James Aitken Wylie who visited the Jericho region in 1883, tells us that of a copious spring known as the Fountain of Elisha, and that "It bubbles up in a gravely basin at the foot of the mountain, and as we drank its waters at table, we can attest that they are still sweet." Reverend James Aitken Wylie, LLD., *Over the Holy Land* (London: James Nisbet & CO, 1883) p. 191.
33 *Sefer Hatzyonūt*, pp. 90–96.
34 Tabenkin, Vol. I, p. 146.
35 Arlozoroff, pp. 131–132.
36 Ben Yerucham, p. 546.
37 Qaḍīyat shirā' al-arāḍi, pp. 33–34.
38 Elath, pp. 108–109, 112.
39 Nordau, pp. 152–153.
40 Bashīr, pp.11–12.
41 Gilbert, p. 536.
42 Mohammed Izzat Darwazeh, 97 Years Autobiography: A long side with Arab movements and Palestinian cause, Memories and Registrations, Vol. V, *Arabic text with title in English* (Beirut: Dār al-Gharb al-Islāmi, 1993), p. 532.
43 Muhammad 'Ali al-Sawirki, *Al-Kurd wa-al Hashemiyyūn: Tarikh hāfil bil-sadāqa wa-al wafā'* (The Kurds and the Hashemites: A History Replete with Friendship and Faithfulness) Arabic text, *Sardam al-'Arabi*, Vol. 6, No. 24 (Summer 2009), pp.76–86.
44 Cited in Linda L. Layne, "National Representations of Tribal Life in Jordan," *Urban Anthropology and Studies of Cultural Systems and World Economic Development*, Vol. 16, No. 2 (Summer 1987), p. 187.
45 Layan Fuleihan, "Urban Nomads in Petra: An Alternative Interpretation of the Bedoul Bedouin's Relationship with History and Space," *Consilience: The Journal of Sustainable Development*, Vol. 6, No. 1 (2011), p. 102.
46 Cited in Layne, "National Representation," p. 190.
47 Linda L. Layne, *Home and Homeland: The Dialogics of Tribal Identities in Jordan* (Princeton, NJ: Princeton University Press, 1994), p. 103.
48 Alec Seath Kirkbride, "Changes in Tribal Life in Trans-Jordan," *Man*, Vol. 45 (March–April 1945), p. 40. http://www.jstore.org/stable/2792948.
49 Waṣfi Zakarīya, *'Ashā'ir al-Shām* (The Tribes of Syria), Arabic text (Dimashq: Maṭba'at Dār al-Hilāl, 1945), pp. 128–135.
50 Zahr al-'Annābī (Fāṭimah al-Zahrah Ghrabī), *Urdun, al-Bashāir fī 'ūyūn al-badaw wa-al-'Ashāir* (Jordan, the Auguries in the eyes of the Bedouins and the Tribes), Arabic text, Vol. I (Irbīd: al-Rumantīk lil-Abḥath wa-al-Ḥirāsāt, 2004), pp. 56–57.
51 Aḥmad 'Uwaydi al-'Abbādī, *Al-'Ashā'ir al-Urdunīyah: al-ard wa-al- insān wa al-tarīkh: Jawlāwa-liqā'at ma'a ba'ḍ al-'ashā'ir al-Urdunīyah fī 'ami 1985, 1986* (The Jordanian Tribes: The Land, the People and the History: Meetings with some Jordanian Tribes in the years 1985, 1986), Arabic text ('Amman: Al-Dār al-'Arabīyah lil-tawzī' wa-al-nashr, 1988), pp. 10–11.
52 Abdul-Rahim Abu-Husayn, *Provincial Leadership in Syria, 1575–1650* (Beirut: The American University of Beirut, 1985), pp. 161–164.
53 *Ibid*, pp. 154–160.
54 *Ibid*, p. 173.
55 *Ibid*, pp. 176–178.

56 Benjamin Shwadran, *Jordan: A State of Tension* (New York: Council for Middle Eastern Affairs, 1959), p. 84, n. 4.
57 Schirin H. Fathi, *Jordan-An Invented Nation?: Tribe-State Dynamics and the Formation of National Identity* (Hamburg: Deutsches Orient-Institut, 1994), pp. 74, 79.
58 M. Freiherr von Oppenheim, *Die Beduinen-stämme in Palästina, Transjordan, Sinai, Hedjâz* (The Bedouin Tribes in Palestine, Transjordan, Sinai, Hejaz), German text (Leipzig: Otto Harrassowitz, 1943) Band II, p. 177. Cited in Fathi, p. 74.
59 Musa, p. 90.
60 Mordechai Ben-Hillel Hacohen, *Wars of the Nations: An Eretz Israel Diary 1914–1918, Vol. II, Hebrew Text with Title in English* (Jerusalem: Yad Yizhak Ben Zvi Publications, 1985), p. 683. Entry for July 23, 1917. [Parentheses are mine].
61 Nāhiḍ Ḥattar, *Taḥāwwulāt Jidhrīyah fī al-Urdun 1994–2004* (Radical Transformations in Jordan), Arabic text (Al-Qāhirah-al-maḥrūsah lil-nashr wa-al-khadamāt al-ṣaḥafīyah wa-al-ma'lumāt, 2004), p. 111.
62 *Ibid*, pp. 112–113.
63 *Ibid*, p. 114.
64 Christina Phelps Grant, *The Syrian Desert: Caravans, Travel and Exploration* (London: A&C Black Ltd., 1937), pp. 214–215.
65 Joseph M. Hiatt, "State Formation and the Incorporation of Nomads: Local Change and Continuity among Jordanian Bedouin," *Outwitting the State*, Edited by Peter Skalník (New Brunswick, NJ: Transaction Publishers, 1989), p. 78. Cited in Renate Dieterich, *Transformation oder Stagnation? Die jordanische Demokratisierungspolitik seit 1989* (Hamburg: Deutsches Orient-Institut, 1999), p. 119.
66 Fathi, p. 92.
67 *Ibid*, p. 94.
68 Cited *Ibid*, p. 182.
69 Toby Dodge, An Arabian Prince, English Gentleman and the Tribes East of the Jordan River: Abdullah and the Creation and Consolidation of the Trans-Jordanian state, Occasional Paper 13, Center of Near and Middle Eastern Studies (SOAS), University of London, May 1994, p. 28.
70 Zahr al-'Annābī (Fāṭimah al-Zahrah Ghrabī), *Silsilah fī bunyat al-'aql al-Urdunī* (A Series in the Structure of the Jordanian Mentality), Arabic text (Irbīb: Zahr al-'Annābī, 2003), p. 135.
71 Ibn Khadûn, *An Introduction to History: The Muqaddimah*, translated from the Arabic by Franz Rozenthal, Abridged and Edited by Nessim Joseph Dawood (London: Routledge and Kegan Paul, 1967), p. 93.
72 Lu'ayy Fāyiz al-Nu'aymāt, *Al-Ṭayyib al-kabīr: jawānib min ḥayāt al-Ḥusayn* (The Great Good: Aspects from Al-Hussein's Life), Arabic text ('Ammān: Da'irat al-Maktabah al-Waṭanīyah, 2003), p. 89.
73 *Jordan Times*, July 4, 1998.
74 Ṣalāḥ Musṭafā al-Fawwāl, *Al-Badāwah al-'Arabīyah wa-al-Tanmīyah* (The Arab Bedouins and the Development), Arabic text (Maktabat al-Qāhirah al-ḥadīthah, 1967), pp. 332–334.
75 Muhammad Abū Hasān, *Al-Qadh'a al-'ashāïri fi al-Urdun* (Leaders of the Tribes in Jordan), Arabic text ('Ammān: Lajnat tarīkh al-Urdun, 1993), pp. 19–20.
76 Ya'qūb Ziyādin, *Sḥāhid 'ala al-'aṣr* (Looking at the Decade), Arabic text ('Ammān: Dār al-Karmal lil-nashr wa-al-tawzī,' 2003), pp.145–147.
77 Ḥattar, p. 116.
78 Fathi, p. 9.
79 Andrew Shryock, *Nationalism and the Geneological Imagination: Oral History and Textual Authority in Tribal Jordan* (Berkeley: University of California Press, 1997), p. 7.
80 Linda L. Layne, "The Dialogies of Tribal Self-Representation in Jordan," *American Ethnologist*, Vol. 16, No. 1 (February 1989), p. 35.

VIII The formative years of the Hashemite Kingdom

Jordan experienced unusual hardships during the late Ottoman period. The Young Turks had brazenly demonstrated their hostility toward the country's population and taxes were raised to finance the Balkan wars. The country's participation in World War I and the forced recruitment of the inhabitants of the region added to the popular discontent. The Turkish authorities confiscated food supplies to feed their soldiers, and even the beasts of burden were taken. The inhabitants of Ajlun complained bitterly against the recruitment and death of many of their young men. The year 1910 marks the apogee of Turkish tyrannical rule. Sami Pasha al-Faruqi embarked on a campaign aimed at disarming the population in the Hawran and he taxed them heavily. The inhabitants of Transjordan expressed their sympathy toward the Hawranis and the Druze and when he tried to impose similar measures on the people of Karak, they immediately rebelled. When the state announced the conscription on the Saturday of 13 August 1914, the country went through a rough period having to supply all the army's needs.

This period became ingrained in the memory of the local inhabitants as the "Safar Birlak days." It was named after a village where these draconian measures were applied with utmost severity. Young men were conscripted and those who attempted to escape were severely punished. People were robbed and their possessions were confiscated. Corruption increased and chaos prevailed. The *Jandarma* followed those who refused to hand over their belongings to the war effort. Furthermore, the Turkish government attempted to prevent the Bedouins from taking *khuwah* from those whom they protected.

On July 1918, the Turkish army under the German commander Liman Von Sanders withdrew and the end of the Ottoman state in Syria was announced. Jemal Pasha, the Turkish commander who led the Eighth Regiment, left Damascus on his way to Istanbul. When the Entente forces entered Damascus the city's notables gathered, they agreed to form a provisional national government, and hoisted the Arab flags on the government's buildings. This was done in the name of Sharif Hussein bin Ali King of the Hejaz. They asked Amir Sa'id al-Abd al-Qadir al-Jaza'iri to take control and establish order with Faişal's help. Sa'id took control and declared himself head of the Provisional Government. However, Faişal who was on his way to Damascus sent Sharif Naşir bin Ali a message to nominate Ali Riddah

DOI: 10.4324/9781003450313-9

Pasha al-Rikabi as military governor of the northern region, and Transjordan was incorporated to it. Faişal arrived in Damascus in October 1918, and was warmly received by its inhabitants. Syria was organized into eight provinces, three of which were in Transjordan; Karak, Balqa, and Hawran. This was the first attempt to establish an Arab state with Damascus as its capital.

Following their arrival to Damascus, the Arab armies conquered the northern part of the country. They entered Ḥims on October 10, 1918, Ḥama on October 16, and Aleppo on 25. These areas were considered part of the eastern region of the conquered enemy land. Transjordan and Jabal Druze were added as part of the region that came under Faişal's Arab government. The attempt to incorporate Lebanon failed and Faişal's government dominated modern-day Syria and Transjordan. In November 1918, General Edmund Allenby divided Syria into three military regions: the southern region that included Jerusalem, Acre, and Nablus was placed under British administration; the northern or western region that included the Lebanon Mountain and the coastal region from Acre to Iskanderun was placed under French administration, and the eastern region that included Damascus, Ḥama, Ḥawran, Karak, and southern Aleppo was placed under Arab control. However, Faişal was not content with this arrangement and he began planning to establish a new state.

Such were the conditions when Faişal's government took over. His government expanded the bureaucracy and nominated officials to carry out its orders and maintain security. The need to establish security brought the military governor to establish order by himself. The government began the task of reconstruction, particularly in al-Salt and its villages. It had to interfere in order to settle disputes between the inhabitants of the village al-Faḥis and the Turcomans who fought over land. When the *qaimaqam* of al-Salt asked that the government provide seeds to the inhabitants it promptly responded to his call. The government resorted to harsh measures such as confiscation of property from those who violated the law. Measures to secure peace on the route to the *hajj* were introduced, roads were maintained, and new ones were built. Special attention was paid to the Hejaz Railway project, and in 1900, it passed through 26 stations starting with at Mafraq and ending in Ma'an. The government began rebuilding the Hejaz railroad between Amman and Dar'a. The Qatranah Bridge was rebuilt, and both the telegraph and the postal systems began operating regularly throughout the country. In 1919, the railway was connected to the Hejaz and Egypt. Efforts were made to establish health facilities and to help eradicate pestilence, which had a devastating effect on agriculture. More schools were built and the education for girls expanded.

During that time, the Jordanians remained relatively unaffected by the events that took place in Greater Syria. The British Chief of Staff announced that his forces would start withdrawing from the Occupied Enemy Territory Administration by the beginning of November, except for Dera'a, Amfres and al-Salt, and stated that the British government was compelled to accept French advisors.[1] Events in other parts of Greater Syria were of little interest to the inhabitants of Transjordan as Richard Meinertzhagen told Lord George Nathaniel Curzon in a telegram from November 10, 1919:

> Trans-Jordan has remained remarkably apathetic to events in Syria. Beyond the normal inter-tribal and inter-village quarrels, which often involve the loss of life, there has been no untoward incident during the last two months. The country is very loosely administered, and the local responsibilities depend considerably on the advice of political officers.[2]

The Arab representatives who met in Damascus included several members from Transjordan. These were Sa'id al-Salibi and Sa'id Ibn Jabir from al-Salt; Abd a-Rahman Rashidat and Sulayman al-Sawdi from Ajlun; Khalil al-Talhawani from Ma'an; Abd al-Mahdi Maḥmud al-Marafi from Tafila; and Isa al-Midanat from Karak. When the Syrian conference met for the first time, a delegation from its members was elected to contact the Entente powers in Damascus. It included Khalil al-Talhuni, the representative from Ma'an. The members of this delegation maintained contact with British, French and Italian representatives in an effort to prevent the division of Syria. On November 7, 1919, the notables of Ajlun sent a telegram expressing concern about the division of Syria. It read as follows:

> Rumors had spread regarding the division of the state, which caused great excitement among us. We, heads of the tribes, notables and all the people of the Ajlun district protest with all our vigor against any attempt to divide our state. We are ready to defend [ourselves] to death until we, like the nations that benefited from the last victory…[obtain] absolute independence.[3]

The protest expanded to all the parts of Transjordan. It started in Ajlun and expanded to al-Salt, Karak, Ma'an, Tafila, and the desert regions. Amir Nawaf al-Fa'iz the head of Banu Sakhr sent a letter signed by 30,000 Bedouins to the British liaison officer in al-Salt, protesting the agreement between Britain and France regarding the division of the country, and demanded absolute independence to all Arab lands in the region. He also expressed his objection to the immigration of Jews to Palestine. The newspaper *Al-Aşimah* quoted him saying,

> We have a firm belief that the Allied countries will look into our demands in fairness, justice and the pursuit of self-determination for our country. We would not be responsible if we did not resist the hostility on our nation. We are against meddling in our country's affairs and we will not be deterred by any force that comes to the battlefield.[4]

All over Transjordan demonstrations had taken place and petitions were drafted and sent to the representatives of the Allies. The tribes of Balqa wrote a petition to the military Governor General, which read as follows:

> We the Arab tribes of the Balqa protest any measure that divides our country, deprives it from its total independence, and grants its southern part to the

> Jews. We also protest the recent agreement reached between England and France, and we announce to all that we are ready to shed blood in order to defend our country, and to preserve its unity, and we are asking the Allied powers who announced the principles of justice and the freedom all peoples to live up to their legal obligations and not to ignite the fire of dissension by violating our rights and colonizing our country or dividing it. Now, with all our might, our tongues and our hands that hold our shining swords we demand: first that the latest decision be rescinded; second that Syria remain undivided and completely independent; and third, that Wilson's principles be adhered to.[5]

Similar protests were heard in other parts of Transjordan. The issue was debated fervently in many areas, special committees were set up to discuss it, and preparations were made to create military units, to act if necessary. Funds were raised all over the country, to provide for that purpose. However, the campaign in Maysalun, which took place on July 24, 1920, and ended in French victory over the forces of the Syrian nationalists, put an end to all these dreams and Faişal had to leave Damascus.

Transjordan remained outside the stormy events that took place in the region. It was Damascus rather than Amman that underwent upheavals during the Arab Revolt and after. The most vocal voice in the region came from Damascus where the Syrian congress met in July 1919, and called for Faisal's recognition as king of an independent Syria. Living up to their promises to the French according to the Sykes-Picot Agreement, which gave Britain control over Palestine, Iraq, and Transjordan and allowed for French domination of Syria and Lebanon, the British evacuated their forces from Syria and compensated Faişal by crowning him king of Iraq. What remained thereafter was the need to compensate his brother Abdallah who suffered a major defeat by the Saudi Islamic Brotherhood (*Ikhwan*) at the Battle of Turaba in May 1919.

The new administrative changes were not conducive to centralization of power and the Bedouin tribes continued to live according to their old habits. Representatives from every part in the country came with the intension of promoting the idea of Syria's unity under Faişal and new organizations were established with that end in mind. One of these was the Arab Istiqlal, the successor of the party known as Jam'iyah al-Arabiyah al-Fatah, which was the pioneer of the idea of Syrian unity. The new party was created on December 20, 1919, and it had 40,000 members who came from all walks of life. The party platform called for total independence for the Arab states and the inclusion of Iraq and Syria in a federal union. The order envisaged by the party was decentralized. The party eliminated the influence of the notables and the local aristocracy, and when they tried to enroll, the party refused their admission.

The party members had differences with Faişal and they opposed most of his plans. They did not wish to cooperate with the French, and they helped Kemal Mustafa Atatürk in his war against the French in Cilicia. Likewise, they supported the campaign against the French at Mysalun. However, some notables who had taken the opportunity to improve relations with France. Among these were

Muhammad Fawzi al-Aẓam, Abd al-Rahman al-Yusuf, Shaikh Mithqal al-Fa'iz, and others from the Anza tribes. The people of Hawran attacked Prime Minister Ala-Din al-Darubi and Abd al-Rahman al-Yusuf, head of the Consultative Council for their cooperation with France. In Transjordan, the *qaimaqam* of Ma'an was imprisoned for hoisting the French flag on the local government house, and he wrote to Sharif Hussein asking for help. Meanwhile, the supporters of France in Hawran expressed their willingness to rebel and they obtained support in Transjordan. They sent a message to Sharif Hussein requesting that he send one of his sons to lead them in Syria in order "to hoist the French flag" there. However, after the Battle of Maysalun, the Istiqlal sent its emissaries to Egypt and the European countries to obtain their support for the party's desiderata. Some of the party members remained at home to maintain order, while others went to Transjordan and sent a telegram to Sharif Hussein, asking his help to bring Syria under Sharifi rule.

The early negotiations with Britain

Studies on the rise of the Hashemite Kingdom of Jordan consider the year 1921 a turning point and the beginning of the state. The period between the end of Turkish rule and the formation of the Emirate of Transjordan is often ignored. It was during that period that King Faiṣal laid the foundations for a large state that he believed would be under his control and it was then that Amir Abdallah arrived in Ma'an, and claimed the throne of Greater Syria. However, the British government had other plans in mind, which altered the course of Jordanian history.

The San Remo Convention of 1920 allocated Palestine to Britain. This territory included the lands east of the Jordan River, which came to be known collectively as Transjordan. This area was much larger than Palestine in the west. It was a desert inhabited by some 300,000 Arabs, with virtually no Jewish settlers. Transjordan constituted part of Faiṣal's dominions during the brief period in which he was King of Syria, until he was evicted by the French. It was this area that his bother Abdallah claimed as his kingdom. Feeling that he was unable to control Transjordan in addition to Palestine, the Commander of the Egyptian Expeditionary Force, General W. Congreve, informed Winston Churchill that without additional troops, the British advisors in Transjordan were incapable of maintaining order, since the local gendarmerie was practically useless. He said that in order to send a detachment of troops to Transjordan, it was necessary to increase the number of troops under his command, and he recommended that Britain give up the entire region east of the Jordan, in order to reduce the cost of maintaining the Palestine Mandate.[6] One of Britain's main concerns was that the Arabs would use the British territories in the Middle East, as a base for military operations against the French. When Lord Curzon expressed his concern that the Arabs might use the Britain's territories in Iraq and Transjordan to mount assaults on the French in Syria, Churchill replied that he would endeavor to devise a policy, whereby Britain would be in a position "to promise the French no attack through Trans Jordania upon them in consequence of the friendly relations we are establishing with Hussein & Sons Ltd."[7]

Fearing that Transjordan would turn into a place of opposition to their rule in Syria, the French appealed to the British to allow them to occupy the country. Reluctant to do so, the British began the process of establishing a local government in it. The High Commissioner for Palestine Herbert Samuel reassured the Jordanian notables that the British government had no intension to incorporate the country into the Palestine administration. However, the attempt failed and the local governments in this region disintegrated due to tribal dissensions. In August 1920, Sharif Hussein sent Abdallah to Ma'an, which was part of the Hejaz at that time, with a small force, which included members of the Istiqlal and some leaders and *shaikh*s from Transjordan. Abdallah and the Istiqlal regarded this cooperation as natural. Abdallah sought to restore the Hashemite regime in Syria and to evict the French from it. The Hashemites did not abandon their hope that the British would play a positive role in fulfilling their aspirations, especially in country's northern regions, and Abdallah encouraged the Istiqlal's efforts to obtain the support and cooperation of the Kemalists in Turkey. Likewise, the Istiqlal acknowledged the positive role that the Hashemite family played in Syria. The Istiqlal supported the goals of the Turkish nationalists, and did not exclude the possibility of cooperation with Britain, but it opposed any kind of assistance from France.

Three separate administrations were formed in Transjordan in September 1920: Irbid, al-Salt, and Karak. Ma'an and Aqaba were part of the Hejaz. The attempt to establish peace and order in these areas failed, since the local notables did not recognize the division, and were not loyal to it. Chaos ensued as a result. The Bedouins continued their time-honored raids on the villages and took their cattle. In the village of Ramtha, at least 80 men from both sides were killed. Peace was eventually restored until the Emirate of Transjordan was formed; however, Abdallah did not renounce his claim to Greater Syria.

Following his arrival to Ma'an, Abdallah announced that he was the king of Syria, and called the members of the Syrian conference to come to Ma'an with their troops to liberate the country. He nominated Amir Ghalib Beg al-Sha'lan to establish contact with Atatürk, with a view to obtain Turkish cooperation. Atatürk responded positively to his overture. Abdallah refused to give the country to Syrian control, especially since the French came to occupy that region.

However, after consulting with his brother Faişal, he realized that he was not in a position to fight the French, and therefore he was inclined to come to terms with them. He also contacted Churchill to learn about his attitude toward the French objectives in Syria. Meanwhile, the armed uprising against the French continued with help from the Istiqlal in Transjordan. The Arab assaults on the French forces were so frequent and unrelenting that General Henri Gouraud who commanded them, admitted that he was dealing with substantial resistance that he could not possibly contain. As it turned out, the rebellion against the French did not remain confined to the area under their control, and it spread to Transjordan, the Hawran and Jerusalem.

The Resistance to French rule in Syria began soon after the Battle of Maysalun in July 1920. The villagers in Hawran participated in the uprising, and they held a meeting where they decided to appeal to Sharif Hussein to send one of his sons to lead the resistance movement. In one of the telegrams sent to Sharif Hussein, they said, "We are the young men of Syria. We were compelled to come to this region. There is nothing that we need other than a leader to lead us."[8] This is how Abdallah arrived in Ma'an on November 11, 1920. The reason why Sharif Hussein sent his son to Ma'an was that he regarded that city as part of the Hejaz. Moreover, Abdallah saw himself taking revenge on the British who did not allow him to go to Iraq, and assume the throne after the Iraqis accepted him as king, and the Syrians agreed to his brother's Faisal's coronation in Syria. Abdallah was the only person capable of undertaking such task because Amir Ali was the crown prince of the Hejaz, while Faiṣal was in Europe with his brother after their departure from Damascus.[9] Describing the conditions in Transjordan upon Abdallah's arrival, Khayr al-Din al-Zirikli who was an eyewitness to the events writes:

> There were governments, governors, and trustworthy British civil servants in the region but…their confusion came to be dominated by ways of reason after Abdallah, who bore an official title, entered Transjordan…. There were disturbances, however, they did not take the form of a civil war. There were governments but their power was severely curtailed, and there was chaos, but it did not last long, because those who were concerned about Syria and Palestine realized that chaos will cause them money and men, and it could not last.[10]

Intense pressure on the part of the French led the British to pressure Abdallah to give up his intension to bring Greater Syria under Hashemite control. Furthermore, the governors of al-Salt and Karak informed him that they would oppose his move northward, if it was carried out "for political aims."[11] The fear that France would invade Transjordan with a view to incorporate it into its sphere of influence, and as compensation for eastern Iraq, which Britain prevented it from acquiring, spread panic among the public in Transjordan. At the same time, however, Britain's promise that a government separate from the area allocated to the Jews in the Balfour Declaration would be established in Transjordan left the public optimistic about the country's future. Moreover, Britain promised not to recruit the inhabitants of this region into their army nor to disarm them, and last but not the least, the British reassured them that they will install one of Sharif Hussein's sons as the country's leader.

When the issue of establishing a separate administration for Transjordan was discussed in the Middle East Department, most British officials agreed that there was justification for such step. In a memorandum, which they drew for use by the Cairo Conference in February 1921, Sir John Shuckburgh, Major Hubert Young, and T.E. Lawrence wrote to Churchill saying,

> The Mandate itself supplies the answer. In the first place, the preamble provides that nothing shall be done which may prejudice the civil and religious rights of existing non-Jewish communities. In the second place, article 3 obliges the mandatory to encourage the widest measure of self-Government

> for localities consistent with the prevailing conditions. We consider that these two clauses, taken in conjunction, afford adequate justification for setting up in Trans-Jordan a political system somewhat different from that in force on the other side of the river. If British promises are to stand, this system must be Arab in character. We consider that it should preferably be centralized under an Arab ruler acceptable to His Majesty's Government and acting in important matters under their advice.[12]

The local governments formed in Transjordan managed to survive, and on April 1, 1921, they were replaced by a unified administration and Abdallah became the king. Churchill who became Colonial Secretary on January 4, 1921, assumed responsibility for the British areas in the Middle East. A Middle East department was set up with T.E. Lawrence as its advisor on Arab affairs. Churchill summoned his staff to a conference, which held its meeting in Cairo on March 12, 1921. The conference members were not inclined to appoint Abdallah as king of Transjordan. Samuel believed that this was a desirable solution, while Lawrence preferred to nominate a governor for Transjordan. Lawrence feared that the French might approach Abdallah and offer him the crown in Syria, and that Transjordan would fall into French hands as a result. Major Hubert Young was also in favor of an alternative to Abdallah. However, by then, Abdallah was already established in Amman with his followers. Both Wyndham Deedes, and Major Somerset called attention to the *fait accompli*. After considering all the alternatives, Churchill told David Lloyd George,

> I have no doubt whatever that occupation of Transjordania on basis of an arrangement with Abdullah is right policy for us to adopt, and that it will afford best prospect of discharge of our responsibilities with future reductions of expense.[13]

At the Cairo Conference, Churchill confirmed Faiṣal as king of Iraq, while Abdallah was installed in in Transjordan. The arrangement was to be temporary and Abdallah was granted an annual subsidy.[14] Moreover, it was agreed that a British representative would be assigned to assist him, and that he would receive British protection when needed. Abdallah promised goodwill toward the French and the subsidy that he obtained from the British amounted to £180,000 for the fiscal year 1921–1922.[15]

The future of Abdallah and his country took a different turn following the Cairo Conference, in which Churchill announced that Transjordan would turn into an Arab annex of Palestine to be ruled by an Arab governor appointed by the High Commissioner. Abdallah told Churchill that he was incapable of discussing his country's future without consulting its leaders and their parties. Following his talks with the leaders, both sides agreed on the following:

a A nationalist government led by Amir Abdallah would be formed in Transjordan.
b Within a short time period, both sides will hold meeting with a view to accelerate the process by which the country would become independent.

- c The government would seek guidance from a commissioner whose residence would be in Amman.
- d The British government will provide the means to guarantee the country's protection.
- e Great Britain would endeavor to improve the relations between Amir Abdallah and the French. Rebels operating against the French in Syria would not be allowed to operate from Transjordan.
- f Britain will obtain a military base and an airfield in Amman.
- g This agreement would be considered limited to six months, and be extended if beneficial to both sides.[16]

The opposition to the treaty with Britain was immense and Abdallah had to introduce changes into it. However, these amendments did not change the main clauses, which safeguarded Britain's interests, and which many regarded as detrimental to Transjordan. One of the amendments changed the title "The High Commissioner" to "The British representative." While the formation of a new Transjordanian entity was being discussed, the Zionist leaders were exerting pressure on the British government to extend the boundaries of Palestine eastward, and to include Transjordan as part of the Jewish National Home. In a letter to Churchill, the Jewish leader Chaim Weizmann writes,

> It is upon these fields now that the rich plains to the north have been taken away from Palestine and given to France, that the success of the Jewish National Home must largely rest. Trans-Jordania has from the earliest time been an integral and vital part of Palestine.... The climate of Trans-Jordania is invigorating; the soil is rich; irrigation would be easy; and hills are covered with forests. There Jewish settlement could proceed on a large scale without friction with the local population. The economic progress of Cis-Jordania itself is dependent upon the development of these Trans-Jordania plains, for they form the natural granary of all Palestine and without them Palestine can never become a self-sustaining, economic unit and a real National Home.[17]

Weizmann asked Churchill to extend the southern boundary of Palestine to the Gulf of Aqaba. He regarded these areas as compensation for the loss of the northern territory, which prevented the Jews from having access to the Litani River. In addition, he attempted to persuade Churchill to incorporate the Negev in the Jewish Nation Home. However, Churchill who already decided to separate Transjordan from Palestine, remained unconvinced. The only concession that he was ready to make was to include the Negev in the Palestine Mandate.[18] However, it was Samuel who was most critical of Churchill's decision to separate Transjordan from the Palestine Mandate, arguing that crowning Abdallah as king in that region might encourage the Arabs to continue fighting against the French as well as the Zionists. Nevertheless, Churchill remained adamant, insisting that Britain's policy toward Transjordan should not differ from its policy in Iraq, and that it was essential to place a Sharifi candidate in both countries. He argued that supporting Faişal in Iraq while depriving his brother Abdallah of Transjordan "would be courting trouble."[19] Furthermore, he argued that Britain could obtain peace in Arabia only by subsidizing their father Sharif Hussein, and paying Ibn Saud to refrain from attacking the Hejaz. Moreover, he said that the decisions of the Cairo Conference were aimed at installing the entire Sharifi family "under an obligation to His Majesty's Government in one sphere or another."[20]

Like Lawrence, Churchill believed that with financial support and adequate troops Abdallah could be persuaded to convince his tribesmen to refrain from anti-Zionist activities. Neither Samuel nor his Chief Secretary, Wyndham Deedes managed to change the decision made by the Middle East Department, or dissuade Churchill who insisted that with a small force and British support Abdallah would be capable of setting up a stable government and help prevent hostile actions against the French and the Zionists.[21] When the British Cabinet met to discuss the matter on March 22, 1921, Abdallah's candidature was confirmed but there was considerable opposition to the proposal to send British troops to Transjordan. Henry Wilson noted in his diary, "We discussed Winston's proposal sent from Cairo to occupy Amman & Trans-Jordania. I was opposed-& won-on the grounds of expense and further commitment."[22]

In his meeting with Abdallah on March 27, 1921, Churchill raised the issue of the tribesmen's assault on the French police border saying, "I hear there was an attack by a band of brigands…and murder was committed. My government attributes this to your influence, but luckily I have two broad shoulders to carry the Government protest to you." Abdallah replied that he knew nothing of the incident but added, "I cannot ever, of course, prevent people from defending their own country."[23] Then Churchill told Abdallah that since Transjordan was too small to stand alone, it ought to turn into an Arab province under a governor responsible to the High Commissioner for Palestine. However, Abdallah proposed another solution, telling Churchill that if Britain was amenable to the idea that an Arab emir rule both Palestine and Transjordan, the difficulties between Arabs and Jews could be easily overcome. While Churchill was reluctant to accept Abdallah's proposal, he went out of his way to promise that the British government would not apply the Zionist clauses of the Mandate, and would not expect Transjordan to adopt any measures promoting Jewish immigration and colonization. By doing so, Churchill put an end to the hopes of the Zionists to settle the Transjordan's lands of the Bashan and the Gilead.[24]

Upon his return from the Middle East, Churchill defended his decisions regarding Transjordan, explaining that with a subsidy and a small force, Britain could obtain a stable government in that country, and that Abdallah had agreed to cooperate by preventing assaults on French and Zionist interests. Furthermore, to appease "air enthusiasts" such as Air Marshal Trenchard and others who believed that the aircraft was the most decisive weapon of the future, he said that Abdallah agreed to provide three aerodromes, and that this would enable the RAF to fly regularly between Ludd in Palestine and Amman. This arrangement, he said, would substantially reduce the cost of maintaining peace in the country.[25] Nevertheless, both the Zionists and some members of the British administration in Palestine continued to regard Churchill's plan for Transjordan unfavorably. Meinertzhagen criticized Samuel's appointment of Hajj Amin al-Ḥusseini as Mufti of Jerusalem, and argued that the separation of Transjordan from Palestine was a betrayal of Britain's pledge to the Jews. He protested directly to Churchill saying:

> I told him it was grossly unfair to the Jews, that it was yet another promise broken and that it was a most dishonest act, that the Balfour Declaration was being torn up by degrees and that the official policy of H.M.G. to establish a Home for the Jews in Biblical Palestine was being sabotaged; that I found the Middle East Department whose business it was to implement the Mandate, almost one hundred per cent hebraphobe and could not the duration of Abdallah's Emirate in Transjordan be of a temporary nature, say for seven years, and a guarantee given that Abdullah should never be given sovereign powers over what was in fact Jewish territory. Churchill listened and said he saw the force of my argument and would consider the question. He thought it was too late to alter but a time to limit Abdullah's Emirate in Transjordan might work.[26]

Although he listened carefully to those who criticized his policy regarding Transjordan, Churchill did not change his mind. Herbert Sidebotham who had a meeting with him had this to say:

> He has very high opinion of Abdullah, and his idea is that Trans-Jordania should be part of Palestine, but with a special Regime under Abdullah, analogous to Kurdistan. I said this was serious and asked what about liberty of Jewish Colonization there. There would, I understood him to say, be such liberty, but he hoped nothing would be said about it. Faire sans dire? I inquired. That would be the ideal, he said but he recognized the difficulty the Z.O. was under. They had to make propaganda in order to get funds for their work. Only he hoped that they would recognize *his* difficulty. He was enthusiast about the Jewish colonies and said that he meant to say a great deal about them in his speeches. Splendid open air men, he exclaimed, beautiful women; and they have the desert blossom like the rose.[27]

Following the collapse of the Ottoman Empire, the British faced several major problems. Chaos prevailed in Transjordan. The place was turning into a hotbed of resistance to French rule in Syria, and Abdallah who had just arrived in the country was not recognized yet as leader, despite his father's charisma and his brother's Faiṣal's fame. Furthermore, the British did not seem to have substitute for Abdallah and it was not clear whether Transjordan would be part of the Palestine mandate under the High Commissioner's purview. There were other concerns such as what would be the nature of Abdallah's relations with the French and the Syrian nationalists and there was fear that his actions might cause friction between London and Paris. There were other scenarios, which caused concern in Whitehall, such as the specter that Abdallah might insist that Transjordan was a Hejazi province, which he was liable to claim if he were to succeed his father as king. Nevertheless, the negotiations with Abdallah went on with a view to reach an agreement.

Since the very beginning of the discourse regarding the creation of a Hashemite Kingdom the British sought to exclude Palestine from the area promised to the Hashemites. Prime Minister Lloyd George instructed Mark Sykes who negotiated the agreement to divide the Arab regions of the collapsing Ottoman Empire with the French, and to secure Britain's hold on Palestine. Both Lloyd George and Lord Curzon urged Sykes to make it possible for Britain to develop Palestine under Britain's auspices. Even Sykes became convinced that the best solution was to exclude Palestine from the area given to the Hashemites, and he believed that they realized that they could not expect to incorporate it to their kingdom. He was the one who designed the general outline separating the two countries and Sir Herbert Young adjusted the political boundaries separating the two countries. Even though Transjordan was grafted on the Palestine Mandate, the British treated it as a separate entity. Only minor changes in the boundaries could be made as result of strategic, administrative, or economic considerations. The boundary change that was made in 1946 came primarily as result of the growing strategic importance of Aqaba in British eyes.[28]

The birth of the Hashemite Kingdom can be traced back to the agreement between Abdallah and Churchill, signed in March 1921, and in one of its clauses, Britain agreed to act as mediator between him and the French. In return, Abdallah pledged to refrain from supporting the military organizations in Syria and Lebanon against the French. This was made possible by convincing those who surrounded him, and especially by negotiating with the members of the Istiqlal who had considerable influence in Transjordan.

Both the British and the French authorities in Transjordan stirred conflicts among the tribes; the British in Azraq and the French in Jabal Druze. By supporting a group led by Abd al-Qadir al-Atrash, the British sought to incorporate that region to their Mandate. They also sought to incorporate Hawran into Transjordan. Basing their claim on the Sykes-Picot Agreement signed in 1916, the British sought to incorporate the southern part of the country, especially Azraq to their mandate. However, neither the great powers nor the Jordanian notables managed to reach an agreement regarding the borders. This did not seem to have negative impact on the relations between Abdallah and the Istiqlal members. Following his return from the meeting with Churchill, Abdallah nominated the Istiqlal member, Rashid Tali' to form a governing body for the emirate. Tali' assumed the title 'President of the Consultative Council' and the "Administrative Officer." He accepted the nomination on the proviso that the government would be constitutional, and that he would remain in charge of the rebellion in Hawran. On April 11, 1921, the first central government in Transjordan was born. Abdallah chose Amman as the capital of the newly established emirate, which included Ajlun, Balqa, and Moab within its boundaries. This territory turned into a refuge for those Arabs who fought against the French in Syria and the British in Palestine. The agreement between the

British government and Transjordan obligated Abdallah to accept the following provisos:

a To refrain from appointing any official who is not of a Jordanian nationality, unless the British government approves it.
b To refrain from adopting any law that prevents Britain from fulfilling its international responsibilities and obligations.
c To accept Britain's guidance and follow its advice in all administrative and financial matters
d To accept any reasonable judicial provisions introduced by Britain, with a view to protect foreign nationals
e To share the cost of maintaining the army, and accept any law that Britain introduces that affects the country's defense.
f To provide every facility to the British armed forces.
g To accept Britain's guidance in matters relating to concessions, exploitation of natural resources, construction of railways, and loan raising.
h To refrain from ceding or leasing any part of his territory to foreign powers.
i To accept Britain's regulations regarding the imposition of martial law, when such step becomes necessary.

In addition, the agreement included the following terms:

a Great Britain will be represented by a resident who will act on behalf of the High Commissioner for Transjordan who will be hosted and paid for by the Transjordan government.
b The British government will exercise the legislative powers entrusted to it under the Mandate in Transjordan through a constitutional government.
c There will be no custom barriers between Palestine and Transjordan, except by agreement.
d Transjordan will have the right to form any association, customs or otherwise, with neighboring Arab states.
e Britain will have the right to maintain armed forces in Transjordan and the Amir agrees not to raise an army without its consent.
f Britain agrees to help pay Transjordan's military and administrative expenses by occasional grants.
g Britain will have the right to exercise jurisdiction over all members of the armed forces.
h The extradition treaties between the two counties will remain valid.
i The contracting parties will be able to revise the agreement when they see fit.
j The agreement will be drawn in English and Arabic, both of which will be valid but in case of doubt or contradiction, the English version shall prevail.[29]

The Emirate's first conflict was with the British who insisted that they should have four representatives in Transjordan. Tali' nominated only one representative in Amman. This new government of Transjordan included a majority of Istiqlal members who played an important role in the anti-French position that it adopted. Khayr al-Din al-Zarkali became chief of intelligence and head of the government's council; Ghada Adil Arslan became advisor to the amir; Fuad Beg became the army chief of staff, along with Abd al-Qadir Basha al-Jundi, and Muhammad Ali Beg al-Ajluni.

By June 1921, senior officials in the Palestine administration and the Colonial Office, except Churchill, were convinced that Abdallah was not the right choice to rule Transjordan. As for Lawrence, he summarized his views regarding Transjordan as follows:

a It was desirable to leave Abdallah in charge "for the present" with a British representative, but without an infrastructure of British politicians or direct supervision from Jerusalem. This was despite of his conviction that Abdallah was coward, "lazy and by no means dominating."[30]
b Transjordan had to receive grants, including a personal allowance to be given to Abdallah, the amount of which to be determined by the degree of his cooperation.
c Abdallah's authority should be confined to the central al-Salt-Amman axis.
d Ma'an ought to be severed from the Hejaz.
e British influence ought to be expanded to Wadi Sirḥan, from Azraq to Jauf, in cooperation with the government of Transjordan. This ought to be done in order to protect the Baghdad air route, a task made difficult by the French intrigues in Rualla, and the occupation of Hail by Ibn Saud.
f Transjordan ought to be united with Palestine.
g The union with Palestine can be achieved without strong military presence in Transjordan.
h Any resistance from the Bedouins east of the Hejaz Railway ought to be dealt with a few armored cars and airplanes.
i The armored cars ought to be used in conjunction with aircraft, all under the direction of the RAF.
j The Amman-al-Salt road ought to be repaired in order to insure safe communication with Jerusalem under any weather conditions.
k The Amman-Qatrana section of the Hejaz Railway ought to be repaired and Karak occupied.
l The Reserve Force ought to be expanded and improved.[31]

Abdallah's aspirations to become the king of Greater Syria continued to stand on the way to understanding with Britain. He believed that he could use the members of the Istiqlal to achieve his ultimate objective. In 1921, he asked Tali' to assemble the members in Amman and to elect new leadership to the party. He stipulated that the party should not interfere in Transjordan's affairs. He was also in touch with Michel Lutf-Allah of the Istiqlal whose members organized a conference in Geneva on August 25, 1921 to discuss the party's objectives. The members established the organ *La Tribune de Geneve* where they published their party's desiderata. The Istiqlal members in Transjordan were determined to establish a state in Damascus under Hashemite rule. They encouraged resistance to France in Syria, and thereby put Abdallah in an uncomfortable position.

On August 12, 1921, Asad al-Atrash returned from Amman to Suwaida and hoisted the Sharifi flag on it. The French advisor in the town left immediately for Damascus. Negotiations between Paris and London ensued, and the French prime minister asked the British ambassador to bring the matter of Abdallah's violation of French Mandatory rights to the attention of the British government. Meanwhile, the resistance organized by al-Atrash caused turmoil in other parts of Syria but the French managed to suppress all the attempts to rebel. Al-Atrash did not return to Transjordan after the failure of his uprising, and he surrendered to the French. This brought Tali' to resign from his office. The Istiqlal members encouraged hostility against France and provided refuge to those who were involved in the attempts to undermine its authority in Syria. This led to friction between them and Abdallah, especially since the British were not willing to overlook any attempts to undermine French rule, fearing that this would encourage rebellions in Iraq and Palestine, which they controlled. One of the incidents, which increased the tension between Abdallah and the members of the Istiqlal, was the attempt on the life of the French High Commissioner Henri Gouraud on June 23, 1921, when he was on his way to Madaba. Gouraud's companion was killed in the attack on his vehicle. The perpetrators belonged a group led by Aḥmad Maryud who was one of the three ministers in the government of Miẓhar Arslan, and the representative of the Istiqlal in Amman. This incident made the French more determined to oppose Abdallah's attempt to rule over Greater Syria, even though the British advised them that the best way to resolve the issue was by crowning him instead of his brother. Moreover, this incident brought the French to complain about what they regarded as British attempt to reduce their influence in the Middle East. Based on the information provided by the intelligence office in Beirut, the French blamed Abdallah for the attempt, and Gouraud did not respond to Samuel's attempt to obtain their consent to Abdallah's visit to Damascus.

The incident had adverse effect on Abdallah's claim to the Syrian throne, and it tarnished his image in the eyes of the British. Clearly, Abdallah gave the impression that he could not be trusted. The chief commander of the British army in Egypt and Palestine remarked "that Abdallah of Transjordan is an imposter…and that if we wanted to make him useful we ought to provide him with a competent and strong Englishman who would administer all his affairs, and British forces to support him."[32] Lawrence was the only one who saw that it was possible to benefit from Abdallah "on the proviso that he enjoy great popularity and would not be too competent."[33] After meeting Abdallah for the first time, Lawrence was impressed by his personality but suspicious of his aims. He writes:

> The Arabs thought Abdullah a far-seeing statesman, and an astute politician. Astute he certainly was, but I suspected some insincerity throughout our talk. His ambition was patent. Rumour made him the brain of his father, and of the Arab Revolt: but he seemed too easy for that. His object was of course the

> winning of Arab independence and the building up of Arab nations, but in these states Abdullah meant to secure the pre-eminence at least of his family, quite possibly of himself. He was watching us and playing subtly for effect all the time.[34]

From the beginning, Abdallah appeared more conciliatory that his father. Léon Krajevski, who was the consul of France in Jeddah at that time, remarked that after a meeting with Faişal in which he insisted on total independence for the Arabs, his brother Abdallah "wanted to intervene in order to attenuate the content of his declarations, but his father imposed silence on him."[35] Abdallah had a vision of Greater Syria that would include Palestine and Transjordan. Syria, his insisted, could not be independent and divided at the same time.[36] Commenting on Abdallah's strategy and his ultimate goal, Ali Muḥafiẓah writes:

> Abdallah did not hide his political ambition. He regarded the government of Transjordan as no more than a temporary phase on the road to the unity of Greater Syria, and he considered the unity of the four Syrian cities as an important stage toward Arab unity. He reached the political leaders in Syria, Lebanon and Palestine, regardless of their party affiliation and political inclination, exhorting them to unity. And when the proponents of Syrian unity blamed him of cupidity, he denied the accusation and expressed his willingness to accept the opinion of the inhabitants of the Syrian cities regarding the form of government that they would choose, whether it was a kingdom or a republic.[37]

Abdallah relied on British force to establish peace and stability. This helped him control the ambitions of the shaikhs who competed with him. With help from the RAF, he managed to suppress rebellions in al-Kawrah, Balqa, Karak and Tafila. During this period, his commanders managed to suppress a rebellion in Kurrah, which was led by Shaikh Kalib al-Sharida. During the first two years of the Emirate's establishment, the nationalists constituted the majority of the government ministers and advisors, and Amman turned into refuge for militants from Syria and Palestine. They regarded their duty as helping Abdallah establish his rule in the Emirate in order to turn it into a base of opposition to French rule.

In 1922, Shaikh Mustafa al-Ghalayni arrived at the Emirate, after being accused by the French of taking part in the murder of As'ad Khurshid, head of the interior ministry in Lebanon. Not only did Abdallah provide him refuge but he also hired him as a tutor for his son. According to memoirs published by the name *Turkish Officer*, the nationalists gathered to discuss ways and means to start a rebellion in Jabal Druze. According to the same source, Abdallah tended to support such rebellion, and he encouraged Ibrahim Hanu to transfer his movement from northern Syria to Jabal Druze.[38]

The nationalists' plan to turn the Emirate into a base of operation against French rule in Syria brought the government in Paris to ask the British to pressure Abdallah to stop stirring troubles in Syria. Abdallah made strenuous efforts to control the

Istiqlal, but he did not wish to eliminate them as this would have made his role as a mediator and a power broker irrelevant. Besides, the fact that the Istiqlal members were comparatively well-educated, and that they served the Hashemite family in Damascus, provided Abdallah with a pool of skilled labor, which he could use when needed. The fact that Abdallah's first administration consisted entirely of Faişal's former advisors and ministers demonstrates the influence of that party. For example, Abdallah's prime minister Tali' was Faisal's *mutasarrif* of Aleppo. Another member of that party who had considerable influence at that time was Ali Khulki Bey who had the authority to recruit soldiers into the Arab Legion. Another party member, whose activities caused turmoil during that time, was Ibrahim Hanano whom the French sought to arrest but Abdallah feared that his capture would lead to riots due to his popularity among the public, and in the Arab Legion in particular. It was not until 1924, that the Istiqlal lost its power, when the British replaced its members with personnel from the British administration in Palestine.

Abdallah's attitude toward the Istiqlal was not entirely hostile. Although he did not wish to be dominated by its members, their links with the Arab Revolt and their ardent nationalism supported his claim to the leadership over a pan-Arab state. Furthermore, they constituted a reservoir of talented manpower on which he could rely. Though it was his nemesis, Abdallah saw the Istiqlal as an asset to counter British influence. He could always argue that they prevented him from yielding to British demands, and that he was a better alternative to their rule. He used the Istiqlal against Prime Minister Ali Riddah Pasha, which the British imposed on him. Furthermore, by supporting to the Istiqlal, he was in a position to play a mediating role between the government imposed by the British and the restless populace.[39]

Seeking to curb their pan-Arab ambitions, the British exploited every opportunity to lay obstacles for Abdallah and the nationalists. This attempt manifested itself in the efforts to capture Adham Khanjar and his comrades who found refuge in Transjordan. However, the Transjordanian government did not cooperate and decided not to hand them over to the British authorities. The agitators, Adham Khanjar and Shakib Wahab were sent to Sultan Pasha al-Atrash who agreed to provide them shelter. But when Khanjar arrived on July 17, 1922, Sultan al-Atrash was not there. He was caught by the French and arrested in Suwaida prison.

The British continuously pressured Abdallah to rid himself of his nationalist supporters, and to refrain from supporting the rebels in Suwaida. At the same time, al-Atrash took advantage of Khanjar's incarceration to ignite a rebellion. However, he did not find much support for his efforts. He began attacking French targets and when pursued, he fled and found shelter in Transjordan where the government allowed him entry, and sent a delegation to Sharif Hussein to discuss with him means by which the rebellion could spread. However, Sharif Hussein was occupied in discussions with Abd al-Aziz al-Saud, and found it difficult to promote a rebellion in Transjordan. Moreover, the British and the French agreed to cooperate on pressuring the Transjordanian government not to lend support to the rebels. The upshot was that the conflict between some of the leaders and the officers in Transjordan intensified. At the same time, the British and the French cooperated in pursuing the rebels in Transjordan and preventing them from infiltrating Suwaida.

When the government of Ali Riddah al-Rikkabi began dealing with the British, with a view to reach an agreement regarding the future of Anglo-Transjordanian relations, the British agreed on the proviso that he would expel the Istiqlal officers. Despite the fact that the second government of Mudhir Arslan, which took office in February 1922, limited the number of Istiqlal ministers to two, the British government insisted that all of them be dismissed, and decided to counter the influence of the nationalists by appointing Frederick Beg as commander of the Arab army, and John Philby as the British representative in Amman.

In March 1922, the boundaries of Transjordan were defined. Abdallah obtained control over the southern region that later became part of his kingdom. This included Ma'an, Aqaba, and Tabbuk. On September 1922, the League of Nations excluded Transjordan from the Mandate for Palestine. Many saw Britain's creation of the Emirate of Transjordan as an imperialist ploy designed to enable them to maintain their influence in the region. Thus, for example, Maḥmoud al-Ja'fari writes:

> The Sykes-Picot Agreement divided the Arab regions of Greater Syria between Britain and France. Like Palestine and Iraq, the region that lies east of the Jordan River came under British rule, except that it was not a part of Palestine or Iraq. But what lies behind this is that the British did not say what role the Hashemites played in the conspiracy against the Arabs, and they sought to hunt two birds in one stone. The strongest voices in the Colonial Ministry aimed at compensating the Hashemites with a small part of that region, after they dealt a major blow to their dream of establishing an "Arab kingdom."[40]

By the end of 1922, the idea of an Arab confederation led by the Hashemite regime was being discussed in Whitehall. This seemed a possible solution that would allow the Jewish community in Palestine a measure of limited autonomy, and thereby lessen the resistance of the Arab states to the Zionist enterprise. Promoted by Samuel and Deedes, this idea was put to rest by Lord Curzon.[41] Pressed by the French to crack down on the rebels in their domains the British deemed it necessary to curb Abdallah whom they continued to regard as a rabble rouser and an accessory to the assassination attempt on Gouraud. Churchill even agreed to increase the subsidy to Sharif Hussein, on the proviso that he and his son Abdallah maintain an attitude of goodwill toward the British government and dissociate themselves from anti-French propaganda.[42] Another affair, which complicated matters even more, was the raid of Sultan al-Atrash on a French force in Jabal Druze where a French officer was killed. Like many rebels who sought to undermine French rule in Syria, al-Atrash crossed the border to Transjordan where he found refuge.

Meanwhile, Britain's negotiations with Abdallah continued. G.F. Clayton who was the spokesman of the Colonial Office and Riddah Pasha al-Rikabi who served as Faiṣal's prime minister eventually agreed on a settlement, which gave Transjordan autonomy within the Palestine Mandate, with British assistance and membership in the UN. Britain was to provide aid to Abdallah and to appoint a representative in Amman, answerable to the High Commissioner in Jerusalem. These were the terms of the agreement, which was not signed yet. Concerned about the French reaction, the Foreign Office insisted that Atrash and other assailants be caught before publishing Clayton's promises to Abdallah. This caused considerable delays in the negotiations.

Transjordan became independent on May 15, 1923, and Britain recognized its existence. The Arab Legion was created, and Peake was entrusted with its command. When Ibn Saud forced Sharif Hussein's son Ali to abdicate his throne as King of the Hejaz, Abdallah exploited the opportunity of the defeat of a Saudi-Wahhabi force by Banu Sakhr and other tribesmen to incorporate Ma'an and Aqaba to his emirate.[43] Unable to compensate the disgruntled amir, the British found it better and less complicated to leave him where he was, and the incorporation of Ma'an and Aqaba became *fait accompli.* On May 25, 1923, the High Commissioner gave assurance to Abdallah and his sons that the British government will recognize an independent government in Transjordan, on the proviso that it was constitutional, and that it allow the British "to fulfill their international obligations in respect to the territory by means of an agreement to be concluded between the two governments."[44] Although Abdallah accepted the constitutional requirement and established formal procedures for the elections of a representative assembly, he did nothing to convince the British that these would lead to a genuine constitutional government. The British regarded Abdallah as a tyrannical and extravagant ruler lacking administrative talent. Neither Peake nor Philby were impressed by his personality. Moreover, Abdallah was still under the influence of the Syrian nationalists who pressed him to pursue a hostile policy toward Britain. Abdallah found himself between the hammer and anvil; even if he wished to reach a modus vivendi with his British masters, he could hardly afford to have the reputation of one who betrayed Faişal's companions, and therefore could not ignore them.

In 1923, the British intensified their efforts to purge Abdallah's government from pan-Arab militants. British officials dismissed Fuad Salim, Hasib Dhibyan, Naşri Salim, Adil Arslan, and Subḥi al-Khaḍrah, all of whom had links with the Istiqlal. Britain applied tremendous pressure on Abdallah to contain the influence of the pan-Arab members of his government. Urged by the British to crack down on the dissenters, Abdallah delivered a speech to his government members where he said, "whoever tampers with the security in Syria and Palestine by calling for dissension we will consider him not one of us."[45] This was followed by an official announcement by the government on August 21, 1923, regarding "the eviction of some notables whose presence in the region is said to have led to an unfriendly policy toward the Allied government in Syria."[46] Several more members, including Aḥmad Maryud, Nabi al-Aẓmah, Sami al-Sarraj, Uthman Qasim, Aḥmad Ḥilmi, and Mahmoud al-Hindi, were dismissed from their positions. This marked the end of the Istiqlal's influence in Abdallah's government.

Throughout the entire period, the cooperation between Abdallah and the Istiqlal members ebbed and flowed according to the needs of the moment. Learning from the bitter experience of his brother Faişal in Damascus, Abdallah agreed to cooperate with the British. However, when the country faced foreign enemies, cooperation with the Istiqlal seemed imperative in Abdallah's eyes. It was doubtful from the beginning that the Istiqlal could have contributed to the emergence of a stronger and more substantial Jordanian state. This was largely because it did not manage to bring unity among the Jordanians. Nor was it capable of settling the differences among many groups in the society. Though educated, the party members were detached from the people and therefore there was practically no reaction on the part of the public to their dismissal.

Both Churchill and Lawrence favored the idea of allowing Abdallah to remain in power after the allotted six-month period. However, when they were no longer in office, this issue presented a dilemma for their followers. The British government recognized Transjordan as an independent government under Abdallah, but not a state. The separation of Transjordan from Palestine was not a *fait accompli* yet, but Abdallah preferred to regard the agreement of May 25, 1923 as a grant of independence. As it turned out, he did not manage to put his house in order. Inefficiency, corruption, and mismanagement led to crises. Both Peake Pasha who commanded the Arab Legion, and Philby the chief representative in Amman became critical and hostile toward him. Another one of his nemeses was Colonel Henry Cox who came from Palestine to discipline him. In August 1924, Abdallah received an ultimatum to submit to Cox's tutelage or resign, and he yielded.[47] Furthermore, Abdallah's status suffered a major blow as result of his father's trip to Transjordan in early 1924, and in the eyes of many Jordanians, Sharif Hussein cast a giant shadow over his son.

More changes and adjustments were introduced into the agreement as time went by and the process of forming a robust constitutional government was painfully slow. Initially, the government of Transjordan was to be constitutional, although it was not clearly stated how the system would operate. Nor were there any remarks about the kind of elections that ought to take place. Peake was promoted as major general of the Reserve Force. It was not decided yet who were his superiors or to whom he was accountable. It was decided that the section of the Hejaz Railway that passed through Jordanian territory would belong to the government of Transjordan whereas its management would be in the hands of the Palestine Railways. Railway policy was to be determined by three board members, two of them were to be Muslims. The town police, the country gendarmerie, and the Reserve Force, which became known as the Arab Legion, were placed under Peake's command, and he was to be accountable to Abdallah. In addition, a customs agreement was signed between the two parties. Jauf was occupied by Ibn Sa'ud's forces but the status of the land bridge between Transjordan and Iraq was not discussed until the Haddah Agreement that was negotiated between Calyton and Ibn Saud in 1925.[48]

The fact that Ma'an was a Hejazi *vilayet* at that time brought the British to insist on wresting it from Sharif Hussein and incorporating it, along with the port of Aqaba to Transjordan. However, there was a crisis in British-Jordanian relations in 1924, and the nomination of Cox as Britain's representative in Transjordan did little to improve the relations. Cox sought to impose stricter financial regulations on Abdallah's government. Abdallah refused the new measures, and Cox called for his dismissal. The British government was left with virtually no alternatives but to recognize the status quo. One alternative for Britain was to let Transjordan be incorporated into the Hejaz or into Palestine, but there was no support for such measure. On the other hand, punitive measures against Abdallah could have adverse effect on the Arab Legion and the civilian administration, which might have collapsed as a result. Furthermore, there was pressure on the British government not to make any changes without Washington's consent.

Upon his return from his journey to Mecca, Clayton presented a letter to Abdallah through Cox, which included several conditions, which he had to agree upon: (a) That the air officer in command of the imperial forces Palestine be allowed to inspect and direct the Arab Legion; (b) that seven more Syrian nationalists be expelled; (c) that the Tribal Administration Department under Sharif Shakir bin Zayd be abolished; and (d) that Abdallah agree to British financial control. On August 14, 1924, the Wahhabis advanced toward Amman. Seeing the specter of a puritan Islamic regime replacing the newly formed Emirate of Transjordan, the British decided to act. Clayton sent a small force, which was sufficient to deter further aggression. Believing that this was done to his benefit, Abdallah accepted the British conditions and the crisis was averted.

Setting Transjordan's borders

Transjordan was located between 34–39 longitudes and 29–32 latitudes. Its size is 89, 875 square kilometers. It extends eastwards to the Syrian Desert, and then to Wadi Sirḥan and the Iraqi border. In the west, the country bordered a mountain chains extending from the Jordan River to the Egyptian border. In the north, it reached the Yarmouk River and the Ḥawran region bordering Syria. Southward, the country extended to Aqaba and the Saudi desert.

During the Ottoman period, the British consul in Palestine had jurisdiction over Palestine whose borders reached Sidon in present-day Lebanon and the Ottoman authorities recognized his authority. The German consul general had jurisdiction over the Ottoman districts of Nablus-Balqa, and Acre. The Ottoman authorities confirmed the jurisdiction of the consul general and thereby recognized that Palestine included Transjordan in the east and Acre in the north.[49]

Following the establishment of the Emirate of Transjordan, the Revisionist wing of the Zionist movement was especially enraged at Britain's decision to separate Transjordan from the Jewish National Home. Jabotinsky was one of the first critics who disapproved of tearing Transjordan from the Jewish National Home, and he regarded it as violation of the Balfour Declaration.[50]

The term "Transjordan" can be described as the area that extended from Damascus to Mount Hermon in the north; from the Gulf of Eilat to the Arab desert in the south; the Jordan Valley's Rift, the Dead Sea and Araba in the west, and the Syrian Arab Desert in the east. This area was identical to modern Transjordan that obtained its independence in 1946. It bordered Syria in the north and its southern border was a line that started two miles south of Aqaba and extended eastward to the Iraqi border. Theoretically, this area was detached from the area that His Majesty's government was committed to establish a National Home for the Jews in Palestine according to the Balfour Declaration. On September 23, 1922, the Council of the

League of Nations confirmed that the clauses pertaining to the establishment of a National Home for the Jews in Palestine will not apply to Transjordan, and that Britain will rule it separately.

There are those who argue that Churchill' s White Paper of 1922 specified that Palestine west of the Jordan River was excluded from the areas that McMahon promised Sharif Hussein of Mecca in the famous correspondence at the beginning of World War I. Others insist that Transjordan was included in the area promised to the Arabs, and that it was later separated from Palestine. Most scholars, however, hold the view that the decision to separate Transjordan from Palestine was made at the Cairo Conference, which took place in March 1921. The explanation given to that decision was that the British had to pacify Amir Abdallah who threatened to attack the French forces in Syria, and therefore agreed to hand Transjordan to him, on the proviso that he would not attack the French. Moreover, there were those who argued that Britain's decision to separate Transjordan was motivated by its desire to reduce its financial obligations, while others maintain that Britain sought to fulfill its obligations to the Arabs in line with the original McMahon-Sharif Hussein correspondence. There is another interpretation, which maintains that the separation was not a "historical accident" but part of a deliberate policy, which the British government adopted at the beginning of August 1920.[51] For example, in article published in the daily *Ha'aretz*, a commentator writes:

> Britain's policy toward Palestine was, in matters affecting us, absolutely clear already in the month of August 1920, during Sir Herbert Samuel's first visit to Al-Salt, and all the events that followed-granting Emir Abdallah rule overt that district, abolition of the 'Jewish clauses' in the Mandate regarding Transjordan, and the announcement of the High Commissioner in the month of April 1923-none of these were loud novelties.[52]

One of the scholars who explored the topic in depth, using British archival material to prove his point is Yizthak Gil-Har who argued that the idea of separating Transjordan from Palestine was began taking shape since October 1915, and there is no certainty that his Majesty's government included Transjordan in the areas promised to the Zionists in the Balfour Declaration.

Gil-Har goes on to argue that already at the time of the Sykes-Picot Agreement of 1916, British officials began making the distinction between "Palestine proper" that lies west of the Jordan River, and Transjordan to the east. The geographical separation between Transjordan and Palestine was done, seven months prior the Balfour Declaration. Therefore, according to Gil-Har, the assumption that Palestine under the British Mandate included eastern Transjordan cannot be substantiated by evidence. Moreover, the eastern border of the Palestine Mandate was determined at the Huda Agreement of November 2, 1925. During World War I, Allenby was the supreme commander in Palestine and the Foreign Office determined that the areas east of the Jordan River and Syria, from Ma'an in the south to Damascus in the north, would be controlled by an Arab administration with the assistance of British and French officers.

The establishment of a military regime in Transjordan in October 1918 was a manifestation of a policy that was conceived and crystalized during the war. There was a suggestion, which was raised in August 1919, and several times during 1919–1920, to grant the Mandate over Transjordan to France. This suggestion did not negate the assumption that Transjordan would be part of an independent Arab state. Moreover, the willingness of British officials to consider the idea of moving the eastern border of Palestine to the Jordan River and the Dead Sea did not mean that the fate of this area remained undetermined. According to the military arrangements made in October 1918, Transjordan's western border was Wadi Araba, from the southern edge of the Dead Sea to Aqaba. It was determined that the area east of that line would belong to the Arabs. In the talks, which British officials had with Sharif Hussein of Mecca this border was recognized as temporary, but since he did not sign the peace treaty on time this became Palestine's *de facto* border.

At the San Remo convention of April 25, 1920, Palestine's borders were defined as the area extending from the Mediterranean in the west to several kilometers east of the Jordan River. At the same time, the term "Syria" included Transjordan, and was under the purview of an Arab regime in Damascus. In reality, Transjordan was left without a government. There was chaos in the country and the fear that the French would take it over prevailed. At the same time, the debate over the jurisdictional status of Transjordan continued. According to clause 132 of the Treaty of Sevres, Transjordan was part of an area, which Turkey gave to the Allies. The British had no desire to bring the issue to the peace conference, and since the India Office was not in favor of incorporating Transjordan to Mesopotamia, they had no other alternative, but to assume that it was incorporated into the area of the Palestine Mandate, and at the same time to treat it as separate from Palestine. The British remained determined to include Transjordan in the promised Arab state, and therefore they rejected Samuel's proposal to reconquer it in 1920.[53] Initially, the Foreign Office decided to form three separate and autonomous Arab entities to be ruled with the help of British advisors. However, since Transjordan's inhabitants lacked the sense of national unity and self-government the attempt failed. The chaotic conditions in the country were of major concern to the British who therefore decided to establish one regime headed by an Arab leader who would be able to accommodate the different ethnic groups and provide security for the region. It was then that Abdallah appeared in Transjordan as his father's emissary, with a view to attack the French in Syria.

The agenda of the Cairo Conference determined Britain's intention to distinguish between Palestine and Transjordan and to conduct different policy in each region. However, Abdallah's appearance disrupted the British plan. He was not considered to be the best candidate to rule Transjordan, but it was impossible to ignore him once he appeared. As the British saw it, cooperation with the Sheriff Hussein's family seemed the only way to avoid conflict. Therefore, on March 27, 1921, he was called to meet Churchill in Jerusalem where he agreed to rule Transjordan for a six months trial period. In addition, he agreed not to attack the French in Syria and not to act against British policy in regards to the Balfour Declaration.

According to Gil-Har, there is no evidence for the assumption that Abdallah agreed to renounce his big political ambitions. Ruling Transjordan was only a small part in his big plan to be the ruler the territories that extended from the Turkey's border with Syria, to the tip of the Arabian Peninsula. He wished to succeed where his father and brother failed. As it turned out, Abdallah was far from being content with the deal. Transjordan was no more than a tiny portion of the territories that he aspired to. Besides, by agreeing not to fight the French, he alienated his father. In his talks with Churchill, he proposed that Palestine and Transjordan become one state, and that a Muslim emir would be its leader. Churchill rejected the proposal, arguing that it contradicted the terms of the British Mandate.

In addition to the meager results that he achieved in his negotiations with Churchill, the Amir's attempt to convince the French to the crown him over Damascus failed. He was faced with a *fait accompli* when his brother was crowned king of Iraq, despite the fact that he was the candidate whom the All Syrian Congress chose in Damascus on March 8, 1920.

Abdallah brought several proposals that he thought could help him come closer to his grandiose goals. In addition to his proposals to combine Palestine and Jordan, he talked about a union between Transjordan and the Hejaz. Unwilling to interfere in the Sharifi-Saudi family feuds the British rejected the proposals. Moreover, such plans ran counter to Britain's policy as a Mandatory power in Palestine. Though important, fiscal considerations did not play a major role in the decision to separate Transjordan from Palestine. British involvement in Transjordan demanded not only deployment of troops whenever needed but also financial assistance, which the taxpayers in Palestine had to help pay.

Abdallah did not prove to be an effective leader. His ministers and the senior officers were foreigners from the neighboring Arab countries and did not gain popularity among the local population. Moreover, his council of ministers was inefficient, the taxing system was flawed and the Bedouin tribes did not cooperate. Therefore, the British thought about replacing him with another Arab leader. There were also proposals to conquer the country or to combine it with Palestine under one ruler. Moreover, Abdallah himself expressed his willingness to relinquish power. Nevertheless, both Churchill and Lawrence were convinced that with proper assistance and guidance, he would be able to rule and Samuel believed that he was popular in the eyes of the Jordanian public. As it turned out, his term was renewed without specifying when it would end and he remained in power indefinitely.

Abdallah made an effort to fortify his position in Transjordan and he sought British assurances to treat his country as a separate entity. The British gave him such assurance in May 1923, and on February 20, 1928, Transjordan's prime minister signed a treaty with the High Commissioner for Palestine which determined that Transjordan will become a separate entity, and that the amir would cooperate with Britain and help it fulfill its obligations according the Mandate's requirements. Furthermore, the treaty determined that Transjordan would be under the purview of the High Commissioner who would be guide it in matters affecting foreign affairs, international finances and issues affecting British interests, and that the country would have a separate constitution.

Gil-Har's conclusions are that the idea of separating Transjordan from Palestine occurred during World War I, and that British policy makers had constantly sought coordination with the French, the Arabs, and the Zionists. It was already in the summer of 1917 that the British determined that Transjordan's future would take a different turn than Palestine. The establishment of a separate military regime in Transjordan in October 1918 was the first step of applying the policy that was conceived in 1917. In September 1919, Transjordan became a Syrian-Arab entity, but its juridical status had yet to be determined by the peace conference. The fall of Faisal's government and the conquest of Syria brought back the juridical status of Transjordan to the fore. The Cairo Conference made it clear that Transjordan would become an Arab entity. Transjordan became part of the Palestinian Mandate whose Arab character would not have adverse effect on Britain's obligations to the Jews. Some Zionist leaders viewed with favor the separation of Transjordan in 1918–1919, and generally, they expected that the border with Transjordan would be adjusted in favor of the Jewish National Home. The inclusion of Transjordan in the framework of the British Mandate tempted some Zionist leaders who ceased their attempts to change the border, and thought that it was included in Palestine, without being able to distinguish between the political and juridical status, until Transjordan became independent in 1946.[54]

The Muslim fundamentalist Ikhwan movement that spread into the region of Transjordan at that time posed a serious dilemma for the British. The Ikhwan's domination of Jauf and Wadi Sirḥan prompted the British who believed that their raids constituted a dangerous invasion that could have put their mandate in Palestine in jeopardy, to assist Abdallah in conquering al-Kaf, which guarded that location.[55]

Senior British politicians, including Lord Curzon and Lloyd George, took into consideration the demands of the Zionists and both urged Sykes to enable the government to obtain a mandate for Palestine on their behalf, and to help them develop the country under British guidance. Eventually, Sykes himself became convinced that this was the right path to follow. The boundaries separating Palestine and Transjordan were initially created as an outcome Britain's wartime commitments. While the general outline of the borders was designed by Sykes in May 1917, it was Sir Herbert Young who determined the exact lines. Even though Transjordan was administered as part of the Palestine Mandate the British government always treated it as a separate political unit. As the British government saw it, the boundaries were largely determined in September 1922, and then again in February 1928, and only minor changes could be made, based on strategic, administrative, economic, or other considerations, which affected its interest in the region. The last border adjustment that was introduced in 1946 was largely a result of a change in Britain's perception regarding the strategic importance of Aqaba.[56]

The political and military developments, which took place in the Arabian Peninsula in the early 1920s, forced upon the British the need to modify Transjordan's southern borders. It was primarily the occupation of Hail and the overthrow of the Shamar Emirate by the Ikhwan forces led by Ibn Saud, Sultan of the Najd in November 1921 that brought the British to the conclusion that Iraq, Palestine and Transjordan were under threat. Ibn Saud's intension to occupy Jauf was viewed by the British as compromising the security of the British Empire, and a threat to their strategic interests in the region. Moreover, the advance of the Ikhwan forces toward Wadi Sirḥan was seen as undermining the stability of Transjordan and Palestine. Ikhwani raids of the villages of Tanaib and Umm al-Ahmad in August 1922, and the raid of the railway at Ziza in 1924, prompted the British to act against the invaders. It was largely the proximity of these areas to Amman that caused concern in Whitehall. Soon after the British forces faced the invaders and inflicted heavy losses on them, negotiations got under way. Abdallah contributed to the peaceful negotiations by giving up his claim to Jauf. Thereupon, the British drew a provisional line starting either in Tabbuk or at Mudawarra on the Hejaz Railway, thence to the East, along the 38E longitude until it reached the northern part of Kaf, and then followed a northeasterly direction until the Iraqi frontier. Realizing that they could not demand the inclusion of the entire Wadi Sirḥan into Transjordan, the British sought to include Kaf, which was a stronghold controlling the way from central Arabia into Transjordan and Southern Syria.

Concerned about the possibility that Ibn Saud was about to occupy Kaf, the British sent him a warning him that such move would not be regarded favorably, and provided a plan that they believed would satisfy the demands of all contestants in the region. According to the plan, Transjordan would cede a big part of Wadi Sirḥan, including Kaf to Najd; Najd would cede Khurma and Turabah to the Hejaz; the Hejaz would move its northern frontier up to Mudawarra, while Transjordan would obtain the territory up to the Aqaba-Mudawarra line in the south, and would thereby be able to access the Red Sea.

Neither Ibn Saud who already occupied the entire territory that was about to be granted to Najd nor Abdallah who already occupied Transjordan were satisfied with the British proposal. Since Ibn Saud demanded the entire Sirḥan Valley and the Nefud Desert, the conference dissolved without an agreement. When Hussein was proclaimed caliph, Ibn Saud declared a Holy War against the Hejaz. When Hussein proclaimed the establishment of the Ma'an Vilayet Administration, which the British considered part of the Palestine Mandate, they decided to restore their control over that district. The Hadda Agreement of 1925 determined the frontiers between the Najd and Transjordan. The Jeddah Agreement of May 1927 determined the frontiers between the Hejaz and Transjordan, and while General Clayton rejected Ibn Saud's demands for more territory along the border with Transjordan, he agreed to cede Kaf to the Najd. In exchange, Saudi Arabia committed itself to cooperate with Transjordan in order to prevent subversive religious activities, to facilitate trade, and to form an organization for arbitration of feuds among Bedouins. In the final analysis, it was primarily due to strategic reasons and considerations of imperial defense that Britain intervened in the border conflicts along Transjordan's southern frontiers.[57]

The Anglo-Jordanian treaty of 1928

In 1925, the villagers of north Irbid assembled in Wadi Shallala. They were led by Shaikh Mustafa al-Khalali and Ḍayf Allah al-Ṣaliḥ al-Shabul. Among them, there were 500 horsemen who entered Syria and occupied several strongholds. The French army advanced toward them from Dar'a, and their aircraft razed Damascus. The campaign took place in Da'il. The Jordanians, according to accounts of eye-witnesses, were ingenious. They jumped from their horses, landed on the French armored cars, and fired on the soldiers. Nevertheless, the campaign ended with numerous Jordanian casualties some of whom died and others imprisoned. The Jordanian commanders fled to Ma'an after the Druze guaranteed their safety. They continued to fight the French in guerrilla style campaigns. The French authorities pressured the Jordanian government to hand over the rebels to them. Abdallah collaborated and arrested rebels whom he turned over to the French but the prisoners fled and al-Shabul found shelter with Ṭallal al-Mufliḥ al-Zu'bi. When the commander of the district of Irbid came to arrest him, Ṭallal refused to surrender and Dayf Allah enabled him to flee to Wadi al-Shallala after nightfall. Accompanied by three armed rebels, Ḍayf Allah passed through the Abbab tribes who cordially received him and sent him to Banu Sakhr, until he reached Zizya where he was caught.[58]

In 1928, a treaty was signed, which left the country under British control. A constitution called the Organic Law allowed the establishment of a Legislative Council, which consisted of 14 elected members, two tribal representatives, and a chief minister, in addition to four Executive Council members who fulfilled an advisory role. The Bedouins, Circassians, and Christian communities were over-represented, and the appointment of their representatives depended on the regime's goodwill.

After the amendments introduced in 1939 and 1946, the Organic Law became the basis of Jordan's constitution of 1952. It was based of the British model and was similar to the Iraqi constitution. In addition to legislative councils and the Amir's cabinet, it established a judiciary and an independent court system, which included civil and religious courts. However, neither the recognition of Transjordan's independence nor the treaty that was signed in February 20, 1928, satisfied the demands of the Jordanian nationalists. On July 25, 1928, a meeting was held in which the local dignitaries took part. The participants in that convention were regarded as legitimate representatives of the Jordanian people. The National Covenant that was drafted for that occasion became the first political document with a definite program. This covenant constituted a political landmark in the history of the Jordanian national and political struggle. Its main points were:

- a The Emirate of Transjordan is an independent Arab state with sovereignty in its recognized natural boundaries. It will be led by a constitutional government headed by His Highness Amir Abdallah Ibn Hussein and his successors.
- b Rejection of the Mandate, except as a means by which the British agree to provide assistance to the country.

c The ties between the Emirate and Great Britain ought to be regulated by a treaty based on the mutual needs and respect for Jordanian sovereignty.
d The Balfour Declaration, which promised the Jews a homeland in Palestine, contradicts the British promises to the Arabs.
e The British authorities ought to facilitate the election of a representative body that reflects the wishes of the electorate.
f Recruitment of soldiers, taxes, or any other duties will not be legal without the consent of the constitutional government of the Emirate.[59]

According to the terms of the treaty, Britain obtained the right to maintain armed presence in the country. In addition to the Arab Legion, the British formed the Transjordan Frontier Force (TJFF) whose purpose was to guard the borders against invasions by foreign powers, and Bedouin tribes. The country was to be ruled by an executive and legislative councils on the national and local levels. According to the treaty, Transjordan's border with the Hejaz, which was incorporated into the Saudi state, was determined. The British were to determine the appointment of non-Jordanian officials. This stipulation came as result of fear that the Syrian nationalists might try to turn the Emirate into a base of operations against France. This was a fear shared by Britain and Abdallah. In return for its willingness to provide financial assistance, Britain had the freedom of stationing forces in Transjordan as it saw fit. In addition, Britain promised not to oppose any attempt by Transjordan to seek alliances with other Middle Eastern countries. Abdallah was to be the head of state whose form of government was to be a constitutional, with a unicameral legislative council, and an executive council or a cabinet. The Executive Council consisted of nationalists who served his brother Faişal in Damascus.

Nevertheless, the tension between Britain and Abdallah did not subside. This was primarily because the British advisers endeavored to include local representatives in order to reduce the influence of the nationalists who were suspected of seeking the incorporation of Transjordan into Greater Syria, and neither the amir nor the nationalists in Damascus were willing to forfeit what they regarded as their right to expand the country's borders. The agreement also stated that the amir could be succeeded by a family member and that the chief minister was to preside over the meeting of the legislature.

The system provided the amir with more powers vis-à-vis the other branches of government. He could issue decrees and ordinances, which could turn into laws and veto bills passed by the legislature. The Council of Ministers had more power than those of the legislature. The Organic Law was later supplemented by the Election Law, which set the principle of universal male suffrage. It divided the settled country into districts, which had a certain number of representatives-Muslim, Circassians and Christians. The Bedouins participated in the system by sending two members who were elected by two committees of shaikhs that were selected by the amir. One was to represent the north and one the south. The first elections took place on April 2, 1929, and the agreement was ratified after a long debate. It was later amended three times.[60]

Contrary to Abdallah's wishes, the British insisted on referring to his territory not as an emirate but as a district. During the period between the establishment of the Emirate and the outbreak of World War II, Britain provided one-third of the total yearly income. Initially, they provided £150,000 per year. Abdallah's administration, however, was subjected to strict control, which reduced the amount that he received. This happened during the years 1923–1926, when the amount was reduced from £36,000 to £12,000.[61] To secure his position in the country, the British formed the Arab Legion, which had 1,300 men and the Transjordanian Frontier Force (TJEF), which provided security to the newly created emirate and both were commanded by British officers. In addition, the British made use of the RAF to repel raids by Wahhabis from Saudi Arabia and prevent unrest in the frontiers.

At the time of the state's establishment, the population of Jordan, excluding Ma'an and Aqaba, was around 225,000, more than a half of which (54 percent) was sedentary and the rest nomads. The total number of people with these two areas was in the neighborhood of 300,000 most of whom (94 percent) were Muslim Arabs. The Circassians, who were also Sunni Muslims, were just under 5 percent and 10 percent of the populations were Christians, most of whom were Greek Orthodox.[62] Generally, the individual's ties were to the tribe or the clan, rather than to the state. No sense of national identity or loyalty to the state of Jordan existed yet. Most of the population lived in small towns. The population in al-Salt, which was the biggest city in 1920, was about 20,000 and Amman had no more than 2,400, but its population increased rapidly when Abdallah turned it into the state's capital. The cities were inhabited by a mixture of nomads and sedentary people. The city's expansion was limited by the rugged nature of the terrain that left little area for cultivation, except in the Jordan Valley region, and a small area in the east. Water came mainly from the Jordan River and its tributaries, the Zarqa and the Yarmouk. The limited rainfall ranged from 40 cm in Ajlun to 5 cm in Badia, in the eastern desert.

Jordan's political institutions did not develop independently. Its institutions were established by the British Mandatory authorities in Palestine. Abdallah's representatives had a little say in the development of Jordan's political structure. Cox who took part in the establishment of these institutions made all efforts to keep Abdallah as a symbolic head of state. The Emirate absorbed immigrants, which came from Syria, the Hejaz and Palestine. These began to fill important positions in a country where the size of the indigenous personnel was small. The number of immigrants who sought to settle in the country or seek refuge in it increased significantly as result of the instability and warfare that took place in the region. Another important development was the land settlement program that was implemented during the 1930s and early 1940s. The registration of land made it easier and more attractive for its owners to cultivate it. Transjordan was affected by the Arab rebellion, which erupted in 1936 in Palestine. In 1937, preparations were underway in Transjordan to join the Palestinians in opposition to British rule. There were unsuccessful attempts to cut off the pipelines that passed through the country. Three homemade bombs exploded in Irbid and several Jordanians, including Muhammad Ali al-Ajluni met in Damascus in October 1937, where they obtained arms and looked for a hidden passage to transfer them to Palestine. Telephone wires were severed in five areas in Transjordan and there were attempts to cut off pipelines. In November that year, several police stations were exposed to fire and some of their personnel were arrested. In the same month, the telephone line was cut off in Karak and other locations throughout the country. Recalling the efforts to organize resistance against the British, Mohammed Izzat Darwazeh writes:

> It appears that the half dozen that the minister in Damascus mentioned in connection with the disturbances in Transjordan consisted of Muhammad Ali al-Ajjluni and his colleagues…
>
> Together with Ṣubḥi Abi Ghanimah we agreed to establish a resistance movement in Transjordan. We mentioned in our daily our role in escalating the resistance, and the deplorable failure of the operation, for the reasons that we have mentioned. There is no doubt that the British intelligence caught a glimpse of it and the Colonial Secretary alluded to it.[63]

So sensitive were the British to the state of affairs in Transjordan that when former Egyptian Khedive Abbas Ḥilmi proposed to visit Abdallah, the matter had to be discussed between the High Commissioner, Sir Arthur Wauchope and the Colonial Office.[64] The Jordanian government was authorized to appoint consuls but Article 5 of the Agreement of 1928, which stated that the Amir agreed to be guided by Britain through the High Commissioner in matters concerning his country's foreign relations was left unchanged.[65]

Even in matters affecting changes in custom duties, the Amir was required to accept British advice, even though the proposed amendment was simply to eliminate the words "and the customs tariffs in Trans-Jordan shall be approved by His Majesty."[66] The agreement caused major controversy and it was not welcome by the public in Transjordan.[67] According to the High Commissioner the Amir recognized that he was the ultimate authority to determine the existence of a state of emergency.[68] Major General Sir Alfred Knox asked the colonial secretary whether or not to allow the exploration of oil in the Dead Sea. These rights were granted to a British subject known as Dr. Homer in 1938. Knox stressed the need to have access to these oil fields in order to bolster the defense of the British Empire.[69]

British concern for Transjordan's security intensified prior to World War II when it became known that Nazi Germany was expanding its propaganda activities in the country. A German agent by name Herr Geseler Wirsing was reported to have visited Transjordan with a view to spread anti-British propaganda.[70] In an interview which he held with Prime Minister Ramsey MacDonald, the Jordanian envoy Taufiq Pasha Abul-Huda was told that in case the British decided to set up an independent state in Palestine, there would be a statement regarding the position of Transjordan, implying that he would propose granting it greater measure of self-government.[71]

Figure 8.1 King Abdallah I.

Notes

1 Colonel Meinertzhagen to Lord Curzon, Cairo, October 27, 1919. *Documents on British Foreign Policy 1919–1939*, Edited by E.L. Woodward and Rohan Butler, Vol. IV, 1919 (London, Her Majesty's Stationary Office, 1952), No. 345, pp. 499–500.

2 *Ibid*, p. 524.

3 Cited in Hind Ghāṣān Abū al-Shi'ir, "Sharqi al-Urdun fī 'āhd al-ḥūkūmah al-'Arabīyah al-Fayṣalīyah, September 1918-July 1920," (East Jordan during the Faisali-Arab Period) (Arabic text), Min al-ma'ālim al-thaqāfīyah wa-al-ḥaḍāriyah fī-al-Urdun 'abra al-'usūr, Vol. II, p. 425.

4 Cited *Ibid*, p. 425.

5 Cited *Ibid*, p. 426.

6 Martin Gilbert, *Winston S. Churchill, Vol. IV, 1916–1922: The Stricken World* (Boston, MA: Houghton Miflin, 1975), pp. 502–503.

7 Cited *Ibid*, p. 534.

8 Cited in Sulayman Mūsā, *Awrāq min Daftar al-Ayyām: Dhikriyyāt al-Ra'īl al-Awwal* (Papers from the Notebook of Times: Memoirs of the first Generation," Arabic text (Ammān: Matba'at al-Ajyal, 2000), p. 68.

9 Qasim Muhammad al-Durū ', *Sāfāhāt mushtariqah fī masirāt al-Urdun al-hadīth* (Common Pages in the History of Modern Jordan), Arabic text (Irbid: Imādat al-Dirāsāt al-Jami'iyah wa-al-Nashr wa al-Tawzī', 2000), p. 28.

10 Kayr al-Din al-Ziriklī, *Mudhakkirāt 'āmayn fī 'āṣimat Sharq al-Urdun* (Memoirs of Two Years in the Capital of East Jordan), Arabic text (Miṣr: Al-Maṭba'ah al-'Arabīyah, 1925), p. 31.

11 *Cameos: Jordan, Arab Nationalism*, p. 96.
12 Gilbert, p. 538.
13 Cited in Aaron Kleinman, *Foundations of British Policy in the Arab World: The Cairo Conference of 1921* (Baltimore, MD: The Johns Hopkins Press, 1970), p. 120.
14 This arrangement caused much consternation in Zionist circles, particularly when it was followed by a draft of a treaty signed by Sharif Hussein on April 1923, that recognized Britain's special position in Iraq, Palestine, and Transjordan. Leading Zionists figures expressed their concern and there were those who blamed the Zionist leader Chaim Weizmann for not objecting to the treaty. Leon (Ariah) Simon to Asher Ginsberg, *Letter No. 308 Aḥad Ha'am, Mikhtavīm be-'inyanei Eretz Yisrael, 1891–1926* (Ahad Ha'am, Letters pertaining to the Land of Israel), Hebrew text, Edited by Shulamit Laskov (Jerusalem: Yad Ben Tzvi, 2000), p. 593.
15 Uriel Dan, *Studies in the History of Transjordan 1920-1949: The Making of a State* (Boulder, CO: Westview Press, 1984), p. 3.
16 Sulayman Mustafa al-Samādi, *Al-Malik wa-al-Dawlah* (The King and the State), Arabic text (Amman: Dar Al-Khalīj, 2002), p. 22.
17 Gilbert, p. 541.
18 *Ibid.*
19 *Ibid*, p. 553.
20 *Ibid.*
21 *Ibid*, p. 554.
22 *Ibid*, p. 557.
23 *Ibid*, p. 560.
24 Cited *Ibid*, p. 561.
25 *Ibid*, pp. 576–577.
26 *Ibid*, p. 583.
27 *Ibid*, p. 584.
28 Yitzhak Gil-Har, "Boundaries Delimitation: Palestine and Trans-Jordan," *Middle Eastern Studies*, Vol. 36, No. 1 (January 2000), pp. 69, 78.
29 Agreement: The United Kingdom and Transjordan, February 20, 1928. (Great Britain, Parliamentary Papers, 1930, Treaty Series No. 7, Cmd 3488). Jacob Coleman Hurewitz, *Diplomacy in the Near and Middle East: A Documentary Record 1535–1956*, Vol. II, 1914–1956 (Oxford, UK: Archive Edition, 1987), pp. 156–159.
30 Karl E. Meyer and Shireen Blair Brysac, *Kingmakers: The Invention of the Modern Middle East* (New York: W.W. Norton & Company, 2008), pp.160–161.
31 Uriel Dan, pp. 40–43.
32 Cited in 'Ali Shu'ayb, "Anmāt al-'ālāqah bayn al-amīr 'Abdallāh wa-ḥizb al-istiqlāl al- 'Arabi," (Methods of the tie between Amir Abdallah and the Arab Istiqlal Party), Arabic text, Min al-ma'ālim al-thaqāfīyah wa-al-ḥaḍāriyah fī-al- Urdun 'abra al-'usūr ('Ammān: al-Markaz al-Thaqāfi al-Malaki, 2002), Vol. II, p. 40.
33 *Ibid.*
34 Thomas Edward Laurence, *Seven Pillars of Wisdom: A Triumph* (Fordingbridge, UK: Castle Hill Press, 1997), p. 52.
35 Leon Krajevski, *Consul de France à Djeddah à Alexandre Millerand, President du Conseil, Ministre des affaires étrangerés. Djeddah, le 18 Juillet 1920 a 9^h* (The Consul of France in Jeddah to Alexander Millerand, President of the Council, Ministry of Foreign Affairs), French text, Documents diplomatiques française relatifs à l'histoire du Liban et de la Syrie à l'époque *du Mandat, 1914–1946*, Tome II (Paris: L'Harmattan, 2012), # 368, p. 497.
36 'Abdallāh bin al-Ḥusayn, *Mudhakkarāti* (Abdallah ibn Hussein: My Memoirs), Arabic text (Al-Quds: Maṭba'at Bayt al-Muqqādas, 1945), p. 256.
37 'Alī Muḥāfaẓah, "Abdallāh bin al-Ḥusayn: Ḥayātūhū wa-Fikrūhū al-Siyāsī," *The Founder-King Abdullah Ibn al-Hussein*, Arabic text with Title in English (Amman: Ministry of Culture, 1999), p. 126.

38 Shu'ayb, p. 36.
39 Toby Dodge, *An Arabian Prince, English Gentleman and the Tribes East of the Jordan River: Abdullah and the Creation and Consolidation of the Trans-Jordanian State*, Occasional Paper 13, Center of Near and Middle Eastern Studies (SOAS), University of London, May 1994, pp. 29–31.
40 Maḥmoud al-Ja'fari, *Badhrat al-ṭughyān al-Hashimī wa-dawruhā al-ta'āmurī 'alá Filasṭīn* (The Origins of the Hashemite Tyranny and its conspiratorial role in Palestine), Arabic text (No publisher, 1990), p. 25.
41 Uriel Dan, p. 52.
42 Gilbert, p. 551.
43 Beverly Milton-Edwards and Peter Hinchcliffe, *Jordan: A Hashemite Legacy* (London: Routledge, 2001), p. 21.
44 Cited in Uriel Dan, p. 71.
45 Cited in Shu'ayb, p. 42.
46 Cited *Ibid.*
47 Uriel Dan, p. 7.
48 *Ibid*, p. 70.
49 Yitzhak Gil-Har, "The Northern Boundary of Palestine," *Yahadut Zemanenu*, Vol. II (1984), pp. 317–318.
50 Vladimir Jabotinsky, *The Story of the Jewish Legion* (New York: Bernard Ackerman, Inc., 1945), p. 138.
51 Yitzhak Gil-Har, "The Separation of Transjordan from Eretz Israel-Another Angle," *Yahadut Zemanenu*, Vol. I (1983), pp. 163–167.
52 Meron Medzini, "Transjordan, on the Agenda," *Ha'aretz* March 1, 1928, Cited in Yitzhak Gil-Har, "The Separation of Transjordan from Eretz Israel-Another Angle," *Yahadut Zemanenu*, Vol. I (1983), p. 167.
53 Herbert Samuel endeavored to convince the British government of the need to conquer Transjordan. He said explicitly that Dar'a was located outside the Sykes-Picot line, and that it was imperative to conquer Transjordan because, as he put it, "the Jordan River is a poor border strategically, economically and politically for Palestine," TNA FO371/5/21, No. 179, Letter from Sir Herbert Samuel to Earl Curzon, August 7, 1920. Cited in Amjad Aḥmad Sulaymān al-Zu'bi, *Hirbirt Ṣamū'īl: Al-Mandūb al-Sāmi al-Barīṭanī 'ala Filasṭīn wa-Sharqī al-Urdun wa-ta'sīs Imārat Sharqī al-Urdun 1920–1925* (Herbert Samuel: The British High Commissioner for Palestine and Transjordan and the establishment of Transjordan 1920–1925), Arabic text ('Ammān: Markaz al-Kitāb al-Akādīmī, 2002), p. 55.
54 The Separation of Transjordan from Eretz Israel-Another Angle, pp. 172–177.
55 Fatḥi al-'Afīfī, *Mushkilāt al-ḥudūd al-siyasīyah fi al-jazīrah al-'Arabīyah: dirāsah tārikhīyah, siyāsīyah, qānunīyah* (The problem of the political borders in the Arabian Peninsula: A Historical, Political and Legal Study), Arabic text (Jizah: Al-Haram, 2000), p. 318.
56 Yitzhak Gil-Or, "Boundaries Delimitation: Palestine and Trans-Jordan," *Middle Eastern Studies*, Vol. 36, No. 1 (January 2000), pp. 68, 72, 78.
57 Yitzhak Gil-Har, "Delimitation Trans-Jordan and Saudi Arabia," *Middle Eastern Studies*, Vol. 28, No. 2 (April1992). pp. 374–376, 378–379, 382.
58 Aḥmad 'Uwaydī al-'Abbādī, *Fi rubū' al-Urdun: jawlāt wa-mushāhadāt* (In the Quarters of Jordan: Tours and Observations), Arabic text, Vol I. ('Ammān: Dār al-Fikr, 1987), pp. 418–419.
59 Al-Durū', pp.12–13.
60 Uriel Dan, p. 8.
61 Milton-Edwards and Hinchcliffe, p. 23.
62 *Ibid*, p. 21.
63 Mohammed Izzat Darwazeh, *97 Years Autobiography: A long side with Arab movements and Palestinian cause, Memories and Registrations*, Vol. III, Arabic text with title in English (Beirut: Dār al-Gharb al-Islāmi, 1993), p. 534.

64 Williams to Rendel, TNA FO371/17877/E5137, August 8, 1934.
65 Williams to Foreign office, TNA FO371/17877/E270, January 1934.
66 Colonial Office: Proposed Amendment of Trans-Jordanian Agreement of 1928. Minutes by Colonial Office. TNA FO371/17877/E2554, April 24, 1934.
67 Zahr al-ʻAnnābī (Fāṭimah al-Zahrah Ghrabī), *Al-shu'ub muta'alifah: Qira'ā fī ḥarakiyāt al-istrātījī al-Hāshīmī*, Arabic text (Irbīd: Al-Rumantik lil-Abḥāth wa-al-Dirāsāt, 2003), p. 443.
68 Starling to Colonial Office, TNA FO371/21887/E1173, March 3, 1938.
69 Parliamentary Question by Major General Sir Alfred Knox. TNA FO371/21887/E1345, March 9, 1938.
70 Baggallay to Downie, TNA FO371/21887/E21887/E4734/740/31, August 16, 1938.
71 Conference on Palestine, 1939: Note of Informal Conversation with H.E. Taufiq Pasha Abul-Huda, TNA FO371/23247/E1702, March 2, 1939.

IX World War II and the Hashemite quest for national identity

During Abdallah's reign, the country underwent a thorough process of change. When the country was established, the population did not exceed 200,000 in which most were villagers and Bedouin. The villages were small and distant from each other, especially in the southern part of the country. There were no towns to speak of, except for Amman, which Abdallah took as his place of residence and the capital of his kingdom, and it had no more than 6,000 inhabitants at that time.

The Bedouin lived in tents, cultivated the land, and raised sheep, horses, and camels. They were nomads who moved from one place to another seeking water and arable land to cultivate. Some of their tribes, like Abbad and Bani Hassan, were semi-nomadic who tended to settle in certain areas where they cultivated the land and raised sheep and camels. The tribe or the clan was the basic unit of social life, both among the villagers and the Bedouin. The tribe or clan was a unit whose members had a common history, tradition, heritage, and views. This was the traditional system that prevailed in the country where the central government failed to assert its control. With the passage of time, connections among the tribes or clans were established. However, the relations between Bedouin and villagers were often unfriendly. Bedouin tribes raided villages and the central government, with its military forces was rarely in a position to establish order. This state of affairs compelled the villagers to pay *khuwah* to those who protected them from plunder. Even the central government was forced to pay *khuwah* to those who provided protection for the villagers. This was an old practice, which the Ottoman authorities were accustomed to when they paid the tribes who guarded the road to the *hajj*. Bedouin tribes dominated Transjordan to such an extent that no Turkish soldier was capable of restoring order in the country without relying on them. Awdah al-Qasus states in his memoirs that

> the Bedouin used to come to the Karaki farmland when the farmer ploughs the land, telling him that he was interested in becoming his partner, but he would not return until the reaping season to take his part of the harvest.[1]

Izz al-Din al-Tanukhi who lived a month with Banu Sakhr in 1914 said that the Bedouin lived on constant raiding, and that they were harmful to agriculture in the Balqa region.[2] However, despite the raids on agricultural land and the water

DOI: 10.4324/9781003450313-10

resources, there was always commercial interaction between the villagers and the Bedouin. Normally, the Bedouin bought flower and the villager let him use his grindstones for that purpose. The Bedouin used to buy from the villager agricultural items and other things that he needed for his survival in return for cattle, fat, butter, and other products, which he made in his tent. The fact that the Ottoman government was not in a position to control the villages and the Bedouin who often raided them brought the two sides to establish rules that regulated not only the trade but also other areas relating to damages, settlement of disputes, and so forth.

Small families in the villages were incorporated into the bigger ones in order to obtain protection. The shaikh of the family or the clan was the one who came to fill the vacuum, which the Ottoman authorities could not. In most cases, the inhabitants regarded with suspicion the security forces sent from the central government. This was the result of the harsh methods used by the authorities. The successive Arab uprisings provides an example for the brutal methods used by the central government, and the response of the local population. Normally, the Ottoman government, imposed taxes, demanded that the inhabitants disarm, and applied coercive measures to restore order. Such requirements made it difficult for the government to establish trust with the villagers and the Bedouin.

The Ottoman government sought to maintain control over the railroad and the Bedouin whose camels could reach the interior were valuable since they could maintain order in regions, which its forces could not reach. The Ottomans adopted a policy of hostility and cooperation with the Bedouin as the circumstances demanded. The Bedouin who guarded the railway were paid annually. They guarded the line from Dar'a to Medina southward in order to prevent the tribes from destroying the railroad and the stations connecting it. The shaikh was the dominating figure in the tribal society, and his position was determined by his noble origin, and the personal characteristics that he possessed such as bravery, wisdom, and willingness to help others. One of his most important virtues was his willingness to accept visitors and provide food. It was during the hospitality that the shaikh led discussions with members of other tribes on matters affecting life in the village, and it was there that decisions were made. The elders in the tribes were the ones who set the norms of behavior. There were no major cleavages in the society based of affiliation with certain classes. Christians lived with Muslims and there was little that separated ethnic groups. Women had a major role in the society, in the villages as well in as the desert. They participated in the major decisions that were made in the family. They provided hospitality to guests in the absence of their husband, and they enjoyed a large measure of freedom in the household. Furthermore, they were in the habit of accompanying their husbands to the battlefield to encourage them. The ties among the members of the tribes were close and the solidarity was ingrained in their way of life. Values such as "valor," "honor," and "shame" were paramount. Shame had to be cleansed by all members of the tribe who needed to fight against the tribe from which the offender came. Life for both villagers and Bedouin was the on a subsistence level, and the equity among the members was remarkable.

Amir Abdallah was faced with the difficulty of imposing modern standards of living on a traditional society. This led to discontent and dissatisfaction, which caused a rebellion in May 1921. It was only in July 1922 that the government managed to gather a force large enough to deal with the rebels. The suppression of the rebellion did not serve as an example to other *shaikhs* such as Sultan al-Adwan who rebelled later that year. He gathered a large force and after controlling of the regions in the vicinity of Amman, he threatened the city itself. However, the government's army defeated him and he fled to Jabal Druze. These events led to major changes among the tribes who were forced to abandon many of their traditional ways, and to adjust to the needs of the new age. Al-Adwan's arrest had adverse effect on his authority. However, the fact that Abdallah pardoned the leaders of the revolt led to better understanding between the tribes and the Hashemite regime.

Restoring order took a long time. The problem was that the tribes were not only in collision with the regime but also with one another. In addition, there were invasions that came from the Najd, Iraq and Syria, and the Jordanian tribes were raiding each other. There were major raids in 1922 and 1924 by the tribes of the Najd who embraced Wahhabism and raised the banner of the House of Saud. On two occasions, invaders came from the east, and they reached the encampments of Banu Sakhr and other tribes south of Amman. The Jordanian regime managed to inflict a defeat on them with its army and the cooperation of Banu Sakhr and other tribes. The fact that the government forces cooperated with the tribes in the face of these raids had enormous impact on the tribal community. Despite the fact that the government endeavored to establish trust among the Bedouin by forming a tribal council under Shakir bin Zayd in order to settle disputes, the raids did not cease entirely. In 1927, the Hashemite government reached an agreement with some tribes regarding the methods of curbing the raids. A similar agreement was concluded with Syria in 1930. However, the raids from the Najd and the Hejaz did not cease. In February 1928, bands from Rawlah and al-Shararat attacked the clans of Zaban and Haqish of the Bani Sakhr tribes, and they killed seventy men. In addition, al-Shararat attacked the Tawayana clan. Sheep and camels were stolen from Banu Sakhr and al-Ḥuwaiṭat. The raids recurred in 1929 and 1930. Abdallah made efforts to establish peace and agreements to that effect were reached between Huwaiṭat and Banu Sakhr on the one hand, and Jazi and al-Tawayana on the other. Establishing order in the society required the cooperation of the neighboring countries and in 1931, the Jordanian government sent a message to Saudi Arabia regarding this matter.

One of the ways to enhance the country's security was to settle the disputes among the tribes, and this could be accomplished only by encouraging them to meet and discuss the outstanding issues, and the other was to integrate them into the society and the Hashemite regime addressed these issues with remarkable success. In 1930, the Desert Force was formed by John Glubb, and he managed to recruit Bedouin to his force. The force consisted of Bedouin, except for the drivers of the armored vehicles, the soldiers who worked in the wireless network, and the instructors. This was a major step in the social development of Jordan. The Bedouin were incorporated into the defense apparatus, and thus became defenders of the country. Many of them began to settling in the towns and they joined the government's bureaucracy. The introduction of modern technology, the vehicles, and the communication system helped turn the Desert Force into a vital defense organization whose members became proud of their mission.

During Abdallah's reign, Transjordan witnessed an important development in all areas of life; the regime provided greater security and education became more common; transportation and communications improved and; bureaucracy was formed and institutions vital to the country's progress were established. This had an important impact on social life in the country. Free education allowed young men to advance and reach high positions in the government. Girls as well as boys benefitted from this change. In the last years of Abdallah's reign, many Palestinians came to Transjordan and made it their home. The incorporation of the two banks of the Jordan in the aftermath of the Palestine War of 1948 created greater cohesion and had an important impact on social life, and above all, Abdallah's emphasis on the Arab character of his emirate earned him handsome dividends among the neighboring countries. Transjordan turned into a country with solid commercial and cultural ties not only with the Arab countries but also with the West. The outcome was that it became less provincial and less nationalistic than any other Arabs country.[3]

Jordan during World War II

The situation in Transjordan worsened in July 1938, as result of the Arab Rebellion in Palestine. Amman had turned into a hotbed of intense nationalist sentiments that emanated from Damascus and Nablus, while the government officials remained indifferent and had little concern for the country's fate.[4] At the same time, the tribes were busy fighting each other in the countryside and the tension mounted considerably. The main tribes in Wadi Araba and west of it were the Sadiyeen, the Ahaiwat, the Azzamah, and the Terabeen. About a third of the Sadiyeen were Jordanian subjects. They resided in Wadi Araba, owned land in Ma'an, and their water resources were in Gharandal. Some of the Ahaiwat tribesmen lived in Wadi Araba as well, but their grazing areas bordered the Sinai Peninsula, Palestine, and Transjordan—three geographical units that did not easily get along with each other. Under these conditions, incidents among the tribes could hardly be avoided, and the authorities were incapable of settling conflicts, which erupted between the Ahaiwat and the Sadiyeen in September 1938. Moreover, the Palestine government's evacuation of Beersheba brought the conflict among the tribes to resurface. Finding themselves outnumbered by the Ahaiwat, the other tribes crossed to the east side of Wadi Araba to seek protection in Transjordan. Faced with a threat that their water resources at Gharandal would be taken by the Terabeen, the Sadiyeens committed themselves to maintain order in Wadi Araba.[5] What caused further turmoil in the area was the fact that many of the inhabitants of Jabal Druze looked to Transjordan as a place, which they would have liked to settle.[6]

By the end of 1938, Abdallah told British officials that the Iraqi propaganda against Transjordan had reached a dangerous stage.[7] He continued to expressed his desire for unity with Palestine and Syria.[8] Annoyed by the Iraqi broadcasts, he expressed his discontent by ordering his ambassador in Baghdad to protest to King Ghazi.[9] There were also reports that the Ghazzawieh tribes of the Jordan Valley, particularly those under Muhammad Saleh who had taken part in the assaults on Jews in Palestine, opened fire on the Transjordan Frontier Force.[10]

In addition to the fights among the tribes, Abdallah faced numerous issues that he needed to deal with. Seeking to increase the state's revenues, he sought payment from the Iraq Petroleum Company for oil that passed through his territory. According to British sources, he was probably the one who raised the issue, despite his commitment to avoid confrontation with the company.[11] Moreover, he expressed dissatisfaction with the fact that his treaty with Britain restricted his country's sovereignty, and prevented him from having control over the armed forces. Jordanian officials had constantly complained that the financial subsidies that they received from Britain were far too small to cover the expenses; that Abdallah's government did not enjoy sufficient power; and that Transjordan did not receive compensations for guarding the pipeline installed on its territory.[12]

Abdallah's demands from Britain were (a) that they changed his title to "king"; (b) that his annual subsidy be raised to £18,000; (c) that the Executive Council should be called the Council of Ministers and, (d) that Transjordan should have consular representation in the neighboring states.[13] Transjordan was besieged by many sides at that time. The Palestinian leader Hajj Amin al-Husseini and his Arab Higher Committee had made attempts to stir trouble in Transjordan. In addition, politicians such as Muhammad Ali Bey al-Ajluni, Subhi Abu Ghanima, and Suleiman Pasha Sudi who failed to obtain the positions, which they aspired to, stirred trouble in the kingdom.[14] What made matters worse was the fact that many Druze came to Transjordan following the 1925 revolt, and armed bands from Syria were penetrating the country through the Yarmouk Valley. Furthermore, the French authorities in Syria were neither consistent nor determined enough to prevent agitation by Arab nationalists against Transjordan, and Palestinians gangs stirred trouble in the country, practically with impunity.[15]

The Druze leaders continued to maintain a friendly attitude toward the inhabitants of Transjordan. This was largely a result of their disagreement with the leaders in Damascus.[16] However, Abdallah took measures to prevent the Druze leaders who came to find refuge in his country from settling near the Syrian frontier.

In February 1939, the Arab Committee in Damascus embarked on a plan to invite the inhabitants of Transjordan to rebel. This was a bold plan according to which, Hajj Mahmoud al- Shiteiwi (alias, Abu Raswan of Semakh) was to lead the rebellion whose headquarters was to be in Palestine; Mifleh al-Robadan al-Sherari was to operate in the northern part of the Jordan Valley; Abu Sha'ban of Lifta in the Balqa district, west of Amman; Abu Mahmoud Hammam in Jabal Ajlun; Abdallah Abu Sha'ar in Tafila; and Saud al-Yusuf al-Khadhra in the southern half of the Jordan Valley as far as the Dead Sea. All these leaders, except Abdallah Abu Sha'ar, entered Transjordan with their gangs and all the commanders, except Mifleh ash Shevari, were Palestinians.[17]

By 1939, the Germans were becoming more active in the country. In the report on the state of affairs in Transjordan for May 1939, Glubb writes: "It is noticeable that the Germans appear remarkably energetic in approaching the leading personalities in the country, while at the same time showing a meticulous thoroughness in studying the peculiarities of each."[18] According to a document forwarded by the French Commander in Chief to the General Officer Commanding in Palestine, Glubb started a propaganda campaign "with a clear plan of annexing Syria to Transjordan," and a number of Druze villages on Transjordan's frontiers were authorized to start preparations against possible invasion by Transjordan.[19]

Formerly known as the Turkish Petroleum Company (TPC), the Iraqi Petroleum Company had monopoly on the exploration and production of oil in Iraq between 1925 and 1961 until June 1972 when the socialist Ba'th party nationalized it and its operations were taken over by the Iraq National Oil Company. Upon its establishment, in 1912, this company became known by the title the Turkish Petroleum Company (TPC) and it was formed in order to acquire concessions from the Ottoman Empire to explore oil in Mesopotamia. The TPC obtained a promise of a concession from the Ottoman government, but the outbreak of World War I brought all the activities to an end and it was only in 1925 that the TPC began exploring for oil in return for a promise that the Iraqi government would receive a royalty for every ton of oil extracted. The Red Line Agreement divided the oil fields among the companies and this was the manner in which the great powers hoped to reduce the tension among the competing companies. The San Remo Conference of 1920 had stipulated that Iraqi government should be entitled to 20% of the company if it wished to invest in it, but the existing shareholders successfully resisted Iraqi efforts to participate despite pressure by the British government. In 1929 the TPC was renamed the Iraq Petroleum Company. Two pipelines were laid by the company, each with a capacity of two million tons a year. The northern line expanded in 1934 and the pipelines extended from Kirkuk to Al-Hadithah and from there to Tripoli and Haifa. The Kirkuk field was added at the same year. Only in 1938, nine years after the discovery did the IPC begin to export oil in significant quantities. The northern line from Kirkuk to Haifa extended over 532 miles while the southern (Mosul-Haifa pipeline) extended over 620 miles.

On July 21, 1939, the IPC pipeline was cut off about two miles east of Jordan by a gang, which operated in the Yarmouk Valley. Among the rebels who participated in such operations was the Palestinian leader Yusuf Abu Dura. His arrest provided the Arab leaders in Damascus the excuse to meddle in Transjordan's affairs, and plans to assassinate Jordanian officials were being adopted. When Transjordan was invaded by gangs from Syria in February 1939, the Arab Legion was barely capable of repelling them.[20] According to sources in the Arab Legion the vast majority of Transjordan's rural population approved of the British administration and had little desire for a change, and despite the severity of the conditions in Palestine the propaganda spread by the Germans had little appeal. The exception was Amman in which some politically minded government officials had differences with Britain.[21] On the eve of World War II, the French became increasingly involved in the Yarmouk Valley, after a gang of Palestinian rebels clashed with a detachment of

Syrian-Circassian cavalry. French successes were limited and temporary, and the rebels reemerged soon after each operation.[22]

Jordan: The Vichy Era

In his report on the situation in Transjordan, the Commanding Officer of the Arab Legion, al-Farik, stated that during the Vichy period, the border with Syria was controlled far more effectively than afterward, when the Allies recovered Syria. Transjordan's relations with the Deraa region became tenser. Protests by farmers whose houses were looted and their animals stolen could always find redress to their complaints during the Vichy period. Authorities in Irbid complained that since the officers of Free France had taken over, frontier incidents increased and complaints regarding stolen cattle remained largely ignored. He attributed the change to (a) lack of experience of the officials of Free France compared to those of Vichy and their tendency to deny Arab officials a say in the government (b) the fact that during the Vichy era, officials in Transjordan enjoyed greater prestige, and more support from Britain when needed. He argued:

> Nowadays, with British officers sitting beside the French in Deraa and Damascus, Transjordan no longer carries the prestige of a foreign country, and letters from Arab officials in Irbid are treated by the French as they would treat a letter from one of their own Syrian officials.

And (c) The excessive preoccupation of the British and the French with numerous issues connected with the country's occupation, tended to minimize the significance of other grievances.[23]

The British encountered a problem when they attempted to use the Trans-Jordanian Frontier Force for their operations in other Middle Eastern theaters. In one of the cases, a mechanized squadron that operated with the British troops, refused to cross the frontier into Iraq to attack Rutbah. The reason given for the refusal was that the terms of enlistment did not include the requirement that the unit serve outside Palestine. In his telegram to the Secretary of State for Colonies, Sir Harold McMichael attributed the refusal to the impact of Axis propaganda.[24]

During 1940, Abdallah's loyalty wavered, like other leaders during that time who believed that it was better to side with the Axis powers against *Perfidious Albion*, but he did not follow the example of leaders such as al-Ḥusseini in Palestine, Ali Maher in Egypt, or Rashid Ali al-Gaylani in Iraq who were pro-Axis. Moreover, he made the Desert Mechanized Force available to the British in Iraq and Syria in the early summer of 1941. The Arab Legion was involved in the war, whereas a squadron of the Transjordan Frontier Force refused to cross the border into Iraq. The period witnessed the expansion of the Desert Mechanized Force, and more units were created for guard duties, by recruitment from among the indigenous population. For a while, the fall of France encouraged Abdallah to revive his dream of Greater Syria under his leadership, but the British discouraged such thoughts, and even his most ardent supporters doubted that such scheme could be implemented. Abdallah persisted in his hopes until 1947.

Jordan in the aftermath of World War II

During the Arab revolt of 1936–1939, Abdallah portrayed an image of a hesitant and cowardly figure. His image became more robust when his father entrusted him to protect his kingdom from Saudi encroachments. However, his defeat at the battle of Turaba caused him not only embarrassment but also the loss of confidence which his father had in him. Despite marching toward Syria, his dream of talking over all the territories in that region did not materialize and he remained confined to Transjordan. His attempts to gain the territories continued sporadically and ineffectively when he supported the rebels who operated from his territory against the French. These, however, could not last long. Neither the British nor the Jordanian population were receptive to such acts. Abdallah's rule remained precarious and he had to appear supporting the main forces in his country. Apart from the Syrian exiles who exerted enormous influence on his government, there were the traditional tribal *shaikhs* and other notables who promoted their personal agenda, and he was hardly in a position to alienate them. Moreover, there were British officials whom he could not ignore. Abdallah had to maneuver through all these groups by coaxing and cajoling, rewarding and threatening, and by distribution of material benefits.

Abdallah exploited the need of the Syrians in the Istiqlal party for a safe haven from French retribution. However, despite the fact that they obtained high positions in his administration, they could not become a substantial threat to his regime. This was largely because he kept the resentment against them among the local population alive. He was always in a position to warn and put them in their place. At one time, he scolded his chief treasurer for not granting him the money he requested saying, "Those who do not wish to obey me blindly, let them leave me at once, I shall replace you with another treasurer."[25] Moreover, Abdallah resorted to granting titles and honors to those who were loyal to him, and reprimand them when he saw fit. He bound himself to every party member and official in his administration. His goal was not to promote loyalty to government institutions but to tie every official directly to him.[26]

The British saw Abdallah as a ruler, which they could manipulate for their benefit. They believed that with his Hashemite credentials he could be relied upon to mediate with the tribal chiefs whose customs he was familiar with. Furthermore, they thought that he was easy to control, and that his differences with the House of Saud were in line with their 'divide and rule' policy. However, Abdallah proved savvier than they thought. He managed to control the domestic opponents by playing off one against the other, and claiming that the British left him with little power.

The devastation caused by World War II forced the British to begin the process of domestic reconstruction and the process of disengagement from their imperial possessions began in earnest. Accordingly, another round of negotiations with Transjordan began and a second treaty was reached and ratified on June 17, 1946. The British recognized the independence of Transjordan, which became known as the Hashemite Kingdom of Jordan, and on May 25, 1946, the Parliament announced the establishment of an independent state with hereditary constitutional monarchy. Since the British dominated Transjordan, the French did not manage to advance toward that region. The fall of France and the establishment of the Vichy regime made it obvious that France was no longer in a position to maintain its presence in Syria, let alone pursue the nationalists who found refuge in Transjordan. Thus, Britain managed to maintain influence in the country despite the independence, which was given to the country according to the Treaty of London of March 25, 1946. Abdallah's title changed from 'amir' to 'king' and despite the Treaty of Friendship, which Britain signed with Abdallah two years later, it still maintained considerable influence in the country. As one writer put it, "This influence continued entering sometimes through the door, and sometimes from the window, secretly or openly, but it entered."[27]

Pressed by critics who argued that the British government did not move promptly with the negotiations, officials in Whitehall argued that the demands of the war made it impossible and impractical to discuss the Jordanian demand for total independence. Unlike the conditions in Palestine, which caused the British to withdraw after being caught in a crossfire of Arab and Jewish paramilitary forces, Whitehall's abandonment of Transjordan was smooth and peaceful.

Moreover, King Abdallah did not seem to follow the policy pursued by the other Arab states as it became obvious from the meetings, which he had with the Zionists. Jorge Garcia-Granados, who was nominated a member of the United Nations Special Committee on Palestine (UNSCOP) on May 13, 1947, and was charged with the task of contacting the King, had noted that "Abdullah definitely did not wish to associate himself with the other Arab states; and they, for their part, feared what he would say to us and would do all in their power to discourage any conference between us."[28] Abdallah assassination on July 20, 1951, caused much concern in British government circles. More ominous events followed in the early 1950s, which threatened to terminate British influence in the country, yet there was good will toward Britain.

Unlike most Arab countries, the Jordanians were always proud of their willingness to stand besides Britain, as al-Fariq noted in his report,

> Trans-Jordan is the only Arab country where men still stand in queues to enlist and were turned away. Some thirty of these are at this moment standing at the door of the room where this report is being written, clamoring to be accepted in the Arab Legion. When the present writer goes on tour, men pursue the car down the road and cross the fields, waving their cloaks and asking to be enlisted.[29]

Neither the treaty of 1946 nor the dismissal of John Glubb from Jordan in 1956 led to total separation between the two countries. Concerned about its declining influence in Jordan, the British conducted negotiations with the French, and raised the possibility that tension along the Israeli-Jordanian border could mount. Britain even planned to ask the Iraqis to move forces toward the Jordanian border.[30] Abdallah's assassination caused concern not only in London where the British government described him as an outstanding and far-sighted king but also in Israel where Eilath stated that the murder constituted a heavy blow to peace and stability in the Middle East.[31] Abdallah had close connections to the Bedouin tribes and *shaikhs* such as Mithqal al-Fa'iz whose release from prison he obtained immediately after Banu Sakhr demanded it. Mithqal who detested Glubb and did not consult him on any matter went directly to Abdallah. Shaikh Awad al-Saṭam al-Fa'iz recalled Mithqal's words to Glubb when he said, "You have cured us from bodily illness and inflicted us with Zionism."[32] Abdallah's assassination was a result of his dedication to Arab unity, whether it was of both banks of the Jordan River, between Jordan and Iraq, or the Greater Syria plan. This was certainly the main motive for the assassination according to most sources. It seems that the accounts regarding Abdallah's assassination are based on one source. Munib al-Maḍi and Sulayman Musa argued that it became obvious during the trial, that the assassination was conceived and planned in Cairo, where Abdallah al-Tal was a political refugee. The other partner to the conspiracy was Musa Muhammad al-Ayyubi who flew from between Cairo and Jerusalem on several occasions to meet Musa al-Husayni and planned the conspiracy. James Lent Kirkbride described the assassin Mustafa Ashuh as a hired terrorist, and argued that the conspiracy included Abdallah al-Tal who was one of the outstanding Arab officers who took part in defending the old city of Jerusalem in 1948. But Abdallah al-Tal denied taking any part in the conspiracy. There are three more accounts of the conspiracy. Naṣir al-Din al-Nashashibi claims that he received a telegram from the former Jordanian ambassador Walid Salih, in which the latter argued that as the attorney general involved in investigating King Abdallah's assassination, he found out that it was part of a conspiracy perpetrated by Faruk, former king of Egypt who sought to control both branches of the Hashemite family, in Amman and Baghdad.[33]

Najib al-Aḥmad argued that Britain was responsible for the assassination. He argued that 40 soldiers were stationed in front of the al-Aqsa Mosque by Glubb's order but their rifles were not loaded with ammunition. When the soldiers inquired why they were not allowed to load their rifles, Glubb said that the sanctity of the mosque would be compromised by loading the rifles with ammunition. Furthermore, he argued that Britain did not entrust an Arab unit, whether Jordanian or Iraqi with that mission. King Hussein did not see any connection between the assassination of the Lebanese politician, Riyad al-Ṣulḥ and that of grandfather Abdallah. This was the first time that Jordan experienced such an event. The public outrage was not against a certain perpetrator or a group of conspirators, but against the British who still maintained influence in the country. King Hussein stated that he was aware of the fact that Egypt shared part of the responsibility for the assassination because King Abdallah had many enemies there and the purpose of the conspiracy was aimed at dismembering Jordan. He added, however, that "the Egyptians had nothing to do with it. I lived among them and I know them."[34]

Abdallah's army was in Palestine during the Deir Yasin campaign on the road to Jerusalem where Palestinians were massacred by the Jewish fighters. He led his army to Palestine and called upon the Arab states to follow suit. Ṭahah Pasha al-Hashemi called for a meeting with Abdallah and Amir Abd al-Illah. At the meeting, Ṭahah said that it was inappropriate to conduct a war for political motives, hinting that Abdallah was seeking to dominate Palestine. This became abundantly clear in the first meeting, which Abdallah had with the Syrian prime minister.[35]

The short reign of King Talal

Talal who was crowned king in the aftermath of his father Abdallah's death, on July 20, 1951, was a tragic figure. Many were convinced of his mental illness, which they believed disqualified him from becoming king. His short reign of seven months during which he showed positive signs that he was about to follow his father's policy of moderation and discretion, came to a tragic end when he was judged to be mentally ill and unfit to rule. There are clear indications that he made sincere attempts to please his subjects. For example, he dismissed Justice Minister Fallaḥ Madadha who was not popular among the Palestinians, and nominated the popular opposition leader Abd al-Ḥalim al-Nimr as finance minister. Furthermore, in 1951, he gave amnesty to all prisoners, abolished censorship, and introduced a new constitution based on the principle that sovereignty emanates from the people. Unlike the constitution of 1946, which determined that the monarch was the supreme leader, the new document guaranteed freedom of speech, and determined that both the executive and legislative bodies were independent. Similarly, Ṭalal's foreign relations were marked by a since attempts to mend fences with the Arab states. He traveled to Riyadh to improve his relations with King Abd al-Aziz Ibn Saud. He approached King Faruk of Egypt who was known for his hostility to his father, and agreed to join the Egyptian-led Arab Collective Security Pact. In 1952, he contacted the Syrian government, met General Adib al-Shishakli, and agreed to open a Syrian embassy in Amman. Among his numerous guests were al-Husseini, and former Syria's Prime Minister Jamil Mardam Bey. However, his meetings with Egyptian officials caused concern in Jordanian government circles and he was eventually transferred from Egypt to Turkey on August 15, 1953. Eventually, Ṭalal's sympathy toward Nasser and his pan-Arab plans in 1956 caused tension between him and his son Hussein who refused to adopt a pro-Nasser orientation. After his failure to overthrow his son with the support from former loyal officers, Ṭalal approached his cousin Abdul Illah for support and when the latter declined, he approached a Kuwaiti business to help him return home.[36]

The difficulties inherent in forging a Jordanian identity

Following the collapse of the Ottoman Empire, the area that became known as Transjordan had practically nothing that could distinguish it from its neighbors. The inhabitants of the north and the west were associated with Syria, while those of the south had tribal links with the Arabian Peninsula.[37] The problem of creating a national identity remained complex for the Hashemites. There were various sources, from which they could fashion a separate identity for their newly established state, and these were scattered through its history and landscape. Moreover, there were numerous characteristics, local and foreign, from which to create a sense of group solidary. Throughout history, the country's residents were affected by Hellenistic, Christian, Islamic, Ottoman and Arab cultures. There were even common events from which a national identity could be fashioned, such as the Karak Revolt, which the Hashemites found useful in creating a national Arab background to their rule, and while attempted to build a unique common narrative, they left room to adjust it to newly rising circumstances.[38]

Young Hussein who ascended the throne after his father's short reign managed to fashion a unique identity for the state by promoting the uniqueness of the Bedouin tribes and their culture. Bedouin were incorporated not only into the army but also into civilian life and this was achieved by special legislation that promoted and protected them. By making a clear distinction between "native" Jordanian or Transjordanians and Jordanian Palestinians, he made the former stand out as unique, and as representing all that is authentic in his kingdom. In addition, he endeavored to develop a collective memory through education.[39] The debate over Jordan's identity has never ceased. It became part and parcel of the political discourse among both Jordanians and foreigners seeking to understand the state's raison d'étre and the meaning of life in it. Nahid Ḥattar is one of many who challenged the idea that Jordan is an artificial state, and a colonial creation, weak and relying on international support.[40]

According to the Ḥattar, Jordan is far from being an international or regional accident, but a result of a historical cumulative effort, and its resources are far from being limited. On the contrary, it is a state with unlimited resources, except the limits of political decisions. Jordan is not a poor country, except in determination and faith. Moreover, he seeks to refute the notion of Jordan's weakness arguing that the Jordanian state is only a stage for meaningful social or political activities. Jordan, he argues, is it not an outcome of the Sykes-Picot Agreement. Unlike other Jordanians, Ḥattar does not glorify the Nabatean period in Jordanian history. Nor does he dwell on the periods when Jordan was under the Byzantines, the Umayyads, the Abbasids, the Ayubbids, the Fatimids, or the Mamluks to find an identity for Jordan. He looks at Ottoman Jordan as the time when its identity was formed, argues that while the Ottoman administration played a negative role in the social progress in Syria and Lebanon, it played a constructive role in Jordan by encouraging national development. It contributed to the crystallization of Jordanian national entity, which was agricultural at that time, and was heading toward unity with other regions of Greater Syria, in the sociohistorical sense of the word. The Jordanian entity, he argues, was established during the nineteenth century, when the conflict between agriculturalists and Bedouin was raging. This conflict resulted in victory for the agriculturalists and the transformation of the Bedouins into agriculturists or semi-agriculturalists and the Ottomans contributed to this process by safeguarding the pilgrims' road to the holy cities. Therefore, they encouraged the agriculturalists to establish administrative centers and commercial enterprises, agricultural banks and other facilities. The result was that by the end of the nineteenth century, Jordan turned into a self-sufficient agricultural state. It exported barely, butter, desert plants, beasts of burden, sheep and other items to Syria and Europe. Thus, Jordan turned into a stable state and numerous villages emerged throughout the country. There were only three villages in al-Salt by the end of the eighteenth century, but their number increased to 103 by the end of the nineteenth century. During that time, a class of rich farmers emerged and their sons and daughters attended school. Many excelled in their profession and occupied high military and administrative positions in the Ottoman state. Some of the most prominent among them was Ali Khalfi al-Shirayiri who was well-versed in military studies, and taught at the military school in the Ottoman capital. Another personality of distinction was Ali Niyazi al-Tal who became the governor of Diyar Bakr. There were no Bedouins in the social and economic sense of the word in Jordan. The tribes established commercial ties with foreign countries. For example, Banu Sakhr who sought to export desert plants established commercial connections with Europe through Beirut. Agriculture expanded during that time, and part of it was financed by the Ottomans. Agricultural associations and villages were established. All this contributed to the settlement of most Bedouins.

By these means a Jordanian personality, which was semi-agriculturalist and semi-Bedouin began to crystallize and it started expressing itself in the Jordanian dialect, customs and traditions. Thus, the Jordanian nationals became capable of utmost loyalty to Great Syria.

After Greater Syria fell apart, they aimed at establishing a separate Jordanian entity that could unite the semi-agriculturalist and semi-Bedouin inhabitants based on loyalty and the need to struggle for existence. When the development of Jordanian history was interrupted by the British Mandate the Bedouins resumed their traditional way of life. Thus, Jordan's inhabitants turned from agriculturalists, and semi-Bedouins into Bedouins in the political and not in the socio-economical sense of the word. They turned into Bedouin employees whose ties to land and cattle were severed. In the modern economy, they became employees in industry and services, and many of them came to depend on charity and other civil society organizations.[41]

The question of what is Jordan and what criteria can be used to define a Jordanian continues to be vexing. Jordan's population is mixed. There is a large Palestinian majority in addition to Circassians and Chechens who came to the country in the nineteenth century. The country is predominantly, Muslim but there are Christians as well. In addition to villagers and town dwellers, there are Bedouin tribes who originated in the Arabian Peninsula, Iraq, and Palestine. The ruling dynasty is of a Saudi origin. It is for that reason that Jordanian textbooks emphasize the origin of the leadership rather than the country. The difficulty of defining the country stems from the fact that its borders remained unstable. Jordan's borders have altered constantly since its creation. By annexing the West Bank after the Palestine War of 1948, the country's borders changed, and it absorbed Palestinian refugees who became Jordanian refugees. Jordan's borders had changed again after the Six-Day War when it lost the West Bank and East Jerusalem. Then came another change in 1988, when King Hussein renounced all claims to the West Bank. This state of affairs makes it impossible to provide a definition of what Jordan is and who is a Jordanian. As Riad Nasser put it, "Due to the complex ethnic and national composition of Jordanian society, as well as its shifting geographical boundaries, any claim of historical continuity in the land, between the contemporary generations of Jordanians and their alleged ancestors, becomes questionable."[42]

In order to create a sense of national identity, Jordanian textbooks tend to emphasize the connection of the country's rulers to Prophet Muhammad and Jordan's connection to pan-Arabism, which stresses the element of solidarity among the Arabs. Jordan became a legitimate state largely because it is part of the Arab nation, which has no definite boundaries. The textbooks emphasize the role that Jordan had played in major events in the context of the Arab nation. For example, Jordan's role in the Arab Revolt of 1916 is emphasized, with a view to provide legitimacy to the Hashemite regime. The emphasis on Jordan's role in that rebellion is so heavy, that is it often portrayed as an exclusively Jordanian affair, while Syrians and Palestinians are excluded. Jordan's participation in such important pan-Arab events plays a major role in the formulation of national identity. By emphasizing its role in an issue of pan-Arab concern and linking its king to the Prophet, the Hashemites seek to compensate for the lack of historical continuity and the diversity of the country's population.

Riad Nasser argues that although the textbooks discuss the ancient civilizations that flourished on Jordanian territory,

> they do not explicitly claim that contemporary generations of Jordanians are the descendants of those communities. Consequently, the Jordanian narrative leaves contemporary generations of Jordanians without historical roots in the land-without historical continuity in the territory-they claim as their homeland.[43]

The Jordanian narrative overcomes this conflict by stressing the fact that Jordanians are a branch of Arab people, regardless of whether they are Jordanians, Syrians, or Saudis. Textbooks tend to stress the Hashemite origin of the Quraysh family of the Prophet. One of them said:

> *Quraysh* came to Mecca for the first time in the second century C.E. Six generations later, the first generation of *Quraysh* rose to power in Mecca when *Qusai ibn Kelab* took a leadership position in 480 C.E. He was preceded by his grandsons from *bani Hahem*. Thus, they earned the respect of all Arab tribes for the many good things they have done to ensure livelihood, security, and Arab unity.[44]

Discussing the origins of Amir ʻAbdallah, one of the textbooks reads as follows:

> He is *Abdullah ibn Ali ibn Muhammad ibn Abed al-Moa'in ibn 'Awan*. Born to two Hashemite parents in 1882 C.E. in the honorable Mecca; [born to] a noble family that had a title to the Emirate of Mecca. Its kin extends to the Prophet, peace be upon him.[45]

In the textbooks, the Hashemites portray themselves as the custodians of the holy cities of Islam and the pioneers of pan-Arabism. They portray the king as the follower of Ṣalaḥ al-Din who triumphed over the Crusaders, and delivered Jerusalem and the holy places from their domination. The Hashemite regime went to great length to renovate and restore any part of the holy places that were destroyed or fell into disrepair. The most obvious case was the restoration of the al-Aqsa mosque in Jerusalem, after it was attacked by a militant Australian Jew in 1968. This service emphasizes the Hashemites' role as protectors of the holy places not only for Jordan's sake but for all Muslims. Jordan as a geographical unit is not emphasized in the Hashemite campaign to glorify its role as the protector of the holy places. This role is not confined to a specific time-period or to the period of the state formation. It is tied to the role which, the early Hashemite tribe played already since the *jahiliya* period, as the custodian of the holy places.

Jordanian textbooks emphasize the historical role, which Sharif Hussein of Mecca played in Arab history but not for the sake of Jordan as a unique political entity. Furthermore, the Arab revolt is portrayed as an event that benefitted the entire Arab nation and not only Jordan in its modern boundaries. The Hashemites use both pan-Arabism and pan-Islamic ideologies to legitimize their rule. In an effort to explain the relationship between Jordanians and other Arabs the textbooks distinguish between the terms "people" (*sha'b*) and "nation" (*umma*). The term *sha'b* refers to a collective ruled by a state while *umma* is a larger group, with a common language, history, tradition and customs. The Jordanians are regarded as a branch of that large nation. According to this explanation, the nation consists of smaller units called "states." Although the textbooks trace the origins of the Jordanian people to the Arab race, they avoid discussing the ethnic origin of the country's inhabitants due the existence of several ethnic groups, and the complex issues, which such discussion brings up.

The message that the country was ruled throughout history by many conquerors such as Nabateans, Moabites, Edomites, Ammonites, Persians, Greeks, Romans, and others implies that there is lack of homogeneity and that the Jordanians are a conglomeration of foreign elements. The history and achievements of some Arab kingdoms such as the Nabateans are mentioned in the textbook but there is no attempt to link them with modern Jordanians. Moreover, the country is mentioned as a place through which many nations passed, and the only feature which identifies it with Jordan is the fact that it was "liberated" by Muslim Arabs in the seventh century. The description of Jordan's boundaries is not consistent in the textbooks, and the historical sites, which they choose to connect with the Arab nation in the attempt to glorify it are arbitrary. Similarly, the attempt to construct a glorious age for Jordan is problematic, and the textbooks fail to demonstrate a historical past that is wholly Jordanian. Instead, the textbooks mention historical sites where great battles took place, and in which Muslim armies triumphed over their adversaries.

The attempt to glorify the Hashemite family appears far more successful. Neither the Hashemites nor the Jordanians are of Jordanian origin. This makes the task of finding common features that could identify the country or its inhabitants all the more daunting, forcing the state to forge a national identity only by tying its destiny with pan-Islamism, pan-Arabism, and the deeds of the Hashemites.[46]

The difficulty of forging a unique national identity has serious implications on political life in the county. Jordanian political parties find similar difficulties when they try to attract voters. Political parties need raison d'étre, a clear platform and a program that emphasize their uniqueness. During the 1950s, the Jordanian political parties fashioned their platforms from colonial rule and the Palestinian fiasco (*nakbah*), caused by the establishment of the State of Israel. The campaign of the political parties consists of national and foreign issues, which most of the inhabitants can identify with. However, once these issues were no longer relevant, the parties find it more difficult to raise issues that could be regarded as vital and thereby attract many voters. As Muhammad al-Muṣaliḥah put it, "The current political endeavor is in need of supreme ability to integrate the present dangers and resistance movements, and supreme capacity to construct a political speech that could attract the masses."[47]

In his book, *Jordanians, Palestinians, and the Hashemite Kingdom in the Middle East Peace Process*, Adnan Abu Odeh discusses the nature of Jordanian nationalism and its adverse effect on the struggle of the Palestinians for greater equality in the country. He proposes another ideology, which he believes will bring greater unity to the country, while enhancing the status of its Palestinian inhabitants. He argues that "Hashemitism" ought to be the new ideology of the state. As he sees it, this ideology is inextricably connected to Jordan's history and to its Hashemite roots, and it is a flexible term that takes into consideration the demographic changes, which took place in the county. Indeed, Hashemitism has expanded and contracted with the expansion and contraction of the state. Prior to 1948, Jordanian national identity focused on the tribes in the East Bank under Arab Hashemite leadership. From 1948 to 1967, that term was applied to both banks of the Jordan River, and it included both the Jordanians and the Palestinians. Following the loss of the West Bank in the Six-Day War of 1967, the civil war of 1970–1971 and the subsequent renunciation of the West Bank by King Hussein in 1988, the Palestinians were excluded from the Jordanian state.[48] These events are seen by the author as detrimental to the remaining Palestinian population in Jordan, since the national identity shifted back to the East Bank, leaving the Palestinians in an inferior position vis-à-vis the Jordanians in the country.

Another personality who proclaimed himself as "the ideologist of the new Jordanian national identity" is Ahmad Uwaydi al-Abbadi of the Sikarnah, which is one of the less distinguished of the six Afgha clans. Uwaydi was a journalist who published books about the Bedouin tribes and later became a member of the Lower House of Parliament. By the late 1980s, he developed his own theory about Jordan's identity. Central to his political ideology is the conviction that the Jordanian are "sons of tribes." According to his vision, Jordan's national identity ought to be reserved for the descendants and adopted allies of the Arab tribal confederation known as Judham, and whose territory was in present-day Jordan. While oral tradition has it that Uwaydi's clan originated from the West Bank some two hundred years ago, he is convinced that the Sikarnah are actually descendants of Prophet Muhammad who originated from Mecca, lived in the West Bank for no more than two generations, and are distant cousins of the Hashemites. Uwaydi regards the Jordanian national identity as purely tribal, and thereby excludes all non-tribal Jordanians from this identity. As it turned out, his exclusion of the Palestinians and the minorities without tribal affiliation brought him into conflict with King Hussein who constantly portrayed himself as the father of all Jordanians. Andrew Shryock who had worked closely with him and the members of the royal family relates how they felt that "Ahmad was a great disappointment to us" and he heard them describe him as a "dangerous man."[49] The upshot was that Uwaydi was placed under government surveillance, and eventually brought to trial for "undermining national unity" after publishing an article in the organ *Shihan* entitled "I'll be relieved if the Palestinians leave [Jordan]." Defending himself in court he argued that journalists took his statement out of context, and he explained his conviction that if the Palestinians adopt a Jordanian identity, they would be forfeiting their claim to Palestine and thus serving the Zionists who keep on insisting that Jordan in a Palestinian state. It was only due to his tribal al-Abbadi supporters who demonstrated outside the courtroom that the case was dismissed by the judges. On August 22, 1996, King Hussein addressed this matter in a speech to the Parliament in which he said:

> O brothers, democracy has its limits. There is a former colleague of yours who wrote the worst things imaginable against our national unity, in a very clear and vulgar way. He was called to court, and he was able to bring many people to besiege the court, to shout slogans: *'al-l-makshuf, 'al-l-makshuf, falastini ma nashuf* (roughly: "Loud and clear: Loud and clear! Palestine disappear!"). He says overtly that no Palestinians should be in Jordan. Is there anything worse than this? Democracy has limits. We should not destroy national unity in the name of democracy. We are one family. I have said before and I will continue to say for as long as I live, "Anyone who attempts to destroy national unity is my enemy till the Day of Judgement." And he is also the enemy of every Jordanian and every true citizen of this country. Until then, let us protect this achievement, this democracy, this spirit of dialogue, and all our accomplishments. Let us build up and repair what needs to be repaired in any field of endeavor, at any time (Transcript of Royal Address to Parliament, 22 August 1996; from the personal papers of Ahmad Uwaydi al-Abbadi).[50]

The affair ended after the judge acquitted him. The case was dismissed and Ahmad was allowed to continue his political activities, which ended in his election as parliament member. The national identity of the Jordanian inhabitants of the East Bank proved much more robust than those of the Palestinians in that country and it manifested itself clearly following the events of the Arab Spring, when many demonstrated against the regime and demanded reforms, as Pénélope Larzilliere noted:

> A certain consensus emerged among demonstrators on the issue of a constitutional monarchy, even if the Jordanian opposition remains silently wrought and weakened by the lasting opposition between "Jordanians" and Palestinians. It should nevertheless be pointed out that the "Palestinians" did not form an advocacy group as such. The Palestinian camps which remain

> places of memory, are not actually strong arenas of mobilization in Jordan, and they scarcely took part in these movements. On the other hand, political groups formed exclusively on the basis of Transjordanian identity had a strong presence, grouped around tribal personalities, but not only them. Their originality is that they no longer throw their support unconditionally behind the king, no matter how the monarchy tries to exploit this political identity.[51]

Prominent Jordanian personalities continue to offer their definitions of Jordanian identity. According to Dr. Ali Muhafiza, President of Yarmouk University in Irbid, "We can't say that there is a Jordanian identity, or a Syrian, or Lebanese or Palestinian identity…The reason is that our new political entities in this area have been created by Western powers at the beginning of this century."[52] Dr Mazen Armouti, Advisor to H.R.H. Crown Prince Hassan had this to say about the identity issue,

> Here in this area we have different layers of identity. So, the most common demarcation is what we call the three-layer-approach of saying I am a Jordanian, also an Arab and also a Muslim. We have three circles of identity and they are not necessarily contradictory…although politically on certain occasions in history sometimes we have a conflict between a stronger Arab leaning or a stronger national leaning in the smaller sense of nation, *qawmî* and *waṭanî*.[53]

The Jordanian Senator Leila Sharaf was much more specific about this is issue when interviewed in August 14, 1999. She said:

> I think that the national identity of Jordanians started to delineate itself since 1970, when there was a clash between Palestinian and Jordanian identity…It took a legal and more outright status in 1974…[before that] the psyche of the Jordanians was pan-Arab and that is why they were not as free as the other Arabs to say we are strictly Jordanian…The other factor is that the influx of so many Palestinians made it 'ayb [taboo] to say I am Jordanian because it would imply discrimination against the Palestinians.[54]

Hani Hourani, the editor-in-chief of *Al-Jadid* magazine and cultural director of the Shoman Foundation in Amman distinguished between Palestinians and Jordanians when he tried to deal with the issue of national identity. He said on August 10–11, 1991:

> Palestinians, especially, see Jordanian identity only as an expression of loyalty to the king, there is a difference between loyalty to the kingdom and loyalty to the entity…Jordanians often look to the state as a protector, to maintain the internal balance. Since the late 70's, as the society developed more rapidly, a need was created for people to express their own identity.

> The Palestinians already have their national identity, their organizations and representations. But Jordanians only have the king and kingdom and a government which does not express their national identity and nationalism.[55]

Abdel-Raouf Rawabdeh, Member of the Lower House of Parliament representing Irbid, argued that Jordanians have become much more aware of their national identity than they were in the past and "no Jordanization has ever taken place in the sense of thinking of the Jordo-Jordanians [East-Jordanians] as being the owners of their country."[56] Ahmad Uwaydi opined that Jordanianism is simply a transformation of tribalism. He told Fathi on August 14, 1991.

> Tribal organization is very strong in Jordan and you have to know that the Jordanian society is one of the strongest in the world.... But tribalism has now changed into Jordanianism, which means that usually they say I am ʻAbbâdî or Banî Ṣakhr but now we are Jordanian first, [a change] from tribal identity to national identity.[57]

Notes

1 Cited in Sulayman Musa, *Dirasāt fī Tarīkh al-Urdun al-Ḥadith* (ʻAmmān: Wizarat al-Thaqāfah, 1999), p. 134.
2 *Ibid.*
3 *Ibid*, p.141.
4 A Monthly Report on the Administration of the Trans-Jordan Desert from the Months of July and August, 1938. TNA FO371/23246/E639, pp. 4–5.
5 *Ibid.*
6 A Monthly Report on the Administration of the Trans-Jordan Deserts, January 1939. TNA FO371/23246/E3079, p. 4.
7 The High Commissioner for Transjordan to the Colonial Secretary. TNA FO 371/23247/E646, November 17, 1938, p. 28.
8 *Ibid*, p. 37.
9 Report on the Political Situation for the Month of December, 1938. TNA FO371/23247/E1256, p. 2.
10 *Ibid*, p. 3.
11 *Ibid*, p. 5.
12 "Office Arabe, Bulletin hebdomadaire, No. 1, February 12, 1939.TNA FO 371/23247/E1388.
13 Telegram from the High Commissioner for Palestine to Colonial Secretary, February 24, 1939. TNA FO371/23247/E1570.
14 A Monthly Report on the Administration of the Trans-Jordan Deserts, January 1939. TNA FO371/23246/E3585, p. 4.
15 *Ibid*, p. 7.
16 A Monthly Report for the Month of April 1939. Amman, Transjordan, TNA FO371/23246/E4041, p. 5.
17 A Monthly Report for the Month of April 1939. Amman, Transjordan, TNA FO371/23246/E5119, pp. 10–11.
18 *Ibid.*
19 A Monthly Report of July 1939, Amman, Transjordan, TNA FO317/23246/E6663, p. 11.
20 *Ibid*, pp. 19; 21.

21 A Monthly Report for the Month of August 1939. Amman, Transjordan, TNA FO371/23246/E6905, pp. 7–9.
22 A Monthly Report for the Month of October 1939. Amman, Transjordan TNA FO 371/23246/8054, p. 3.
23 MacMichael to Colonial Secretary, TNA FO 371/27143/E2528, May 21, 1941.
24 Cited in Toby Dodge, *An Arabian Prince, English Gentleman and the Tribes East of the Jordan River: Abdullah and the Creation and Consolidation of the Trans-Jordanian State*, Occasional Paper 13, Center of Near and Middle Eastern Studies (SOAS), University of London, May 994, p. 13.
25 *Ibid.*
26 Anīs Ṣāyigh, *Al-Hāshimīyūn wa-al-Thawrah al-'Arabīyah al-Kubrah* (The Hashemites and the Great Arab Revolution), Arabic text (Beirut: Manshurāt Dār al-Ṭalī'a, 1966), p. 262.
27 Jorje García-Granados, *The Birth of Israel: The Drama as I Saw It* (New York: Alfred A. Knopf, 1949), p. 190.
28 Report by Colonel Glubb (February 1–May 31, 1942). TNA FO 371/31383/E4106, p. 17.
29 Meron Medzini, *The Proud Jewess: Golda Meir and the Vision of Israel-A Political Biography*, Hebrew text with Title in English (Tel Aviv: Edanim, 1990), 241.
30 'Ādil Riḍā, *Waṣfī al-Tall: Al-Qātil wa-al-Qatīl, al-Ightiyāl fī al-fikr al-Qānūnī wa-al-siyāsī* (The Assassin and the Assassinated, the Assassination in the Legal and Political Thought), Arabic text (al-Qāhirah: Dār Hīrurdūt, 1972), p. 70.
31 Cited in Ṭal'at Shanāah, *Ayyām Zamān: Al-Tarīkh al-Shafawi lil-Urdun wa-Filasṭīn* (Days Ago: The Oral History of Jordan and Palestine), Arabic text ('Ammān: Al-Ahlīyah, 1993), p. 138.
32 Cited in 'Alī Muḥammad Sa'āda, *Al-Ightiyāl al-Siyāsī fī al-Urdun* (Political Assassination in Jordan) ('Ammān?; Daïrat al-Maktaba al-Waṭṭanīyah, 1999), p. 36.
33 Cited *Ibid*, p. 37.
34 'Ādil Arslan, *Mudhakkirāt al-Amīr 'Ādil Arslan* (The Memoirs of al-Amir 'Ādil Arslan), Arabic text (Beirut: Dār al-Taqaddumīyah, 1994), p. 109. Entry for Thursday, May 2, 1948.
35 Sami Moubayed, "Talal: the Sad Story of the King of Jordan," *Al-Mashriq*, Vol. 4, No. 15 (December 2005, Febuary 21, 2006).
36 Cited in Yitzhak Gil-Har, "British Commitments to the Arabs and Their Application to the Palestine-Trans-Jordan Boundary: The Issue of the Semakh Triangle," *Middle Eastern Studies*, Vol. 29, No. 4 (October 1993), p. 694.
37 Musa Budeiri, "Poor kid on the Bloc: The Importance of Being Jordan," *Die Welt des Islams*, Vol. 36, No. 2 (July 1996), p. 242.
38 Elena D. Corbett, *Competitive Archaeology in Jordan: Narrating Identity from the Ottomans to the Hashemites* (Austin: University of Texas Press, 2014), p. 87.
39 Pénélope Larzilliere, *Activism in Jordan* (London: Zed Books, 1998), pp. 13–14.
40 Nāhiḍ Ḥattar, *Taḥāwwulāt Jadhrīyah fī al-Urdun 1994–2004* (Radical Transformation in Jordan 1994–2004), Arabic text (Al-Qāhirah-al-maḥrūsah lil-nashr wa-al-khadamāt al-ṣaḥafīyah wa-al-ma'lumāt, 2004), pp. 156–157.
41 *Ibid*, pp. 160–161.
42 Riad Nasser, *Recovered Histories and Contested Identities: Jordan, Israel, and Palestine* (Lanham, MD: Lexington Books, 2011), p. 126.
43 *Ibid*, pp. 128–129.
44 Cited *Ibid*, p. 131.
45 Cited *Ibid*, p. 132. [Parentheses by Nasser].
46 *Ibid*, p. 148.
47 Muḥammad al-Muṣāliḥah, *Al-tajribah al-ḥizbīyah al-siyasīyah fī al-Urdun: Dirasāt taḥlilīyah-muqāranah bayna tajribatay al-khamsināt wa-al-tis'ināt* (The Political Trial of the Parties in Jordan: Analytical Studies Comparing between the Trials of the Fifties and the Nineties), Arabic text ('Ammān: Dār Wā'il lil-Nashr, 1999), p. 122.

48 Stefanie Nanes, "Hashemitism National Identity, and the Abu Odeh Episode," *The Arab Studies Journal*, Vol. 18, No. 1 (Spring 2010), p. 163.
49 Andrew Shryock, "Dynastic Modernism and Its Contradictions: Testing the limits of Pluralism, Tribalism, and King Hussein's example in Hashemite Jordan," *Arab Studies Quarterly*, Vol. 22, No. 3 (Summer 2000), p. 68.
50 Cited *Ibid*, p. 69.
51 Larzilliere, pp. 185–186.
52 Cited in Fathi, p. 257.
53 Cited *Ibid.*
54 Cited *Ibid*, pp. 258–259.
55 Cited *Ibid*, p. 259.
56 Cited *Ibid.*
57 Cited *Ibid.*

X King Hussein's challenges

Following the death of King Ṭalal and the rise of his son Hussein in 1952, the county faced numerous challenges. It obtained its independence from Britain, but the Arab Legion was commanded by Glubb, and the British influence was still discernible in all aspects of life. The nationalists in Syria and Iraq had their own grievances, and did not come to terms with the Hashemite family in Jordan. The overthrow of King Faruk and the rise of the Free Officers in Egypt inspired the Arab nationalists in Jordan to terminate the vestiges of colonialism, and they looked at Nasser as the leader who would bring an end to Western influence. In Jordan, many saw the young king as a compromiser and a collaborator with a former colonial power whose objective was to perpetuate its influence in the country even after independence. Above all, however, it was primarily the egalitarian socialist message of the Syrian Ba'th Party and its charismatic leader Michel Aflaq that had enormous influence of on the young generation in Jordan. He inspired them to become active and to form a group dedicated to the mission of rescuing the country from imperialist domination. Abd al-Salam al-Majali who met Aflaq and later joined this Ba'th Party recalled in his memoirs:

> I was still in the association after the first year, when we celebrated the noble holiday of the Prophet's birth. Michel Aflaq was one of the speakers. I was struck with awe. You see? What will a Christian say in the holiday of the Prophet's birth? I sat and waited for his turn. And when he began to speak, he amazed me. All these years I did not hear a speech more beautiful than that of Aflaq, about the sublime Prophet, may peace be upon him....
>
> I went to listen to Aflaq's periodically. We were hearing about his actions and speeches, and I found myself participating in the Ba'th Party. There were other parties that were active in the association, such as the Communist Party and the National Syrian Party, however, Ba'th Party was the one that filled my soul with magic by virtue of its philosophy and thought.[1]

The sense of despair, which resulted from the endemic struggle of the Hashemite family against its opponents in the surrounding Arab states; the shame engendered by the establishment of the State of Israel in the aftermath of the Palestine War of 1948; the influx of numerous Palestinian refugees; and the dire economic conditions

DOI: 10.4324/9781003450313-11

brought many young Jordanians to look for a better future. There is little wonder that the Ba'th Party's agenda had enormous influence on the mind of these young men. The prominent Jordanian politician Jamal Asha'er recalled how attractive was the vision of that party for him, and many of his compatriots. He writes:

> There was nothing unusual or difficult about my association with the Arab Ba'ath Party after my studies in al-Salt, the experiment of the Syrian national party, the events of 1948 and the political atmosphere at the American University in Beirut and Damascus.... The dreams about unity, democracy and progress in all theirs meanings and all their extent occupied the minds of our generation.[2]

The origins of the Free Officers Movement in Jordan can be traced back to the Palestine War of 1948, which left many Jordanians in the society and particularly in the armed forces disillusioned. Among those who participated in the war there was a sense that their commanders were not prepared for the war. The criticism intensified, and culminated in accusations of conspiracy and betrayal. Gradually, the young officers felt that they had a mission to save the country. Among those who led this movement was Abdallah al-Tall, Mahmoud al-Musa, Maḥmoud al-Rawsan, and Ali Abu Nuwar. Undoubtedly, al-Tall was the most deeply involved in politics. He stayed in Jerusalem where he met some of the young enthusiasts. Another factor, which led to frustration among these young men, was the conviction that Glubb prevented the Jordanian army from taking over the entire city of Jerusalem, and that it would have been possible to hold on to the towns of Lod and Ramla after the Palestine War. Sulayman Musa recalled the impact of this sentiment saying, "This conviction was so deeply rooted that I felt that is it still ingrained in the souls of many to this day (1984)."[3]

In 1950, four of these officers joined the Ba'th Party. These were Shahir Yusuf Abu Shaḥut, Mahmoud al-Mu'ayata, Qasim al-Naṣir, and Turki al-Handawi. They formed the nucleus of an organization, which they called The Secret Organization of the National Officers in the Jordanian Army. Soon others joined, and the organization established the weekly magazine *Al-Qunbilah* (The Bomb), which contained articles in their own handwriting. Its editor was Zahir Maṭar and some of his comrades in the artillery corps.

The two main goals of this organization were to free Jordan from British influence and to establish union with Syria. This organization expanded, and included officers from all branches of the army. Moreover, independent officers with political affiliation joined the organization. On the whole however, members such as Shawkat al-Sabul who joined the organization, tended to be closer to the left-of-center. Inspired by the Free Officers Revolution in Egypt and their platform, which led to transformation in that country, they called their organization "The Jordanian Free Officers Movement." Their next move was to form an apparatus for the movement. This apparatus included officers from all branches of the army. Then they chose a small group to lead the movement. Its president was Abu Shaḥut, and its vice president was Qasim al-Naṣir. The deputy in charge of the organization's secrets was Aḥmad Z'arur and the deputy in charge of its finances was al-Handawi.

This organization consisted of young officers whose average age was less than thirty-five, most of them were fairly educated, and it was secretive to the extreme. It consisted of small five independent members units that acted in isolation from each other. Ba'thists did not occupy any positions in these units. Although there were Ba'thists who thought that it was beneficial and prudent to coordinate their activities with their comrades in the Ba'th Party, this organization operated entirely on their own. The organization remained secret, confined to a handful of officers, and it had no supreme commander. The officers of this organization established ties with their comrades in Egypt. For example, in 1948, the Egyptian officer al-Tuhami was in contact with the Jordanian officer Qasim al-Naşir. In 1954, one of the Egyptian officers contacted al-Naşir, and asked for his cooperation in forming military units whose purpose was to operate against Israel. Al-Naşir agreed to cooperate. The Egyptians stirred the Jordanians to carry out operations as they saw fit, and they paid them for their efforts. According to Maḥmoud al-Mu'ayṭa, it was Fuad Hillal, the Egyptian military attaché in Amman in 1957, who incited the Free Officers to act against the Ba'thi influence, and the Egyptian intelligence played a destructive role in the Jordanian army. Ali Abu Nuwar confirmed that Egyptian intelligence officers were behind the Jordanian operations on the Israeli side of the armistice line. These operations led to wide-ranging reprisals by the Israelis.

The Free Officers Movement included members from the towns as well as the villages. It had Circassians, Bedouins, Christians, and other minorities, and all took part in one national mission; to liberate the country from foreign influence. Nadhir Rashid who was one of the prominent members of the movement explained what motivated him to be active saying, "We had deep conviction that the army would not be capable to carry out its national mission as long as it was commanded by British officers."[4] It is worth mentioning that three Circassian officers who belonged to the Ba'th party or adopted Nasserism; these were Musa Mahmoud, Muhammad 'Ali Amin and Ismet Ramzi who held formal nationalist positions.

Despite opposition from Glubb who attempted to weaken the movement by nominating its leaders to different positions, it continued its destructive operations. When the announcement regarding the promotions in the army was pronounced in 1954, the main figure in the movement, Abu Shaḥut found out that he was not promoted. When asked for the reason, Glubb told him that his involvement in politics disqualified him from being a leading member in it. He was then nominated as one of Lawrence's aids, and was thereby promoted.

Being in charge of the desert regions, Glubb worked in order to integrate the Bedouins in the Jordanian society. This was done by recruiting them to the army and by opening schools in it. This gave them the ability to read and write, and to be promoted as a result. Some of them became commanders of regiments. Thus, the Bedouins began to acquire assets that helped them become active in the Jordanian society. Glubb's policy brought many young tribesmen from Iraq, Syria, the Najd, and the Hejaz to cross the desert and join the Jordanian army. Glubb embraced the Bedouins, spoke in their language, and became involved in their lives. They were impressed by his personality, and they called him by endearing terms such *Abu Ḥanik*, *Ṣaḥib*, *Abu Faris*, and *Basha*. In Glubb's eyes, the Bedouin was more reliable than the city dweller or the villager who remained attached to his land, and was less devoted to the army than the Bedouin who had no land to which he could return.

Glubb lived with the Bedouins and followed their customs and traditions. Unlike Peake Pasha who preceded him, and who alienated them following his decision to arrest Mithqal al-Faiz in the hay store, Glubb refrained from such heavy punishments. When the young king Hussein was in Paris, he was accompanied by the military attaché Ali Abu Nuwar, who spoke to him about the dominance of the British officers in the Jordanian army, and about the losses, which the country had as result of the Palestine War. The officer talked about freeing the country from foreign rule, and about the need to Arabize the army and rid the country of British rule, which Glubb represented. He went on saying, that Glubb was operating in the interest of the British who allowed the Jews to come to Palestine. In 1953, Abu Shaḥut visited London for military training. Several Jordanian officers, including Abu Shaḥut and Abu Nuwar, sought to throw a party in the King's honor. At that meeting, Abu Shaḥut spoke about the Free Officers, tried to convince Abu Nuwar to join, and accompanied him on his way to see King Hussein who heard about them and seemed sympathetic to their plans.

The other objective of the Free Officers was to make contacts with Syria. With that objective in mind, Abu Shaḥut went to Damascus on a special mission, in May 1954. During that visit, he met Jamal Ḥamad, the Egyptian military attaché in Damascus, and he spoke to him about the movement. Then he met the Syrian army officer Adil Shahir, and Ba'th Party member Mustafa Ḥamdoun. He spoke to them about the movement and its objectives and about his desire to establish ties with the Syrian army. The upshot was that Ḥamdoun delivered the message to his colleagues in the party. Shortly afterward, Ammad Abd al-Karim came to Amman and informed Abu Shaḥut and his comrade Shawkat al-Suboul that the Syrian military command is asking the members of the Free Officers to prove the seriousness and the sincerity of their intent by executing a few British officers and Jordanian government officials, and bombing several British airplanes at Ma'an airport. Infuriated by the egregiousness of this challenge, Abu Shaḥut and Shawkat responded by saying, "go back to your men and tell them: we are a nationalist movement and not gang of murder and destruction."[5]

The officers gave their blessing to Abu Nuwar's trip to Egypt where he met Nasser and told him about the movement's plan to expel the British officers and Arabize the army. Nasser's reaction was that such step would be too risky. He then said that that he was in favor of a collision with the British, before their forces land at the Suez Canal. At that moment, Abu Nuwar was one of the most prominent military figures, and the point of contact between the King and the Free Officers. Two of the group's members, Mundhir Inab and Mazen al-Ajluni, joined him as military advisors of the king. Gradually, Abu Nuwar began regarding himself as the movement's spokesman. He began challenging the members of the government. He told Abd al-Ḥalim al-Nimr "Why don't your politicians make a decision and we the soldiers will carry it out?" What he meant to say was that the government ought to make a decision to dismiss Glubb. Abd al-Halim's response was "Stay away from me. I can see you hanging in front of the mosque." The same day, he addressed his comrade Ali al-Ḥiyari, told him about his plan, and asked him to join the Free Officers whose aim was to dismiss Glubb and the British soldiers. Al-Ḥiyari's response was "You are playing with your blood. I am a professional soldier and I don't meddle in politics."[6]

Abu Nuwar and his comrades in the Free Officers movement continued in their efforts to convince others to join, and to bring about the dismissal of the British officers, and Glubb in particular. They met Raḍi al-Handawi Ṣaliḥ al-Shar' and his brother Ṣadik, but they did not respond to the call. According to Abu Nuwar, Ṣaliḥ told Shar' that the Jordanian officers were not skilled enough to carry out the military mission. Later, Ṣaliḥ denied, and said that this matter was not discussed at all. Abu Nuwar said specifically that he had no rancor against Glubb. He added, however, that Glubb pursued Britain's interests and not those of the Kingdom of Jordan. Hazza' al-Majali mentions in his memoirs that he heard from some of the ministers that Abu Nuwar was in touch with the Americans, with a view to establish a pact with them, apart from the one that Jordan had with Britain. He asked the ministry to establish contacts with the Americans regarding that matter. Al-Majali also said that he heard from several representatives that Abu Nuwar told them that it was sheer lunacy to substitute Arab financial assistance for the British because there was no guarantee that the Arab countries would be able to continue sending it. According to other sources, Abu Nuwar exploited his position to convince the King to dismiss Glubb. Abu Nuwar organized a group of officers whose mission was to expel Glubb. He asked for financial assistance for him and his colleagues to carry out the operation, but he did not give them anything from the sum that he obtained.[7]

Seeing that Abu Nuwar's movement did not carry out its mission, an organization within army took matters in its hands and planned a military coup. This group was led by Maḥmoud al-Rawsan, and included members such as Ibrahim al-Ḥadidi, Abd al-Rahman Muhadayn who represented the Ba'th Party, Mundhir Inab and Mahmoud al-Tall. Ibrahim al-Ḥadidi was the liaison officer with the Ba'th Party. Waḥdan Uways was nominated as a liaison officer who contacted other members of the organization through al-Ḥadidi whom he visited in his home in Zarqa in May 1958. Muhadayn who had a major role in the organization joined the debates but the leadership was in al-Rawsan's hands. A telegram from the Ba'th Party in Damascus arrived in Jordan, saying that the Iraqis were inclining to introduce changes with the collaboration of the Ba'th Party. The telegram sent to the organization asked the Jordanian branch of the Ba'th to be ready for action against the British officers. Another telegram was sent to the organization through an officer who was connected with Mahmoud al-Musa who found shelter in Damascus. The telegram repeated the request that the organization in Jordan be ready for action as soon as they hear from Baghdad.

On July 14, 1958, Abd al-Karim Qasim and his followers carried out the coup, which toppled the Hashemite monarchy in Iraq, and brutally executed

Prime Minister Nuri al-Sa'id. Wahdan Uways recalled the excitement, which the news regarding the Iraqi take-over created among the Jordanian officers in the organization. He writes:

> Three weeks went by after the meeting without contact with the organization. On the morning of July 14, 1958 Radio Baghdad made the first announcement regarding a military coup, as it was agreed upon. I rushed to Bahjat Abu Ghuraybah. This was a great joy for all of us, and we agreed that something similar will take place in Jordan. However, nothing like that took place. By the second day Bahjat asked me to contact Ibrahim al-Ḥadidi and to find out why there was no movement according to the agreement.[8]

According to al-Musa, the reason why the Jordanian officers did not move was the fear that the Israelis might intervene. Waḥdan Uways noted in memoirs that he carried a telegram to Salim Musa'dah, which called for a popular rebellion in the north that would take place at the same time that the army mobilized.[9] Shortly afterward, the entire group was caught and arrested. Meanwhile, members of the Jordanian delegation were killed during the Iraqi coup. The most prominent among these was Sulayman Ṭawqan. The impact of the Iraqi coup among the Jordanian public was a mixture of joy and expectation. However, King Hussein was not at ease. The council of ministers met in Amman airport in order to discuss the developments. This was out of fear that a similar coup might take place in Jordan.

Bahjat Abu Ghuraybah told Uways that he heard from Rifa'at Awdah that al-Shar' had an organization in the army, which included his brother, and planned to overthrow the regime, and that Rifa'at 'Awdah wanted to know the party's position in the matter. Uways met Rifa'at from whom he learned that the organization was ready to act, and to assist him in this matter. Uways learned that contacts were made with the tribes in the north, with a view to start the rebellion at the same time that the army moved. He told him that he would introduce him to al-Shar' and the leader who was to start the rebellion. When Uways told Bahjat about that plan, the latter asked for financial assistance from Damascus. In the end, the King survived one of the most important challenges of his regime after Uways was caught and taken to prison.

The debate over the Baghdad Pact

Another major challenge that the young king had to face emerged in 1955, when the British started negotiations regarding Jordan's entry into the Baghdad Pact. This was dangerous issue, which put the king on the horns of a dilemma; cooperating with Britain's attempt to include Jordan in the proposed defense pact would have benefitted the king by gaining greater support against the nationalists, who found every opportunity to condemn his connection with what they saw as a Western ploy, designed to prolong the subordination of the Arab peoples to exploitation. One the other hand, however, the King feared the opponents of Britain, and Nasser in particular. Besides, joining such pact meant taking side in the Cold War conflict, which could have earned Jordan the friendship of the United States, but alienate the Soviet Union, which was a potential ally and an arms supplier.

A British delegation under General Gerald Templar arrived in Amman that year. He proposed to increase the size of the Jordanian armed forces by sixty percent, on the proviso that Jordan join the proposed Baghdad Pact with Britain, Turkey, Iran, and Pakistan. This was an attractive offer, which promised Jordan the support of several countries in the West. In the beginning, it seemed as if the government tended to accept it. However, opposition by Egypt and Saudi Arabia accompanied by intense propaganda campaign, led to intense opposition within Jordan. The opposition culminated in the resignation of four ministers, which forced Prime Minister Sa'id al-Mufti to resign. The demonstrations that ensued did not cease until the new Prime Minister Hazza' al-Majali resigned as well. Meanwhile, the Free Officers called a meeting to discuss the matter, and the decision was that Jordan should not join the pact because it targeted the Soviet Union as the enemy. Abu Shaḥut argues in his memoirs that the Egyptian media played a major role inciting against the pact. The Free Officers made that decision primarily because as members of the Ba'th Party, they opposed the pact but they were also carried away by the intense Egyptian propaganda campaign that swept the Arab world at that time.

The controversy over the Baghdad Pact stirred the Jordanian public. Not only Egypt but also Saudi Arabia and Syria were vocal against the pact. While encouraging Iraq, Turkey, Iran, and Pakistan to join the pact, Washington refrained from pressuring the Jordanian government to join the pact, believing that there was no strategic imperative at stake. This is little doubt that Washington's policy in this matter stemmed from its special relationship with Israel. The King and his ministers continued the debate. The prospects of gaining the support of Britain and the other members of the Baghdad Pact continued to tempt the young monarch, especially after Turkey's President Jalal Bayar stated during his visit to Jerusalem, that it was not inconceivable that the Turkish army would join the Jordanian army in defending that city.[10] Nevertheless, faced by all these domestic and external pressures, the King was compelled to reject the British proposal.

It became clear at the same time that Jordan's relations with Britain were tense. The Jordanian army had to disperse the demonstrations but many of its officers sympathized with the demonstrators. For those who demonstrated in the streets of Amman and other cities, Glubb was the culprit, and the British officer Peter Lloyd who was in charge of dispersing the demonstrators in Qaraqa was killed. The hostility toward Britain had deep roots in the past. When the Palestine War erupted, the Jordanians became convinced that the British did not supply them the necessary weapons to defend themselves. This led to rancor against Glubb and the British officers and many demanded that the pact with Britain be terminated. Glubb made the effort to convince the Jordanian officers not to provide Israel an excuse to expand it military actions. Only a few were convinced. One of the events, which further alienated Glubb from the Jordanian public, was the Israeli operation on October 14, 1953, in Qibyah village, in which 66 people died and 75 injured. The public blamed Glubb and the British officers for being indifferent to the death of many innocent Jordanians. Furthermore, the Parliament met to discuss the issue and there was a proposal to court-marshal Glubb and to dismiss the British officers. A ministerial commission of inquiry was formed and its conclusion was that several British senior officers neglected their duty, and did not take the necessary action against the enemy. Matters became worse during the parliamentary elections of 1954, when many Jordanians demonstrated. The tension mounted to such an extent that al-Shar' stated his conviction that Glubb was responsible for the massacre in Qibyah, and therefore had to resign. The tension mounted further when the leader of the opposition, Sulayman al-Nabulsi, told the Interior Minister Abbas Mirza Hazza' who served in al-Majali's first government, to leave Amman and go to his farm in Ḥisban. Hazza' responded by saying, "Are you asking me to leave Amman? This is impossible. I cannot leave the city and its inhabitants. Should I give it to Glubb? I tell you: it is either me or Glubb in this city."[11]

The King's feelings of unease increased further after the Suez Affair of 1956, when Nasser's claimed that Western countries colluded with Israel in a colonial conspiracy aimed at dominating the Arab world. The danger to the Hashemite regime did not subside even after the King refused to join the Baghdad Pact and dismissed Glubb from his position as commander of the Arab Legion. In 1957, there was talk in Jordan about an imminent coup. Prime Minister Sulayman Nabulsi was regarded as the man who would be most likely to stage such coup. Attempting to deny the rumors he told Sulayman Musa:

> The talk about a coup in 1957 is not true.... we were all loyal to the regime. The only thing I would like to see in Jordan is a peaceful experiment in democracy that Syria and Iraq would imitate. I do not like a democracy of the Lebanese style because it is not genuine. And why a coup? Would I carry out a coup against myself? Am I crazy to do what Ali Sabri had done in Egypt? I was a prime minister and the people cooperated with me. What more do I want? There was no conspiracy there. This is certain in regard to me and the council of ministers. We believed that the presence of King Hussein as the head of state is best for Jordan.[12]

The Islamist challenge

The Islamist challenge to King Hussein was not as difficult to meet as in other Arab countries. Two factors contributed to the King's ability to control the Islamic movement; first, his claim to linage from Prophet Muhammad, which was widely accepted by the public; second, the moderate character of the movement and the pacifist approach of its leaders; and third, his political acumen and ability to manipulate the election system to his advantage.

Founded in 1945, the Muslim Brotherhood in Jordan was unique in the Arab world. Although its members were inspired by Ḥasan al-Banna who founded the first such organization Egypt in 1928, they followed a moderate and gradual approach to change. This becomes evident from statements made by the group's leaders. For example, in an interview published by *Amman Al-Safir* on January

4, 1997, the movement's leader 'Abd al-Thunaybat described his group's *modus operandi* saying:

> Our approach to education is to begin with the individual and then move on to the family and then ultimately the Islamic government that rules as provided for in God's *sharia*. Our mission does not envisage an overthrow of the regime in the sense of holding the reigns of power regardless of people's temperament or whether they approve of this regime or not.... We denounce violence and say that the alternative is political reform and respect for the Islamic *sharia*, which constitute the base of powers as approved by all Arab and Islamic constitutions.[13]

The rise of the Islamists in Jordan occurred in several stages. The establishment of the movement occurred during the 1940s, when King Abdallah welcomed the members of the Muslim Brotherhood who came to spread the organization's message. Abdallah nominated one of them to be the Minister of Culture and Education. This phase constituted the general acceptance of the Muslim Brotherhood, and no significant practical steps were taken by the group or by the government. During the second phase of the 1950s, the message began spreading and many joined the movement, but it remained general, and no particular encounters took place between the group and the government. However, in 1953, the Muslim Brotherhood held an Islamic conference in Jerusalem where its members called upon the scholars of the entire Muslim world, and warned about the danger to the city of Jerusalem. In addition to this general conference, they held another one that dealt with the holy sites, and decided to publish their special organ *The Islamic Campaign* in which they began expressing their views. Furthermore, the Islamists demonstrated against the Baghdad Pact. In 1958, representatives of the group called upon the Parliament to rescind the Anglo-Jordanian Treaty, and expel all foreign troops from Jordan. They spread leaflets in which they expressed their opposition to the Eisenhower Doctrine. Furthermore, they refused to take part in the government and protested against its decision to allow British troops into the country following Qasim's coup in Iraq, which took place in that year.

During the third phase, the movement began participating in charity and grassroots activities. An Islamic charity center was opened in Amman in 1964, with branches in other cities. An Islamic secondary school was opened in Irbid and other cities. Another center opened in Zarqa, clinics were established, and an Islamic hospital opened its doors to those in need of medical care in Amman and Aqaba.

During the fourth phase, which started in the 1980s, the Brotherhood became active in the trade unions and among the students in the campuses. But the members realized that their involvement in charity work was insufficient, and did not pave the way to their rise to positions of power. Like other Islamist movements, such as al-Nahda in Tunisia, they began operating among the trade unions where they obtained leadership positions. This was an area, in which only leftists participated until that point. During the fifth stage, in the 1990s the movement became involved in politics and its members took part in the parliamentary elections of

1989. Their influence in the Eleventh Parliament increased, and they managed to obtain positions of leadership in it. When the Political Parties Law was enacted in 1992, they established the Islamic Labor Front, which included independent members, in addition to those who belonged to the Muslim Brotherhood. This party participated in the parliamentary elections to the Twelfth Parliament in 1993. Despite restrictions that were imposed on the movement, 17 members of that party managed to enter the Parliament. The party participated in all parliamentary activities and it expressed its opposition to the Wadi Araba Agreement of 1994, between Israel and Jordan, and to American policy in the Middle East. Despite the fact that they were called upon to resign, they remained steadfast and continued their activities. In addition, the party participated in the city governments where many of them reached positions of power in 1999.

Feeling uneasy about the rise of the Islamists, King Hussein decided to reduce their appeal by fulfilling the Islamic tasks, which they performed. Consequently, many abandoned their positions but the movement managed to survive due to its ability to pursue a carefully studied and moderate approach, based on mediation and positive resistance that kept fighting for its goals without resort to violence. By using such methods, in addition to wide-ranging grass root activities, the movement managed to have influence in the Jordanian street. One of the main reasons for the success of the movement lies in the fact that it embraced Islam, which the Jordanian people could identify with. The first requirement, which the party had in order to give its vote of confidence to Muḍar Badran's government, was to follow the *sharia* and change the laws that conflicted with the second clause of the Jordanian constitution. The Islamic direction, which the party took, attracted many supporters among the public.

The general approach of the Muslim Brotherhood in Jordan was persistent but moderate, and despite occasional clash of interests with the government, it never aimed at overthrowing the Hashemite regime. The relations between the Brotherhood and the state can best be described as marriage of convenience. What made this cooperation possible was primarily the ever-present Hashemite quest for legitimacy. On the other hand, the Brotherhood needed to survive in a moderate country highly influenced by Western ideas of reform and democracy. Undoubtedly, there were numerous bones of contention between the Muslim Brotherhood and the government but even the most militant among them did not call for a revolution against the regime, nor cast doubt about its legitimacy. The fact that the Muslim Brotherhood was allowed to operate under the regime of King Abdallah II laid a solid foundation for cooperation. The regime's policy remained consistent, and the attempt to co-opt the Muslim Brotherhood rather than to oppose it and thereby cause it to go the underground, never wavered. What contributed to the tolerance, which the regime had toward the Muslim Brotherhood, was that both sides tended to agree on the political issues of the day, particularly on matters of foreign relations. For example, both sides had sympathy to the Algerian liberation movement, both were anti-Communist and both opposed Nasser's intervention in the Yemeni civil war.[14]

Since the very beginning, the regime refrained from outlawing the Muslim Brotherhood. One the contrary, many of its members were absorbed in the state's bureaucracy and some reached positions of substantial power. There were Muslim brothers in major government ministries, and when elections were permitted, there were several parliament members who came from among their ranks. As for the Muslim Brotherhood, its main occupation was not to organize resistance to the government but to demonstrate its concern for the society. Thus, its members became occupied with peaceful grassroots activities, such as providing Qur'anic education, medical care, and other services in areas where the government failed to provide them. The regime's conciliatory attitude emanated from the fact that there was need to fight against leftists and communists, which were regarded as the real threat to the regime. This was particularly the case when Nasserism and Soviet influence spread in the country during the 1950s and 1960s. According to Emile Sahliyeh, four factors made it possible for King Hussein to tolerate the activities of the Muslim Brotherhood during that time:

- a The need for containing the Communists, the Islamic militants, and the Palestinian radicals;
- b Hussein's lineage from the Prophet brought them to regard him as a legitimate ruler;
- c the fact that the Muslim Brotherhood proved itself pragmatic and reformist, reduced the King's fear that they would challenge his rule; and
- d the cordial relations between Muslims and Christians prevented the former from becoming radical.[15]

A closer look reveals that the conflict between the Muslim Brotherhood and the Jordanian government during Sulayman al-Nabulsi's premiership (October 1956-April 1957) was a result of several factors, the most important of which were:

- a The theoretical and doctrinal competition between the Islamists and other parties who participated in the government. These were parties with Marxist and national convictions and their interests were diametrically opposed to those of the Islamists with whom they could not cooperate. This doctrinal division led to opposing views regarding major issues.
- b Since 1954, Jordan came under Egyptian influence and Nasser gained popularity in the country. The relations between Nasser and the Muslim Brotherhood were tense. The Brotherhood was blamed for attempting to assassinate Nasser during the famous Manshiya affair on October 26, 1954. This event had significant impact on Jordan where the King was concerned about the Muslim Brotherhood's intentions and the clash with the government intensified.
- c The political contest between the leftist parties and the Islamists over the parliamentary elections in the years 1954 and 1956, and over other domestic matters.
- d The political equation between the government and the opposition, which was created following al-Nabulsi's rise to the premiership. This equation accentuated

> the differences and the disagreements when the government had to deal with serious issues.[16]

The Muslim Brotherhood's popularity stemmed from its ability to portray an image of a party that can provide solutions to the individual's problems. As Pascaline Eury put it,

> The Association of the Muslim Brotherhood offers an image of a political party in the western sense of the term, that will be renewed with a past, a tradition and a proper culture for the Jordanian society, which suffers from a thousand and one problems for which no solution has been found until the present by those officials who assumed the high tasks of the state.[17]

Ḥattar calls our attention to the fact that the numerical majority of the nationalists-leftists and the liberals was distributed over several small parties and independent associations. They were far from being united, whereas the Muslims continued to be in one party with tight organization and ample financial resources. Thus, the Islamic party was in a better position to organize. Moreover, the national-progressive forces suffered from differences among their members who were mostly of petty-bourgeoisie background, and who were detached from the Jordanian street and from the commoners whom they despised.[18]

The Muslim Brotherhood had differences with the regime in numerous cases such as when the King did not follow the hard line of the rejectionist Arab states who called for Egypt's expulsion from the Arab League following the signing of the Camp David Accord with Israel. The Muslim Brotherhood had a similar view regarding the Jordanian peace treaty with Israel. Nevertheless, there were no demonstrations, nor acts of violence against the Hashemites, and there was never real danger that the regime was about to collapse as result of an initiative on the part of the Muslim Brotherhood. In order to obtain legitimacy for its actions the Muslim Brotherhood operated through Islamic nongovernment organizations (NGO's) such as the Islamic Center Charity Society and the Society for the Preservation of the Qur'an. These tactics were known to the government, which provided considerable freedom for these societies to operate despite its awareness that the Muslim Brotherhood was using the NGOs to implement their program. Clearly, the experience of the Muslim Brotherhood in Jordan proved that not all Islamist movements were enemies of the regime.[19]

Yet the relations between the Hashemites and Muslim Brotherhood ebbed and flowed over the years. A particular set of circumstances provided the Muslim Brotherhood the opportunity to rise. The bankruptcy of the leftist and Communist parties which was accentuated by the Arab defeat in the Six Days' War of and the Islamic revolution in Iran left room for the Islamists in Jordan to rise with virtually no competition from other parties. As for the liberals and democrats, not only were they regarded as un-Islamic, but also as collaborators and puppets of the West. Moreover, they appeared too compromising, hesitant and incapable of providing a robust program of change or reform. Thus, when the electoral law of 1989 allowed the Islamists to participate they made significant gains. Another factor, which allowed the Islamists to rise was the dire state of the economy, which was made worse in the 1980s, due to the recession, the rise in unemployment, the decline in investments, the removal of subsidies, the devaluation of the coin and the austerity measures all of which contributed to the demand for change.

The ban on political parties continued to be in effect and that meant that in the 1989 elections candidates had to run as individuals. It was largely due to its internal cohesion and the popularity of its message that the Islamic Action Front (IAF) managed to obtain 32 of the 80 seats in the Parliament. Given the fact that the Christians, Circassians and Chechens had a guaranteed quota of 12 seats, this actually meant that the IAF won 32 out of the remaining 68 or nearly half of the seats. The IAF won 20 seats while the independent Islamist candidates won 12. The tribes, the independents, the centrists, and the minorities won 35 seat, while the leftists won 13 only. The Islamists obtained seven portfolios in Prime Minister Badran's government. The ministers of Education, Health, Justice, Social Development, Islamic Endowments, Transport and Agriculture were all Islamists.[20] Particularly important was the education portfolio, which meant that the Islamists could have decisive influence on the education of the country's youth, and the Hashemites were uneasy about letting them exert such influence. Therefore, when the IAF announced that it would use the education portfolio in order to segregate all schools by gender the King decided to dissolve the cabinet.

The restrictive measures taken against the Muslim Brotherhood demonstrate clearly that the Hashemites sought to curtail its influence. However, the fear that the Muslim Brotherhood and the IAF constituted a threat to democracy cannot be substantiated, In his study on the linkage between the Islamists and democracy in Jordan, Glen Robinson demonstrates that the IAF not only refrained from opposing the democratic trend in the country but also promoted its growth since the liberalization process, which began in 1989, and this was largely because such development was in the party's interest.[21] The elections of 1989, which followed the bread riots, came as a concession by the regime, and a response to the vicissitudes of the late 1980s, which the Jordanian public experienced, and it was calculated to contain the impact of the crisis.

The Parliament of 1989 discussed several controversial issues the most outstanding among them was: the legalization of political parties; the ratification of the International Monetary Fund (IMF) agreement for economic restructuring; the lifting of martial law; the passing the Press and Publications Law and; the adoption of the National Charter. The last was the most important one that the Islamists supported. The opposition of the Islamists to government policies such as the normalization of relations with Israel brought the King to introduce a new electoral law in 1993, aimed at forming a more docile parliament, which meant that the power of the Islamists had to be curtailed. The new law was designed to give the tribes, which traditionally supported the Hashemites, greater weight in the elections. Not unexpectedly, this law reduced the number of Islamists seats from 32 to 22 of which 16 were won by the IAF. By winning 46 seats out of the 80 the independents and those without party affiliation, the pro-Hashemite parties dominated the

Parliament, even though the Islamist representation was not reduced substantially. Yet despite their rancor over the new electoral law and their opposition to policy measures such as the peace negotiations with Israel, the Islamists played according the rules of the game just as The Political and Justice Development Party (AKP) in Turkey and Al-Nahda in Tunisia.

Introduced in 1992, the IAF platform of 1992 was conservative in nature. It guaranteed basic freedoms for the individual, called for the elimination of corruption, tax reform, increased investments, a more just distribution of wealth, increased exports, and job creation. It gave equal rights to women within the limits of the *sharia*, introduced measures against what it regarded as indecent places of gathering, and prohibited alcohol consumption. In foreign affairs, the party called for the liberation of Palestine, and peaceful coexistence with other Arab countries. As for that party's stand on democracy, its leaders stated explicitly that it was only an interim stage that will lead to the establishment of a theocratic regime following their rise to power. The IAF leader Isḥaq Farhan stated that his party believed in gradual reform and opposed violence. He saw neither Iran nor Saudi Arabia as a model that his party sought to emulate. As for the Golden Age of the Rashidun caliphs, he regarded it as a utopia that his party did not aspire to. Similar views were expressed by Ziyad Abu Ghanima, both of whom harbored suspicion of the West.[22]

Major restrictions were imposed on the Islamists in the wake of their criticism of King Hussein's peace with Israel, his contacts with the West and the deteriorating state of the economy. The King's introduction of the one-man-one-vote in 1993, which reduced the number of Islamic parliamentary seats, result in the IAF's boycott of the parliamentary elections of 1997, when its demands to revoke the restrictions on voting were not met. King Hussein's attempt to reconcile the Islamists in 1999, ended in failure due to their resentment over the expulsion of three Hamas activists from Jordan in July 1999, the outbreak of the Intifada al-Aqṣa in the Israeli occupied territories in September 2000, the rise of hawkish leader Ariel Sharon in Israel, and the U.S. war against Iraq. Fearing that all these events would result in an Islamist victory the King postponed the elections from September 2002 to the spring of 2003. In addition, he introduced further regulations increasing the number of parliamentary seats to 110, but the one-man one-vote law, which reduces their prospects of winning remained in place and further restrictions on freedom of assembly were impose. Again, the upshot was that the IAF boycotted the 2003 elections but later decided to participate in them, out of fear that its influence was about to diminish, and it won 17 seats out of the 110. Moreover, the IAF proved itself willing to cooperate with the opposition parties, except in matters affecting the *sharia*. This became obvious in the mid-1990s when its members joined the Higher Committee for the Coordination of the National Opposition Parties. When the committee debated the introduction of three amendments: Law 340, pertaining to honor-crimes; an amendment setting quota for women seats in the parliament; and the Personal Status Law, granting women divorce rights, the IAF cooperated with the other parties only on the latter issue and since the other measures were likely to contradict the *sharia*, it refused to discuss them.[23]

The Salafia movement

Despite what its name implies, the Salafia movement did not constitute a menace to the regime. This is largely due to the fact that many members of this group are moderate and do not favor violence, despite their fundamentalist beliefs. Even the militants among them were kept under control by manipulation and co-optation, and like the Muslim Brotherhood they responded relatively well to the regime's attempt to accommodate them, despite the resentment that they still harbored.

Like other Muslim countries, Jordan has Sunni Muslims and activists some of whom are scholars who belong to the Salafi branch of Islam. Many of them are not radical. Among these there is an apolitical quietist branch whose leaders became loyal to the regime after a process of "domestication" took place.[24] Many of the Salafists are ideologically inclined to aspire to the Golden Age of Islam, while maintaining a regular and practical lifestyle. Salafis hold the view that the concept of "oneness" (*tawḥid*) is central in Islam. They reject popular religion with its tendency to saint worship. Like the Christian Calvinists in the West, they regard themselves as strangers in a sinning world and consider themselves "saved." They also avoid introducing innovations (*bid'a*), attempt to remain pure and highly respectful of the terms "faith" (*iman*) and "apostasy" (*kufr*). They consider the believer's motivation as highly important. One can distinguish among three branches of Salafism; (a) quietists, who refrain from political action and focus on studying and spreading the faith; (b) politicos, who become active politically; and (c) jihadists who believe that *jihad* should be waged against unbelievers, and deviant Muslims alike. The last category believes in overthrowing regimes led by apostates, who do not apply the *sharia*.

Quietists can be further divided into 'aloofists' who oppose the regime but cooperate with it, and propagandists who are active praising the regime and even willing to fight against its opponents. The most prominent quietist was Muhammad Naṣr al-Din al-Albani who led the Salafi community in the 1980s and 1990s. His view was that unlike belief in the heart or speech with the tongue, acts could not decrease the faith or take it away altogether, but could only increase it. Both Muhammad Abu Ruhayyim and Muhammad Ibrahim Shaqra opposed this view, saying that it is akin to the belief of the Murji'ites who believed that God alone has the right to judge. Their pupil Ali al-Ḥalabi defended their position. The quietists tend to delay political action and to emphasize collaboration with the regime. This is the reason why they did not seem to pose a threat to the monarchy in Jordan. Quietists also reject democracy, and they regard elections only as a way to prevent the rise of the worst candidate. Salafism did not become a popular trend in Jordan, until Ibrahim Shaqra and Aḥmad al-Salik embraced it. The Salafi message spread faster after al-Albani's arrival. Unlike their Gulf counterparts, the Jordanian quietists tended to remain apolitical. They were critical of the Muslim Brotherhood whose ideas contributed to the development of political Salafism. The quietists were later led by al-Ḥalabi who remained more loyalist than al-Albani and Shaqra toward the regime. Al-Halabi's position became firmer in 2001, when the government founded the Imam al-Albani Center in Amman, which he was in charge of, and he was thereby in full cooperation with it.

Despite the quiet nature of this movement, the Hashemite monarchy found it prudent to accommodate its members and have them take part in its activities. The government's ability to co-opt the quietists allowed it to combat terrorism, particularly following the terrorist attack of New York's World Trade Center in September 11, 2001. They became the government's right hand in combatting terrorism. The Salafis remained respected throughout the country despite accusations that al-Ḥalabi plagiarized from other scholars. There is no well-defined hierarchy among the quietists, but their high stature grants them recognition. The Salafi movement does not have more than a few tens of thousands, and most of them are from lower middle-class background, both Jordanian and Palestinians. Some of them are members of the Muslim Brotherhood or Jama'at al-Tabligh, but they are quietists nevertheless.[25] Even among the Jihadi-Salafists, there is a split. The faction led by the Palestinian Abu Muhammad al-Maqdisi was Salafi and anti-regime, but at the same time he was critical of extremism. The other faction was led by Abu-Mus'ab al-Zarqawi who was far more radical. The quietists suffered from another split following the rise of the Islamic State of Iraq and Syria (ISIS). There were those who supported it and those who opposed.

The Salafi quietists remained split from the Jihadi-Salafis whom they call *Khawarij*.[26] Another trend among the quietists were the "Reformist" Salafis who emerged in 1993, when the Jam'iyyat al-Kitab wa-l-Sunna (Book and Sunna Association) was founded. This group focuses on social and political issues. It is willing to act now and has more favorable attitude toward party politics. The attitude of the quietists and the government toward this group has remained negative, and the government is constantly trying to prevent them from political action by engaging them in governmental positions and thereby controlling them.[27]

The Salafis refrain from establishing formal organizations. Instead, Salafi *shaikhs* and other mentors prefer to lecture in private houses, in mosques and in informal gatherings. The Salafis have no established hierarchies, even though some of them are considered greater scholars than others. The movement's recruiting methods are informal as well. Students who attend their lectures bring others and spread the word in an informal manner. According to Quintan Wiktorowicz, the informal manner in which the Salafis spread their beliefs is not accidental. It is a clear choice made by the leaders of the movement, to avoid detection and repression by the government. The decentralized and haphazard structure of the movement make it hard for the regime to act against it, and the absence of a formal administrative center or leader to whom the entire movement owes allegiance shields the movement from harassment. The movement's tendency to refrain from formal organization increased substantially since the 1990s, as a result of the repression exercised by the regime against the militant Islamists. The only registered Salafi organization in Jordan is the Qur'an and Sunna Society, which became inactive as a result of the group's determination to maintain low profile and avoid government detection.[28] The quietist nature of this movement led to its toleration by the monarchy, which does not show signs of alarm by what its members do and what they preach.

The Palestinian factor

A greater challenge to the regime in Jordan had been the existence of a large population of Palestinians. The Jordanian public had demonstrated its solidarity with the Palestinian people immediately following the collapse of the Ottoman Empire. In April 1920, Jordanians raided Palestine as a measure of solidarity with the Palestinians, and protested against Britain's policy which they considered to be pro-Zionist. Ten men were killed during that incident where the British used airplanes. However, it was not until the Palestine War of 1948 that the Jordanians began learning about the severity of the Palestinian refugee problem. Many Palestinians fled to Jordan in the aftermath of that war, and they had to be integrated into the Jordanian economy. The enormous difficulties, which the process entailed, made the Jordanians more acquainted with the Palestinian refugee problem, and more hostile to the Jewish state that was established on their border.

The term "Palestinian identity" (*al-kiyyan al-filasṭini*), which became a slogan of the pan-Arabists during the 1960s, was in all likelihood coined by Egyptian President Nasser. This development took place in March 1959, when the union between Egypt and Syria, which became known as the United Arab Republic (UAR), was formed and thereby triggered a hostile reaction from Iraq's President Qasim. In his speech in Damascus on March 8, 1959, Nasser condemned his Iraqi rival, and both leaders attempted to show greater solidarity to the Palestinian cause, without specific commitment.[29] However, the Jordanian tribes had demonstrated their sympathy with the Palestinian cause long before. Recalling the events that took place in Palestine in 1936, Mohammed Izzat Darwazeh writes:

> In Transjordan, Mithqal al-Fa'iz, leader of Bani Sakhr called upon his brothers, leaders of the tribes to assemble in order to find out what needs to be done to help the people of Palestine and to support them. The pipelines in Transjordan were damaged by enemies. The British and Amir Abdallah were concerned about these matters. One the one hand, the amir exerted efforts to abort the meeting of the chiefs of the tribes. One the other hand, he cooperated with the British authorities in the effort to strengthen the defense of the pipelines that pass through Jordan.[30]

Following the Palestine War of 1948, which caused many Palestinians to flee, the King's fear of being inundated with refugees, which his country had difficulties accommodating increased.

Moreover, when the Palestinians began infiltrating Israel and engaging in terrorist activities, which triggered Israeli retaliation, the Jordanian government had to control their activities.

The King instructed his prime minister to confront Yasser Arafat regarding the free manner in which he acted in Jordan. Nabulsi was reported to have told Arafat on one occasion, "listen Abu 'Ammar, you are behaving as invaders in Jordan. This is not acceptable because Jordan is not place for your invasion."[31] According to those who knew him, Wasfi al-Tal had a definite position regarding the Palestinian presence in Jordan. He called for negotiations with them and sought to convince them to evacuate Amman with all their armed forces and arsenals. He believed that he could convince them that this was a necessary step. They agreed eventually to leave but their arsenals remained as they were and the search for them ceased.[32]

King Hussein was faced with difficult choices following the Six Days' War when some 250,000 Palestinians joined those who came in 1948. Although number of refugees that fled after the Six Days' War was no more than third of those who left Palestine in 1948, the problem intensified, especially in the West Bank, which had a large number of Palestinians. Arafat's methods of fighting Israel from Jordanian territory and the Israel's policy of holding Jordan responsible for his actions brought harsh reprisals, which the King was not willing to tolerate.

The most active and most daring of the Palestinian resistance was Black September. The operations of the militant group intensified in the early 1970s. Its members had little tolerance toward King Hussein whom they regarded as an agent of the West, and a traitor to the Palestinian cause and the news that he was conspiring against the Palestinian people by collaborating with the West and Israel in particular were not to their liking. In July 1971, Black September declared a total war against him and his Hashemite regime, and in November that year four of its members assassinated the Jordanian Prime Minister, Wasfi Tal in his hotel in Cairo. Like King Hussein, he was accused by the group's members as a traitor and a collaborator. Early the following year, the group was engaged in operations against Israel in foreign countries when it claimed responsibility for the murder of five Jordanians living in West Germany who were accused of spying for Israel. Moreover, the group made an attempt on the life of Jordan's ambassador to London, broke into a factory in West Germany that made electric generators for the Israeli Air Force, and attacked an oil refinery complex at Trieste, Italy, that processed oil for what they called "pro-Zionist" interests. Gradually, Black September turned into an elite arm of Fatah's secret service, and it had between 400 and 600 members. According to American sources the group had between 100 and 200 young fighters who were formerly members of the Palestinian Fatah movement. The members of Black September were young and most of whom were born in refugee camps and attended European or Middle Eastern universities. Some of them originated from North Africa and some were employed by foreign technical companies that offered them high wages. Muhammad Mustafa Syein who served as a deputy of Chairman Yasir Arafat was the movement's first leader and he was killed in July 1971.[33]

Black September had four main operating units in charge of various regions of the world such as Europe, the Middle East, Africa and the Americas. Black September operated secretly and it had no official symbols, no special ceremonies, and no offices.

The conflict with the Palestinian came to a head in September 1970, when King Hussein decided to use the Arab Legion against them. The Palestinian forces were crushed, and forced to leave the country to Lebanon. One of the most notorious activities of Black September was the murder of 11 Israeli athletes in the Olympic games, which took place in September 1972. This brought an angry response from the Israeli government and Prime Minister Gold Meir vowed to avenge their murder. In a pursuit that followed, most of the assassins were killed by members of the Israeli Mossad intelligence.

The persistence of the Israeli-Palestinian conflict and the growing discontent among Jordan's Palestinian population led King Hussein to disengage from the West Bank on July 31, 1988. Prior to that decision, the Jordanian government made the following decisions: (a) to abolish the development plan for the West Bank and all the administrative bodies connected with it. This included all the purchasing and selling activities that were carried out for that purpose; (b) to stress the uniqueness of the Palestinian identity, and call upon the liberation organizations to take responsibility for their affairs; and (c) to call upon the Palestinians to limit their goal of liberating their land, and to aspire for the establishment of a Palestinian state in the West Bank and the Gaza Strip.

After making the decision King Hussein said,

> The intention of the steps that Jordan has taken is to support the Palestinian movement and to put an emphasis on the Palestinian identity....Jordan believes that the tie with the West Bank does not constitute an obstacle in the way of the liberation of the conquered Palestinian land. However, it became obvious recently that there is a Palestinian and pan-Arab trend that believes in the necessity of putting an emphasis on the Palestinian identity in a complete manner, and it became incumbent on Jordan to respond to that trend.[34]

One of the reasons for the emergence of the Jordanian national identity was the development of a similar phenomenon among the Palestinians following the Six Days' War. The concentration on the Palestinian struggle against Israel caused the Jordanian national identity to be overshadowed, and it lost much of its appeal. Jordan's identity was absorbed, fused or replaced by the Palestinian nationalist movement, which was represented by the PLO.[35] Since 1967, the Jordanian government was compelled to cooperate with the political institutions, which had support among the Palestinians in Jordan as well as those under Israeli occupation. For quite some time, the government managed to cooperate with the Palestinian resistance movement, without alienating the Jordanians. However, the fact that Jordan was exposed to pressure by other Arab countries such as Egypt under Nasser and Syria under the Ba'th had a negative impact on the modus vivendi, which the Jordanian regime achieved with the Palestinian organizations. This was largely because the ties which the Palestinians in Jordan had with the resistance movement were based not merely on doctrine, Egyptian or Ba'thist, but on real, active and corporeal ground.

The Jordanian political parties suffered a major blow by the end of the 1950s. They had to adjust themselves to the radical atmosphere, which prevailed in the country in the aftermath of Qasim's coup in Iraq and the formation of the UAR.[36] Then came the Six Days' War, which forced them to adjust to yet another reality. Before the war, the objective of the political parties was to achieve democratic gains, and to introduce reforms in the government structure. The parties became exposed to persecution and their members were imprisoned. They remained weak and incapable of pursuing their goals. This state of affair compelled them to amalgamate in the Palestinian organizations where they could continue to pursue their goals. The Palestinian resistance movement took advantage of this state of affairs, knowing that the parties became dependent on it, and it became the leader and the vanguard not only of its people but also of the rest of the Jordanians. Its slogan called for struggle against the bourgeois classes. This state of affairs brought the Jordanian national movement to realize that its struggling methods were different from those of the Palestinians. The difference between the Jordanian and the Palestinian national movements became all the more obvious when the latter insisted on overthrowing the regime by force of arms. This goal stood in stark contrast to what the Jordanian national movement aimed for. The upshot was that the Jordanian national movement was in despair, and it began seeking to overthrow the Palestinian yoke. During the period between 1967 and 1970, the Jordanian political parties had given up their daily struggle, and turned into liberation organizations in a political framework. By doing so, they lost their political identity, and became a mere echo of the Palestinian liberation movement.[37]

> The Hashemite regime had constantly expressed its solidarity with the Palestinian cause. Thus, for example, when Prime Minister al-Muhandis Ali Abu al-Raghib (2000–2003) addressed the parliament with a view to gain the confidence of its members, he said: It is imperative to ascertain that the Palestinian problem will remain Jordan's first problem and that we will exert all possible efforts, with the cooperation and coordination of the Palestinian national authority, and the Palestinian government in order to support our Palestinian brethren, until they are capable of obtaining their legal rights and establish their independent state on their national land and Jerusalem its noble capital.[38]

The participation of the Palestinians in the country's political life demonstrated that they sided with the forces of the opposition, whether it was Islamist of leftist. One of the main beneficiaries was the Muslim Brotherhood, which distributed charity in refugee camps and rejected the peace process with Israel. In addition, the number of Palestinian representatives in the parliament and the number of voters increased considerably.[39]

The Arab Legion

The Arab Legion played a crucial role in state-building in Transjordan. In addition to instilling a sense of pride and devotion to the country rather than to the tribe, it fulfilled a major role in educating and integrating the citizens into the society.[40] Building such military force was a major challenge to the King who depended on the assistance of a colonial power. Furthermore, the fact that the Arab Legion was commanded by British officers constituted a major dilemma for the King, since it was regarded by many as an instrument of Western domination, and it was this pressure that led him to dismiss Glubb in 1956.

Following the defeat of the Ottoman forces, three Occupied Enemy Territory Administrations (OETA) were formed by General Allenby in 1918. Transjordan was part of the OETA/ East. Its capital was Damascus and by Amir Faiṣal was its governor. Following the Arab defeat by the French at the Battle of Maysalun in 1920, the lines between the areas of French and British influence became firm. However, the British who began establishing the foundation of their military presence in Palestine were hardly inclined to have a substantial military presence in Transjordan, despite Samuel's conviction that stationing troops in this area was desirable. Lord Curzon made that point clear when he told Samuel that it was worthwhile to send a few British officers to al-Salt and Karak, to act as advisors and prepare the population to self-government. The officers chosen for the task were young veterans who participated in the British occupation on 1918–1919. These were Lieutenant Colonel F.G. Peake, Major I.N. Camp, Major F.R. Somerset, Captain C. Dunbar Brunton, Captain Alec S. Kirkbride, Alan L. Kirkbride, and Captain R.F.P. Monkton. They were given posts in the major towns as representatives, secretaries and inspectors. The existing defense force for the region was the gendarmerie, which remained from the days when the area was administered from Damascus. There was need to create a new unit whose soldiers were well-trained and imbued with *esprit de corps* to maintain order in a region where the lack of security was of main concern for the British.

On September 11, 1920, Captain Brunton submitted his recommendation to establish a small reserve force that would supplement and reinforce the gendarmerie when necessary. His proposal included a detailed list of the number of officers and soldiers, and their monthly pay. Seven officers from the rank of second lieutenant to major, ten non-commissioned officers, and 200 men were to be recruited. Each man had to bring his horse and a British rifle, to agree to serve anywhere and the service was to last two years. The rough annual estimate for salaries was £30,000 in addition £4,000 for apparel. The force was to be equipped with four machine guns and eight mules. What Brunton had in mind was the creation of two mounted squadrons supported by a machine gun section with mule transport. The force's headquarters were stationed in Amman, close to the Hejaz Railway, and in Jerusalem. Brunton managed to obtain the support of the local *shaikhs* and on October 3, 1920, he reported that 30 Arab machine gunners and two officers from the troops that remained in Jordan after Maysalun had been recruited. Under Brunton's supervision, the Reserve Force was organized into one squadron (75 mounted gendarmes and 25 machine guns) under Lieutenant Umar Luṭfi, and five field officers.

The first test of the new force was at the village of Sahab, eight miles southeast of Amman where the local settlers who originated from Egypt refused to pay their taxes. When the new force arrived, the village was reduced to submission. Then Captain Brunton moved the force from Amman to al-Salt following Abdallah's arrival to Ma'an and the disorder that ensued.[41]

This reserve force constituted the nucleus of the Arab Legion. After Abdallah's army suffered a major disaster in May 1921, at the hands of the tribesmen of the Kura region in Ajlun, the force was enlarged to five times its size. Incapable of supporting his army on the small subsidy, which the British provided, Abdallah increased the taxes that were levied from the peasants and the Bedouins. The result was a major uprising, which only the British could suppress by superior arms. Meanwhile, the need to provide Transjordan with a well-trained army became more obvious as result of the Saudi-Wahhabi invasion. By then, Ibn Saud had already acquired Jabal Shamar with Wadi Sirḥan, which gave him access to the heart of Transjordan. This brought him close to Amman, and it was impossible to stop the advance of the Wahabi forces without assistance from the RAF.[42]

In 1926, the Arab Legion was transformed into a police force and its size was reduced. This was largely because the Legion did not demonstrate spectacular military achievements. In fact, the real combatant was the TJFF. The TJFF was a Palestinian force even though its headquarters were in Zarqa, and Abdallah was its honorary colonel. Moreover, the commander of the TJFF was subordinated to the commanding officer in Palestine and Transjordan, who in turn was accountable to the High Commissioner.[43] When Glubb arrived in Transjordan in 1930 and began to organize the Desert Patrol, which consisted of Bedouins of the Arab Legion, the response from Peake who sought to protect the peasants from the Bedouin raids, was not favorable. Yet, Glubb managed to recruit Bedouins and thereby turned the Desert Patrol into a political and social integrating force in the country. The Desert Patrol not only enabled the Bedouins to find an occupation, it also instilled in them a sense of pride and service to the country. The Desert Patrol and the Arab Legion, which followed it, became instruments of integration where all tribes fought for the same cause. The tribal allegiance was gradually transferred from the chief of the tribe to whom the Bedouins had loyalty, to the commander and then to the monarchy. By these means, Abdallah turned into the ultimate *shaikh* to whom all had loyalty. The fact that Abdallah connected with the tribes by going to different locations and participating in local traditional Bedouin ceremonies, helped enhance his position as the ultimate political figure in the country. Yet, it is not certain that the Bedouin soldiers regarded themselves as the country's citizens. It was military loyalty rather than allegiance state authority that motivated the Bedouin soldier in the Arab Legion.[44]

The patrol's mission was to secure peace in Transjordan and along the frontier of the Najd and the Hejaz. The force consisted of less than a hundred men some of whom were Glubb's personal guard. Glubb's force assumed greater importance when the IPC pipeline from Kirkuk to Haifa was laid across Transjordan, and its northern parts needed protection. When the Arab Revolt in Palestine erupted in 1936, the Desert Mechanized Force was expanded and its soldiers became more devoted. When Peake retired in 1939, Glubb became the commander of the Arab Legion that was to play an important role in Jordan's history.

Glubb's dismissal and the Arabization of the Jordanian army

The Jordanian army was led by British officers since the very beginning. Glubb entered the ranks of the Jordanian army in 1930, as an adviser to the Desert Force, which was formed in order to control the south-eastern borders, with the rank of major. Following Peake's resignation, he became the chief of staff. As such, he was the representative of the British government in Jordan. He remained in his position following the country's independence. However, in the eyes of the Jordanian public he became the symbol of British colonial rule in the country. Moreover, he was regarded not only as the one who prevented the Jordanian army from conquering West Jerusalem, and allowed the towns of Lod and Ramla to fall into Jewish hands during the Palestine War, but also as collaborator who helped the Jews conquer the southern Negev desert and the region close to Aqaba. Thus, he was identified as a collaborator with the Jews, and became unpopular in the eyes of the public. On the other hand, however, he played a major role after 1951, in the service of King Talal and his struggle for the unification of both banks of the Jordan River. Nevertheless, the majority of the Jordanians resented his meddling in Jordan's domestic affairs, particularly in the parliamentary elections. The parliamentary legislation allowed for military intervention and that enabled him to have influence over the election process. Furthermore, the incidents along the Israeli-Jordanian border in the early 1950s led to resentment and allegations of conspiracy. The constitutional reforms that were introduced at the time of King Hussein and Prime Minister Fauzi al-Mulqi (April 1953–March 1954) were exploited by the opposition parties to organize demonstrations against the regime, and the British who were regarded as collaborators. In addition, some parliament members from the West Bank sought to separate the police from the army, in order to reduce the influence, which Glubb wielded in the country, and the Egyptian penetration intensified the hostility toward what the public regarded as imperialism and which Glubb became its symbol. In the meantime, King Hussein established ties with the young officers in the years 1953–1955. One of these officers was Ali Abu Nuwar who was the military attaché in Paris. This officer took it upon himself to present the officers' views to the King. This is what brought the King to understand that Glubb controlled the political life in the country. Accordingly, he maintained closer contacts with all politicians and senior public officials.

According to Glubb, the army had to be professional and it had to include Bedouins and peasants. On the other hand, the opposition sought to turn the army into a professional national force led by Arab officers with strong qualifications and high political culture. Glubb was opposed to the nomination of Jordanian officers to high positions in the army.[45] He refused to honor the King Talal's request to dismiss fifteen officers, saying that he could not dispense with them.[46]

King Hussein saw himself as a leader of a nationalistic country whose vision had considerable impact on the young officers. While these developments were taking place, the tension between the King and his Chief of Staff mounted and Nasser's campaign to gain supporters for his pan-Arab goals intensified. In addition, the suppression of the demonstrations against the regime contributed to the tension. Motivated by these developments, the officers spread leaflets accusing the British officers of siding with the enemies of the Arab people. This pressure compelled the King to ask the Council of Ministers to dismiss Glubb, and three other senior British officers.[47]

Glubb's dismissal can be better understood if one takes into consideration the mood that prevailed in the Jordanian army at that time. Abu Nuwar had this to say about the Glubb's dismissal:

> Glubb regarded the Jordanian army as his private army into which he could introduce any changes that he saw fit, that he could bring closer to him any officers he wished, and ignore others. We, the officers, felt that the people looked at us as if they were looking at individuals having no other concern but to march in a procession of duplicity and tyranny. My colleagues and I were despondent about this state of affairs. [48]

The news about Glubb's dismissal were received with dismay in Whitehall. For quite some time the Arab Legion's role in defending Britain's interests in the region was highly appreciated in Whitehall. For example, in a telegram to the Foreign Office from February 4, 1942, a British minister writes:

> The grant during the war of Syrian and Lebanese independence was dictated by political expediency and they had done nothing to assist the Allied cause. On the other hand, Trans-Jordan's attitude had been constantly helpful and the Arab Legion played a useful part in Iraq and Syria. We must look after our friends.[49]

The Arab Legion was used to pacify the unruly tribes. One of the cases noted by the British administration was that of Banu Sakhr and the occupation of their villages by the Mechanized Regiment of the Arab Legion on June 26, 1943. According to a report by the High Commissioner Harold McMichael, the movement appeared to have taken Banu Sakhr completely by surprise, and the overwhelming force used by the Legion crushed all resistance.[50] Incidents along the border continued to occur during the war. In April 1943, Transjordan was invaded by Druze cavalry and a patrol of the Arab Legion was fired upon. Sultan al-Atrash had written a letter to Abdallah deploring the incidents but the High Commissioner had noted, "the degree of sincerity of the letter is difficult to assess."[51]Another incident that occupied the Arab Legion occurred in July 3, 1943, when a fight broke out between the Syrian members of the Ruallah tribe and those of the Iraqi Dahamsha over a water resource. When the tribes camped near Burqa, the Third Mechanized Regiment of the Arab Legion was sent to restore order in the area.[52]

After 1948, Glubb was no longer the Arab Legion's commander and he became chief of the general staff. By then, the Arab Legion had three brigades. The TJFF was disbanded and its personnel joined the Arab Legion. Supplies for the Legion were coordinated through the British headquarters in the Middle East. The Arab Legion continued to be regarded as an effective force and the Israelis who met its soldiers in the battlefield could attest to its robustness. In the Israeli literature of the Independence War of 1948, the Arab soldier is depicted as arrogant, coward, and helpless at the same time. The Arab Legion, however, is depicted in a much more positive fashion. Its warriors are described as dedicated to their mission, and they are noted for their bravery.[53] The Jordanian army continues to play an important role in civilian life. It is a major consumer of raw materials and products offered by the civilian sector of the society. Moreover, the Arab Legion encourages investments and production and it employs civilians in various industries.[54]

The quest for national security

One of King Hussein's major challenges from the very beginning of his reign was to modernize the Arab Legion, and supply it with the most up-to-date weaponry and equipment.

This was also Abdallah's prime concern. The tendency to establish a strong defense force was quite apparent in Transjordan from the early days, and it became much more obvious on the eve of World War II. In his report to Malcolm MacDonald, the Colonial Secretary writes:

> The Trans-Jordan government has worked out what is believed to be a somewhat grandiose and expensive scheme, which clearly will be impossible of acceptance. They certainly cannot afford it and His Majesty's Government are unlikely to wish to pay for it. In any case the matter must, of course, await settlement of the issue regarding the ultimate disposition of the Trans-Jordan Frontier Force.[55]

Defense matters loomed large during the negotiations, which led to the signing of the treaty of 1928. Article 10 of the agreement read as follows:

> His Britannic Majesty may maintain forces in trans-Jordan and may raise, organize and control in trans-Jordan such armed forces, as may in his opinion be necessary for the defense of the country and to assist His Highness the Emir in the preservation of peace and order. His Highness the Emir agrees that he will not raise or maintain in Trans-Jordan or allow to be raised or maintained any military forces without the consent of his Britannic Majesty.[56]

Abdallah's pressure on the British to allow him greater control on the armed forces yielded results. Thus, the supplementary to the agreement gave him greater control over the armed forces. Its Article 10 was cancelled and substituted on July 19, 1941, by another that said:

> His Britannic Majesty may maintain armed forces in Trans-Jordan, and may raise, organize and control in Trans-Jordan such armed forces as may in his opinion be necessary for the defense of the country and to assist His Highness the Amir in the preservation of peace and order.[57]

According to a report on the political situation in Transjordan from July 1939, the rumors regarding the impending invasion of the country by infiltrators continued but little had happened except for the damage to the I.P.C pipeline near

Makhraba village, which was probably perpetrated by arms smugglers in Deraa. Operations carried out by the British and the French authorities yielded significant results, and the exile of Suleiman Pasha Sudi from Damascus to Aleppo helped curb the activities of the Transjordanian dissidents in Syria. Occasional arrests of Palestinian activists had taken place, but little else happened to upset the existing order.[58]

The amendment to the Transjordan Organic Law, which was introduced in the summer of 1939, stated that "The Emir is the head of the State and the Commander in Chief of its military force. He sanctions and promulgates all the laws and supervises their execution." Yet, it limited his power by saying that "he is not entitled to modify or suspend laws or to give dispensation in their execution except in the circumstances and in the manner prescribed by law."[59]

The outbreak of World War II had little impact on the country. Rebel activities remained confined to a small region in the Yarmouk Valley. Abdallah pledged loyalty to Britain and the emergency measures imposed by the British authorities were generally accepted by the public, with only few complaints. The only factor, which led to tension in the kingdom was the rumor that Ibn Saud had struck a deal with Nazi Germany stipulating, that if the war ended with its victory, he would be allowed to extend his rule to Transjordan and Palestine, and evict all the Jews from the country. The fact that reinforcements were seen on the Saudi borders gave credence to this rumor.[60] Abdallah was pleased to hear that Britain concluded an agreement with France and Turkey. This agreement allayed his fear of Communist penetration into the region. In addition, the rumors regarding a Saudi attack proved to be false, and the relations between the two monarchs improved. Deserters of the French Foreign Legion who fled from Jabal Druze to Transjordan were sent to Palestine. In this manner, Abdallah managed to avoid complications.[61]

When the issue of Jordan's incorporation into the Baghdad Pact was discussed at the National Party, the members reached a consensus not to join, arguing that Zionism and not communism was the enemy of the Arabs.[62] During the Suez Affair of 1956, King Hussein refrained from embarking on a war against Israel. Recalling the decision to refrain from war against Israel, when Britain and France joined it in a war against Egypt, Nabulsi boasted,

> I did not consent to Jordan's entry into a war against Israel because Britain and France were threatening Egypt, and Israel had the ability to send its entire army to confront Jordan. I take pride of this stand because I saved my country from great danger.[63]

As the quest for security continued to remain a major issue for Jordan, the government explored all possibilities of acquiring news weapons. In one of his meetings with King Hussein, Nabulsi proposed the creation of a big army of reserve soldiers, similar to IDF, Israel's Defense Force, where Israeli soldiers were required to serve after their military service ended, but Wasfi al-Tal rejected the proposal.[64] King Hussein continued to face the security dilemma. Therefore, he sought to improve

Figure 10.1 King Hussein.

his relations with Washington and avoid rupture of his relations with the Soviet Union.

Notes

1 *'Abd al-Salām al-Majālī, Riḥlat al-umr: Min bayt al-sha'er ila sadat al-ḥukm* (Journey of a Lifetime: From the House of the Poet to Leadership), Arabic text (Beirut: Shirkat al-Maṭbu'āt lil-Tawzī' wa-al-Nashr, 2003), pp. 63–64.
2 Jamāl Alshā'er, *A politician Remembers: Commentary on My Political Experience*, Arabic text with title in English (London: Riad El-Rayyes, 1987), p. 51.
3 Sulayman Musa, *Dirasāt fī tarīkh al-Urdun al-Ḥadīth* ('Ammāṇ: Wizarat al-Thaqāfah, 1999), p. 11.
4 *Ibid*, p. 17.
5 Cited *Ibid*, p. 28.
6 Cited *Ibid*, p. 31.
7 Hazzā' al-Majālī, *Mudhakkirātī* (Hazzā' al-Majālī, My Memoirs), Arabic text ('Ammān: No Publisher listed, 1960), pp. 214–215.
8 Wahdān 'Uways, *Al-'Awdah ila al-"had'ah": Riḥlāt ul-'Umr* (Returning to Tranquility: A Journey of a Lifetime), Arabic text (Beirut: al-Mu'assasah al-'Arabīyah lil-Dirāsāt wa-al-Nashr, 2003), p. 87.
9 *Ibid*, p. 88.
10 Dirasāt fī tarīkh al-Urdun al-Ḥadīth, p. 33.
11 Cited *Ibid*, pp. 36–37.

12 Sulayman Musa, *Awrāq min Daftar al-Ayyām: Dhikriyyāt al-Ra'īl al-Awwal* (Papers from the Notebook of the Days: Memories of the first Generation), Arabic text (Ammān: Matba'at al-Ajyal), 2000, p. 87.
13 Cited in Quintan Wiktorowicz, "Islamists, the State, and Cooperation in Jordan," *Arab Studies Quarterly*, Vol. 21, No. 4 (Fall 1999), p. 3.
14 Shmuel Bar, *The Muslim Brotherhood in Jordan* (Tel Aviv: The Moshe Dayan Center for Middle Eastern and African Studies, Tel Aviv University, 2000), p. 18.
15 Emile F. Sahliyeh, "The State and the Islamic Movement," *Journal of Church and State*, Vol. 47, No. 1 (Winter 2005), p. 113.
16 "Ṣamiḥ al-Mu'āyṭah, "Al-tayyār al-Islāmi wa-ḥūkūmat al-Nabulsī," (The Islamic Movement and Nabulsi's Government), Arabic text, *Ḥukūmat Sulaymān al-Nābulsi, 1956–1957, a'māl nadwah/ishraf Hāni al-Ḥūrānī*, [taḥrīr] Maḥmūd al-Rimāwi wa-al-Ḥusayn Abū Rummān ('Ammān: Markaz al-Urduni al-Jadīd lil-Dirāsāt: Dār Sindibād, 1999), pp. 149–150.
17 Pascaline Eury, "Les Élections Législatives du 8 Novembre 1989, Paris 1991," (The Legislative Elections of November 8, 1989), French text, Cited in Renate Dieterich, Transformation oder Stagnation? Die jordanisch Demokratisierungspolitik seit 1989 (Hamburg: Deutsches Orient-Institut, 1999), p. 216.
18 Ḥattar, pp. 153–154.
19 "Islamists, the State and Cooperation in Jordan," p. 2.
20 Sahliyeh, p. 117.
21 Glen E. Robinson, "Can Islamists be Democrats," *Middle East Journal*, Vol. 51, No. 3 (Summer 1997), p. 374.
22 *Ibid*, p. 379.
23 Janine A. Clark, "The Conditions of Islamist Moderation: Unpacking Cross-Ideological Cooperation in Jordan," *International Journal of Middle East Studies*, Vol. 38, No. 4 (November 2006), pp. 539–540.
24 Joas Wagemakers, *Salafism in Jordan: Political Islam in a Quietist Community* (Cambridge, UK: Cambridge University Press, 2016), p. 227.
25 *Ibid*, p. 232.
26 Named after the Kharijites who left 'Ali's Shi'i camp because of his failure to defeat Muāwiya's army at the Battle of Siffin, which took place in 657 AD and his acceptance of arbitration as a way to resolve the conflict over the succession to the Prophet.
27 Wagemakers, p. 234.
28 Quintan Wiktorowicz, "The Salafi movement in Jordan," *International Journal of Middle East Studies*, Vol. 32, No. 2 (May 2000), pp. 236–237.
29 Eliezer Be'eri, *The Palestinians under Jordanian Rule*, Hebrew text with title in English (Jerusalem: The Magnes Press, 1978), p. 12.
30 Mohammed Izzat Darwazeh, *97 Years Autobiography: A Long Side with Arab Movements and Palestinian Cause, Memories and Registrations*, Vol. II, Arabic text with title in English (Beirut: Dār al-Gharb al-Islāmi, 1993), p. 88.
31 Awrāq min Daftar al-Ayyām, p. 89.
32 Waṣfi al-Tall: fikruhu wa-mawāqifahu (waqā' al-nadwah) (Wasfi al-Tall: His Thoughts and His Positions), Arabic text (Ammān: al-Markaz al-Urduni wa-al-Islāmi lil-dirasāt wa-al-ma'lumāt, 1996), pp.72–73.
33 John B. Wolf, "Black September: Militant Palestinianism," *Current History*, Vol. 64, No. 377 (January, 1973), p. 8.
34 Cited in Sulaymān Muṣtafa al-Ṣamādī, *Al-Urdun: mi'at 'ām min al-taḥaddī wa-al-'aṭā* (Irbīd: Maṭba'at al-Ruzanah, 1999), p. 111.
35 Sulayman H. Nuṣayrat, *Al-Shakhsīyah al-Urdunīyah bayn al-bu'ud al-waṭanī wa-al-bu'ud al Qawmī* (The Jordanian personality between the national and the nationalistic Dimensions), Arabic text ('Ammān: Sulayman Nuṣayrat, 2002), p. 42.
36 The United Arab Republic (UAR) was the union between Egypt and Syria, which was formed in 1958 and ended at Syria's initiative in 1961.

37 Khālīl Ibrahīm al-Ḥajjāj, *Tarīkh al-aḥzāb al-Urdunīyah 1946–1970* (History of the Jordanian Parties), Arabic text ('Ammān: Da'irat al-Maktabah al-Waṭaniyah, 2001), pp. 351–352.
38 "Ra'īs al-wuzarah al-Muhandis 'Alī Abū al-Rāghib yalqi bayān al-ḥūkūmah al-wizāri amāma majlis nuwwāb li-nil al-Thiqqa, August 6, 2003." (Prime Minister al-Muhandis Ali Abu al-Raghib reads the ministerial announcement to the House of Representatives to obtain their vote of confidence), Arabic text, *Ḥūkūmat al-Sayd 'Alī Abū al-Rāghib* ('Ammān: Da'irat al-Maṭbu'āt al-Nashr, 2004), p. 135.
39 Muḥammad 'Abd a-Karīm 'Akkūr, Al-'awāmil al-mu'athirah 'ala al-waẓīfah al-raqābīyah li-*majlis al-nuwāb al-Urduni* (Factors affecting the task of overseeing the Jordanian House of Representatives), Arabic text (Irbid: Dai'rat al-Maktaba al-Waṭaniyah, 2003), pp. 202–203.
40 Toby Dodge, An Arabian Prince, English Gentleman and the Tribes East of the Jordan River: Abdullah and the Creation and Consolidation of the Trans-Jordanian state, Occasional Paper 13, Center of Near and Middle Eastern Studies (SOAS), University of London, May 1994, p. 28.
41 Uriel Dan, pp. 22–23, 26–27.
42 *Ibid*, pp. 2, 5.
43 *Ibid*, p. 9.
44 Fathi, p. 97.
45 Suhaylā Sulaymān al-Shalabī, *Al-'Alāqāt al-Urdunīyah al-Barīṭanīyah: 1951–1967* (Anglo-Jordanian Relations: 1951–1967), Arabic text (Beirut: Markaz Dirāsāt al-Waḥdah al-'Arabīyah, 2006), p. 71.
46 Mamdūḥ Riḍā, *Mudhakkirāt al-Malik Ṭalāl* (Memoirs of King Talal), Arabic text (Al-Qāhirah: Mu'assasat Rūz al-Yūsuf, 1962), p.132.
47 'Alī al-Muḥafaẓah, *Al-'Alāqāt al-Urdunīyah al-Barīṭanīyah: Min ta'sīs al-imārah ḥattā' ilghā' al-mu'āhadah, 1921–1958* (Anglo-Jordanian relations: From the foundation of the Emirate until the Abrogation of the Organic Law, 1921–1958/), Arabic text (Beirut: Dār al-Nahār lil-Nashr, 1973), pp. 243–244.
48 Cited in Riyād Aḥmad Bunduqjī, *Al-Urdun fi 'ahd Klubb* (Jordan in Glubb's Time), Arabic text ('Ammān: Maṭābi' Ṣafādī, 195?), p. 43.
49 Minister of State Cairo to Foreign Office. TNA FO371/31381/E901, February 4, 1942.
50 Situation Report on Trans-Jordan for the Month of June, 1943, TNA FO 371/35045/ E4678, p.1.
51 Situation Report on Trans-Jordan for April and June 1943, TNA FO 371/35045/E4648, pp. 2–3.
52 Situation Report on Trans-Jordan for the Month of July 1943. TNA FO 371/3545/5902, pp. 2–3.
53 Avner Wishnitzer, "A Fortress of Ignorance and Cowardice-The image of the Arab fighter in the Eyes of the Israeli Fighters in 1948," Hebrew text, *Jama'a*, Vol. 14 (2005), pp. 91, 110.
54 Muḥammad Ibrahīm al-Tarawinah, *Athr al-iṣlāḥ al-idārī fī al-tanmīyah: Al-tajrībah al-Urdunīyah* (The impact of administrative reform on development: The Jordanian trial), Arabic text ('Ammān: Dār al-Yarā', 2006), pp. 213–214.
55 McMichael to MacDonald, June 10, 1939. TNA FO/371, 23247/ E5015.
56 Trans-Jordan: Agreement between the United Kingdom and Transjordan signed in Jerusalem, February 20, 1928. Cmd 3069, London: His Majesty's Stationary office, 1928. TNA FO 371/27138/E6016.
57 Agreement between His Britannic Majesty and His Highness the Emir of Trans-Jordan Supplementary to the Agreement signed on the 20 February, 1928, TNA FO/371/27138/ E1168.
58 Report on the Political Situation for the Month of July, 1939. TNA FO 371/23248/ E5970.

59 "A Law to amend the Organic Law of Transjordan, 1939." TNA FO 371/23248/E6688.
60 Report on the Political Situation for the Month of September 1939. TNA FO 371/23248/E7205.
61 Report on the Political Situation for the Month of October 1939. TNA FO 371/23248/E7713.
62 Awrāq min Daftar al-Ayyām, p. 86.
63 *Ibid.*
64 *Ibid*, p. 87.

XI Jordan, the West Bank, and Jewish settlement plans

King Hussein's foreign policy developed in response to three main aspects: Jordan's dependence on British imperial power; the challenge of the radical Arab nationalist forces, and the conflict with Israel.[1] Jordan's foreign policy as defined by King Hussein was linked to the Hashemite vision, which sought to promote democracy, cooperation and openness to the outside world.[2] There is little doubt that Jordanian foreign policy took a different turn when King Hussein ascended throne on August 11, 1952. Commenting on this change Musa Braizat writes:

> If the observer ventures to go as far as looking at the King's first speech to the parliament, he or she will find it containing the basic themes of Jordanian foreign policy at that time. These manifested themselves in the relations with Britain and the other great power, the situation in Palestine, the Israeli threat, and the rights of the Palestinians. There was lack of continuity with the policy of King Abdallah, blessed be his name, which manifested itself in the quest for a diplomatic solution to the conflict with Israel.[3]

The main objectives of Jordan's foreign relations remained basically unchanged. They included the preservation of the country's independence, its territorial integrity, and the perpetuation of the existing monarchial Hashemite order. In order to achieve these objectives, the Hashemite regime endeavored to keep the sources of foreign danger at bay, and strengthen the loyalty to the monarchial regime by building a strong military force to defend the kingdom. In addition, the regime sought guardianship of the places holy to Islam, and participation in Islamic affairs. It was committed to take part in all national events. The regime aspired to maintain a policy of positive neutralism, nonalignment and commitment to abide by the resolutions of the UN and its covenant, to guarantee that Jordan remain an independent contributing state, having the right to be a member of the family of nations. And last but not the least, the regime was committed to the preservation of world peace and security.[4] However, for a country with limited resources achieving all these goals always presented as serious challenge.

DOI: 10.4324/9781003450313-12

Ḥattar's observation regarding the limitation of Jordan's foreign policy is revealing. Though lengthy, is pertinent to quote. He writes:

> Perhaps it is realistic for us to realize that we do not possess the Egyptian or the Saudi weight in the U.S., and even they are not capable of anything. We do not dictate policies in the Palestinian affair, and we do not take part in dictating it....The Jordanian state is not entirely marginal, but it is not central on the Arab level, and even on that level it has weight [only] as a supporter of policies [dictated by others], and it is in no position to dictate such policies. The geographical, historical and political dictatorship made us part of the Fertile Crescent, we are incapable of allying ourselves with Syria or with Iraq, and we are incapable of being indefinitely outside a Syrian-Iraqi alliance.... Our place is with Palestine-the problem on our borders-which the Syrian-Iraqi "center" dictates.... the regional and international margin of maneuverability facing Amman is far greater than the policy-makers think.[5]

As one of the weakest and poorest countries in the Middle East, Jordan plays a role disproportionate to its resources. This, in a large measure is a result of its geographical location, at the heart of the Middle East. Surrounded by Syria, Iraq, Saudi Arabia, and Israel, the country's only access to the sea is at the Gulf of Aqaba. Its meager resources and its location had always compelled it to conduct a highly aggressive foreign policy. Moreover, domestic instability caused by the existence of aggressive Bedouin tribes, and a large population of Palestinians, made it necessary to maintain a robust army, and supply it with sophisticated weapons and equipment. Such objectives, could not be achieved unless the country's leaders were ready and willing to engage in an active foreign policy. The country continues to face major challenges, living in an environment surrounded by countries with territorial ambitions, and the Hashemites are compelled to establish relations with their neighboring countries with a view to secure the country's survival.

Above all, the lack of resources continues to determine the course of Jordanian foreign policy and the country continues to depend on foreign sources for help. Oil from Egypt and financial assistance from Saudi Arabia are needed more than ever before, especially as the demands for reconstruction and reforms increase. The resentment against Bedouins, who are regarded as parasites milking the system, and the Syrian refugees, which lately came to the country constitute intense pressure on the regime to tap foreign sources of aid. Given these economic and social woes, one can better understand the demonstrations of many Islamists and leftists who disapprove of the King's connections with the West and demand that Jordan revoke its peace treaty with Israel. These dire conditions only increase Jordan's dependence on its donors.[6]

Another component that had an impact of Jordan's foreign policy throughout the country's independent existence was the quest for Arab unity. This has been a component, which could not be ignored by the Hashemites. In addition to their need to promote the idea of Palestinian sovereignty, the Hashemites were compelled to tolerate the manifestations of the pan-Arab ideology, which spread in the country during the Nasser era, and constituted a severe limitation on Hashemite foreign policy.

The most prominent figure who promoted Arab unity at that time was Prime Minister Wasfi al-Tall (1962–1963), a firm believer in the Fertile Crescent concept, and a proponent of an alliance with the West. He promoted the idea of unity within the Arab nation, which in his view constituted four parts: the Arabian Peninsula; Syria and Iraq; Egypt and Sudan, and the Maghreb states.[7] The attempts at Arab unity began in Jordan, and had a major impact of the regime's foreign policy. King Abdallah called for Arab unity and his grandson Hussein assumed the task, which Sharif Hussein of Mecca began with the great Arab rebellion. It is widely assumed that the Jordanian-Iraqi union of February 1958 came in response to Egypt's union with Syria, which took place in that year, and there are many who argue that Jordan's quest to unity with Iraq stemmed from the King's natural aspiration to Arab unity.[8]

Jordan's foreign policy continued to be affected by the idea of Arab unity and it made it virtually impossible for the Hashemites to stay out of the conflict with Israel, and that reality manifested itself clearly during the Six-Day War. Nevertheless, King Hussein had proven that despite his commitment to the pan-Arab sentiment, he was unwilling to let it limit the scope of his foreign policy, and his campaign against the Palestinians in 1972–1973 constituted a proof of his determination.

The West Bank

The stature of the traditional political elite in the West Bank, which consisted of notables of the historically prominent families that had long dominated Palestinian politics, declined considerably in the years 1947–1949. The Jordanian occupation that followed in 1950 decreased their influence even further, since they relied on Hashemite support. Their authority continued to depend on their ability to act as mediators between the West Bankers and the Jordanian government. As it turned out, the Hashemites' relations with the West Bank were marred by distrust, which the Palestinians had toward them from the very beginning. The West Bank Palestinians held a grudge toward King Abdallah due to his connections with the Israelis, and the fact that he gave them areas held by the Arabs at the Rhodes Armistice in 1949, with the sole purpose of promoting his family's interests.[9] The Hashemites were blamed not only for their collusion with Israel and its Western allies, but also for curbing the activities of the Palestinians and limiting their access to the army and to senior positions in the regime's bureaucracy. Furthermore, the Hashemites were blamed for preventing the Palestinians from expressing their views and giving preference to the East Bank.

The restrictions on PLO activities caused so such resentment among the public that in the autumn of 1966, violent demonstrations erupted in the West Bank, and brought down two cabinets. Moreover, the circumstances, which caused Jordan to lose the West Bank and East Jerusalem during the Six-Day War, caused many to suspect that the King concentrated his main forces in the East Bank, leaving the West Bank and East Jerusalem exposed. Among those who blamed the King for such neglect was Hebron's Mayor Shaikh Muhammad Ali al-Ja'bari who was quoted as saying, "Jordan proved unable to defend the West Bank, consequently, we owe her nothing."[10]

Many Palestinians continued to blame King Hussein for his determination to keep the East Bank for himself and for his neglect of the West Bank.[11] Generally, notables who occupied senior positions in the Hashemite establishment and benefited from this connection refrained from criticizing it. This group included Anwar al-Khatib who was the governor of the Jerusalem district; former cabinet minister Anwar Nusaybah; former governor of the Nablus district Abd al-Raḥim al-Sharif; the entrepreneur Ḥajj Ma'zuz al-Maşri from Nablus, and the Arshayd family of Jenin one of whose daughters married King Hussein's brother Prince Muhammad. There were also Palestinians who genuinely felt that under the circumstances, which prevailed at that time, the Hashemites did their best, and should not be held responsible for Palestinians' predicament.[12]

The uncertainty over the future of the West Bank, allowed the Hashemites to continue exerting influence in that region. Soon after the Six-Day War, the notables tried to negotiate with Israel with a view to establish an independent Arab state in the West Bank, but the negotiations reached an impasse. Israel left the mayors as the only leaders in the West Bank who could actually wield power, leaving many other officials unemployed, and many of them called for ending the Israeli occupation. Aware of their position as representatives of the West Bankers and recognizing that they had the most to lose from the severing the connection with Jordan, they protested and called for return to the status quo. As the war ended and the occupation of the West Bank began, Israel's Defense Minister Moshe Dayan called for "Open Bridges Policy," which enabled Jordan to perpetuate its penetration of the West Bank and to extend the rule of the traditional elite. The continuation of the Israeli occupation caused many West Bankers to believe that returning to Hashemite control was still an option. Following the Six-Day War, the notables continued to benefit from Jordanian largesse, while the opposition elite began to identify with the PLO and its nationalist ideology. Moreover, while the Hashemites continued to exert influence on the West Bank the counter elite became frustrated over the issue of allocation of benefits from Amman, and pointed to the Israeli occupation as their major cause of dissatisfaction. The outcome was that West Bank politics turned into a podium where the traditional elite lived in an uneasy working relationship with the counter elite.[13]

Generally, the traditional political elite in the West Bank acted with moderation throughout the years, despite the extreme nature of its pronouncements, and it rarely resorted to violence. Just like the Israelis and the PLO, the Hashemites held the view that the political future of the West Bank will be determined by external elements and not by the indigenous leaders. The Hashemites continued to regard both banks of the Jordan River as part of their state, while the political elite in the West Bank was disillusioned, distrusting all sides and seeking to change the status quo by military means if necessary.[14] Realizing that connection with Jordan was beneficial for them, the West Bank leaders did not sever the ties. They convinced themselves and their opponents by arguing that this was only a temporary arrangement. Although the veteran leaders in the West Bank spoke in favor of the Palestinians, they tended to stifle the young intellectual group that sought immediate action against Israel, and promoted cooperation with it.

In 1970, the policy of the West Bank elite was similar to that of Jordan and the PLO in that they were all in favor of activities on the local level, and sought to avoid a military encounter with Israel. This policy of restraint kept the extremists in check even under Israeli rule. The Jordanian government pursued a policy of restraint by opposing any attempt to organize a large-scale opposition movement against Israel. On the other hand, however it discouraged the mayors of the West Bank cities from establishing a meaningful cooperation with Israel. Following the civil war of 1970–1971, the Jordanian government reconciled itself to the freedom of action that the mayors had taken, and only sought to prevent them from coming up with political initiatives that could affect the West Bank as a whole.[15] Both Israel and Jordan had interests in the West Bank but while Israel's main concern was to normalize the daily life in the area, Jordan sought to prevent the emergence of a new political reality there. It was under these circumstances that Israel and Jordan operated with a tacit understanding that while Israel ought to be allowed to facilitate normalization of daily life, nothing would be done that could change the overall political status of the West Bank. Consequently, the West Bank elite managed to cooperate with Israel and Jordan at the same time, and continued to benefit from its power and freedom of action.

In 1970–1971, King Hussein succeeded in crushing the PLO in the East Bank and thereby intensified the resentment in the West Bank. The PLO's expulsion to Lebanon and Hussein's support for Syria's intervention in that country, which led to the fall of Tall al-Za'tar in 1976, strained the relations even further but the West Bankers were in no position to sever the ties with Amman, which provided them access to the outside world. They had to carry Jordanian passports and to pass Jordanian examinations, if they intended to work or study in other Arab countries.

Since the mid-1972, and especially after the Arab Summit Meeting in Rabat in October 1974, which recognized the PLO as the sole representative of the Palestinian people, its influence in Jordan increased, and thereby caused the veteran West Bank leadership to lose power, to a point where its existence was threatened and the new generation of West Bank leaders became more nationalistic and more inclined to cooperate with the PLO than their predecessors.[16]

Even though the West Bank was no longer part of Jordan, the connection was not easy to sever nor was it desirable. To begin with, there was an economic necessity to maintain the ties between the two banks, since the West Bank became a significant exporter of agricultural produce to Jordan. In 1976, its agricultural exports were estimated at over one hundred million dollars.[17] Moreover, there were numerous employees paid by the Jordanian government, in addition to funds given to key personnel in the West Bank, to maintain their loyalty and discourage them from developing ties with Israel. In addition, numerous institutions were supported by Jordan, including the municipalities, which obtained about 25 percent of their budgets from Amman. This connection was seen by the West Bank's leaders as deterring Israeli annexation. They did not wish to become part of the Israeli military establishment, nor did they want its judicial system to replace the Jordanian one even after the stormy events of 1970–1971. With the exception of the Mayor of Nablus, Ḥamdi Kan'an who recommended severing the ties with Amman, most West Bank leader were in favor of maintaining them. When the Arab League debated the "Open Bridge" between the two banks in September 1972 and recommended that the connection be severed, the mayors raised strong objection, saying that "the continuation of this link is vital and indispensable for political, economic and humanitarian reasons."[18]

Several proposals for solving the West Bank's problem were raised over the years. The first known as the "Palestine Entity" was to recognize Israel in its pre–Six-Day War borders and establish a Palestinian state in the West Bank, independent or under UN trusteeship. This proposal was rejected by Jordan, the PLO, and many of the West Bank leaders and was eventually dropped from the agenda.[19] The second proposal called for maintaining the connection with Jordan while introducing reforms that would raise the West Bank's stature. The radical members of the Ba'th parties and the Arab National Movement were in favor of transferring power to the Palestinian majority in Jordan. They insisted on a democratic political system and a universal military service, which would replace the Bedouin predominance in the army with a Palestinian one. Moreover, they demanded that Jordan's foreign policy would no longer be pro-Western. In 1969, Kan'an called for the establishment of a federation that would unite both banks on an equal basis. Although some of the King's close supporters such as Abd al-Raḥim al-Sharif and Anwar Nusseiba were in favor of the plan the King never officially accepted it. Following the elimination of the Palestinian guerrilla, the King believed that such plan would actually help him retain his influence in the West Bank. He therefore promoted his federation plan, and announced the formation of the United Arab Kingdom, which called for two autonomous provinces and a joint army, while major decisions affecting the two entities were to be made by the central government in Amman. This proposal was more popular than the first; however, there were too many Palestinians who opposed Hussein's rule or had reservations about it.[20] The third alternative was to sever the ties with Jordan and it came as a result of Hussein's unpopularity in the aftermath of the Yom Kippur War of 1973 in which he opted to stay out. Arafat's address to the UN General Assembly and the subsequent recognition of the PLO as the sole representative of the Palestinian people at the Arab Summit Meeting in Rabat in 1974 brought many to consider that option. However, when the PLO began losing popularity following Israel's war in Lebanon, the leaders of the West Bank and the Arab world in general came to the conclusion that severing the ties with Jordan would not be a wise move. By contrast, Jordan's image in the West improved and its military power was considered an asset if used coordination with Syria in case of a clash with Israel.[21] The fourth alternative was to establish a Palestinian state led by the PLO and linked with Jordan. Egyptian President Anwar Sadat made this proposal in 1973, and had many supporters who believe that the PLO would benefit from Jordan's diplomatic connections in the effort to end the occupation. There were still many supports of the idea of connection with Jordan despite the events that took place in 1970–1971. This is largely King Hussein's lineage to Prophet Muhammad and to the media's tendency to portray the monarchy in a positive light. Besides, Jordan enjoyed some years of prosperity under Hashemite rule, which helped bolster Hussein's image as a popular monarch. This helped King Hussein to maintain his influence in the West Bank as well despite the fact that both Jordan and Israel collaborated in the effort to control that region.[22]

In his study of the bicommunal perspective on Israeli-Palestinian relations, Shmuel Sandler argues that the Israeli-Jordanian combined effort to control the West Bank had adverse effect on the rise of an effective political leadership in that region. According to this analysis, Jordan's relationship to the West Bank prior to the Six-Day War of 1967 was a center-periphery in which the Hashemite Kingdom controlled that part of the country. The agreement between Jordan to jointly control the West Bank created a new kind of relationship in which two centers started controlling one periphery; Israel dominated the coercive resources, while Jordan provided an institutional-legal identity for the inhabitants, and both countries controlled the utilitarian resources. This left no room for self-expression in the West Bank since neither of the two centers was capable of providing a central value system with which the Palestinians could identify. Thus, sharing control with Israel had reduced the possibility that the population in the West Bank would agree to such arrangement.[23] Yet, some leaders did emerge in the West Bank. A new type of pragmatic leaders emerged in the West Bank in the early 1980s. Some of them came from the traditional elite and some from the supporters of the PLO. This group consisted of younger and more educated individuals with diverse professional backgrounds. It was markedly different from the once that controlled the political arena between 1967 and 1973. The new group tended to identify more closely with the PLO, and was inspired by intense Palestinian nationalism. Their opposition to Israel and Jordan was far more pronounced than their predecessors, and they constituted the leadership that was in power between 1973 and 1980. The young leaders were inspired by the PLO's gains in the regional and international levels.

The rise of the right-wing Likud government in Israel ushered in a new era of iron-fist policy which began in 1979, with the resignation of the last moderate leaders such as Moshe Dayan and Ezer Weizman. The Likud government's hardline policy toward the West Bank began on May 2, 1979, after the murder of six Israelis in Hebron, which the PLO supported. In retaliation, the Israeli government decided to deport the mayors of Hebron and Ḥalḥul. Several assassination attempts followed, resulting in the maiming of the mayors of Ramallah and Nablus. Begin's second government, which came to power in 1981, continued the hardliner policy, which intensified in the wake of his war against Lebanon. Further restrictions on the West Bank were introduced following Sharon's appointment as defense minister. Israel's policy of undermining the urban leaders of the West Bank by encouraging a new rural-based leadership failed. In the aftermath of Israel's war in Lebanon President Reagan began the initiative which jumpstarted the Jordanian-PLO dialogue and thereby brought the Jordanian government to play an essential role in West Bank politics. This initiative attracted many West Bank politicians.

It allowed for the rise of a pro-Jordanian elite, and facilitated the emergence of a different class of pragmatic politicians many of whom remained sympathetic to the PLO.[24]

Like Israel, Jordan sought to create alternative leadership in the West Bank. Hussein's development plan for the West Bank, which was unveiled in mid-July 1986, was designed to provide $1.2 billion for projects that would allow Jordan to increase its influence and neutralize the PLO. King Hussein who obtained the sum of $4.5 million for West Bank development continued to lobby Washington to finance the plan but many blamed him for colluding with Israel in the attempt to neutralize the PLO.[25]

It is difficult to predict the outcome of the Israeli-Palestinian conflict; however, the land surveys and registration undertaken by the Jordanian government after its annexation of the West Bank in 1950 had a significant impact on claims to land ownership, registration and taxation and is likely to have impact on future negotiations regarding the West Bank's fate.[26]

The Jewish settlement plans

During the Mandatory period, the German Jewish entrepreneur Pinhas Ruthenberg discussed the possibility of establishing a Jewish settlement in Transjordan, and his plan was debated in British government circles. The High Commissioner for Palestine John Chancellor and other British politicians such as Lord Reading supported the plan.[27] However, the response from officials in Transjordan was fast and furious. For example, Shams al-Din Sami, one of the pioneers of Jordan's struggle for independence, said at a meeting of the Legislative Assembly on June 4, 1929, that Ruthenberg's Plan was an illegal Zionist enterprise, and that the government of Transjordan ought to reject it.[28]

According to Moshe Sharett, the Arab notable Taufik Ghussayn who met King Abdallah was genuinely interested in the country's partition between Arabs and Jews.[29] Abdallah did not seem to follow the rejectionist policy pursued by the other Arab states. Jorge Garcia-Granados who was nominated member of the United Nations Special Committee on Palestine (UNSCOP) on May 13, 1947, and was charged with the task of contacting Abdallah had this to say about him:

> Abdullah definitely did not wish to associate himself with the other Arab states; and they, for their part, feared what he would say to us and would do all in their power to discourage any conference between us.[30]

The status quo that followed the Palestine War of 1948 was convenient to Israel and Jordan and both realized that they were threatened by the Palestinian nationalists, and felt that they had to prevent them from achieving self-determination on their land. Despite the difference between the two countries and the disagreement on the borders, this was the wide strategic framework to which they adhered, and they chose not to document that tacit agreement.[31] According to Sharett, Ben Gurion considered the possibility of invading Jordan and occupying it. To a large extent, this was his reaction to the Scorpion Pass Incident (*Ma'alei Akrabim*) on March 17, 1954, in which 11 Israelis were ambushed and massacred. Sharett rejected the idea as flashy and dangerous. He said:

> I have heard that after Ma'alei Akrabim you have expressed an opinion that we ought to capture an area in Jordan. In my opinion, such step would have immediately brought us to war with Jordan, with England fighting on her side and the United States screaming and condemning us in front of the entire world, and treating us as aggressors.[32]

Abdallah's decision to capture the West Bank caused tension not only in his relations with the Palestinian nationalists but also with Israel. Yet he was open to the possibility of a settlement. At a meeting with Abdallah in 1949, Dayan agreed to drive the Egyptians out of the Strip Gaza, and hand it over to Jordan with its 300,000 Palestinian refugees. For that purpose, Israel agreed to give up a strip of land that would provide a corridor linking Hebron to the Gaza.[33] However, the plan did not materialize, and when Abdallah decided to annex the West Bank to Jordan, on April 24, 1950, the response from the Israeli government was stern and unequivocal. The Israeli government spokesman issued the following statement:

> The decision to annex the Arab areas west of the River Jordan to the Hashemite Kingdom of Jordan is a unilateral step to which Israel is not a party in any way. We are connected with the Hashemite Kingdom of Jordan through the Armistice Agreement, which we will uphold rigorously. This agreement does not include any final political settlement, however, and no such settlement is possible without negotiations and a peace treaty between the sides. It must be evident, therefore, that the question of the status of the Arab areas west of the River Jordan remains open as far as we are concerned.[34]

Following an intense debate over the issue the Knesset adopted a resolution rejecting the annexation on the ground that the territory was part of Palestine; that it belonged to the Jewish people; and that the decision to annex it constituted a violation the Armistice Agreement.[35] The infiltration of Jordanians into Israeli territory and the reprisal that ensued, led to controversy among those who argued that it provoked Israel to retaliate, and those who blamed Israel for aggressive intensions toward the Hashemite Kingdom. For example, Glubb noted:

> In the five years since the Rhodes Armistice was signed in April 1949, not one single incursion into Israeli-held territory has been either planned or executed or even connived at by the Arab Legion, or by any other armed force controlled by the Jordan government. This is a fact.[36]

Nevertheless, contacts between Israel and Abdallah did take place and the documentary evidence shows that he sincerely tried to reach an agreement. Aware of his advanced age, Abdallah sought to end the conflict with Israel in a peaceful manner.

It is possible that his dream of reconquering Hejaz caused him to be moderate in his ties with Israel. What made this agreement impossible to achieve was the difference of opinion between Abdallah and his cabinet ministers who refused to reach a separate agreement with Israel. Abdallah made efforts not only to convince his ministers of the value of such agreement but also to find a prime minister receptive to such idea. The Palestinian-born Prime Minister Tewfik Abu al-Huda resigned in March 1950, precisely because he did not wish to be identified with Abdallah's peace talks with Israel. When Abdallah asked the Palestinian Samir al-Rifa'i to form a new cabinet he failed to do so. Therefore, Abdallah was compelled to reinstate al-Huda and suspended the negotiations with Israel until the elections of April 4, 1950. This brought an end to all serious negotiations with Israel. Abdallah continued to pressure the successive prime ministers to keep the negotiations going but neither Sa'id al-Mufti, nor this follower al-Rifa'i were willing to pursue direct negotiations with Israel. In fact, al-Mufti threatened to resign and his refusal to accept direct negotiation with Israel was overwhelmingly supported by both houses of parliament. The attempts by Sir Alec Kirkbride, the British minister in Jordan, to intervene in order to reach an agreement on that issue failed. Al-Mufti preferred to resign rather than become associated with this matter. After failing to find a prime minister willing to accept his view regarding direct negotiations with Israel, the King admitted his failure and asked al-Rifai to form a new cabinet, which refused to accept his proposal, and he was obliged to inform Israel that his government would not cooperate. After dismissing the cabinet, he recalled al-Rifa'i who agreed to cooperate this time. The King met the Israeli representative Reuven Shiloah, but the meetings reached an impasse because Israel did not meet his requirements. One of the bones of contention between the two countries was Abdallah's demand that Israel provide him with an outlet to the Mediterranean, by granting him sovereignty over a wide, two-kilometers corridor, but all the Israelis were willing to offer was a narrow road. Moreover, there were numerous opponents who were reluctant to agree to a separate peace with Israel. These were not only government officials and parliament members but also Palestinians and nationalists. Nevertheless, one cannot cast doubt on Abdallah's sincere efforts to reach an agreement with Israel. As Mordechai Gazit who explored this topic put is, "Abdallah's determination to achieve peace with Israel is borne out by documents numerous enough to convince the most confirmed sceptic."[37]

In June 1954, Abraham Ruthenberg conceived of a plan to purchase the shares and the installations of the Israel Electrical Company in Jordan and transfer the Jordanian part to a British company that would maintain ties to the Israeli company. Sharett opposed the plan fearing that the British company's connection with Israel was likely to be discovered. Nevertheless, he was willing to support such initiative, hoping that the connection with the British company would give Israel economic leverage in Jordan when peace comes.

This issue resurfaced in September when Ruthenberg tried to obtain Sharett's consent to purchase the entire Balfour-Beatty Company, with a view to divide it to an Israeli and Jordanian parts and to sell the Jordanian part to a British company that would continue to maintain ties with Israel. At the same time, Balfour-Beatty

Company planned to divide the company and to sell its part to Israel. Once more, Sharett opposed the plan fearing that Jordan might consider such act as an economic and political infiltration by Israel, and take measures against the company with a view to bring to its liquidation. Nevertheless, Ruthenberg was convinced that the Jordanian prime minister would be receptive to such plan. The upshot was that Sharett eventually agreed to implement the scheme, on the proviso that all the means to achieve it were legal, and that neither the British Exchequer nor the Foreign Office objected.[38]

An issue of major concern to both Israel and Jordan was related to water distribution and Johnston who proposed the water-sharing project faced enormous difficulties. Yet King Hussein was willing to listen. Recalling Johnston's experience Sharett writes,

> Nevertheless, he found the King of Jordan- whose influence in his country is growing constantly-willing to listen to words of virtue, and to agree that hatred never solved any problem, and that real policy making requires a positive approach to problems affecting the destiny of multitudes of humans. Among all Jordanian statesmen there are 2–3 whose hearts are for peace with Israel, but there are those who believe the complete opposite. It all depends on the push that would come from the negotiations table on the water issue-whether it would lead to an agreement or to a messier dispute.[39]

Tension along the Israeli-Jordanian border increased considerably in July 1956, and the media reported on concentration of Iraqi forces on the Jordanian border. This measure was taken with a view to counter Egyptian penetration, but Iraq justified it arguing that its purpose was to come to Jordan's defense against Israel. At the same time, the Arab media spread news regarding the concentration of Israel forces on the Jordanian border. Disgruntled by the rumors, Sharett said, "I am isolated and paralyzed and all I have to do is to eat my heart out."[40] Unlike Sharett, Ben Gurion started thinking about ways to prevent Iraq from threatening the stability in the region. He warned that if Jordan collapsed the neighboring Arab countries would intervene to grab its territory and Israel would have to act.[41] The tension increased when Transjordan's National Covenant was drafted. Those who drafted the Covenant stated categorically that they regarded the Balfour Declaration as contradictory to the promises made to the Arabs and a violation of international laws.[42] Nevertheless, the Iraqi threat did not seem to abate. On the contrary, the Israeli raid on the Palestinian city of Qalqilya on October 11, 1956, caused many casualties and led the King to ask the Iraqis to send a division to Jordan. Concerned about the outcome of his decision Golda Meir told the Knesset members:

> The entry of Iraqi units is part of a design aimed at promoting Iraqi territorial ambitions and bringing a drastic change in the status quo in the region. This constitutes a direct threat to Israel's territorial integrity on the part of an Arab state that invaded Israel in 1948, and then refused to sign the armistice

> with it. Committed to its obligation to its people, the Israeli government is determined to face this threat.[43]

The Israeli security doctrine adopted during the 1950s determined that the stability of the Hashemite regime was a strategic asset in the struggle against Arab radicalism sponsored and supported by Egypt and Syria. The prevailing attitude in Israel was that despite the fact that the Jordanian regime refused to let Jews have access to the holy sites and failed to adhere to the Armistice, it was essential to defend the Hashemite regime against the threat of Pan-Arabism, radicalism and the Palestinian national movement. In sum, the Israeli government could reasonably assume that despite its verbal support and the freedom of action that the Hashemites gave to the Palestinians to operate against Israel from its territory, it would not cross the 'red line' and allow the status quo to continue. From Israel's viewpoint the Hashemite regime provided a certain guarantee that no major Arab assault would come from Jordanian territory. Likewise, the Hashemites came to the realization that Israel was essential for Jordan's survival. This explains the reason for the strategic talks, which they held with senior Israeli officials. A British source quoted the head of Jordan's intelligence as saying that "an agreement with Israel is Jordan's only hope."[44] These contacts laid the foundations for wider understanding between the two countries, with a view, to keep the status quo and to expand its dimensions. The Israeli government made it clear to the western countries that if the Hashemite regime collapsed, it reserved the right to invade the West Bank and conquer it partially, or in its entirety. In one of his addresses to the cabinet, Ben Gurion informed its members that he told UN Secretary Dag Hammarskjöld:

> You need to understand that according to the UN Charter, Jordan has no right to Mount Scopus and the West Bank. The only right according to the armistice agreement between us, that there has to be an independent state in the West Bank, not Jordan. If it was not for clause 8 in which the Jordanians agreed in principle to free access to Mount Scopus and the Wailing Wall, we would not have signed the armistice agreement. We would not have agreed not to have access to the Wailing Wall, which is an emotional matter for world Jewry ...They [the Jordanians] have no right whatsoever to Mount Scopus and the West Bank. You know that Jordan is an unstable state. I am not sure if it will survive. It is true that few of us say that it is necessary to conquer the West Bank [but] most of us think that we cannot afford to add another million Arabs who might destroy the state of Israel. Mount Scopus is a different matter....We will not agree to let others take Mount Scopus.[45]

Following the coup of 1958, which brought Qasim to power in Iraq, the Israeli government agreed, albeit reluctantly, to let the British fly their troops and equipment through Israeli air space, in order to save King Hussein's regime from collapse. Qasim's rise to power, the turmoil in Jordan and the civil war in Lebanon necessitated a British intervention in Jordan. During the first decade of Israel's existence, Ben Gurion considered the border with Jordan as indefensible but his view changed in 1958, and he began regarding its independent existence as an important factor that contributed to Israel's defense. Until that year, he maintained the view that Israel reserved the right in intervene in the event of a foreign invasion of Jordanian territory. However, following the coup in Iraq, which caught him when he was contemplating the establishing a Peripheral Alliance with Turkey, Iran, and Ethiopia in order to contain Nasser's influence and to obtain nuclear capability, his thinking began to change. Fearing negative reaction from France and the United States on whose assistance he was counting to achieve both objectives, he no longer thought about invading Jordan. Already in October 1956, President Eisenhower warned him to resist pressure by extremists to invade the territory west of the Jordan River. It was at that time that he proposed to the French Prime Minister Guy Mollet the partitioning of Jordan by annexing the West Bank to Israel, and the East Bank to Iraq, on the proviso that the latter sign a peace treaty with Israel, and agree to absorb a large number of Palestinian refugees. Yet, Ben Gurion sought to acquire the West Bank, or at least turn it into an autonomous zone linked to Israel, and he still considered the possibility of a limited action to change Israel's border with Jordan. On August 12, 1958, Israel's Foreign Minister Golda Meir informed the British Foreign Secretary Selwyn Lloyd that Jordan was on the verge of collapse, and that Israel might have to intervene. However, she stressed that Israel had no desire to annex territory inhabited by many Arabs. According to Lloyd, she stated that Israel was likely to accept Jordan in its current borders, if the great powers would guarantee its independence.

During the crisis of 1958, Ben Gurion rejected the proposals for military action against Jordan, arguing that it would jeopardize his plan to forge an anti-Nasser alliance and to obtain a nuclear reactor. During the second crisis, which erupted in 1960, following the assassination of Jordan's Prime Minister Wasfi al-Tal, a meeting between General Chaim Herzog and a representative of the Jordanian intelligence took place, and they discussed the possible steps that could be taken, in order to react to the danger, which Nasser and the Pan-Arabists posed for Jordan. Shortly afterward, Ben Gurion informed the King that his country's independence was in Israel's interest. By the time of the third crisis of 1963, caused by the threat of pro-Nasserite elements to the Hashemite regime, Israel not only used diplomatic channels in order to obtain foreign support for Jordan's independence but also concentrated its forces along its border as a warning to Egypt and Syria.[46] The threat of the pro-Nasserite forces compelled the King to call upon Britain, the United States, and Israel for help. Concerned that the danger to stability of Jordan would have adverse effect on Israel's security, Ben Gurion made strenuous efforts to convince the great powers to conclude a security alliance with Israel.[47]

By the end of 1965, King Hussein asked for a meeting with the Israeli representative Ya'acov Herzog who was the head of Israel's Prime Minister's Office and he communicated the message to its ambassador to Paris, Walter Eithan. Shortly afterward, a meeting between King Hussein and Golda Meir was held at the house of a Jewish family in Paris, in November that year. At the meeting, the King expressed his concern that his country was in a precarious position, and that it was a target of threats from Nasser, Syria, and the PLO. He asked that the Israeli government give its consent to the Jordan's purchase of tanks from the United States, which the Israel already agreed to. He promised that the tanks will not cross the Jordan River, and that he will not use them against Israel. Furthermore, he agreed to provide President Johnson a written guarantee to that effect, and said that he will not sabotage Israel's efforts to expand its water projects, while Meir promised that the amount of water that Israel would pump from the Jordan River would not exceed the allotment agreed upon according the Johnston Plan of 1955. King Hussein had also asked that Israel exercise restraint and avoid retaliating against the Palestinians commando fighters across the Jordanian border. He blamed Syria for causing incidents along the border and asked that Israel understand his predicament. However, Israel's retaliation campaign against the Palestinian guerrillas who operated from Samu' in Mount Hebron in November 1966, resulted in the death of many Jordanians, and caused tension in the bilateral relations and in Israel's ties with the Western countries. Historians tend to regard the raid on Samu' as a turning point in the relations between the two countries. The attack convinced the King that Israel's aim was nothing less than the invasion and occupation of the West Bank. The pressure exerted by the Palestinians who demanded that King Hussein join Nasser's coalition played a major role in his decision to join the war against Israel in June 1967.[48] The King decided to join Egypt and Syria despite previous Israeli warning. Neither the Israelis nor the Arabs were certain that Jordan would join. The Ba'athist founding member Sami al-Jundi argued that the Syrians believed that Jordan will not become involved, and that the conflict will end with Egypt and Israel exhausting each other, until they would come to the rescue.[49]

As it turned out, King Hussein yielded to the pan-Arab sentiment that reached one of its crescendos at that time, and he lost the West Bank and East Jerusalem to Israel. Scores of American tanks fell into the hands of the IDF in the West Bank during the Six-Day War. The Israelis who hoped that the King would keep his promise not to use them against the IDF had a good reason to be disillusioned.[50] The impact of Israel's decision to annex East Jerusalem immediately after the war was devastating for Jordan. Anwar al-Khatib al-Tamimi who was the governor of Jerusalem district at that time, mentioned in his memoirs that the Jordanians were concerned about the impact of the Israeli annexation on the legal status of the holy places and the Islamic institutions. He recalled how furious and frustrated the Jordanian officials were and how vigorously they protested. He writes:

> We protested to the military governor general regarding the annexation of Jerusalem, which we refused to accept. We regarded Jerusalem as part of the West Bank, which constitutes a part of the Hashemite Kingdom of Jordan, and [we said] that the Israeli decision was in violation of the fourth paragraph of the second clause of the United Nation's Covenant. Those who were present announced that the inhabitants of Jerusalem had already exercised all their full rights to self-determination by declaring the unity of the two banks, based on the historical resolution that was adopted by the Jordanian parliament on April 24, 1950.[51]

Following the Six-Day War, the Israelis began discussing the possibility of reaching an agreement with the Arab states. One of the most talked about peace plans was that of Yigal Allon, the former celebrated commander the Palmach, the elite force of the Yishuv prior to independence. Allon suggested that Israel and Jordan would divide the West Bank between them, and nearly all the cabinet members supported his plan. Even Dayan did not rule out the possibility of sharing these territories with Jordan. However, Allon's plan was not on the cabinet's agenda and neither the head of the opposition Herut Party, Menachem Begin nor Joseph Sappir who joined his right-wing coalition GAHAL (Herut-Liberal Bloc) had the opportunity to express their opposition to it at a cabinet meeting.

The encounter between Israel and Jordan during the Karameh Campaign in March 1968, where Israel sought to hit Palestinian targets in Jordan but ended up suffering severe casualties, increased the tension between the two countries. The Jordanian press celebrated the operation by paying homage to the commander who led the campaign. The weekly magazine *Al-Sabil* praised Lieutenant General Mashhur Ḥaditah al-Jazi as the one who destroyed the legend regarding Israel's invincibility.[52]

Begin who led the Herut opposition party was unwilling to recognize Jordan from the very beginning. His party's daily *Herut* mentioned Jordan's name in quotation marks, in order to demonstrate its refusal to recognize the country's legitimacy. This was in line with Jabotinsky's lyrics of the song *The Jordan River has two banks, and both belong to us*! It was not until the mid-1950s that Begin started changing his attitude and gradually Jordan was no longer mentioned in the party's publications. Even the publications of the Revisionist, Betar youth movement, stopped mentioning Jordan as part of the Jewish homeland. This change in Herut's ideology became more obvious when GAHAL was formed. Seeking to attract middle-class supporters and to accommodate the Liberals in his party, Begin deemed it wiser to downplay his desire to annex Jordan. The change manifested itself with greater force, after he joined the National Unity Government on eve of the Six-Day War and even more so thereafter. Not only did he not propose that the IDF cross the Jordan but also supported Dayan's 'Open Bridge' policy with Jordan. Moreover, he was aware of the meetings which the leaders of the Labor coalition had with King Hussein, and did not raise objection. His position became less ambitious and more realistic, and he stated that Israel should not give up what it had and not demand what it did not have. By the beginning of 1970, Begin shared Dayan's attitude, which opposed Soviet influence in Jordan, and even the aid that Israel provided Jordan during Golda Meir ministry was met with his approval. By 1973, it became abundantly clear that his party gave up its claim to Jordan and his successors in the Likud party, which supplanted GAHAL, became accustomed to refer to the Jordan River as Israel's boundary.[53] Jordan's name no longer appeared in quotation marks, and when Begin came to power in 1977, he called upon King Hussein to embark on negotiations for peace.[54] Yitzhak Shamir who succeeded Begin as prime minister, adopted a similar attitude of suspicion and distrust toward the King, and maintain the conviction that Israel should not rush to conclude peace with him. On the eve of the elections to the Knesset, he said:

> In my eyes it is extremely important to start negotiations with the leaders of the neighboring countries in matters of mutual concern. As for Hussein, for example, there are numerous topics requiring co-existence in our region; for example, [sharing] the waters of the Jordan River. This is a gigantic problem.... or the phosphate enterprise in the Dead Sea; we have a huge common resource here; or the ports of Eilat-Aqaba with their ecological problems, and other issues such as, Jordan's outlet to the sea and its oil pipeline. These are the issues on which there is need to reach an agreement with Hussein in order to create and better atmosphere that would enable us to start negotiations on the main issues. Meanwhile, they only 'grind water'. Hussein keeps on expressing the most extreme position. They always ask, what are we going to offer but it is always possible to ask what does he offer us?.... It is better to start negotiations about coexistence, because destiny determined that we live in the same region, close to each other, and sharing common problems.[55]

The way to obtain peace, according to Shamir, was to convince King Hussein that an accommodation with Israel would not only earn his country material and practical benefits such as technical assistance and economic prosperity, but also political stability. Such attitude triggered a critical response from politicians and scholars alike. Former secretary of the Likud Party Arye Naor writes:

> The assumption that it is possible to negotiate with Jordan in an inverted order reflects disregard to reality. We cannot hope to reach a set of international agreements with Jordan prior to the conclusion of a peace treaty. It is necessary that Jordan agree to that and there is need for Arab legitimacy to such step.[56]

According to Shamir, Jordan's legitimacy derives from the fact that it is a Palestinian state. He once told Lord Hugh Foot Caradon who crafted the UN 242 Resolution, which required Israel to withdraw from Arab territories that it occupied in Six-Day War, "As far as I am concerned, the national aspirations of the Palestinian people had already found their expression in Jordan."[57] General Ariel Sharon who later became Israel's prime minister had repeatedly argued that King Hussein was the real threat to peace in the region, and that he would rather see the PLO leader Yasser Arafat rule Jordan. His rationale was that converting Hussein's kingdom from Jordan into Palestine would invalidate the Palestinian claim for another state at Israel's expense. In one of his meetings in the Knesset lounge in 1982, he went as far as saying that he was willing to help the Palestinians overthrow King Hussein and turn Jordan into a Palestinian state. Sharon's plan became more concrete after Israel's war in Lebanon. He hoped that the destruction of the PLO's infrastructure in Lebanon would cause the Palestinians to leave the country and since Syria was not going to allow them entry, they would return to Jordan and overthrow King

Hussein's regime. This is how the slogan "Jordan is Palestine" became common in Israel and popular in the right-wing parties.[58] The attitude of the Israeli leaders underwent drastic change over time, and even Dayan who promoted the "Open Bridge" policy rejected King Hussein's insistence that Israel ought to withdraw from all the territories it conquered in the Six-Day War. By 1973, he became a proponent of Greater Israel that includes Judea and Samaria. He made statements to that effect in his press interviews and speeches to audiences. For example, in his address at the ceremony on the peak of Masada, he stated his conviction that victory in the Six-Day War provided Israel the opportunity to redefine its borders, that the Jews have a right to settle in the West Bank, and that the state's boundaries should extend from Jordan to the Suez Canal.[59] The Israeli right-wing continued to regard Jordan as the homeland of the Palestinians and Benjamin Netanyahu, who later became the Likud prime minister, repeated the same argument saying:

> For over the years, nearly all the refugees *have* been absorbed into the economies and societies of the countries of their residence. Indeed, most Palestinian Arabs have home. Many of them, in fact, live as full citizens in eastern Palestine today called the Hashemite Kingdom of Jordan.[60]

One of the proposals to resolve the Israeli-Palestinian conflict was to establish a confederation that would allow both Israelis and Palestinians to have in independent state within the confederation. King Hussein was in favor of such plan and it resonated in the Israeli Labor Camp. For example, Labor leader Shimon Peres writes:

> The political logic of a functional compromise might lead us, in the framework of peace, to the concept of a confederation between "a Jewish Israel" and a "Palestinian Jordan"; the Jewish settlements in Judea and Samaria will have a special status, within Jordan. At the same time, the city of Gaza will have a special status. Under Israeli sovereignty united Jerusalem might be not only Israel's capital but also that of the confederation, while Amman will be the capital of Palestinian Jordan.[61]

The idea of a confederation was not well received by the right-wing opposition parties and Begin made it abundantly clear that all the Palestinians could hope for was "home rule" or autonomy.[62] Labor Prime Minister, Yitzhak Rabin met King Hussein on several occasions. The first meeting according to his wife Leah, took place in 1975 or 1976. On that occasion, he traveled to Eilat and from there to an undisclosed location at sea, or in the desert. Shortly afterward, Israeli newspapers published a cartoon depicting the two leaders playing tennis.[63]

King Hussein has reluctantly accepted the Oslo accord signed between Israel and the Palestinians in 1993. The negotiators did not consul him and did not inform him about the details of the accord. Nevertheless, he accepted it as a basis for a viable peace. He told Hinchcliffe that this was the "only game in town."[64] King Hussein proceeded with the peace talks which culminated in the Wadi Araba peace treaty signed on October 26, 1994. What motivated him to establish peace was the fact that Syria was in the process of negotiating peace with Israel, and he did not wish to fall behind. He regraded the negotiations as an opportunity to mend fences with Washington. Moreover, he believed that Labor Prime Minister Rabin was a better partner for peace than any Israeli right-wing prime minister, and given the fact that Jordan lost much of the Iraqi market when the UN sanctions were in force, and its relations with the Gulf countries went sour, he had little choice but to move ahead with the normalization process. King Hussein realized that his country needed to attract investment and to obtain more water, and that peace could earn him the good will of the Americans who could supply F16 aircraft to the Jordanian air force. Moreover, by making peace with Israel the King could hope to obtain Britain's promise to write off Jordan's loans, and provide credit for exports.[65]

The peace treaty between Jordan and Israel was in jeopardy in 1996, when Netanyahu decided to retaliate for the killing of some 60 Israelis by Hamas. On September 25, Mossad agents made an attempt on the life of Hamas leader Khaled Meshaal by injecting him with fentanyl, a painkiller, which could kill within 48 hours. King Hussein demanded that Israel provide the antidote, threatening that if Meshaal dies he would revoke the peace treaty. He even called President Clinton to intervene. Eventually, Israel yielded, Meshaal was saved, and Netanyahu flew to Amman to apologize for the incident.[66]

Time will tell whether or not Jordan will ever be willing to live in peace and accept an Israeli state on its western border. Occasionally, Jordanian politicians raise the issue and they still do not seem willing to come to terms with Israel. An example for such recalcitrant attitude was provided on August 18, 2018, when former Jordan's prime minister Abd al-Salam al Majali who signed the peace treaty with Israel told the Jordanian television that the Arabs ought to capture Haifa by force, and that he opted for peace only in order to prevent bloodshed.[67]

Notes

1 Jaimie Allinson, *The Struggle for the State in Jordan: The Social Origins of Alliances in the Middle East* (London: I.B. Tauris, 2016), p. 15.
2 Bahgat Korany and Ali E. Hillal Dessouki, (Eds.), *The Foreign Policies of Arab States: The Challenge of Globalization*, (Cairo: The American University in Cairo Press, 2008), p. 263.
3 Musā Brayzat, "Sulaymān al-Nabūlsi wa-'alaqāt al-Urdun al'Arabiyya," (Sulayman al-Nabulsi and Jordan's Arab Ties), Arabic text. Sulaymān al-Nabulsi: Qirā'ah fī sirātahu wa-tajribātahu, *Waqā'i nadwat 1997* (Ammān: Al-Markaz al-Urduni lil-Dirasāt wa-al-Ma'lumāt, 1997), p. 145.
4 Amīn al-Mushāqaba, "Al-Siyasīyah al-Kharijīyah al-Urdunīyah: Thawabith wu-murtakazāt," (Jordan's Foreign Policy: Constants and Pivots), Arabic text, *Al-Siyāsah al-Kharijīyah al-*Urdunīyah wa-duwal Majlis al-Ta'āwūn al-Khalījī: Awrāq wa-Wathā'iq al-Mu'tamar al-*Thālith 3-4 Nisān, 2001*, 'Ammān-Irbīd, 2002 ('Ammān: Dār al-Kāmil, 2002), pp. 19–20.
5 Nāhiḍ Ḥattar, *Taḥāwwulāt Jadhrīyah fī al-Urdun 1994–2004* (Al-Qāhirah-al-maḥrūsah lil-Nashr wa-al-khadamāt al-ṣaḥafīyah wa-al-ma'lumāt, 2004), pp. 646–648.
6 "Jordan's mukhabarat and 'careless' Monarch set back Reform?," *Democracy Digest*, http://www.demdigest.net May 4, 2012.

7 Awrāq min Daftar al-Ayyām, p. 88.
8 Muḥammad Aḥmad Ṣāliḥ, "Al-Ḥusayn wa-al-waḥdah al-'Arabīyah-al-Ittiḥād al-'Arabi bayna mamlakatay al-Urdun wa-al-'Irāq," (Al Husayn and the Arab Unity: The Arab Unity between the kingdoms of Jordan and Iraq), Arabic text with title in English, *A Series on: National Culture Research and Dialogues* (4), King Hussein and the Arab Regional System: Papers from "Studies on King Hussein's Thought and Intellectual Legacy Conference" 8–10/4/2002 (Amman: Al-Hussein Bin Talal University, 2004), p. 237.
9 Clinton Bailey, "Changing Attitudes Towards Jordan in the West Bank," *Middle East Journal*, Vol. 32, No. 2 (Spring 1978), p. 155.
10 Cited *Ibid*, p. 156.
11 Marjorie Miller, "Palestinians Love and Loathe King Hussein," *Los Angeles Times*, February 7, 1999.
12 Bailey, p. 156.
13 Mark Heller, "Political and Social Change in the West Bank Since 1967," *Palestinian Society and Politics*, Edited by Joel S. Migdal (Princeton, NJ: Princeton University Press, 1980), pp. 185, 187, 200–204, 207–211.
14 Shaul Mishal, "Nationalism through Localism: Some Observations on the West Bank Political Elite," *Middle Eastern Studies*, Vol. 17, No. 4 (October 1981), p. 479.
15 *Ibid*, pp. 484–485.
16 *Ibid*, pp. 486, 488–489.
17 Bailey, p. 157.
18 Cited *Ibid*, p. 158.
19 *Ibid*, pp. 158–159.
20 *Ibid*, pp. 159–161.
21 *Ibid*, pp. 162–164.
22 Shmuel Sandler and Hillel Frisch, *Israel, the Palestinians and the West Bank: A Study in Intercommunal Conflict* (Lexington, MA: LexigtonBooks, 1984), p. 67.
23 Shmuel Sandler, "Israel and the West Bank Palestinians," *Publius*, Vol. 18, No. 2 (Spring 1988), p. 53, https://jstor.org/stable/3330460.
24 Emile Sahliyeh, "The West Bank Pragmatic Elite: The Uncertain Future," *Journal of Palestine Studies*, Vol. 15, No. 4 (Summer 1986), pp. 34–35, 37–38, 44.
25 Kevin Kelly, "Jordan's Plan for the West Bank," *Middle East Report*, No. 144 (January–February, 1987), p. 44.
26 Michael R. Fischbach, "The Implications of the Jordanian Land Policy for the West Bank," *Middle East Journal*, Vol. 48, No. 3 (Summer 1994), p. 509.
27 Yoav Gelber, *Jewish Transjordanian Relations 1921–48* (London: Frank Cass, 1997), p. 51.
28 Details regarding his arguments are discussed in Fawzī al-Khutabā, *Shams al-Dīn Sāmi: al-rajul, wa-al-tajribah, wa-al-ru'yah* ('Ammān: Dār al-Manāhij, 2002), pp. 77–81.
29 *Making of Policy: The Diaries of Moshe Sharett, 1938*, Vol. III [Hebrew] (Tel Aviv: Am Oved, 1972), p. 32.
30 Jorje García-Granados, *The Birth of Israel: The Drama as I Saw It* (New York: Alfred A. Knopf, 1949), p. 190.
31 Zaki Shalom, *Diplomacy in the Shadow of War: Myth and Reality in Advance of the Six Day War*, Hebrew text with title in English (Tel-Aviv: Ministry of Defense Publishing House, 2007), p. 73.
32 Sharett to Ben Gurion, April 4, 1954. Moshe Sharett, *Yoman Ishī* (Personal Diary), Hebrew text (Tel Aviv: Sifriyat Ma'ariv, 1978), Vol. II, p. 436.
33 Eric Rouleau, "Crisis in Jordan," *The World Today*, Vol. 23, No. 2 (February 1967), p. 67.
34 "Annexation of the West Bank by the Hashemite Kingdom; Sitting 135–May 3, 1950. The Constituent Assembly, First Knesset/1949–1951 (Jerusalem: Center for Public Affairs), http://www.jcpa.org/art/kne.

35 Ibid.
36 John Bagot Glubb, "Violence on the Jordan-Israeli Border," *Foreign Affairs*, Vol. 32, No. 4 (July 1954), p. 562.
37 Mordechai Gazit, "The Israel-Jordan Negotiations (1949–51): King Abdallah's Lonely Efforts," *Journal of Contemporary History*, Vol. 23, No. 3 (July 1988), pp. 410–411, 413, 433.
38 Moshe, Sharett, *Yoman Ishī* (Tel Aviv: Sifriyat Ma'ariv, 1978), Vol. II, pp. 530–531, 540.
39 *Ibid*, Vol. III, p. 745.
40 *Ibid*, Vol. VI, pp. 1540–1541.
41 *Ibid*, p. 1617.
42 *Mādhā taraka al-amīr lil-asatīr* (What did the Amir leave for Legends), Arabic text (Ammān?: Maktab al-Di'āyah wa-al-Nashr lil Qadīyah al-Urdunīyah, 1938), p. 129.
43 Golda Meir's speech in the Knesset, October 13, 1956. Cited in Medzini, pp. 243–244.
44 Shalom, p. 80.
45 Cited *Ibid*, pp. 78–79.
46 Moshe Zak and Yosef Yaacov, "The Shift in Ben Gurion's Attitude toward the Kingdom of Jordan," *Israel Studies*, Vo. I, No. 2 (Fall 1996), pp. 140–143, 146, 150-152, 158.
47 Ben Gurion's conviction that the Jordanian regime could not be relied upon to provide security for Israel convinced him to search for alternative security arrangements. After witnessing the demise of the pro-Western regime of Nuri al-Sa'id in Iraq, the civil war in Lebanon and the unrest in Jordan, he proposed to US President Dwight Eisenhower the formation of a peripheral alliance, including Israel, Turkey, Iran, and Ethiopia. See "Text of a Letter by Prime Minister Ben-Gurion to the President of the United States of America," Eisenhower Papers, International Series, Box 35, Mid East, July 1958 (4). Eisenhower Library, Abilene, Kansas.
48 Moshe Shemesh, "The IDF Raid on Samu': The Turning-Point in Jordan's Relations with Israel and the West Bank Palestinians," *Israel Studies*, Vol. 7, No. 1 (Spring 2002), pp. 161, 164.
49 Fouad Ajami, *The Arab Predicament: Arab Political Thought and Practice since 1967* (Cambridge, UK: Cambridge University Press), p. 45. (Sami al-Jundi, *Al-Ba'th…*).
50 Medzini, p. 295.
51 Anwar al-Khātīb al-Tamīmī, *Ma'a Ṣalāḥ al-Din fī al-Quds: ta'ammulāt wa-dhikrayāt* (With Salah al-Din in Jerusalem: Deals and Memoirs), Arabic text (Al-Quds: Dār al-Ṭibā'a al-Arābīyah, 1989), p. 179.
52 Al-Dhikrá al-sanawīyah al-ūlá li-raḥīl Fāris al-Karāmah al-Farīq al-Rukn Mashhūr Ḥadītah *al-Jāzi* (The First Annual Memorial to the Passing of Fāris al-Karāmah al-Farīq al-Rukn Mashhūr Ḥadītah al-Jāzi), Arabic text ('Ammān: Maṭābi' al-Dustūr al-Tijāriyah, 2002), p. 63.
53 Nadav G. Shelef, "From 'Both Banks of the Jordan' to the 'Whole Land of Israel': Ideological Change in Revisionist Zionism," *Israel Studies*, Vol. 9, No. 1 (Spring 2004), p. 135.
54 Arye Naor, *Writing of the Wall: Where the Likud Leading To?*, Hebrew text (Tel Aviv: Edanim, 1988), p. 40.
55 Cited *Ibid*, p. 37.
56 *Ibid*, p. 38.
57 Cited *Ibid*, p. 39.
58 *Ibid*, pp. 41–42.
59 Abba Eban, *An Autobiography* (New York: Random House, 1977), p. 487.
60 Benjamin Netanyahu, *A Durable Peace: Israel and its Place among the Nations* (New York: Warner Books, 2000), p. 156. [Italics are in the original].
61 Shimon Peres and Haggai Eshed, *Tomorrow Is Now*, [Hebrew text] (Jerusalem: Keter, 1978), p. 257.

62 David Kimche, *The Last Option: After Nasser, Arafat & Hussein: The Quest for Peace in the Middle East* (London: Weidenfeld and Nicolson, 1991), p. 251.
63 Leah Rabin, *Rabin: Our Life, His Legacy* (New York: G.P. Putnam's Sons, 1977), pp. 192–193.
64 Hinchcliffe, p. 346.
65 *Ibid*, pp. 346–347.
66 King Abdullah II, *Our Last Best Chance: The Pursuit of Peace in a Time of Peril* (New York: Viking Penguin, 2011), pp. 132–133.
67 "The Jordanian Prime Minister who signed the Peace Treaty with Israel says that Haifa should be taken by Force," *Times of Israel* (Arabic), September 8, 2018.

XII Jordan and its Muslim neighbors

Jordan's relations with its surrounding neighbors were far from smooth over the years. This was largely the result of the Hashemites' tendency to rely on Western support. The Arab nationalists in Jordan disapproved of King Hussein's moderate approach toward the West, and particularly the efforts that he exerted in order to develop a close relationship with the United States. The Palestinian population of Jordan, which constituted more than half of the country's population, felt betrayed by his inability to integrate them into the society, and resented his tendency to favor the East Bank over the West Bank, in which most of them resided.

By the late 1950s, King Hussein found himself surrounded by Arab countries whose leaders were inspired by radical ideas such as independence from foreign rule and Arab socialism, and were therefore committed to combat colonialism. Elements loyal to Nasser's Pan-Arab ideology pressured the government to adopt a radical anti-Western approach. They regarded King Hussein as a weak monarch committed not only to serve Western interests but also to prolong the Hashemite rule over the country. Others blamed him for what they regarded as lack of commitment to the Arab cause. Pressured by his radical neighbors and the Palestinian population, which expected him to fight for their cause, King Hussein lost their trust. His attempt to accommodate the demands of the Arab nationalists culminated in the loss of East Jerusalem in the Six-Day War of 1967, which everyone regarded as one of the greatest calamities, which befell the Muslim world. Furthermore, the attempts of the Palestinian guerrilla organizations to dominate the country, ended with their expulsion three years later. This chapter analyzes the course of Jordan's relations with its neighboring Muslim counties and attempts to explain how the King dealt with each crisis.

Syria

Jordan's relations with Syria fluctuated over the years. Jordan shares a common border with Syria, and the events in that country had a major impact on the Hashemite regime. The first contact between the two countries was in 1925, when the French authorities who attempted to suppress the Druze Rebellion, pursued the Syrian nationalists who sympathized with the rebels and found refuge in Transjordan. The attempts to pursue the nationalists brought the French to Transjordan and thereby

DOI: 10.4324/9781003450313-13

put the regime in a serious dilemma; handing them over meant a betrayal of the Arab cause, greater French influence, and interference in the Kingdom's affairs. Among the several dozen who fled to Transjordan were prominent nationalists some of whom played a major role in Syria's fight for independence. Munir al-Rayyis who participated in the flight to Transjordan recalled in his memoirs:

> The Syrian foreigners decided to travel to Amman to where Dr. al-Shahbandar and Jamil Mardam already fled. After lengthy preparations we hired camels from village of 'Anz....we came primarily to bear arms alongside our brethren the Druzes, and to fight with them against the common enemy [France]. After midnight... several dozen men hired beasts of burden and a guide to show them the way. Some of them went by foot because they did not have the means to hire the beasts to carry them to Amman.[1]

Another serious dilemma that clouded the bilateral relations was the suspicion that Amir Abdallah did not abandon his dream to rule Greater Syria. This kept Transjordan's relations with the Syrian republic tense. Adil Arslan recalled in his memoirs:

> For a long time our brother Shukri [al-Quwatli] is accompanied by violent fear of Greater Syria. He constantly trembled and was afraid to sleep, seeing the Jordanian army in his sleep, moving toward Damascus, and King Abdallah on Achilles' tendon and under its hoofs the body of 'Abd al-Karim al-'A'idi the governor of Hawran and the defender of the republic's borders.[2]

What further complicated the relations between the two countries was the presence of Ba'thi loyalists in Jordan. The connection between the Syrian and Jordanian members of the Ba'th can be traced back to the days when these young men attended the same schools. Munif al-Razaz who led the Ba'th movement in Jordan and then went to Syria noted in his memoirs how his connections with the Jordanians were formed. He writes:

> Friendships were established or former friendships were deepened between me and the Jordanians, Riyaḍ al-Khaṭib, 'Abd al-Ḥamid Sarraj, Waṣfi al-Tal, Ḥamad al-Farḥan, 'Abd al-Raḥim al-Ḥamoud, Kamil al-Ḥamarnah, and between me and my colleagues in the medical school, and in particular Ḥasan Far'un, 'Abdallah Ṣaliḥ and Naji Bishnaq, and between me and my friends George Tu'amah Niqulah Dibb, Burhan al-Dajani, and between me and my colleauges in the national organization, Khalid Muti' and Ṣaliḥ al-'Anbatawi.[3]

The possibility of union between Jordan and Syria did not seem to vanish during the 1930s. When 'Abd al-Mun'im al-Rifa'i sought to be transferred to the Jordanian consulate which opened in Damascus, Prime Minister Tawfiq al-Hadi asked him why did he wish to do so, his answer was: "It seems to me that the conditions in Jordan and Syria are likely to prioritize the union between the two countries and I wish to be closer in order to witness that and to become familiar with this field."[4] Between 1941 and 1947, King Abdallh persisted in his efforts to convince Syria and Lebanon to form a union with his country, however, both rejected his appeal. Syria made it clear that if the king wished to form a union, he must agree to incorporate his country to it, and not vice versa, and that the new form of government must be republican.[5]

Both Jordan and Syria participated in the Palestine War of 1948 against Israel. Although the war ended in Israeli victory, the sense of camaraderie fostered by the war had a positive impact of the bilateral relations. However, the turmoil which prevailed during the 1950s and early 1960s, as a result of the pan-Arab sentiment, and Nasser's expanding influence, caused anxiety in Jordan, leaving the Hashemite regime on the horns of a dilemma, which led to the rise of pro-Nasser politicians such as Nabulsi, and was bound to have its impact on Jordan's relations with the Arab countries. François Quilici's description of the events is vivid and pertinent to quote. He writes:

> The young king, however, underestimated the hold, which this Egyptian "hero" [Nasser] had on his people. He was not in a position to form a cabinet without Nabulsi as his foreign minister. "Death to traitors!" and "Down with Eisenhower!" proclaim the banners that were carried by the hitherto victorious masses who "descend to the street" every day, with many curses in their mouths. The assault is taking place on April 24. In the intersections the police encourage the 3,000 protesters who march toward the Parliament. The Bedouins of the Legion are there. Hussein is taking refuge at the Philadelphia Hotel. Glubb's mercenaries had saved him, and in order not to be recognized and to prevent vengeance, which until then was lying in the street corners, their faces were covered with grease. Martial law, dissolution of political parties and Nabulsi's imprisonment....The Americans had taken the "Big Stick" which they had snatched from the French and the British....With great zeal the little king denounce the "plot of international communism." But he claims loyalty to the Arab plot, which was his real priest. He could not and did not wish to detach himself from it. An airplane always awaits him in Amman's airport for the moment that he would need to flee.[6]

When Egypt, Syria, and Yemen formed the United Arab Republic in February 1958, the King felt insecure and announced the creation of a Hashemite union with Iraq. Surprisingly, Nasser refrained from criticizing these countries. In fact, he sent telegrams to both congratulating them on their success.[7] It became obvious, however, that the Arab Cold War reached one of its crescendos, and the tension between Jordan one the one hand, and Egypt and Syria on the other mounted considerably. Describing the Jordanian reaction to the Egyptian attempt to establish a triple federation with Syria and Iraq, Nasser' confidant and the celebrated editor of the semi-official organ *Al-Ahram*, Muhammad Hassanien Heikal, writes:

> In Jordan the reaction was frenzied. The changes that took place in Baghdad and then in Damascus, and the triple federation negotiations, which took place in Cairo afterwards, caused a stir among the public in Jordan. Demonstrations began in Amman and in the big cities of the West Bank, demanding that the government take part in the negotiations in Cairo…and there were clashes and skirmishes, which led to many deaths and injuries. Wasfi al Tall's government resigned and Samir al-Rifa'i was entrusted with forming a new government that had to face a tense situation.[8]

The tension in Jordan's relations with Syria mounted prior to 1958. In the summer of 1957, Jordan complained about the virulent Syrian press campaign, warning that it could result in an armed clash between the two countries. According to Syrian sources, Jordan's Foreign Minister Rifa'i warned the Syrian *chargé d'affaires* Ahmad Rahby that if the press campaign did not stop, Jordan would sever its relations with Syria, and take "any other action necessary" to end it. He added that if the press campaign did not cease "we shall check you and we are able to sacrifice victims on your border as we did on the Israeli border."[9]

The verbal campaign did not cease, despite the warnings, and the Syrians exploited every opportunity to intensify their hostile activities against Jordan. Syria's hostility to Israel acted as a catalyst to its intervention in Jordan, particularly since it sought to use its territory for hostile acts against the Jewish state. In a special memorandum from the CIA the author warned about King Hussein's inability to control the Palestinians, and Israel's retaliatory acts against their positions in Jordan. He added: "The Syrians, on the other hand, can be expected to continue to train saboteurs and dispatch them to Israel through Jordan. They are intent on causing troubles in both countries."[10]

The hostile rhetoric did not cease, and when Nasser challenged Israel to start a war in May 1967, the tension in Jordan's relations with Syria mounted ever further. Feeling uneasy about the timing of war, the King was far less enthusiastic about challenging Israel. On the other hand, both Egypt and Syria were determined to exploit what they regarded as a fortuitous moment to attack Israel. Explaining why Egypt decided to not the delay the attack on Israel, Field Marshal Mohamed Abdel Ghani El-Gamasy writes:

> We felt that any extension of the stalemate would lead to a weakened sense of urgency amongst the Arab states and a sense of loss of confidence in Egypt and Syria's commitment to war. First signs of this had already appeared with the collapse of the eastern front (Syria, Jordan and Iraq), with Jordan distancing itself from Syria and other Arabs.[11]

Following Hussein's crackdown on the Palestinians in 1970–1971, Syria tried to exploit the opportunity to invade the country and increase its influence there. Both

Israel and Jordan were alarmed at that prospect. U.S. Secretary of State Henry Kissinger called Yitzhak Rabin who was Israel's ambassador to Washington at that time and said, "King Hussein has approached us, describing the situation of his forces, and asked me to transmit his request that your air forces attack the Syrians in northern Jordan. I need an immediate reply."[12] It was only after Israel reinforced its forces in Irbid, close to the Syrian border and on the Golan Heights, and the Jordanian small air force and army managed to stop the advance of the Syrian tanks that the threat was over. Washington's response was that the action taken was insufficient. Assistant Secretary of State Joseph Sisco warned the Soviet *chargé d'affaires* Yuly Vorontsov that a failure to put a stop to Syrian hostilities might result in a joint U.S.-Israeli action aimed at rescuing Jordan.[13]

By the mid-1970s, the relations between the two countries improved and they agreed to cooperate, particularly on defense matters. However, American officials who visited the region came out with the impression that the Jordanians remained apprehensive and suspicious toward Syria's intentions.[14] When Iran-Iraq War began in 1980, Jordan supported Iraq and thereby alienated Syria, which supported Iran in the conflict. However, neither Syria nor Jordan wished to stop the process of rapprochement, which began in the mid-1970s. This rapprochement stemmed from King Hussein's desire to drive a wedge between Syria and the Palestinians whom he sought to control. On the other hand, Syria's willingness to improve its relations with Jordan stemmed from a desire to minimize the PLO's influence in the region. Moreover, Syria's President Hafiz Assad was concerned about the possibility that King Hussein would sign a peace treaty with Israel. Witnessing the rapprochement between Sadat's regime in Egypt and the United States, the Syrian leader had little hope that another war in the Middle East would result in Israeli defeat, and it became clear to him that the prospects of liberating the Golan Heights were quite slim. He therefore considered it prudent to remain on good terms with Jordan. Probably, the most common interest shared by the two countries was that both feared a PLO domination anywhere in the Middle East, and especially in Lebanon, which was embroiled in a civil war in 1975. In addition to these culculations, both countries sought to continue the commercial exchange that helped boost their economies.

The tension in the bilateral relations increased again during the Gulf War of 1991, when Jordan opposed the intervention of the U.S.-led coalition against Iraq, while Syria joined it. Once again, however, neither country let the relations deteriorate and another period of normalization ensued, until the King's decision to sign a peace treaty with Israel in 1994, which caused the relations to deteriorate once more, but not beyond repair. Syria's response to the peace treaty was mild compared to its reaction to Sadat's peace initiative and unlike Egypt, Jordan was not expelled from the Arab League. The reason for Syria's restraint was that Jordan's peace treaty with Israel came at a time when the negotiations between Israel and the Palestinians were still going on, and therefore King Hussein's initiative seemed part of the general peace process that was underway at that time. Minor incidents along the border occurred at Syria's initiative thereafter.

By 2003, Jordanian officials expressed frustration with Syria's violations of the truce along the border. They complained that Syria was unwilling to discuss the demarcation of the border, and that even Jordanian trading activities were subject to Syrian obstructions and unreasonable demands. Furthermore, they argued that Syria tolerated smuggling along the border, and that frequent shooting and numerous acts of violation were perpetrated by its soldiers. Indeed, the border was far from being quiet. Some tracts of land along the border were occupied by Syria and in return, the Jordanians occupied Syrian land. Yet despite these incidents, the construction work on the Al-Wihdeh Dam, along the border, continued without obstructions or delays.[15]

Despite the fact that the two countries had differences on the political level, the bilateral trade continued and even increased by the end of the twentieth century, after King Abdallah II and Bashar Assad came to power.

By the mid-1990s, the two countries concluded several trade agreements, which reduced the tariffs. The weakness of the Jordanian economy and the fact that its GDP averaged no more than three percent in the second half of the 1990s, led King Hussein to seek outside help and improve the country's trade relations with foreign countries. Pressure from foreign donners and contributors acted as another incentive for better trade relations with Syria. Moreover, the fall of Saddam Hussein had an adverse effect on Jordan's trade with its Iraqi neighbor and forced King Hussein to seek better economic relations with Syria. Similar pressure operated on the Syrian regime, which had long been isolated, and criticized by many who were in favor of liberalizing the economy.

Trade between Jordan and Syria remained modest over the years but was still important for both. In 1996, trade with Syria constituted 3.2 percent of Jordan's foreign trade, while Syria's trade with Jordan amounted to no more than 2.3 of Syria's. On the whole, the rise and fall in the volume of trade between the two countries was relatively insignificant but sometimes it made considerable difference. For example, from 1996 to 1999, Jordan's exports of building materials to Syria fell by over four-fifths, and the metal exports declined as well. On the other hand, Syrian purchases of Jordanian chemicals and resins rose during that period. Syria's exports to Jordan were mainly fabrics and chickpeas, and they constituted 51 percent of its total exports to Jordan in 1999, while the rest were textile agricultural and manufactured products. During that period, Syrian exports of grains to Jordan, which was valued $110 million in 1996, declined sharply. Seeking to boost the bilateral trade, the two countries signed a trade agreement in August 1999, which eliminated tariffs on many items. However, its impact on the bilateral trade was negligible.

By 1999, Jordan's major exports to Syria were potash, pharmaceuticals, phosphates, garments, phosphoric acid, chemicals, processed foods, metal products, such as aluminum, iron pipes, agricultural raw materials, and vehicles, all of which amounted to 58 percent of the Jordanian exports to Syria, and the rest were manufactured goods. Jordan's major imports from Syria included machines, spare parts, textiles, pharmaceuticals and oil, which constituted 61 percent of Syria's total exports to Jordan. While Jordanian exports to Syria rose in 2000, those of Syria fell, and the total for both countries was only slightly higher than the previous year.[16] In 2000, the bilateral trade declined considerably. Jordan's trade with Syria amounted to $68 million or 1.1 percent of Jordanian trade, while Syria's trade with Jordan was merely 0.8 percent of its foreign trade.

With King Hussein's death on February 7, 1999, another period in the bilateral relations began. Assad's speech on that occasion was replete with words of good will and cooperation. An article published in the Syrian daily *Tishrin* stated that

> Syria does not wish anything for Jordan, its sister country, except for glory and stability, and she is a source of strength and support for Jordan. The brotherly ties between the two countries block the way to Israeli attempts to fish in sordid waters.[17]

Now the two young leaders found much more in common. Neither King Abdallah II nor Bashar Assad were interested in a conflict at a time when both were striving to consolidate power in their hands. There was no personal rivalry between them, especially after Jordan became more detached from the conflict in the region, due to King Hussein's decision in 1988 to disown the West Bank. And once the Gulf War came to an end, it became easier to move toward rapprochement. Despite occasional periods of anti-Jordanian propaganda, the two countries saw benefit in maintaining cordial relations. Being dependent on water from Israel, which sometimes could not supply Jordan's needs, forced Abdallah to rely on Syria as an alternative source. By the early 2000, the two countries had more in common than ever. They both supported the Palestinian Intifada and opposed U.S. intervention in Iraq. Furthermore, the fall of the Soviet Union and the end of the Cold War reduced the tension of yesteryears.[18] When Bashar Assad began cracking down on his opponents, the King observed the unfolding events and it was only after it seemed clear that the Syrian opposition was about to win the civil war, that he called upon Assad to step down. In an interview to the BBC on November 14, 2011, he said:

> If Bashar has the interest of his country, he would step down, but he would also create an ability to reach out and start a new phase of Syrian political life…If I was in his position, I would—if it was me—I would step down and make sure whoever comes behind me has the ability to change the status quo that we're seeing.[19]

Iraq

Jordan and Iraq were ruled by the Hashemite family since 1921, when Amir Abdallah became king of the newly established Kingdom of Transjordan, while his brother Amir Faisal was crowned in Iraq. It is hardly surprising therefore, that the bilateral relations were cordial in the early years. In May 1941, Rashid Ali al-Gaylani rebelled against the British in Iraq, but his pro-Nazi coup was immediately crushed. This coup attempt brought a large influx of refugees into Transjordan. The Iraqi regime blamed many of the refugees for being collaborators with the British. This was happening at a time when the pro-Nazi sentiment in Iraq was strong and had serious impact on Transjordan. In his report on the events in Transjordan for October 1941, the officer commanding the Arab Legion, al-Fariq, mentioned how the pro-Nazi sentiment in Iraq affected his country. He writes:

> Throughout the months of September and October 1941 an average of perhaps 20 to 30 Iraqi tribesmen has been in Amman every night…they have frequently been abused and taunted by Iraqi officials with the charge of being pro-British…the sudden flood of visitors which has poured across from Iraq to Amman in the last three months, seems to emphasize both the repressive and the anti-British Iraq governments since 1930, and also the amazing and unprecedented change which has taken place in the last three or four months in Iraq.[20]

The pro-Nazi sentiment in Iraq caused tension in the bilateral relations and many Iraqis had little sympathy for the Hashemite regime in Jordan, which they regarded as a tool of imperialism and a collaborator with *Perfidious Albion*. During the Palestine War of 1948, Iraq sent 3,000 troops to support Abdallah, but they refrained from attacking the area allotted to the Jews in the Partition Plan of 1947. Iraq later sent another contingent of 10,000 troops to protect the Hashemite Kingdom. Nuri al-Sa'id who later became Iraq's prime minister had gone to Jordan to lead a contingent of Iraqi troops in the fight against the Jews, in coordination with Abdallah.[21] However, Abdallah's determination to incorporate the West Bank to his kingdom two years later strained the relations between the two countries once again.[22]

In 1949, the National Socialist Party in Jordan was renamed The Jordanian National Front Party. Its members included Hazza' al-Majali, 'Abd al-Halim al-Nimr, Anwar al-Khatib, Ḥikmet al-Masri, and Shafiq Arshidat, among others. The party's platform stated the Jordan was part of the Arab nation, that its goal was to preserve the constitutional monarchy and to protect the people from poverty, sickness and foreign influence. The party's goal according to its platform was to establish a unified Arab regime. Its objective was to introduce social reforms based on the Marxist model. Spokesmen for the party argued that since Jordan had no natural resources to rely on, it ought to seek unity with Iraq, as a first step toward general Arab unity. The party's spokesmen justified its preference for unity with Iraq, arguing that its economic resources were more plentiful that those of Jordan. In addition, they argued the foreign relations of both countries were similar; that both were ruled by the Hashemite family; and that the combined forces of their armies constituted a formidable deterrent against Israel.[23] Like Syria, the Iraqi regime showed little enthusiasm for such project. However, the rise of Nasser in Egypt and the expansion of pan-Arabism brought the cooperation between the two Hashemite regimes to a new height on February 14, 1958, when they formed the Arab Federation with a view to counter Egyptian domination. As it turned out, the overthrow of the Iraqi monarchy and the rise of Qasim on July 14, 1958, brought this "honeymoon" to an end, and the bilateral relations were marked by constant changes thereafter, from open hostility to restraint, until the rise of the Ba'th party ten year later. Following the unity between Syria and Egypt, which led to the establishment of the UAR, secret talks about a Hashemite unity between Jordan and Iraq resumed. The Jordanian delegation sent to Baghdad consisted of Prime Minister al-Rifa'i, the army commander, and the ministers Khalusi al-Khayri and Ahmad al-Tarawnah. While they were in Baghdad, an assassination attempt took place, when a bomb exploded prematurely, but there were no casualties. Suspicion fell on Nuri al-Sa'id and his comrades. His opponents blamed him for the attempt to form a union with Jordan, which in their eyes was aimed at weakening the UAR. In his speech to Nuri al-Sa'id's government, the opposition leader Colonel Kamil Shabib said:

> You Nuri, the mere mentioning of your name causes trembling and fear in every house throughout Iraq. Why did you become a prime minister? Is there a conspiracy here against the Arabs and against Egypt and Syria? Naturally, you will not answer my question, but I tell you yes, you are the trusted and obedient servant of British imperialism. You came to conspire against our people, our Arab brethren and against Syria and Egypt in particular. You ought to tender your resignation so that the people will be reassured and not mourn you. And no, no union with Jordan, because you are forming this union as an uprising, and in order to weaken the union between Egypt and Syria.[24]

Jordan's close relations with the Britain and later with the United States were detrimental to its relations with the radical Arab states, particularly Egypt and Syria. This was particularly the case during the Nasser era, when King Hussein felt compelled to enter the Six-Day War against Israel. The common hostility toward Israel brought Jordan and Iraq to greater cooperation; however, the feeling of solidarity ebbed shortly afterward. The political platform of the Ba'th party, which came to power in Iraq as result of the humiliation of the Arab states in the Six-Day War, was so radical that its leaders called for supporting the Palestinian resistance, which King Hussein had no desire to encourage. Moreover, the Iraqi Ba'th party embarked on an intense propaganda campaign against the Jordanian monarchy. Nevertheless, Iraq's hostility to Jordan was not constant, and there were even periods in which the Ba'th leaders endeavored to reach an accommodation with King Hussein.[25]

Though not always amicable, Jordan's relations with Iraq were significantly less tense than with Syria and even Qasim's coup did not cause a serious rupture in the bilateral relations. The common commercial interests played a major role in maintaining the two countries on friendly terms. However, the relations ebbed and flowed depending on the foreign policy alternatives pursued by the two regimes. A sharp turn for the worse took place in the autumn of 1970, when King Hussein began his campaign to crush the Palestinians in his country. Iraq's attempt to mediate between the King and the Palestinians failed. Fearing that its 25,000 troops stationed in Jordan would become embroiled in conflict with the Jordanian army, and maybe with the IDF, the Iraqi government decided not to intervene. However, an intense propaganda campaign in which the Iraqi regime blamed King Hussein for killing Palestinians and acting as an agent of Zionism and the United States began in earnest. The relations deteriorated further in 1975, when Jordan mended fences with Syria, Iraq's deadly enemy, and even more so the following year, when Abu Nidal's commandos stationed in Iraq raided the Intercontinental Hotel in Amman, and demanded that King Hussein make concessions to Iraq.[26] Nevertheless, despite the growing hostility between the two countries, the Iraqi regime was reluctant to alienate Jordan. There were several reasons for that. Primarily it was the fear that extreme hostility toward Jordan might throw the King into Syria's arms. Besides, the Iraqi regime sought to maintain the option of using the Aqaba sea route, after Syria closed most of its land routes to the Mediterranean. Aqaba became more desirable after the Six-Day War, which brought to the closure of the Suez Canal. These factors weighed heavily in Baghdad during the early 1970s, when the hostility reached its zenith, but even at that time, we find Iraqis involved in various development projects in Jordan. We hear about cooperation agreements in various fields, and Iraqi financial support by powerful persons such as Saddam Hussein, who was in charge of national security under President Ahmad Hasan al-Bakr. From King Hussein's viewpoint, it was desirable to maintain ties with Iraq, in order to secure the supply of oil, and to continue benefitting from its market. The fact that the King's relations with Syria were strained for most the period, except for the mid-1970, when he became disillusioned with Egypt and Saudi Arabia, who recognized the PLO as the only legitimate representative of the Palestinians at the Arab summit meeting in Rabat in October 1974, forced him to decide who his ally should be. King Hussein concluded that being close to Syria was riskier than to Iraq, and more likely to trigger Israeli reaction. Israel was less likely to be concerned about a Jordanian-Iraqi rapprochement as long as the latter did not station military force in Jordan, particularly since it had no medium-range missiles. Besides, Saddam's efforts to improve the ties with Iran and the conservative states of the Middle East encouraged King Hussein who became convinced that Iraq was a political and economic asset for his country. The final factor, which brought Jordan and Iraq closer, was that the Saudis made their financial aid to Jordan contingent upon keeping distance from Syria. Egypt' isolation, which came as result of the Camp David accord of 1979, made it impossible for King Hussein to have closer ties with Sadat. Consequently, the remaining alternative was to come closer to Iraq. Furthermore, King Hussein had good reason to hope that he could mediate between Iraq and Egypt, and thereby become a major player in the region and a reliable mediator for a U.S.-sponsored Middle East peace plan. As King Hussein saw it, Iraq was more likely than any country to recognize his rule over Jerusalem.[27]

The outbreak of the war with Iran in 1980 left Iraq without a secure outlet to the Persian Gulf. Therefore, the Iraqi regime had to rely on the port of Aqaba and thereby increased Jordan's profits. Iraq's role in the Jordanian economy increased considerably thereafter. Jordanian exports increased, and arms badly needed for the war against Iran were transferred to Iraq through Jordan. When the war began, Iraq became were highly involved in Jordan, which turned into its primary economic partner. Workshops and service institutions were established in order to serve Iraqi needs, and the economic partnership included both the public and the private sectors. By these means, the Iraqi regime penetrated Jordan and became part of it. Moreover, Iraq solidified its position by grants and oil shipments. Despite the fact that the official contacts were not always cordial the partnership continued. The reason for this is that this partnership remained embedded in institutions and organizations, which followed the same practices for years, despite changes in the official diplomatic discourse. Forty percent of all Jordan's commercial transactions were with Iraq. The countries were tied to each other commercially as well as politically, and they had similar interests and viewpoints.[28]

Following the Camp David Accord of 1979 between Egypt and Israel, the Iraqi government became more interested in cordial relations with Jordan. It seemed that the Iraqis noticed that there were many Ba'thi ministers and others with such tendencies in the Jordanian government and its agencies. This constituted a base for close cooperation between the Iraqi popular sector and that of Jordan. Besides, Iraq provided a loan of $189.2 million to Jordan.[29] They cooperated in many areas and sectors in which Jordan employed the sons of the tribes, whether they were government employees, or occupied in lower positions, particularly in transportation and shipping. This cooperation became extremely important due to the losses that Iraq suffered during its war with Iran. The closure of the ports of Basra and Um Qasr made Iraq increasingly dependent on the Gulf of Aqaba.

One of Jordan's challenges during the Iran-Iraq War was how to support Iraq without alienating Iran. In his speech at the International Conference in Amman, on March 25, 1986, which discussed the possibility of ending the conflict, Crown Prince Hasan bin Talal had this to say:

> I will speak frankly. Our support of Iraq whose territory was violated is a stand against aggression, and not against the Iranian people. Our standing beside Iraq, when the Iranian government announced its impossible conditions to put an end to the armed conflict, is merely a stand against the imposition of foreign domination, regardless of its origins or justifications. We would take the same position toward Iran, from the very beginning, if its people fall under foreign domination. Jordan is still a victim of aggression schemes and foreign domination. Moreover, the entire Arab nation is still a victim of aggression schemes and foreign domination. For us in Jordan the issue of national independence in the region is undisputable.[30]

Saddam's invasion to Kuwait in 1990 was a serious setback to the Jordanian economy, especially after the Iraqi forces were defeated and sanctions were imposed on the country.[31] The Iraqi invasion had such profound impact on the Hashemites that even a *persona non grata* like George Habash, leader of the Popular Front for the Liberation of Palestine was allowed to meet the King, and they stated that their feelings about the Iraqi leader was similar.[32] When faced by his critics regarding his hesitant and ambivalent stand during Saddam's invasion, King Hussein insisted that he merely responded to the popular sentiment, which left him no choice but to refrain from opposing the Iraqi leader. Furthermore, he argued that Jordan had vital interests, both strategic and economic, in maintaining normal relationship with Iraq. He argued, for example, that Jordan shared a long border with Iraq, and was therefore vulnerable to attack, which could adversely affect the Jordanian economy.

During the Gulf War, the Jordanian government assumed the task of a mediator. There were several reasons for that position: Jordan's geographical position and its economic and social contacts with Iraq, Kuwait and all the Gulf countries made it risky for the King to take sides. It goes without saying then, that the Hashemites had a sense of belonging to the family of Arab nations. Besides, the fact that Jordan presided over the Gulf Cooperation Council (GCC) alongside Egypt and Yemen in 1990, had considerable impact on Jordan's policy. These factors were the primary motives affecting the Jordanian decision makers, as the conflict was unfolding.[33]

It was during the incumbency of Zayd bin Shakir as Jordan's prime minister that the United States sought to impose sanctions on Iraq, and blamed Jordan for violating its terms. When Washington pressed Jordan to agree to the stationing of U.S. observers along its border with Iraq, bin Shakir refused to comply.[34] Then came a drastic and unexpected change in Jordan's policy; in May 1993, King Hussein severed his relations with Iraq. The official explanation for the move was that Iraqi "practices" deeply harmed Jordan's interests.[35] It was mainly the fear of alienating the United States and the Gulf states on which he depended for financial assistance, which brought King Hussein to such drastic decision.

In sum, the bilateral relations fluctuated according the developments of the moment in the Middle East and the international arena, and the main reason why the two countries maintained contacts, despite the absence of diplomatic ties, was economic. During the early years, Iraqi-Jordanian relations were cordial due to close family ties. This state of affairs changed following Qasim's coup. The bilateral relations improved until the Islamic revolution in Iran and the subsequent Iran-Iraq War. A rapprochement took place afterward, and the relations remained cordial throughout the Gulf War. All this time, the two countries benefitted from the alliance. During the war with Iran, Saddam needed Jordanian support. He relied on the Gulf of Aqaba through which much of the food and supplied arrived into Iraq. As for Jordan, the alliance was indispensable mainly for its economic needs. It was primarily Jordan's dependence on Iraqi oil, which made the alliance so vital. Moreover, King Hussein's fear that Iran's expansion into the Gulf countries would have adverse effect on their ability to provide him aid played an important role in his determination to maintain the alliance with Iraq. Furthermore, King Hussein viewed Iran's militancy as a threat to the pro-Western Hashemite regime.

Saddam invasion of Kuwait put Jordan in a serious dilemma. Supporting him was risky and likely to impair Jordan's relations with the United States, while taking part in the Western coalition meant a grave economic loss to Jordan, and a danger to its security in the east, especially when Syria was less than a reliable ally, and Israel was not yet in peace with Jordan. King Hussein was also aware of the danger that supporting Saddam might cause harm to his relations with Kuwait, Saudi Arabia and other regimes in the Gulf, where hundreds of thousands of Jordanians worked and sent their remittances home. He was in dire need of diplomacy that would not alienate the United States while keeping Iraq as an ally. Therefore, he chose not to join the U.S.-led coalition and at the same time called for Iraqi withdrawal from

Kuwait. This policy was by no means beneficial to Jordan, and it eventually forced King Hussein to consider opening dialogue with Israel.

Following the Gulf War, the King took the initiative to mend fences with Iraq as he had done with the United States. In April 1991, he visited Syria and reached an agreement with Assad on two fundamental points: that Iraq's territorial integrity was a strategic necessity that must be maintained, and that Syria will not deal with the United States nor with Israel, without including Jordan in the negotiations about a solution to the Arab-Israeli conflict.[36]

Several factors led to deterioration in the bilateral relations in the mid-1990s; Jordan severed its relations with Iraq; gave asylum to Iraqi opposition groups, including members of Saddam's family who defected from Iraq, and there were even rumors that the King revived his grandfather's claim to Iraq, which he emphatically denied.[37] Nevertheless, the bilateral trade did not stop and the two countries still maintained commercial relations. The relations improved significantly following King Hussein's death in 1999. King Abdallah II lifted the embargo and although the two countries did not form an alliance, the ties resumed their normal course. Jordan's dependence or Iraqi oil and the Iraqi dependence on the port of Aqaba helped normalize the bilateral relations as time went by.

Lebanon

Jordan's relations with Lebanon were cordial from the very beginning. The two countries do not share a common border, and there were no serious issues that could cause conflict between them. The two countries maintained commercial relations, which hardly ever caused disputes. The first time that Lebanon began to loom large in Jordan's foreign policy was in the aftermath of the Israeli invasion to Lebanon in 1982. King Hussein feared that the Palestinians whom he expelled from the country in 1970 might be tempted to return from Lebanon where they found shelter, and it was not until the Tunisian government announced its willingness to host the Palestinians who were evicted from Beirut by the IDF that the he sighed with relief.

In September 1999, King Abdallah II visited Lebanon where he met President Emile Lahoud and discussed cooperation in common projects and ways to enhance trade. This was the first visit to that country by a Hashemite monarch in more than 30 years.[38] In March 2001, the two countries agreed to install a gas pipeline and planned to establish a free trade area between them. However, the plans did not materialize due to the unrest in Lebanon. Both sides exchanged visits in 2005, and established the Lebanon-Jordan Higher Committee with a view to increase the cooperation. The improvement in Jordan's relations with Syria open the way for greater cooperation between the two countries. In December 2009, Jordan's Foreign Minister Nasser Judeh arrived in Lebanon, and they discussed the possibility of Jordanian cooperation in training the Lebanese armed forces.[39]

Egypt and Libya

Jordan's relations with Egypt fluctuated over the years. Both countries took part in the Palestine War of 1948, and both were members of the Arab League and other organizations that dealt with general Arab concerns. Tension in the bilateral relations started when Nasser came to power and promoted his vision of pan-Arabism. His call for a struggle against colonialism and Western influence resonated with many Jordanians who began criticizing the Hashemite regime for its connections with Britain and the United States. Pressured to response to Pan-Arab ideology and its many supporters, King Hussein was no longer at liberty to openly approach the Western powers or join defense treaties that they initiated.

In September 2, 1954, an Egyptian delegation visited Jordan. At a meeting with its members, King Hussein stated that he will not join any military alliance with foreign powers, and that he would support the efforts to establish a robust joint Arab defense treaty.[40] The Great Powers still maintained considerable influence in the Middle East at that time, and they often conducted their negotiations in secret. For example, according to the secret ALPHA Plan conceived by the United States and Britain at that time, it was agreed that a settlement with Arab states will include adjustments along the Israeli-Jordanian border, with a view to compensate the Arab farmers whose land remained part of Israel according to the Armistice that concluded the Palestine War 1948. According to the plan, Jordan was to regain most of the militarized, zone in return for allowing Israel to pave the old road leading from Jerusalem to Tel Aviv. In addition, the plan stipulated that Israel would give up the southern Negev, which constituted a triangular whose base bordered Egypt, and whose summit bordered Jordan, in order to establish connection between the Arab countries.[41] The Egyptians, who had long sought an access to their Arab neighbors, regarded the proposal with favor, while King Hussein was concerned about the expansion of Egyptian influence into his country.

King Hussein's decision not to join the Baghdad Pact ushered in a new era in his relations with Egypt. He took accommodating steps to satisfy the nationalists who were loyal to Nasser. These included the expulsion of Glubb, entry into the Arab Collective Security Pact, and the termination of the Anglo-Jordanian Treaty of 1948. The Suez Affair of 1956 put the Jordanian government on the horns of a dilemma. While the Palace was in favor of joining the Egyptian struggle against Colonialism and Zionism, Nabulsi's government opposed direct intervention, arguing that such step would be detrimental to Jordan.[42] Meanwhile, the activities of the pro-Nasser elements caused mayhem in Jordan, and by the summer of 1957, the King decided to bring the era of accommodation to an end. He accused the Egyptian military attaché in Amman, Major Fu'ad Hilal, and the consul in Jerusalem and expelled from Jordan. It was also in 1957, that Jordan formed an alliance with Saudi Arabia and thereby brought the tension to one of its highest crescendos.

The confrontation with Nasser continued through 1958, and after the union between Egypt and Syria was formed and became known as the United Arab Republic (UAR), the King decided to establish the Arab Federation with Iraq, which came to an abrupt end with Qasim's coup. Then the King decided on a policy of accommodation with Nasser, by replacing Samir al-Rifa'i who was critical of Egypt. Nasser agreed to restore the diplomatic relations on August 15 1959, primarily because he sought support from Jordan and Saudi Arabia in the Arab League in order to isolate Qasim who embarked on a virulent anti-Egyptian campaign.[43] This episode of rapprochement ended in 1961, when Syria decided to dismantle the

UAR. However, when King Hussein recognized the secessionist Syrian government of Ma'mun al-Kuzbari, Nasser decided to sever the relations once again. This move threw Jordan into Saudi hands and the two countries decided to establish a military union. Furthermore, the Hashemite regime decided to support the Royalists in the Yemeni civil war, and thereby infuriated Nasser. However, the King's fear of being surrounded by radical countries, which increased significantly in April 1963, after Egypt, Syria and Iraq announced their decision to form a federal union, convinced him to move toward accommodation once again.

The King's initial response was to give its blessing to idea of Arab unity. However, he made it clear that while he was ready to cooperate with the new union, he was not about to join it. Known for his hostility to Egypt, Prime Minister Wasfi al-Tall resigned from his position and a new government was formed under Samir al-Rifa'i and politicians such as Sa'id al-Mufti and Bahjat al-Talhuni. The new government embarked on a policy of mending fences with Egypt and even promised to introduce reforms, but the tension did not cease. Demonstrations in the Jordanian cities by crowds who were in favor of Arab unity and those who had grievances against the Hashemite regime were followed by riots in which many Palestinians participated. Palestinian deputies from the West Bank were among those who demanded Jordan's participation in the union. The upshot was that the government lost its popularity and the confidence of the parliament. Rifa'i was forced to resign, and the King who was against joining the union ordered his uncle Sharif Hussein bin Nasir to form a caretaker government, which brought some stability in Jordan.[44]

In January 1964, Nasser who felt isolated as result of the collapse of his union with Yemen and the deterioration of his relations with the United States was more willing to accommodate the conservative regimes of Jordan and Saudi Arabia. Both responded willingly and the Arab summit meeting, which took place in 1964, ushered in a period of peaceful coexistence between the conservative and revolutionary regimes. However, when Jordan sided with Saudi Arabia in January 1966, during the struggle between the revolutionary and the Islamic camps, the relations souered again, until May 30, 1967, when King Hussein agreed to sign a defense pact with Egypt, in preparation to the war against Israel, which erupted a week later. The King's decision to choose Egypt over Saudi Arabia emanated from his fear of the nationalists many of whom were Nasser's loyalists. As it turned out, this decision ended up costing him half of his kingdom in the Six-Day War.[45]

The aftermath of the Six-Day War was such that it brought the two countries together once more, since both lost territories to Israel, and Nasser understood that only with improved relations with the moderate monarchies could he hope to convince the United States. to pressure Israel to withdraw from the territories that it occupied. The alliance benefited the King who was determined to crush the Palestinians, and since Nasser committed himself to accepting the Rogers peace initiative on July 23, 1970, he had no alternative but to maintain ties with the King rather than the Palestinians. The upshot was that Nasser lost much of his credibility in Jordan and the King was free to crush the Palestinian resistance. Unlike Qaddafi, who expressed his outrage at the King's suppression of the Palestinians the Egyptian response was critical but mild.

After Nasser's death in 1970, the pressure on Jordan eased considerably. However, on April 6, 1972, Egypt severed its relations with Jordan in protest over the King's federation plan for the West Bank, and it was only on September 11, 1973, that they were restored. This move came largely as result of Sadat's plan to attack Israel, which he implemented with coordination with Syria in the following month. This time, the King did not join the coalition, which confronted Israel in the Yom Kippur War, and his decision did not seem to affect the relations between the two countries. The Jordanian government tended not to criticize or interfere in Egyptian affairs. In an interview with Sulayman Musa in 1974, Nabulsi said,

> I am one of the greatest Nasserites, and Sadat has his own faults, but we cannot dictate a policy to him. If we were to criticize his mistakes, this has to be within reason. I find that it is incumbent on me to criticize the mistakes in my country not in another country.[46]

The ties between the two countries were severed again in 1979, due to Sadat's decision to sign the Camp David accords with Israel, and they were not restored until September 25, 1984. Jordan's relations with Egypt have been cordial since Egypt was readmitted into the Arab fold and they lasted without major changes. In August 2016, King Abdallah II visited Egypt and therby brought the bilateral ties to new heights, when he met President Abd al-Fattah al-Sisi and both agreed to expand the cooperation, and discussed the possibility of strategic cooperation.

Jordan's relations with Libya were far less intense than with Egypt. Nevertheless, Qaddafi was critical of all the moderate regimes in the Middle East, and called upon the Arabs to overthrow them.[47] He sought to assassinate King Hussein and even encouraged the Palestinians to kill Kissinger.[48] This was largely due to his infatuation with the Palestinian problem, which he regarded as the main problem in the region. According to Heikal, Qaddafi raised strong objection to include King Hussein in the proposed conference that was scheduled to take place, in order to end the Jordanian-Palestinian conflict. Qaddafi was reported to have said, "What's the use of getting him? He's crazy. He's mad."[49] On September 1, 1980, he proposed a union with Syria, and said that if his proposal was rejected he would become a *fedayee* for the Palestinian cause.[50] Jordan's relations with Libya improved three years later when Qaddafi arrived in Amman on June 10, 1983. King Hussein invited him to stay before continuing his journey to Syria. Commenting on King Hussein's hospitality Abdallah II noted in his memoirs. "To an outsider, this might seem like an odd way to treat a man who the year before had tried to kill you. But my father always believed in keeping one's friends close and one's enemies even closer."[51]

Jordanian diplomats regarded Qaddafi as unpredictable and cast doubt on his ability to survive. Yet, they argued that the relationship between the two countries had improved considerably, despite the tension caused by the fire that Libyans set to the Jordanian Embassy in 1986, when King Hussein was on his way to Washington at the time of the U.S. bombing of Libya. Seeking to mend fences with Jordan, the Libyan government decided to rebuild the embassy six years later. Although the relations improved, the Jordanians remained dissatisfied with the slow implementation of the commercial agreements, and the limited opportunities that were available to them in Libya.[52] During the Libyan conflict, which brought to Qaddafi's downfall, Jordan contributed to the operation along with the UAE and Qatar.[53]

On September 21, 1987, Jordan renewed the diplomatic relations with Libya that were severed as result of the fire set to the Jordanian embassy. This move was possible largely because Libya restored its diplomatic relations with Iraq, after supporting Iran in the Iran-Iraq War, while Jordan supported Iraq in that conflict. Jordan's relations with Libya could not be restored immediately, due to King Hussein's efforts to reach an agreement with Israel and restore the diplomatic relations with Egypt.[54]

Jordan is one of the few Middle Eastern countries that maintained normal relations with Libya even though the two countries differed on main political issues, such as the Middle East peace process. According to the Jordanian Embassy's representative Nash'at al-Hasid, the relationship with Libya was fraught with difficulties, despite the commercial agreements that were signed between the two countries in September of 2009, when King Abdallah II passed through Libya to attend the celebration Qaddafi's 40th anniversary in power, en route to Morocco to meet the Saudi Prince Sultan.

Despite Qaddafi's criticism, Jordan's foreign policy under Hussein and Abdallah II remained unchanged. Both were determined to keep the peace treaty with Israel despite enormous pressure to cancel it. Moreover, King Abdallah's determination to concentrate on economic reconstruction and his "Jordan First" policy strengthened his resolve to keep the peace treaty. He noted in his memoirs, "The only role we will play is to continue to work for regional peace by helping the Palestinians in their effort to establish a viable independent state that will live in peace side by side with a secure Israel."[55] Unlike Qaddafi, who promoted the idea that only Jews of Arab origin have the right to remain in Palestine, neither Hussein nor Abdallah II made such distinction, and both favored an agreement with Israel. In fact, King Abdallah II went to the extent of challenging Israel to start the normalization process. He writes:

> Israel has a clear choice. Does it want to remain fortress Israel, peering over the ramparts at increasingly hostile and aggressive neighbors? Or is it prepared to accept the hand of peace offered by all fifty-seven Muslim states and finally integrate itself into its region, accepted and accepting?[56]

Saudi Arabia

Jordan's frontiers with Saudi Arabia were unstable from the beginning since the Trans-Jordanian tribes were accustomed to moving into its territory in search of grazing land for their cattle, and the Saudi tax collectors harassed them in the process. This was an endemic phenomenon, which caused tension in the bilateral relations. What complicated matters even further was that the relations between the Banu Sakhr and the Christian villagers in Madaba were tense. In order to safeguard the border with Palestine and protect Ma'an, the Tranjordanian government was compelled to recruit soldiers from the desert.[57] In August 1938, Saudi soldiers had crossed the border with Transjordan near Tutun, 15 miles southeast of Aqaba, causing the Bedouins in the region to flee in an effort to avoid the Saudi tax collectors. At the same time, Saudi tribes penetrated south Tubaiq to graze, without having to pay taxes to the Jordanian government.[58]

The first attempt to define border between the two countries was made in 1918. It was followed by the Hadda Agreement of November 1925, which did not meet the Jordanian demands, and was revised again in 1938. At a meeting with Glubb and Kirkbride, which took place at Mughaira on February 6–8, 1941, the Jordanian negotiator, Amir Abdul Aziz as Sudairi, made strenuous efforts to gain more territory. First, he insisted that the frontier should be at Bair, but after meeting resistance, he settled for Imshash Hadraj. The dispute was limited to a narrow strip of territory between the frontier marked in 1918, and that of 1938. Ibn Saud had a claim to the entire districts of Ma'an and Aqaba. Although he respected the boundary south of these regions, he still claimed both Ma'an and Aqaba.[59]

Al-Sudairi seemed willing to accept the British proposals at the Mughaira meeting. A British officer who witnessed the events along the border noted in his report:

> In spite of the abortive nature of the meeting with Abdul Aziz as-Sudairi, on the 6th February 1941, Saudi patrol seems to have been more careful in their observance of the frontier since the meeting. Perhaps Sudairi formerly had the impression that we were on the run, and that he would soon be able to take over large slice of Trans-Jordan territory. Our firm attitude at the Mughaira meeting may have convinced him that he would not bluff us as easily as he hoped.[60]

The Saudi conflict with Transjordan eased considerably during the World War II and as the Commanding Officer of the Arab Legion stated in his report in late spring 1942, "The [Saudi] King has apparently given orders to his provincial governors that all prevarications with the British or with Transjordan are to cease for the duration of the war."[61] However, the border issue continued to be controversial. The British report on the situation in Transjordan read in part:

> Investigations showed that the military surveyors have disregarded the pre-arranged line up to which they were to carry their work, a line well short of the true frontier, and had gone up to the line, hitherto undemarcated, according to the geographical coordinates given in the Hadda Agreement. One of their trig points was south of a line which purported to mark the frontier but coincided with no interpretation of the boundary and which appears to have been drawn by some one from the Trans-Jordan side. This cairn was demolished by the Saudis from their post at Haditha. Later a further cairn was demolished by the Saudis, this time west of the T.J. track and well within Trans-Jordan territory under any definition of the frontier. The principle trouble appears to arise from the fact that the Saudis believe that a unilateral demarcation of the frontier is in progress.[62]

Reports that the Saudis were helping finance anti-government gangs in Transjordan through their consulate in Damascus, began to circulate soon afterward. This was largely due to the competition between the Saudis and the Hashemites over the Syrian throne.[63] The tension in Jordan-Saudi relations intensified when Druze leaders who found refuge in Transjordan were often expelled and forced to move into Saudi Arabia.[64] The Jordanian government had constantly found itself besieged by complaints of Saudi merchants whose goods were robbed while crossing into Transjordan.[65] There were also reports that the Saudis were supporting a rebel organization in Damascus, whose purpose was to undermine the regime in Transjordan. One of the individuals involved in the attempt was Izzet el-Darwaza who had been caught with £3,000 worth of gold that was allocated to that purpose.[66]

In one of the border incidents, the commander of the Saudi post at Haditha, located some 30 miles southwest of Azraq, moved toward Wadi Makhruq inside Transjordan in an attempt to tax Banu Sakhr. Then the Saudi force moved to Hazim where it collected taxes from the Ruwalla tribesmen. Even though the British allowed the Saudis to remain close to the Hazim post and use its water resources, they did not renounce their claim, and the incidents along the border did not cease.[67]

During the early 1950s, Jordan was one of the revisionist countries in the Arab world. Abdallah called for the establishment of Greater Syria under his rule, and at the same time, Iraq aspired to unity with Syria. This state of affairs was not convenient for the Saudi regime whose king was uneasy about a possible alliance between the Iraq and Jordan. Saudi Arabia had taken advantage of the differences between them, in order to prevent their expansion southward. It gathered all the forces that opposed Abdallah in Jordan and Abd al-Illah in Iraq. Saudi Arabia continued to oppose any attempt to implement the Greater Syria or the Fertile Crescent plans.[68] Consequently, Jordan's relations with Saudi Arabia were not as cordial as the young King Hussein expected. There were mutual visits in the early years, but there was lack of enthusiasm on both sides. Moreover, Saudi financial aid to Jordan remained small. Apart from £50,000 that Saudi Arabia gave to the Jordanian National Guard, little was done to promote good will. King Saud's visit to Badna, on the border with Jordan, left the Hashemites unimpressed. Jordan's Prime Minister Fauzi al-Mulki expressed his disappointment, saying that the visit did not bring substantial results, neither in the political or the economic spheres. Moreover, the Jordanian government's hope that the Saudis would agree to purchase its grain and repair the Hejaz railroad did not materialize.

King Hussein's hope for better relations with Saudi Arabia did not materialize. There was lack of harmony between the two countries, and there were no agreements between the two sides despite the absence of major disputes. By the mid-1950s, Jordan was closer to Iraq than to Saudi Arabia. Jordan obtained British support, and there was even talk about the possibility that it would join the Baghdad Pact. At the same time, the Saudis were vehemently opposed to a union between Jordan and Iraq or Syria. Ibn Saud went to the extent of warning the British not to promote such unions because, as he put it, this would deny King Abdallah's sons the right to inherit their fathers' land.

The Saudis promoted union between Jordan and Syria, while the Iraqis were leaning, but not enthusiastic about union with Jordan. At the same time, the Egyptians attempted to prevent a Jordanian-Palestinian union, and supported the creation of a Palestinian state. As for the British, they sought to prevent a strategic union between Jordan and any Arab state, except for Iraq, which in most cases was not enthusiastic about such union.[69] The Saudis interfered in Jordan's affairs and tried to incite its politicians against Fauzi al-Mulki who in their eyes was close to Iraq. According to Braizat, al-Mulki's first government collapsed due to a Saudi-British collusion with a Jordanian organization led by Tawfiq Abu al-Huda when they agreed to overthrow that government to his benefit.[70]

Another phase of Saudi-Jordanian relations started after the issue of joining the Baghdad Pact was shelved. During that phase, there was talk about Saudi aid to the opposition in Jordan, which included the National Socialist Party led by Nabulsi. At that juncture, Saudi objectives coincided with those of Egypt and Syria who sought to curb the Communist expansion, and the Jordanian opposition, which opposed the British assistance to Jordan. The Saudis feared that the possibility of Jordan's entry into the Baghdad Pact, or the formation of an Iraqi-Jordanian union would increase Hashemite influence in that region. This was a prospect, which Egypt and Syria sought to prevent as well. Consequently, the three countries coordinated their actions against such possibility. This was done by supporting the opposition in Jordan, inciting against Britain, and promising to supplant Britain as Jordan's benefactor.

The state of Jordan's relations with Saudi Arabia began to change by the end of 1957, as result of the signing of the Arab Solidarity Pact by Saudi Arabia, Egypt and Syria in November of that year in Cairo. This caused Jordan to distance itself from Iraq and Britain, and come closer to Egypt-Syria-Saudi axis and naturally, to a Saudi-Jordanian rapprochement. Considering Communism to be the real threat, the Saudis desisted from supporting the opposition parties in Jordan, which included the National Socialist Party, in addition to the Ba'thists and Communists, and began supporting the monarchy.[71] Jordan's relations with Saudi Arabia continued to be cordial as both remained moderate, and improved their relations with the United States, and it was not until the Second Gulf War that a major crisis emerged, after Jordan's decision not to alienate Iraq. Naturally, Jordan' stand had adverse effect on the relations between the two countries and it alienated many of the senior officers in the Saudi army. The Saudi general Khaled Bin Sultan recalled in his memoirs how he and he colleagues felt at that time. He writes:

> Certainly, Saddam's invasion allowed us to recognize our friends, and identify our enemies. Rightly or wrongly, we came to believe that Jordan, the PLO, Yemen and even Sudan had conspired with Saddam to control the Gulf. The reluctance of King Hussein, Chairman Yasser Arafat and President Ali Abdallah Salih to condemn Iraq aroused our deepest suspicions.[72]

Iran

Jordan's relations with Iran were cordial during the reign of Shah Muhammad Reza Pahlavi. When Ayatollah Khomeini came to power in 1979, the relations with the Islamic Republic of Iran cooled off and reached their nadir in 1980, due to Jordan's support for Saddam Hussein during the Iran-Iraq War, which eruopted at that year, and lasted more than eight years. Jordan's relations with Iran deteriorated further, when King Hussein supported Iraq, both during the summit meeting of the Arab states in Fez on September 6–9, 1980, and the one that took place in Tunis on November 27, 1980, where the Arabs states expressed their willingness to call upon Iran to end the hostilities. During these meetings, King Hussein called upon the Arab states to support Iraq against Iran. He warned the participants that Iran constituted a danger to the Arabs and their unity.[73] This attitude increased the tension, which brought the Iranian regime to sever its relations with Jordan in 1981.

Jordan's relations with Iran did not improve until 1991, when Ahmed Dastmalchian, who founded the Hezbollah organization, which operated illegally in Jordan, became the first ambassador to Amman. However, when Jordan signed a peace treaty with Israel in 1994, Iran expressed its disapproval, and became hostile again. Several incidents occurred in that year that strained the relations even further. Angered by the assassination of a Jordanian diplomat, which occurred in Beirut in that year, the Jordanian government cast the blame on Iran, and expelled 21 Iranian diplomats from the country. On the one hand, Iranian officials expressed their dismay at Jordan's tolerance of Mujahedin-e Khalq's presence in Jordan. Mujahedin-e Khalq was a militant exile organization formed with the expressed purpose of overthrowing Ayatollah Khameini and Iran regarded its presence in Jordan as a provocation and danger to its regime.

King Hussein's concern about the growing power of the Islamic Republic was one of the reasons that led to his request to join the Gulf Security Council. Yet, he had no desire to bring the ties to the brink of collapse, and he maintained a lukewarm level of cordiality toward Iran. King Abdallah II followed the same policy, and when the issue of Iran's nuclear threat was discussed among the Arab leaders, he refrained from advocating a military solution to the problem. Moreover, he argued that Iran has a right to pursue its nuclear programs for peaceful purposes. At a meeting with Manouchehr Mottaki on May 17, 2006, he said, "Force will lead to catastrophic consequences for the security and the stability of the region."[74] At the same time, however, he expressed his objection to Iran's support of Hamas. A Jordanian official was reported to have said, "We are very concerned about Tehran's support for radical groups that seek to wreck peace accords and push the region toward greater bloodshed."[75]

On November 16, 2009, King Abdallah II told a delegation of the American Israel Public Affairs Committee (AIPAC) that his country was opposed to military strikes against Iran and stressed the need for resolving the dispute over its nuclear program by negotiations. Moreover, King Abdallah II argued that a solution to the Palestinian problem would bring the Iranian regime to realize that there is no need to develop nuclear weapons. In an interview with CNN on February 7, 2010, he said,

> Today, Iran is putting itself as the defenders of the Palestinian cause… If we solve the Israeli-Palestinian problem, why would Iranians want to spend so much money on a military program? It makes no sense. I mean, the country has social challenges. It has economic challenges. Why push the envelope in

getting to a military program? For what cause? If you solve the problem, you don't need to pursue that path.[76]

On October 13, 2010: Iranian President Mahmoud Ahmadinejad told King Abdallah II that "Iran welcomes further growth in the relations between the two countries and assumes reinvigoration and continuation of consultations that serve the interests of both nations and the region."[77] Despite the tension caused by Iran's nuclear project the Jordanian government continued to welcome economic cooperation. The two sides discussed ways of promoting cooperation but when news that Iran was about to supply Jordan with natural gas began to circulate in July 2011, Teheran was quick to deny them.

Meanwhile, the Iranian press continued to maintain a hostile attitude toward King Abdallah II and this trend led to tension in the bilateral relations. On March 16, 2011, Iran cancelled the king's visit, which was going to take place during the Nowruz celebrations. Iranian officials attributed the cancellation to "intense popular opposition and the opposition of decision-making institutions," and a member of the National Security and Foreign Policy Commission of Iran's Parliament, Mahmoud Ahmadi Bighash added, "Malik Abdullah's trip, which... has been cancelled, could delay the downfall of Jordan's dictatorial regime."[78] On May 11, 2011, the GCC began discussing Jordan's request to join the organization. According to many sources, Jordan's request to join the GCC came in the wake of the Iranian threat to the region.[79]

Turkey

The relations between the Hahemites and the Turkish state are marked by cordiality over the years even though Jordan fought alongside the British during World War I, in an effort to carve out the moribund Ottoman Empire.[80] While Jordan did not join the Baghdad Pact in 1955, it became a partner of the Israeli-Turkish alignment of 1996, and on January 7, 1998, it agreed to take part in the naval maneuvers that both countries conducted, despite Arab objections. Especially critical was the Syrian government, which spread propaganda that portrayed Jordan as a traitor to the Arab cause. Faced by severe criticism from Syria and Egypt, which failed to convince it to reject the Turkish proposal, the Jordanian government had to respond. It argued that the invitation did not come from Israel but from Turkey; that the outgoing government already accepted it; that its participation was only symbolic, since it pledged to send only one observer; and that these maneuvers were not aimed at any country. The Jordanian writer Al-Farik, Farid who originally was against the government's decision to send the observer responded to Syria's criticism by attacking its decision to support Iran against Iraq, and for its alliance with the United States against Saddam in the Second Gulf War. Moreover, he argued that Jordan had every right to establish relations with Turkey, if such step served its interest.[81]

The bilateral relations became warmer toward the end of the century. This was largely because both countries tended to be pro-Western, and they shared a common enemy; the Jordanians never forgot Syria's aggression, when it concentrated forces along their border in the aftermath of the Palestinian showdown with King Hussein in 1970–1971. Nor did Turkey forget Syria's encouragement of the Kurds living in Turkey, and since both collaborated with Israel in the maneuvers of 1998, there was nothing to stop the rapprochement. It was at that time, that both sides decided allow their senior officers to exchange visits and King Hussein gave a medal to the Turkey's Deputy Commander in Chief Cevik Bir.[82]

Oman and the Gulf Cooperation Council

Following the abdication of his father Sa'id Bin Taymur (1932–1972), Sultan Qabbus came to power in Oman on July 23, 1970. Oman of those days was country with little to offer to its inhabitants and there were very few educational institutions and medical facilities in the country. In 1970, Jordan supported Oman's entry to the Arab League and to the UN in the following year. In 1972, a Jordanian embassy opened in Muscat. Muhammad Khalil Abd al-Dayim became the first Jordanian ambassador. Jordan was one of the first Arab countries to establish diplomatic relations with Oman in 1973. The cooperation between the two countries began in earnest, and expanded to the economic field. In 1973, the Jordanian Arab Bank opened a branch in Muscat, and in 1974, Gulf Air opened a direct weekly flight between the two countries. The trade between the two countries expanded significantly over the years. Jordan contributed to peace and security in Oman in which there was a symbolic Jordanian military presence in order to help contain the Dhofari rebels. Jordan provided traing to young Omanis, an Omani embassy opened in Amman in 1975, after the sultan's visit, and the two countries signed a cultural agreement in 1976. The first Omani ambassador to Jordan was Badr Bin Sa'ud Bin Ḥarib al-Busa'idi. The cooperation between the two countries expanded over the years and in 1974–1976, several agreements were signed to exchange information in many areas from religion to labor exchange.

In 1979, Oman imported goods from Jordan valued at 832,000 Omani rials, but it exported very little to Jordan. By 1999, however, Oman's imports reached 3,851,000 rials, and its exports to Jordan amounted to 8,932,000.[83] The Jordanian army continued to support the Sultan when faced the Dhofari rebellion. In addition to engineers and instructors, Jordan sent 31 airplanes and 150 soldiers to fight against the rebels who were supported by South Yemen and Arab countries such as Iraq, Libya and several Palestinian factions. Both the Jordanian and the Omani armed forces were established according to the British model, which made it easier for Jordan to play an important role in training the Omani armed forces.

Jordan sought membership in the GCC since the formation of this organization in the early 1980s. The contacts between Jordan the Gulf countries can be traced back to their time of independence, and both sides benefited from the cooperation. The quest for membership in the GCC stemmed not only from hope that the rich countries of the Gulf would help Jordan economically, but also from the fact that Jordan became isolated following Saddam's demise. Jordan's success in joining the

GCC was regarded as was one of the pinnacles of its foreign policy. Tobias Buck and Eileen Byrne summarized the way that this major feat was achieved by saying:

> Now, after decades of canny diplomacy and shifting loyalties, Jordan is finally preparing to enter what many in the country see as the safest harbor in the entire Middle East: the Gulf Co-operation Council, the alliance formed by the conservative, oil-drenched monarchies along the Persian Gulf.[84]

King Abdallah's quest was motivated by commercial reasons as well; primarily to enable Jordanians to find employment opportunities in the Gulf countries, and to promote tourism.

However, Jordan's quest to the join the GCC was far from being smooth. Many cast doubt on the appropriateness of Jordan's inclusion in that organization, and Jordan's request to join raised eyebrows in many quarters. One of the critics writes:

> GCC member countries agreed to consider Jordan and Morocco's requests to join the council!!... I do not see any relation between Jordan and the Gulf... If Jordan and Morocco become GCC members, we will have the MCC not the GCC as MCC stands for Monarchies cooperation council!![85]

Observers regarded Jordan's move as an attempt to cement its ties with the monarchies in the region, particularly in the face of domestic unrest, which the Jordanian regime had to face.[86] Moreover, this move was designed to bolster Jordan's position vis-a-vis the United States and the West.

One might wonder what motivated the GCC to accommodate Jordan's request. It was primarily the constructive role that Jordan played in defending the Saudi border, which mattered the most to the GCC countries who agreed to its incorporation. By joining the GCC, King Abdallah hoped to have a say in Gulf affairs, and bolster the public's confidence that it could rely on wealthy group of states and combat unrest in the country.[87] The economic benefits of joining the GCC became clear immediately. While considering Jordan and Morocco's request, the GCC ministers met to discuss a five-year assistance program for the two countries.[88]

The hesitation of the GCC to accept Jordan's membership can be better understood if one considers other concerns, which its members had. Saudi Arabia, Bahrain, Qatar, and the UAE were important markets for Jordanian fruits and vegetables, and any fluctuation in prices, which such exports entailed, was a source of concern for the council's members. Joining the GCC had negative impact on Jordan as well. Many Jordanians flocked to these oil-rich countries and never returned to their country. By the late 1980s, some 350,000 Jordanians came to these countries as immigrants in search of economic opportunities. Many worked and sent their remittances home, which amounted to \$1.3 billion, or roughly the same amount that Jordan earned from all its exports. The fragile Jordanian economy deteriorated further in 1989, when the government defaulted on its debts and forced to devalue the dinar. These conditions made it imperative that Jordan continue to rely on financial support from Saudi Arabia and Kuwait. Although these commercial contacts benefitted Jordan, they led to tension, which had adverse effect on the ties with these countries. The distrust and suspicions, which the Gulf countries, had toward Jordan increased considerably over the years. There were lingering suspicions that the Jordanian monarchy held a grudge against Saudi Arabia for the loss of the Hejaz and the custodianship of the Holy shrines of Mecca and Medina. A Kuwaiti friend told Peter Hinchcliffe, a veteran of the British Diplomatic Service, who served as an ambassador to Jordan from 1993 to 1997, that King Hussein "sided with" Saddam Hussein hoping that he would liberate the Hejaz and reinstate the Hashemites in their old patrimony.[89] Jordanian arms found after Saddam's invasion convinced the Kuwaitis that they were intended to help Iraq conquer the Gulf region, rather than help in the war against Iran.

In the eyes of ordinary Jordanians, the Kuwaitis are autocratic, arrogant, and exploitive. This image strained the relations between the two countries for quite some time. Moreover, the fact that Kuwaiti aid to Jordan was reduced by the late 1980s, added to the tension, even though the Kuwaitis explained that they were compelled to reduce the amount due to the devastating impact of the Iran-Iraq War on their economy. It was not only King Hussein's failure to condemn Saddam for the invasion, but also the fact that many Jordanians rejoiced at Kuwait's fall in the Gulf War, which exacerbated the already existing tension between the two countries. The consequences of Jordan's attitude during the war were grave. Kuwaitis and Saudis refused to continue trading with Jordan and the subsidies were reduced substantially. Furthermore, the expulsion of some 300,000 Palestinians of Jordanian origins from Kuwait constituted an additional burden on the economy.[90]

Jordan's stand in the conflict was carefully calculated to earn the Arabs' good will, while avoiding conflict with Iraq. In his Address to the Oxford University Jordanian Society in November 1990, Crown Prince Hassan said,

> Unconditionality in the language of diplomacy does not exclude prior understandings about subsequent arrangements. In other words, the justifiable concern that aggressors should not reap the benefits of their aggression should not obscure the need to address outstanding issues nor to implement existing obligations if these obligations stand on their own.[91]

In his attempt to convince Saddam to resolve the conflict amicably, King Hussein linked the Iraqi occupation of Kuwait to the Israeli occupation. In his letter to the Iraqi leader, he noted,

> Certainly, you Excellency know that we are committed to the principle of inadmissibility of the acquisition of territory by force, not only because this is an internationally accepted principle, but also because of the Israeli occupation of Arab territories. Failure to apply this principle-especially in our area-will constitute a dangerous precedent of which Israel will take advantage, with all that implies in terms of threats to the security and existence of Jordan and to our national security in General.[92]

Jordan's quest for security and economic stability led its leaders to take part in another organization, which proved ephemeral. This was King Hussein's decision to join the Arab Cooperation Council (ACC) with Egypt, Iraq and North Yemen. This organization was established on February 16, 1989 but the Gulf War of 1990–1991, brought an end to it. Considerations of security and strategy were undoubtedly involved in the Hashemite decision to join the ACC, particularly following King Hussein's decision to disengage from the West Bank in 1988, which left the Israeli-Palestinian conflict out of his hands, and he aspired to continue playing a role in inter-Arab affairs. Moreover, he believed that an alliance with Iraq provided his country strategic depth in case of a military encounter with Israel, and Egyptian support still loomed large in his calculations, particularly given the fact that his relations with Syria were tense. Nevertheless, the overwhelming concern of the Jordanian government were economic, and joining ACC was primarily motivated by the events that took place in Jordan during the 1980s, when the economic difficulties mounted, and the country suffered from sharp decline in revenues due to the oil glut, which caused the Gulf countries to lose revenues. Consequently, they substantially reduce their grants to Jordan, which in turn caused economic difficulties and brought the Hashemites to lose their legitimacy. King Hussein tried to allay Syria's concern regarding his decision to join the ACC, and to convince Hafiz Assad to join it. In fact, all ACC members tried to reassure their neighbors such as Kuwait, Saudi Arabia and Syria by reiterating that the objectives of this organization were not military and encouraged them to apply for membership.

From the Hashemite point of view, joining the ACC was a way to improve the state of the national economy, and thereby to regain legitimacy. Consequently, joining this organization was regarded not as military or strategic step, but as an economic measure designed to bring prosperity and legitimacy. To begin with, the members of the ACC drafted a charter, which defined their goal, which was primarily economic, rather than ideological or defensive. This was certainly the case with Jordan, as Curtis Ryan stated in his study on the ACC that "Its Jordanian architects intended to move beyond the banalities of many inter-Arab alliances by immediately stressing the importance of economic ties."[93] Moreover, the agreement to form the ACC did not include military provisions. The bread riots and the disturbances that took place in Jordan in April 1989 spread to the East Bank, to places like Ma'an in the south. These were places, which the Hashemites regarded as the bastion of their power, and it was where that they could count on the popular support. Thererfore the King deemed it prudent to embark on major reforms, which included the legalization of political parties, limiting censorship, and other liberal measures. However, these measures were by no means sufficient to satisfy the regime's critics. There was a need for showing substantial results, particularly to the most vocal of the regime's critics. As the Hashemites saw it, the ACC provided an opportunity to put the Jordanian economy on the right track. The regime had to provide economic opportunities to entrpreneurs who resided in the East Bank and to Palestinians in the West Bank. It provided a channel and a structure through which producers could increase their exports and profits. Besides, it provided an opportunity for those who were engaged in construction, both civilians and those who served in the military, to make profit. This was a way in which the Hashemites endeavored to restore their legitimacy, which was seriously eroded as result of the economic difficulties.

By the end of 2017, the Gulf countries decreased the aid provided to Jordan by $1 billion a year. While they claimed that the decline in oil revenues was the reason for their decision, there are clear indications that they were not pleased with Jordan's conduct. It seems, however, that this step was taken largely as result of Jordan's refusal to impose a trade embargo on Qatar, after they decided to impose sanctions of that country. Moreover, the Gulf countries have recently become more interested in obtaining aid from the United States and tacitly from Israel, in order to counter the Iranian nuclear threat, rather than to become involved in supporting the Palestinians.[94]

Notes

1 Munīr al-Rayyis, *Al Kitāb al-Dhahabi lil-thawrāt al-waṭaniyah fī al-Māshriq al-'Arabī: Vol. I, Al-Thawrah al-Suryah al-Kubrah* (The Golden Book of the Nationalist Revolutions in the Arab East, Vol. 1, The Great Syrian Revolt), Arabic text (Beirut: Dār al-Ṭalī'āh, 1969), pp. 232–233.

2 'Ādil Arslan, *Mudhakkirāt al-Amīr 'Ādil Arslan* (The Memoirs of Amir 'Ādil Arslan), Arabic Text (Beirut: Dār al-Taqaddumīyah, 1994), p. 122. Entry for Monday June 7, 1948.

3 Munif Razzāz, *Rasā'il ila Awlādī* (Messages to My Children), Arabic text ('Ammān: Markaz al-Urdun al-Jadīd lil-Dirasāt, Dār Sindībād, 1995), p. 113.

4 'Abd al-Mun'im al-Rifā'ī, *Al-Amwāj: Ṣafaḥāt min riḥlat al-ḥayah* (The Waves: Pages from the Voyage of Life), Arabic text ('Ammān; Wizārat al-Thaqāfah, 2001), p. 47.

5 Reeva S. Simon, "The Hashemite 'Conspiracy': Hashemite Unity Attempts, 1921–1958," *International Journal of Middle East Studies*, Vol. 5, No. 3 (June 1974), p. 317.

6 François Quilici, *Le Pétrole et La Haine: Choses vues Terres d'Islam* (The Oil and the Hatred: Things seen in the Lands of Islam), French text (Paris: Librarie Arthème Fayard, 1957), p. 156.

7 Mamduḥ Anīs Fatḥi, *Misr min al-Thwra ila al-Nāksah: Muqaddamāt Ḥarb Huzairān/ Yunyu 1967* (Egypt from the Revolution to the Setback: Introduction to the War of June 1967), Arabic text (Abu Dhabi: Markaz al-Imarāt lil Dirasāt wa-al Buḥūth al-Istratijīya, 2003), p. 159.

8 Muḥammad Hassanein Heikal, *Sanawāt al-Ghalyān* (The Boiling Years), Arabic text (Al-Qāhira: Markaz al-Ahrām lil-Tarjama wa al-Nashr, Mu'assassat al-Ahrām, 1988), p. 702.

9 Cited in "Jordan Warns Syria Blasts in Press May Cause Armed Clash," *The Milwaukee Journal*, August 3, 1957.

10 "Special Memorandum Prepared in the Central Intelligence Agency," *FRUS, Vol. XVIII: Arab-Israeli Dispute, 1964–1967*, Edited by Harriet Dashiell Schwar and David S. Patterson (Washington, DC: United States Government Printing Office, 2000), p. 668.

11 *The October War: Memoirs of Field marshal El Gamasy of Egypt* (Cairo: The American University in Cairo Press, 1989), p. 174. [Parentheses are in the original].

12 Yitzhak Rabin, *The Rabin Memoirs* (Boston, MA: Little Brown and Company, 1979), p. 187.

13 Gideon Rafael, *Destination Peace: Three Decades of Israeli Foreign Policy-A Personal Memoir* (New York: Stein and Day, 1981), pp. 245–246.

14 Yitzhak Rabin and Dov Goldstein, *Pinkas Sherut* (Service Diary), Hebrew text (Tel Aviv: Ma'ariv, 1979), Vol. II, p. 444.

15 Cable from U.S. Embassy in Amman, December 17, 2003, http://www.cablegatesearch.net/cable.php?id=03AMMAN8242.
16 Riad al-Khouri, *Jordan Times* (Amman), August 30, 2001.
17 Cited in Jordanian *Foreign Policy Trends under King Abdallah II*, Arabic text with title in English (Amman: Middle East Studies Center, May 1999), p. 41.
18 Ryan Curtis, "'Jordan First' : Jordan's inter-Arab Relations and Foreign Policy under King Abdallah II,"*Arab Studies Quarterly*, Vol. 26 (Summer 2004), p. 51.
19 http://www.foxnews.com/world/2011/11/14/jordans-king-urges-syrias-assad-to step-down/#ixzz1sXzMSOq5.
20 "A Monthly Report on Transjordan for the Month of October 1941 by Headquarters of the Arab Legion. TNA FO 371/31383/E925.
21 'Abd al-Majīd Ḥussein al-Qāysi, *Al-Tarīkh yūktabu ghadan: hawāmish 'ala tarīkh al-'Irāq al-ḥadīth* (The History will be written Tomorrow: Marginal Notes on the History of Modern Iraq), Arabic text (London: Dar Al-Ḥikma, 1993), p. 720.
22 Juan Cole, "Iraq and the Israeli-Palestinian Conflict in the Twentieth Century," *Macalester International*, Vol. 23 (2009), pp. 9–10.
23 Juan Cole, "Iraq and the Mūsa 'Akkūr, *Hazz'a al-Majālī wa-dawruhu fī al-siyāsh al-Urdunīyah 1948–1960* (Hazz'a al-Majālī and his Role in Jordanian Politics 1948–1960), Arabic text ('Ammān: Wizārat al-Thaqāfah, 2002), pp. 58–59.
24 'Ali Muḥammad Sa'ādah, *Al-Ightiyāl al-Siyāsī fī al-Urdun* (Political Assassination in Jordan), Arabic text (Amman? Da'irat al-Maktaba al-Waṭṭanīyah, 1999), pp. 45–46.
25 Amatzia Baram, "Baathi Iraq and Hashemite Jordan: From Hostility to Alignment," *Middle East Journal*, Vol. 45, No. 1 (Winter 1991), p. 52.
26 *Ibid*, p. 53.
27 *Ibid*, p. 56.
28 Ḥattar, p. 117.
29 Baram, p. 56.
30 Ḥasan Ibn Talāl, Ta'ḥāddīyāt, *Afkār wa-Ru'yah mustaqbalīyah: Al-majmūāh al-rābi'ah li-khiṭabāt sūmū'al-Amīr al-Ḥasan wāli al-'ahd 1986* (Challenges, Thoughts and Views of the Future: The Third Collection of the Speeches of His Highness, Crown Prince Amir al-Hassan 1986), Arabic text, Edited by Bassām al-Sākit and'Alī Ṭāhir al-Dajāni ('Ammān: Maṭba'at Kitābukum, 1986), pp. 78–79.
31 Hinchcliffe, p. 344.
32 *The Baltimore Sun*, September 19, 1990.
33 Yāsir Quṭayshāt, *Al-Siyāsah al-Kharijīyah al-Urdunīyah wa-al-Miṣrīyah tujāha azmat al-Khalīj al-Thānīyah 1990–1991* (The foreign policy of Jordan and Egypt toward the Second Gulf Crisis 1990–1991), Arabic text ('Ammān: Dār al-Kindī lil-Nashr wa-al-Tawzī', 2002), p. 86.
34 Ḥasan Muḥammad al-Zabin, *Al-Amīr Zayd bin Shākir: Siyāsīyon wa-Ijtimā'īyon wa-'Askārīyon* (Al Amir Zayd bin Shakir: Politician, Companion and Soldier), Arabic text ('Ammān: Markaz al-Fāris lil-Ṭaṣmīm wa-al-Ṭibā'ah, 2002), p. 25.
35 *The New York Times*, May 27, 1993.
36 Jamil E. Jreisat and Hanna Y. Freij, "Jordan, the United States, and the Gulf Crisis," *Arab Studies Quarterly*, Vol. 13, No. 1/2 (Winter/Spring 1991), pp. 113–114.
37 Curtis, p. 53.
38 "King Abdullah calls for stronger Jordanian-Lebanese relations," *Jordan Times*, September 14, 1999.
39 Faisal Al Rfouh, "Jordan-Lebanese Ties," *Jordan Times*, January 13, 2010.
40 Fatḥi, p. 83.
41 *Ibid*, p. 85.
42 Faisal al-Rafū', "Sulaymān al-Nabulsi-Qirāah fi sulūkuhu al-siyāsi," (Sulayman al-Nabulsi-A Reading in his Political Method), Arabic text, *Sulaymān al-Nabulsi: Qirā'ah fī sirātahu wa-tajribātahu, Waqā'i nadwat 1997* (Ammān: Al-Markaz al-Urduni lil-Dirasāt wa-al-Ma'lumāt, 1997), p. 87.

43 Salloukh, p. 50.
44 Elie Podeh, "To Unite or Not to Unite: That Is Not the Question: The 1963 Tripartite Unity Talks Reassed," *Middle Eastern Studies*, Vol. 39, No. 1. (January 2003), p. 154.
45 Salloukh, p. 51.
46 Awrāq min Daftar al-Ayyām, p. 90.
47 *Washington Times*, April 2, 1985.
48 Geoff Simons, *Libya: The Struggle for Survival* (London: St. Martin's Press, 1981), p. 114.
49 Mohamed Hassanein Heikal, *The Cairo Documents: The Inside Story of Nasser and his Relationship with World Leaders, Rebels, and Statesmen* (Garden City, New York: Doubleday & Company, Inc., 1973), p. 3.
50 Martin Sicker, *The Making of a Pariah State: The Adventurist Politics of Muammar Qaddafi* (New York: 1987), p. 59.
51 King Abdullah II, *Our Last Best Chance: The Pursuit of Peace in a Time of Peril* (New York: Viking Penguin, 2011), p. 150.
52 "Jordan's Perspective on Libyan Regime and their Bilateral Relationship Tripoli," January 31, 2010, http://telegraph.co.uk.
53 Rebah Ghezali, "The Arab Spring's Implications for NATO," *Huff Post World*, The Internet Newspaper: New Blog Community. May 8, 2012, http://www.huffingtonpost.
54 "Jordan Plans to Revive Its Relations with Libya," *The New York Times*, September 24, 1987.
55 Our Last Best Chance, pp. 326–327.
56 *Ibid*, p. 327.
57 A Monthly Report of the Administration of the Trans-Jordanian desert for the Month of November 1938. TNA FO371/23246/E184, January 7, 1939, pp. 1–2; 12.
58 A Monthly Report on the Administration of the Trans-Jordan Desert from the Months of July and August, 1938. TNA FO371/23246/E639, pp. 1–2.
59 A Monthly Report on Trans-Jordan for the Month of February 1941. TNA FO 371 /27136/E1774.
60 A Monthly Report on Transjordan for the Month of March 1941, TNA FO371/27136. E1774/323/31.
61 Periodic Report on Transjordan by Colonel Glubb for the Period 1st February to 31st May 1942. TNA FO371/31383/E4106, p. 1.
62 Situation Report on trans-Jordan for the Month of February, 1943 by the British Resident, TNA FO371/35045/E2548, Amman, March 4, 1943.
63 A Monthly Report for the Month of April 1939. Amman, Transjordan, TNA FO371/23246/E4041, p. 3.
64 *Ibid*, p. 7.
65 A Monthly Report of July 1939, Amman, Transjordan, TNA FO317/23246/E6663, p. 10.
66 Report on the Political Situation for the Month of June 1939. TNA FO371/23247/E5212, p. 2.
67 A Report on Trans-Jordan for the Month of December 1941. TNA FO 371/31383/E2014.
68 'Umar al-Ḥaḍrami, *Al-'Alāqāt al-Urdunīyah al-Sa'ūdīyah* (Jordanian-Saudi Relations) Arabic text ('Ammān: Dār al-Majdalāwi, 2003), p. 21.
69 Musā Braizat, "Sulaymān al-Nabūlsi wa-'alaqāt al-Urdun al'Arabiyya," (Sulayman al-Nabulsi and the Jordanian Arab Relations), Arabic text, *Sulaymān al-Nabulsi: Qirā'ah*, p. 147.
70 *Ibid*, p. 148.
71 *Ibid*, pp. 149–150.
72 HRH General Khaled Bin Sultan, with Patrick Seale, *Desert Warrior: A Personal View of the Gulf War by the Joint Forces Commander* (London: HarperCollins Publishers, 1995), p. 180.
73 Awjīni Tanūri, "All-Malik Ḥusayn wa-jāmi'at al-duwal al-Arabīyah," (King Hussein and the Arab League), Arabic text with title in English, *A Series on: National Culture*

Research and Dialogues (4), King Hussein and the Arab Regional System: Papers from "Studies on King Hussein's Thought and Intellectual Legacy Conference" 8–10/4/2002 (Amman: Al-Hussein Bin Talal University, 2004), p. 43.

74 Cited in Will Fulton, Ariel Farrar-Wellman, and Robert Frasco, August 11, 2011. "Jordan-Iran Relations," http//www.irantracker.org/foreign relations/Jordan-iran-foreign-relations.

75 Cited *Ibid.*

76 Cited *Ibid.*

77 Cited *Ibid.*

78 Cited *Ibid.*

79 Cited *Ibid.*

80 Michael Bishku, "Turkey's Relations with Lebanon and Jordan," *Journal of South Asian and Middle Eastern Studies*, Vol. XXXV, No. 4 (Summer 2012), p. 70.

81 Ofra Bengio and Gencer Özcan, "Old Grievences, New Fears: Arab Perceptions of Turkey and Its Alighnment with Israel," *Middle Eastern Studies*, Vol. 37, No. 2 (April 2001), p. 74.

82 *Turkey's New World: Changing Dynamics in Turkish Foreign Policy*, Edited by Alan Makovsky and Sabri Sayari. (Wshington, DC: The Washington Institute for Near East Policy, 2000), p. 48.

83 Sa'īd Bin Muhammad Bin Sa'īd al-Hāshemi, "Jawānib min al-'Alaqāt al-'Umanīyah-al-Urdunīyah khilāla al-thulth al-ākhir min al-qarn al-'ishrīn," (Aspects of Omani-Jordanian Relations during the last third of the twentieth century), *A Series on: National Culture Research and Dialogues*, p. 217.

84 Tobias Buck and Eileen Byrne, "Gulf States' Overtures delight Jordan," May 12, 2011, http://www.ft.com/cms/s/0/fd0d2fce-7cbb-11e0-994d-.

85 "GCC to Include Jordan and Morocco: The Neo Royal Baghdad Pact !!!," *Egyptian Chronicles*, May 11, 2011.

86 "Morocco and Jordan ask to join the GCC," May 11, 2011, http://thenational.ae/n. An interesting outcome of this move was that women of the Gulf countries expressed concern that Gulf men would look for wives in Jordan and Morocco. "Gulf Women fear Jordan, Morocco entry into GCC," *Emirates 24/7 News*, May 13, 2011, http://www.emirates247/com/ne.

87 Randa Habib, "Jordan, Morocco could boost GCC 'monarchy club'," May 11, 2011, http://google.com/hos.

88 "Morocco, Jordan attend first GCC Ministerial Meeting in Jedda," *Al-Arabiya*, September, 11, 2011, http://www.alarbiya.net/art; "Morrocco, Jordan inch closer to GCC," September 11, 2009. http://arabnews.com.

89 Hinchcliffe, p. 344.

90 *Ibid.*

91 "Address by His Royal Highness Crown Prince Hassan to the Oxford University Jordanian Society, November 22, 1990. White Paper: Jordan and the Gulf Crisis: August 1990–March 1991," *The Government of the Hashemite Kingdom of Jordan*, Amman, August 1991, p. 28.

92 A Letter from His Majesty King Hussein to H.E. President Saddam Hussein of Iraq. Excerpts. *Ibid.*, p. 32.

93 Byan Curtis, "Jordan and the Fall of the Arab Cooperation Council," *Middle East Journal*, Vol. 52, No. 3 (Summer 1998), p. 388.

94 Rana F. Sweis, "Jordan's Prime Minister Quits as Protesters Demand an end to Austerity," *The New York Times*, June 4, 2018.

XIII Jordan's global reach

Jordan's foreign policy had always reflected the country needs. Consequently, the Hashemites' effort concentrated on establishing strong ties with wealthy and powerful countries, capable of providing foreign aid. Primarily, Jordan's foreign policy focused mainly on strong ties with the United States, the countries of Western Europe, the Persian Gulf, the Russian Federation, and more recently, China. Very little effort was made to reach out to African and Asian or Latin American nations, especially the poor among them. Unlike Israel, whose policy was to reach as many countries in these continents as possible, in order to obtain legitimacy and political support, the Hashemites felt no need to seek recognition throughout the world community. Even their staunchest enemies found it difficult to construct a narrative capable of denying the conviction that they are the descendants of Prophet Muhammad. Moreover, unlike Israel, Jordan never possessed the technical expertise and the scientific knowhow necessary to help the small and counties in these continents. Consequently, Jordan's foreign policy remained constrained by the regime's inability to offer much in return.

The United States and Canada

Jordan's relations with the United States have been cordial since World War II. The American consul general in Jerusalem was also the representative of the United States in Amman. In February 1941, Lowell C. Pinkerton was nominated as consul. U.S. interests in that country were confined at that time to educational, military, and petroleum affairs. The United States had 23.75 percent share in the Iraq Petroleum Company's revenues and keen interest in ARAMCO's plan to lay a pipeline passing through Jordanian territory. Plans for the Trans-Arabian Pipeline Company (Tapline) were being discussed in July 1945. Moreover, U.S. officials indicated that they were considering the possibility of becoming involved in Jordan's defense. When asked by the Counsellor at the British embassy Michael Right whether Washington had objection to stationing troops in the country, Loy Handerson, the director of the Near Eastern and African Affairs Office, said that his government will not object if the request came from the government of Transjordan.

A press release by the State Department on April 23, 1946, stated, "The department considers, however, that it would be premature for this government to take

DOI: 10.4324/9781003450313-14

any decision at the present time with respect to the question of its recognition of Transjordan as an independent state."[1] Washington did not rush to grant Jordan recognition without assurances that King Abdallah I would fulfill all his international obligations, including an agreement with the British. A memorandum from June 3, 1946, sheds light on Washington's concerns at that time. It read in part:

> It seems likely that eventually we shall accord full recognition… we should not, in our opinion, take definite steps in this direction until we have an opportunity to observe how the new arrangement between Great Britain and Transjordan works out, to make sure that the country is in fact independent, and to satisfy ourselves that it has the intension and ability to carry out its international obligations…The Zionists of course are pressing us not to recognize Transjordan.[2]

In addition to the uncertainty regarding Abdallah's intensions toward Britain, there was intense pressure from Zionists all over the world, particularly from right-wing organizations such as the Hebrew Committee of National Liberation and Jabotinsky's New Zionist Organization, not to recognize Transjordan. Prominent American Zionist leaders such as Abba Hillel Silver and Stephen Wise joined the opponents' chorus. Among the most vocal Congressmen who opposed Jordan's recognition were Andrew L. Somers and Emanuel Celler, both Democrats from New York; Dean M. Gillespie, a Republican from Colorado, and the Democratic senator from Pennsylvania Francis J. Myers. Three resolutions were passed regarding that issue. The Senate's resolution of July 2, 1946, asked the government not to recognize any part of Palestine as a separate state, and insisted that the status of Transjordan remain as it is, until the fate of Palestine was determined. Although he spoke about his desire to maintain good relations with the United States, Abdallah did not seem to stress the issue of recognition in his correspondence with U.S. officials. On August 8, 1946, he gave Tapline the right to build a pipeline through his territory, in return for an annual payment of $250,000. Washington supported Transjordan's application for UN membership at the vote that took place in the Security Council on August 29, 1946. Abdallah's cautious approach stemmed from his reluctance to alienate his British ally. Therefore, it was not before the second half of 1947, that he began intensifying his campaign to obtain Washington's recognition. Jordanian officials told their U.S. counterparts that such step would be in line with their strategic interests, and that their country could play a positive role in the Cold War.

On October 23, 1947, Umar Dajani contacted the Office of Near Eastern and African Affairs in the State Department with a view to discuss recognition. His argument that Transjordan could play an important role as a "bulwark against the Soviet Union" convinced Loy Henderson who began advocating recognition and the establishment normal relations. He suggested two preconditions to such recognition: that Transjordan adhere to the UN Charter and refrain from using force to obtain the liberation of Palestine or Greater Syria, and that the terms of the 1924 convention regarding the protection of U.S. interests remain valid. Handerson opined that Ibn Saud's cooperation in this matter could be achieved with an explanation, and that Sharett did not oppose recognition, on the proviso that Transjordan will not use its troops against the Yishuv.[3] However, since the Jewish resistance was unrelenting Handerson failed to convince the U.S. government. The British abandonment of the Mandate and the intensification in the Cold War, which brought the Truman Doctrine in its wake, played their role as well, and it was not until August 1948 that a change in Washington's attitude occurred. On July 29, the U.S. representative at the UN Philip C. Jesup sent a memorandum to Secretary George Marshall, which called for reassessment of U.S. policy in the Middle East. He stated that Transjordan had become an important factor in that region, and that even the Yishuv would not object to recognition. Truman, who sought to obtain the Jewish vote in the presidential elections of 1948, exploited the recognition issue to curry favor with the Jews. The fact that the United States recognized Israel de facto but not de jure was an advantage to the president who accepted the idea that such recognition should be granted to Israel and Transjordan simultaneously. Abdallah's confidante Samir Pasha al-Rifa'i went to Washington to ask that Transjordan obtain recognition by the United States before Israel. However, unwilling to alienate the Jewish constituency, the White House refrained from granting equal diplomatic status to the two countries. On January 26, 1949, Abdallah was told that the matter was being debated in Washington, and on January 31, the United States gave de jure recognition to Israel.[4] The United States granted recognition de facto to Transjordan on the same day, but the de jure recognition was delayed for almost three years.

American policy toward Transjordan was laid out in a secret memorandum circulated by the Near Eastern Affairs Division of the Office of Near Eastern and African Affairs in the State Department on February 26, 1946. According to the memorandum, U.S. policy was based on two principles; (a) that the United States recognized Britain's responsibility to administer the Palestine Mandate, which included Transjordan, and gave its consent during the American-British Mandate Convention of December 3, 1924, and; (b) that the Convention granted the United States special rights that were indirectly confirmed by the Anglo-Transjordanian Agreement of February 20, 1928.

According to the memorandum the British recognized an independent government in Transjordan in 1923. This status was confirmed by the League of Nations, and when the United States signed the Convention of 1924, it tacitly accepted it. According to the memorandum, the Convention guaranteed the United States the right to maintain property in Transjordan, and to obtain consular and extraterritorial privileges. In addition, U.S. nationals were free to establish any organizations or institutions that they saw fit. The memorandum mentioned the strategic location of Transjordan and its importance to the United States, particularly since any pipeline connecting Saudi Arabia to the Mediterranean had to pass through its territory. Moreover, it stated that the United States was in favor of recognizing Transjordan's independence, and that it would not approve of any treaty between Britain and Transjordan that does not grants its nationals special privileges.

One of the plans conceived in Washington at that time was based on the notion that the United States could play an important role in the development of the Jordan Valley and the distribution of water between Jordan and Israel. Asked to comment about his plan to send Johnston to discuss the issue, Eisenhower said, "It is my conviction that acceptance of a comprehensive plan for the development of the Jordan Valley could contribute to the stability in the Near East and to the general economic progress in the region."[5]

When asked to comment about Glubb's dismissal by King Hussein, Eisenhower was reluctant to interfere in this matter, and preferred to leave it for the British government to react. He stated that he was in a delicate position; that his goal was to promote better relations with both sides and said, "Now, when you come down to the example of Jordan it is a matter that I would rather hear discussed from London rather than from here."[6]

Jordan benefited from the Cold War by siding with the United States. At the same time however, King Hussein preferred not to alienate the Soviet Union and therefore maintained his connection with Washington in a low-profile manner. Even Nabulsi preferred to exercise caution at that time. At a meeting with the U.S. ambassador in 1958, the latter said that the United States was willing to provide Jordan with a $100 million grant if it agreed to accept the Eisenhower Doctrine. Unwilling to commit his country to side with the United States in the Cold War, Nabulsi's response was, "We have only recently achieved our independence. It is in its infancy. Wait until our rod becomes tougher."[7] On January 2, 1957, he told the Parliament, "There are dangerous American political objectives there and we oppose them."[8] In addition to its efforts to draw Jordan to the Western camp, there was talk at that time that Washington was discussing a plan to divide Jordan into two parts. According to that plan, the West Bank was to be taken by Israel and the East Bank by Iraq.[9]

In an Address to the Nation, Eisenhower stated his conviction that Jordan must receive American financial aid in order to fight Communist influence. He praised King Hussein's successful struggle against Communism saying, "Yet this victory would surely be lost without economic aid from outside Jordan. Jordan's armed forces must be paid, the nation's utilities must function. And, above all, the people must have hope."[10] The events in the Middle East loomed large in U.S. foreign policy in 1958, when several events seemed to threaten the region's stability. Qasim came to power after overthrowing the Hashemite dynasty in Iraq, and Syria merged with Egypt to form the UAR. Moreover, tension in Lebanon increased and it seems that the Christian regime was in danger. These changes caused Eisenhower to be concerned about the region's future, and after ordering the U.S. Marines to land in Lebanon, he said:

> Yesterday a day of grave developments in the Middle East. In Iraq a highly organized military blow struck down the duly constituted government.... At about the same time there was discovered a highly organized plot to overthrow the lawful government in Jordan....It seemed, last week, that the situation was moving toward a peaceful solution which would preserve

> the integrity of Lebanon…These hopes, however, dashed by the events of yesterday in Iraq and Jordan.[11]

Eisenhower feared that turmoil in small countries like Jordan and Lebanon would lead to instability in the region as a whole.[12] Yet despite statements made by Eisenhower and other U.S. officials, a close look at Washington's attitude toward Jordan reveals that it was far less committed to Jordan's security than the official correspondence suggest. The British seemed far more determined to come to King Hussein's rescue at that point. Moreover, the Eisenhower Administration seemed more committed to rescue Lebanon than Jordan. When approached by King Hussein and the British to plan a rescue operation, John Foster Dulles stated explicitly that the United States would not be able to honor Jordan's request. He argued, that he did not know whether the United States had troops available for such mission, despite what Eisenhower told congressional leaders, and that there were no plans for sending forces anywhere, except for Lebanon.[13]

Asked to comment about his plan to send Johnston to discuss water and natural resources distribution between Jordan and Israel, Eisenhower said that acceptance of a comprehensive plan for the development of the Jordan Valley was the only thing that could contribute to the stability and the general economic progress in the region.[14] After realizing the difficulties, which implementing this plan involved, he remarked that neither side to the conflict wished to accept its political consequence.[15] In a message to the Congress on March 13, 1959, he said that in order to maintain its stability, Jordan will continue to need substantial foreign aid.[16]

U.S. foreign policy toward the region did not change when John Kennedy became president. He declared his support for both Israel and Jordan, and stated that U.S. policy was aimed at stopping the arms race in the region.[17] U.S. officials continued to treat the Johnston Plan as binding on both sides. A memorandum from the State Department to the President's Special Assistant for National Security Affairs stated that any departure from Johnston's allocation was a serious matter.[18]

President Lyndon Johnson who became president in the aftermath of Kennedy's assassination saw no reason to alter U.S. policy in the Middle East. In his remarks on the occasion of King Hussein's visit on April 14, 1964, he promised that U.S. aid to Jordan will continue.[19] The amount of U.S. aid to Jordan was quite significant compared to other recipients. This becomes evident from Johnson's speech to the Congress on January 14, 1965, when he said that eighty-eight percent of the $369 million that he requested will go to Vietnam, Laos, Korea, and Jordan.[20] Supplying arms to Jordan had always presented a problem to U.S. officials. For example, when Jordan asked for arms in 1965, the American negotiators were in a serious dilemma, largely due to pressure by the Jewish community, and the pro-Israeli organizations. This become evident from a memorandum sent by Robert K. Komer of the National Council Staff to Johnson in which he writes:

> Of course, the underlying decision to be made is whether we should now sell arms to Israel as well as Jordan, as the only way to buy off the Israelis and protect your domestic flank. This would raise hob with the Arabs, but is probably necessary sooner or later anyway.[21]

In another telegram from the State Department to the American Embassy in Jordan, George Ball noted that any plan to send aid to Jordan required prior discussion with the Israelis.[22]

The rise of a radical regime in Syria following the coup of February 1966 caused much alarm in Amman, and there was danger that the Hashemites might become a victim of Syrian militant nationalism. Jordan appealed the United States to prevent the new regime from ensconcing itself in power. While officials in Washington were not convinced that the new regime would pose a threat to Jordan, there was growing concern that a coup in Syria could endanger the vital interests of the United States in the region.[23] On November 1966, King Hussein found himself in a desperate situation after facing disturbances in his county, when Israel attacked Palestinians who operated against it from his kingdom. In meetings with U.S. officials, he said that the unwritten agreement that he had with Israel to neutralize the border between the two countries has "now been permanently shattered" and that the only way to fulfill his obligation to his people was to strengthen his army and procure arms, hopefully from the United States but also from "the Devil himself" if necessary. Moreover, he told his interlocutors that he was facing pressure from his people, particularly from junior officers in the army, to retaliate against Israel and that Syria was inciting them to overthrow his regime. So strong was the reaction of the personnel in the U.S. Embassy in Amman that they favored condemnation of Israel at the UN, and the suspension of military aid to it. They were particularly angry to learn that Israel had used the United States made Patton tanks in the operation against Jordan. In a memorandum to the President's Special Assistant, a member of the National Security Council's staff stated:

> NEA (Office of Near Eastern Affairs) and IO (Bureau of international Organization Affairs) have recommended a resolution that condemns Israel ....If we confirms charges that US Patton were used in the Israeli attacks, we will almost certainly have to suspend further shipments to Israel. Most of the tanks have gone, but we still have 80–85% of the refitting kits. Also, the Israelis have urgently requested some ammunitions and we can be clumsy about meeting their demand on that....We'll either have to give in to Hussein's expensive new arms requests or try to rebuild what the King today feels is "permanently shattered."[24]

While Washington seemed serious about taking action against Israel, King Hussein was dismayed at the fact that it did not exert pressure on Israel to withdraw from the occupied territories. Nevertheless, the contacts with the United States were not severed, and he alerted his listeners to the urgency of finding solution to the Arab-Israeli conflict. During his visit to the White House on April 8, 1969, he told President Richard Nixon and his guests:

> The area from which I come sire is a troubled area...within the very near future we can either move towards our objectives-a just and honorable peace in that area-or we might, indeed, lose the chance and the opportunity to establish peace, a just and lasting peace, there.[25]

In a joint statement following the discussion, King Hussein was more specific, saying that peace could be achieved only by Israel's withdrawal from all the territories it occupied in the Six-Day War.[26]

Following King Hussein's suppression of the Palestinians in September 1970, and the subsequent danger of Syrian invasion the U.S. government was extremely concerned that the recent developments would enhance the Soviet position in the region, and lead to the triumph of radical forces hostile to Western interests. Referring to that incident Kissinger noted in his memoirs:

> I had no doubt that this challenge had to be met. If we failed to act, the Middle East crisis would deepen as radicals and their Soviet sponsors seized the initiative. If we succeeded, the Arab moderates would receive a new lease on life.[27]

Consequently, Nixon asked for Israeli assistance in order to stop the Syrian advance toward the Jordanian border and on November 17, 1970, he asked the Congress provide $30 million financial aid to King Hussein.[28] Satisfied with the outcome of his decision, he wrote in his report to the Congress on February 25, 1971, "We took a firm stand against the Syrian intervention....The Syrians withdrew, the Government of Jordan established order, and a fragile agreement was reached on the future role of the organized Palestinians."[29]

While it is tempting to conclude that the American unwavering commitment saved Jordan from the Syrian danger, there are indications that Washington did not act in a resolute manner. In his study on U.S. decision-making during that crisis, Adam Garfinkle has conclusively demonstrated that after Israel agreed to mobilize its forces to protect Hussein's regime, the Nixon Administration failed to provide it with guarantees of American military intervention in case of need. Furthermore, he argues that it was primarily King Hussein's use of his own aircraft that scattered the Syrian forces and not the U.S. forces, and that the Syrians refrained from using their air force against the Israeli troops.[30]

Following the Yom Kippur War of 1973, in which Egypt and Syria invaded Israel while Jordan remained out of the conflict, King Hussein agreed to attend the Geneva peace conference, in an effort to recover his lost territories but his attempts failed. Believing that the United States was the only power capable of moving the peace process forward, he continued to cultivate his ties with it. At a meeting with King Hussein on August 16, 1974, President Gerald Ford said that regardless of which party was in power, U.S. policy toward Jordan stood on a firm and friendly ground, and that his administration will continue supporting all diplomatic efforts in the Middle East.[31] In a message to the Congress on October 30, 1975, he announced that Jordan will receive $100 million in military assistance grants, $78 million in security supporting assistance, and $75 million in military credit sales.[32]

The bilateral relations became tense when President Jimmy Carter took office. It was primarily because the Jordanians found it difficult to deal with his hawkish national security adviser, Zbigniev Brzezinski.[33] Moreover, Carter corresponded with Sadat and he had no intention to involve King Hussein in the Israeli-Egyptian peace negotiations, which led to the Camp David accords. In respond to reporters who raised the issue of including King Hussein in the negotiations, he said on January 6, 1978, "all of us feel for now until Sadat specifically requests it, that Hussein should stay out of the direct negotiations."[34]

The peace treaty between Israel and Egypt ushered in a period of coolness in U.S.-Jordanian relations, when King Hussein decided to join the rejectionist countries of the Middle East in opposition to the treaty, despite Washington's request. Jordan remained dependent of U.S arms but King Hussein made efforts to diversify his sources, and made it clear that if the United States failed to supply him the weapons he needed to defend his country, he will turn to the Soviet Union. He acquired *Mirage* aircraft from France, and anti-aircraft weapons from the Soviet Union.

In order to mend fences with the United States, the King had even made concessions in his negotiations with Israel. He was aware of the fact that his ties with the United States could not improve unless he moved with the peace process and sign a treaty with Israel. He therefore agreed to the idea of meeting the Israelis in an international conference, and reassured Secretary of State James Baker that Jordan will participate, even if Syria remained out of it. Furthermore, he agreed to Israel's Prime Minister Yitzhak Shamir's proposal that a joint Jordanian-Palestinian delegation participate in the proposed conference, and he even endorsed Baker's compromise regarding the observer status that the Palestinian delegation was about to obtain in the UN. Moreover, he promised to convince the PLO to keep a low-profile, and to remain committed to the peace process. Confident that he won a significant diplomatic victory, Baker called Shamir and stated his conviction that the King would be much more accommodating than Syria's President Assad.[35]

Once again, King Hussein put his relationship with Washington to the test, asking the Reagan Administration to pressure the Israeli government to cease the settlement activities. Pressured by the Israelis on the one hand, and the Jordanians on the other, Reagan formulated a new plan. Known as the Reagan Plan, this was essentially an expression of principles, which former U.S. governments adhered to over the years. Although the plan confirmed the right of the Palestinians to self-government, it stated explicitly that the U.S. government will not support the creation on an independent state for them. Furthermore, the Reagan Administration made it clear that future negotiations will be made only with a combined Jordanian-Palestinian representative body. This made it imperative for the King to communicate with Arafat. However, mutual suspicions and disagreement brought the negotiations to a halt, and by 1983, it became clear that the King decided to abandon the plan.

Jordan's relations with the United States reached their nadir in that year. Reagan failed to stop the Israeli settlement building and when the King sponsored a resolution at the UN declaring the Israeli settlement activities to be illegal, the United States opposed the measure. Moreover, Israel's request to purchase F-16 aircraft was approved in Washington in that year. This state of affairs forced the King to re-examine his country's position. His alliance with Iraq had little strategic value. Not only did Jordan alienate Iran by supporting Saddam during the Iran-Iraq War, but it also showed how weak and unreliable the Iraqi regime was. Isolated in the face of growing Syrian influence, which intensified after the war in Lebanon, the King was compelled to reassess his foreign policy objectives. A new campaign for rapprochement with Egypt began in 1983, and culminated in the establishment of diplomatic relations between the two countries in 1984, a move that was not well-received in Damascus.

Once more, Jordan's relations with the United States underwent a serious crisis as a result of King Hussein's support of Saddam during the Second Gulf War. However, the King moved quickly toward reconciliation. Finding himself in dire need of American support, he sought to patch up the differences, and tried to find justification for his behavior. He made the effort to assure the American public that despite its close relations with Iraq, his country had no prior knowledge nor any form of involvement in the Iraqi plan to act militarily against Kuwait.[36] Baker who met him at that time recalled in his memoirs:

> The King showed me some recent photographs of equipment seized from terrorists who entered Jordan to kill him. He said that he, too, was committed to peace and to repairing his tattered ties with Washington. He made no attempt to justify his support for Saddam with me. During lunch, however, he launched into an extensive rationalization of his behavior during the war, which our delegation found wholly unconvincing. At one point he even claimed that Saddam was now contemplating a more democratic political system for Iraq.[37]

The United States remained cautious about pushing Jordan on the issue of political reform, as the Middle East analyst Jeremey M. Sharp said in a report to the Congress on June 15, 2006,

> With Jordan facing a terrorist threat emanating from Iraq in the east, and with Hamas in control of parts of the bordering West Bank, the United States seems willing to accept whatever pace the government sets for the political process.[38]

Though cordial for the most part, Jordan's relations with the United States ebbed and flowed. Although King Hussein never went to the extent of distancing his country from the United States, he was often disenchanted with its policy, especially when it came to arms procurement. A report from the U.S. embassy in Amman sent on November 25, 2009, stated that the military relationship between Jordan and the United States was close and substantive; that Jordan was receiving about $300 million annually; and that the Jordanian forces were being deployed in missions led by the United States, throughout the world, including Afghanistan and Somalia.[39] However, Jordan's request for weapons often fell on deaf ears in Washington. Prompted by Washington's refusal to provide him a sophisticated air defense system, the King approached the Soviet Union and other countries. Concerned about the impact of this turn in Hussein's policy the United States agreed to supply Jordan with weapons, albeit more obsolete than he hoped.

Jordan's relations with the United States constitute the most important aspect of King Abdallah's foreign policy. One of Washington's conditions for supporting Jordan was the demand that he introduce reforms. However, officials in Washington cautioned that given his predicament at that time, pressuring him in that direction could prove counterproductive. Though cordial for the most part, Jordan's relations with the United States continued to ebb and flow. King Abdallah never went to the extent of distancing his country from the United States even though he was often disenchanted with its policy, especially when it came to arms procurement. However, given his commitment to promote economic growth and encourage foreign investments, he came to realize that the United States remained the only global power he could rely on to supply his needs.

Jordan's efforts to expand its commercial network led to increased contacts with Canada in recent years. For quite some time, Jordan acted as a mediator between Canada and the states in the Middle Eastern countries. The ties between the two countries extended to numerous shared interests such as education, trade, landmines and peacekeeping operations. At the conclusion of a visit to Canada by King Abdullah in 2007, a Free-Trade Agreement, a Foreign Investment Promotion and Protection Agreement, and a new Air Transport Agreement were signed. Another significant bilateral achievement has been the signing of a Nuclear Cooperation Agreement in February 2009. Negotiations on these agreements were completed expeditiously, and were signed by Canada's Trade Minister Stockwell Day, during a visit to Jordan in June that year. The two countries are consistent supporters of the UN's efforts to promote peace and security, and Jordan was one of the first countries to sign the Ottawa Convention banning anti-personnel mines.

Jordan benefited from Canada's expertise in modernizing its educational system and its labor market management systems, two areas where the Canadian International Development Agency (CIDA) has been active for a number of years, with considerable measure of success.

The CIDA has become a leader in supporting Jordan's educational system. It helped Jordan develop skills for expanding employment opportunities. Its programs focused on educational reform, women's empowerment and job skills development. In May 2010, the CIDA announced a $20 million investment in the second phase of the Education Reform for a Knowledge Economy project, which sought to improve the schools' environment, upgrade curricula, and set up a unit that guarantees gender equality at the Ministry of Education.

Canadian firms have achieved increasing success in trade with Jordan, particularly in the potash and phosphate industries. The expanding Jordanian economy, and the country's growing importance as a regional commercial and transportation hub, particularly for exports to Iraq, continue to provide opportunities for Canadian companies. In 2010, Canada's exports to Jordan were valued at $66 million, and imports from Jordan at $19.9 million. Jordan is an important model for the Middle East as a country that has been able to foster economic growth despite the paucity of its natural resources and the severe shortage of agricultural land and water. Its rising importance as a regional shipping and transportation hub and its proximity to Iraq have made it increasingly attractive to Canadian companies. The two countries continue to take part in joint infrastructure projects, including water management, nuclear power generation, and desalination.

The Russian federation, China, India, Japan, and South Korea

Jordan's relations with the former Soviet Union were marred by difficulties since the early days of the Hashemite regime, and it was not until 1948 that Moscow recognized it as an independent state, and supported its membership to the UN. Diplomatic relations between the two countries were established on August 21, 1963 but it was at Jordan's initiative. Since Jordan sided with the West during the Cold War, there were barely any contacts between the two countries during King Hussein's reign. This pattern has drastically changed since the fall of the Soviet Union, and King Abdallah II visited the country on numerous occasions since. However, the King did not throw himself into Putin's arms, out of fear that he might alienate his Western allies and the United States in particular. Attempting to end the influx of Syrian refugees into his country, the King sought Russia's help to end the civil war in that country. King Abdallah's efforts to reach Moscow should be regarded as part of his overall effort to expand his global reach to major powers such as China and India. His primary goal was to obtain Russia's support for his modernization plan and the restructuring of Jordan's economy.

The bilateral trade between the two countries expanded significantly since 2007. It reached $169 million (for the period of ten months in 2007) in comparison to only $64.8 million in 2006. Among the Russian companies that obtained contracts in Jordan are *Russian Railways* to build the Amman-Zarqa railway line; *Tekhnopromexort* to construct thermal power plants and hydroelectric power stations on the River Yarmuk; *AvtoVAZ* to manufacture cars; *Stroitransgaz* to lay out a pipeline connecting oilfields in Iraq (Kirkuk); and petroleum refinery in Zarqa and *EnergoEngineeringEnterprises* to generate electricity. Russian and Jordanian artists and students in every field exchange visits on a regular basis.[40]

Jordan's diaspora of about 10,000 Chechens was a source of concern for Moscow since many of them identified with their brethren in Russia, and some called to help them in their effort to obtain independence. On December 28, 1991, Jordan recognized the sovereignty and independence of the Russian Federation. The mutual visits intensified to such as extent that King Abdallah became the Middle Eastern leader who visited Moscow the most. He met Putin almost every year since the beginning of the millennium, and Putin visited Jordan on February 12–13, 2007. This was in addition to other high-ranking officials from both sides who exchanged visits. The two countries share similar and even identical views regarding numerous issues such as combatting terrorism, nuclear disarmament, and human rights.

From Abdallah's standpoint, Russia's intervention in Syria in 2015 was a blessing and he expressed his approval, largely since he hoped that it would help stop, or at least substantially reduce the influx of Syrian refugees, which his country could no longer absorb. Moreover, his hope was that the Russian intervention would prevent Turkey and Iran from penetrating Syria, especially in areas close to the border with Jordan. King Abdallah II had no desire to see Syria turn into an Islamist country subservient to Iran, nor did he want to see its militias such as the Lebanese Hezbollah, continue to engage in drug trafficking in the region. Moreover, he welcomed the possibility of greater stability in the region, which would help bolster the ties with Syria, and thereby boost the trade between the two countries. From Abdallah's viewpoint, improved relations with Russia had a salutary effect on Jordan's security. This became evident in 2017, when Russia joined the United States in establishing a de-escalation zone in southern Syria.

King Abdallah II found himself on the horns of a dilemma in 2022, when Putin decided to invade Ukraine. Unlike many countries who criticized the invasion, the King called for negotiations to solve the problem, without mentioning Russia. His main concern was to return the Jordanian students who studied in Ukraine and whose number exceeded 1,700. On March 2, 2022, he voted against Russia in the UN General Assembly, but again he avoided referring to Russia as the aggressor.

Jordan's contacts with China did not become substantial until 1977, when the two countries established diplomatic relations. The King was largely motivated by the commercial benefits that such relations could bring. Ever since, the commercial contacts increased by leaps and bounds, and China has become Jordan's second largest trading partner. The bilateral trade volume hit about $1.92 billion in 2008, and the cooperation intensified thereafter.[41] On June 24, 2009, China's Communist Party member He Guoqiang met with Jordan's Prince Ali bin al-Hussein in Amman. He said that China-Jordan relations have made continued progress since the two countries established diplomatic ties, and even more so since Abdallah II ascended the throne.

Unlike its relations with China, Jordan's relations with India were marked by occasional periods of tension. Jordan's nonaligned stand in the Cold War brought it to identify with India, which adopted a similar policy. In addition, a common colonial heritage and history caused the bilateral relations to develop and brought the two countries to cooperate in numerous areas.

There were also similarities in their foreign policy. Jordan supported India in its struggle against China in 1962, and maintained a cautious attitude in the Indo-Pakistani conflict ever since. At the same time, India maintained distance from Israel and supported Jordan in the conflict. However, the relations suffered a setback at the end of the 1960s. According to Nabulsi, the tension was caused by Jordan's refusal to admit Indian representatives to the Islamic Conference, which debated the consequences of the fire at the Al-Aqsa Mosque set by the Australian Denis Michael Rohan on August 21, 1969. At the same time, Lebanon with much smaller Muslim population was allowed to send delegates to the conference. Moreover, Jordan's sale of phosphates to Pakistan was not well received in India.[42] It was only after the Simla Agreement with Pakistan in 1972, and the nuclear explosion in Pokaran, that India began paying attention to Jordan. Despite the tension caused by Jordan's support of Kashmir's right to independence, its approval of the Simla Agreement was viewed with favor in Delhi. The bilateral relations resumed their cordial course, culminating in Crown Prince Al-Hassan's visit to India in 1976.

The commercial ties increased as well and brought the two countries closer. Jordan gradually became a major exporter of phosphate and potash to India, and it began employing many of its workers.[43]

The bilateral trade amounted to $2 billion, and India has become the largest importer of phosphates.[44]

Diplomatic relations between Jordan and Japan were established in 1954, and in 1974, the two countries opened embassies in their respective countries. In 2005, Japan granted Jordan $23.6 million in Development Aid. It also took part in a project aimed at saving the Dead Sea and its resources from extinction. Trade balance between the two countries reached JD 288 million, JD 17 million of which were Jordanian exports to Japan. The volume of Japanese investment in Jordan reached JD 31 million.[45] In April 2009, Abdallah visited Japan and the two sides agreed to expand their cooperation to numerous areas such as land reclamation, desalination, and expansion of water resources.

Another Asian country that attracted Jordan's attention was South Korea. Jordan and South Korea first established ties in 1962, but the Korean embassy in Amman was not inaugurated, until 1975, and Jordan opened its embassy in Seoul fifteen years later. During Abdullah's visit to South Korea, the two countries signed a memorandum of understanding aimed at intensifying the cooperation. Korea's Ambassador to Jordan Shin Hyun-suk boasted that his country has taken important steps in that direction. He said:

> We started our financial contribution in the mid-1990s in the form of government soft loans and grants. By now, we have provided $200 million in soft loans, mainly in wastewater management and the nuclear research and training reactor currently under construction at the Jordan University of Science and Technology. We also provide more than $20 million in grants consumed in various projects. Four million dollars per year are now allocated in grants for Jordan.[46]

The bilateral relations continued to develop. However, the volume of trade remained low compared to Jordan's trade with the major powers in the region.

The European countries

Concerned about its declining influence in Jordan, which became obvious after Glubb's dismissal in 1956, Britain conducted negotiations with the French with a view to maintain its influence in that country. Among the plans discussed at that time was the possibility of creating unrest along the Israeli-Jordanian border, and calling upon the Iraqi government to move its forces to the Jordanian border. This plan was aimed at allowing Britain to react, and thereby maintain its credibility in the Arab world. Proposed by the French, this plan did not see the light of day.[47] Nevertheless, Britain maintained and even tightened its economic links to Jordan. In 1957, both sides agreed to terminate the Anglo-Jordanian Treaty of 1948, however, despite mutual visits and occasional purchases of arms by Jordan the relations between the two countries remained cold.

Fearful of Nasser ambitions in the Middle East and in Jordan in particular, the British government prepared for a show of force, which culminated in what became known as Operation Vantage, which was meant to save King Hussein's regime from collapse. According to Dulles, the revelation regarding a plot to assassinate King Hussein "came from the British who gave a digest of it to Hussein."[48] Harold Macmillan stated in memoirs how "Nuri Pasha came to see me…He is full of plans-some of them rather dangerously vague-for detaching Syria from Egypt. He wants us to get the Ruler of Kuwait to join, in some form, the Iraqi-Jordanian union."[49] Macmillan recalled how he received "a message from the King…a further plea, still stronger and more poignant from almost the last survivor of the Hashemite family."[50] The King felt threatened by the talk of an impending union between Egypt and Syria, which became frequent in 1958. The situation in Jordan worried the British, particularly following Qasim's coup, and the subsequent talks between Egypt and Syria about forming a united republic. They began flying from Cyprus over Israel's air space before they obtained permission to do so.[51] These were the last political and strategic maneuvers in which the British were involved and afterward, the ties between the two countries remained confined to trade. Between 1977 and 1980, British exports to Jordan reached $100 million in addition to arms.[52] In 1988, Britain supplies Tornado aircraft to Jordan, however by then, the King was accustomed to obtain his supply of sophisticated weapons from the United States.

Through its missionaries and its educational institutes, France was involved in Jordan long before the country's creation. Both the Catholic Church and the French government, which sought to increase its political influence in the Levant, encouraged the spread of French culture on both banks of the Jordan River. Missionary orders such as Brothers of Christian Schools and Sisters of Saint Joseph, operated in Amman and throughout the West Bank. Collèges des Frères opened in Jaffa and the Old City of Jerusalem, and a Catholic seminary was opened in Bet Jala, near Bethlehem.[53]

The relations between Transjordan and France were strained since the beginning of the French Mandate in Syria. The reason for the tension was that many Arab nationalists who opposed the French fled to Transjordan, to avoid arrest by their representatives in Syria. Jordanian officials had constantly raised the issue and their resentment did not cease.

They discussed the matter with the British on numerous occasions, to no avail. In an interview with Secretary Malcolm Macdonald, which was held in March 13, 1939, the Jordanian Chief Minister Abul Huda complained that France did not take the necessary steps to prevent the entry of armed bands who penetrated Transjordan from Syria. The British Colonial Secretary promised to take the matter with the Foreign Office, with a view to approach the French government on that issue.[54]

While the French tended to arrest smugglers who brought arms from Transjordan to Syria, they seemed to have done little to prevent smugglers and armed bands from crossing the areas under their control. In his report on the political situation in Transjordan, from February 1939, the British Resident says:

> The French authorities in Syria are acting in a manner which at the best must be described as most unfriendly in allowing the Palestinian leaders in Syria

> to organize rebellions and assassinations in Palestine and the beginnings of a similar condition in Transjordan. If these leaders must be given asylum as political refugees then at least they should be segregated effectively and neutralized.[55]

In a telegram from April 17, 1939, to the colonial secretary, the high commissioner writes:

> Reliable information available in Transjordan that the ravines of the River Yarmouk lying north of Transjordan, Syria and the boundary running into Palestine are used as important depôts for supplies and as bases and routes for gangs wishing to operate in Palestine or Transjordan. British Resident and Trans-Jordan authorities urge that cleaning out this system by the French authorities is essential to prevention of gang activities in Palestine and Trans-Jordan and I concur in this view. I shall be grateful if urgent representations may be made to the French authorities. I understand that the question had already brought up to the notice of the French Frontier authorities by the British Resident but without concrete results.[56]

In a more specific telegram to the Colonial Office, Consul Gilbert Mackereth stated that he had requested from the French that Suleiman al-Sudi, who was responsible for causing revolt in Transjordan, be removed from the frontier region. He complained that on five occasions he asked the French to prevent the Zawiya area of the Gulf of Fiq from being used by brigands against British bases in Transjordan and Palestine.[57]

On June 26, 1939, the French foreign office sent a memorandum in response to Britain's request. It described the measures taken by the French high commissioner in Syria to prevent the infiltration of armed bands into Transjordan. Its argument was that the Palestinian leaders in Syria were under surveillance. Furthermore, it stated that a joint Anglo-French plan to put an end to the practice of using the ravines of the Yarmouk Valley as supply depots for the gangs was being considered, and that al-Sudi was imprisoned in Aleppo. The memorandum's author concluded by saying that the French authorities complied with the request of the British consul general to expel the Palestinian agitator Mouin al-Madi from Syria.[58] Part of the reason why the French were not sympathetic to the British request to arrest al-Sudi was that he was not charged with any crime in Transjordan, and there was no warrant for his arrest.[59]

According to a report by an agent sent by the French authorities to Amman, the British sought to undermine French position in the country, and when a revolt erupted in Syria, Peake Pasha asked the Syrian rebel Sultan al-Atrash and his comrades to occupy Dera'a, and promised that he would supply them arms and money for that purpose. He also ordered Colonel Stafford to occupy that region with a contingent of cavalry and tanks that he had in al-Ramtha. The pretext that was given to this attempt was the need to protect the railway line and the frontier.[60] The French authorities sent a Druze cavalry force into Transjordan in order to prevent the rebels from carrying out their mission, arguing that the operation was in line with the 'hot pursuit' policy, which the Good Neighborhood Agreement between Transjordan and Syria permitted.[61]

On June 9, 1941 several Jordanian notables, tribal chiefs, and parliament members sent a telegram to General de Gaulle, saying that they thanked France for ending the Mandate and that they looked forward to cooperate with France. Moreover, they announced that Transjordan was an indivisible part of Syria, into which they wished to be incorporated. The telegram was signed by Shaikh Banu Sakhr Mithqal al-Fa'iz, Shaikh of the Balqa tribes, Majid al-Adwan, the parliament member and head of the Chamber of Commerce Muhammad Ṣabri al-Ṭaba', the mufti of Amman Amr Luṭfi, the deputy of Amman's mayor Ḥamdi Manku, the pharmacist Muhammad Salim al-Ṣabagh, and the parliament member Sa'ud al-Nabulsi.[62]

When the Partition Plan for Palestine was brought to discussion at the UN on November 29, 1947, France was hesitant but pressured by the United States, it voted for the resolution. After the Suez Affair and the Algerian crisis, De Gaulle noted,

> In the Middle East our affairs are at an all-time low. The Algerian crisis and the Suez incident have closed off our access to the Arab states...Naturally, I intend to reestablish our position in this region of the world, where France has always been active.[63]

Following the Six-Day War, De Gaulle responded by imposing an embargo on Israel.

He harshly criticized Israel for the occupation and denounced the "scandalous fate of the refugees in Jordan".[64] France continued to support the Palestinian demand for a homeland and when President Giscard d'Estaing referred to the Arab-Israeli conflict on March 1980, he stressed that negotiations must include all parties. France hoped that the Jordanian-Palestinian coordination would eventually lead to the establishment of a Jordanian-Palestinian confederation. The French position was that any attempt to solve the Palestinian problem ought to be based on cooperation with Jordan. On August 8, 1986, Prime Minister Jacques Chirac told journalists, that he was not in favor of an independent Palestinian state, and yet believed that they must have a homeland. He added that he did not believe that the PLO was the sole representative of the Palestinian people and that "the problem should be resolved within the framework of a solution negotiated with Jordan."[65]

France continued to show interest in Middle Eastern affairs and the cooperation between the two countries intensified in 1988, when it agreed to sell Jordan 20 Mirage aircraft.[66] Jordan's relations with France continued to improve. Both countries agreed on the need to fight terrorism, to find a solution to the Syrian crisis, and a comprehensive solution to the Israeli-Palestinian conflict based on the two-state formula.[67] During his visit to France, Abdallah II met Prime Minister Emanuel Macron, and the two leaders agreed on strategic partnership. Macron pledged his support to the "two states solution" and agreed to involve his country in the Jordanian struggle to absorb the Syrian immigrants.[68]

At the same time, Abdallah II continued to expand his country's relations with other European countries. Jordan's relations with Germany were mostly confined to trade. Since 2001, Germany provided Jordan €234 million in numerous development projects, particularly in water resources management and construction of primary schools. The German government had also agreed to grant Jordan debt cancellations, amounting to a total of €1million. By 2007, Germany's development assistance to Jordan reached €1.2 billion.

At a meeting between Abdallah and Germany's Federal Chancellor Angela Merkel, which took place on November 14, 2007, the two sides agreed to expand the cooperation. They expressed their support to the Middle East peace process, and for a two-state-solution to the Israeli-Palestinian conflict. By then, the total value of the bilateral trade was €839 million. Moreover, Germany encouraged its companies to participate in rebuilding the Iraq Fair in Amman, and a new German Investment Protection Agreement was signed. In addition, the German government agreed to continue helping Jordan repay its debts to foreign creditors.[69] Three German NGOs currently operate in Jordan: Friedrich Ebert Stifftung, Friedrich Naumann Stifftung, and Konrad Adenauer, all of which coordinate numerous aspects of business and joint projects in many fields.[70]

Italy showed interest in Jordan already during Mussolini's time with a view to spread Axis propaganda. The Jordanian members involved in this attempt were Muhammad al-Assali and Muhammad Attiya. Both were in contact with Dr. Fausto Tesio whose Syrian agents were former members of the Istiqlal Party in Transjordan, such as Adel and Nabih al-Azmeh. In addition, there was a Lebanese journalist, who spread pro-Italian propaganda and traveled between Palestine, Transjordan, and Egypt. Another person who was involved in such activities was Shaikh Jassar from Bethlehem, who offered Amir Abdallah £30,000 to help the Palestinian rebels stir troubles along the Kingdom's borders with Syria, and spread pro-Italian propaganda. However, Abdallah rejected the offer, and ordered his visitor to leave Transjordan.[71] Jordan's relations with Italy were not confined to such nefarious acts. Both countries cooperated in the medical field and Italian physicians helped establish hospitals in the country. Thanks to Dr Tesio, hospitals were opened in Amman in 1927 and Karak in 1935. Following Jordan's independence, the two countries began trading but the exchange remained modest.

Trade exchange statistics reveal that in 2015 Italy exported 10.6 percent more than the previous year compared to a decrease of 15.5 percent in Jordanian exports to Italy.[72] The two countries began cooperating since Jordan's independence, and by 2017, Italy's investments in Jordan amounted to 2JD million. Jordan's connections increased over the years in numerous areas from commerce to cultural events.[73] Several cultural events were included in the "Italia, Culture, Mediterraneo" in 2018. The program included exhibits by artists, archaeologists and photographers from both countries, and the events continued in 2019.[74] Italy also plans to take part in the Red Sea-Dead Sea Water Conveyance Project as well as in the Human Resources Development Strategy.[75] What is most remarkable about the bilateral relations as that in 2022, Italy allocated $286 million for Jordan.[76]

King Hussein was keen on maintaining cordial relations with the Vatican as well. Contacts between Jordan and Holy See date back to King Abdullah I who exchanged messages with Pope John Paul XII regarding shrines in Jerusalem, and the status of the Christians in it. In 1964, Paul VI was the first pope to visit the city. King Hussein took the opportunity to express his willingness to protect the Christian holy sites and the pilgrims, and the Vatican appointed Michel Sabbaḥ as the first Arab Latin patriarch of Jerusalem.

Convinced that Jordan is a moderate country that values freedom of religion the Vatican opened its first embassy in Jordan in 1994.[77] Commenting of that move, *The Spokesman's Review* said, "The diplomatic moves reflect the Vatican's desire to play a role in the Middle East Peace process, especially regarding Jerusalem. The Vatican seeks an internationally backed status regarding freedom of worship in Jerusalem."[78] In 2000, Pope John Paul II visited Jordan. In 2006, Prince Ghazi Bin Mohammad had presented the Vatican a Qur'anic verse signed by 138 Muslim scholars, which highlighted the significance of Muslim-Christian dialogue. In May 2009, Pope Benedict XVI visited the holy sites.[79]

Australia

Despite the normalization in the Israeli-Jordanian relations, the Hashemites' relations with Australia remained marred by the positive role, which Australia played in the establishment of Israel. Both the Liberal and the Labor Party in Australia tended to be sympathetic to Israel. However, it was the Liberal Party, which introduced the trend of maintaining an even-handed policy toward the Arab-Israeli conflict, and therefore promoted better relations with Jordan. Nevertheless, the sympathy toward Israel remained strong. Australian forces participated in the Anzac campaign in the Middle East during World War I, and they faced stiff opposition by Turkish and German forces in Amman.[80] Not only was Australia a member in the UNSCOP, which recommended the partition of Palestine in 1947, but also it sent forces to the war front and enthusiastically supported Israel.[81]

Although King Hussein never went to extent of severing relations with Australia as Nasser had done in 1959, the relations remained cool. Australia was one of Israel's most ardent supporters during the entire period in which the Liberal Party was in power (1949–1972). It supported Israel during the Six-Day War of 1967. During the October War of 1973, it remained sympathetic to Israel, despite the fact that its ambassador to the UN Laurence Macintyre declared his country's determination to pursue an evenhanded policy toward the Middle East. Australia's even-handed policy in the Middle East began result of Liberal Prime Minister Malcolm Frazer's decision to benefit from better relations with the Arab world. Although the traditional pro-Israel policy remained dominant, the Labor Party, which came to power in 1983, felt the need to continue the evenhanded trend begun by the Liberal Party.

In 1983, Labor's Foreign Minister Bill Hayden stated that his government recognized the need to find a solution to the Palestinian problem; that the Palestinians have a right to self-determination; and that the PLO is their sole representative. At the same time, the Australian government set conditions for these concessions: that the PLO recognize Israel's right to exist, in addition to accepting the 242 and 338 UN Resolutions, and that the terrorist activities cease. On the other hand,

Australia asked that Israel freeze its settlement activities in the occupied territories. The Australian government made more concessions to the Palestinians after they announced their peace program in 1988, and the Oslo accords that followed. On the whole, however, Australia's policy remained sympathetic to Israel under both parties, and this position had a cooling effect of its relations with Jordan. The pro-Israeli tendency intensifies when John Howard's Liberal government came to power 1996, and the Labor government under Kevin Rudd that followed in 2007 continued that trend.[82]

In recent years, Jordan has shown interest in expanding its global reach. However, so far Jordan's contacts with the countries of Latin American remained limited, apart from occasional meetings, such as when Abdallah met Peru's President Alejandro Toledo on May 30, 2005, and asked his country's support for the peace process, and the two-state solution to the Israeli-Palestinian dispute; there were virtually no contacts with the countries in that region.[83] Similarly, Jordan's contacts with the Africa remained confined to pivotal countries such as South Africa, with which it established full diplomatic relations with in 1993, and was the first Arab country to do so. In the following year, South Africa established a resident mission in Amman. In April 1996, King Hussein headed a delegation on a visit to Pretoria, and in October 1999, former President Nelson Mandela reciprocated with a visit to Amman. Although Jordan is striving to expand it contacts with the African states, these efforts pale in comparison with those of Israel, whose diplomatic efforts to acquire more friends in Africa have no parallel in Jordan or any Arab country, with the possible exception of Egypt, simply because its inability to offer much to these countries.

Jordan's quest for security made it imperative to establish contacts with defense organizations as well. It was largely due to pressure by nationalists and pro-Nasser elements that the Hashemites found it impossible to join the Baghdad Pact. Cooperation with NATO provided the Hashemites an opportunity to bolster the country's security. However, unwilling to be blamed by their opponents who could claim that they were conspiring with Western imperialists, they sought to avoid contacts with NATO, and it was not until the early 1990s that such contacts were made, when King Hussein cooperated with NATO forces in an effort to restore peace in the Balkans. In return, NATO established special funds to help Jordan eliminate explosives and mines, which remained in its territory after the wars. Educational centers were established for that purpose in Ajlun, Jarash, and Zarqa.[84] Abdallah II continued the trend and sought to cooperate with any defense organization that could enhance the country's security. Moreover, he was keen on taking part in peacekeeping operations throughout the world. In a speech at the Jordanian Defense College from January 10, 2009, NATO's General Secretary Jaap de Hoop Scheffer praised Abdallah for his commitment to maintain peace in many countries and his support for in human rights operations in the Balkans and Afghanistan. He also noted that Jordan signed the Memorandum of Understanding with NATO's Maintenance and Supply Agency.[85] Jordan has expressed its ambition to build a nuclear reactor and to complete the project by 2019. However, this plan raised opposition by many experts who warned that such step could be detrimental to the country's security and environment.[86]

Notes

1 Cited in Uriel Dan, p. 98.
2 Memorandum from Henderson to Byrnes, June 3, 1946. Cited *Ibid*, pp. 99–100.
3 *Ibid*, p. 107.
4 *Ibid*, pp. 111–112.
5 Statement by the President on Eric Johnston's Mission to the Middle East, October 16, 1953, Public Papers of the Presidents of the United States, Dwight D. Eisenhower, 1953(Washington, DC: United States Government Printing Press), No. 217, p. 678.
6 The President's News Conference of April 23 1956, *Public Papers of the Presidents of the United States*, Dwight D. Eisenhower, 1956, No. 53, p. 294.
7 Awrāq min Daftar al-Ayyām, p. 87.
8 'Abdallāh Hamūda, "Sulayman al-Nabulsi—Qirā'ah fi al-Qawanīn alati asdaraha," (Sulayman al-Nabulsi—A Reading in the Laws that he Introduced), Arabic text, *Sulaymān al-Nabulsi:* Qirā'ah, p. 108.
9 Muḥammad al-'Izabī, Kayfa sana'al-Injlīz al-Urdun: Al-mufawāḍāt al-siriyya bayn al-*Ṣahyuniyīn wa-al-bayt al-Hāshemi* (How did the British establish Jordan: The Secret Negotiations between the Zionists and the Hashemites), Arabic text (Al-Qāhirah: Dar al-Qawmiyyah lil-Ṭibā'ah wa-al-Nashr, 1960), p. 43.
10 Radio and Television Address to the American People on the Need for Mutual Security in Waging the Peace, May 21, 1957. Public Papers of the Presidents of the United States, Dwight D. Eisenhower, 1957, No. 91, p. 394.
11 Statement by the President Following the Landing of United States Marines at Beirut. July 15, 1958. *Ibid*, No. 173, pp. 553–554.
12 Letter to Nikita Khrushchev Chairman, Council of Ministers, U.S.S.R July 25, 1958. *Ibid*, No. 179, pp. 565–566.
13 Ritchie Ovendale, "Great Britain and the Anglo-American Invasion of Jordan and Lebanon in 1958," *The International History Review*, Vol. 16, No. 2 (May 1994), p. 294.
14 "Statement by the President on Eric Johnston's Mission to the Middle East" October 16, 1953, Public Papers of the Presidents of the United States, Dwight D. Eisenhower, 1953. (Washington, DC: United States Government Printing Press), No. 217, p. 678.
15 Public Papers of the Presidents of the United States, Dwight D. Eisenhower, 1958, No. 198, p. 593.
16 "Special Message to the Congress on the Mutual Security Program, March 13, 1959," Public Papers of the Presidents of the United States, Dwight D. Eisenhower, 1959, No. 55, p. 264.
17 President's News Conference of May 8, 1963 (Washington, DC: United States Government Printing Press, 1964), p. 373. Public Papers of the Presidents of the United States, John F. *Kennedy*, No. 169, p. 373.
18 Memorandum From the Department of State Executive Secretary (Brubeck) to the President's Special Assistant for National Security Affairs (Bundy), Washington, August 30, 1962. *FRUS*, Vol XVIII, Nina J. Norings and Glenn W. LaFantasie (Washington, DC: Government Printing Office, 1995). No. 33, p. 80.
19 Remarks of Welcome at the White House to Hussein I, King of Jordan, April 14, 1964. *Public Papers of the Presidents of the United States, Lyndon Johnson* (Washington, DC: United States Government Printing Press, 1965), No. 258, p. 373.
20 Special Message to the Congress on Foreign Aid, January 14, 1965. *Public Papers of the Presidents of the United States, Lyndon Johnson Book I* (Washington, DC: United States Government Printing Press, Washington, 1966), No. 18, p. 45.
21 Memorandum from Robert W. Komer of the National Security Council to President Johnson, February 9, 1965. *FRUS*, Vol. XVIII, Edited by Harriet Dashiell Schawar and David S. Patterson. (Washington, DC: United States Government Printing office, 2000) No. 143, p. 318.

22 Telegram From the department of State to the Embassy in Jordan, February 9, 1965, *Ibid*, No. 145, p. 322.
23 Shalom, p. 82.
24 Memorandum from W. Howard Wriggins and Harold H. Saunders of the National Security Council Staff to the President's Special Assistant (Rostwo), Washington, November 16, 1966. *FRUS*, Vol. XVIII, p. 665.
25 Remarks of Welcome at the White House to King Hussein I, The Hashemite Kingdom of Jordan. April 8, 1969, Public Papers of the Presidents of the United States, Richard *Nixon* (Washington, DC: United States Government Printing Press, 1971), No. 142, p. 268.
26 Joint Statement following the Discussions with King Hussein I of Jordan. April 10, 1969, *Ibid*, No. 146, p. 277.
27 Henry Kissinger, *Henry Kissinger: White House Years* (Boston, MA: Little Brown and Company, 1979), pp. 618–619.
28 Special Message to the Congress Proposing Supplemental Foreign Assistance Appropriations, November 18, 1970, *Public Papers of the Presidents of the United States, Richard Nixon* (Washington, DC: Government Printing Press, 1972), No. 438, p. 1076.
29 Second Annual Report to the Congress on United States Foreign Policy, February 25, 1971, *Ibid*, No. 75, p. 289.
30 Adam M. Garfinkle, "U.S. Decision Making in the Jordan Crisis: Correcting the Record," *Political Science Quarterly*, Vol. 100, No. 1 (Spring 1985), p. 135.
31 Toast to the President and King Hussein on August 16, 1974, *Public Papers of the Presidents of the United States*, Gerald Ford (Washington, DC: United States Government Printing Press, 1975), No. 12, p. 17.
32 Special Message to the Congress Proposing Legislation to Fund Security Assistance Programs, October 30, 1975, *Public Papers of the Presidents of the United States, Gerald Ford* (Washington, DC: United States Government Printing Press, 1977), No. 649, p. 1758.
33 Robert Stephens, "Jordan and the Powers," *The Shaping of an Arab Statesman: Sharif Abd al-Hamid Sharaf and the Modern Arab World*, Edited by Patrick Seale (London: Quartet Books, 1983), p. 40.
34 The President's Overseas trip: Question-and-Answer Session with Reporters on Board Air Force One on Route to the United States, January 6, 1978. *Public Papers of the Presidents of the United States, Jimmy Carter* (Washington, DC: United States Government Printing Press, Washington, 1979), p. 46.
35 James A. Baker, III with Thomas M. Defrank, *The Politics of Diplomacy: Revolution, War and Peace 1989–1992* (New York: G.P. Putnam's Sons, 1995), pp. 451–452.
36 "Message to the American Public from His Majesty King Hussein, September 1990," *Ibid*, p. 37.
37 The Politics of Diplomacy, p. 451.
38 CRS Report for Congress: Received through the CRS Web: "U.S. Democracy Promotion Policy in Middle East: The Islamist Dilemma," Jeremy M. Sharp, *Middle East Policy Analyst, Foreign Affairs, Defense and Trade Division*. June 15, 2006, p. 26, http://www.fas.org/sgp/csr/mideast/RL33486.pdf.
39 Cable from the U.S.Embassy in Amman. Reference id 09AMMAN257, November 25, 2009, http://wikileak.org/cable/2009/11/09AMMAN2579.html.
40 Russian Jordanian Business Council, http://russian-jordanian-bc.org/en/russian-jordanian-relations/.
41 *Xinhua*, http://paper.people.com.cn/rmrb/html/2009-06/26/content_283041.htm; Ministry of Foreign Affairs of the People's Republic of China, http://www.fmprc.gov.cn/en August 22, 2011.
42 Min Daftar al-Ayyām, p. 88.

43 Sayel Zaki Hamid Khataybeh, *Indo-Jordan Relations* (Amman: Published by the Author, 1996), pp. 162–165.
44 Batool Ghaith, "India Aims to Enhance Trade, IT Cooperation with Jordan-Ambassador," *Jordan Times*, January 25, 2022.
45 "Economic and Trade Relations between Jordan and Japan," July 13, 2005, http://www.albawaba.com/r.
46 "Jordan an 'oasis of stability, model of reform," *Jordan Times*, April 19, 2012.
47 Meron Medzini, *The Proud Jewess: Golda Meir and the Vision of Israel-A Political Biography*, Hebrew text with title in English (Tel Aviv: Edanim, 1990), p. 241.
48 Eisenhower Papers; Ann Whitman file, DDE diary series, box 35, Conference with the President, July 16, 1958. Cited in Nigel John Ashton, "A Microcosm of Decline: British Loss of Nerve and Military Intervention in Jordan and Kuwait, 1958 and 1961," *The Historical Journal*, Vol. 40, No. 40 (December 1997), p. 1074.
49 Catteral Peter, (Ed.), *The Macmillan Diaries: Prime Minister and After, 1957–66* (London: Macmillan, 2011), Entry for February 17, 1958, p. 95.
50 *Ibid*, Entry for July 16, 1958, p. 134.
51 *Ibid*, Entry for July 17, 1958, p. 136.
52 Stephens, p. 41.
53 William F.S. Miles, "Minoritarian Francophonie-The case of Israel, with Special reference to the Palestinians Territories," *International Migration Review*, Vol. 29, No. 4 (Winter 1995), p. 1036.
54 MacDonald's interview with Taufiq Pasha Abdul-Huda, March 13, 1939. TNA FO 371/23247/E2262.
55 Transjordan: Report on the Political Situation for the Month of February 1939. March 28, 1939. TNA FO371/23247/E2262, pp. 2–3.
56 Telegram from the High Commissioner for Trans-Jordan to the Colonial Secretary, April a7, 1939. TNA FO 371/23247/E2874.
57 Reference to Telegram No. 33 Addressed to the Colonial Office by His Majesty's High Commissioner Palestine, April 19, 1939. TNA FO371/23247/E2875.
58 Letter from the French Foreign Ministry to the British Ambassador in Paris, June 26, 1939. TNA FO 23247/E4667.
59 Mackereth to Glubb, June 29, 1939. TNA FO 371/23247/E5146.
60 Mackereh to Baxter, Secret Report, August 2, 1939. TNA FO371, 23248/E5448.
61 Situation Report on Trans-Jordan for the Month of April 1943, Enclosure III, may 17, 1943. TNA FO 371/35045/4678.
62 "Rijalāt Sharq al-Urdun yuṭalibūn al-iltiḥāq bi-Suryah," (East Jordanians ask to join a Union with Syria), Arabic text, Awrāq wa-Mudhakkirāt Fakhri al-Bārūdī 1887–1966: *Khamsūn 'āman min ḥayāt al-waṭṭan*, Vol. II (Dimashq: Wizārat al-Thaqāfah, 1999), pp. 269–270.
63 Cited in Philippe Rondot, "France and Palestine: From Charles de Gaulle to François Mitterand," *Journal of Palestine Studies*, Vol. 16, No. 3 (Spring 1987), p. 87.
64 Cited *Ibid*, p. 89.
65 Cited *Ibid*, p. 98.
66 "Jordan an 'Oasis of Stability, Model of Reform," *Jordan Times*, April 19, 2012.
67 Diplomatie, https://www.diplomatie.gouv.fr/en/country-files/Jordan/France-and-jordan/.
68 "Jordan, France Keen on Strategic Partnership," *Jordan Times*, June 20, 2017.
69 *Ibid*, November 15, 2007.
70 Jawad Anani, "Jordan-Germany Connection," *Ibid*, February 8, 2016.
71 Gilbert Mackereth to Baxter, Interview with Emir 'Abdallāh, TNA FO 371/23247/E2142, March 1939, p. 5.
72 "Jordan and Italy 'Restore Bridges, not Create Walls'," *Jordan Times*, May 30, 2016.
73 Suzanna Goussous, "Jordan, Italy extend further than political arena-Ambassador," *Ibid*, May 31, 2017.

74 "'Italia, Culture, Mediterraneo': A Yearly Italian Cultural Programme in Jordan," *Ibid*, February 3, 2018.
75 "Openness, Humanity Distinctive Features of National Identities of Jordan, Italy," *Ibid*, June 18, 2018.
76 "Italy Commits $286 m in aid to Jordan," *Arab News*, arabnews.com/node/1865856.
77 *The New York Times*, March 4, 1994.
78 *The Spokesman Review* (Spokane), March 4, 1994.
79 Jordanian News Agency, April 18, 2009, http://www.breitbart.com/article.php?id=upi20090418-172507-5989&show_article=1.
80 Peter Firkins, *The Australians in Nine Wars: Waikto to Long Tan* (New York: McGraw-Hill Book Company, 1971), p. 146.
81 Thomas Bruce Millar, *Australia in Peace and War 1788–1977* (New York: St Martin's Press, 1978), p. 360.
82 "Australia's Political View of the Middle East," *Australia and the Arab World* (Arabic Text), Edited by 'Ali al-Qazq (Abu Dhābi: The Emirates Center for Strategic Studies and Research, 2009), pp. 156–163.
83 *Jordan Times*, June 1, 2005.
84 Lt Gen Wolf-Dieter Loeser, "NATO and the Middle East after the Lisbon Summit: Implications form the New Strategic Concept," *The Jordanian Diplomat: Cultural Quarterly*, Vol. II, No. 2 (March–June, 2011), p. 25.
85 Speech by NATO's General Secretary Jaap de Hoop Scheffer at the Jordanian Defence College, January 10, 2009, http://nato.int/cps.en.
86 "Experts Urge Jordan to abandon Nuclear Energy Quest," *NTI: Global Security Newswire*, April 15, 2011, http://www.nti.org/gsn/artic.

XIV The reign of King Abdallah II

The rise of King Abdallah II in 1999, ushered in a new period in the history of modern Jordan. The new monarch set his priorities clearly from the very beginning. His vision was to turn Jordan into a new Western-oriented model state, with a view to gain greater support in the international community, and this had to be achieved by introducing greater economic liberalization and attracting foreign investment. The establishment of the Ministry of Political Development was one of the first steps taken by Abdallah II in 2003, with a view to accelerate the country's economic development. At the same time, however, his objective was to reinforce the power of the monarchy, at the expense of slowing down the progress toward democracy. His first response to the public disenchantment was to introduce a measure known as "Jordan First" and the other was to announce the National Agenda 2006–2015, the emphasis of which was economic rather than political. These measures were to be carried out without adverse effect on the regime's freedom of action, even though the progress toward democracy slowed down. In order to achieve these goals, King Abdallah II opted for combining economic development with restrictions on political freedom and occasional use of coercive measures. The political organs continued to function, but he intervened whenever there was a threat to the regime, justifying his action by arguing that the country's security was at stake. One of the events that demonstrated his determination to strengthen the monarchy's power was his decision to dissolve the Parliament on March 2, 2007, and to delay the national elections.

Background

In response to the riots triggered by price increase on staples and the restrictions imposed by the International Monetary Fund, King Hussein made concessions that brought greater democratization to the country. The general elections that were suspended since 1967 were restored, the martial law imposed in 1957 were ended, the restrictions on the press were relaxed, and the political parties legalized.

King Hussein's decision not to join the U.S.-led coalition against Iraq during the Second Gulf War brought unprecedented hardships to the Jordanians. This was largely due to the sanctions that were imposed on Iraq, and adversely affected the Jordanian economy. The reaction of the Gulf countries, which suspended the

DOI: 10.4324/9781003450313-15

debts owed to Jordan and dismissed many of its expatriate workers from their positions, compounded the difficulties, and it was not until the Oslo Accords of 1993, that King Hussein was free to move toward peace with Israel. The Oslo Accords helped to improve Jordan's relations with the U.S. King Hussein agreed to call for a change of regime in Iraq, and even allowed the CIA-backed opposition in that country to open offices in Amman. However, the introduction of free market in 1996, which resulted in sever cuts in subsidies and price increases, led to unrest, which he was determined to suppress by repressive measures. These measures caused much resentment in the opposition parties, particularly among the conservatives and the tribal deputies.[1]

King Hussein's death was followed by a struggle between his brother Hassan who was prepared for taking over the reins of power, and chief of the General Intelligence Department General Samih Battikhi who collaborated with former Prime Minister Abdul Karim al-Kabariti to prevent Hassan from becoming the successor. Moreover, there were rumors that Kabariti was in cahoots with Queen Nur in an effort to replace Hassan with her son Ḥamza. However, King Hussein decided to designate his son Abdallah as the successor. The reasons given to Hussein's change of heart vary. There are those who believe that he feared that his brother did not have enough support among the tribes, while others opine that Hassan's prejudice against the Palestinians led Hussein to fear that the plans to allow them greater representation were likely to be jeopardized. King Hussein's choice came apparently as result of a natural tendency to see his son in power. Furthermore, the fact that Abdallah had military experience and maintained good relations with the Gulf states, the Americans and even the Israelis, made him a more attractive choice.[2]

Several trends became obvious with the rise of Abdallah II to power; greater efforts to incorporate the country in the global economy; greater willingness to become part of the American-led endeavor to bring peace into the region; and a slowdown and even reversal of the democratization process.[3] Abdallah II continued the pro-Western tradition of his father and he sought to further disengage from the Palestinian legacy of the Hashemites, their heavy reliance on the tribes and their tendency to inflate the bureaucracy. Abdallah's major goal was to concentrate on the East Bank, keep the West Bank separate, and concentrate on economic development. To promote economic growth, he began concentrating on building robust commercial ties with Washington, privatizing the economy, and developing the private sector while reducing the size of the public one.

Free from the burden of controlling the West Bank, the young king put the Arab-Israeli conflict and the Palestinian problem on the back burner, while pursuing his goal of finding a place for his country in a U.S.-dominated world, and promoting economic growth by increasing investments, privatization and technological development. He maintained a low profile in foreign policy, and apart from occasional statements such as his call for NATO intervention in order to end the war in Kosovo, he refrained from making controversial statements regarding the Palestinian struggle for statehood. Unlike his father who was compelled to operate in a bipolar Cold War environment, Abdallah felt free to become closely associated with the United States, which he regarded as the backbone of his country's security and prosperity. Moreover, he was not compelled to promote Arab nationalism in order to gain legitimacy to his rule. In order to concentrate on turning the country into a regional commercial center with strong ties to the United States, Abdallah sought to mend fences with his Arab neighbors whose leaders had demonstrated good will following his father's death. Despite the tension over Jordan's position during the Gulf War and the peace accord with Israel, the Arab leaders did not call for overthrowing Hashemites, nor did they insist on evicting Jordan from the Arab League.

The Arab states' desire to survive and play a constructive role in the global economy facilitated greater cooperation with Jordan, particularly when Abdallah II displayed his diplomatic skills with great caution, by supporting and lobbying for Bashar Assad to succeed his father as president in Syria. By emphasizing the need for cooperation in a globalized market, Abdallah II managed to mend fences with the Gulf states as well. Unlike his father, he refrained from referring to Arab nationalism as a sentiment uniting all Arab countries. Discourse about economy and prosperity replaced the old nationalist rhetoric about *jihad*, and even Israel did not loom large in his speeches. Not only did he exert considerable efforts to promote trade talks with all Jordan's neighbors but also kept the peace treaty with Israel and sought security partnership with its leaders.[4]

The establishment of the Qualified Industrial Zones in which Israeli, Jordanian, and American products were to be sold freely was one of the first steps taken by Abdallah II to stimulate the economy. Inefficient practices were ceased, the private sector was expanded significantly, investments increased, and Jordan obtained membership in the World Trade Organization. Though modest, these achievements helped bolster the stability of Abdallah's regime. Abdallah's emphasis on cooperation with the United States led him to combat terrorism and intensify his campaign against the Islamic militants who opposed his peace treaty with Israel. Another step in that direction was taken in 1999, when he decided to deport the Hamas leaders from his country.

The resiliency of Abdallah's regime

Abdallah's regime proved to be as stable as his father's. Like his father, he continued to bolster his regime by emphasizing his lineage to Prophet Muhammad. Besides, there were other factors in favor his regime. The influence of the Jordanian left and the Islamic opposition remained limited, and they were not in a position to exert significant pressure on the government's policy toward the Palestinians. The government's ability to balance the domestic and external forces, curtailed the linkage between them and thereby managed to limit the influence of the opposition groups. The government adopted a pragmatic approach in dealing with the Palestinians and demonstrated sympathy to their struggle, but it rejected the radical methods of the left and the Islamists, and refrained from encouraging violent solutions. Moreover, it did not confront the opposition groups violently, but chose to compromise with them. It recruited many of the opposition members to high positions in the administration and made the effort to prevent them from uniting against its policy. Constant attempts were made to convince the PLO to accept the government's foreign policy and King Abdallah II did not refrain from exploiting the rift between the leftist groups and the Muslim Brotherhood, in order to bring its members to cooperate with the regime.[5]

Undoubtedly, the Hashemite regime benefited from the solid foundations laid by King Hussein who coopted the Bedouin tribes and increased his influence in the East Bank, and Abdallah continued that trend. He continued to remain in power due to his ability to manipulate the state's institutions in order to counter the opposition groups, and prevent them from building a powerful front. As in Hussein's days, the government manipulated the constitutional rules in such a way that the opposition could not build a power base against it. The Jordanian regime managed to stifle the opposition through a strategy of controlling the political parties, the Parliament, and the press. Even though the National Charter and the Political Parties Act of 1992 reintroduced democratic life into Jordan, none of the parties, with the exception of the Muslim Brotherhood, became popular among the public. Moreover, none of the parties was allowed to make contacts with non-Jordanian organizations. The government's meddling in the electoral law in 1993 resulted in the establishment of a loyal parliament, and the 1997 amendments to the Press and Publication Law enabled the regime to control the Parliament and public opinion.[6]

Under Abdallah the Jordanian regime continued to use the civil society organizations in order to enhance its control. Civil society groups were coerced into becoming formal organizations where collective action was taking place and these were monitored directly by the government bureaucracy. This was done mainly by forcing all working groups and those who were involved in collective action, to register at a ministry, which monitored their action and regulated their activities.[7]

The Hashemite regime managed to restrain the Muslim Brotherhood by various methods of cooperation, rewards as well as punishments when necessary. It established rules for political behavior, which were designed to bring the Brotherhood to cooperate. Until the 1980s, the Jordanian government had to deal with opposition forces such as the pan-Arabists who were loyal to Nasser, the Palestinians and a variety of leftist groups. When the Islamists appeared on the scene the government, which by then had experience dealing with dissident groups was ready to face the challenge. Its security and intelligence forces penetrated the Muslim Brotherhood and the terrorist organizations that were beginning to form. Through discourse and accommodation methods, the Jordanian regime managed to control these organizations and they were allowed to operate as long as they willing to accept its rules.[8]

From 1921 to at least until 1989, the Jordanian state relied heavily on foreign aid since the domestic sources were inadequate. However, this option was limited as well, especially since the regime aspired to sovereignty and sought the limit the pressure applied by foreign donners. Therefore, it had to resort to higher taxation. At the same time, the rentier elite in the private sector enjoyed increase in remittances paid by those renting their facilities. Consequently, there was a conflict of interests between the government and the rentier elite whose members were expected to pay the bulk of the tax payments.[9]

The rise of Abdallah II has led observers to speculate regarding his ability to remain in power. Like Bashar Assad who came to power in Syria, without previous knowledge or substantial experience, Abdallah II assumed power in a period of uncertainty, against a background of instability caused by severe economic crisis, and growing opposition to the Jordanian-Israeli peace accord. The young king's major dilemma was how to establish an authoritarian regime, while facing such challenges. The conclusions reached by Oliver Schlumberger and André Bank provide partial answer to that question. According to their findings, Abdallah II managed to remain in power due to three main factors; his ability to enhance the regime's legitimacy; his practice of constantly changing the composition of the political elite, and his reliance on inherited instruments of authoritarian control. While accomplishing these tasks, the King managed to keep all domestic pressure for liberalization in check. The survival and stability, according to these authors, depended on legitimacy, repression, or a combination of both. Abdallah managed to not only obtain the loyalty of the political elites but also maintain control over domestic affairs. His descent from Prophet Muhammad lent legitimacy to his rule and consequently, he was less vulnerable to criticism. This aspect of political legitimacy was termed by these authors as "religious-traditional legitimacy" since it consists of both religion and tradition. Although this type of legitimacy did not play crucial role in everyday life, it could be invoked by the monarch in time of crisis, as King Hussein had done in 1990–1991, when he demanded that that all participants in the political game sign a document, stating that the political system in Jordan is "Hashemite" and "dynastic."

Theorists classify Jordan as a "rentier state of the second order" or "semi-rentier" and its reliance on foreign donors provides legitimacy since donors insist on restructuring of the economy and the imposition of retrenchment measures, which the regime must carry out, in order to obtain loans or grants. Therefore, the state can apply control measures that help stabilize the regime, except in times of economic crisis such as the Second Gulf War when King Hussein supported Saddam Hussein. When King Hussein was compelled to resort to greater dependence on foreign donors, he was compelled to introduce political liberalization measures. The decline of legitimacy that ensued after King Hussein's death left Abdallah II with a serious challenge, especially in the wake of the severe economic crisis and the discontent, which emanated from the opposition to the peace treaty, which his father signed with Israel. The opposition to the treaty with Israel came particularly from groups that suffered the most from the economic crisis of the late 1990s.

Abdallah's ability to manipulate the existing elites enabled him to control the political system more effectively. He resorted to radical measures such as dismissal and transfer of officials from their positions in order to prevent anyone from building a power base. The example of the royal adviser Samih Baṭṭikhi is revealing. He accumulated so much power that Abdallah II found it necessary to replace him with his second in command, Major General Sa'd Khayr in the fall of 2000. Battikhi was later appointed member of the upper house of Parliament. Similar experience happened to Mustafa Hamarneh, director of the Center of Strategic Studies at the University of Amman who was dismissed from his position, and later was not only reinstated but also nominated as board member of the newly established Committee for the Privatization of the Jordanian Media. There were numerous replacements of key personnel, especially in sensitive positions in the military, the police, and the intelligence apparatus. Similarly, the creation of the Economic Consultative Council (ECC) whose members were mostly entrepreneurs in their mid-thirties or early forties, and the dismissal of Prime Minister Abd al-Ra'uf Rawabda who opposed the regime's policies, is indicative of Abdallah's guard-changing strategy. The most powerful figure in the council was Basim Abdallah who was not only a member but also a liaison between the council and the royal court. Despite its economic nature, this council was charged with numerous developmental and educational projects, and its members occupied other top positions in the royal administration.

These young men have become so influential that the old members of the governmental bodies such as the Senate in Hussein's time lost much of their influence. In fact, these measures brought a new political elite to power. The ECC had turned into an institution on which the king relies upon in questions of strategy and policy-making, and only he determines its composition. Basically, the entire public sector is under government control and there are no agencies that can be called autonomous, including the media. Not only does the regime keeps close censorship on the press, but he also monitors the MP's closely, and whereas the degree of liberalization in the parliament in 1989–1993 was high and included a significant number of Islamists, the parliament of 1993 was dissolved shortly after the introduction of a pro-government electoral law. In 2001, the government postponed the elections and thereby obtained another respite in which it could consolidate its power. Overall, however, it seems that the level of repression did not increase since Hussein's time. Abdallah's ability to appear as a reformist king whose goal is to bring prosperity to every class in the kingdom provides him considerable legitimization. Moreover, he was able to convince the public to believe that once the country achieves a high level of economic development and technological progress, the democratization of the political system would follow. Unfortunately, numerous symptoms of neo-patrimonial rule such as clientelism, nepotism, and corruption remained in Jordan, and there is still need for some measure of control and repression. However, unlike his father who introduced a measure of democratization and then had to resort to its curtailment, Abdallah II managed to eliminate it entirely from the scene, by insisting that greater political freedom is contingent upon the country's economic prosperity.[10]

The political parties

The development of Jordan's political parties can be divided into several phases:

The first phase (1920–1928), which began with the arrival of Amir Abdallah to Jordan in November 1920, was characterized by instability. Amir Abdallah was engaged in negotiations with the British regarding the terms of the Mandate, and the formation of the nucleus of the Jordanian army. During that phase, the

People's Party (*ḥizb al sha'b*) and the Independence Party (*hizb al-istiqlal*) were active in Transjordan. These parties reflected the views and aspirations of Amir Abdallah, the most prominent among which were the objectives of the great Arab revolt and the aspirations for Syria's territorial integrity. During that phase, the first national conference met in Amman, on July 25, 1927. Its deliberation resulted in the drafting of the National Covenant, which demanded independence for Transjordan, and the formation of a constitutional regime. The participants rejected the Mandate, and demanded the establishment of parliamentary practices. This was the first popular development in Transjordan's political life. The Istiqlal Party and its members who came from Syria, Iraq and Palestine turned into a formidable opposition to Amir Abdallah who dismissed them from their positions. The regime regarded them as traitors, and they lost their Jordanian citizenship. Nevertheless, the parties continued to be active.

The second phase (1928–1946) began with the Organic Law of April 16 1928, which consisted of 72 clauses. This resulted in the formation of a legislative council in 1929. The treaty with Britain was the main issue of debate at that time. The council included fourteen members, nine of whom were Muslims, three Christians and two Circassians. Two Bedouin leaders had joined the council later. Four legislative councils were elected, the first was dissolved in 1931 and the last in 1946, when the country became independent. Two additional parties were formed during the 1930s; the Solidarity Party (*al-taḍamun*) and The National Convention (*al-mu'tamar al-waṭani*). However, these parties had no clear platform that could attract voters and did not last for more than five years.

The third phase: On May 25, 1946, Amir Abdallah became the king of Transjordan and a new constitution was drafted in February 1948. The constitution called for legislating a new electoral law and establishing a parliament. It was at that point that Amir Abdallah became less interested in his Greater Syria scheme and began paying more attention to the Palestine issue. The change had a significant impact on political life in Transjordan. The Palestine War that followed the establishment of Israel in 1948 brought the Arab Legion to keep the West Bank, and after a short period of struggle with the Palestinian leader al-Husseini, the Jericho Convention of April 24, 1950, determined that the West Bank was part of Transjordan.

Following Abdallah's assassination in 1951, King Talal ascended the throne. The new king introduced a constitution in 1952, which aimed at regulating the political life in the country. On May 2, 1953, Hussein ascended the throne and thereby ushered in a new period in the country's history. The country underwent a traumatic period during the years 1955–1958 when the nationalist movement, which emanated from Cairo, swept through the region. The Iraqi revolution of 1958 and the subsequent unification between Egypt and Syria had a profound impact on the country. Moreover, the Six-Day War and the clashes between the regime and the Palestinian organizations constituted another serious threat to the fragile state. Nevertheless, political life followed its natural course. King Hussein continued to play his role as head of state and the executive branch of the government, and the prime ministers operated like their Western counterparts. During that time, however, the regime regarded the political parties as a threat to its existence. Although the King sought to turn the Parliament into a vibrant forum of open discourse it remained marginal in the country's political life. The executive made all the decisions and it was above the other branches. However, the executive faced major problems in the following decades, and the economic crisis of 1989 convinced the regime to make changes and introduce reforms. At the same time that the public began expressing its discontent, calls for democratizations and reforms became more frequent. Consequently, a new period of greater democracy ensued and the parties resumed their activities.

Though banned during the entire period between 1958 and 1992, the parties operated clandestinely. When the government removed the ban, some of the old parties resumed their activities in the open, and several central parties emerged, but they remained weak and did not attract many voters. The parties of the earlier period were engaged in critical issues such as independence from Turkish rule, opposition to the British mandate, and the struggle against colonialism and thereby captivated large segments of the public whereas the parties that emerged after 1992 were less likely to call for a major Arab revolution and were therefore less capable of attracting the masses.[11] Nevertheless, the number of the political parties increased significantly over the years. The new parties have clear agenda and their platforms are more specific: the Islamic wing consists of the Labor Front Party (*ḥizb jabhat al-'amal*); the Invocation Movement (*ḥarakat du'a*) and The Central Islamic Party (*ḥizb al-wasat al-islami*). the left wing consists of: the Jordanian Communist Party (*al-ḥizb al-shuyu'i al-urduni*); the Progressive Party (*al-ḥizb al-taqqadumi*); the Jordanian Democratic Union Party (*al-ḥizb al-dimuqraṭi al-waḥdawi al-urduni*); the Democratic United People's Party (*ḥizb al-waḥdah al-sha'biyah al-dimuqraṭiyah al-urduniyah*); and the Democratic People's Party (*ḥizb al-sh'ab al-dimuqraṭi al-urduni*).

The nationalist wing consists of the Jordanian Arab Socialist Renaissance Party (*ḥizb al-ba'th al-'Arabi al-ishtiraki al-urduni*); the Progressive Arab Renaissance Party (*ḥizb al-ba'th al-'arabi al-taqqadumi*); the National Labor Front Party (*ḥizb jabhat al-'amal al-qawmi, "ḥaq"*); the Jordanian Constitutional Arab Front (*ḥizb al-jabha al-arabiyah al-dusturiyah*); the Jordanian Land Party (*ḥizb al-arḍ al-'arabiyah*); the Arab Helpers Party (*ḥizb al-anṣar al-'arabi*); the National Democratic People's Movement Party (*ḥizb al-ḥaraka al-qawmiyah al-dimuqraṭiyah al-sha'biyah*); and the Jordanian Arab Party (*ḥizb al-Arabi al-urduni*).

The central wing consists of the National Constitutional Party (*al-ḥizb al-waṭani al-dusturi*); the Freedom Party (*ḥizb al-aḥrar*); the Future's Party (*ḥizb al-mustaqbal*); the Revival Party (*ḥizb al-nahḍah*); and the Jordanian Welfare Party (*ḥizb al-rifah al-urduni*).

Dominated by traditional values, such as piety, heroism, and generosity according to which humans are judged, the Jordanian society was far from ready to embrace an egalitarian ideology such as communism. However, the radical changes, which took place following the establishment of the new state, made the ground fertile for new ideas. The dire political and economic conditions exacerbated by the rapid population growth caused mainly by the incorporation of the Palestinian refugees in 1948, the Cold War rivalry of the superpowers in the Middle East, and the attraction of Pan-Arabism in the 1950s, were some of the factors that contributed to a climate receptive to the communist idea. It was in the Independence (*Istiqlal*) Party in Palestine that the idea began to take root. One of its members, Subḥi Abu Ghanima founded the *Ittiḥadu'il 'ummal al-urduniyin* (Union of the Jordanian Workers). Established in the early 1930s, this organization had less than two thousand workers, but there were several militant Communists among them. Nevertheless, this organization did not crystalize into an effective force. In 1936, the political activist Qasim Milhin, made another attempt to revive the Communist agenda but his success was limited. Other such groups emerged during World War II, and they tried to attract members by addressing the country's most pressing problems. For example, they called for an end to British mandatory rule, and for the establishment of independent institutions and free elections. These groups however, remained small largely because educated Marxists thought that Jordan was not industrialized, and therefore not fit for revolution. According to the Marxist intellectual elite, this condition was a sine qua non for a communist revolution. Even those who believed that the Jordanian peasantry could fulfill the role of a proletariat remained hopeless, since they were indifferent, and did not seem willing to start a revolution. Even more vexing was the absence of an intelligentsia to spearhead such revolution.

A change came in 1949, when several leading Palestinian Communists headed by Fuad Naşir and Rushdi Shahin were appointed to lead their followers in Jordan. Optimists among the Communists were encouraged by the influx of the Palestinian Arabs who came in the aftermath of the Palestine War. Many of them believed that the Palestinian refugee camps provided favorable conditions for a Communist revolution. The newly created League for National Liberation managed to adjust its strategy according to the prevailing circumstances. Its cadres were mainly teachers, physicians, journalists, and other free professions. Being realists, they gave up the rhetoric regarding mass struggle and other communist concepts, which they believed were incomprehensible to their followers. They simplified their rhetoric over time. They denounced the West; called for the toppling what they regarded as a "feudal regime"; and demanded reforms, development, and industrialization. The League pointed to the Soviet Union as a model and the place where its ideals were likely to materialize. It founded the organ The Popular Resistance (*al-muqawama al-sha'biya*), spoke in favor of the idea of partitioning Palestine according the 1947 UN Partition Plan, and promoted the internationalization of Jerusalem as the Soviet Union had done. The League established cells and operated in major urban areas. It also attempted to penetrate the Arab-Palestine Workers' Association in Jerusalem but with little success.

By the early 1950, the League became militant. It protested against the proposals to establish the Middle East Command and a Jordanian 'national guard' on the border with Israel. It also called on the population of Arab Palestine to refrain from voting in the elections of April 1950. However, after deciding to boycott the

1951 elections in Jordan, the League changed its tactic, and found it beneficial to participate in the political game. Two of its candidates Rushdi Shahin and Abdul Majid Abu Hajla won 25 percent of the total votes in Nablus, while its candidate in Amman, Mahmoud Mutlag, won 15 percent. In June 1951, the League changed its name to Jordan's Communist Party. By the end of 1951, the party had 700 members, and it attracted prominent members such as Nabulsi.

As it turned out, the party's activities led to the arrest of its secretary-general Naşir, and in 1953, the government introduced a law against Communism. Nevertheless, the party continued to appeal to the public, and in 1954, its leaders took the opportunity to establish a movement known as The National Front (*al jabha al-wataniya*). Among the sponsors of this movement were figures such as Qadri Tukan and Abdul Qadir Saliḥ. This movement was active in the elections of that year. The government's decision to control the activities of the opposition parties brought the Ba'th party to join the movement, and there were incidents and riots throughout the country in which Communists fell victim to violence and arrest. The Communists proved pragmatic enough to ally themselves with other opposition parties, including the Ba'th. In the beginning, they appeared as no more than a fringe group. In time, however, they became the mainstay of the opposition parties. This was in large measure due to the tight discipline within the party and its efficient management. By that time, the mixed Jordan-Arab-Palestine opposition group known as the National-Socialist Party under Nabulsi cooperated with the Communists. The Communist Party attracted many middle-class members and it called for reform, which made it appealing to the public. Since Islam was no longer the spiritual force that used to be and there was no Jordanian nationalism to speak of, the ground was fertile for a new doctrine that called for greater equality. However, like all Communist parties in the Middle East, the Jordanian Communist Party was a movement of the intelligentsia and not of the masses. The Communist Party remained illegal. Its aim was to undermine the King's authority and rid the country of foreign influence, but it had no overall plan to overthrow the government.[12] Nevertheless, the party continued to attract young men who were eager to spread the communist message. Yusuf al-'Aẓm, a parliament member and one of the symbols of the Islamist movement, recalled in his memoirs the unrelenting efforts of the young Communists to convince him of the validity of their doctrine. He writes:

> In the boisterous atmosphere, which attracts the new generation of young men, several traps were laid for me, to attract and include me in the left-wing. The first trap was laid by a Communist teacher.... He led me to think that Communism is our salvation from the difficulties of life and from imperialism...He began asking me when we were sitting: "where are you spending the days of your short vacation in Cairo?" I said, "in the mosque with some young men, and at the general center of the Muslim Brotherhood."
>
> He responded with astonishment and disapproval..."With the Muslim Brotherhood?" I said, "yes", he said, "your words are amazing, I said: what is so amazing about them? He said, the economic conditions in our country

> are deteriorating and the poverty kills the people, and you don't think about going in the direction of an economic thought or an organization that could save the people from their suffering…I plead with you to remain in touch with us…" I drank the tea and I returned to the room where I lived, and I was happy for that victory."[13]

Commenting about the change that he saw taking place in Jordan in the mid-1960s ,Ya'qub Ziyadin, one of the Jordanian Communist Party's most prominent members, writes:

> The new imperialism under the leadership of the United States managed to alter Jordan's demographic character. The tribal and feudal leadership, which for many years was the pillar of the regime, turned into smallest one. It was replaced by a bourgeoisie, big and small, a ruling bureaucracy of hundreds and thousands of officers, senior employees and retirees whose hands are always stretched toward the state's funds from which they steal. The government and those behind it have vested interest in all this. Moreover, they facilitate the creation of such parasitic classes and the expansion of American imperialistic influence in particular.[14]

Aiming to maintain its hold on the country and improve its relations with the United States the Hashemite regime suppressed any manifestation of Communist thought. Despite the renewal of political life in Jordan, the democratization process remained slow and cumbersome. The way that the government managed the parliamentary elections of 1997 shows that the electoral process was seriously flawed. Neither the management nor the supervision of the elections were sound. The fact that the executive branch of the government was in charge of supervising the elections was a cause for concern because by assuming that role the government became involved in the process, without the ability to supervise the elections. The elections had demonstrated that the relative weakness of the parliament left it out of the election process, without the ability to play a positive role in it, or to offer remedies. Moreover, the Palestinian factor as well as the acute problems, which the country was facing, such as privatization, unemployment, and poverty, all contributed to its inability to conduct meaningful elections.[15]

One of Abdallah's first priorities was to deal with social reforms. He noted in his memoirs: "One of my top priorities was to carry out a broad program of social reforms, and in particular to provide more support for the weakest members of our society."[16] Similarly, he felt obliged to be proactive on foreign relations, soon after his rise to power. He writes:

> I knew I would have to build personal relations with my fellow Arab leaders. The centers of power in the Middle East are Egypt, Saudi Arabia, Syria, and Iraq, due to their size and historical importance, and the Gulf countries, because of their wealth and influence. I would need to meet the leaders of all these nations to establish good relations.[17]

Coercive measures and political stagnation

Abdallah II came to power at a crucial time in the development of democracy in Jordan. The democratization process, which resumed in 1989, ushered in a new period in the country's political development. Elections were held every four years since 1989, and they were generally free and fair, with the exception of with those of 2020, which did not attract many voters due to the COVID-19 epidemic.[18] Other developments such as the promulgation of the National Charter, which provided for democratic reform; the legalization of political parties and the lifting of martial law, turned Jordan into one of the most democratic countries in the Middle East. Yet at the same time, the Hashemite regime imposed strict measures to control the country's NGOs, reduce the number of public demonstrations, and limit the freedom of the press. These measures led one observer to state that "There is a disconnect between democratic principles and actual reform."[19]

King Hussein's decisions to hold elections in November 1989 was a compensation to those who traditionally supported the regime and suffered the consequences of the austerity measures. It was a strategy adopted by the regime to ensure its survival. Since the very beginning, the state invested efforts in preventing voluntary organizations from playing a political role. This was the purpose of the Law of Societies and Social Organizations of 1966, and the Political Party Law of 1992, which limited such organizations to benevolent activities, without gaining political benefits. Of course, the state took the liberty of defining what activity was political and what was not, and often these organizations insisted that they were only involved in cultural matters. The upshot was that often there was a conflict between these organizations and the state, which often resorted to coercive measures aimed at curtailing their activities.

The regime continued to prohibit, or at least limit demonstrations, particularly if they had political implications. To do so, it requires individuals and organizations to obtain permits, which the government gives sparingly and only after a thorough investigation. Even moderate opposition organizations, such as those of the Islamic Action Front Party, encountered difficulties when it sought to protest. The regime's typical response was that the security of the state was at stake. For example, when the party asked to hold a "hungry million march" to protest the reduction of the subsidies during the bread riots of 1996, the government denied their request on the ground that the march could lead to disturbances and instability. In the following year, the Progressive Ba'th Party asked for permission to hold a rally in Irbid, in protest against the U.S. military preparations to go to war against Iraq. Once again, the government denied its request.[20] Instead, it allowed the party to hold a much smaller rally in Amman afterward, which made it easier to monitor its activities and when opposition groups such as the IAF attempted to demonstrate prior to the American invasion of Iraq, the government arrested 60 people, including members of the Muslim Brotherhood.[21]

Under King Abdallah II, the regime tends to allow demonstrations without an explicit political message, such as a march against smoking cigarettes, which causes cancer, but even such events require permits from the district governor who normally sends an administrator to ascertain that the protesters do not violate the permit's conditions. Otherwise, King Hussein's approach did not change drastically when Abdallah II came to power.

In addition to these measures, the government restricts the freedom of the press, particularly if they publish articles criticizing the royal family. Heavy fines were imposed on violators. Introduced in May 1997, the new amendment to the 1993 Press and Publications Law demanded that weekly newspapers will have to deposit the sum of JD 300.000 (US$210.000) at the Ministry and Trade and Industry instead of the JD 50.000 (US$35.000) required by the 1993 law. When the weeklies sued the government, the Higher Court of Justice protected the state's right to control the press "in accordance with the national interest."[22] Although the press obtained the cancellation of the amendment in January 1998, the government remained vigilant and continued to monitor its activities. The new Press and Publications Law, which was introduced in September, reduced the amount of deposit required by dailies to JD 500.000 and by weeklies to JD 100.000, but the restrictions remained unchanged. Newspapers are prohibited from publishing anything critical of the royal family or affecting national security. Furthermore, they are not allowed to publish anything that may have adverse effect of the country's relations with foreign countries. These measures were introduced mainly in order to prevent criticism of the peace accord with Israel, opposition to Arafat or to the Middle East peace process.[23]

The political parties in Jordan are currently weak. More than half of the parliament members are representatives of the tribes and not the parties. In addition, the allocation of seats in the Chamber of Deputies is designed to provide greater weight to the supporters of the regime. Thus, rural and urban areas, particularly in the southern districts and Bedouin tribes, receive greater number of seats. For example, Irbid which had a population of 390,685 in the mid-1990s was given nine seats while Amman, which had a population of 391,849 had only three. King Hussein's decision to introduce an amendment to the electoral law was specifically meant to weaken the opposition groups. He changed the electoral system from block-voting to a one-person-one-vote system. Now voters were given only one vote regardless of the number of seats in their district. The new election system reduced the number of the Islamists from 32 to 22 in the elections of 1993. Another amendment to the 1955 law regulating municipal elections was introduced in 1995, and it determined that the mayor of Amman and half of its Municipal Council were to be appointed by the Council of Ministers, and since Amman constitutes about a third of the kingdom's population, this constitutes a serious limitation on democracy. In addition to these restrictions, the crown continues to maintain power by virtue of the fact that only the Chamber of Deputies is a representative institution, while the King appoints the Senate, the Prime Minister, and the Council of Ministers. The constitution provides the King the ability to dissolve the Parliament, call for new elections and declare martial law. These powers allow him to apply his agenda with little opposition.[24]

These arrangements did not change when Abdallah II ascended the throne. His emphasis on economic development and his "Jordan First" agenda became the hallmark of his reign, and the coercive methods continued with a view to protect the Hashemite family from criticism. Abdallah II saw no reason to change the laws that enabled his family to maintain strict control over his people, and the regulations regarding the freedom of the press continue to serve the regime. For example, on June 18, 2015, the Jordanian supreme court of cassation convicted the journalist Husam Abdallat for trying to undermine the regime by criticizing the officials and friends of King Abdallah II.[25] The king continued to monitor the activities of the Islamists and in the elections held in 2016 the IAF and all other Islamist parties won no more than 16 seats in the Parliament.[26]

Ever since the outbreak of the Syrian civil war, Jordan was burdened with the need to support the refugees who came from that country. Attempting to console the Jordanian people, he once promised that for every job given to the refugees, he will create five for his countrymen. This, however, was no more than an attempt to comfort his listeners and as Senator Jawad Anani stated, did not have to be taken literally.[27] One of the steps taken by King Abdallah II was to modernize the armed forces. For that purpose, he established the Design and Development Bureau (KADDB), which turned into the military-industrial arm of the armed forces. This organ coordinates the joint ventures, which the armed forces are involved in, with cooperation with foreign defense companies. According to one study, at least 26 companies are currently collaborating with the Jordanian armed forces in the production of numerous sophisticated military devices, which help enhance their fighting capabilities.[28]

The national economy

Jordan has virtually no natural resources, except for phosphate and potash. Water is in short supply and inadequate rainfall has adverse effect on agriculture. In the early years after its independence, Jordan had a shortage of technically trained personnel and no infrastructure that could facilitate economic growth. The vast expenses needed for transporting merchandise, maintaining an army for defense, and absorbing numerous refugees had stifled the country's economic development, and in the early years of its independence, the *per capita* income did not exceed \$60 to \$70 per year. Approximately 300,000 Palestinian refugees arrived at the country in the aftermath of the Palestine War of 1948. It is amazing, however, that during the period between the Palestine War and the Six-Day War of 1967, Jordan experienced a remarkable economic growth. The Six-Day War resulted in the loss of east Jerusalem and the West Bank, and brought additional 355,000 Palestinian refugees. Jordan lost a significant portion of its trade, one-third of its agricultural land, and about three-quarters of its income from tourism.

A glance at the statistics available on Jordan's economic development show that a remarkable growth had taken place in the first sixteen years of its independent existence. Its gross domestic product jumped from JD (Jordanian dinar) 51 million in 1954 to JD 118 in 1961, and to about JD 140 in 1964. Jordan's economic growth was made possible due to its political stability, the ingenuity of its economic planners, the industry of its people, and above all, the foreign aid, which it obtained from the United States, Britain, West Germany, Kuwait, and some of the United Nations' agencies. According to the budget for 1963–1964, only 46 percent of the country's revenue came from taxes, and the rest from foreign aid.[29] The following data show the remarkable expansion of the Jordanian economy during the decade between 1954 and 1964: the GNP had risen from JD 52.4 million to JD 159.6; the per capita product had increased from JD 37 million to JD 82; the total available resources increased from JD 71.1 million to JD 204.6; consumption expenditures increased from JD 59.1 million to JD 159.4; the ratio of exports of goods and services increased from 30.8 percent to 43.4 and; the GDP increased from JD 47.7 million to JD 134.7. Income from agriculture, industry, mining, tourism, and other industries show similar growth.[30]

Despite the fact that Washington was keen on assisting Jordan due the moderation of the Hashemite monarchy, its pro-Western outlook, and the country's geographical location, which turned it into a strategic asset in the late 1950s and the early 1960s, when the Cold War reached one of its crescendos. Nevertheless, there were often issues, which caused disagreements between Amman and Washington that sometimes led to failures to implement major projects. For example, on October 16, 1961, King Hussein opened the floodgates of the East Ghor Canal, letting the waters of the Yarmouk River flow into a channel that ran parallel to the Jordan River for about 23 kilometers. This project was financed mostly by Washington in an effort to irrigate the eastern bank of the river and distribute land to small farmers and Palestinians in particular. Apart from symbolically granting titles of ownership to a few farmers, King Hussein regarded the project not as a measure intended to solve the Palestinian refugee problem as Washington wanted, but as a way to accumulate capital for industrial development. This was one of the numerous cases where U.S. goals clashed with those of the Hashemites and they led to tension between the two countries.[31]

Another recovery period ensued following the Six-Day War, between 1968 and 1970, but it was interrupted by the Hashemite crackdown on the Palestinian guerrillas and the clashes with Syria, and it was not until 1972, when states like Libya and Kuwait resumed their commercial activities that financial aid from the Arab states began flowing into Jordan. Robust economic growth began thereafter. The GDP grew by 9 percent per annum between 1971 and 1981, and nearly 13 percent between 1975 and 1981. The economy took off by the middle of the decade, and by 1979 the Arab League pledged to provide Jordan an annual grant of $1.25 billion. Moreover, the reopening of the Suez Canal in 1975 stimulated the trade that passed from the east through the port of Aqaba, and the outbreak of the Lebanese Civil War in 1976 brought investors to Jordan and thereby ushered in a new period of construction boom. The Iran-Iraq War, which erupted in 1980, had a similar effect on the Jordanian economy, which benefited not only from the arrival of Iraqi investors but also from import dues paid for Jordanian products.[32]

Like its neighbors, Jordan employed foreign workers, particularly from Egypt who worked in the construction industry, in agriculture and numerous services, including tourism. According to one estimate, their number increased from 803 in 1975 to 153, and then to 519 in 1984.[33]

During 1969–1989, the Jordanian economy experienced growth but external shocks stood on the way of greater progress. The devastating impact of the Six-Day War continued to have adverse effect on the economy. The change in the price of oil and the labor unrest which took place had their negative impact as well. Consequently, The efficiency of the overall economy between 1969 and 1989 declined at an average annual rate of 2.6 percent. Dividing this period into two (1969–1979 and 1980–1989) can better explain the impact of these changes. The first period was marked by the reconstruction of the economy in the aftermath of the Six-Day War. This was also a period in which a substantial number of the Jordanian labor force left for the Arab Gulf states that enjoyed a boom after the oil price increase of 1973–1974. During the second period from 1980 to 1989, many of Jordan's migrating labor force returned home due to the falling oil prices, and the government had to provide the means by which they could resettle, which included not only providing jobs in the public sector but also basic services such as education and health. Moreover, providing jobs to those who returned had aggravated the problem of disguised unemployment, causing a reduction in labor productivity.[34]

By the end of the 1980s, the country's population was about three million, excluding the West Bank, and the average Jordanian lived a better life than his neighbor in the surrounding Arab countries. Jordan's GDP was estimated at $5.5 billion. According to UN statistics, the annual growth rate averaged almost 16.5 percent between 1972 and 1975. Then it fell to 8.5 between 1976 and 1979, and reached 18 percent in 1980. By the end of the decade, the GDP was estimated to have been no more than 2 or 3 percent.[35] Jordan's economy could have performed better if not for the enormous defense expenditure which was estimated in 1987 to have reached $635 million of the total government spending. Jordan's economy changed drastically following the arrival of the Palestinian refugees who were driven out of Kuwait in the aftermath of Saddam Hussein's invasion in August 1990. While the arrival of the refugees was a burden on the Jordanian economy, they helped usher in a new period in Jordan's economic development. Among the refugees, there were Palestinians with liberal tendencies who believed that privatization would be a panacea to Jordan's economy. Upon their arrival into the country, they changed the composition of the existing government coalition and immediately began advocating liberal reforms. Their arrival in Jordan led to expansion of the labor force that reached 12 percent and constituted 27 percent of the unemployed population on 1991. According to the estimate provided by the government, the GDP declined by 30 percent in the last five months of 1991, but it was at that stage that the regime decided to introduce liberalization and privatization in order to secure its existence.[36]

In the early 1990s, there was less demand for Jordanian exports, aid from the Gulf countries decreased and there was less demand for workers. Remittances decreased as well and a sudden devaluation led to severe inflationary pressures. More Jordanian women started looking for jobs. However, high external debt and high male unemployment brought the government to discourage women from applying for work. Unemployment among women was about 20 percent in 2000, significantly less than it was in the beginning of the decade. In the mid-1990s, the unemployment rate among women was more than double that of men and was highest among the youngest age groups. Some 70–75 percent of unemployed women had post-secondary qualifications, compared with 25 percent of unemployed men. Educated women were more likely to be unemployed than educated men or less-educated women. It is possible that the women's high unemployment was a result of the increase in jobs that did not require higher education. However, it is also possible that gender bias played a role, given that educated men's unemployment rates were not very high. Yet despite the growing unemployment among men and rising prices the participation of women in the work force remained very low. In the late 1990s, it reached about 12 percent. The women's rate of participation in the agricultural work force did not exceed 18 percent. In addition to gender bias, traditional values such as the husband's pride and his duty to protect her dignity played a role in limiting the number of women seeking employment. Moreover, social policies and labor laws allowed working women to exit the market easily. The wage inequality between the genders and the absence of minimum wage were additional factors discouraging women from seeking employment. A 1987 survey of the state sector indicates that men received 28 percent more than women of equal education, age, and experience. In the manufacturing sector, women's wages were only 57 percent of men, and this discrepancy left them unmotivated to seek employment.

Among the women who went to work most were employed in agriculture and the textile industry and there were relatively few who engaged in sales and services. In the late 1980s, significant social changes took place and women became employed in a wider variety of jobs such as chemicals, electronics, and food processing. Between 1994 and 1997, women became employed in 38.4 percent of the new employment opportunities. This was due to improvement in education and training practices, increased government spending on the promotion of women in the economy, and a more favorable public attitude toward female career.[37]

Major changes were introduced by the end of the 1980s. Liberalization, restructuring, and privatization measures were introduced and the Jordanian regime has been encouraging investments that it hoped would eventually lead to less reliance on foreign aid. Nevertheless, foreign aid and remittances remained the mainstays of the economy. The emphasis on attracting investors brought the government to introduce new legislation aimed at reducing risks and guaranteeing handsome returns. Corporate and income taxes were reduced and bank regulations were simplified. Major companies and agencies began hiring new managers some of whom were transferred into the private sector. Profound changes were introduced in major enterprises such as the glass industry, the telecommunication facilities, the radio and television, the cinema and the electricity, and other service providing agencies. Other measures introduced by the government were an increase in the value added tax from 7 to 10 percent, reduction in subsidies, an increase in the prices of fuel, water, and other essential commodities. Extreme saving measures were introduced and the government began making the effort to educate the public to consume while saving the country's resources.

There is a consensus among economists that robust economic growth depends among other variables, on healthy cooperation between the business community and the state. As it turned out, the Jordanian economy rarely benefited from such cooperation. The Jordanian business association failed not only in influencing economic policy productively but also in working with state officials in a common effort to solve problems. Unfortunately, Jordan had no strong business community on which the government could rely. This had a negative impact on the prospects of economic reforms. Besides, by the late 1990s, the Jordanian bureaucracy became extremely corrupt and disorganized. The result was disastrous and had the U.S. government not forgiven Jordan's external debt following the Madrid 1991 peace conference, the country would have likely been on the verge of economic collapse.[38]

During 1994 and 1995, the GDP reached 6 percent, inflation was held at 3.0–3.5 percent, the deficit declined by 7 percent, and in 1995 exports were reduced by 14 percent. Steps were taken by the government to negotiate with foreign companies in order to modernize the phosphate industry, to accelerate the production of pharmaceuticals, textiles, and other industries. One of the most important of these joint ventures has been with an Indian firm, the Indo-Jordan Chemicals Company, which started operating in 1993, with a view to increase the country's phosphate production. Estimated to have cost $160 million the project was completed at the end of 1996.[39]

The economic situation continued to deteriorate following Saddam's invasion of Kuwait. Many of the Palestinians sought to return to Jordan and found it difficult to be integrated in the economy. Prices continued to rise and many observers began talking about the disappearance of the Jordanian middle class.[40] The outbreak of the Syrian Civil War in 2011 brought as many as 1.3 million refugees thereby compounding the difficulties and at the time of this writing optimism is in short supply in Jordan and the news regarding the king's secret account in a Swiss bank intensified the discontent.[41]

Figure 14.1 King Abdallah II.

Notes

1 Lamis Andoni, "King Abdallah: In His Father's Footsteps?," *Journal of Palestine Studies*, Vol. 29, No. 3 (Spring 2000), pp. 77–89.
2 *Ibid*, p. 80.
3 *Ibid*, p. 77.
4 *Ibid*, p. 84.
5 Sami Al-Khazerendar, *Jordan and the Palestine Question: The Role of Islamic and Left Forces in Foreign Policy Making* (Reading, UK: Ithaca Press, 1997), pp. 176, 184.
6 Russel E. Lucas, *Institutions and Politics of Survival in Jordan: Domestic Responses to External Challenges, 1980–2001* (Albany: University of New York Press, 2005), pp. 155, 138–139.
7 Quintan Wiktorowicz, "Civil Society as Social Control: State Power in Jordan," *Comparative Politics*, Vol. 33, No. 1 (October 2000), pp. 49, 57.
8 Nachman Tal, *Radical Islam in Egypt and Jordan* (Brighton, UK: Sussex Academic Press, 2005), pp. 233, 234–235.
9 Warwick Knowles, *Jordan Since 1989: A Study in Political Economy* (London: I.B. Tauris, 2005), pp. 210–211.
10 Oliver Schlumberger and André Bank, "Succession, Legitimacy, and the Regime Stability in Jordan," *The Arab Studies Journal*, Vol. 9/10, No. 2/1 (Fall 2001/Spring 2002), pp. 50, 51–54, 56, 59, 61–62, 65.
11 'Abd al-Hādi al-Majāli, "Al-ḥayāt al-siyasīyah wa-tāḥāddiyāt bina' al-aḥzāb fī al-Urdun," (Political life and the Challenges among the Parties in Jordan," *Arabic text, Al-aḥzāb wa-al-ta'addudīyah al-siyasīyah fī al-Urdun* ('Ammān: Mu'assasat 'Abd al-Ḥamīd Shūmān al-'Arabiyah lil-dirasāt wa-al-Nashr, 1999), Edited by 'Alī Maḥafiẓah, pp. 86–87.
12 W.Z.L. "Communism in Jordan," *The World Today*, Vol. 12, No. 3 (March 1956), p. 118.
13 Yūsuf al-'Aẓm, *Mudhakkirāt thalāthat arbā'qarn* (Memoirs of Three Quarters of a Century), Arabic text ('Ammān: Dār al-Ḍiyā', 2004), pp. 199, 203, 204, 205.
14 Ya'qūb Ziyadīn, *Al-Bidāyāt: Sīrah Dhatīyah, Arba'ūn sanah fī al-Ḥarakah al-Waṭanīyah al-Urdunīyah* (The Beginnings: A Curriculum vitae, Forty years in the Jordanian National Movement), Arabic text ('Al-Quds: Manshurāt Ṣalāḥ al-Dīn, 1981), p. 131.
15 Mūsā Shatyāwi, "Al-intikhabāt al-niyabīyah al-Urdunīyah li-'am 1997: Taḥlīl susyulūjī," (The Jordanian Parliamentary Elections of the year 1997: A Sociological Analysis), Arabic text, *Dirāsāt fī al-intikhābāt al-niyabīyah al-Urdunīyah 1997* ('Ammān: Dār Sindbad lil-Nashr, 2002), pp. 45–46.
16 Our Last Best Chance, p. 137.
17 *Ibid*, p. 145.
18 Kristen Kao and Ezra J. Karmel, "The Pandemic Compromised Jordan's Parliamentary Elections," *The Washington Post*, November 20, 2020.
19 Quintan Wiktorowicz, "The Limit of Democracy in the Middle East: The Case of Jordan," *Middle East Journal*, Vol. 53, No. 4 (Autumn 1999), p. 607.
20 *Ibid*, p. 612.
21 *Ibid*, p. 613.
22 *Ibid*, p. 616.
23 *Ibid*, p. 617.
24 *Ibid*, pp. 619–620.
25 Ali Younes, "Jordanian Supreme Court Imprisons Journalist for criticizing Corruption," *The Arab Daily News*, September 22, 2015. http://the arabdailynews.com/tag/king-abdullah-ii.
26 Rana F. Sweis, "The Islamic Action Front Wins Seats in Jordan's Parliament," *The New York Times*, September 22, 2016.

27 Rana F. Sweis, "Jordan Struggle Under a Wave of Syrian Refugees," *The New York Times*, Februray 13, 2016.
28 Shana Marshall, "Jordan's Military-Industrial Complex and the Middle East's New Model Army," *Middle East Report*, No. 267 (Summer 2013), p. 42.
29 D.R. Campbell, "Jordan: The Economic of Survival," *International Journal*, Vol. 23, No. 1 (Winter 1967/1968), pp.109, 111–113.
30 See H. Talal's article, "Growth and Stability in the Jordan Economy," *The Middle East Journal*, Vol. 21, No. 1 (Winter 1967) pp. 92–100.
31 Nathan J. Citino, "The Ghosts of Development: The United States and Jordan's East Ghor Canal," *Journal of Cold War Studies*, Vol. 16, No. 4 (Fall 2014), pp. 160–161.
32 John Roberts, "Jordan's Economic Growth in the 1970s: Policies for Responding to External Stimulus," *Development Policy Review*, Vol. 2 No. 2 (November 1984), p. 154.
33 Pierre-Nicholas Baussand, "Jordanie: L'utilisation de l'immigration pour stabiliser une économie postrentiére en crise," *Revu Tiers Monde*, Vol. 41, No. 163 (Juillet–Septembre 2000), p. 647.
34 Khairy Tourk, "Sources of Economic Growth in Jordan" 1969-1989," *The Journal of Energy and Development*, Vol. 27, No. 1 (Autumn 2001), p. 91.
35 "Jordan-The Economy-Structure and Dynamics," https//countrystudies.us/Jordan/46/htm.
36 Alex Nowrasteh, Andrew Forrester, and Cole Blondin, "How Mass Immigration Affects Countries with Weak Economic Institutions: A natural Experiment in Jordan," *Cato Working Paper No. 51*, Cato Institute, March 20, 2018, pp. 24, 26.
37 Valentine M. Moghadam, "Women's Economic Participation in the Middle East: What Difference Has the Neoliberal Policy Turn Made," *Journal of Middle East Women Studies*, Vol. I, No. 1 (Winter 2005), pp. 134–135.
38 Pete W. Moore, "What Makes Successful Business Lobbies: Business Associations and the Rentier State in Jordan and Kuwait," *Comparative Politics*, Vol. 33, No. 2 (January 2001), pp. 143–144.
39 Muhammad Azhar, "Indo-Jordanian Trade: Performance and Prospects," *Middle Eastern Studies*, Vol. 36, No. 3 (July 2000), p. 208.
40 K. Luisa Gandolfo, "Bridging the Economic Gap: The Rise and Fall of the Middle Class in Jordan," *The Arab Studies Journal*, Vol. 15–16, No. 2/1 (Fall 2007/Spring 2008), p. 114.
41 Patrick Kingsley, "Jordan's King Among Leaders Accused of Amassing Secret Property Empire," *The New York Times*, October 3, 2021.

XV Vernacular and culture in modern Jordan

Culture can be defined as the total sum of human ideas and their products at a given time. J. Duncan and D. Ley define it as "a conflict between empowered and marginalized ideological and political interpretations of place." Others argue that culture is a dynamic concept that changes over time. Anthropologists differentiate between "vernacular culture," which includes the use of language that is different from the literary language or from that of official news broadcasts. The term tells us that the "vernacular" is one aspect or portion of the total culture. It is native to or common in a certain region or a group. It does not mean that the term suggests primitive or traditional but rather something that is "of one's house."[1] In literature, the term "vernacular" is used to contrast the predominantly used and recognized language of a specific region with the formal language of the court, or the elite. Some use the term in connection with forms and apply it to architecture.[2] It is possible to say that the word "vernacular" implies a relationship of power and subordination between the officially recognized authorities and the indigenous ones. This kind of relationship is in a state of flux, and it is constantly redefined.[3] Vernacular items and phenomena exist in numerous areas such as architecture, music, literature, and food. They are slowly adopted and incorporated into the elitist cultural canon. The vernacular evolves organically from the bottom up rather than imposed from the top-town by what David Byrne called "designated experts."[4]

An analysis of Jordan's culture ought to differentiate between the vernacular aspect, which includes practices that emanate from religion, and common beliefs that develop on the regional level, and the high culture promoted by the state. Thus, common practices such as *wasta* (mediation), polygamy, and femicide are among the numerous phenomena that can be classified as vernacular, whereas achievements in areas such as modern literature, cinema, or music can be classified as high culture. This chapter deals with several cultural phenomena that can be defined as vernacular-oriented and continue to pose a challenge for the Hashemite regime. Also, the chapter assesses Jordan's achievements in the main areas of high culture.

The *Wasta* in Jordanian culture

One of the most prominent features of Jordanian culture is the concept of *wasta*, which Aseel al-Ramahi defines as "the well-connected, personal intermediary-intervener

DOI: 10.4324/9781003450313-16

and the process of intermediation-intervention."[5] This practice played a major role in Jordan's history during the 1930s and 1940s, and it continues today. In his work on disputing systems, O.G. Chase argued that "Dispute processes are in large part a reflection of the culture in which they are embedded; they are not an autonomous system that is predominately the product of insulated specialists and expert."[6] This conclusion applies to Jordan as to other traditional societies. The individual's need for *wasta* continues to dominate Jordanian thinking. The individual needs to rely on help from a mediator in numerous daily needs such as protection against exorbitant prices in the market place, finding employment, resolving a conflict, accelerating the pace of the government bureaucracy's response to one's application or request, and even finding a bride. Originally, the term *wasta* means "mediation" and its purpose was to resolve disputes among warring tribes. The person practicing *wasta* endeavors to end a conflict by coaxing and cajoling, in order to safeguard the honor of an injured person, and to absolve him or her from the duty of taking revenge by violent means. The urbanization and modernization processes, which the country experienced, did not cause this practice to end; they merely transformed it a utilitarian instrument aimed at achieving personal benefits, particularly from the state's bureaucracy. For example, Amir Abdallah who became the country's first monarch made effective use of *wasta* by using the leaders of the tribes as mediators. He obtained their service by numerous gifts, which included land grants, honorary titles, tax exemptions, deductions, and other kinds of benefits and when the modern state began to function he placed them in key positions in its bureaucracy. Some tribal leaders became mediators between the government and the tribes. They fulfilled important positions in areas related to national security, law enforcement, and so forth. The best example of a successful mediator who made wide use of *wasta* was no other than Mithqal al-Fayiz who became one of Abdallah's confidantes. As a mediator, he obtained numerous privileges, which included not only material benefits and protection, but also judicial and administration rights. His enormous fortune enabled his to become Abdallah's right hand. By these means, the tribes became the regime's backbone and consequently they had interest in the state's survival and prosperity.[7] Reliance on the tribes continued under King Hussein and King Abdallah II who valued their contribution, especially in matters relating to national security. Thus, their main bases of power became the Arab Legion and the intelligence apparatus.

In inter-tribal conflict resolution, a group of notables known as *jaha* became involved in the conflict resolution process, and its aim was to reach a compromise solution that absolved the victim from having to take revenge, while preserving his or her honor. The *jaha* members were usually elders whose judgment was accepted by both tribes and the Jordanians, especially villagers followed the unwritten tribal law.[8] This tradition existed despite the process of modernization and the expansion of the state's power and today *wasta* is widely used in order to gain personal benefits. The persistence of this practice constitutes a major impediment to modernization. Jordanians using such practice must justify their actions to others who tend to regard them as corruption. Similarly, the state's campaign for better business practices and transparency is adversely affected by the persistence of this practice. Abdallah II continues to face this dilemma in his campaign to introduce ethical standards into the economy. At a meeting with Jordanian editors in 2000, he addressed this issue by saying, "I stand against cronyism. Everyone who works on consolidating it or ignoring its existence is my personal enemy… government should establish a code of honour to put an end to *wasta*, favouritism and cliques."[9] However, it was not until 2005 that the Anti-Corruption Commission law, which provides a clear strategy for combatting corruption, that *wasta* was officially criminalized.[10] It would be too optimistic to assume that such time-honored institution would simply come to an end in a society where *wasta* has been so prominent, particularly since it began as an honorable way to settle disputes.

Polygamy, honor killing, and male supremacy in Jordanian culture

Polygamy, honor killing, and the notion of male superiority are all part of a vernacular culture that the modern state seeks to suppress. While the state had been successful in limiting the number of honor-killing, combatting polygamy is an impossible task, especially since the practice is not forbidden in Islam, and even though the educational curriculum is under state control, textbooks at the elementary level are still male-biased.

Like in all Muslim countries, man is the head of the household in Jordan, even though many reforms were introduced to promote the woman's position. A study from 2010 demonstrates that in the textbooks used for teaching history and civics at the eighth, ninth, and tenth grades, the students were addressed in a gender-balanced style. However, the outcomes of the units addressed only male students.[11] Despite numerous attempts at reform, legislation by the Parliament is still conservative, and the tendency to regard male as superior still persists in Jordan. Moreover, the traditional attitude continues to manifest itself in polygamy and honor killing. Studies show that even the onset of industrialization did not have as much impact on the country's social and cultural values, as it had on employment values.[12]

As a Muslim country, the regulations for marriage and polygamy in Jordan are similar to other Arab countries. This cultural attitude however, continues to face numerous challenges in the modern age, and the number of people who oppose the practice of polygamy has increased dramatically in recent years. Islam does not force a woman to get married, even to a single man who is not her choice. Yet, polygamy exists and allowed for both the husband and the first wife, if she suffers from infertility or serious health conditions and believes that polygamy is preferable to divorce. Moreover, the first wife has the right to divorce a husband who marries another woman, provided the marriage agreement grants her the right of a unilateral divorce.

Polygamy is accepted, yet the one practicing it faces a challenge from the rest of the society, which tolerates it but does not encourage it. Critics of the practice argue that polygamy has adverse effect on the children, and that often the man is not in a position to provide the material conditions that a woman might need in the modern age of materialism, that obliges him to provide much more than men provided in the past. Basing their argument on the statement in the Qur'an that "You are never able to be fair and just between women even if it is your passionate desire" (The Qur'an 4:3), there were many opponents of such practice since the early days of Islam. The rationale behind polygamy when it originated was not to satisfy to man's sexual and sensual desires, but to provide a solution to the problem of widows and orphans who were incapable of proving for themselves. The Islamic rules regarding polygamy came at a time when men married even more than four wives, and therefore they can be regarded as eliminating the adverse conditions in which many women experienced when they were married to a man with multiple wives. The Qur'an is clear about the fundamental issue involving polygamy when it states that if the husband cannot satisfy all his women's needs, he should "get married to no more than one" (The Qur'an, 4:3). Moreover, the woman is allowed to take her husband to court in case of maltreatment. Since divorce is not regarded with favor, polygamy became accepted because neither the widow nor the orphans remain uncared for. Moreover, the fear that the husband might fornicate if his wife was sick or somehow incapable of satisfying his desires, led to greater tolerance toward polygamy. Studies on the impact of polygamy show that neither the women nor the children felt that polygamy had adverse effect on their wellbeing.[13] Nevertheless, the increasing power, which women constantly acquire in the Jordanian society, increases the opposition to this practice and its popularity continues to decline.

Like in every Arab country honor killing is an integral part of Jordanian culture and it is closely connected with the subordination of women and domestic violence. Jordan can be classified as 'neo-patriarchal'. Gender, class and proximity to the regime all determine the individual's position in the society.[14] Traditionally, the family occupies an important place in Jordanian society. A man's honor is closely tied to the conduct of the females in his household and among the relatives. The young women in the family are the responsibility of the father until they get married and become the responsibility of their husbands. Just like in all Arab countries, it is expected that women keep low profile, avoid being in public unless it is absolutely necessary, and stay hidden in the house. The Arabic term used for such woman is *mastura*, the connotation of which is not only "hidden" but also "decent," "dignified," and "honorable." In the family's view, *mastura* is a woman who did not lose her virginity, and once she is married must remain chaste, and there has to be a punishment if this honor code is violated.

If a violation was committed the honor of the family was at stake and the male members must take action against the perpetrator. The family's honor cannot be restored unless the woman who committed the violation is punished. On most occasions, the brothers take the initiative to punish the woman. Sometimes, the father goes after the perpetrator and sometimes a nephew. Knowledge about such violation normally occurs through rumors and the desire to maintain the family's reputation plays a role as well. Most the honor killings went unpunished even in modern times because the Penal Code was lenient toward the killers, and in many cases, sentences were commuted or reduced. The cultural environment in Jordan has always been such that the family had the absolute right to restore its honor, and killing the offender was the only way to achieve that. A married woman who committed adultery was delivered to her husband for punishment and if he killed her he was exercising his right.

Promulgated in 1953 Article 6 in the constitution guarantees the rights of all Jordanian citizens, regardless of gender. However, it stood in contrast to Article 340 of the Penal Code, which stated that "he who discovers his wife or one of his female relatives committing adultery with another, and he kills, wounds or injures one of both of them, is exempt from any penalty."[15]

Despite all attempts by feminists and liberals to resolve that issue, there was strong resistance on the part of Islamist Parliament members who feared that the abolition of this article in the penal code would lead to promiscuity and laxity of morals.

Other types of violence against women such as sexual assault and beating by husbands are common in Jordan and many of them are not reported. Most women are afraid of losing their rights to housing or custody, and therefore withdraw the charge before the case goes to court. So strong is the concept of family honor that it stands in the way of meaningful reform. The purity of women is not only a family value but a national one as well. Any attempt to change the status quo met stiff resistance by the Islamists. For example, the head of the Islamic Action, Abdul Latif Arabiyyat, once argued that those who raised the issue of honor killing are influenced by Western countries wishing to impose their values om Jordan.[16] Many Jordanians shared his view.

It is clear, however, that the judicial system was not willing to take the matter lightly and allow the perpetrators to go unpunished. One cannot find a single case between 1953 and 1965 in which article 340 of the Penal Code was applied. Moreover, we find many cases in which the Court of Cassation argued against the application of Article 98, which stated that the killer's sentence can be reduced if he killed in a "fit of fury."[17]

Statistics show that on average between 15 and 20 women are killed in Jordan every year.

It was not until the end of 2016 that the government decided to take actions against honor killing. In a landmark ruling on honor killing judge Muhammad Tarawneh of the Court of Cassation said, "We want to send a strong message to the people that killing women in the name of family honor will no longer be tolerated by the court."[18] This ruling doubled the sentences for two brothers who killed their sister with poison, after she fell in love and fled, from 7.5 years imprisonment to 15 for one, and from 10 years to 20 for the other. This ruling came as a result of a religious edict (*fatwa*) from December 2016, declaring for the first time that honor killing is against the *Sharia*. In July 2017, the Parliament abolished Article 98. However, Article 340 remained and it still allows a reduced sentence in certain cases.

Archaeological conservation and vernacular culture

Heritage conservation is dynamic process initiated by the state and in order to understand it one must take into consideration the political, social and economic dimensions of cultural change caused by that process. Heritage conservation can be defined as the ongoing management of change in the social environment.[19] The Jordanian state's attempt to extend its control over the country's modernization brought to a clash not only with entrepreneurs that sought to benefit from the process but also with local communities who were affected by the state's actions. Fearing that the state's projects and their impact on the national treasures, local and transnational civil society organizations began mobilizing in order to challenge the state's plans.[20]

Critics of Jordan's archaeological preservation argue that the government's projects are being approached as ordinary conservation plans, with no consideration to the local inhabitants or their culture; that the management of cultural resources has only recently been integrated into the scope of municipal planning practice; and that there are no clear guidelines that could avoid the adverse effect of the municipal planning on the local culture. They argue that the results of the government's policy was that during the 1980s, the previously harmonious coexistence of different cultures in places like Umm Qais was disrupted because some scholars and authority figures decided to prioritize one period of history at the expense of another.[21] Furthermore, they argued that during the process of reconstruction and renovation, the local inhabitants lost their occupations, and much of their land, and that all they received as compensation were low-paying jobs in the touristic spots, which they used to reside. There were those who argued that the government's reconstruction projects deprived the locals of their water, their animals, crops, and sometimes even their access to close relatives, and that this process led to the locals' alienation from their villages. Others argued that school closures forced the locals to move and seek other jobs; that there was no balanced interaction between the living cultural heritage and the new investment in tourism; that the profit motive caused the government to ignore their needs; that only powerful individuals with the ability to invest in the new structures could benefit; and that by doing so, the government sacrificed the authenticity and the continuity of the old culture.[22]

In their anthropological study on the impact of historical sites on Jordan's cultural heritage Shatha Abu-Khafajah and Shaher Rababeh argue that cultural heritage is created through the intangible. People's knowledge, feelings, memories and stories about the archaeological sites and their interaction with them, turn them into tangible experiences which become integrated into their cultural heritage.[23] Inhabitants living close to these sites told about their experience and the authors provide a few examples proving their point. When speaking about the Roman theater in Amman locals referred to it as *Darajat Fer'on* (Pharaoh's Steps). When asked by the authors why he called the site by that name, an old man replied:

> We know the Room [the Roman as mentioned in the Koran; the holy book of Islam] were here too. *Fer'on* had his cities and theatres built in Egypt and maybe Palestine, but not in here. We call in [in reference to the theatre] *daraj* [steps] because it looks like *daraj*, and we ascribe it to *Fer'on* because we know *Fer'on* more than we know the Romans…we know him very well…he is mentioned a lot in the Koran, and he was oppressive and if he built *daraj* [steps] they would be like these you see here.[24]

Similarly, a monument in Petra called by the locals *Qasr el-Bint* (the girl's palace) is associated with a story told by a middle-aged woman who told the authors that the girl was pharaoh's daughter who was married to a Nabatean king, and the palace was her wedding gift. She went on saying:

> The girl was so beautiful and the king has to impress her by building a palace for her that was not very different from her father's...We have lot of stories about the girl and her palace and servants and cloths, we tell them to our children. You might not agree, I know you won't. You people [scholars] have your own sources that are different from ours, but for us this place is about this pharaoh's daughter...just like nowadays, the girl must marry from someone who is as rich as her father, otherwise the husband will feel less and the marriage will crumble.[25]

Similar memories are associated with a bridge named after the al-Khalaeleh family that lived in Amman in the beginning of the twentieth century. The bridge was destroyed when the city expanded in the 1980s. Even though no one knows about that family the memory of the bridge became so ingrained in the minds of the local people. An old woman who was interviewed by the authors recalled vividly that there was abundance of rain at that time, and that there was a river where she and her family used to fish and added in a sad tone, "It is all gone Even the bridge is gone."[26]

Similarly, for the Circassian community in Amman, the Roman theater became a symbol of their heritage. An old Circassian told the authors,

> we [the Circassians] carried our culture, our religion, and fled Russia where we were oppressed, we settled first in here [Amman and the theatre] and established our culture in Jordan and as part of Jordan, this is our *turath* [heritage]...the theatre has special place in our hearts not because it is the theatre you see, but because it is part of our *turath*.[27]

Thus through their memories and their stories the Circassians turned an archaeological site into their cultural heritage.[28] This is a major problem which the Jordanian government continues to face when it attempts to preserve the country's cultural heritage. Its plans stand in contrast to the vernacular culture, which the inhabitants seek to preserve.

The reconstruction of tribal culture

Just like its attempt to use archeological sites in order to foster national identity capable of uniting the people, the government makes use of the tribal culture and its symbols to bolster its position in the country and to create a national identity. This is a continuous effort which often poses a challenge to the government. According to Linda Layne, the Jordanian tribes of the Jordan Valley respond to the denigration of their culture and its appropriation by the state as a key element of the national heritage, by reevaluating what their culture is, and by doing so, they use some of the same practices used by the state and the Jordanian intelligentsia in constructing the tribal representations of Jordan's past.[29] Cultural identity can be created by attaching special meaning to special items used by the tribes such as a certain type of dress or a certain kind of food, which is constantly put on display. One of the ways to establish a unique cultural identity is by attributing meaning to the *dilug*, the traditional embroidered dress of the tribes in the Jordan Valley. Over the years, this dress acquired a new meaning for the tribes and it defines the status of the woman wearing it. The more elaborate is the embroidery on the dress the greater is the respect that she gains in the eyes of the tribe. Thus, the *dilug* acquired a new meaning; it symbolizes the Arab character of the tribe and by extension, its Jordaniannes. Young women tend to wear it, and the positive response of the tribe encourages them to continue the practice. The same applies to other articles of clothing such as the scarf (*kufiyya*). Another method of culture reconstruction common among the tribes in this region is the customs of presenting cultural items in an exhibition. Large exhibitions such as the one held in the annual Jerash festival provides the right venue to present such items. This is also the place where members of the royal family appear, mainly in order to increase the power and prestige of the Hashemite family, and the country as a whole. Another method of reconstructing culture is by recounting the genealogies and the deeds of the past.[30]

The young generation of the tribes are aware of the danger that their cultural heritage might be lost, and therefore they use modern technology and the press in particular, in order to tell their history, which hitherto was transmitted by stories told orally. A case in point is Muhammad Hamdan, a member of the Adwan tribe of the Balqa, who tried to overthrow the Hashemites in 1923. Recalling how powerful was this tribe in the early days, he told Andrew Shryock:

> Today, Adwanis sit decorously in government councils, but in the not-so-distant past their grandfathers cut off the heads of Turkish Pashas, routed Bedouin armies ten times their size, and collected tribute to "the gates of Syria."[31] Hamdan regards himself as one who documents the tribe's spoken tradition, and thus serves as a preserver of Adwan culture. In this case as well, the indigenous or vernacular culture faces a situation where it is being appropriated by the state for its own benefit, and not for the tribes, and this continues to create tension between them and the royal culture.

The tent as a mirror of Bedouin vernacular culture

The tribes' identity continues to manifest itself not only in the manner in which they behave, but also in their belongings that shed light on their unique culture. Tribal culture can be understood by examining the manner in which the tribes construct their tents. The shape of their tent is a manifestation of the strength of the tribe's vernacular culture, which stood the test of time. Basing their argument on H. Lefebvre's assertion that space is a complex social product based on values and the social production of meanings, and D. Turton's argument that a place is inextricably tied to people's identity, Mahmoud Na'amneh, Mohammed Shunnaq, and Aysegul Tasbasi examined the unique features of the tent inhabited by the Huwaitat Bedouin community in southern Jordan and their conclusion was as follows:

> The Bedouin tent lies at the heart of the Bedouin lifestyle. Indeed, it is more than a simple shelter and place to sleep or meet guests. It is a whole sphere where sociocultural values are constantly produced and reproduced...the physical features of the tent reflect many aspects of the Bedouin socioeconomic realms and reveal many elements of the Bedouin culture in general.[32]

Anthropologists argue that people tend to shape building according to their cultural concepts and in turn are also affected by these shapes. Field research carried out by the authors concentrated on the tent and its structure among the Huwaitat tribe in of Wadi Rum and Petra. The Huwaitat tribe with its various branches constitute approximately 70 percent of the Bedouins in Jordan. The black tent is made of goat's hair which provide insulation from the desert's harsh environment. It has a roof, walls, poles, and guy ropes. The roof is a rectangular cloth supported in the center and at the edges by poles and anchored by guy ropes. The tent is normally divided into two sections by a woven curtain, which is suspended from the tent's poles. The tent consists of one or more poles, according to the size of the family. Most tents have two or three poles. The tent's blackness is a symbolical indication of detachment from Western culture.[33] While the location and the material from which the tent is built reflect pragmatic considerations such as adverse geographical and climatic conditions, the tent's interior is a reflection of the tribe's culture and social worldview. The first section is the place where men entertain visitors and it is usually left open during the day. The men's section has a fireplace with various utensils used to serve coffee to guests. Cushions, rugs and mattresses which are stored in the women's section are spread for the guests to lean on.

The other section belongs to the women where they prepare food, take care of the children and entertain friends. It is usually kept closed when strangers are likely to be around. The entire family sleeps in this section. Cooking utensils are usually kept in the women's section. The mattresses, quilts, and other items used for sleeping are usually piled up on the dividing wall of the tent.[34] This arrangement reflects the tribe's culture. This is clearly a patriarchal culture where men are at the top of the social pyramid. One of the most important cultural characteristics of the Bedouin tribe is hospitality and entertainment of guests. This is clearly seen in the men's section and the availability of the utensils necessary for serving the guests. The second section confines the women in their complimentary and traditional role as mothers and homemakers. Their section is isolated and strangers have no access to it. The tent's shape demonstrates the tribe's preference for privacy, and the nature of gender relations becomes clear. The dividing curtain is clearly an attempt to control the interaction between men and women. It is in the men's section that the discussions take place, and the flow of information proceeds from there. Women usually hear from men but not vice versa. Only older women can serve the men in their section. It is only in the evening that both men and women spend time together in the men's section.

The vernacular culture is represented by numerous items such as the coffee pot, the camel, and whatever else is used by the Bedouins. Even though many Bedouins try to adjust their lifestyle with modern equipment, they tend to maintain traditional customs. These items represent their old way of life, and one of the ways in which the state deal with the vernacular concepts of the tribes is to display them as national symbols.

Ceremonies and the adaptation of vernacular culture

Attempting to create a sense of national identity the Jordanian government has made a serious attempt to show respect to education. The way to achieve that was to have the state become involved in graduation ceremonies, to hold banquets and shower gifts on those whose educational achievements were the highest. Respect for knowledge is rooted in the vernacular culture since the early days of Islam. One of the chapters in the Qur'an reads as follows:

> Recite! And Your Lord is the Most Generous. Who has taught by the pen. He has taught man that which he knew not. (Qur'an, 96, Clot : 4–5).

Holding graduation ceremonies is one of the methods which the Jordanian crown is utilizing as an important component of the vernacular culture in order to acquire greater legitimacy and bolster its position in the country, and by doing so it transforms the vernacular into high culture.

The graduation ceremonies of the two oldest and best private secondary schools, the Aliya School for Girls and the Bishop School for boys, which serve about five percent of the Christian minority and the Muslim elite, serve as examples of the state's attempt to capitalize on an existing component of vernacular culture and take possession of it. The presence of the royal family, the high expenses invested in the rituals, and all the publicity given to these events attest to the great value that education occupies in Jordanian culture. The rituals attest not only to the knowledge but also to the social status that one obtains by acquiring education and this phenomenon manifests itself in the education of girls who are educated not necessarily in order to be prepared for the job market, but primarily to obtain a social status. The names of royal figures such as Princess Basma, King Hussein, and Prince Hassan were all mentioned in the ceremonies, which took place in 2006. These ceremonies, according to Willy Jansen who attended them, help enhance the social status of the family, especially for girls. Dressing the daughter for the events sends a message regarding the family's social status. Families go to a great length in order to educate their daughters and have them participate in such events, which associates them with royalty, and thereby makes their daughters no only more desirable as brides but also place them in a higher position on the social scale.[35] This is also another one of the myriad ways in which the Hashemite regime makes use of the vernacular culture by appropriating one of its most salient features.

Vernacular culture and the national economy

Vernacular culture has negative sides as well and these are often at odds with modern business practices. The clash between the vernacular features of the society and the requirements of modern life causes numerous problems. One of the areas in the economy that is mostly affected by vernacular elements is the banking system. Recently, the Jordanian banking sector has introduced the international Business Continuity Management (BCM) as a criterion and a way to improve the bank's operation, reduce risk, and avoid disaster or crisis. The application of this tool constitutes a serious problem for Jordanian banks. Primarily, because Islamic banks operate according to Islamic principles, and often they are reluctant to adopt regulations, which are incompatible with their tradition, particularly when these come from Western countries. Generally, Arab organizations are highly centralized, they have a clear hierarchy and there is little autonomy at the lower level. This is part of the vernacular culture which stands in the way of adopting such Western tool that requires employees at the lower level of the organization to assume greater responsibility, which makes it imperative to allow them greater autonomy.

In an interview designed to demonstrate the impact of cultural factor on the adoption of the BCM a respondent from a local Jordanian bank said, "We cannot operate in isolation from local traditions and the larger context of Arab culture, not just in terms of BCM, but also in terms of many other processes and banking services." Another respondent from a local Islamic bank argued in the similar vein saying, "The majority of our operations and banking services, including many aspects of BCM are conducted within an Islamic framework and according to Islamic principles and guidelines…such principles are considered as best practice in our bank."[36]

According to interviews conducted by Ihab Hanna S. Sawalha, John R. Anchor, and Julia Meaton, Arab culture and the local traditions affected not only application of the BCM but other banking services as well, such as international transactions and corporate communications. The conclusion that can be reached from these interviews is that vernacular Arab culture has considerable impact on Arab organizations, including financial ones. Similar conclusion was reached by the researchers R. Ababaneh, H. Sabri, A. Al-Rashid and G. Hofstede.[37]

The traditional background and the differences between the vernacular culture and the requirements of modern life had significant impact on the process by which the BCM was implemented. Other factors relating to the failure to implement the BCM were

> gender; CBJ (Central Bank of Jordan) and government-imposed restrictions; nature of corporate communications; level of financial openness; liberalization of banking operations and services; institutional environment and bureaucracy; geographical location of the branches of the bank in Jordan; religion; and the legal traditions of Jordan.[38]

Clearly, there are numerous customs and beliefs inherent in the vernacular culture that makes the attempt to introduce better banking practices by adhering to a modern criterion such as the BCM an impossible task.

The dilemma of disseminating the English Language

Another major problem, which the Jordanian government has to struggle with, is the English language whose widespread use has adverse effect on the vernacular culture. The consequences of heavy emphasis on the English language is that Arabic, which had been a vital component of the vernacular culture and which had been in use for many generations is adversely affected.

Interviews with Jordanian students have demonstrated that they regarded the use of English primarily as a way to achieve personal goals, and that they tried to reduce its influence on their children. They explained the necessity of using English by arguing that the need for advance technology forced them to learn foreign languages. At the same time, however, they complained that the widespread diffusion of the English language had adverse effect on their relationship to Arabic.[39] English occupies a prominent place in the Jordan's curriculum. Initially taught at schools in the beginning at the fifth grade, the current tendency is to begin teaching it at the first grade. The English language is widely used in higher education. Due to the paucity of educational opportunities, students seeking terminal degrees tend to pursue their studies overseas, primarily in English speaking countries. They justify their choice to pursue their education overseas by saying that degrees from foreign universities are more prestigious and that the demands that such schools have are far more rigorous than in Jordanian institutions. Furthermore, they rightfully argue that there are not too many schools in Jordan offering terminal degrees. As for the professors who participated in the study, they argued that publishing their works in English has greater impact on their career, since they have to reach the wider scholarly community overseas.

Recognizing the importance of the English language the government placed greater emphasis on its instruction and candidates at the MA level who wish to be accepted to doctoral programs must pass the Test of English for Foreign Language (TOEFL). Even those who do not continue their studies overseas spend considerable amount of time learning English. There is a keen awareness that the interaction with the West on which the Jordanian economy depends makes it imperative to know English, especially in areas such as engineering and other fields connected with high-tech. Besides, only a few books are published in Arabic, and the lack of textbooks makes it imperative to learn English. Even students who did not leave to country for their terminal degrees were exposed to their fields of study by instructors who studied overseas and there are numerous concepts that they need to become familiar with, which require knowledge of English. The fact that the government rewards English speakers and manifests itself by the rule that requires schools to give extra credit for publications in foreign journals, thereby forcing the students to gain better command of the English language. An archaeologist who was interviewed by Anne-Marie Pedersen expressed his view in the following words:

> So when you want to publish, you should publish in a refereed journal, and this journal should be listed in the international journals. I searched this one.

> I found a few related to my field of study. About 70% of your articles should be published in these things. And these are either in English or German or French, and a few are in Arabic, but in archaeology, all of them [are] in English. So if you want to be promoted, I'm assistant professor now, and I want [to be] promoted to be associated professor, I have to publish about 70% of my works in these journals in English. So they don't publish in Arabic. So it's a necessity.[40]

All the participants in the study felt that English enabled them to share their work with the academic community everywhere, and some even argued that they have a moral obligation to share their findings with foreign scholars. As one of the participants said,

> This is a science, and everyone has the right to take a look to this science, and to be sure that it will be available for at least 95% of the people who…[are] interested in this subject, I have to write in English.[41]

The results of the schools' requirements are that Arabic sources are less cited, and therefore are less likely to be listed among the international journals. One of the respondents described the cultural dilemma, saying that it creates a "closed circle whereby the scientist will find it easier to read, write, and teach in English, and hence avoid Arabic as much as possible and, in turn, never improve his mastery of the native language."[42] One of the participants admitted that he does not use Arabic as a language of communication with the scholarly community or even with his friends. He explicitly said,

> I don't know how to type in Arabic, and I am not interested in learning. My phone is…all the setting are in English. You will see a lot of people [with] the setting in Arabic. I can't. I don't understand it, operating systems in Arabic.[43]

Housewives find it difficult to resist their children's tendency to be spoken to in English. One of the respondents explained that her attempts to limit the incursion of English did not succeed, because all their favorite television programs are in English, and the nanny who spends most of the time with them is an English speaker. The dominance of the English language constitutes a cultural dilemma for many Jordanians who wish to preserve the Arabic language that constitutes an essential part of their culture. This dilemma is especially acute for those who left the country to obtain a terminal degree and were faced with the need to return home with their children. One of the respondents who decided to return with his children explained the dilemma saying:

> A lot of my friends, when I left America and decided to come home here, thought that I am weird because I always expressed to them the reason I left America is for… my kids. I want to give them the gift of Arabic language. Are you crazy? Who cares about the Arabic language? What did it do for you

> and things like that. I ...just can't comprehend such arguments because it's a beautiful language. I enjoy it and...so...so yes I came for my kids, and I came to give them the Arabic language.[44]

The response of each participant varied. Some argued that communicating in English does not mean accepting Western values. However, the vast majority were concerned that greater reliance on English had adverse effect on Arabic and clearly saw the connection between Arabic and Arab cultural identity. All the 14 who were interviewed, however, justified the use of the English language by saying that this was merely a utilitarian practice that does necessarily imply accepting British or American values, and that they are using a language adopted by the scholarly community. Many stated that communicating with other scholars in their field would simply be impossible without English. Given the fact that Arabic is a main component of the vernacular culture, which all Jordanians seek to preserve, the discourse regarding the use of English is unlikely to end.

High culture in Jordan

Jordan's achievements in high culture are quite impressive for a country with limited resources. The Hashemite regime, which faced numerous challenges since the very beginning, was hardly in a position to support cultural centers or to provide financial assistance to talented men and women. The area allotted to the Hashemite family by Great Britain was mostly desert. The country's primary need was to establish a national economy and to build an army, literally from scratch. Given the hostility of the Arab nationalist movement in Syria, which did not regard the Hashemites as the rightful owners of the country, and the hostility of powerful tribes such as the Adwan, the imperative of the moment was to invest in building a loyal and powerful military force and little was left for investment in culture. Besides, the British who were instrumental in building the Arab Legion were in no position to provide substantial financial aid and the revenues from commerce were meager. This state of affairs continued and even worsened following the establishment of the state of Israel, which brought the Hashemites to invest more resources in national defense. This explains why the investment in culture remained minimal, and it took many years until the kingdom developed keen interest in the arts. Nevertheless, achievements were made in a few areas of high culture and poetry in particular. There were some achievements in arts and crafts, but there was little progress in cinema or in music, and these are the fields to which the following section is devoted.

The Jordanian theater

The Jordanian theater began prior to the country's independence and was meant to entertain the public, without serious messages or criticism, and it was only later that playwrights began exploiting this medium to make political or social statements. One of the reasons for the slow development of the critical theater was the strict censorship imposed by the authorities. Generally, the official censor is the Ministry of Culture but the playwrights, the directors, the press and the audience, all take part in the process. Any play considered indecent, anti-religious, or offensive to the public is banned. Plays that raise political or social issues, which might compromise national security, are banned as well. For example, plays that dealt with the events that took place in 1970, when King Hussein unleashed his campaign against the PLO, were not allowed to be performed. Likewise, plays that demonstrated sympathy toward Egyptian President Nasser, the Ba'th regimes of Syria and Iraq, or those that portrayed socialism in a positive light were censored heavily. The same can be said about Russian plays. Particularly sensitive were the censors when it came to plays that portrayed the Hashemite monarchy in a negative light.

Playwrights had virtually no way to express themselves freely until 1989, when democracy was restored but even then, the entire personnel involved in the production had to be vigilant, especially when the issue affected the country's defense and foreign relations. For example, when Iraq invaded Kuwait in 1990, the government did not allow criticism of Saddam Hussein. Nevertheless, the march toward democracy left its mark on the theater and the artists became more open and daring in their criticism. In 1991, Mohammed al-Shwaqfeh wrote the play *Zaman al-Shaqlabah* (The Epoch of Chaos), which dared to criticize the government. In 1993, he wrote the play *Hi America*, which criticized the Jordanian public for being hypocritical, showing those who demonstrated against the United States standing on line at its embassy to obtain a visa. Produced in 1994, his next play *Hi Muwatin* (Hi Citizen) presented his view of the peace treaty with Israel, which was different from that of the government. Written in 1996, his play *Muwatin Hasab al-Talab* (Citizens by Order) criticized the manner in which the government dealt with the bread riots, and in the play *Ila man La Yahummou al-amr* (To Whom It May Not Concern), which he wrote in 1998, he concentrated on the economic distress and criticized Israel's procrastination in signing the peace treaty with Jordan.[45]

Criticism of the society and the government is obvious in the performance of small groups of performers. The most prominent examples of such performances of the duo Nabil and Hisham in which Nabil Swalha and Hisham Yunis poke fun at institutions and individuals. Their best known works are *'Alami Jadid* (A New World Order), *Barlaman wa Mizaniya* (Parliament and Budget), *Ahlan, Mu'tamar Arabi* (Wecome, An Arab Conference), and *La Tadḥak Nahnu Urduniyun* (Don't Lough: We Are Jordanians). They discuss numerous topics and democratization looms large in their performances.[46]

Literature, cinema, arts, and music

Discussing Jordanian literature in isolation from the rest of the Arab world, especially Palestine, is an impossible task since many Jordanians are of Palestinian origin, and Jordan's culture is very similar to its Arab neighbors. For the sake of convenience however, one needs to include literary figures on both banks of the Jordan River. One of the main themes portrayed by Jordanian poets and novelists is the eviction from Palestine, the suffering that accompanied the departure, life outside this country, and the yearning to return to it. Just like the rest of the Arab world the dominant literary genre is poetry. Jordan's early poetry consisted of old melodies recited in numerous events such as wedding, funerals and so forth. Many of them are told in coffee shops, markets, and other public places, and often in private meetings. These poems deal with numerous issues such as love for the country or the tribe, love of a man to a woman, or simply stories about the tribe's ancestors and their heroic deeds. One of the most popular are old love poems such as *Antar and 'Abla* written by the sixth-century poet 'Antarah Ibn Shaddad ('Antar). This is a poem about 'Antar, a black slave who was prevented from marrying his beloved Abla and it describes his agony and yearning to reunite with his sweetheart Abla. The poem reads in part:

> O dwelling of Abla in the valley of Gawa
> speak to me for my camel and I salute you
> White and purple are the lilies of the valley
> but Abla is a branch of flowers
> Who will guide me to the dwelling of Abla?

Such stories constituted material for the traditional poetry, which was transmitted orally and rarely written down. It was only during the first half of the twentieth century that modern poetry in Jordan evolved. Foremost among the Jordanian poets was Ibrahim Tuqan (1905–1941), the modernist who wrote love poems as well as nationalist ones. His poems express themes such as disdain of corrupt politicians, and despair caused by the Palestinian tragedy. Published in 1955, his *Diwan* is a manifestation of his ardent love for his country, and his genuine concern for its future. Known as the "The poet of Palestine" he enjoyed wide reputation both in Jordan and outside.[47] His daughter and follower Fadwa Tuqan (b. 1917) was a fiery poetess known for her collection *Alone with Days* (1952), which vividly expresses her feeling of dispossession, anxiety, emptiness, and hope. One of the most well-known of her poems is *Perplexed Nostalgia*, which reads in part

> My soul is torn, tortured
> in its longing, in its enigmatic desire,
> Driven by a nostalgia for the unknown
> through the walls of its solitude,
> Nostalgia for what I do not comprehend
> calls in it the soundless isolation,
> It is nature which is calling?
> Is it life urging her daughter?
> What do I feel? This feeling of a lost
> soul, suffering in her perplexity

Important innovations in poetry took place when she was active. Among these were the use of irregular feet and the abandonment of monorhyme (in which every single line of the poem has the same rhyming sound at the end of the verse) that was used extensively in the classical verse. Her second volume *I found It*, includes similar themes and symbols.[48] Her subsequent volumes such as *Give Us Love* and *Before the Closed Door* were written in 1967 and, The *Night and the Knights* in 1969. Another famous poetess was her friend Salma al-Khaḍra al-Jayyusi who was influenced by foreign poets such George Eliot, Dylan Thomas, Garcia Lorca, Charles Baudelaire, and St-John Perse, and she used more new technics than her older friend. One of her best collection is *Returning from the Dreaming Spring* (1960), which includes the poem *Without Roots* in which she describes the dilemma of a Palestinian refugee who was left abandoned and was yearning for repatriation. Her poetry, as Alwan noted, is more similar to the Tamuziyyun poets of Syria, Lebanon, an Iraq than to her Jordanian compatriot.

Another poet who was highly preoccupied with the Palestine refugee theme was Harun Hashim Rashid. Some of his themes written in the middle and late 1950s, included *With the Stranger*; *The Return of the Stranger*; *Gaza in the Firing Line*; *The Land Revolutions*; *Until our People Return*; and *The Ship of Anger*. According to Alwan, his poetry is traditional and its lacks the depth and vision of his contemporary poets. Other poets of note are Ali Hashim Rashid whose *Candle on the Way* is worthy of note and Abd al-Karim al-Karmi known as Abu Salma who is famous for his poem *The Refugee* (1953). According to Alwan, he is capable of writing splendid lyrical poems. Other poets who dealt with the Palestine refugee theme were Ahmad Fahmi whose work *The Dream of Return* (1957); Mahmoud al-Ḥut's *Arab Comedy*, and Kamal Naṣir's *The Wounds Are Stinging* are also worthy of note.[49]

In the aftermath of the Six-Day War of 1967 in which Jordan lost East Jerusalem to Israel, a different type of poetry emerged. It was dubbed "The Poetry of Resistance" and defined at as "an expression of rejection of the status quo." The young poets who embraced this kind of poetry include Samiḥ al-Qasim, Maḥmoud Darwish, Tawfiq Zayyad, Mu'in Basisu, Rashid Ḥusayn, Salim Jubran, Fawzi Jirayyis, and others. Al-Qasim is one of the most outstanding in this group. He uses images from the Hebrew and the Christian scriptures. In his poem, *In the Twentieth Century* from *Songs of the Trails* he writes: "Many centuries ago/I was a poet/ in the circle of dervishes/but I am a rebellious volcano/in the twentieth century." In Alwan's estimation, his long poem *Iram* is an impressive tour de force. After a prolog, the poem is followed by four songs: *The Song of the Age—The Search for Paradise*; *The Song of the Priests—The Heroes with Banners*; *The Song of War—Hiroshima*, and *The Song of the New Man*, which was highly inspired by the existentialist Jean Paul Sartre and the surrealist Pablo Neruda. This is essentially a poetic narration of world history, and the utopia that would follow.[50] In other poems, such as *On the Memory of al-Ma'taṣim*, *Layla of Aden*, *From the Diary of Job*, and *Pslam, Iskanderun and Children of Rafah*, al-Qasim relies on myths from ancient Egyptian, Babylonian, and mythologies.[51] Another poet who had written poems against the existing order was Tawfiq Zayyad who used Palestinian expressions and proverbs in his fiery poems. However, aside from the three volumes *Warmly I Shake Your Hands*, *Bury Your Dead* and *Songs of Revolution and Anger* written in 1969 and 1970, there was little interest in them.

Mahmoud Darwish is known for his beautiful love poems such as *Birds without Wings, My Beloved Wakes from Her Sleep* or his revolutionary ones such as *A Lover from Palestine* and *Wing by the Light of the Gun* but he is best known best for poems such as *Quatrains, Lorca*, and *Diary of a Palestinian Wound.* Another fiery poet whose work did not obtain much appreciation was Tawfiq Sayigh who published his *Thirty Poems* (1954) in a free verse style, which was difficult for the general public to identify with. Also important to mention is the poet and novelist Jabra Ibrahim. He translated many works of European origin and his poems have symbolic and Christian content. However, his main contribution to Arab literature was in fiction. His earliest novelette *Scream in a Long Night* (1955) about the life of a Palestinian young man shows the impact, which foreign literary figures such as James Joyce and Virginia Woolf had on him, and it constitutes the first time that the stream-of-consciousness technique was used in Arabic. His second novel *Hunters in the Narrow Street* is about an Arab Christian from Jerusalem who goes to Baghdad to tutor Sulafa, a young woman with whom he falls in love but at the same time he was seduced by her aunt Salma. In addition to the love story, the novel portrays life in Baghdad in great detail. Another one of his novels is *The Ship*, which tells a similar love story that takes place on a ship cruising the Mediterranean, and sheds light on the Arab society and its values.

According to Alwan, Jordan did not produce many novels and the collection of shorts stories such as Nabil Khuri's *Blasphemy* (1952), Muhammad Adib al-Amiri's *Ray of Light* (1953), and Muhmoud Sayf ad-Din al-Irani's *With the People* (1955) and *How Cheap* (1962) are mediocre and have little artistic merit. There are a few exceptions, such as the works of Najati Sidqi, Isa an-Nauri, Samirah Azzam, and Ghassan Kanafani, most of which tell about the Palestinian refugees and their tribulations, incorporating a love story against that background.[52]

Muhammad Fanatil al-Hajaya is one of the most popular poets in Jordan today. More than any other poet, his poetry expresses the frustrations and fears of the contemporary Arab world. His poem *The West's Crafty Men* expresses anger at foreign rulers whom he regards as making policy that ignores the Arabs. It sheds lights on the main events and personalities causing anxiety among the Arabs such as the Russian leader Vladimir Putin who in the poet's opinion was tricked by the West to intervene on Syria's behalf and prop Bashar al-Assad's regime. The poet's message is that Israel is the beneficiary of all the chaos in the Middle East. Moreover, he vents his anger at Iran whose leaders exploit Arab weakness and intervene in Lebanon in support of Hezbollah and in Yemen in support of the Houthis. Above all, he is angry about the loss of Jerusalem, and at the Security Council, which in his view does not fulfill its duty to bring justice. Though lengthy, this poem is worthwhile to quote:

> The West crafty men laid a trap, and Putin fell in
> They messed with his mind the way Spaniards mess with bulls
> Putin went to save a man who slaughtered half his people
> And the chaos is helping out the Balfour Declaration
> The Persians are playing the same game
> Divvying up the land and the work and the roles

A conspiracy against the Arabs, so hard for us to bear
A dish of politics cooked up by one thousand specialists
For them we're just a plate of food, their greed for which has increased
With our divided opinions and broken power
The Arabs' Baghdad? A Zoroastrian hyena-wolf is tearing it to pieces
The Levant? Now a rabid bear's slice of the pie
Lebanon? Nasrallah and Hezbollah are mangling it
Yemen? Contracted out to the Houthis
Every form of evil has been sowed in the Arabs' lands
Sectarian strife has increased, and blood is being spilled in vain
Jerusalem? Our generation haven't even heard of it
An old nakba is waiting for a cast of falcons
A world of injustice, convinced we Arabs have no rights
For that world, injustice is the principle, a way, a constitution
Oh Security Council, you're also just a game
And I hereby witness that you're a council of injustice and oppression

Contemporary Jordanian poets seek to express their feelings freely on foreign and domestic issues and sometimes risk arrest by the government. One of the most famous cases demonstrating that risk was the poet Ibrahim Nasrallah (b. 1954) who was accused by the government for writing on themes relating to national security. His reference to the events of September 1970, when King Hussein crushed the Palestinians, triggered a quick response by the government. Published in 1984, his poetry collection *Nu'man Yastariddu Lawnahu* (Nu'man Regains Its Color) was banned. And when he published his novel *Tuyur al-Hadhar* (Birds of Caution) in 1996, the censor decided to ban it as well because it mentioned the events of Black September.[53] In 2006, he was charged for insulting the state. It was only after intervention from literary groups in Jordan and overseas that he survived the accusations. Another poet facing the same problem is Aysha el-Shamayleh who was born in Jordan and went to study in the United States where she became engaged in slamming poetry criticizing her country for issues such as sexual harassment and domestic violence.

Other literary figures include Elias Farkouh (b. 1948) whose *The Land of Purgatory* is regarded as one of the best Arabic novels. Jamal Naji (b. 1954) is well-known for his novel *When the Wolves Grow Old*; Ahmad Nasser (b.1955) is known for his poem collection *Shepherd of Solitude* and his novel, *Land of no Rain*; Fadia Faqir (b. 1956) is known for her novel *Nisanit*, which discusses the impact of the Israeli-Palestinian conflict, *Pillars of Salt* which deals with Jordan in the colonial era, and her most famous novel is *My name Is Salma* describing the life of an Arab woman who was forced to flee to the West. One should also mention Hisham Bustani (b. 1975) whose three collections of short fiction *Of Love and Death, The Monotonous Chaos of Existence* and *The Perception of Meaning* turned him into one of the most talented writers of the young generation.

Haider Mahmoud's poem about violations of human rights and social injustices led to unrest in Jordan in 1989. Samer Raimouny's poem *Of Strength and Sakina* extolls the virtues of the terminally ill patients who suffer from disease that cannot be treated. His poem *Diaspora of the Soul: The Taboo of Allau Akbar*, which he had written in 2005 and was not allowed to be recited, was about human rights violation in Jordan. He also describes the attitudes that people have toward the country that he loves. His poem *Green Palms...Ode to the Land* reads in part:

Some say it is the Holyland.
Others say it is the Middle East's lifeline,
The paradigm of achievable expanses…
While others remain in doubt of all its realistic stances.
Others not really forming an opinion...
Not hot-spotted enough to be given their glances.

The poet and political activist from Jerash, Ali Taha Alnobani (b. 1968) was inspired by a cosmopolitan vision of peace and camaraderie and therefore his poems lack the excessive emphasis on Arab nationalism, which characterizes the poems written by others. The major themes in his poetry are love, brotherhood and democracy, which he aspires to spread throughout the world. His poem *I'm to Leave Now* reads in part:

I'm to leave now.
Can I have a deep look at your eyes?
Can I take my dreams, your smile
And my dried red rose?
Can I keep your image in my mind?

Nesma Alnsour is a contemporary poet and human rights activist who shares her thoughts and beliefs in a better and more humane society. She writes in her poem *Thoughts* how she hopes that her poetry would move people to act for the benefit of the society. It reads in part:

Many times I've seen a dream
Tonight I give the world my sight
Paper and ink will be my knight
Hazy visions of the night
Help me see the light
Words carved in my heart
Sky bleeding in my eyes
Feather is my soul
Ink is my path
Paper is my life

There are many more Jordanian poets such as Mustafa Wahbi al-Tal and younger ones such as Rasha Awale, Rula Hijazi, Ammar Khammash, Mohannad Khufash, Sayf Mahasneh, Hayfa Nuyu, Samar Saleh, Dalia Shahein, and most of them portray their inner struggle for personal desires as well as for the good of the society.

Films made in the Arab world were popular in Jordan from the very beginning. They dealt not only with political and cultural themes of the time, but also with the ideological and intellectual trends that dominated the Arab world since at the beginning of the nineteenth century.[54] Cinema did not begin in Jordan until recently. Aged Jordanians are accustomed to watch movies produced mainly in Egypt and Lebanon, while the youth watch imported Western movies, mainly from the United States. Also popular are Palestinian films, particularly those dealing with the tragedy of the Palestinian people. In fact, the Palestinians were the ones that stimulated the development of the Jordanian cinema. There are indications that the Palestinian producer Ibrahim Hassan Sirḥan directed, filmed, or participated in a film production in 1957, but there is no definite proof for that. The film *The Struggle in Jarash* that was produced in that year in Jordan was an adventure that did not relate to the Palestinian issue. However, the government prohibited its release believing that it defamed the city of Jarash. It was released later and became the first Jordanian film. The second film *My Home, My Love* was released in 1964 and its producer was the Palestinian Abdallah Ka'wash. It played in Jordan's main cities.[55] Palestinian producers like Mustafa Abu-Ali and Hani Johariya lived and worked in Jordan where they met Sulafa Jadallah Mirsal. Both worked for the Jordanian television from which they obtained cameras and other filming equipment. Following the battle in al-Karameh in 1968, they presented photographs showing the fighting that took place in al-Wahdat refugee camp in Amman.[56]

Palestinian films first made their appearance in Jordan shortly after the Six-Day War. The film *Say No to the Peaceful Solution* (1968) was screened in Amman to an audience of top Fatah members. The film was screened in an attempt to have the opinion of the political leaders before releasing it to the general public. Many of the films screened in Jordan are foreign importation. The bulk of these films come from Western countries, and the United States in particular. Prior to screening, all films must obtain the approval of a censorship board appointed by the prime minister. The Amman Filmmakers Cooperative has been promoting filmmaking until 2003, when the Royal Film Commission was established. Three of the ten films produced in Jordan in 2007 were Jordanian. In the following year, Jordan established the Red Sea Institute of Cinematic Arts and it offers an MA degree in cinema and fine arts. The outstanding film *Theeb* was produced in Jordan in 2015. It was directed by Naji Abu Nowar and it portrays a young man guiding a British officer in Hejaz during World War I.

Jordan cannot be treated as a unique country in the Middle East. This is largely because it had been part of Syria. Its language is Arabic which is spoken in the rest of the Middle East and just like all Arab countries, its tradition is based on Islam, the Qur'an, and oral tradition. Therefore, Jordanian culture can be regarded as just another shade of the common Arab tradition. Jordanians read Arab literature written in neighboring countries such as the West Bank, Gaza, Iraq, Syria, and the Gulf states. Similarly, they watch films produced in other Arab countries and their art works are similar to theirs. Consequently, it is nearly impossible to identify an art work as purely Jordanian. This is particularly the case in popular arts and in objects made of pottery, glasswork, tapestry, and weaving, which are similar to those produced in Syria, Palestine, and other places along the Mediterranean shore.[57] Numerous works of metal are made for daily use such as pots, coffeepots, trays, or jewelry items such bracelets, earrings, pendants, and even glass works bear strong Syrian influence. Most of these works are used by ordinary people and not only by the elites. Tapestry works made on traditional looms as well as leather works tend to have a similar design to that of Syria. Also common are shell works used for decoration. Numerous such works are made in traditional workshops, and many of them bear signs of the cultural impact that the West have on Jordan.

The modern art movement began in Jordan in the late 1950s, when students of the Russian artist George Aleef such as Rafiq Lahham, Muhanna al-Dura, and Suha Katibah Noursi learned the basic technics of watercolor and painting, and inspired others such Princess Wijdan Ali, Nawal Abdallah, and Khalid Khreis. Some of them were inspired by the European artistic trends, while others such as Wijdan tended to paint in the traditional Islamic style.

Traditional songs and tunes are still popular in Jordan. Many of them are sung on special occasions such as weddings, funerals, holidays and so forth. It is difficult to trace the origins of these songs and some of them are popular in other countries throughout the Arab world. While Western music is built on full tone and half tone intervals, Arab music has quarter tones and three-quarter tones, and the unlike Western music, the emphasis is not on harmony but on rhythm and melody. A special feature of Jordanian music was the *hajin*, which are songs composed by camel drivers, which are set according to the camel's movement rhythm. Another musical style is known as the *shruqi*, which is probably Lebanese in origin, and used to accompany a dance. Other types of folk songs are the *ataba*, *mijana*, *qasida*, and *mana*. Also popular are religious songs, which are recited during services and celebrations. The musical instruments used for these purposes are the traditional ones used throughout the Arab world such as a reed flute (*nay*), a one string violin (*rababa*), a lute (*ud*), a harp (*qanun*), and percussion instruments such as *daff*, *riqq*, and *darbaka*.[58]

Following the colonial age, Egypt became the musical center of the Arab world. Egyptian artists such as Muhammad Abd al-Wahhab, Umm Kulthum, Fairuz, Asmahan, and Abd al-Halim Hafiz became popular in Jordan, as they did throughout the entire Arab world. However, Jordan did not have artists of such high caliber. During the 1970s, a new blend of Western and Arab songs became known as Arabic pop. These were Western style songs with Arab instruments and lyrics. By the 1980s, Western instruments were added such as the electric guitar and drums. The availability of discs and other Western innovations such as the walkman and better recording devices increased the popularity of Western music, and it is quite rare to hear the new generation of the twenty-first century singing Arabic songs. There are numerous artists in every field in Jordan. Given the fact that the country's resources are limited, its cultural achievements are by no means negligible.

Notes

1 Margaret Lantis, "Vernacular Culture," *American Anthropology*, Vol. 62, No. 2 (April 1960), p. 202.

2 Kingston Wm. Heath, "Defining the Nature of Vernacular," *Material Culture*, Vol. 35, No. 2 (Fall 2003), p. 48.

3 Cofin Nicholson, "Vernacular Poetry," *The Edinburgh Introduction to Studying English Literature*, Edited by Dermot Cavanagh, Alan Gillis, Michelle Keown, James Loxley and Randall Stevenson (Edinburgh: Edinburgh University Press, 2014), p. 88.
4 David Byrne, "Vernacular Culture and Nationalism," http://davidbyrne.com/journal/vernacular-culture-and-Nationalism, February 22, 2016.
5 Aseel Al-Ramahi, "*Wasta* in Jordan: A Distinct Feature of (and Benefit for) Middle Eastern Society," *Arab Law Quarterly*, Vol. 22 (2008), p. 35.
6 Cited *Ibid*, p. 25.
7 Yoav Alon, *The Making of Jordan: Tribes, Colonialism and the Modern State* (London: I.B. Tauris, 2007), p. 1. Cited in Al-Ramahi, p. 43.
8 Al-Ramahi, pp. 47–48.
9 Basem Skijha and Sa'eda Kilani, *Wasta in Jordan: The Declared Secret* (Amman: Jordan Press Foundation, 2002). Cited in Al-Ramahi, p. 52.
10 Al-Ramahi, p. 55.
11 Samira Alayan and Naseema Al-Khalidi, "Gender and Agency in History, Civics, and National Education Textbooks of Jordan and Palestine," *Journal of Educational Media, Memory and Society*, Vol. 2, No. 1 (Spring 2010), p. 90.
12 Robert B. Cunningham, "Dimensions of Family Loyalty un the Arab Middle East: The Case of Jordan," *The Journal of Developing Areas*, Vol. 8, No. 1 (October 1973), p. 60.
13 Omar M. Khasawneh, Abdul Kareem Yacin Hijazi and Nassmat Hassan Salman, "Polygamy and Its Impact on the Upbringing of Children," *Journal of Comparative Family Studies*, Vol. 42, No. 4 (2011), p. 573.
14 Fadia Faqir, "Interfamily Femicide in Defence of Honour: The Case in Jordan," *Third World Quarterly*, Vol. 22, No. 1 (2001), p. 65.
15 Cited *Ibid*, p. 72.
16 *Ibid*, p. 77.
17 Lama Abu Odeh, "Honor Killing and the Construction of Gender in Arab Societies," *The American Journal of Comparative Law*, Vol. 58, No. 4 (Fall 2010), p. 924.
18 Rothna Begum, "How to End 'Honor' Killing in Jordan," https://www.hrw.org/news/2017/04/03/how-end-honor-killings-jordan April 3, 2017.
19 Rami Farouk Daher, "Centrification and the Politics of Power, Capital and Culture in an Emerging Jordanian Heritage Industry," *Traditional Dwellings and Settlements Review*, Vol. 10, No. 2 (Spring 1999), p. 33.
20 Waleed Hazbun, *Beaches, Ruins, Resorts: The Politics of Tourism in the Arab World* (Minneapolis: University of Minnesota Press, 2008), p. 134.
21 Daher, p. 37.
22 *Ibid*, pp. 42–43.
23 Shatha Abu-Khafarjah and Shaher Rababeh, "The Silence of Meanings in Conventional Approaches to Cultural Heritage in Jordan," *Safeguarding Intangible Cultural Heritage*, Edited by Michelle L. Stefano, Peter Davis and Gerard Corsane (Suffolk, UK: Boydel & Brewer, 2012), p. 81.
24 Cited *Ibid*, p. 77. [Parentheses are in the text].
25 Cited *Ibid*, p. 78. [Parentheses are in the text].
26 Cited *Ibid*, p. 79.
27 Cited *Ibid*, p. 80.
28 *Ibid*, p. 80.
29 Linda L. Payne, "Reconstructing Culture and Tradition in the Valley," *Home and Homeland: The Dialogue of Tribal and National Identities in Jordan* (Princeton, NJ: Princeton University Press, 1994), p. 128.
30 *Ibid*, pp. 130, 135.
31 Andrew Shryock, "Tribes and the Print Trade: Notes from the Margins of Literature in Jordan," *American Anthropologist*, Vol. 98, No. 1 (March 1996), p. 28.
32 Mahmoud Na'amneh, Mohammed Shunnaq and Aysegul Tasbasi, "The Modern Sociocultural Significance of the Bedouin Tent," *Nomadic Peoples*, Vol. 12, No. 1 (2008), p. 150.

33 *Ibid*, p. 154.
34 *Ibid*, p. 155.
35 Willy Jansen, "Ceremonies of Learning and Status in Jordan," *Cultural Styles of Knowledge Transformation: Essays in Honor of Ad Borsboom*, Edited by Jean Kommers and Eric Venbrux (Amesterdam, The Netherlands: Amsterdam University Press, 2008), p. 63.
36 Ihab Hanna S. Sawalha, John R. Anchor and Julia Meaton, "Business Continuity Management in Jordanian Banks: Some Cultural Considerations," *Risk Management*, Vol. 14, No. 4 (November 2012), pp. 316–317.
37 *Ibid*, p. 317.
38 *Ibid*, p. 321.
39 Anne-Marie Pedersen, "Negotiating Cultural Identities through Language: Academic English in Jordan," *College Composition and Communication*, Vol. 62, No. 2 (December 2010), p. 286.
40 Cited *Ibid*, p. 294.
41 Cited *Ibid*, p. 292.
42 Cited *Ibid*, p. 295.
43 Cited *Ibid*, p. 296.
44 Cited *Ibid*, p. 298.
45 Muhammad Qasem al-Hamad, *Translation and Censorship with Special Reference to Jordan*, Unpublished Dissertation, University of Edinburgh, 2001. pp. 170–172.
46 *Ibid*, pp. 172–173.
47 M. Bakir Alwan, "Contemporary and Jordanian Literature: Fractured Vision," *Books Abroad*, Vol. 46, No. 2 (Spring 1972), p. 219.
48 *Ibid.*
49 *Ibid*, p. 220.
50 *Ibid*, p. 221.
51 *Ibid*, p. 222.
52 *Ibid*, p. 225.
53 Richard Lee, "Writing of Jordan, Dreaming of Palestine," *The Guardian*, January 29, 2007.
54 Malek Khoury, "Origins and Patterns in the Discourse of New Arab Cinema," *Arab Studies Quarterly*, Vol. 27 (Winter/Spring 2005), p. 1.
55 Nurith Gertz and George Khleifi, *Palestinian Cinema: Landscape, Trauma and Memory* (Edinburgh, Scotland: Edinburgh University Press, 2008), pp. 19–20.
56 *Ibid*, pp. 20–21.
57 Raphael Patai, *Kingdom of Jordan* (Princeton, NJ: Princeton University Press, 1958), p. 263.
58 *Ibid*, pp. 265–267.

Selected Bibliography

Abdullah II, King of Jordan, *Our Last Best Chance: A Story of War and Peace* (London: King's Academy, Inc., 2011).

Abu Lebdeh, Hatem Shareef, *Conflict and Peace in the Middle East: National Perceptions and United States-Jordan Relations* (Lanham, MD: University Press of America, 1997).

Abu Nowar, Maan, *The Development of Trans-Jordan 1929-1939: A History of the Hashemite Kingdom of Jordan* (Reading, Berkshire, UK: Ithaca Press, 1999).

Abu- Nowar, Maan, *The Jordanian-Israeli War, 1948–1951: A History of the Hashemite Kingdom of Jordan* (Reading, Berkshire, UK: Ithaca Press, 1999).

Abu Nowar, Maan, *The Struggle for Independence 1939–1947: A History of the Hashemite Kingdom of Jordan* (Reading, Berkshire, UK: Ithaca Press, 2001).

Abu-Odeh, Adnan, *Jordanians, Palestinians & the Hashemite Kingdom in the Middle East Peace Process* (Washington, DC: United States Institute of Peace Press, 1999).

Allinson, Jamie, *The Struggle for the State in Jordan: The Social Origins of Alliances in the Middle East* (London: I.B. Tauris, 2016).

Alon, Yoav, *The Making of Jordan: Tribes, Colonialism and the Modern State* (London: I.B. Tauris, 2009).

Alon, Yoav, *The Shaykh of Shaykhs: Mithqal al-Fayiz and Tribal Leadership in Modern Jordan* (Stanford, CA: Stanford University Press, 2016).

Anderson, S. Betty, *Nationalist Voices in Jordan: The Street and the State* (Austin: University of Texas Press, 2005).

Ashton, Nigel, *King Hussein of Jordan: A Political Life* (New Haven, CT: Yale University Press, 2008).

Bacik, Gokhan, *Hybrid Sovereignty in the Arab Middle East: The Cases of Kuwait, Jordan, and Iraq* (New York: Palgrave Macmillan, 2008).

Bailey, Clinton, *Jordan's Palestinian Challenge, 1948–1983: A Political History* (New York: Routledge, 1984).

Ben-Zvi, Abraham, *The Origins of the American-Israeli Alliance: The Jordanian Factor* (New York: Routledge, 2007).

Berdine, Michael D., *Redrawing the Middle East: Sir Mark Sykes, Imperialism and the Sykes-Picot Agreement* (London: I.B. Tauris, 2018).

Bienkowski, Piotr, *Early Edom and Moab* (Sheffield, UK: Sheffield Academic Press, 1992).

Blackwell, Stephen, *British Military Intervention and the Struggle for Jordan* (New York: Routledge, 2009).

Bradshaw, Tancred, *Britain and Jordan: Imperial Strategy, King Abdullah I and the Zionist Movement* (London: I.B. Tauris, 2012).

Clark, Janine A., *Local Politics in Jordan and Morocco: Strategies of Centralization and Decentralization* (New York: Columbia University Press, 2018).

Curtis, R. Ryan, *Jordan and the Arab Uprisings: Regime Survival and Politics Beyond the State* (New York: Columbia University Press, 2018).

Dallas, Ronald, *King Hussein: A Life on the Edge* (London: Profile Books, 1999).

Faulkner, Neil, *Lawrence of Arabia's War: The Arabs, the British and the Remaking of the Middle East in WWI* (New Haven, CT: Yale University Press, 2016).

Fromkin, David, *A Peace to End All Peace: The Fall of the Ottoman Empire and the Creation of the Middle East* (New York: Henry Holt and Company, 1989).

Havrelock, Rachel, *River Jordan: The Mythology of a Dividing Line* (Chicago: University of Chicago Press, 2011).

Hubbard, Laurence, *A History of Aqaba in the Hashemite Kingdom of Jordan: From The Edomites to the Resurgence of the Church in Modern Times 2000 BC -2000 AD* (London: Choir Press, 2020).

Hussein, King, *Uneasy Lies the Head: The Autobiography of His Majesty King Hussein I of the Hashemite Kingdom of Jordan* (New York: Bernard Geis Associates, 1962).

Jevon, Graham, *Glubb Pasha and the Arab Legion: Britain, Jordan and the End of Empire in the Middle East* (Cambridge, UK: Cambridge University Press, 2017).

Joyce, Miriam, *Anglo-American Support for Jordan: The Career of King Hussein* (New York: Palgrave Macmillan, 2008).

Jureidini, A. Paul, *Jordan: The Impact of Social Change on the Role of the Tribes* (New York: Prager, 1984).

Karsh, Ephraim and Kumaraswamy, P.R., *Israel, the Hashemites and the Palestinians* (London: Routledge, 2003).

Kennedy, David and Hodges, Richard, *Gerasa and the Decapolis: A "Virtual Island" in Northwest Jordan* (London: Bloomsbury, 2007).

Khouri, Norma, *Honor Lost: Love and Death in Modern Day Jordan* (New York: Simon & Schuster, 2003).

Kirdis, Esen, *The Rise of Islamic Political Movements and Parties: Morocco, Turkey and Jordan* (Edinburgh, UK: Edinburgh University Press, 2019).

Kumaraswamy, P.R. (Ed.), *The Palgrave Handbook of the Hashemite Kingdom of Jordan* (Singapore: Palgrave Macmillan, 2019).

Lewis, N. Norman, *Nomads and Settlers in Syria and Jordan, 1800–1980* (Cambridge, UK: Cambridge University Press, 1987).

Lipchin, Clive, Sandler, Deborah and Cushman, Emily (Eds.), *The Jordan River and the Dead Sea Basin: Cooperation amid Conflict* (Dordrecht, ND: Springer 2007).

Lowi, R. Miriam, *Water and Power: The Politics of a Scarce Resource in the Jordan River Basin* (Cambridge, UK: Cambridge University Press, 1993).

Madanat, Philip Odeh, *Framing the Friday Sermon to Shape Opinion: The Case of Jordan* (Lanham, MD: Lexington Books, 2019).

Markoe, Glenn, *Petra Rediscovered: Lost City of the Nabateans* (New York: Harry N. Abrams, 2003).

Massad, A. Joseph, *Colonial Effects: The Making of National Identity in Jordan* (New York: Columbia University Press, 2001).

Melman, Yossi and Raviv, Dan, *Behind the Uprising: Israelis Jordanians, and Palestinians* (New York: Shlaim Avi, *Lion of Jordan: The Life of King Hussein in War and Peace* (New York: Alfred Knopf, 2008). Praeger, 1989).

Milton-Edwards, Beverley and Hinchcliffe, Peter, *Jordan: A Hashemite Legacy* (London: Routledge, 2009).

Mishal, Shaul, *East Bank/West Bank: The Palestinians in Jordan, 1949–1967* (New Haven, CT: Yale University Press, 1978).

Morris, Benny, *The Road to Jerusalem: Glubb Pasha, Palestine and the Jews* (London: I.B. Tauris, 2002).

Morris, James, *The Hashemite Kings* (London: Faber & Faber, 1959).

Nevo, Joseph, *King Abdullah and Palestine: A Territorial Ambition* (London: Palgrave Macmillan, 1997).

Nevo, Joseph, *King Hussein and Jordan's Perception of a Political Settlement with Israel, 1967–1988* (Sussex UK: Sussex Academic Press, 2006).

Nevo, Joseph and Pappe, Ilan, *Jordan in the Middle East: The Making of a Pivotal State, 1948–1988* (London: Routledge, 1994).

Nour, Queen, *Leap of Faith: Memoirs of an Unexpected Life* (New York: Miramax, 2003).

O'Connell, Jack, *King's Council: A Memoir of War, Espionage, and Diplomacy in the Middle East* (New York: W.W. Norton & Company, 2011).

Patai, Raphael, *The Kingdom of Jordan* (Princeton: Princeton University Press, 2016).

Piro, J. Timothy, *The Political Economy of Market Reform in Jordan* (New York: Rowman & Littlefield, 1998).

Plascov, Avi, *The Palestinian Refugees in Jordan 1948–1957* (New York: Routledge, 2017).

Pratt, Nicola, *Embodying Geopolitics: Generations of Women's Activism in Egypt, Jordan and Lebanon* (Oakland: University of California Press, 2020).

Report by His Majesty's Government in the United Kingdom of Great Britain and Ireland to the Council of the League of Nations on the Administration of Palestine and Trans-Jordan for the Year 1930 (London: His Majesty's Stationary Office, January 1, 1931).

Raz, Avi, *The Bride and the Dowry: Israel, Jordan and the Palestinians in the Aftermath of the June 1967 War* (New Haven, CT: Yale University Press, 2012).

Robins, Philip, *A History of Jordan* (Cambridge, UK: Cambridge University Press, 2004).

Salibi, S. Kemal, *The Modern History of Jordan* (London: I.B. Tauris, 1993).

Satloff, B. Robert, *From Abdullah to Hussein: Jordan in Transition* (New York: Oxford University Press, 1994).

Shlaim, Avi, *Collusion Across the Jordan: King Abdullah, the Zionist Movement, and the Partition of Palestine* (New York: Columbia University Press, 1988).

Shlaim, Avi, *Lion of Jordan: The Life of King Hussein in War and Peace* (New York: Alfred Knopf, 2008).

Shlaim, Avi, *The Politics of Partition: King Abdullah, the Zionists and Palestine 1921–1951* (New York: Oxford University Press, 1999).

Shoup A. John, *Culture and Customs of Jordan* (Westport, CT: Greenwood Press, 2006).

Sinai, Anne and Pollack, Allen, *The Hashemite Kingdom of Jordan and the West Bank: A Handbook* (New York: American Academic Association for Peace in the Middle East, 1977).

Smith, Darryl, *The Royal Family of the Hashemite Kingdom of Jordan: History of the Royal Family of the Hashemite Kingdom of Jordan* (London: True Stories Press, 2019).

Sonbol, El-Azhary, Amira, *Women of Jordan: Islam, Labor, and the Law* (New York: Syracuse University Press, 2003).

Susser, Asher, *Israel, Jordan, and Palestine: The Two-State Imperative* (Waltham, MA: Brandeis University Press, 2011).

Susser, Asher, *Jordan: The Hashemites in the Modern Arab World: Essays in honor of the Late Professor Uriel Dan* (London: Frank Cass, 1995).

Tawara al-Mohamed Mahmoud, *The Hashemite Kingdom of Jordan: From Abdullah I to Abdullah II* (London: No Publisher, 2017).

Taylor, Jane, *Petra and the Lost Kingdom of the Nabateans* (London: I.B. Tauris, 2012).

Tobin, A. Sarah, *Everyday Piety: Islam an Economy in Jordan* (New York: Cornell University Press, 2016).

Vine, Peter, *Jewels of the Kingdom: The heritage of Jordan* (London: Immel Publishing, 1987).

Warrick, Catherine, *Law in the Service of Legitimacy: Gender and Politics in Jordan* (London: Routledge, 2016).

Wiktorowicz, Quintan, *The Management of Islamic Activism: Salafis, the Muslim Brotherhood, and State Power in Jordan* (New York: SUNY Press, 2000).

Wilson Mary, *King Abdullah and the Making of Jordan* (Cambridge, UK: Cambridge University Press, 1988).

Yesilbursa, Behcet Kemal, *The Baghdad Pact: Anglo-American Defence Policies in the Middle East, 1950–1959* (London: Frank Cass, 2005).

Index

Abbad 193, 238
Abbadi 256
Abbasid Caliphate 2, 10, 56, 57, 60, 189, 249
Abd al-Aziz bin al-Sultan, al-Zahir, Barquq 87
Abd al-Dayim, Muhammad Khalil 332
Abd al-Hadi 147, 148
Abd al-Hadi, Mahmoud 148–149
Abd al-Hamid I 146
Abd al-Hamid II 127
Abd al-Hamid, Ibn ʿAissa al-Kharushahi ibn al-Qoff 105
Abd al-Illah 247, 248, 328
Abd al-Karim, Ammad 261
Abd al-Karim, Qasim 147, 267, 275, 277, 300, 317, 318, 321, 323, 343, 353
Abd al-Latif, Subhi 129
Abd al-Marwan 53
Abd al-Mu'min, Sharif 159
Abd al-Nabi 124
Abd al-Nasser, Gamal 174, 248, 259, 261, 264, 266, 268, 269, 275, 277, 281, 301, 302, 310, 312, 313, 323, 324, 357, 397
Abd al-Qadir al-Jazairi 204
Abd al-Qadir, Shaikh al-Ashir 77
Abd al-Rahman, al-Baba 81
Abd al-Rahman, al-Mihtar 83, 84
Abd al-Rahman, al-Yusuf 186
Abd al-Salam, bin Daud bin Uthman al-Ajluni 107, 163
Abd al-Samad, bin Abdallah 71
Abd al-Thunaybat 267
Abd al-Wahhab, Muhammad 404
Abdallah, I bin Hussein, (Amir and King of Jordan) 2, 7–9, 122, 134, 186, 195–197, 208–210, 212–227, 229–232, 238, 240–242, 244–247, 267, 275, 277, 280, 282–284, 289, 291, 296–298, 311, 312, 315, 317, 328, 341, 342, 356, 358, 368, 384; Abd al-Illah of Iraq 247; al-Husseini, Haj Amin 244; Anglo-Jordanian Treaty (1928) 230–231; assassination of 246–248; Balfour Declaration 226; Border claims and Saudi encroachments 228–229; Britain's conditions 224; British opposition to his crowning as king 217, 218, 223, 226; Claim to Iraq 210; Fall of France 244; Iraq Petroleum Company 242; Istiqlal 209, 215, 217, 220, 222, 245; Negotiations with Britan 211–212, 213, 215, 216, 221–222, 223, 229–231; Notables of the tribes 245, 247; Quest to restore Hashemite rule in Syria 209, 217, 218, 227; Rebellion of May 1921 240; resistance to French rule in Syria 209, 214, 215, 219, 226; Treaty of London (1946) 247
Abdallah II, King 10, 268, 315, 316, 322, 325, 326, 330, 331, 333, 349–352, 355, 356, 363–368, 373–376, 384, 385; Anti-Corruption Commission Law 385; call for a new regime in Iraq 364; civil society 366; collaboration with the tribes 365; Economic Consultative Council (ECC) 367; Integration of the Palestinians 366; 'Jordan First' Policy 363, 375; Membership in the World Trade Organization 364; Muslim Brotherhood 366; National Agenda for 2006–2015 363; NGO's 374; Nomination as successor 364; Press Control 374; Qualified Industrial Zones 364; reliance on the tribes 364; resilience of the regime 367; social reforms 373; women in the work force 378–379

Abdallah, Ali Salih 28, 189, 311, 329
Abdallah, Basim 368
Abdallah, Nawal 404
Abdallah, Pasha 147
Abdullat, Husam 376
Abi, al-Abbas 55
Abi Sa'id 77
Abila (Tel Abil) 25, 27, 37
Abraham, (patriarch) 143
Abu Abdallah al-Ajluni 106
Abu Abdallah Muhammad bin Salama al-Nuwayri al-Karaki 105
Abu Abdallah Muhammad bin Salama al-Tawzari al-Karaki 105
Abu Albani, Mouhammad Nasr al-Din 273
Abu al-Dhahab 146
Abu al-Fadail, Danyal bin Mankali al-Karaki 108
Abu al-Faraj bin Ya'qub bin Ishaq, bin al-Kaf al- Karaki 104
Abu al-Fida 13
Abu al-Ghanam, Salim 198
Abu al-Hadi 186
Abu al-Huda, Tawfiq 298, 329
Abu Ali, Mustafa 403
Abu al-Lason 154
Abu al-Raghib, Ali al-Muhandis 278
Abu al-Sh'r, Najib 198
Abu Bakr 44, 45, 48
Abu Dura, Yusuf 243
Abu Ghanima, Subhi 242, 371
Abu Ghanima, Ziya 272
Abu Ghuraybah, Bahjat 263, 264
Abu Hajla, Abdul Majid 372
Abu Hamid al-Ghazzali 107
Abu Irgeig 162
Abu Khafajah, Shatha 388
Abu Lissan 160
Abu Mahmoud, Hamman 242
Abu Musa, Mahmoud 260
Abu Muslim al Khurasani 54, 56
Abu Nowar, Naji 403
Abu Nuwar, Ali 260, 262, 263, 281, 282
Abu Odeh, Adnan 253
Abu Ruhayyim, Muhammad 273
Abu Safyan 190
Abu Sha'ban of Lifta 242
Abu Shahut, Shahir Yusuf 260–262, 265
Abu Sh'ar, Abdallah 242
Abu Tarfa 159
Abu Tayeh, Audeh 122, 123, 153, 154, 157, 160, 163
Abu Ubaidah 42, 45, 46, 50
Abul Abbas al-Saffah 56
Abul-Huda, Taufiq Pasha 233, 353
Acre (Akkah) 73, 74, 119, 146, 147, 189, 224
Actium, Battle of 28
ad-Darriyah 143
ad-Dur, Shajara 62
Aden 102
Adenauer, Konrad 356
Adhrah 55, 59, 189, 199
Adhriat 47, 49, 112
Adib al-Amiri, Muhammad 400
Adil Arslan, Ghada 217
Adwan 122, 130, 136, 137, 174, 193, 196, 390, 396
Adyghe Xabze 177
Afdal 67
Affendi, Taqi al-Din 154
Afgha 253
Afghanistan 348
Afiq 47
Aflaq, Michel 259
Agha Kardu, Faris 174
Agha Muhammad, Sai'd 174
Ahab, (King of Israel) 22
Ahaiwat 241
Ahl Ali 86
Ahl al-Mara'i 109, 110, 112
Ahmad al-Din al-Karaki 105
Ahmad al-Qalqashandi 78
Ahmad, bin Aways 85
Ahmad bin Ismail al Hasbani 106
Ahmad Effendi Salim 136
Ahmad, Ibn Arabsha 86
Ahmadinijad, Mahmoud 331
Ain al-Tamr 46
Ain Jalut 62, 67, 69–71, 86
Aintab 116
Aisha bint Usuf bin Ahmad bin Nasir al-Ba'uniyya 108
Ajlun 2, 18, 19, 21, 29, 62, 67, 69–72, 77, 78, 80, 84–90, 95, 99–101, 103, 104, 106, 112, 114–118, 120, 121, 122–124, 125–127, 130, 133–138, 140, 141, 145, 146, 164, 165, 170–174, 179, 181, 183, 189–192, 194, 195, 200, 204, 206, 216, 232, 242, 279, 358
Ajnadayn 46, 48
Ajwa, Battle of 117
Akidir 44
Akkah, (Acre) 39, 40, 50
Akkar 73
Akrad 130

Ala 97, 101, 130
Ala al-Din, al-Bandaqdar 71
Ala al-Din Ali bin Isa bin Hamid al-Azraqi al-Karaki al-Azraqi al- Shafi'i 105
Ala al-Din, Aqbaghah al-Safawi 79, 82
al-Abbadi Ahmad Uwaydi of Sikarnah 253, 254
al-Abbasi, Abdallah Ibn Muhammad 56
Ala-Din Ibn, Qadi Ajlun 108
al-Adwan, Majid 355
al-Adwan, Sultan 196, 240
al-'Aidi, Abd al-Karim 311
al-Ajluni, Mazen 262
al-Ajluni, Muhammad Ali Bey 217, 233, 242
al-Ajrami, Naufal 130
Alam al-Din Sanjar al-Halabi 71
al-Anbatawi 311
al-Aqra, Ahmad 191
al-Arab, Wadi 122
al-Ashraf Shaiban 111
al-Askari, Ja'far 163, 186
al-Asqalani, Ibn Hajar 85, 86, 103, 104, 106
al-Assad, Bashar 315, 316, 322, 365, 367, 400
al-Assad, Hafiz 314, 335, 347
al-Assali, Muhamad 356
al-Atrash, Abd al-Qadir 215
al-Atrash, Asad 218
al-Atrash, Sultan Pasha 220–222, 232, 354
al-Awdan, Salih 198
al-Ayid 191
al-Ayyubi Musa, Mouhammad 247
al-Ayyubi, Salah al-Din 2, 125, 251
al-Azam, Muhammad Fauzi 208
al-Azm, Yusuf 372
al-Azmeh, Adel 356
al-Azmeh, Nabih 356
al-Azraq 159, 160
al-Azraq, Wadi 50, 57, 101
al-Badr al-Ayni 87
al-Bahali, Abu Amamah 45
al-Bakhith, Muhammad Adnan 116
al-Bakr, Ahmad Hasan 319
al-Bakri, Nasib 153, 159
al-Baladhuri, Ahamd Ibn Yahya, Ibn Jabir 39, 47
al-Banna, Hasan 266
al-Barzani, Khalid 186
al-Barzani, Mullah Mustafa 186
al-Basta 157
al-Batush 158
al-Bauniya 95
al-Budayri Ahamad 121
al-Bukhari 107
al-Burhan al-Karaki 105
al-Dahaq ibn Qays 52
al-Dajani, Burhan 311
al-Dalil 95, 112
al-Damur, Ibrahim 126
al-Damur, Shaikh Hussein 159
al-Darabi, Ala-Din 208
al-Darri, Tamir 143
al-Darwish, Jarf 163
al-Dhamour, Ibrahim 193
al-Din Salah al-Ayyubi 60–62
al-Din Sami, Shams 198
al-Din Sanjar al-Halabi 71
al-Din, Zehir 60
al-Dubbaya 45
al-Dura, Muhanna 404
Aleef, George 404
Aleppo 71, 73, 76, 79, 82, 85, 86, 88, 89, 94, 96, 102, 104, 110, 114, 115, 117, 190, 205, 220, 354
Alesina, Alberto 3
Alexander the Great 24
Alexandria 52, 61, 75, 79, 104
al-Fahis 205
al-Faiz, Mithqal 275
al-Far'a 15
al-Farhan, Hamad 311
al-Fariq 317
al-Fariq, Fahd 246, 331
al-Farouki, Sami 132, 170, 204
al-Farukqi, Sami 139
al-Farzah 199
al-Fasi 87
al-Fatah, Jam'iyah al-Arabiyah 207
al-Fatimi, al-Mu'izz 58
al-Fayiz, Mithqal 196, 198, 208, 247, 355, 384
al-Fayz, Satam 142
al-Fuhays 142, 167, 178
al-Gaylan 316
al-Gaylani, Rashid Ali 244
al-Ghadaf, Wadi 159
al-Ghalayni, Mustafa 219
al-Ghanimah, Subbhi 233
al-Ghazali, Janbirdi 190
al-Ghazawi 82
al-Ghôr 14, 16
al-Hadi, Tawfiq 312
al-Hadidi, Ibrahim 263, 264
al-Haditha 243
al-Hafiz, Ahmad Pasha 191

al-Hajaya 158, 160, 196
al-Halabi 273, 274
al-Hamarnah, Kamil 311
al-Hamima (Hawra) 53–55
al-Hamoud, Abd al-Rahim 311
al-Hamuri, Musa 186
al-Handawi, Radi, Salih al-Shar' 264, 265, 363
al-Handawi, Salih 263
al-Handawi, Turki 260
al-Harfush, Yunus 117, 191
al-Harithi, Ali 159
al-Harithi, Sharif Ali al-Hussein 163
al-Harrah 78
al-Hasan, Wadi 16
al-Hashemi, Taha Pasha 242, 247
al-Hashim, Izat 115
al-Hasid, Nash'at 226
al-Hassan, (Crown Prince) 351
al-Hayar 192
al-Haysha 157
al-Hinawi, Sami 186
al-Hindi, Mahmoud 222
al-Hiyari, Ali 263
al-Humud, Dhiab 174
al-Hussein, Muhammad 198
al-Husseini, Haj Amin 214, 242, 244, 248, 369
al-Husseini, Musa 247
al-Hut, Muhammad 399
al-Huwaytat 240
Ali al-Kurdi, Muhammad 186
Ali al-Kurdi, Saydu 186
Ali, Amir 210
Ali Bey, al-Kabir 133, 146
Ali bin Ibrahim, al-Rabawi al Karaki 106
Ali, Dali 191
Ali Ibn Arid, al-Sharif 158
Ali Ibn Sharif Husein 222
Ali, Imam 50, 53
al-Irani, Mahmoud Saif al-Din 400
al-Iraq 166
al-Isa 196
al-Jabiyah 45
al-Ja'fari, Mahmoud 221
al-Jafn 95
al-Jamali, Badr 59
al-Jarah 59
al-Jarba 42
al-Jazari 98
al-Jazi, Mashhur Haditah 303
al-Jazzar 147
al-Jiy 128
al-Jundi 44
al-Jundi, Sami 302
al-Kabariti, Abdul Karim 364
al-Kaf 228
al-Kalbi, Sinan Bin Alyan 59
al-Kamil 62
al-Karmi, Abd al-Karim (Abu Salma) 399
al-Kaswah 96
al-Kawrah 154
al-Khadhra, Saud al-Yusuf 242
al-Khadim, Munir 59
al-Khadra, Salma al-Jayyusi 399
al-Khalaeleh 389
al-Khalali, Shaikh Mustafa 230
al-Khalil 69, 78
al-Kharar 42
al-Khardash, Subhi 222
al-Kharisha, Naif 158, 200
al-Khatib, Anwar 317
al-Khatib, Riyad 311
al-Khawra 219
al-Khayri, Khalusi 318
al-Kujkani 80, 82
al-Kurdi, Ahmad 186
al-Kurdi, Faiz 186
al-Kurdi, Hosni Saydu 186
al-Kurdi, Walid 186
al-Kurdi, Yahya 186
al-Kurdi, Zayd Sa'd al-Din Jum'a 186
al-Kuzbari, Ma'mun 324
Allenby, Edmund 160–163, 205, 225, 279
Allon, Yigal 303
al-Madi, Mouin 354
al-Madi, Munib 247
al-Mafraq 95, 101
al-Mahdi, Abdallah Ibn al-Mansur 56, 57
al-Mahmoudi 87, 88
al-Majali, Abd al-Salam 259, 306
al-Majali, Hazza' 263, 265, 266, 317
al-Majali, Qadr Pasha 198
al-Majali, Rufayfan 196
al-Majali, Salih 129
al-Majaliyah 158
al-Malik al Ashraf, Musa al Ayyubi 69
al-Malik al-Adil 60, 61
al-Malik al-Ashraf Abu al-Nasir Qa'itbay 105
al-Malik al-Mansur, Ali ibn Aybak Izz al-Din Nur al-Din 70
al-Malik al-Mansur, Amir Haji 82
al-Malik al-Mu'ayyad, Shaikh al-Mahmoudi 110
al-Malik al-Mu'zam Isa 97, 112

al-Malik al-Nasir Dawud 13, 111
al-Malik al-Nasir, Muhammad 111
al-Malik al-Nasir Yusuf 70
al-Malik al-Zahir Sayf Jarbak al-Khushqadam 100
al-Man'in 160
Almansour, Nesma 402
al-Mansur, Haji 81, 82
al-Maqdisi, Abu Muhammad 274
al-Maqrizi 84, 104, 112
al-Mara 98
al-Marafi, Abd al-Mahdi Mahmoud 206
al-Marar, Salih 179
al-Masri, Hajj Ma'zuz 292
al-Mas'udi 49
al-Matir 159
al-Midanat Isa 206
al-Midfa'i, Jamil 126
al-Midfa'i, Rashid Pasha 186
Almoravids 51
al-Muayid, Shaikh al Mahmoudi 102
al-Mu'ayta, Mahmoud 260, 261
al-Mu'azzam Isa 62
al-Mudawara 13
al-Mufrij 59
al-Mufti, Sa'id 186, 198, 224, 263, 298
al-Mughith, Umar 68, 69, 71
al-Mulki, Fauzi 328, 329
al-Mulqi, Fauzi 281
al-Muntasir bi'Ilah 59
al-Muqqadisi 59, 60
al-Musalihah, Mouhammad 252
al-Musta'rib, Faris al-Din 68
al-Muttaqi Billah 57
al-Nabulsi, Saud 355
al-Nabulsi, Sulayman 266, 269
al-Nahda (Tunisia) 267, 272
al-Nashashibi, Nasr al-Din 247
al-Nasir Daud 68, 76, 103–105
al-Nasir, Muhammad, bin Qalaun 73, 76, 77, 103, 104, 109, 112, 143
al-Nasir, Qasim 260, 261
al-Nasiri 79, 80
al-Nasr, Farraj, Ibn Barquq 84
al-Nasser, Abd 5, 6, 9
al-Nimr 147, 148
al-Nimr, Abd al-Halim 248, 262, 263, 317
Alnobani, Ali Taha 402
al-Nu'aymat 158
al-Nu'aymat Fayz, Lu'ayy 198
al-Omari 108
ALPHA Plan 323
al-Qadha 158
al-Qalqashandi, Ahmad 78, 94, 96, 112
al-Qasim, Samih 399
al-Qasus, Awda 198, 238
al-Qawirah 163, 199
al-Qurrah, Wadi 45
al-Quwatli, Shukri 311
al-Raayyis, Munir 311
al-Ramahi, Aseel 383
al-Rashid, A. 393
al-Rawsan, Mahmoud 260, 263
al-Rayyan 147
al-Razzaz, Munif 311
al-Rifa'i, Abd al-Mun'im 311, 318
al-Rifa'i, Samir 298, 313, 323, 324, 342
al-Rikabi, Ali Riddah 221
al-Rikabi, al-Riddah 204–205
al-Ruman 141
al-Rumaymin 142, 167
al-Ruwalah 159
al-Rwasan, Sulayman 198
al-Sabul, Shawkat 260
al-Sadun, Agha Salim 186
al-Sahimat, Atallah 198
al-Sa'id Ibn Baybars 77
al-Sa'id, Nuri 159, 263, 317, 318, 353
al-Sa'idi, Abd al-Muta'al 44
al-Saidiyeen 196
al-Sajjad, Ali 56
al-Sakhawi 89, 103
al-Salibi, Sa'id 206
al-Salih, Abd al-Qadir 154
al-Salih al-Shabul Daif Alla 230
al-Salih, Ayyub 68
al-Salih, Haji bin al-Malik al Ashraf (Malik al-Mansur) 80
al-Salih, Riad 247
al-Salik, Ahmad 273
al-Salt 14, 22, 57, 59, 60, 62, 67, 69, 70, 72, 77, 78, 94, 95, 104, 105, 116, 120–123, 126, 129, 130, 132–137, 140–142, 159, 162, 166, 167, 170, 172, 174, 178, 181, 198, 200, 205, 206, 209, 217, 225, 232, 249, 279
al-Sanmin 96
al-Sanz, Abd al-Aziz 220
al-Sarayrah 158
al-Sarraj, Sami 222
al-Satam al-Faiz Awad 247
al-Sawdi Sulayman 206
al-Shahbandar, Abd al-Rahman 311
al-Shalala, Wadi 123
al-Sh'alan Ghalib Beg 209
al-Shamiya (Al-Maghara) 128

al-Shararat 196, 240
al-Sharida Kalib 219
al-Sharif, Abd al-Rahim 292, 294
al-Sharq, Nasir 159
al-Sherari, Mifleh al-Robadan 242
al-Shihab Ahmad al-Baridi 80, 81
al-Shirayiri, Ali Khalfi 250
al-Shiteiwi, Haj Mahmoud (Abu Redhwan of Semakh) 242
al-Shwaqfeh, Muhammad 397
al-Sir, Wadi 133, 134
al-Sisi, Abd al-Fatah 325
al-Suboul, Shawkat 262
al-Sudi, Suleiman 354
al-Taba' Sabri, Muhammad 355
al-Tabari 45
al-Tal, Abdallah 247, 260
al-Tal, Ali Niyazi 250
al-Tal, Wasfi 224, 275, 284, 290, 301, 311
al-Talhuni, Bahjat 224
al-Talhuni, Khalil 206
al-Tall, Mahmoud 263
al-Tamimi, Anwar al-Khatib 302
Alṭamish 85
al-Tanukhi, Izz al-Din 238
al-Tarawana, Ahmad 158, 318
al-Tarawanah, Hussein 198
al-Tawana 160
al-Tim, Wadi 133
al-Tuhami 261
al-Turki, Baltakin 59
al-Turkmani, Muhammad 87
al-Turkomani al-Aṣfahid 60
al-Umari 109
al-Wahdat 403
Alwan M. Bakir 399, 400
al-Waqidi 46
al-Wihdeh 315
al-Yusuf, Abd al-Rahman 208
al-Zahra, Fatima 56
al-Zahri, Khalil 133
al-Zarkali, Khayr al-Din 186
al-Zarqawi, Abu Mus'ab 274
al-Zirikli, Khayr al-Din 210, 217
al-Zu'bi, Tallal al-Mulih 220
Amalek, King of Kadar 22
Amamiyah 125
Amaziah 22
American Israel Public Affairs Committee, (AIPAC) 330
Amin al-Din Musa Ibn al-Turkumani 72
Amin, Muhammad Ali 261
Amir al-Hajj 190
Amman 21, 39, 50, 51, 57, 59–61, 95, 122, 130, 132, 133, 139, 141, 142, 155, 159–163, 166, 175, 176, 178, 181–183, 193, 194, 196, 205, 211, 213, 215, 217–219, 221, 224, 229, 232, 238–242, 248, 261, 264–266, 276, 279, 280, 290, 292–294, 306, 311–313, 317, 319, 320, 323, 325, 330, 332, 340, 345, 348, 352–358, 364, 367, 369, 372, 374, 377, 388, 389, 403
Ammon 16–22, 24, 104
Amorites 175
Amr bin al-Hadhbani 84
Amr bin Fadl al-Jerami 85, 87
Amr Shah al-Tukmani 91
Amr, Shaikh 190, 192
Amru 125, 145
Amru Elkis (Amorkesos) 38
Anani, Jawad 376
Anasah 193
Anastasius 43
Anatolia 114, 141, 175
Anaza 208
Anchor R. John 393
Andalusia 51
Anderson, Lisa 4
Anga bin Shati 80
Anglo-Jordanian Treaty 267, 323, 352
Anglo-Transjordanian Agreement (1928) 342
Anti-Corruption Commission Law 385
Antigonus, The One Eyed 26
Antioch 43, 117, 180
Antiochus I, King of the Seleucids 26
Antiochus III, King of the Seleucids 24, 25
Antiochus IV, King of the Seleucids 24
Antipas, Herod 28
Antipater the Idumean 27
Antonius, Martyr 14
Anz 311
Aqaba 13, 25, 53, 55, 58, 60, 61, 67, 73, 96–98, 112, 120, 121, 123, 131, 132, 154–157, 159–163, 166, 167, 193, 209, 215, 221–223, 226, 228, 232, 281, 319, 322, 327
Aqabat as-Sawam 95, 101
Aqbagha al-Lakash al-Zahiri 91
Aqbagha al-Turkmani 89, 91
Aqbardi al-Dawadar 89
Aqbardi bin Bakhshaish al-Inali 89
Aqil 59
Ara, Wadi 118
Arab Collective Security Pact 248

Arab Cooperation Council (ACC) 335
Arab Frontier Force 232
Arab Helpers Party 370
Arab Higher Committee 242
Arab League 314, 322, 323, 332, 377
Arab Legion 177, 196, 220, 222–224, 231, 232, 243, 244, 246, 276, 278–283, 312, 316, 327, 369, 384
Arab Revolt 218, 220, 245, 251
Arab Revolt (1916) 207
Arab Spring 254
Arab Summit Meeting, (Rabat: 1974) 293, 319
Arab Summit Meeting, (Tunis: 1980) 330
Araba, Wadi 6, 13, 23, 37, 39, 45, 46, 95, 96, 99, 101, 149, 162, 163, 224, 226, 241, 305
Araba Wadi Accord, (Jordan's peace accord with Israel: 1994) 268
Arabia Felix 26
Arabia Petrea 29–31, 38, 39
Arabian Peninsula 1, 17, 28, 67, 100
Arabiyyat, Abdul Latif 387
Arab-Palestine Workers Association 371
Arafat, Yasser 85, 275, 276, 304, 329, 347, 375
Aram 21, 22
ARAMCO 340
Araq el-Amir 17
Arava 3
Arbela (Irbid) 26
Areopoils (Er-Rabba) 37
Aretas III, King of the Nabateans 27, 55
Aretas IV, King of the Nabateans 17, 28, 55
Arindela (Gharandel) 37, 39
Aristobulus Judah 27
Aristodicides of Issus 26
Arlozoroff, Chaim 140, 184
Armouti, Mazen 255
Arnon 18, 20, 21, 23, 183
Arshayd 292
Arshidat. Shafiq 317
Arslan, Adil 222, 311
Arslan, Amir 166
Arslan, Mizhar 218
Arslan, Mudhir 221
Arsuf 73
Asabiyya 6, 7
As'ad al-Ayyubi 186
Asha'er, Jamal 260
'Ash'iryya (Tribalism) 187
Ashkenazi Malkiel, Rabbi 143
Ash-Shevari, Mifleh 242
Ash-Shrayda, Klayb 195
Ashteret, Farnin 124
Ashterot 18
Ashurbanipal, King of Assyria 22
Asir 96, 131
Asmahan 404
as-Sarat 125
as-Sudairi, Abdul Aziz 327
Assyrian Empire 17
Ataturk, Mustafa Kemal 207, 209
Atiya, S. Aziz 75
Atlit 118
Attiya, Muhammad 356
Augustopolis (Udruh) 37
Auja 185
Australia 357–358
Avignon 75
Avila 29
Avila de Lisianias 30
Awale, Rasha 402
Awamila 130
Awdah, Rifa'at 197, 264
Aydun 95
Ayisha 186
Ayl 199
Ayla (Eilat, Aqaba) 14, 19, 20, 29, 30, 37–39, 42, 45, 51, 59, 67, 95, 101, 102, 125, 131
Aynal (Anil) 111
Ayyubid Caliphate 2, 61, 67, 68, 71, 77, 114
Azebaijan 175
Azraq 62, 162, 163, 215, 217
Azzam, Samirah 400
Azzamah 241

Baallbek 50, 71, 79, 86, 108, 191
Bab al-Jabiya 97
Baba Raba 43
Baban, Jalal 186
Babatha 29
Badia 232
Badina 328
Badr al-Din, al-Ayni 85, 91
Badr al-Din, Muhammad bin al-Haj al-Nahidh Bakr al-Atabaki 69
Badr al-Din, Muhammad bin Wahaybiyh al-Salti 108
Badr Bin Sa'ud, Bin Harib al-Busaidi 332
Badran, Mudar 268, 271
Baghdad 52, 85, 96, 217, 247, 263, 264, 313, 317, 319, 400, 401
Baghdad Pact 264–267, 284, 323, 328, 329, 331, 358

Bahr al-Qulzum 125
Bahra 41
Bahrain 333
Bahri (Mamluks) 67, 68, 79, 97, 98, 104, 106, 110
Bahsana 86
Bair 327
Baker, James III 347, 348
Bakhit, Adnan 196
Bakjar 59
Balak Ben Tzipor 58
Balda 73
Baldwin I, (King of Jerusalem) 14, 61
Baldwin II, (King of Jerusalem) 61
Baldwin III, (King of Jerusalem) 61
Balfour Declaration 2, 224–226, 231
Balfour-Beatty Company 298
Bali, Asli 2
Bali U. Ash 4
Balkan Peninsula 140, 141
Balkans 175, 184, 204
Ball, George 345
Balqa 19, 44, 46, 50, 51, 54, 57–61, 68–71, 78, 87, 95, 108, 109, 112, 125, 127, 129, 130–131, 135–137, 139–143, 153, 164, 165, 172–175, 179, 183, 185, 189, 196, 205, 206, 216, 219, 238, 242, 355, 390
Balqawiya Confederation 41, 176
Bani Hajaya 128
Bani Hamida 125, 126, 142, 179
Bani Hashem 251
Bani Hassan 238
Bani Kalb 41, 57
Bani Masila 56
Bani Udhra 57
Bankes, John 165
Bankes, William 14
Banki, Mustafa 192
Banu al-Asar 138
Banu al-Sar 171, 172
Banu Atiya 152, 196
Banu Gham 112
Banu Ghassan 189
Banu Hasan 193, 198
Banu Jam 138, 171, 172
Banu Karafat 133
Banu Khalid 110, 196
Banu Kilab 136, 173
Banu Kinanah 171
Banu Lakhm 189
Banu Lam 110, 111
Banu Mahdi 110, 112
Banu Sakhr 112, 122, 124–126, 129, 130, 136, 137, 154, 157–163, 173, 174, 176, 178, 183, 184, 193, 196, 200, 206, 222, 238, 240, 247, 250, 256, 275, 282, 326, 328, 355
Banu Uqba 109–112
Banu Wanudin 51
Baqawiyya 142
Bar Kokhba 29
Barquq 76, 79–83, 85, 105–107, 110–112
Barquq al-Shaqhab 82, 83
Barzani 186
Basha al-Jundi Abd al-Qadir 217
Bashan 18, 19, 29, 30, 213
Bashir Shihab II 147
Basira 159
Basisu, Mu'in 399
Basma 186, 392
Basra 57, 95, 320
Ba'th Party 199, 259–263, 265, 277, 282, 311, 318, 372, 397
Battikhi, Samih 367
Baudelaire, Charles 399
Bayar, Jalal 265
Baybars al-Malik al-Zahir 68–73, 76, 77, 87
Baybars, Rukn ad-Din 62, 143
Bayir 50
Bayr 101
Bayt Jibril 68
Bayt Ram 60
Bayt Ras (Capitolius) 24, 47, 50
Baztagham Qutb al-Dawlah 59
Bedeli Askeri 132
Bedouin Control Law (1929) 196
Bedoul 187, 188
Beersheba 241
Be'ezer-Ye'ezer 30
Beg al-Abid, Mustafa 127
Begin, Menachem 2, 4, 295, 303, 305
Beidah 16
Beirut 116, 121, 218, 250, 260, 322, 330
Beisan, (Beit Sh'an, Skitopolis) 14, 37, 39, 47, 49, 50, 85, 87, 96, 130
Beit Sh'an 16, 23, 25
Beja 16
Ben Avinoam, Barak 182
Ben Gurion, David 2, 296, 299–301
Ben Hillel Hacohen, Mordechai 194
Ben Hillel, Mordechai 141, 185
Ben Ner Abner 144
Ben Pe'or Balaam 20, 58
Beni Abid 123
Beni Aqaba 98
Beni Auf 61
Beni Hadhim 90
Beni Hasan 136, 174
Beni Juhma 123
Beni Mahdi 82, 85, 86, 88

Beni Ubayd 126
Beni Uqba 81, 84
Benjamin 19
Benjamin of Tudela 182
Ben-Tabeal 22
Beqaa 117, 120
Bet Jala 353
Betar 141, 185, 303
Bethlehem 38, 144, 180, 353, 356
Bettorus, (Lajjun) 37
Bey Arefi, Mehmet 166
Bey, Ishaq 166
Bighash, Mahmoud Ahmadi 331
Billi 41, 155
Bin Abd al-Malik, Hisham 53
Bin Abd al-Malik, Sylayman 52, 53
Bin Abd al-Mutalib, Ḥamza 42
Bin Abdallah al-Abbasi, Muhammad 54
Bin Abdallah, Bakr 175
Bin Abi Jahl, Ikrimah 48
Bin al-Abbas, Saliḥ bin Abdallah 53
Bin al-Hussein, Ali, (Crown Prince) 352
Bin Ali Al-Abbasi, Muhammad 54
Bin al-Khatibi 292
Bin al-Muhalab Yazid 53
Bin Amir, Aṭiyyh 49
Bin Amr, al-Qa'qaa' 48
Bin Amr, Khattab 89
Bin Amr, Sarrakh 175
Bin Armiya, Yahya 57
Bin Fallaḥ, Ja'far 58
Bin Ghazi, Hamd 163
Bin Haiza' Muhammad 88
Bin Hamza, Abadallah 158, 164
Bin Hazim, Badr 59
Bin Hussein, Muhammad (Crown Prince) 292
Bin Jumhur Mansur 51
Bin Mahan Bakir 56
Bin Muhammad, Amir Ghazi, (prince) 198, 357
Bin Muhammad, Ibrahim 54, 55
Bin Muhammad, Marwan 53–55
Bin Muslim, al Bahali Qutaybah 52
Bin Nasir, Sharif Hussein 324
Bin Rabi'a, Abd al-Rahman 175
Bin Sa'id, Khalid 44
Bin Shadid, Jalal 125
Bin Shakir, Zayd 321
Bin Shati 80
Bin Sulaim, Sulayman 51
Bin Sultan, Khaled 329
Bin Taymur, Sa'id 332
Bin Zayd Shakir, Sharif 221, 240
Bir al-Sabi 131
Bir, Cevik 332
Birecik 116
Birket Zizya 68, 70
Bishnaq, Naji 311
Black September 276, 401
Bonaparte, Napoleon 14, 126, 133, 146
Book and Sunna Association 274
Boṣra 17, 19, 23, 28–30, 36, 37, 39, 40, 44–46, 55, 78, 100, 101, 125
Bourji (Mamluks) 67–69, 76, 85, 98, 104, 110
Braizat, Musa 289, 329
British Mandate 134, 179, 186, 198, 208, 210, 214–216, 221, 225–230, 232, 250, 368–371
Brothers of Christian Schools and Sisters of Saint Joseph 353
Brunton, Captain 279
Brzezinski, Zbigniev 346
Buck, Tobias 333
Buckingham, Silk James 14, 165
Burckhardt, Lewis John 14, 31, 172
Burha 94
Burhan al-Din Ibrahim Ibn Abd al-Rahman bin Muhammad bin al-Majd al-Karaki 106
Buri, Taj al-Muluk 61
Burqa 282
Bursa Eski, Sham 166
Business Continuity Management 393
Bustani, Hisham 401
Byrne, David 383
Byrne, Eileen 333

Caesarea 37
Cairo 61, 70, 71, 73, 84, 87–89, 94, 97, 99, 105, 115, 134, 213, 247, 276, 313, 369, 372
Cairo Conference 210, 211, 213, 225, 228
Calbo, Lorenzo 102
Calicut 98
Camp David Accord 320, 325, 347
Camp, I.N. 279
Canaan 19
Canada 349; Air Transport Agreement 349; Canadian International Development Agency, (CIDA) 349; Foreign Investment Promotion and Protection Agreement 349; Free Trade Agreement 349; Nuclear Cooperation Agreement 349; Ottawa Convention 349
Capitolia, (Bat Ras) 26, 37
Carmel Mount 42, 118, 146
Carter, Jimmy 346
Caucasus 175, 181

Celebi Evliya 118
Celler, Emanuel 341
Central Intelligence Agency (CIA) 313
Central Islamic Party 370
Chancellor, John 304
Characmoba, (Karak) 29, 37
Charles II of Anjou 75
Chase, O.G. 384
Chechens 137, 141, 164, 170, 175, 177, 250, 271, 350
China 96, 98, 340, 351
Chirac, Jacques 355
Churchill, Winston 2, 141, 208–217, 221, 223, 225–227
CIA (Central Intelligence Agency) 364
Cilicia 207
Circassians 80, 81, 122, 134, 137, 141, 142, 153, 164, 170, 174–177, 179, 230, 232, 250, 261, 271, 369, 389
Clayton, G.F. 221–224, 229
Clematius 38
Cleopatra VII, Queen of Egypt 28
Clinton, Bill 306
Codrenus George 39
Coele Syria 27, 29, 31
Cold War 264, 312, 341–343, 350
Colleges des Freres 353
Committee for the Privatization of the Jordanian Media 368
Conder, Regnier Claude 141, 185
Congreve W. General 208
Constantine the Great 37
Constantine VII, Porphyrogennetes 39
Constantinople 43, 68, 117, 129, 137, 170
Constantius II 38
Corals Island 38
Cordoba 51
Council of Nicaea 31, 38
Cox, Henry 223, 224
Crac de Chevalier 73
Cubicularius Vicerius, Theodore 39
Curzon, George Nathaniel 206, 208, 215, 221, 228, 279
Cyprus 74, 75, 353
Cyrenaica 25, 29
Cyril of Skitopolis 39
Cyrus, The Great, Emperor of Persia 17

da Gama Vasco 98
Da'amah 57
Daghastan 175
Dahamsha 282
Da'il 230
Dajani, Umar 341
Damardash 86, 89
Damascus (Dimashq) 14, 26, 27, 30, 39, 45, 47, 48, 50–54, 56–58, 60–62, 68, 70, 71, 73, 78–80, 82–84, 86–88, 94–97, 100–102, 104, 107, 108, 110, 111, 115–118, 121, 124, 126, 128, 132, 135, 136, 138, 145–147, 154, 155, 160–162, 171, 173, 186, 190–192, 195, 204–207, 218, 222, 224, 225, 227, 230, 231, 233, 241, 243, 260, 262, 264, 279, 283, 312, 313, 328, 348
Damietta 74, 104
Dara Amram 43
Dar'aa, (Dera'a) 100, 121, 132, 205, 239, 244
Darwazeh, Izzat 233, 275
Darwish, Mahmoud 399, 400
Dastmalchian, Ahmed 330
Dath al-Manar 45
Dathna 45
Daumat al-Jandal (Jauf) 40–42, 44–46, 50, 55–57
David, (King of Israel) 1, 21, 143
Day, Stockwell 349
Dayan, Moshe 292, 295, 297, 303, 305
de Gaulle, Charles 355
de Milly, Philip 61
Decapolis 25, 27, 47, 114
Decius 43
Deedes, Wyndham 211, 213, 221
Deir Ayyub 48
Deir Yasin 247
Delhi 351
Demetrius 26
Democratic People's Party 370
Democratic United People's Party 370
Dera'a 50, 154–156, 161, 162, 354
Derbend 175, 190
Desert Patrol 195
D'Estaing, Giscard 355
Dharb al-Hajj 166
Dharb al-Sultani 166
Dhiab al-Humud 136
Dhiban 1, 17, 18, 113, 166
Dhibyan, Hasib 222
Dhiyab al-Awdan, Shaikh 157
Dhofari Rebellion 332
Dhyab al-Awran 163
Diocletian 37, 43, 55
Diodorus of Sicily 26
Dion, (Tel As'ari) 37
Dir Hanna 146
Diu, Battle of 98
Divon 18, 20, 23
Diyar Bakr 116, 250
Diyum, (Edôm) 26, 27

Dothan, Plain of 118
Drat Atlah 41
Druz Rebellion (1925) 242, 310
Dubois, Peter 75
Dulles, John Foster 353

East Jerusalem 13
East Jordan 22
Easterly, William 3
Economic Consultative Council 368
Edhra'at 137, 138, 171
Edom 1, 16, 17, 19–23, 27, 29, 30, 161
Edomites 143, 252
Education Reform for a Knowledge Economy 349
Egypt 1, 2, 6, 8, 9, 17, 21, 57, 58, 61, 62, 67, 68, 70, 76, 80, 81, 83–87, 95, 96, 98, 100, 107, 108, 114, 118, 120, 126, 129–131, 135, 156, 163, 165, 167, 173, 186, 190, 205, 208, 218, 247, 248, 259, 262, 265, 266, 275, 277, 284, 290, 300–302, 312–314, 317, 318, 322–326, 329, 331, 335, 343, 347, 348, 353, 356, 358, 369, 373, 388, 403
Ehud, Ben Gera 20
Eilat 224, 305
Eilath, Eliahu 141, 185
Ein Gedi 29
Eisenhower Doctrine 267, 343
Eisenhower, Dwight 301, 343, 344
Eithan, Walter 301
Elana 30
El-Arish 23
El-Darwaza, Izzet 328
Election Law (1928) 182
El-Gamasi, Mohamed Abdel Ghani 313
Eliot, George 399
Elonei Mamrai 144
El-Shamayleh, Aysha 401
Elthemos 28
Ephraim 18, 19
Ephron the Hittite 143
Esau 1
Esbos (Ḥeshbon, Tel Ḥishan) 27, 29, 30, 37
Essaa Pasha 137, 171
Ethiopia 301
Eusebius 29
Ezôr 16
Ezra 24

Fairuz 404
Faisal, Amir 153, 155, 157–161, 163, 167, 204, 205, 207–209, 211, 212, 214, 219–222, 228, 231, 316
Fakhr al-Din al-Ma'ani 117, 118, 146, 191
Fakhr al-Din II 117
Fakhri, Hamid 157, 163
Falk of Anjou 61
Family Law (1951) 179
Fanatil al-Hajaya, Muhammad 400
Faqir, Fadia 401
Faraj, Sultan 83, 84, 86, 87, 91, 96
Farhan, Ishaq 272
Faris, Agha Kardu 136
Faroukh, Elias 401
Farrukh Ibn Abdallah 145
Farrukhs 117, 191
Faruk, (King of Egypt) 247, 248, 259
Far'un, Hasan 311
Fatah 276, 403
Fatimids 57, 59–61
Fejr 155
Fenyan, Wadi 1, 15, 16
Ferrea 30
Fidenzio 75
Fiḥl (Pella) 46, 47, 49, 50
Flavius, Josephus 23, 27, 28
Ford, Gerald 346
Foreign Legion 284
France 207–209, 219, 221, 244, 246, 284, 301, 347, 353, 355
Frazer, Malcolm 357
Frederick II 99, 112
Frederick, Beg 221
Free France 244
Free Officers Movement (Egypt) 260
Freedom Party 370
Fuleh (Afula) 147
Fuleihan, Layan 187
Furayhat 124
Furaykh Kormaz 191
Furukh, Mansur 191

Gabaon 178
Gad 18–20
Gadara, (Umm Qays) 24–27, 30, 31, 37
GAHAL (Herut-Liberal Coalition) 303
Gaius, Ceasar 28
Galaditis 27
Gal-Ed 19
Galilee 30, 31, 37, 40, 161
Gamala 28
Garcia-Granados, Jorge 246, 296
Gatti, Don 142, 178
Gaza 23, 45, 61, 69, 77, 79, 83, 85–88, 90, 96, 102–104, 108, 110, 111, 114–116, 118, 128, 145–147, 191, 277, 297, 403
Gazit, Mordechai 298
Gedor (Ain Jedur) 27
Geneva 217, 346

George of Cyras 38
George, St 172
Gerasha, (Gharza, Jarash) 26, 27, 36, 37
Gerizim, Mount 39, 43, 183
Germany 356; And, German Investment Protection Agreement 356
Germany, Nazi 284
Geshem, the Arab 17
Ghadir Abu Safah 163
Ghanem al-Ghazawi 89
Gharaba 125
Gharandal 50, 241
Ghassan, Mahmoud 41, 67, 77, 78
Ghassanids 124
Ghawarini 140, 184
Ghawta 103, 133
Ghazawi 85, 86
Ghazi, King 242
Ghazzawieh 242
Ghor al-Muzara'a 157
Ghor Seisaban 149, 184
Ghussayn, Taufik 296
Ghuwayr, Wadi 15
Gibbon Edward 36, 37, 39
Gilead 13, 18–20, 22, 24, 29, 30, 139–141, 183–185
Gillespie, M. Dean 341
Glubb, John 197, 198, 240, 243, 246, 247, 260–262, 265, 266, 281, 282, 312, 323, 327, 343, 352; dismissal of 263, 280–283, 297
Golan 14, 27, 29, 30, 141
Gordon R. Michael 4, 8
Gouraud, Henri 209, 218, 221
Greater Syria 4, 8, 40, 41, 45–47, 49–51, 53, 54, 59–61, 69–71, 76–80, 85–88, 91, 94–98, 101–104, 106, 115, 116, 120, 164, 168, 173, 176, 181, 186, 194, 195, 205, 208, 209, 217, 219, 221, 231, 244, 247–250, 311, 328, 341, 369
Gujarat 98
Gulf Cooperation Council (GCC) 321, 331–333
Gulf Security Council 330
Gulf War I 314, 316, 321, 322, 334, 335
Gulf War II 329, 331, 348, 363, 367
Guoqiang, He 351

Habash, George 182, 320
Habbus (al-Hasan) 26
Habras 95
Haddah Agreement 223, 229, 327
Haditha 328
Hafiz, Abd al-Halim 404
Haider, Mahmoud 401
Haifa 118, 132, 243, 280, 306
Hail 217, 228
Haj Iyal, al-Jakmi 91
Hajar 128
Hajaya 125
Haji Ibn Musa, Ahmad al-Sa'di al-Hasbani 107
Haldon, John 39
Halevi Eliezer, Rabbi 183
Halhul 295
Hama 68, 71, 73, 85, 86, 94, 104, 108, 110, 186, 205
Hamad, Jamal 262
Hamarneh, Mustafa 367
Hamas 272, 306, 330, 348, 365
Hamdan, Muhammad 390
Hamdi Effendi, Ahmad 166
Hamdoun, Mustafa 262
Hamid 124
Ḥamima 55–57
Hammam as-Sarakh 50
Hammarskjold, Dag 300
Hamza 364
Hanano, Ibrahim 220
Handerson, Loy 340, 342
Hanu, Ibrahim 219
Haqish 240
Ḥaran 53, 56
Harfush 117
Har-Gil, Yitzhak 225, 227, 228
Hartha 85, 86
Harun, Mount 73
Hasa 97, 98, 101, 110, 115, 128, 130, 154, 159, 193, 199
Hasan, al-Azraq 101
Hasan al-Din, bin Bakish 81
Hasan al-Din, Tarntai al-Mansuri 72
Hashem, Ibrahim 185
Hashem Rashid, Ali 399
Hashem Rashid, Harun 399
Hashemite Kingdom of Jordan 1–6, 8, 9, 13
Hashemites 2, 3, 5–8, 10, 163, 165, 170, 174, 175, 181, 186–188, 196, 198, 200, 209, 210, 215, 220, 221, 240, 245, 247, 249, 252, 253, 259, 266, 268, 271, 274, 278, 289, 290, 292, 295, 297, 300, 302, 305, 310, 312, 316–318, 321–324, 328, 329, 334, 336, 340, 343, 345, 350, 353, 358, 365, 366, 373, 374, 376, 377, 383, 390, 392, 396, 397
Hashmonean 20

Hassan, bin-Talal (Crown Prince) 8, 255, 320, 334, 364, 392
Hattar, Nahid 194, 249, 270, 290
Ḥattin 61, 74
Hausa 40
Hawara 119
Hawirat 189
Hawra (Khirbet al-Khaldeh) 38, 55
Hawran 30, 49, 59, 61, 78, 84, 86, 90, 97, 103, 109, 117, 121–123, 124–125, 126, 127, 129, 132, 133, 136–138, 145, 146, 156, 162, 166, 171, 174, 190–192, 204, 205, 208, 215, 216, 224, 311
Hayaris 192
Haydarah 59
Hayden, Bill 357
Haytham bin Khater 81
Haytham bin Khatir 110
Hazim 328
Hazza', Abbas Mirza 265
Hebrew Committee of National Liberation 341
Ḥebron 21, 61, 68, 72, 77, 96, 101, 104, 126, 128, 143, 145, 295, 297, 302
Hegra (Mada'in Salih) 29
Heikal, Muhammad, Hassanein 313, 325
Ḥejaz 40, 42, 51, 54, 55, 60, 72, 75, 96–98, 101, 102, 110, 117, 119, 121, 122, 127, 128, 131, 133, 135, 140, 153–155, 160, 162, 164–167, 173, 176, 183, 186, 189, 193, 204, 205, 209, 210, 213, 217, 222–224, 227, 229, 231, 232, 240, 261, 279, 280, 298, 328, 334, 403
Henry II de Lusignan 75
Heracles 24
Heraclides of Cumae 26
Heraclius 39–41, 46
Herbat Masad 38
Hermon 14
Herod the Great, (King of Judah) 27, 28, 124
Herut Party 303
Herzog, Chaim 301, 302
Ḥeshbon, (Hisban) 18, 23, 28, 57, 95, 99, 104, 105, 107, 166, 174, 266
Hezbollah, (of Lebanon) 330, 351, 400, 401
Hierocles 38
Higher Committee for the Coordination of the National Opposition Parties 272
Hijazi, Rula 402
Hilal, Fuad 261, 323
Hill Gray 123
Hilmi, Abbas, Khedive 233
Hilmi, Ahmad 222
Hilmi, Hussein Pasha 125, 126
Ḥims 39, 45, 46, 50, 59, 68, 72, 77, 85, 86, 104, 108, 116, 205
Hinchcliffe, Peter 305, 334
Hippos, (Sussita) 27, 30
Hira 49, 51
Hisham al-Din Bakyash 79
Hisham al-Din bin Bakish 80
Histadrut 184
Hofstede G. 393
Homer, Dr 233
Hoskins E. Franklin 119
Hospitallers 73
Hourani, Hani 255
House of Saud 240, 245
Houthis 400, 401
Howard, John 358
Hulegu, Khan 68–70
Husayn, Rashid 399
Hussein, bin Bakish 82
Hussein, Ibn Talal, (King) 3, 4, 6, 9, 10, 186, 188, 198, 247–251, 254, 262, 264, 266, 268–270, 272, 276, 277, 281, 283, 284, 289, 292–294, 296, 299–301, 303, 305, 306, 310, 313–316, 318–326, 328–330, 332, 334, 335, 343–348, 350, 353, 356–358, 363, 364, 367–369, 374, 375, 377, 384, 392, 397, 401; Arab Legion 259, 278–280; Baghdad Pact 264–265; Ba'th Party 259, 260; Bedouin tribes 366; Black September 276; CIA (Central Intelligence Agency) 364; constitutional reforms 281; death of 364; democratization 363; Disengagement from the West Bank (1988) 277, 335; Establishment of Israel 259, 260; Fear of an Egyptian inspired coup 266; Foreign Donners 367; Gamal Abd al-Nasser 264, 269; Glubb's Dismissal 259, 260, 265, 266, 280–283; Hamas 272; Hazza' al-Majali 265; Influx of the Palestinian Refugees 259; Iraqi Coup, (1958) 264; Islamic Challenge 266–274; Israel's operation in Qibya 265; Jordanian Free Officers Movement 260–262; Muslim Brotherhood 270; Nasser's influence 266, 369; National Economy 376–380; Oslo Accord 364; Palestine War of 1948 259, 260, 265; Palestinian Challenge 275–278; political parties 370, 374; Political Parties Law (1992) 268; public works 377;

Quest for National Security 283–285; Saddam Hussein 367; Salafia Movement 273–274; Six-Day War 276, 277; Suez Affair 284; Syrian Ba'th Party 259, 260; Turkey 265; Wadi Araba Peace Accord 268
Hussein, Saddam 314, 319–322, 329, 331, 332, 334, 348, 378, 380, 397
Hussein, Sharif of Mecca 3, 8, 208–210, 213, 220, 223, 225, 226
Huwaytat 125, 126, 128, 131, 154, 160, 163, 193, 196, 197
Hyrcanus, John I 27
Hyun-suk, Shin 352

Ibad 130
Ibn Abd al-Aziz, Umar 52
Ibn Abd al-Malik, Akidir 40, 42
Ibn Abd al-Malik Muhammad 51
Ibn Abd al-Malik, Yazid II 50, 53
Ibn Abdallah Ali 53, 57
Ibn Abdallah Aybak 62
Ibn Abdallah, Talal, (King) 248
Ibn Abi Asib'a 104
Ibn Abi Sufyan Mu'awiya 50, 52
Ibn Abi Sufyan, Yazid 45–47, 50
Ibn Abi Talib, Ali 56
Ibn Abi Waqqas, Sa'd 42
Ibn Abu Talif Ja'far 41
Ibn al-'As Amr 42, 45, 46, 48, 49
Ibn al-Atar al-Saghir 90
Ibn al-Fakih al-Ḥamdani 39
Ibn al-Furat 72, 81
Ibn al-Hussein, Talal (King) 259, 281
Ibn Ali al-Abbasi Muhammad 56
Ibn al-Jaraḥ Daghfal 59
Ibn al-Khattab, Umar 46
Ibn al-Mahdi Ibrahim 57
Ibn al-Muhmandar 83
Ibn al-Qalanisi 60
Ibn al-Qan al-Ghazawi 85, 86
Ibn al-Shaikh, Yusuf Fakhr-al-Din 62
Ibn al-Sirafi 98
Ibn al-Sumayda bin Hazbar al-Imliqi 189
Ibn al-Walid Khalid 42, 44–46, 48, 49
Ibn al-Wardi 68
Ibn 'Amr Farwa 41
Ibn 'Amr Isbagh 41
Ibn 'Amr Shuraḥbil 41, 46, 49
Ibn 'Auf Abd al-Raḥman 4
Ibn Aybak al-Dawadari 78
Ibn Ayyas 103
Ibn Baḥdal, Khas 52
Ibn Fadl, al-Jarmi 87
Ibn Farukh, Muhammad 145
Ibn Fayz Sattam 176
Ibn Hajar, al-Asqalani 77, 84
Ibn Harith, Zayd 41
Ibn Haritha, al-Muthanna 44
Ibn Hasanah, Shurahbil 45, 47, 48
Ibn Hazim Badr 59
Ibn Ismail, Shaikh 90
Ibn Iyas 89
Ibn Jabir, Sa'id 206
Ibn Jabr, Amr 190, 191
Ibn Jad 131
Ibn Jahsh Abdallah 42
Ibn Jarraḥ, Abu Ubaidah 45–48, 50
Ibn Khaldan 199
Ibn Khaldun 6, 7, 46, 187
Ibn Khattab, Umar 175
Ibn Kilis, Ya'qub 59
Ibn Marwan, Abd al-Malik 51, 53, 55
Ibn Muhammad, Abdallah Ibn Hanafiyah 56
Ibn Muhammad, Ibrahim 54, 56
Ibn Naim, Nasrallah 190
Ibn Naim, Salam 190
Ibn Omeir Harith 41
Ibn Qadi Shuhba 82, 91
Ibn Qalaun 192
Ibn Qays Abdallah 47
Ibn Raf'i al-Barzali 106, 108
Ibn Rashid 170
Ibn Ruwaha Abi Abdallah 41
Ibn Ruyah, John 42
Ibn Sa'd, Khalid 44
Ibn Sa'd, Shaikh 90
Ibn Saddal, al-Ghazawi 90
Ibn Sarsa 82
Ibn Saud 125, 217, 223, 229, 280, 284, 327, 328, 342
Ibn Saud, Abd al-Aziz 248
Ibn Shaddad 69
Ibn Shaddad, Antarah 398
Ibn Taymiyya 78
Ibn Tughri Bardi 89
Ibn Tulun Ahmad 57
Ibn Turan, Shah 62
Ibn Yusuf, al-Ḥajjaj 52, 53
Ibn Zayd, Osama 43
Ibn Zayd, Sa'id 48
Ibn Zubayr, Abdallah 51, 55
Ibrahim bin Abd al-Rahman, Ibn Muhammad al-Majid al-Karaki 105
Ibrahim bin Muhammad, bin Isa Abu Ishaq al-Ajluni 106
Ibrahim bin Musa al-Sayid, Burhan al-Din al-Salti 108

Ibrahim bin Shadbak 95
Ibrahim Ibn Muhammad Ali Pasha 118–120, 125, 126, 129, 133, 144, 147, 193, 198
Ibrahim Ibn Musa bin Balal, bin Damj al-Karaki 106
Idhr'at 60, 82, 86, 97, 108, 110
Idumea 27, 37
Ifriqiya 61
Ikhshidids 58, 59
Ikhwan 228, 229
Ilkhan of Persia 79
Ilyas al-Jarkasi 83
Imad al-Din Ahmad Bin Isa al-Azraqi al-Ameri al-Karaki al-Shafi'I 106
Imad al-Din Ahmad Bin Isa al-Karaki 105
Imad al-Din Ahmad Isa al-Muqairi al-Karaki 80, 81, 84
Imad al-Din al-Haisbani 106, 107
Imad al-Din Yusuf bin Ahmad al-Ba'uni 106, 108
Imshah, Hadraj 327
Inab, Mundhir 262, 263
India 39, 95, 96, 98, 350–352
Intifada, Al-Aqsa 272
Invocation Movement 370
Iqbardi Tawghan al-Mun'qar 87
Iran 77, 265, 272, 301, 314, 320, 321, 329–331, 350, 400
Iran-Iraq War 321, 326, 329, 347, 377
Iraq 2, 3, 6, 8, 54, 85, 95, 96, 100, 103, 199, 200, 207, 208, 212, 218, 221, 223, 240, 244, 250, 261, 263, 267, 272, 277, 282, 290, 291, 301, 312, 314, 316–321, 328–332, 335, 343, 348, 349, 363, 364, 369, 373–375, 397, 399, 403
Iraq, al-Amir 123, 139
Iraq National Oil Company 243
Iraq Petroleum Company (IPC) 242, 243, 280, 283, 340
Iraqi Revolution (1958) 369
Irbid (Arbela) 18, 50, 70, 84, 86, 95, 96, 98, 119, 123, 134, 136, 154, 166, 172, 173, 181, 209, 230, 256, 267, 374
Irby, Leonard 14, 165
Irfan Shahid 39
Irgun 2
Isa bin Ahmad bin Mansur al-Ajluni 106
Isa bin-Fadl 82, 86
Isaac 1
Ishmael 17
Iskander, Beg 116
Islamic Action Front Party 271, 374
Islamic Center Charity Society 270
Islamic Labor Front 268
Islamic State of Iraq and Syria (ISIS) 274
Israel 3, 6, 8–10, 22, 143, 182, 184–186, 253, 259, 261, 265, 266, 268, 272, 276, 278, 284, 290, 291, 293–295, 297–300, 302–306, 312–314, 320, 322, 324, 326, 330, 331, 334, 340, 342–347, 351, 355, 357, 358, 364, 365, 371, 397
Israel Defense Force (IDF) 284, 302, 318, 322
Issachar Heights 118
Istanbul 149, 191, 204, 221, 222
Istiqlal, (Party) 207, 209, 215, 217, 218, 220, 245, 356, 369, 371
Italy 144, 356
Izz al-Din Aybak bin Abdallah al Alani 70
Izz al-Din Aydamar al-Zahiri 72
Izz al-Din Usama 62, 70
Izzat Pasha al-Abid 127

Jabal al-Druz 13, 28, 29, 122, 127, 132, 138, 155, 157, 159, 191, 205, 215, 219, 221, 240, 241, 284
Jabal al-Shara 100
Jabal al-Tuneiq 13
Jabal Arafat 97
Jabal Awf (Ajlun) 60
Jabal Hamida 116
Jabala 44, 116
Ja'bari 143
Jabbôk 18, 20, 140, 183
Jabin Beni Uqbah 91
Jabir 89
Jabiyah 45
Jabotinsky, Vladimir 141, 185, 224, 303, 341
Jacob, (Patriarch) 1, 143
Jaddham 41, 189
Jaffa 50, 146, 162, 167, 353
Jafr 101
Jaha 384
Jahiliya 252
Jamal al-Makawi 85, 86
James, de Molay 74, 75
Janbulad, Muhammad Ali 134
Jannaeus, Alexander 25, 27
Jansen, Willy 392
Jantmar 82
Japan 352
Jaqmaq 89
Jaragh 402
Jarah 58
Jaram 85
Jarash 24, 25, 28–30, 37–39, 47, 49, 58, 60, 95, 123, 141, 142, 175–177, 181, 358, 403

Jarbak al-Daraki 100
Jardunah 160
Jarf al-Darawish 157, 158, 160
Jarkas al-Khalili 79
Jarkas al-Sawduni 84
Jarm 81, 87, 89
Jarrar 147–149
Jashulad, Ali 191
Jassar, Shaikh 356
Jaun 77
Jawf, (Jauf) 28, 40, 42, 44, 125, 129, 229
Jawlan, (Golan) 47, 50, 71, 121, 176
Jazi 240
Jazzar, Pasha 145–147
Jeddah 98, 102, 229
Jeddah Agreement (1927) 229
Jehoram, (King of Israel) 22
Jemal Pasha 138, 167, 170, 194
Jenin 72
Jericho 14–16, 22, 31, 38, 60, 72, 141, 156, 166, 167, 185, 195
Jericho Convention (1950) 369
Jeroboam I, King of Israel 21, 22
Jeroboam II, King of Israel 22
Jerusalem 16, 17, 42, 43, 61, 72, 74, 77, 85, 87, 88, 90, 96, 103, 104, 108, 110, 111, 114, 116, 117, 122, 125, 126, 129, 143, 145–149, 158, 167, 181, 184, 195, 214, 217, 221, 226, 260, 265, 267, 281, 292, 302, 319, 323, 353, 356, 357, 371, 376, 399–401
Jesup, C. Philip 342
Jewish Agency 185
Jezreel Valley 115, 118, 145
Jirayyis, Fauzi 399
Jisr al-Majami' 96
Joash, (King of Israel) 22
Job, Brian 6
Johariya, Hani 403
John and Theodore of Palestine 39
Johnson, Lyndon 302, 344
Johnston 343
Johnston Plan 9, 299, 344
Jordan 14, 15, 18, 22–24, 27–31, 36, 37, 39–41, 47, 51–53, 57–62, 68, 70, 71, 73, 75–80, 83, 85–87, 94, 96–101, 103, 104, 107, 108, 110–112, 114, 116–120, 122–126, 131, 133–135, 137, 141, 145, 146, 153–155, 160–162, 164–166, 170–172, 174–178, 180, 182–188, 192–201, 204–211, 213–221, 223–229, 232, 233, 240–243, 245–247, 249, 251–254, 259, 263, 265–268, 271–274, 276, 277, 281–284, 289, 291, 292, 294–298, 300, 301, 303–306, 310–313, 315–336, 340–345, 348–350, 352–358, 363–369, 371–373, 377, 378, 380, 383, 384, 388–391, 393, 396, 397, 399–404; Arab Cooperation Council 335; Australia 357–358; Britain 352–353; Canada 349–350; China 351; Egypt 322–325; France 353–355; Germany 355–356; Gulf Cooperation Council 332–333; Gulf Countries 332–336; India 351–352; Iran 329–331; Iraq 316–322; Italy 356; Japan 352; Lebanon 322; Libya 325–326; Oman 322; Russian Federation 350–351; South Korea 352; Syria 310–316; Turkey 331–332; United States 340–349; Vatican 356–357; *see also* Transjordan
'Jordan First' Policy 326, 363
Jordan, River 13, 14, 19, 28, 40, 60, 77, 100, 112
Jordanian Arab Party 370
Jordanian Arab Socialist Renaissance Party 370
Jordanian Communist Party 370, 372
Jordanian Constitutional Arab Front Party 370
Jordanian Democratic Union Party 370
Jordanian Free Officers 199, 260
Jordanian Land Party 370
Jordanian Welfare Party 370
Jotabe Island, (Jazirat Far'un) 38, 61
Jotham, (King of Judah) 22
Joyce, Colonel 161
Joyce, James 400
Jubran, Salim 399
Judah 21, 22, 28, 37, 39, 49, 121, 305
Judeh, Nasser 322
Judzam 41
Jum'a Sa'd 186
Justinian 38, 43

Kadas, (Kadesh Naphthali) 39
Kaf 229
Kafurites 59
Kakun 146
Kamshabgha al-Hamawi 82
Kanafani, Ghassan 400
Kan'an, Hamdi 294
Kanatha (al-Qanawat) 26
Karafat 123
Karak 2, 13, 16, 17, 23, 41, 57, 60, 61, 67–73, 76–85, 87–91, 94–100, 102–106,

108, 110–112, 114, 116, 117, 119–121, 123, 125–127, 128, 132–139, 142, 153, 156–158, 163–166, 170, 172–174, 176, 178, 179, 181, 183, 190, 191, 195, 196, 200, 205, 206, 209, 217, 219, 279
Karak Revolt 248
Karameh Campaign 303, 403
Karj 175
Karkhmuba (Krak Moab) 30
Kaswah 100
Katiba, Noursi Suha 404
Kaura 123
Kavala 176
Kawara 70
Ka'wash, Abdallah 403
Kawkab al-Hawah 61
Kedar 27
Kemankes, Ali Pasha 117
Kennedy, John 344
Khadir 124
Khaibar 72
Khalid, Shaikh 162
Khalid, Wadi 48
Khalidi, Rashid 4
Khalil 125
Khalil bin Shahin al-Zahri 91
Khalutza 37
Khamash, Ammar 402
Khamash, Majd al-Din 177
Khameini, Ayatollah 330
Khamra Beisan 72
Khan Aniza 101
Khan Qatrana 77
Khan Qiyad (Dab'a) 97
Khanjar, Adham 220
Khathrabah 122
Khatir, Amir 78, 91
Khattab bin Amr, bin Mihna bin Yahya al-Ghazawi al-Ajluni 107
Khazandar, Wadi 77
Khilat 68
Khirbet Abur 158
Khirbet Faḥl 25
Khirbet Jama' 21
Khomeini, Ayatollah 329
Khosroes 51
Khreis, Khalid 404
Khubab 171
Khufash, Mohannad 402
Khulki Bey, Ali 220
Khurasan 52, 54, 85
Khuri, Nabil 400
Khurma 229
Khurshid, As'ad 219
Khuwah 122, 128, 129, 131, 132, 135, 172, 193, 204, 243
Khuzira 122
Khyar, Sa'd 367
Kinasrin 50
Kinda 130
Kinglake Alexander William 118
Kir Haroshet 23
Kir Moab 23
Kirkbride L. Alan 279
Kirkbride Lent, Alec 178, 247, 279, 298, 327
Kirkuk 280, 350
Kissinger, Henry 314, 325, 346
Kleber, Jean Paptiste 126
Klirohi 27
Knox, Alfred 233
Komer, K. Robert 344
Kosovo 364
Krajevski, Leon 219
Krak Moab 30
Kufa 54–56
Kufarat 122
Kufriya 124
Kunaitra 122, 125, 146, 176, 183
Kura 124, 126, 279
Kura, (Kurrah) 195, 219
Kurd Hamza 117
Kurdistan 214
Kurds 332
Kurtbai, al-Ahmar 90
Kutuz, Saif al-Din 68
Kuwait 321, 322, 334, 348, 353, 377, 378, 380, 397

Labor Front Party 370
Labor Zionism 141
Lahman, Rafiq 404
Lahoud, Emile 322
Lajjun 72, 88, 101, 115, 118, 145, 189
Lakhm 41
Land Law (1858) 164
Lanners Donald 5
Laos 344
Larzilliere, Penelope 254
Latakia 176
Laterculus Veronesis 37
Law of Societies and Social Organizations 374
Lawrence, T.E. 153, 155, 156, 161, 162, 210, 211, 217, 218, 223, 227, 261
Layne Linda 200, 389
Lazi 37

League for National Liberation 371
Lebanese Civil War 377
Lebanon 135, 145, 173, 180, 186, 207, 215, 219, 249, 293, 295, 300, 304, 312, 314, 322, 343, 344, 348, 351, 399, 400, 403
Lefebvre, H. 390
Leja 137, 138, 171
Levy, Jack 4, 5
Ley, D. 383
Libanius of Antioch 38
Libbey William 119
Libya 325, 326, 332, 377
Likud Party 4, 295, 304, 305
Livias (Julias) 27, 38
Lloyd George, David 211, 215, 228
Lloyd, Peter 265
Lloyd, Selwyn 301
London 214, 218, 246, 262, 276
London Convention (1840) 126
Lorca, Garcia 399
Lot 14
Lovers of Zion 185
Ludd, (Lod) 213, 260, 281
Lu'la 110
Lull, Raymond 75
Lutf-Allah, Michel 217
Lutfi, Amr 355
Lutfi, Umar 279
Luxor 20
Lynch, W.F. 165

Ma'ab 45, 49, 59, 60
Ma'an 30, 39, 41, 53, 59, 61, 96–98, 101, 103, 110, 114, 117–121, 123, 126, 127–130, 128, 129, 131, 132, 134, 135, 137, 145, 154, 155, 157–160, 163–167, 170, 172–174, 180–182, 206, 208–210, 217, 221–223, 225, 229, 232, 241, 262, 326, 327, 335
Ma'an, Ali 191
Ma'an, Fakhr al-Din 192, 193, 200
Maccabi, Judah 143
MacDonald, Malcom 283, 353
MacDonald, Ramsey 233
Macintyre, Laurence 357
Mackereth, Gilbert 354
MacMahon, Henry 155
Macmillan, Harold 353
Macron, Emanuel 355
Madaba 18, 20–22, 25, 27–30, 37, 112, 117, 122, 137, 142, 143, 153, 159, 166, 167, 170, 178–182, 200, 218, 326
Madadha, Fallah 248
Mada'in, Mathew 28, 168
Madin 59, 189
Madrid Peace Conference (1991) 380
Mafarrija 190, 191
Mafraq 121, 166, 181
Maghreb 51, 52
Magles 165
Mahasneh, Sayf 402
Mahdawiya 130
Mahdi 52
Maher, Ali 244
Mahmoud, Musa 261
Mahmoudi, Shaikh 85, 88, 91
Majala 122
Majalis 125, 126, 129, 142, 159, 178
Majdal Bani Fadhil 144
Majmau' al-Muraj 77
Makhraba 284
Makhrug, wadi 328
Malchus of Philadelphia 38
Mali al-Mughith Amr 111
Malichus I, (King of the Nabateans) 28
Malik al-Ashraf Sha'ban 79
Malik Shah 61
Maltiya 86
Mamluk Sultanate, I 2, 10, 15
Mandela, Nelson 358
Mandeville, John 178
Mangles, James 13
Manku, Hamdi 355
Manshiya Affair 269
Manual II, Paleologus 75
Mapai Party (Israel) 140
Maqna 42
Maqrizi 86, 91, 103, 111
Marar, Shaikh 142, 143
Marcellinus Ammianus 29
Mardam Bey, Jamil 248
Mardin 89
Marga 73
Marhala 60
Marj 103
Marj Dabiq 2, 114
Marj Rahit 46, 52
Markaz Jisr al-Hasa 102
Marshall, George 342
Marwan II 56
Maryud, Ahamd 217, 222
Masada 395
Masaylun 207–209, 279
Mashlab, Amir 111
Masjid Du al-Jifa 40
Mastura 386
Mas'ud Ibn Baybars 77
Matar, Zahir 260

Matuszeski Janina 3
Maundrell Henry 139, 183
Mavia 38
Mayer, Arno 4, 5
Mazirib 97
McMahon, Henry 225
McMichael, Harold 244, 282
Meaton, Julia 393
Mecca 40, 42, 55–57, 61, 87, 97, 100, 101, 103, 111, 123, 162, 191, 194, 224, 226, 251, 253, 334
Medain Saleh 120, 126
Medina 40, 55–57, 78, 87, 97, 101, 110, 131, 132, 155, 160, 162, 239, 334
Meinertzhagen, Richard 206, 214
Meir, Golda 277, 299, 301–303
Meleagrus 26
Merill Saleh 122
Merkel, Angela 356
Mesha, (King of Moab) 1, 16–18, 21, 22
Meshaal, Khaled 306
Meshetta 50
Meshulam of Voltaira, Rabbi 144
Mesopotamia 226, 243
Michael, Rohan Denis 351
Michael the Syrian 40
Midhat, Pasha 142
Midhat, Sefik Ahmad 165
Midianites 128
Migdal, Joel 5, 7
Mihtar 84
Milhin, Qasim 371
Mintash 80–82
Miran, Shah 86
Mirsal, Sulafa Jadallah 403
Moab 1, 13, 16–22, 24, 29, 37, 60, 95, 99, 137, 141, 185, 216
Moabites 175, 253
Moahib 155
Mollet, Guy 301
Momsen, Theodor 31
Mongols 67, 97, 102, 112, 143
Monkton, RFP 274
Montreal Castle 14
Moretain Jean 142, 178
Morocco 326, 333
Moscow 350
Mossad 277, 306
Mosul 243
Mottaki Manouchehr 330
Mseibah 140, 184
Mu'ata 100
Mu'ayyad, Shaikh 89
Mubarak Shaikh (Banu Uqba) 110
Mudawara 157, 161, 229
Mughaira 327
Muha'dayn, Abd al-Rahman 263
Muhafiza, Ali 219, 255
Muhammad Ali Pasha, (Governor of Egypt) 118, 120, 125, 126, 131
Muhammad bin Abbas al-Salti 108
Muhammad bin Abi al-Jawd Nasir al-Din al-Karaki 90–91
Muhammad bin Ali bin Ja'far al-Ajluni 106
Muhammad bin Hamad bin Ma'tuq al-Karaki 106
Muhammad bin Khalil al-Asadi 103
Muhammad bin Khaydar bin Daud al-Balqawi 108
Muhammad bin Muhammad, bin Abi al-Jawad al-Karaki 106
Muhammad bin Qalaun 109
Muhammad bin Yusuf, bin Ali al-Ajluni 106
Muhammad Ibn Abdallah bin Ahmad al-Hakari al Salti 107
Muhammad Ibn Ibraham bin Radi al-Salti 107
Muhammad Sa'id, Agha 137
Mujahedin-e Khalq 330
Mujib Wadi, River 95
Mumaniya 130
Munib al-Madi 133
Munjid bin Khatir 84
Murad III 191
Murad IV 117
Musa, Shaikh 134
Musa, Sulayman 324
Musa, Wadi 156, 160, 163, 166
Musa'dah, Salim 264
Muscat 332
Musli, Alois 127
Muslim Brotherhood 266, 268–271, 273, 274, 278, 365, 366, 372, 374
Mustafa III 146
Mu'ta 196
Mu'tah 2, 39, 41, 42
Muti', Khalid 311
Mutlag, Mahmoud 372
Muzairib 100
Myers, J. Francis 341

Na'amneh, Mahmoud 391
Nabaioh 17
Nabatean Kingdom 1, 17, 23–26, 28, 124, 175, 249, 252, 389
Nabatia 37
Nablus 14, 15, 24, 60, 68, 77, 84–87, 89, 90, 108, 114–118, 120, 121, 126, 127,

130, 137, 145–148, 176, 182, 191, 205, 241, 292, 293, 295, 372
Nabonidus 16
Nabulsi, Sulayman 275, 289, 312, 323, 329, 343, 351, 372
Naḥash, (King of Ammôn) 21
Nahr al-Ihrayr 25
Na'ir Amir 81, 103
Najd 229, 240, 280
Naji, Jamal 401
Najm al-Din, Ayyub 71
Najm al-Din, Ibn Qadi Ajlun 107
Nakhl 88
Nakhla 42
Namla, Wadi 16
Nanteuil, de Philippe 73
Naor, Arye 304
Napolis, (Shechem, Nablus) 31
Nasir, (Son of Sharif Hussein of Mecca) 122, 153
Nasir al-Din, Abd Allah 83
Nasir al-Din, bin Mubarak 83
Nasir al-Din, Muhammad 81, 82
Nasir al-Din, Muhammad Ibn Abi Sayf Mudallal (Ibn Sa'id al-Ghazawi) 190
Nasir bin Ali, Sharif 204
Nasir Faraj bin Barquq 78, 88
Nasir, Fuad 371
Nasir, Kamal 399
Nasr al-Din, al Shaikh Ali 82
Nasrallah, Hasan 401
Nasrallah, Ibrahim 401
Nasser, Ahmad 401
Nasserism 261
National Charter 271, 374
National Constitutional Party 370
National Democratic People's Movement Party 370
National Front 372
National Labor Front Party 317, 370
National Socialist Party 329, 372
National Syrian Party 259
NATO (North Atlantic Treaty Organization) 358, 369
Na'ur 133, 142, 175
Nauruz 84, 87, 88, 91
Nawawi 107
Nazareth 104, 126
Nebo, Mount 22
Nebuchadnezzar, (King of Babylon) 17, 23
Negev 29, 30, 36, 37, 96, 281, 323
Negus 51
Nehemiah 24
Neo Babylonian Empire 16
Neruda, Pablo 399
Netanyahu, Benjamin 305
Neveh Vaadraa (Edrei) 29
Nicholas IV 75
Nicopolis 75
Nixon, Richard 345, 346
Nordau, Max 141, 185
North Yemen 335
Novach 19
Nuh 117
Nu'man 57
Nur al-Din 60
Nur, Queen 364
Nusseiba, Anwar 294

Obodas 27
Occupied Enemy Territory Administration (OETA) 279
Octavian 28
Odruh (Adroh) 30
Oliphant, Laurence 139–141, 176, 183–185
Oman 323
Omri, King of Israel 21
Onomasticon 29. 30
Organic Law (1928) 230, 231, 369
Oslo Accord 364
Osman, Nuri Pasha 129
Ottawa Convention 349
Ovadia of Bartnura 144

Pahlavi, Muhammad Reza Shah 329
Pakistan 265, 351
Palawan 77
Palestina Prima 37, 38
Palestina Salutaris 37
Palestina Secunda 37
Palestina Tertia 15, 37, 39
Palestine 17, 21, 24, 27, 29–31, 36–38, 40, 45, 46, 53, 57, 59, 61, 70, 103, 117–121, 125, 131, 145, 149, 155, 160–162, 176, 180, 184, 185, 193, 206–208, 210, 212, 213, 215–225, 227, 229, 232, 233, 241, 242, 244, 246, 250, 272, 275, 276, 297, 305, 326, 341, 342, 354, 356, 369, 388, 397, 403
Palestine Liberation Organization (PLO) 3, 277, 291–296, 301, 304, 314, 319, 347, 355, 357, 397
Palestine War (1948) 13, 174, 181, 182, 184, 199, 241, 247, 250, 259, 260, 262, 265, 275, 281, 282, 284, 296, 299, 312, 317, 322, 323, 369, 371, 376
Palma, Cornelius 28
Palmach 303

Palmyra, (Tadmor) 2, 43, 44, 88, 117
Pan Arabism 310, 312, 323, 366, 371
Paris 214, 218, 262, 301
Partition Plan (Palestine: 1947) 317, 355, 371
Paulus VI 181
Peake, Frederick 197, 222, 223, 262, 279, 281, 354
Pechel 25
Pedersen, Anne-Marie 394
Pekaḥ Ben Remaliahu 22
Pella, (Fiḥl) 1, 18, 25–27, 30, 37, 58
Penuel 21
People's Party 368, 369
Peres, Shimon 305
Peripheral Plan 301
Perse St-John 399
Persia 39, 43, 46, 85, 100
Persians 67
Personal Status Law 272
Peru 358
Pescenius 42
Peter I, de Lusignan 74, 75
Petra 1, 16, 17, 25, 26, 28–30, 36, 37, 55, 76, 128, 154, 160, 166, 187, 188, 389, 391
Phelps Grant, Christina 195
Philadelphia, (Amman) 17, 26–30, 36, 37, 176
Philby, John 197, 221–223
Philip IV 74, 75
Philip of Mesieres 75
Philip, the Tetrarch 28
Philipolis 30
Phoenicia 38
Pinkerton C. Lowell 340
Pisa 102
Pliny the Younger 26, 28
Pokaran 351
Political and Justice Development Party 272
Political Parties Law (1992) 268, 366, 374
Polybius 24
Pompey, Gnaeus 27
Pope, Benedict XVI 357
Pope, John Paul XII 356
Pope, Paul II 357
Pope, Paul VI 357
Popular Democratic Front for the Liberation of Palestine 182
Popular Front for the Liberation of Palestine 320
Popular Resistance 371
Porte 115, 117, 120
Portuguese 98
Possot, Denis 14
Praeses 37
Press and Publications Law 271, 366, 375
Pretoria 358
Procopius 43, 44
Progressive Arab Renaissance Party 370
Progressive Ba'th Party 374
Progressive Party 370
Ptolemaic dynasty 24
Ptolemaus, Claudius 30
Ptolemy 55
Ptolemy II, Philadelphus 24
Ptolemy III Euergetes 24
Putin, Vladimir 350, 351, 400

Qabb Ilyas 117
Qabbus, Sultan 332
Qadda'a 58
Qaddafi, Mu'amar 324–326
Qadi Abd al-Basit 100
Qadi Ala-Din Ali, al-Muqayri al Karaki al-Shafi'i 105
Qadi Ismail bin Khalifa, bin Abd al-Hasbani 107
Qalaun 72, 143
Qalqashandi 109
Qalqilya 21, 299
Qani Bai al-Muhammadi 88
Qansu (family) 189–192
Qansu Ahmad 191, 192
Qansu al-Ghuri 98, 114
Qansu, Bashir 192
Qansu, Hamdan 192
Qansu Hamdun, Ibn Ahmad 189–191
Qansu Ibn Musta'ida, Ibn MuslimIbn al-Ghazawi 190
Qansu, Saif 192
Qanswa al-Yahyawi 90
Qaramatians 58
Qasim al-Ahmad 125
Qasim al-Harathi 82
Qasim bin Ali Bakr al-Ajluni 106
Qasim Muhammad al-Irbid al-Shafi'i 108
Qasim, Uthman 222
Qasr al-Azraq 51
Qasr al-Majali 132, 133
Qasr al-Taubi 51
Qasr al-Tuba 50
Qasr Shabib 90
Qastel 50
Qatar 326, 333, 336
Qatishat 130
Qatrana 128, 157, 158, 167, 192, 199, 205, 217

Qayn 41
Qays and Yaman 52–54, 84, 91, 147, 148
Qaytabi al-Thamadani 90
Qibyah 265, 266
Qinasrin 59
Qualified International Zone 365
Quilici, Francois 312
Qur'an and Sunna Society 274
Quraysh 251
Qutb al-Din al-Nahrawali 127
Qutuz 69, 70
Quweilbeth 58

Rababeh, Shaher 388
Rabbath Ammon, (Biblical Amman) 15, 16, 20, 21, 23, 29
Rabbathmoba 29
Rabbel II, King of the Nabateans 28
Rabin, Leah 305
Rabin, Yitzhak 305, 306
Radha 130
Rahbi, Ahmad 313
Raimouny, Samer 401
Rajab, Raghib Mahmoud 154
Ram Wadi 137, 170
Ramallah 181, 185, 295
Ramat Matred 42
Ramla 58, 59, 74, 103, 110, 128, 141, 260, 281
Ramses II, (King of Ancient Egypt) 19, 20
Ramtha 95, 97, 101, 123, 126, 166, 209, 354
Ramzi, Ismet 261
Raof Pasha 129
Raqim 60
Rashadiyah 156, 158, 160
Rashid, Nadhir 261
Rashid Paha, Mehmet 136
Rashid Pasha 127, 129, 137, 171
Rashid Pasha, Mehmet 174
Rashid, Shaikh 192
Rashidat, Abd al-Rahman 206
Rashidun, (The First Four Rightly Guided Caliphs) 46, 272
Rawabda, Abd al-Ra'uf 256, 368
Rawlah 240
Raydaniyah 115
Rayyan 148
Reading, Lord 296
Reagan Plan 347
Reagan, Ronald 295, 347
Red Line Agreement 243
Reuben, (Hebrew Tribe) 18–20
Revival Party 370
Reynold of Karak 61
Rezin, King of Aram-Damascus 22
Rhodes, Armistice 297
Riad, Nasser 105
Riddah Ali, Pasha 220
Riddah Wars 46
Right, Michael 340
Riyadh 248
Robinson, Glen 271
Robinson Lees 122
Robinson, Ronald 118
Roderick, (King of the Visigoths) 51
Rogers, William 324
Roman Empire 1, 15, 28
Rome 36
Rosenau, James 4
Rosencrance, Richard 4
Rothchild, de Edmond 141, 185
Rudd, Kevin 357
Rum, Wadi 391
Rumaynin 178
Rusafa 142
Rusayfa 175, 177
Rushdam 124
Russia 180, 350, 351; *see also* Russian Federation
Russian Federation 340, 350, 351
Rutbah 244
Ruthenberg, Abraham 298, 299
Ruthenberg, Pinhas 141, 185
Ruthenberg Plan 296
Ruwalla 129, 136, 154, 155, 162, 174, 217, 282, 328
Ryan, Curtis 335

Sabbah, Michel 357
Sabri, Ali 266
Sabri, H. 393
Sa'd al-Din Ibn Ghurab 87
Sa'd, Shaikh 137, 171
Sadat, Anwar 9, 294, 314, 319, 325, 346, 347
Sa'di 122
Sadiq Pasha 127
Sadiyeen 241
Safad, (Safed) 89, 95, 104, 107, 191
Safar Barlik 154, 204
Safavid Persia 114
Sahab 279
Sahliya 80
Sahliyeh, Emile 269
Saif al-Din, al-Qablawi 91
Saif al-Din, Bakhtamar al-Hasami 105

Saif al-Din Barquq, al-Zahir 78
Saif al-Din, Bitkas al-Sawduni 84
Saif al-Din, Ma'mun al-Qalmatawi 79
Saint Hilarion 31
Sakhab 20
Sakhra 85, 90
Salafia 273
Salah al-Din Yusuf, al-Malik al-Nasir 68–70
Salah, Muhammad 242
Salamash 87
Salame, Ghassan 6
Salamish 85
Salayt 128
Salibi 146
Salih, Abdul Qadir 372
Salim al-Sabagh, Muhammad 355
Salim, Fuad 222
Salim Mhmad Effendi 173
Salim, Nasri 222
Salkhad 116
Salkhat 155
Salloukh, Bassel 5
Salome, Alexandra 27
Samar, Salih 402
Samaria (Nablus, Sebastia) 39, 40, 115, 121, 145, 305
Samarqand 98
Samu' 302
Samuel, Herbert 209, 213, 218, 221, 225, 226, 279
San Remo Convention, (1920) 208, 243
Sanamin 100
Sanbalat of Samaria 17
Sandler, Shmuel 2, 295
Sanjar Bin Abdallah al Jawali 103, 104, 108
Santo Feniro 102
Sanur 147
Sapir, Joseph 303
Sara 144
Sardiya 130, 136, 174, 193
Sarim al-Din Qaimag al-Nasir 69
Sar'in 117
Sarkhad 77, 80, 88
Sarraj, Abd al-Hamid 311
Sartre, Jean Paul 399
Saru 126
Sassanid Persians 2, 124
Sattam, Faiz 179
Saudi Arabia 3, 6, 8, 240, 265, 272, 290, 319, 321, 323, 324, 326–329, 333, 334, 342, 373
Saudi Islamic Brotherhood 207
Saul, King of Israel 1, 21
Sawad 60
Sawalha, Hanna S. Ihab 393
Sawan 101
Sawdan al-Hamzawi 87
Sawdan al-Mizfari 79
Sawdun al-Jalb 87–89
Sawdun al-Muhammadi 87, 88
Sawdun al-Zarif 83, 84
Sawdun Baqja 88
Scaurus, Emilius Marcus 27
Scheffer, Jaap de Hoop 358
Schirin, Fathi 196
Schlumberger, Oliver 367
Schumacher, Gottlieb 194
Scorpion Pass 297
Sebastia 31, 43; *see also* Shomron
Secret Organization of the National Officers in the Jordanian Army 260
Seetzen Jasper, Ulrich 14
Seir Mountain 14, 17, 19
Seleucia 25
Seleucids 24, 124
Selim I 114, 115
Seljuks 61, 178
Sellah 23
Seoul 352
Severus, Septimius 42
Sevres, Treaty of 226
Sha'alan, Nuri 155
Sha'alan, Trad 162
Shaba 72
Sha'ban 75
Sha'ban Azbak Dawadar al-Amir Nauruz 87
Sha'ban bin Abi al-Abbas 84
Shabib bin Maki 101
Shabib, Kamil 318
Shabsugh 176
Shafar'am 146
Shahein, Dalia 402
Shahin al-Zardakash 88
Shahin, Rushdi 371, 372
Shahir, Adil 262
Shahrzw Kurds 68
Sh'aib, Nabbi 128
Shaikh Sa'd, (village) 125
Shakespeare, Captain 123
Shallala, Wadi 230
Shalmaneser III 124
Shamar Emirate 229
Shamar, Jabal 280
Shamir, Itzhak 303, 304, 347
Shams al-Din, Abu Abdallah Muhammad bin Sa'id al-Ajluni 107

Shams al-Din, al-Akhnai 88
Shams al-Din, Ibn Tulun 95
Shams al-Din, Muhammad bin Abbas bin Muhammad bin Abbas al-Salti 108
Shams al-Din, Sami 296
Shams al-Din Sawab al-Sahily 94
Shamsdin Muhammad Ali, Agha 136, 173
Shanin, Amir 110
Shaqhab, (Battle of Marj al-Saffar) 78, 82
Shara 99, 118, 128
Sharaf al-Din, al-Kafiri al-Ajluni 107
Sharaf al-Din, al-Qashtamri 83
Sharaf al-Din, al-Samaqi 109
Sharaf al-Din, bin Musa bin Ahmad al-Ramthawi 108
Sharaf al-Din, Musa bin Qadi al-Oudh 84
Sharaf, Leila 255
Sharett, Moshe 296–299, 342
Sharif Hussein of Mecca 121, 155, 158, 160, 186, 204, 291
Sharon, Ariel 4, 272, 304
Sharon, Plain of 118
Sharp, M. Jeremy 348
Sharqa 125, 126
Shati bin Uqbah 109
Shawbak 61, 69, 72, 73, 77–79, 81, 88, 94, 97, 99, 108, 110, 112, 116, 127, 128, 154, 156, 158–160
Sheba 16
Shechem 21, 42; *see also* Nablus; Samaria
Sherah Hills 16, 50, 53, 59, 60
Shihab al-Din, Abu al-Abbas Ahamd bin Rashid bin Tarkhan al-Malkawi 108
Shihab al-Din, Ahmad al-Hasbani 107
Shihab al-Din, Ahmad bin Abd al-Wahhab al-Nuwayri 82, 88, 97
Shihab al-Din, Ahmad bin al-Shaikh 85, 86
Shihab al-Din, al-Bau'ni 108
Shihab al-Din, al-Habbab 108
Shihab al-Din, al-Halabi 85, 86, 108
Shiloah, Reuven 298
Shiraz 98
Shirwan 175
Shkarat Msaied 16
Shomron 21–23, 30, 146; *see also* Nablus
Shryock, Andew 254, 390
Shuckburgh, John 210
Shunnaq, Muhammad 391
Shurayda, Yusuf 135, 172
Sibai 90
Sicily 112
Sidon 50, 116, 117, 146–148
Sidqi, Najati 400
Siḥon 18, 21, 23
Sijilmasa 51
Silver, Abba Hillel 341
Simla Agreement, (1972) 351
Sinai 29, 61
Sinan, Pasha 190
Sir, Wadi 141, 175, 176
Sirhan, Hasan Ibrahim 403
Sirhan Wadi 40, 46, 57, 126, 130, 136, 153, 170, 174, 196, 217, 224, 229, 280
Sisco, Joseph 314
Six-Day War 3, 4, 13, 174, 186, 253, 276, 277, 291, 292, 294, 295, 302–305, 310, 318, 319, 324, 345, 355, 369, 374, 378, 399, 403
Skytopolis (Beisan, Beit Sh'an) 26, 30
Sloot 138
Society for the Preservation of the Qur'an 270
Solidarity Party 369
Solomon, (King of Israel) 21
Somalia 348
Somer, L. Andrew 341
Somerset, E. R. 211, 279
Sons of Ammôn 20
South Africa 358
South Korea 344, 352
South Yemen 332
Soviet Union 265, 316, 343, 347, 348, 350, 371
Spafford, Vester Bertha 167
Stafford, Colonel 354
Stephanus of Byzantium 24
Stifftung, Frederick Ebert 356
Stifftung, Frederick Newmann 356
Subiba 87
Sudan 291, 329
Sudi, Suleiman Pasha 242, 284
Suez Affair 266, 284, 323, 355
Sukhna 142, 175, 177
Sulayman, Musa 133, 247, 260, 266
Suleiman II 115
Suleiman (Sulayman) the Magnificent 116
Ṣur (Tyre) 39, 40, 123
Suraq 85
Susiyah 47
Suwada 220
Suwaylih 142, 175
Suwayt 61, 95
Swalha, Nabil 397
Syein Muhammad, Mustafa 276
Sykes, Mark 215, 228
Sykes-Picot Agreement, (1916) 2, 207, 215, 221, 225, 249
Syria 1–3, 6, 8, 9, 21, 23, 30, 31, 47, 57, 67, 70, 76, 83, 85–87, 89, 94–96, 100, 112, 116, 120, 121, 124, 129, 132, 137,

143, 145, 155, 158, 162, 165, 170, 175, 186, 189, 193, 194, 199, 200, 204–207, 209, 210, 212, 214–216, 218, 219, 222, 224–227, 232, 240, 242–245, 249, 259, 261, 262, 275, 277, 290, 291, 294, 300–302, 304, 306, 323–325, 328, 329, 331, 332, 335, 343, 345–347, 350, 351, 353, 355, 356, 365, 367, 369, 373, 377, 390, 396, 399, 400, 403, 404; *see also* Greater Syria
Syrian Civil War, (2011) 380

Ta'amrah 145
Taba, Wadi 131
Tabbuk 40–42, 45, 59, 97, 101, 120, 126, 128, 167, 189, 221, 229
Tabenkin, Yitzhak 184
Tabor, Battle of 147
Tabriz 85
Tadmuri 143
Tafas 162
Tafila 50, 61, 114, 119, 123, 126, 129, 132, 137, 154, 156–160, 162, 163, 166, 167, 170, 179, 195, 200, 206, 219, 242
Taghai Tamr al-Qablawi 78
Taghitmar Ibn Abd Allah, al-Ala al Qablawi 83
Tahama 96
Taif 42
Taifat Arab 116
Taiman 23
Taj al-Din, bin al-Salti 108
Taj al-Din, Rizq Allah 88
Tal, Wasfi 199, 276
Talal, (King) 369
Tali, Rashid 216–218, 220
Tall al- Umari 1
Tall, Salih 166
Tallal, al-Khair al-Din 162
Tamerlane 77, 79, 84–87, 101
Tamriya 86
Tanaib 229
Tanukhids 38
Tanzimat 120, 164, 179
Taqi al-Din, Ibn Qadi Ajlun 107
Tarawaneh, Muhammad 126, 387
Tarqi, Wadi 130
Tasbasi, Aysegul 391
Tawana 158, 163
Tawayana 240
Tawjan al-Sayfi 91
Tawqan, Sulayman 264
Tay 59
Taym, Wadi 96
Taz 82
Teheran 330, 331
Tel Abil 25
Tel al-Ash'ari 25
Tel al-Sarim 16
Tel Aviv 184, 323
Tel Umm-al-Ammad 25
Teleilat Ghassul 1, 15
Tell al-Sa'diyeh 18, 23
Tell Ammata 27
Tell Mazar 23
Templar, Gerald 265
Terabeen 241
Tesio, Fausto 356
Thaddeus of Naples 75
Thamud 41
Thaniyat al-Okab 46
Thebes 31
Theodorus 46, 48
Theophanes the Confessor 39
Theophilus of Edessa 40
Thevenot de Jean 118
Thomas, Dylan 399
Thomas, Lowell 160
Thomas, Peter 75
Tiberias, (Tabariyyah) 14, 28, 39, 49, 50, 121, 126, 146, 189
Tiberius 28
Tiglat-Pileser III, King of Assyria 22
Timurids 85, 97
Tirzah 21
TJFF 280, 282
Tobias the Ammonite 17, 24
Toledo, Alejandro 358
Tomadhir 41
Trachon 29
Trachtenberg, Marc 5
Trajan 28, 31, 37, 55
Trans Jordanem 13
Trans-Arabian Pipeline, (Tapline) 340, 341
Transjordan Frontier Force 231, 242, 244
Transjordan National Covenant 299
Transjordan Organic Law 284
Treaty of London (1946) 246
Trenchard, Hugh 213
Tripoli 83, 88, 89, 94, 103, 104, 108, 118, 133, 243
Truman Doctrine 342
Truman, Harry 242
Tu'amah, George Niqulah Dibb 310
Tubaiq 327
Tughri Bardi 89
Tughtikin, Zahir al-Din 60
Tukan, Qadri 372
Tukkan, Mustafa 146
Tul Karem 141, 185

Tuma bin Ibrahim al-Tayib al-Shawbaki 108
Tunis 330
Tunisia 267, 272
Tunun 327
Tuqan 147–149
Tuqan, Fadwa 398
Tuqan, Ibrahim 398
Turabah, (Battle of) 229, 245
Turabay, Ahmad 145
Turabay, bin Karajah 115, 117
Turk Rukn al-Din Khass 68
Turkey 68, 208, 227, 248, 265, 284, 301, 331–332, 350
Turkish Petroleum Company (TPC) 243
Turkoman 142
Turton, D. 391
Twilan 17

Udhrah 42
Ukraine 351
Ula 95
Umar II 42, 47, 50
Umayyads 50–54, 56, 57, 128, 189, 249
Umm al Rasas 58, 140, 177, 184
Umm al-Ahmad 229
Umm al-Jamal 95
Umm al-Jimal 58
Umm Kulthum 404
Umm Qais 58, 388
Umm Qasr 320
United Arab Emirates (UAE) 326, 333
United Arab Republic 275, 277, 294, 312, 314, 318, 323, 324, 326, 343
United Nations 242 Resolution 304, 338, 357
United Nations 338 Resolution 357
United Nations Special Committee on Palestine, (UNSCOP) 246, 296, 357
United States 265, 272, 297, 301, 310, 318, 321–324, 333, 336, 340–351, 353, 355, 363–364, 372, 374, 377, 397, 401, 403
Uqab 190
Uriah 60
Usama, Izz al-Din 62
Uways, Wahdan 264
Uyun al-Tujjar 115
Uzayzat 142, 178, 179

Vambery, Arminius 85
Van Floten 52
Van, Lake 68
Vatican 181, 356, 357
Vatikiotis, P. J. 133
Venic 98, 102
Veterocaria (Vetrocania) 38
Via Maris 21
Via Regis 14, 18, 21
Via Traiana 28
Vichy France 144, 244, 246
Vietnam 344
Vilayet Law (1864) 136, 173
Villaret 75
Von Oppenheim, Freiherr 193
Von Sanders, Liman 167, 204
Vorontsov, Yuly 314

Wadd 57
Wadi ʻAraba accord 10
Wahab Shakib 220
Wahbi al-Tal, Mustafa 402
Wahhabis 125, 199, 200, 224, 232
Wahhabism 240
Wahirah 163
Walid II 50–54
Walker, Bethany 76, 103
Wallin George, August 128
Waqi'at Lib 130
Wasfi Pasha, Mirza 176
Washington 265, 296, 306, 314, 325, 341, 343–345, 347–349, 377
Wasta 383–385
Wauchope, Arthur 233
Weber, Max 5, 7
Weizman, Ezer 295
Weizmann, Chaim 212
Wellhausen, Julius 52
Wenger, A.D. 144
West Bank 4, 10, 42, 143, 174, 180, 199, 250, 253, 276, 277, 281, 291–296, 297, 300–303, 305, 316, 317, 324, 325, 335, 343, 348, 364, 369, 376, 378, 403
West Germany 276, 377
White Paper (1922) 225
Whittow, Mark 48
Wijdan, Ali 404
Wiktorowicz, Quintan 7, 274
William of Nogaret 75
William of Tyre 13
Willibald, Saint 14
Wilson, Henry 213
Wingate, Orde 163
Wirsing, Geseler 233
Wise, Stephen 341
Woolf, Virginia 400
World Trade Center Attack, (September 11, 2001) 274

World War I 2, 5, 10, 243, 331, 357, 403
World War II 241–244, 245, 283, 327, 340, 371
World Zionist Organization 214
Wuld Ali 136, 174
Wustiyya 123, 126

Yahatz 22
Yaïri 19
Yaktiel 22
Yalbugha al-Amri, al Khaski 75, 80
Yalbugha al-Nasiri 79
Yalbughawiya Turks 79
Yaman *vs.* Qays 52, 53, 84, 91, 144
Yamun 189
Yarmouk 2, 3, 13, 14, 18, 28, 46, 48, 49, 61, 80, 95, 124, 175, 224, 232, 242, 243, 284, 350, 354
Yashbak al-Mawsumi 87
Yashbak bin Azdmar 88
Yatam, Wadi 98
Yavesh Gilead 21, 30
Yazid II 177
Yazid III 50, 51, 53
Year of the Ashes 50
Yemen 96, 131, 312, 324, 400, 401
Yemeni Civil War 268, 324
Yibna (Yavneh) 44
Yishai 144
Yishuv 303, 342
Yom Kippur War 294, 325, 346
Young, Herbert 210, 211, 215, 228
Young Turks 132, 138, 170, 204
Yunis, Agha 166
Yunis al-Nawruzi al-Dawdar 79
Yunis, Hisham 397
Yusha' Nabi 135, 172
Yusuf al-Turmani 85
Yusuf Bin al-Jayushi 89
Yusuf bin Danyal, bin Mankali al-Karaki 106
Yusuf Bin Israil, Bin al-Karaki 106

Zaban 124, 240
Zaccaria, Benedict 75
Zadocatha (Khirbet el Sadaqa) 38
Zaghr 94, 99, 100
Zahar 96
Zahir al-Umar 146
Zahr 96
Zaizah al-Lajjun 101
Zamzam 56
Zamzumim 20
Zarqa 18, 59, 60, 78, 82, 95, 97, 101, 112, 121, 123, 126, 135, 139, 142, 166, 167, 172, 175, 180, 183, 198, 232, 263, 267, 350, 358
Z'arur 280
Zayd al-Din, Abd al-Rahman bin Ahamad al-Hasbani 105, 107, 108, 154, 156, 157, 159, 160
Zayd al-Zabit, Abdallah al-Dalimi 158, 163, 164, 166
Zaytun 189
Zayyad, Taufiq 399
Zeno 43
Zered 20, 23
Zionism 284, 318, 323
Zippori 146
Ziya, Bey 148
Ziyadin, Ya'qub 373
Ziza 184, 229
Zizya 44, 46, 59, 97, 140, 160, 230
Zizya Resan 101
Zoar 29
Zoara 39
Zobah 124
Zughar 68
Zvi, Shabtai 144

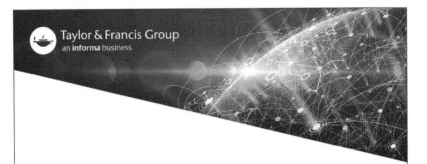

Printed in the United States
by Baker & Taylor Publisher Services